AF530548

GLOBALIZATION : MYTH AND REALITY

About the Editors

Govind Prasad is working as a Reader in the Department of Commerce, Hindu College, Delhi. Besides having a brilliant academic career he has a teaching experience of more than thirty six years in Indian and foreign universities. He has worked as Associate Professor in the Department of Accounting, Addis Ababa University, Ethiopia, during 1978-80 and in the same department of the South Pacific, Fiji in 1998. He has presented a number of articles and papers in national and international conferences/ seminars in India and abroad. He has written several books for the students of graduate levels. He is the life member of large number of academic bodies/associations. Recently, he has been offered the position of Professor in Accounting in Asmara University, Eriteria.

Anil Dutta Mishra started his career as an Assistant Professor in the Department of Nonviolence and Peace Studies, Jain Vishva Bharati Institute (Deemed University), Ladnun, Rajasthan. His area of specialization includes, Indian Government and Politics, Grass-root Politics, Women's Studies, Ecology and Human Rights.

He has been associated with a number of national and international organizations in various capacities like- Editor of Indian Society of Gandhian Studies, General Secretary of Alliance for Sarvodaya, Secretary General of Delhi School of Nonviolence and Member Board of Studies, Punjab University, Chandigarh.

He has authored/edited twelve books and published a number of research papers in leading professional journals. His earlier books Problems and Prospects of Working Women in Urban India (1994); Fundamentals of Gandhism (1995); Gandhian Approach to Contemporary Problems (1996); Decentralised Planning in India: A Study of Objectives and Operational Framework (1999); Gender Perspectives: Participation, Empowerment and Development (1999); Perspectives on Human Rights (2002); Rediscovering Gandhi (2002); Patterns of Gender Violence in India (2002) and Challenges of Twenty First Century And Gandhian Alternative (2002) were well received and widely acclaimed. Presently, he is working "On The Footsteps of Gandhi" which is part of twenty volume series of Rediscovering Gandhi.

GLOBALIZATION : MYTH AND REALITY

Govind Prasad
Anil Dutta Mishra

CONCEPT PUBLISHING COMPANY, NEW DELHI-110059

ISBN: 81-8069-128-4

First Published 2004

Published and Printed by
Ashok Kumar Mittal
Concept Publishing Company
A/15-16, Commercial Block, Mohan Garden
New Delhi-110059 (INDIA)

Phones : 25351460, 25351794
Fax : 091-11-25357103
Email : publishing@conceptpub.com

Preface

The book entitled *Globalization: Myth and Reality* is one of the most focused and challenging topic of 'globalization'. Globalization is a difficult subject to be dealt with. It is difficult because views on its positive and negative impact on society differ. One view is that globalization is integrating trade, commerce, people, etc., and that it is for the benefits of poor people and development of nations. The other view is that it is a neo-imperialism and a domination of few rich countries over poor and developing countries and that it is not beneficial for the developing nations. It is said that the policy of globalization and liberalization adopted by most of the developing nations in the recent past may create the problems of equity and ecology. Available data from China, India and other developing countries point to serious problems ahead. In India only a few states have benefited from the policy of globalization and liberalization. However, today globalization is considered as a reality.

Every nation has to introduce it with human face. Even Gandhiji, the father of the nation, who was fond of and always emphasized for 'Swadeshi' set tone of globalization as early as in *Young India*, June 1, 1921, when he said that "*I do not want my house to be walled in on all sides and my window to be stuffed. I want the cultures of all lands to be blown about my house as freely as possible. But I refuse to be blown off my feet.*"

The book *Globalization: Myth and Reality* is a modest attempt to deal with such a debatable subject. It contains 28 chapters on various social, political and economic aspects. These articles have been written by the scholars, who have active involvement and deep commitment on social issues concerning human beings, of different disciplines. The book provides sufficient matters to the readers for understanding globalization, liberalization and privatization.

In this endeavour we have received helps from a number of organizations and individuals. We shall be failing in our duty if we do not record our gratitude and thanks to them.

We have constantly received the encouragement and help from the Canadian High Commission, the Shastri-Indo Canadian Institute, friends and well wishers. There are number of persons hehind the scene whose ideas and comments, which have been incorporated in the present work, have been of immense help. We would like to place on record our deep sense of appreciation for them.

We are especially indebted to His Excellency, Padam Vibhushan, Shri T.N. Chaturvedi, the present Governor of Karnataka, who has blessed us with his comments and suggestions from time to time.

We express our thanks to Prof. Om P. Kamra, President, Shastri Indo Canadian Institute, New Delhi, for his help. Our friends have been a great source of inspiration for us. We are grateful to all of them. It is difficult to mention the names of all of them but few names which may be mentioned are of Prof. K.R.G. Nair, Dr. Om P. Juneja, Dr. Raj Kumari Kubba, Dr. Usha Pathania, Dr. Kavita Sharma, Dr. Jameela Begum, Dr. Devendra Kakkar, Dr. K.K. Kaushik, Dr. Vimal Dhawan, Dr. R.K. Dhawan and Prof. A.S. Narang.

We are also grateful to Dr. Chandra Mohan, President, IACS for his help and constant incouragement.

The contributors have taken utmost pains in writing their articles and encouraging us in our academic pursuits. Some of them obliged us by sending their articles much before scheduled dates inspite of their academic, social and political commitments. We acknowledge our deep sense of gratitude to each one of them.

The librarians and staffs of Indian Institute of Public Administration, Shastri Indo-Canadian Institute, National Gandhi Museum, Institute of Economic Growth, Planning Commission, Sapru House, British Council, American Centre, Hindu College and Ratan Tata Library, Delhi School of Economics have given their valuable help and support in the completion of this book. We express our heartfelt thanks to all of them.

Our life partners and children have shown a lot of patience and have always been a source of encouragement for the entire period we were busy. We appreciate and thank them for their support.

Last but not the least, we are grateful to Mr. Ashok Mittal of Concept Publishing Company, New Delhi for bringing out the book in its present form and that too within minimum possible time.

New Delhi
13th January, 2004

Govind Prasad
Anil Dutta Mishra

Contents

Preface v

About the Contributors xi

Introduction xxi
Govind Prasad and *Anil Dutta Mishra*

Part I : CONCEPTUAL PARADIGM

1. Globalization: Concept and Nature 3
Anil Dutta Mishra

2. Globalization: The Nature and its Dynamics 24
Hassan Rangriz

3. Contradictions and Challenges of Globalization: Need for an Alternative 36
Saroj Malik

4. Changing Complexion of Public Administration in the Globalization Era: Some Emerging Issues 49
Uma Medury

5. Globalization: Its Clashes, Contents and Discontents 69
A.A. Shaikh

Part II: ISSUES AND IMPACT

6. India Under Globalization: Facing an Unequal World 93
Pushpa Bisht

7. Role of Civil Society Organizations in the Era of Globalization 113
Alka Dhameja

8. Globalization, Sovereignty and Human Rights: A Perspective 133
Arun Kumar Singh

9. Economic Prospects and Environmental Problems of Globalization 155
T.V. Muralivallabhan

10. Globalization and Gender Issues in India 167
Sweta Mishra

11. Globalization and Child Labour 178
Sushma Yadav

12. Globalization and Consumerism: A Study of its Impact 188
Manoj Sinha

13. Consumer in the Globalized World 198
Jai Narain Sharma

14. The Female Consumer in the Globalised World 210
Ashu Pasricha

Part III: COMPARATIVE PERSPECTIVE

15. Globalizing Tribal Economy 223
Priyanka Priyadarshini and *M.C. Behera*

16. Current Trends in Canadian Economy in the Era of Globalization: A Third Millennium Perspective 241
B. Rahamathulla

17. Globalization and Foreign Direct Investment: India and Canada 252
Govind Prasad

18. Impact of Globalization: India and Canada 273
Naina Shaik Mohamed

19. Rhyme, Retham: Cultural Globalization in India and Canada 279
I. Francis Gnana Sekar

20. Globalization and Advertising: A Comparative Study of Television Advertising and their Effect on Children in India, United States, Japan and China 289
Neeru Kapoor

21. Globalization and Consumerism: A Comparative Study of India and Canada 308
G.Y. Shitole

22. Gender Inequity of the Job Market in a Globalization Era: A Comparative Study of Jobs for Women on Canadian and Indian Job Sites on the Internet 320
Sonia Khan

23. Globalization and the Changing Dynamics of Indo-Canadian Relations 336
C. Vinodan

24. Globalization of Equity Market: The Challenges to Asia Pacific and Indian Stock Exchanges 350
P.M. Meera Mohiadeen

25. Demand for Regional Autonomy in an Era of Globalization: A Comparison of India and Canada 360
A.N. Panda

26. Globalization Poses New Challenges to South-South Solidarity 372
Pramod Mishra

27. Globalization and Regionalism in the Asia Pacific Region 387
Sunil Sondhi

28. Canadian Foreign Policy in a Globalizing World: The Role of Canadian Provinces 432
Nalini Kant Jha

Bibliography 444
Sunita Gulati

Index 475

About the Contributors

A.A. Shaikh has long teaching experience of both undergraduate and post-graduate classes and is, at present, working as a Reader in the Department of Commerce, M.C. Shah Commerce College at Ahmedabad. He has written number of research papers and participated in several national and international conferences. He is the life member of several academic bodies in India.

Alka Dhameja is Reader with the Faculty of Public Administration, Indira Gandhi National Open University, New Delhi. She has done her M.A., M.Phil. in Political Science from University of Delhi. She has twelve years of teaching and research experience and is, currently, involved with the Faculty's Initiative to bring out quality courses in the area of Disaster Management. Her Ph.D was on Police Training from University of Punjab.

Anil Dutta Mishra started his career as an Assistant Professor in the Department of Nonviolence and Peace Studies, Jain Vishva Bharati Institute (Deemed University), Ladnun, Rajasthan. His area of specialization includes, Indian Government and Politics, Grass-root Politics, Women's Studies, Ecology and Human Rights.

He has been associated with a number of national and international organizations in various capacities like- Editor of Indian Society of Gandhian Studies, General Secretary of Alliance for Sarvodaya, Secretary General of Delhi School of Nonviolence and Member Board of Studies, Punjab University, Chandigarh.

He has authored/edited twelve books and published a number of research papers in leading professional journals. His earlier books Problems and Prospects of Working Women in Urban India (1994); Fundamentals of Gandhism (1995); Gandhian Approach to

Contemporary Problems (1996); Decentralised Planning in India: A Study of Objectives and Operational Framework (1999); Gender Perspectives: Participation, Empowerment and Development (1999); Perspectives on Human Rights (2002); Rediscovering Gandhi (2002); Patterns of Gender Violence in India (2002) and Challenges of Twenty First Century And Gandhian Alternative (2002) were well received and widely acclaimed. Presently, he is working "On The Footsteps of Gandhi" which is part of twenty volume series of Rediscovering Gandhi.

Arun Kumar Singh has been working as a Reader, Department of Political Science, Arunachal University, Itanagar since 1993. He has presented several research papers in national and international conferences and has published number of research articles. He has supervised five M.Phil and two Ph.D. scholars. He is the life member of IACS, IIPA, etc. He visited Salzburg, Austria, in 1999. He is a member of Executive Council of Arunachal Pradesh University. He is on the editorial board of Journal of Political Science, Chandigarh, and Arunachal Pradesh University Research Journal.

A:N. Panda is presently working as a Senior Lecturer in the Department of Political Science, at Panchayat (Government Lead) College, Bargarh, Orissa. Previously, he was posted at Rajendra College, Bolangir, Government College, Sundergarh and NSCB College, Sambalpur, Orissa. He got the second position in Political Science Honours alongwith distinction in other subjects in his B.A. Examination and the fourth position in his M.A. Examination in Sambalpur Uuniversity. He completed his Ph.D on'State Politics in Orissa'. He has been engaged in research on' Women Leadership in Orissa'.

He has supervised a number of Ph.D scholars and has written many research articles. He is member of many academic bodies such as IPSA, IIPA, New Delhi, IACS, Hyderabad and IACS. Presently, he is pursuing a UGC sponsored research project on "Administration and Tribal Development."

Ashu Pasricha is working in the Department of Gandhian Studies, Punjab University, Chandigarh. She is a law graduate and has Master degrees in Public Administration, Gandhian and Peace Studies and Defence and Strategic Studies, M.Phil and Ph.D from

Punjab University, Chandigarh. Her works "Gandhian Approach to Integrated Rural Development", "Public Administration : Discipline and Dimensions", "Gender Issues in India: Some Reflections (2003)"; and " Public Governance and Decentralisation (2003)' have been widely acknowledged as scholarly work of lasting value. Her book "Contemporary Debates in Public Administration" is in the press. She has completed her work on Gandhian Concept of State and Power" in twenty volume series "Rediscovering Gandhi". Currently, she is associated with the Department of Gandhian Studies, Punjab University, Chandigarh. She has published a number of research papers/articles on different subjects in various Indian and foreign journals of repute. She is also a regular contributor to various prestigious newspapers in the country and abroad.

B. Rahamathulla is Professor in the Department of Political Science, Aligarh Muslim University, Aligarh. He has specialized in International Relations and International Organizations. He teaches International Law as well. He has authored two books on Indo-American politics and published more than sixty papers and book reviews in the edited books and journals. He has attended a number of international conferences and seminars both in India and abroad. He was twice awarded the Research and Faculty Enrichment Fellowships by the Ministry of Foreign Affairs & International Trade, Canada. He has widely travelled abroad and delivered lectures in the foreign universities.

C. Vinodan is currently a Post-Doctoral Fellow in the Department of Political Science, University of Kerala, Kerala. He worked as faculty in the Post Graduate and Research Department of Political Science, S.N. College, Kollam. He specialises in the area of international relations and Canadian studies. He has published articles on Indo-Canadian relations, South Asian Security, E-Governance, US and Indian Foreign Policies, etc. He attended Fullbright course on foreign policy at the University of Delaware, USA, in 2000. He also representd India in the Summer Workshop on Defence Technology and Cooperative Security in South Asia at Kathmandu, Nepal, in September, 2000, organized by the RCSS, Colombo, Sri Lanka. Dr Vinodan has been selected by the Claremont Graduate University, California, USA, as a Visiting

Scholar under the Fullbright International Partnership Program. Recently, he has been invited to California to deliver lectures at various places. He is the life member of IACS. He has attended several national and international conferences in India and presented several papers in different conferences organized by IACS.

Govind Prasad is working as a Reader in the Department of Commerce, Hindu College, Delhi. Besides having a brilliant academic career he has a teaching experience of more than thirty six years in Indian and foreign universities. He has worked as Associate Professor in the Department of Accounting, Addis Ababa University, Ethiopia, during 1978-80 and in the same department of the South Pacific, Fiji in 1998. He has presented a number of articles and papers in national and international conferences/ seminars in India and abroad. He has written several books for the students of graduate levels. He is the life member of large number of academic bodies/associations. Recently, he has been offered the position of Professor in Accounting in Asmara University, Eriteria.

G.Y. Shitole is working as Reader in Commerce at the P.G. Department of Commerce, S.N.D.T. Women's University, Mumbai . He has done his post graduation in commerce and Ph.D from Shivaji University, Kolhapur. Besides, he has done his M.M.S. with Marketing Management from Pune University. He has twenty one years of teaching experience in various colleges in Mumbai. He has several research papers to his credit. He has attended several national and international conferences and presented a number of research papers.

Hassan Rangiz of Shahid Beheshti University, Tehran, Iran, is presently a Research Scholar, Department of Gandhian Studies, Punjab University, Chandigarh.

I.Francis Gnana Sekar is working as Reader in Commerce, St. Joseph's College, Tiruchirapalli, Tamil Nadu. He has eighteen years of teaching experience both at undergraduate and post-graduate levels. He is the life member of several Associations. He has presented five papers in international and six papers in national conferences in India. He is a recognized guide in Bharathidasan

University and presently guiding two students of M.Phil and two of Ph.D. He is a co-ordinator of Career Guidance And Entrepreneurship Cell in the same college.

Jai Narain Sharma is on the faculty of the Department of Gandhian Studies, Panjab University, Chandigarh. He obtained his Masters Degree from Panjab University, M.Phil from H.P. University, Shimla and Ph.D from Panjab University, Chandigarh. Dr. Sharma's area of specialization includes Gandhian Economics, Political Power, Human Rights and Human Resource Management. Dr. Sharma has distinguished himself as a management expert and Gandhian Scholar. He is connected with number of national and international organizations in various capacities. He is a member of Board of Studies, Nagpur University, Nagpur and Mahatma Gandhi Kashividyapeeth, Varanasi and a member of Research Degree Committee of H.P. University, Shimla. He is also the member of the presidium of Alliance for Sarvodaya. He regularly writes for leading newsapapers and has published a large number of research papers in various journals of repute. His books 'Gandhi's View of Political Power', 'Economics of Defence: A Study of SAARC Countries', 'Economic Thought of Mahatma Gandhi' and 'Human Resource Management' have been well received.

Manoj Sinha is working as a Senior Lecturer in the Department of Political Science in Ram Lal Anand College, University of Delhi, Delhi. He has done his M.A., M.Phil and Ph.D from University of Delhi, Delhi. Besides, working on American political system at the University of California, Berkley, U.S.A., he has several articles in professional journals and books. His research papers have been well received in seminars and conferences. The two books, viz., Cooperative Federalism in India & America (1998) and Modernization & Ecology: A Gandhian Perspective (2004) authored by him have been widely appreciated.

M.C. Behera is a Senior Faculty in the Department of Tribal Studies, Arunachal University, Itanagar.

Nalini Kant Jha is Professor and Dean, School of International Studies and Chairman, Department of Political Science, Pondicherry University. He was formerly Fullbright Scholar at the University of California, Berkley, U.S.A., and a Shastri Scholar at the University of Dalhousie, Halifax, Canada. He has authored five and edited four books and contributed more than fifty research papers in national and international journals of repute.

N. Shaik Mohamed is presently working as a Reader in Commerce, P.G. Research and Department of Commerce, Jamal Mohamed College, Trichy. He has twenty two years of teaching expericcne and twelve years of research experience. He has guided seventeen M.Phil and nine Ph.D. students. He has fifteen research publications in national journals. In addition, he got one book published and reviewed six books. He is the life member of IACS, AICA, IARC and NIPM, and has visited Sri Lanka, and Australia and attended nearly forty national and international conferences.

Neeru Kapoor is Reader in the Department of Commerce, Delhi College of Arts and Commerce, Delhi. She obtained her B.Com (Hons), M.Com., M.Phil and Ph.D degrees from the University of Delhi. She has presented papers in national and international conferences. A number of articles in the field of marketing, commerce and management written by her have been published in reputed journals of India. She specialises in marketing, advertising, sales promotion and public relations. Two of her books titled 'Television Advertising and Consumer Response' and Gandhian Economics are under publication.

Pramod Kumar Mishra graduated with honours in Political Science from Utkal University. He obtained his M.A. degree in Political Science from the University of Delhi and both M.Phil and Ph.D in international studies from Jawahar Lal Nehru University, New Delhi. He has been teaching international politics as a Reader in Delhi University for more than two decades and a half. He has authored ten books and ninety research articles in Indian and American journals. He has served as a Professor of International Relations for two years at Netaji Institute of Asian Studies, Calcutta. He has been Fullbright Visiting Professor on South Asian Studies at the University of West Florida, USA, during 1999. He was a Shastri Indo-Canadian Fellow in Social Sciences at the University of Alberta in 2001. He was also a Salzburg Fellow in 2002. Dr Mishra, has extensively visited USA, Canada, Russia and Europe on lecture tours and conference participation. He has been editor of two research journals (Asian Studies, Calcutta, and Indian Ocean , New Delhi). At present, he is the Honorary Director of an NGO known as Academy for Asian Pacific Studies.

P.M. Meera Mohiadeen is working as a Reader in the Department of Commerce, Jamal Mohamed College, Tiruchirapalli. He did his Master in Commerce from Madras University and M.Phil and Ph.D from Bharathidasan University. During his twenty years of teaching career, he has taught various papers to undergraduate, post graduate and supervised M.Phil students. In addition, he has been actively involved in the preparation of correspondence course study materials (both in Tamil and English) of Bharathidasan University. He is a recognized research advisor to the M.Phil and Ph.D students of Bharathidasan University and Madurai Kamraj University. His articles have been published in leading journals and magazines of India. Besides, he has attended national and international seminars and presented papers.

Priyanka Priyadarshini is a Research Scholar in the Department of Economics, Arunachal University, Itanagar.

Pushpa Bisht, a Senior Lecturer in the Department of Political Science, L.D. Arts College, Ahmedabad, Gujarat, has had an academic career of distinction and has been a recipient of National Merit Scholarship. Her doctoral dissertation on "Relevance of Liberalization in India' has been widely appreciated. Her areas of interest are Political Economy and International Relations. In the past she has been associated with Dateline Delhi and with The Himachal Times as a columnist. She has written widely on social issues and is currently working on a project entitled,' Globalization and Regionalism: Reconciling the Irreconcilable'.

Saroj Malik is Professor of Political Science and Chairperson of Political Science Department in Kurukshetra University, Kurukshetra, Haryana. She has a brilliant academic career and has been the recipient of State Merit Scholarship and UGC Research Scholarship. She has twenty five years of teaching experience and has written a book on "Gandhian Satyagraha & Contemporary World". Besides, she has written at least eighteen research articles and reviewed one book entitled "Globalization, Democracy and Culture: Situating Gandhian Alternatives".

Sonia Khan is presently working as Lecturer in Tourism Administration, H.P. University, Shimla. She completed her Master from H.P.University, Shimla, in 1994 and Master in Leisure Studies from WICE, CHN, The Netherlands, in 1996. She has worked as project assistant and organized various tours for students and foreign tourists. She is the life member of various renowned Associations. So far she has completed three projects, participated in various national and international conferences in and outside India and presented various research papers. Besides, she has co-edited a book entitled "Tourism in the New Millennium: Challenges and New Opportunities".

Sunil Sondhi is working as Reader in the Department of Political Science, Ranjdhani College, University of Delhi, Delhi. He did his doctoral research from the University of Delhi and post-doctoral research at the George Washington University, USA, and University of Toronto, Canada. During his distinguished academic career spanning more than two decades. Dr Sondhi has bagged many research awards. These include: Harry S. Truman Institute Research Award; John F. Kennedy Foundation Research Award; Oliver I. Reddick Award; J. William Fullbright Fellowship; Rockfeller University Research Grant; Gerald R.Ford Foundation Research Grant; and Salzburg Program fellowship. He has been granted the Shastri- Indo Canadian Fellowship twice, in 1990 and 1999. In the year 2000, Dr. Sunil Sondhi was awarded the prestigious Asia-Pacific Award by the Department of Foreign Affairs and International Trade, Government of Canada, for research on Governance and Development in Asia. He is the first Indian to be honoured with this award.

Sondhi has published extensively in scholarly journals on international relations and organisation and has more than one hundred research papers and articles to his credit. His three earlier books are : Science Technology and India's Foreign Policy (1994); United Nations in a Changing World (1998) and Corruption Around the World (2002). Dr. Sondhi has been a Trustee of Indian Association For American Studies, and is now the Secretary-General of Fullbright Alumni Association. A keen mountaineer. Dr. Sondhi has been the President of Delhi Mountaineering Association for six years 1995-2001, and is now a Member of its Governing Council.

Sunita Gulati, holds M.A. (Political Science) and MLISc and M.Phil in Library Science degrees from University of Delhi, Delhi, and CIC from IGNOU. Presently she is working as Deputy Librarian in Indian Institute of Public Administration, New Delhi. She has conducted user education programme for librarians sponsored by British Council Division and DOPT. She has authored several articles and compiled more than sixty bibliographies which have been published in distinguished journals and books.

Sushma Yadav is Reader in the Department of Political Science in Delhi College of Arts and Commerce, University of Delhi, Delhi. She has had a brilliant academic career and participated in and presented papers at a number of national and international conferences. She is the author/editor of about nine books. Her major publications include Justice and Social Order in India, Indira Gandhi's Leadership, Centre-State Relations Indian Tradition (1988), Indira Gandhi and Congress Party, Political Culture in Post-Independent India (1989), Issues in Indian Politics (1994), Culture and Politics (1998), Indian State Origin & Development (2000), etc., and has published more than two dozen articles and research papers in various journals. She is actively associated with a number of professional organizations/institutions in various capacities. Presently, she is working on Gender and Human Rights.

Sweta Mishra, is well-appreciated young, energetic and committed researcher and presently teaching Political Science at Shyama Prasad Mukherjee College, University of Delhi, Delhi. Her areas of specialization are Public Administration and Grass-root Democratic Institutions. Her publications include: Democratic Decentralisation in India (1994), Changing Patterns of District Administration (1996), Theory and Practice of Public Administration (1998), Decentralised Planning and Panchayati Raj (2000), and Decentralised Governance (2002). Besides this, she has to her credit more than two dozen research papers published in reputed professional journals. She is associated with a number of professional organizations in different capacities.

T.V. Muralivallabhan, is working as Deputy Director, School of Distance Education, Mahatma Gandhi University, Kottayam, Kerala. He obtained Master degrees in both Economics and Political Science. His areas of keen interest are : Sustainable Development and Higher Education. He has the distinction of presenting seven papers in international seminars and conferences and thirt four papers in national seminars and conferences. He is the member of Syllabus Restructuring Committee and P.G. Board of Studies (Economics), of Mahatma Gandhi University, Kottayam. Besides, he is the Subject Expert (Economics) and Research Guide of the same university.

Uma Medury is Reader of Public Administration at School of Social Sciences Indira Gandhi National Open University, New Delhi. She did M.A. in Public Administration from Osmania University and Ph.D from Punjab University, Chandigarh, on the topic 'Boards of Management'. She has twelve years of research and teaching experience at IGNOU. She is now working on innovative courses in Disaster Management being conceived and developed by the entire Faculty of Public Administration.

Introduction

GOVIND PRASAD and ANIL DUTTA MISHRA

Twentieth century witnessed various technological changes. New and fast means of transport have reduced the distance of the world. Sophisticated means of communication have revolutionized markets particularly money markets around the world. Today we live in *global age* and *global village* and globalization is the catch phrase. It is difficult to describe and interpret globalization. Views on merits and demerits of globalization differ. Today globalization has become the fact of life in the world. It is an important issue and irreversible though there may be several minus points of globalization.

The book contains 28 articles. Some of the articles throw light on the theoretical aspects of globalization against its historical background. The contributors have narrated the nature of globalization and its positive and negative points and its impacts on society particularly in developing nations. There are articles which highlight the position of consumers in a globalized world. The impact of globalization on advertisement, environment, human rights, gender issues, job opportunities for women, etc., have also been critically examined in some of the articles. This chapter has been devoted to describe salient features, in brief, of each article.

Anil Dutta Mishra in his chapter on "Globalization: Concept and Nature" has made an attempt to analyse the broad concept of globalization and its consequences on people and government. He is of the view that globalization has made the nation-state without boundary. The supporters of globalization are of the view that globalization has become the *mantra* these days to bring happiness all over the world. It is believed that global market, global technology, global ideas and global solidarity would enrich the lives of people all over the world. The era of globalization is opening many opportunities for millions of people around the world. Today we find increased trade, new technologies, foreign investments, expanding media and Internet connections and increased choices of products and services. In future people would be more interdependent and there would be shared values and shared commitment for the human development. It is further believed that the globalization would bring faster economic growth which would reduce poverty and inequality, malnutrition, illiteracy, and disease, etc., and would ultimately remove conflicts. Each individual and community would be so integrated with the world that the benefit of globalization would flow both laterally and vertically so smoothly that no one remains untouched by prosperity.

The rosy picture of globalization as painted by the supporters of globalization is far from being true. In most of the developing countries it has created several problems than what it has really solved. Dr. Mishra has also given the views of the opponents of globalization. The opponents are of the view that, no doubt, globalization has reduced the distance, space and time and within no time money, commodities and manpower can be transferred/transported from one part of the world to the other, there are many who are still devoid of their basic needs and their existence is in danger. It is a fact that vast majority of people in Asia, Africa and Latin American regions are still not part of globalization. The progress in the areas of health, education and other social sectors have suffered due to diversion of precious human resources which are being utilized for combating terrorism and separatist movements. This is being done in the name of national security. Moreover, consumerism is the product of globalization. This has significant impact on nation and society both directly and indirectly. Further, the opponents have raised certain fundamental questions. These are: Who want globalization ? Do people really want globalization? Globalization for what and for whom ? Why is there no globalization of human capital? The conclusion of Dr. Mishra's article is that there are several challenges which have arisen out of globalization. These challenges require total newness in approach on all fronts—from government to NGOs levels—so as to make globalization useful for mankind.

Hassan Rangiz's chapter on "Globalization: The Nature and Its Dynamics" highlights the recent wave of economic policy reforms in the developing countries is due to the wave of globalization which has now provided new challenges and created new opportunities for development. Dr. Hassan has explained globalization in two senses, viz., strong and soft. In the former sense, globalization refers to the presumed emergence of a 'supra-natural' borderless economy with its own laws of motion, encompassing and subordinating the various local economies in a single worldwide division of labour, rendering national governments into municipalities. The softer version treats globalization less as an en-stage and more as a process which the international economy becomes more closely integrated with economic agents increasingly oriented to the global market rather than to particular economic development. In Dr. Hassan's opinion, the origins of economic globalization lie in the rise of capitalism and the process was reinforced by the rise in industrialization in Great Britain. There are phases of economic globalization—one is 'extensive' or 'widening' phase of globalization and the other one is 'intensive' or 'deepening' phase. The former has been completed by the end of the World War I. The latter began with the end of the World War II. The outcome of the World War II was that most of the countries of the world were placed under the military, political and economic hegemony of the U.S. The American coporations set up production centres in many countries, looked for new market in search of higher and larger profits. Later on, these coporations converted themselves into MNCs. The American MNCs were later on joined by MNCs of other allies of the U.S. in the OECD. This process accelerated from the mid 1970s onwards. To day these MNCs are the key agents of intensification and some of them now 'dwarf' some governments in economic power.

Dr. Hassan defines market as a place where buyers and sellers meet for the exchange of goods and services on the basis of relative prices. Dr. Hassan is of the view that the market should be allowed to expand since all would gain eventually and the political boundaries should not be allowed to stand in the way of buyers and sellers. Different political units ought to be brought within the compass of one single market system. Markets as they expanded tended to encompass several states within a single division of labour. They further tend to promote integration between several regional economies of the world.

The main theme of Saroj Malik's chapter on "Contradictions and Challenges of Globalization: Need for an Alternative" is that globalization which is the watchword of the last decade of the twentieth century, reflects the vision of a borderless world dominated by multinationals and financial markets, in the sweep of a homogenized culture shaped by western values. But behind this imagined oneness, it presents a picture of paradoxical contrast. Due to the contradictions, many people all over the world, in general, and India, in particular, perceive threat than as a promise. All paradigms from globalization to communism have failed to solve the basic problems of poverty, hunger and unemployment, on one hand, and alienation, dehumanisation, resource exhaustion, environmental pollution, ecological threat, violence and war, on the other hand. As such, globalization is the centre of diverse intellectual and political agenda and several crucial questions about the usefulness of globalization are being asked. In the backdrop of this scenario, she has highlighted the contradictions, challenges and discontents of globalisation and has tried to find out an alternative model.

The chapter on "Public Administration and Globalisation: Emerging Challenges" by Uma Meduri has focused that globalisation is ushering in far-reaching changes in the society. There is need of redefining the role of the state, making state institutions responsive to the needs of the people and working towards state-market and state-society co-operation. Further, management orientation in public administration and the emergence of civil society as a supplementary democratic model are required to counteract the effects of globalisation. In her view public administration needs to gear up to the challenges of:

- redefining the respective spheres of state and non-state actors, building mechanisms for better interaction, and cooperation;
- framing suitable laws and regulations that provide necessary stability, confidence, enforcement; and
- building a professionalised civil service possessing necessary competence, skills, public service, participatory, and a pro-citizen ethic.

The conclusion of Dr. Medury's chapter is that, in the present administrative scenario, what is needed is not less government, but a better and different government.

A.A. Shaikh in his chapter on "Globalization—Its Clashes, Contents and Discontents" has given a brief history of globalization and then explained the meaning of globalization. According to him globalization is a process of economic, social, cultural and political integration of the world. The major constituents of globalization are trade, commerce, technology, science, information and technology. Today globalization is unstoppable and it has to be accepted by all countries. There are conflicting previews and views on globalization. Dr. Shaikh has divided his chapter into following heads:

1. Clashes of Globalization—A New Paradigm of Political Thinkers.
2. Populist—Fallacious Discontents of Globalization.
3. An Anatomy of Discontents of Globalization in which he discusses the views of Prof. Jagdish Bhagwati.
4. Open Society Endangered—Soros Approach.
5. In Search of Building an Inclusive World Economy: How to overcome the anxieties of globalisation (World Bank Policy Research Report, 2002).

The World Bank, IMF, IFC, WTO and other international institutions and professional economists are making serious efforts to solve problems which arose during post era of globalization. Their major focus is on development, poverty reduction international financial stability and institutional build up at World level. The World Bank Policy Research Report 2002 has classified the countries of the world into four categories, viz., less globalized, globalized, more globalized and global one. The less globalized countries are suffering from marginalization, state failure and rising poverty. The countries in the second category are facing the dilemma of being out of market, environmental degradation, social dislocation, imbalances in power. The rich globalized are facing the problem of terrorism, inequality within rich countries, loss of manufacturing jobs to low wage countries and homogenization. At the moment, there are global anxieties which include mounting inequality, global warming and power of government, labour and capital.

The report suggests seven major areas of actions. The first area is development round of action, the second is improving the investment climate, the third is importance of good delivery of health education, the fourth is social protection, the fifth is greater volume of foreign trade, the sixth is debt relief and the seventh is highlighting the importance of tackling green house gases and global warming. Dr. Shaikh's view is that globalization should have humane face and be better managed.

Pushpa Bisht in her chapter on "India Under Globalization: Facing an Unequal World" has stressed that globalisation has emerged as the new international system that has replaced the cold war system. Although, yet in its infancy, it has like a surge overtaken the world transcending boundaries and borders. While a comprehensive definition of globalisation would include political, economic and social aspects, it is, nevertheless, the economic aspect that is most visible today. The economic sector is the only sector that has succeeded in becoming truly global as country after country leaves autarky in favour of free market economy. The globalisation should imply a uniformity of conditions across countries. But this is not so. In the kind of economic globalisation seen today, the fact is that the key players have emerged. Thus, while the USA, Canada and the European Union move centrestage, eager contenders like China wait in the wings. Globalisation has yet to benefit countries of Africa, Latin America, Middle East and much of Asia.

India's definitive move towards economic globalisation came with the adoption of the New Economic Policy (NEP) following the balance of payment crisis of 1991. The NEP, which was a radical departure from the earlier inward policy, generated debate and dichotomic reaction. However, just as globalisation is a fact not an option, so also liberalisation of the Indian economy is a fact and not an option. No country, certainly not India, can divorce itself from the changes in the world environment that has thrown up globalisation as a pervasive, dynamic phenomenon. It is important, therefore, to move beyond the state-market debate.

At present India faces an unequal equation as its weak economic capabilities not only preclude an international role for it but also place it in the bracket of a minor world power. Since a dynamic economy is an undergrid to political power in today's globalised world India must overcome the problems it has internalised. The state has to reconceptualise itself and India will need extremely prudent diplomacy and smart national policies to capture opportunities in the global world. Many factors ranging from macro-economic policies to micro policies on a multilevel basis must augment the ability of the nation to compete successfully. India's fate and destiny in the globalised world would largely depend upon its ability to determine the acceptable contours between the state and free market economy without sacrificing one for the other. It is necessary to work out a solution wherein liberalisation and the state can be suitably balanced.

Alka Dhamija in her chapter on "The Role of Civil Society Organizations in the Era of Globalization" states that in the era of globalization the state is fast becoming a facilitator of the private sector. The fundamental transformation in the welfare commitment of the state, change in the complexion of sovereignty, addition of supra-territorial constituents, influx of markets in core development areas, and reduction of social security provisions have propelled the search for viable alternatives of governance. This has led to the formation of many organizations that could function as intermediaries between the state and the people and also influence the state and the market. These non-state actors have come to be known as civil society organizations or to use a more contemporary term, the social capital or the third sector of a country.

A term widely analyzed in the seventeenth and eighteenth centuries, the concept of civil society seems to have made a re-emergence in the twenty-first century with conformist, reformist and sometimes radical agenda. The rise of democratic opposition movements in East European countries in the 1990s and Robert Putnam's work on social capital in Italy have reintroduced the issue of civil society to the forefront of development discourse. In the globalization context, the growth of global civil society marks a distinct trend in the study of civil society organizations. Global civil society is networking civic organizations around the globe on issues pertaining to human rights, environment, sustainable development and national boundaries. Moreover, Information Technology has empowered the civil society in many new ways, in order to act as the guardians of democracy and good governance.

The civil society encompasses enormous diversity. Though NGOs are its major constituents, to equate the civil society organizations with merely the NGOs would be totally erroneous. The civil society stands for the entire sphere of public debate and brings out the broad processes of interaction among different types of civic organizations. Nevertheless, the combination of donor, NGOs and UN interest, which provides the background of the civil society grab needs to be looked into in the context of globalization. The revitalization of civil society in the form of citizens' initiatives and social movements represents a renewed model of civil society organizations in the era of globalization.

This new thinking should not be seen as a shift in power from the state and the market to civil society but rather as the natural evolution of the relationship between those who govern and organizations have to play in the global scenario, and in which direction are these heading in the future become crucial to any discussion on civil society organizations.

Dr. Alka Dhamija's article aims at addressing some of these key concerns of those who are governed. The synergies arising out of the emerging relations between the state, private sector, and civil society must, therefore, be put to practical use to realize the essentials of effective governance. The questions such as: Why has the civil society become pertinent in today's context? What is its relationship with the state and the market? Why should it not be equated only with the NGOs? What is a global civil society? What kind of role will the civil society play ?.

Arun Kumar Singh's chapter on "Globalization, Sovereignty and Human Rights: The Asia Pacific Perspective" has examined the impact of globalization on sovereignty and human rights. In the beginning of his chapter, he states that the post-Cold War world politics had generated a lot of hype and hope. The expectations all around the world particularly in the Third World were that the world was going to be safer and more secure as it was perceived that ideological conflicts have come to an end. Francis Fukuyama strengthened this view when he argued in his celebrated work *The End of History*? that 'a remarkable consensus concerning the legitimacy of liberal democracy as a system of government had emerged throughout the world as it conquered rival ideologies like hereditary monarchy, fascism and most recently communism' and that 'liberal democracy may constitute the end point of mankind's ideological evolution'. What he was suggesting was that there existed no alternative to the type of political system which is practiced by the US and its allies in the West and if peace in the world has to stay then every country must adopt and adhere to this brand of liberal democracy. The basic force behind this 'liberal' system has been capitalism.

But the 90s has seen a change in the contours of world politics. Instead of a peaceful world a more violent world system has emerged. The conflicts between and within nation-states have increased. The most disturbing aspect of this has been the increasing challenge to the sovereign states both from within as well as from outside.

The real challenge has come from the forces of globalization. The multinational corporations, reinforced by the global economic and financial institutions like IMF, World Bank and World Trade Organizations, have made serious inroads into the territorial, political, economic and cultural identities of nation-states. This is more visible in case of economically and politically weaker nations of Asia, Africa and South America.

As the world shrinks day by day and interdependence between nation-states increases, the entire discourse on human rights needs a fresh look. Globalization violates sovereignty and, thus, impinges upon the basic rights of nation-states to exist. The increase in consumerism and inequality-economic, social, digital and technological—between and within the nations has compounded the problem of human rights violations.

Muralivallabhan in his chapter on "Economic Prospects and Environment Problems of Globalization" states that international trade is one of the major means of bringing the triad of globalization, liberalization and privatization. Globalization is taking place at a very rapid rate throughout the world and its impacts are obvious at the political, economic, social and environmental levels. When the economic activities like capital investment flows, technological transfers and labour mobility take place, the consequences are still debatable. The most vulnerable area of increased economic activity is the environment. His article is an attempt to throw light on the emerging environmental problems as a result of the globalization process and the steps taken to solve them through international organizations like the WTO.

Sweta Mishra's chapter on "Globalization and Women Empowerment" seeks to define the concepts of globalization and analyse the political participation and empowerment of women in India with a special reference to the changes which have been brought about due to globalization. Her chapter also provides some meaningful suggestions as to how women can cope up with the adverse impact of globalization. In her opinion, globalization is a phenomenon that we cannot deny. All we can do is accept it. Globalization means different things to different people. The term which is used to describe the shape of the world economy today has become fashionable but its meaning and implications, particularly for developing countries, are far from clear. Globalization is transforming trade, finance, employment, migration, technology, communications, the environment, social systems, and ways of living, cultures and patterns of governance.

The process of globalization has been accelerated by economic reforms and the liberalization of trade and investment policies undertaken even by developing countries. Most developing countries have replaced the old import substitution policies by export promotion and openness. Besides economic transformation, globalization involves changes in the social and political structures and status of societies. Politically, globalization entails the loss of national sovereignty or, as some like to dramatize, the demise of the nation-state. Admittedly, the role of the nation-state is changing and it is less autonomous in the sense that national economic and monetary policies are also affected by what happens outside the national boundaries.

Recently is has been realized that women hold the key to sustainable development. In fact, an appreciation of the critical role that women can play arose from the contribution of women in struggles against colonialism and in national wars of independence. After World War II, the concept of the equality of the sexes as one of the basic principles on which a community should be based was incorporated in the UN Charter. Since then, there have been a number of conferences and conventions on the theme of women in development. The adverse impact of Structural Adjustment Programme (SAP) policies on women's livelihoods, employment, education, health, social welfare and political participation have all simultaneously brought out the indomitable determination of women to save themselves and their families through strategies of survival and struggle against the depredations of both domestic and foreign elite.

In her chapter on "Globalization and Child Labour" Sushma Yadav expresses her concerns about child labour in the era of globalization. In her opinion, concerns about child labour have become prominent paradigmatic shifts in the concepts of human rights. The ideals about childhood have contributed to increased attention being paid to the issue of child labour. The chapter explores how demographic and politico-economic pressures generated or compounded by the process of globalization, shape or influence the demand for and supply of child labour as also the child labour standards. It has been observed that in the last wave of globalization, migration reduced the supply of potential adult and child workers in Europe which enhanced the possibility of raising the labour standards in Europe. But the current wave of globalization differs significantly from the last one in terms of global governance and the potential for the movement of labour. Studies show that the decline in the proportion of children in populations and the labour force is greater in countries with a higher Human Development Index and Gender Development Index value. Therefore, the high rates of growth that can potentially be gnerated by the globalization process will need to be accompanied by perceptibly adequate instruments of social protection and the meeting of basic needs if child labour is to be eliminated.

The chapter on "Globalization and Consumerism: A Study of Its Impact" by Manoj Sinha highlights that globalization is no longer a theoretical concept but it is a glaring reality and it encompasses economic, technical, environmental, cultural and other aspects of human existence. The article deals with various stages, characteristics and consequences of globalization. The main issue in the era of globalization is whether globalization is benevolent or malevolent. According to Dr. Sinha, globalization is benevolent for the North including Canada whereas it is malevolent for the poor South Asia including India. Dr. Sinha is of the opininion that the condition of full employment existed in the Keynesian phase and as such capitalism was benevolent to the North. But at the moment the situation has changed and there is no such conditions. Globalization has brought job insecurity, financial volatility, weak state and erosion of welfare benefits. The position of trade unions has weakened and the income inequality has increased. The job market is very rewarding for highly educated people. And the big corporations are the villains of piece for this kind of situation. The environmental problem has been created by the growth of production by the large global or transnational corporations. Dr. Sinha also mentions the role played by WTO and the role played by it. According to Dr. Sinha though developments linked with globalization have opened up boundless possibilities for human development, enormous new opportunities and enhanced the quality of life for many people in the Third World. Globalization has certain negative aspects. Dr. Sinha has divided these negative aspects into six categories, viz., economic aspect, political aspect, social aspect, cultural aspect, impact upon indigenous people and ecological aspect and has discussed the negative effects of these aspects at length.

Quoting the famous lines "The market needs a place, and the market needs to be kept in its place" by Anon Jai Narain Sharma in his chapter on "Consumer in the Globalized World" states that the process of liberalization and globalization has done wonders to consumerism in India. On the one hand, Indian market is big enough with large number of consumers (who are not economic rational) having money power. Most of these consumers are not able to weigh costs and benefits and as such purchase goods/services which give less than optimal satisfaction. On the other hand, there are variety of goods/services in the market. Dr. Sharma has pointed out that before globalization most of the persons coming from foreign country used to bring electronic and other goods from foreign countries. Now-a-days foreign goods are not any more attractive for these Indian consumers as they are available in Indian market. Dr. Sharma is of the view that in future many more products with greater sophistication and added features will be available in the market and the consumers will be getting a feeling that they are getting their money's worth.

As per Dr. Sharma's view market is full of germs. It is a place where the consumers are exposed to false, misleading and decepting advertisements regarding quality, price and guaranties and warranties of the products/services. This situation prevails in India inspite of the recent pro-consumer legislation and education of the consumers. The big players of market who are mostly governed by the profit motive want to sell their products by adopting false and deceptive advertisements. In such a situation, the consumers are confused and it has become difficult for many of them to make a right choice of product for his/her purpose.

Dr. Sharma expresses that consumerism in India differs from consumerism in advanced countries. This is because most of the consumers in advanced countries go for new models of products very frequently whereas it is not so in India. Mere availability of more classes of goods and services after liberlization and globalization, should not mislead us that we have reached the level of consumerism as we find in advanced countries. However, things may change in future and with the availability of funds, the consumers in India would go for newer models/brands of the products very frequently

Dr. Sharma points out that consumer is like a king and he/she must behave as a king. They have money in their pockets which no one can touch. They have full right to choose right quality of goods/services without being guided by the deceptive and false advertisements and must reject cheap and sub-standards stuff so as to force the manufacturer/producers/suppliers to supply the products of quality as per the expectations of the consumers.

Dr. Sharma has suggested that technology is like a steam roller and consumers must accept it as friend and not as an adversary. Further, he suggests that consumers must keep a guard of environment from being polluted and they should keep themselves away from excessive borrowing for newer and attractive products. Traditionally, India is a society of savers and it should not succumb to that maddening American syndrome where people go to counsellors for 'debt therapy' and join 'borrowers anonymous'. The end of Dr. Sharma's article states, "The bottom line for consumers of twenty first century—the true measure of consumerism is improved quality of life through better quality of products and services at competitive prices".

Ashu Pasricha in her chapter "The Female Consumer in the Globalized World" has pointed out that women are not economically powerless and they contribute directly to the workforce and about two-thirds of the archetypal female consumers work in and out of home. Yet, her contribution, though considerable, is subordinate to that of man. In her opinion, in Western society, the phenomenon of female consumption is marked by two principles, i.e., massive and extensive. As the first principle, the expenditure which woman controls directly make up the largest sector in consumers expenditure indices. According to the second principle, woman plays crucial role in the selection of household items for the family. It is estimated that women in Canada and America decide 75-90 per cent of consumer sales. It is also said that without the female consumption, the consumer marketing industry would disintegrate. Dr. Pasricha is of the view that in the era of globalization the relationship between woman and the marketing industry would undergo some fundamental and exciting changes. In most of the cases, the housewife controls a substantial part of her husband's economic resources and here decision in the selection of household goods for the family members has a significant impact on the mental and physical health of several people.

In her article Dr. Pasricha deals with New World Order or corporate globalization and states that the mega corporations are dominating over nations and their people. According to Dr. Pasricha, women take active part in agriculture. Globalization has allowed entry of transnational corporations in agribusiness. These corporations have introduced pesticides, insecticides, fertilizers, etc., in agriculture. The health of women workers are adversely affected. She points out that the agrarian society is vanishing and instead manufacturing and tourism industries are coming up. Most of the male members of the family go out of their villages/native places in search of jobs for higher incomes. This creates a lot of problems for woman at home in the absence of her husband. Further, if the woman takes up a job in manufacturing or tourist industry her modesty and prestige are at stake. In service sector, the women are working till late night and very often she is physically and even sexually abused. Today, super profits are raked at the expense of women and children. We find women working in bars and servicing for men in brothel. The use of high tech like the internet has led to widespread sex trafficking, pornography, prostitution, paedophilia, etc. At the end of her article, Dr. Pasricha says, "*only through solidarity can we ever hope to create alternatives to corporate globalization*".

Priyanka Priyadarshini and M.C. Behera in their chapter on "Globalizing Tribal Economy" have examined the integration of the tribal economy in Arunachal Pradesh with the national economy after Independence through plan programmes. They have also examined the impact of the investment by the MNCs in the process of development of Arunachal Pradesh during the period of globalization. The emphasis of the chapter is whether the economic growth in the state has increased job opportunities and ensured the distributive justice given the experience of some countries, which heavily depended on inflow of foreign capital. The conclusion of the chapter is that MNC investment in tribal economy of Arunachal Pradesh may lead to economic growth without distributive justice.

B. Rahamathulla in his chapter on "Current Trends in Canadian Economy in the Era of Globalization: A Third Millennium Perspective" is of the view that Canada is becoming a more open economy and its policy is to accelerate the economic growth and development by attracting investment both from domestic and international investors. Canada has taken a number of initiatives to promote free trade with the intention to integrate with global economy. This has resulted in improvement in inflow and outflows of FDI.

Dr. Rahamathulla feels that the private companies in Canada are acquiring outward investment through partnership, joint venture, acquisitions, mergers, etc., for penetrating their operations. This, according to him, would fetch Canada abundant growth and export opportunities besides creation of a number of jobs.

Dr. Rahamathulla has also cited that in 1995 Canada and other countries within the 29-member organisations for Economic

Cooperation and Development (OECD) developed negotiations towards a Multilateral Agreement on Investment (MAI). These negotiations have helped Canada in increasing its foreign direct investment in Canada and Canadian investment abroad at a phenomenal rates. The principal aim of the MAI is to establish a broad framework of agreed principle and commitments governing the foreign investment. MAI negotiations are based on two principles: These are non-discrimination and fair protection for investors and their investment. Under the non-discrimination principles both the foreign and domestic investors are treated the same way.

In 1994 Miami Summit of the Americas created a blueprint for great economic, political and social co-operation among the nations of the Americas. An important part of this blueprint was the Free Trade Area of the Americas (FTAA). The second Summit of Americas took place in 1998 at Santiago, Chile. The Canadian Prime Minister Chretien and leaders from 33 other countries launched negotiations. The blueprint of FTAA has provided substantial protection to Canadian investments and opened up new markets for Canadian goods by lowering or eliminating high tariffs or other barriers. Further, it has opened up fast growing economies of Americas to small and medium sized Canadian firms.

Dr. Rahamathulla has given the new trends and currents fiscal position of Canadian economy. He is of the view that Asia Pacific Region is the important market for Canada and half of Canada's export is for this region. In 1997, Canada hosted the Asia-Pacific Economic Co-operation (APEC) Forum. In this Forum APEC leader committed to take initiatives to advance early voluntary sectoral liberalization (EVSL) for a package of 15 sectors. Of these, there are nine priority sectors and six other sectors. The first nine sectors are: environmental goods and services, fish and fish products, forest products, energy, toys, medical equipments and instruments, chemicals, gems and jewellery, and tele-communications. The other six sectors are oilseeds, civil aircrafts, rubber, fertilizers, automotive and foods.

Govind Prasad in his chapter on "Globalization and Foreign Direct Investment: India and Canada" has highlighted the position of foreign direct investment during the post-globalization period in the world, in general, and in India and Canada, in particular. He opines that most of the countries in the world introduced globalization with the hope that it would attract foreign direct investment. In turn, it would bring new technologies and capital for the development and prosperity. As per Dr. Prasad's findings, globalization has helped rich nations in attracting FDI. For various reasons, the developing countries have not been benefited by FDI. The FDI inflow showed increasing trend both in India and Canada during Post-Globalization era. Canada attracted more inflow of FDI from USA and invested more in USA. However, the rank of Canada in attracting has been behind several developed nations. The position of India in attracting inflow of FDI, for various reasons, is far from being satisfactory. India is behind China and some other countries in this respect. At the initial stage of globalization in India, Canadian politicians, entrepreneurs, etc, showed interest for more business and investment in India. As such, the trade between India and Canada increased and it went in favour of India during post-globalization period particularly after 1996-97. However, Canadian FDI in India during the post-globalization period is very small. Necessary initiatives on the part of India are urgently required for the growth and development of the country through inflow of FDI.

Naina Shaik Mohamed in his chapter on "Impact of Globalization: India and Canada" makes an attempt to compare reforms in the two most popular economies of the world: India and Canada. While both Canada and India opted for a gradual approach to reforms., India had to begin with stabilization measures due to the fiscal and balance of payments crisis in 1991. Since Canada's reforms were initiated a little before India's, the latter country could benefit by drawing relevant lessons from the former. Reforms are far from complete in either of the countries. In his opinion, in Canada, further reforms need to concentrate on different issues such as overall productivity, international capital inflow, labour movement, social welfare, insurance and the financial system. In India, continued reform actions are required in the areas of fiscal consolidation, openness of the economy, tax reforms, foreign investment policy and the financial sector. In addition, reforms need to be initiated in areas such as exit policy, labour and land law, decentralization of decision-making power and opening up of the insurance sector. Steps in respect of some of these reforms have been taken in the recent past and other reforms have yet to take place in India.

I. Francis Gnana Sekar's chapter on "Rhyme, Retham: Cultural Globalisation in India and Canada" has highlighted cultural globalisation of India and Canada with a special reference to habits and desires. Globalisation, in his view, is an ongoing economic, technological, social and political integration of the world that began after the Second World War. Acccording to Dr. Sekar globalisation refers primarily to integration of various nations of the world at the economic level. However, even if the primary thrust of globalisation is economic integration it also includes as a significant component cultural extension and emergence of cosmopolitan culture through creation of new habits of thoughts and feelings of new behaviour patterns and attitude which are supposed to be in broad.

The chapter on "Globalization And Advertising: A Comparative Study of Television Advertising and Their Effect on Children in India, United States and China" written by Neeru Kapoor highlights the global children's market which has tremendous potential. Dr. Kapoor contends that marketers in India and other developed countries have recognized children as an important segment of target audience and have attempted to influence the consumer socialisation of the child by advertising heavily on television. The effects of television advertising on children is a matter of great controversy and debate at both national and international levels. Yet little research has been conducted on comparing the international attitudes on this issue. In her article she has tried to find the parents' perception of the possible effects of television advertising on children from early childhood to early adolescence in India. The author compared the perceptions of Indian parents with the parental beliefs in United States, Japan and China in order to increase the understanding of family communication patterns and advertising related parental practices in other nations.

Dr. Kapoor's findings reveal that Indian children, are not as easy a target as advertisers and critics believe. They are able to analyse T.V. ads and develop a realistic approach towards them. It was also found that early parental-child interaction was a key element if parents did not want their child to be effected adversely by TV ads. Majority of the Indian parents accept and appreciate the TV ads that teach their children good consumer values. American mothers, on the contrary, seem to hold negative attitudes towards both advertising, in general, and children's advertising, in particular. They maintain close control over what their children watch. Japanese mothers, in contrast, appear to have a more sanguine or optimistic view of advertising and place fewer controls over their children's viewing habits. Although Chinese parents are viewed by their children as less important than television, they do play major role in assisting their children to grow as consumers by providing them with information about new products. Thus, difference in parental attitudes towards television advertising and children provide practical implications to marketers for global segmentation of markets and formulating effective advertising strategies.

Globalisation is the process of integrationalisation and in the recent past most of the countries in the world have undertaken various steps towards globalisation which has led to change in the nation's environment and cultural conditions. This is the view expressed by G.Y. Shitole in his chapter on "Globalisation and Consumerism—A Comparative Study of India and Canada". He is of the opinion that consumerism is as old as man, who did not know how to produce. But he was endowed with plenty of mother nature to discover, use and consume. Therefore, the ancient consumer moved from place to place to hunt for food. Today, man has evolved into a seasoned producer and consumer of a large number of goods and services. At the same time, the consumers constitute the largest unorganised public body in the country.

Dr. Shitole has dealt with consumerism in the era of globalisation. He has made an attempt to present a comparative picture of consumerism in India and Canada in the context of globalization. According to Dr. Shitole the consumers in India are very heterogeneous in composition. They belong to different religions, speak different languages, use very different products and avail different services and adhere closely to their varied traditions. Most of them are poor, illiterate, ignorant and apathetic, therefore, they remain at the receiving end. Consumers in India need education through demonstration and field activities. Further, they may learn by experience also. There are specialised bodies, social organisation, universities, colleges, etc., providing consumer education. Consumers in India need information about various products in respect of quality, price, handling instructions, after sales services, etc.

On the other hand, the Canadian consumers are realistic and practical in nature. They are slow in decision making but they have firm determination about their choice. They are not hasty or thoughtless while deciding about the product brand. The Canadian people, in general, are not mad about something new as Indians are and at the same time they are not influenced by advertising and exaggeration. The lieracy level of consumers in Canada is much higher as compared to that of India. The expectations and standard of living of consumers in Canada are higher. The Canadian consumers purchase branded products only. The Canadian population is migratory in nature and people from different nations have migrated to Canada. Thus, the cross-country population purchases different products and services to adhere to their varied needs. In Canada, consumer education is a part of social responsibility of business and business conductors provide consumer education to induct the consumers into the new varied products and their effective usage. In Canada consumer guidance becomes a part of the promotion of the product and services itself. The advertising and publicity campaign in Canada largely takes care of consumer guidance with reference to the product quality, price, handling instructions, and after sales services, etc.

In her chapter on "Gender Inequity of the Job Market in a Globalization Era: A Comparative Study of Jobs for Women on Canadian and Indian Job Sites on the Internet", Sonia Khan states that globalization has been identified as one important tool to bridge the gender gap in societies and specially acts as a mode of improving the status of women through opening up economic opportunities for them. The proponents of globalisation have marked out eradication of female gender prejudices in the job markets as one of their primary goals, which they are confident of achieving. She has tried to assess as to what extent the globalisation process has affected the gender aspect of the economies of the world and whether it is more pro-developed or pro-developing countries in terms of justifiably providing opportunities to women/female workforce in various professions in the job market.

On the basis of study of job advertisements appearing on selected Indian and Canadian Job sites on the Internet she has attempted to make a comparative study of Canadian and Indian job market to explore, if in the present globalization era, the job market still associates gender identities and offers gender segregated jobs. The essence of her chapter is to explore if the globalization process is succeeding in providing gender neutral jobs universally and what nature of jobs are advertised for women reflecting upon the status accorded to women in a particular country. In her opinion, gender inequities in any aspect of life are observed to be more characteristic of developing than the developed countries. Gender equity is still considered to be a concept of the western world. On account of better education, opportunities and empowerment of women, equality of genders has been achieved to a significant extent in the developed nations. However, the developing countries still have a long way to go in order to bridge the gender gap in all spheres of life.

The long term trade relation between India and Canada based upon the existence of mutual cooperation, support and help for mutual gains in trade and trade related activities has been emphasized by C. Vinodan in his chapter on "Globalisation and the Changing Dynamics of Indo-Canadian Relations" In the opinion of Dr. Vinodan, Canadian business is extending beyond the United States of America and Canada is now capturing the growing markets of India and other South Asian countries. Canada has drawn her attention towards huge Indian market. The growing middle class population provides and several other favourable conditions exist for Canadian business in India. There are several areas where Canadian businessmen may show their interest to invest.

Dr. Vinodan contends that the position of Canadian trade and investment in India shows a dismal picture particularly during post-globalization period. His finding is that Canadian trade with India is merely one-tenth of its trade with China. In addition, the Canadian investment in India is far from being satisfactory. This is the position when several businessmen and industrialists have shown their interest in several areas such as infrastructures like communication, power and roads, etc. The challenge before India is how to attract more Canadian investment in India. For India it is essential to create more stable political environment in India. The need of the hour is firm determination and strong will on the part of both the countries and to restructure policy options in vital areas of cooperation.

Meera Mohiadeen in his chapter on "Globalisation of Equity Market: The Challenges to Asia Pacific and Indian Stock Exchanges" states that world over the capital market is transforming themselves because of the severe impact of the Information Technology. It is facilitating lot of improvements in the existing securities trading systems and promises to be far more cost-effective than the age-old business modes. The major stock exchanges fear that if they can't make global trading easier and cheaper, their customers will join or create private electronic market. Already some attempts were made by the Morgan Stanley, Swiss Stock Exchange and Merrill Lynch to form a private electronic trading; Jiway, Virt-X and MLX Market Edge respectively. Further, the Tokyo, Toronto, Sydney, Sao Paulo, Hong Kong and Mexico stock exchanges try to establish link with

NYSE, German stock exchange with London Stock Exchange and French, Belgian and Dutch stock exchanges merged and form a EURONEXT. The need for developing a global equity market has been felt by major stock exchanges like LSE, NYSE and NASDAQ and other stock exchanges of the Asia Pacific countries.

The entry of the Indian companies into the global equity market has forced the Indian stock market to thrive on challenges and become internationally competitive by upgrading quality of their services. Hence, the Indian capital market has also felt the impact of the globalization seriously. India is unique amongst other developing countries in respect of the well developed and diversified financial system. But the global financial system has undergone very significant change. All these necessitated the Indian as well as the Asia Pacific capital market to comply with the international standards of security dealings. For this purpose there should be sincere efforts among the countries to harmonise the corporate and securities law. Dr. Meera Mohiadeen's chapter focuses the areas in which the capital markets of Asia Pacific and Indian are focusing their attention to meet requirements of the merging global equity market as well as challenges in the years to come.

Globalisation has reduced the impact of national boundaries and brought the people of different countries closer. It has encouraged a new understanding among the nations and their people. This is the view expressed by A.N. Panda in his chapter on "Demand for Regional Autonomy in an Era of Globalisation: A Comparison of India and Canada". His chapter deals with the division of power between the centre and the regions and the demand for more powers by the regions in both India and Canada. According to Dr. Panda, in spite of this happy development in international field, the people of different regions still nurture a feeling of regionalism and isolation from the national mainstream within a country. Regionalism has affected the unity of the country and very often has been responsible for a demand for secession. It has also bred violence and social disharmony.

Both India and Canada share the same federal form of government which envisages national unity along with regional autonomy. But both the countries face the problem of balancing these two ideas while the regions demand more autonomy from the central government. This demand has posed a threat to national unity in both the countries.

P.K. Mishra in his chapter on "Globalization Poses New Challenges to South-South Solidarity" has made an attempt to look at the theory of globalization from an international perspective. In his opinion, globalization has been an accepted fact of life for the people of the world at the end of the twentieth century. He contends that there are certain misperceptions about the term globalization. First, even if the nomenclature sounds very catchy and has affected most of the nation-states, in the ultimate analysis, it lacks a sound spirit of globalization and a rational international system. Second, it has adversely affected the sound growth and functioning of the United Nations. Third, it has resulted in the erosion of the state sovereignty, by taking away the autonomy of the nation-states, to a large extent. Last, but not the least, globalization has widened the gap between the global centres of power and the rest of the world. Dr. Mishra further contends that the developing world has been the worst victim of globalization in a number of ways. First, the global financial institutions like the World Bank and IMF have systematically curtailed the decision making power of these states because of their increasing dependence on foreign aid. Second, the World Trade Organization (WTO) in place of rationalizing the global trading system, has perpetuated the hegemony of the Group of Seven. Third, because of their crucial depdendence on global finance and capital, a large part of the Third World stands badly divided today. As a result, most of the Third World forums like the NAM, Group of 77 and the South Bank have now become more or less defunct and irrelevant. The ultimate reality is that as a result of globalization a large part of the third world have stopped playing any major role either individually or in concert with other nation-states at the international platforms. Because of their overall dependence and subservience to global financial institutions, their governments are no more responsive to popular demands at home. On the other hand, they have been forced to take many anti-people measures like large scale retrenchment of workers, down sizing the public sector undertakings (PSUs) or even selling them to private sector. The repressive power of these states has also been furthering strength even under the dictates of global centres of power. Because of the erosion of multilateralism in world affairs and the gradual emergence of a single hegemony, the syndrome of dependency has increased thereby sacking the vitality of the newly emerged states. In his views globalization raises several searching queries on the problems and hardships faced by the developing nations as a direct or indirect effect of globalization. Dr. Mishra's article also looks at the possibility of raising a Third World hard effect of globalization.

The chapter on "Globalization and Regionalism in the Asia Pacific Region" by Sunil Sondhi raises concerns about civil society's representation and effectiveness in articulating the different vocalities in Aisa and the Pacific. Dr. Sondhi has presented a critical view of the growth of "new regionalisms" specifically in Asia and the Pacific basin and highlighted how civil society is building countervailing powers to challenge the new state-market nexus. The future international political economy presents a bleak picture considering the turbulent prelude that we see now, thereby fuelling the necessity for what the People's Plan for the twenty-first century call a "transborder participatory democracy".

In the opinion of Dr. Sondhi, participatory democracy is a system of decision making about public affairs in which citizens are directly involved. It is the original type of democracy found in ancient Athens (Held 1995). Transborder/transnational participatory democracy envisages broader social relationships beyond national borders. It is also beyond linking already nationally constituted civil societies. It is about making the people themselves visible. It is a process-oriented approach of attaining global civil governance. In the Asian region, the presence of geo-economic and geopolitical structures poses the necessity and possibility of a regional civil society which will push regional/transnational democratisation through participation.

Dr. Sondhi's chapter, firstly, seeks to articulate the **"underside"** of regional integration efforts in Asia and the Pacific. The article also deals with how groups in civil society are reacting to the emerging regional arrangements. Because regionalism should not only be measured in terms of the actual integration of economic fundamentals (trade, production and net capital flow) but also in terms of sociological factors. Further, the article highlights how organised people view themselves in relation to this phenomenon. Secondly, it discusses the dynamism of currently existing civil society network in the region. Social movements are oftentimes inclined to view their position as the representative view of the majority. In his article, Dr. Sondhi has tried to raise concerns about civil society's representation and effectiveness in articulating the different vocalities in Asia and the Pacific.

Nalini Kant Jha in his chapter on "The Canadian Foreign Policy in a Globalising World: The Role of Canadian Provinces" highlights that in certain areas Canadian Provinces are both active and influential in playing significant role in the international political economy of the globalisation. In addition there are fields of policy where constituant governments are simply not players much less players with influence. Dr. Jha is of the opinion that there are apparent inconsistencies in the levels of activity and influence of provincial governments in foreign policy and it requires re-examination of the issue of jurisdiction where provincial governments may involve in foreign policy areas. There is consensus that both the levels of government-Federal and Provincial, must seek to create common policy to avoid conflict between them. It is widely recognised that the federal government should manage matters involving defence and security of the country whereas the provincial governments must be allowed to mobilise foreign investment and conduct commercial dealings with foreign countries in the era of globalisation and liberalisation.

Globalization is overtaking the standard unit of development, the nation or society. The traditional agent of development, the state, is being overtaken by the international institutions and players of market forces. The impact of globalization can be seen everywhere. Whether it is North or South, developed or developing nations. But its benefits are not the same. Rich nations have benefited from globalization. Their wealth and per capita income have increased. In other way now they are controlling the entire world resources indirectly without any responsibility. Poor nations resources are exploited by rich nations through technological knowhow. In fact, poor countries are becoming as market for advance nations.

There is an end of ideologies and everywhere only capitalism is dominating. Even the social movement is decling everywhere. The media, press, political parties, pressure groups, government and its agencies etc. directly or indirectly are part of globalization of western type—i.e. domination of one culture, one country, one military power and complete hegemony of America and its allies. Where as Ancient Indian type of globalization is different. It is globalization of people instead of commerce only. It is based on the philosophy of whole world is one family. In other words it follows the policy of "*Vasudhaiv Kutumbkam*".

Part I

CONCEPTUAL PARADIGM

1

Globalization:
Concept and Nature

ANIL DUTTA MISHRA

"The real wealth of a nation is its people. And the purpose of development is to create an enabling environment for people to enjoy long, healthy and creative lives. This simple but powerful truth is too often forgotten in the pursuit of material and financial wealth".

—Human Development Report, 1990

Introduction

Globalization is not new but the present era has some distinctive features such as shrinking space, shrinking time and disappearing borders are linking people's lives more deeply, more intensively and more immediately than ever before. Globalization is a process integrating not just the economy but culture, technology and governance. Globalization is considered to be neo-liberal. Its normative base is the celebration of the market. In other words it is a triumph not only over so-called global "historic alternatives" [F. Fukuyama (92), *The End of History and the Last Man*] but also over unions and Keynesian states. In fact, elites on behalf of the states are real authors of globalization.

Globalization has become the current *mantra* or even panacea to solve all human problems. It is believed that the achievements of globalization would make the people all over globe happy, prosperous and contended and that there would be no conflicts, no poverty and inequality, no violation of human rights, no malnutrition, no illiteracy, and no disease, etc. Each individual and community would be so integrated with the world that the benefits would flow both laterally and vertically so smoothly that no one would remain untouched by prosperity. There would be nation-state without boundary. It is said that global markets, global technologies, global ideas and global solidarity can enrich the lives of people everywhere, greatly expanding their choices. The growing interdependence of people's lives calls for shared values and a shared commitment to the human development of all people. This era of globalization is opening many opportunities for millions of people around the world. Increased trade, new technologies, foreign investments, expanding media and Internet connections are fuelling economic growth and human advance. All these offer enormous potential eradicate poverty in the twenty-first century. Today we have more wealth and technology—and more commitment to a global community—than ever before.

But reality is totally different. Recently there has been increasing disillusionment among policy-makers in several parts of the world and some fundamental questions are asked. These are: Who want globalization? Globalization for what and for whom? Why is globalization of human resource not taking place? Do people want globalization? It is said that the issue of globalization is receiving considerable attention but no work is being done on the social costs involved (in terms of poverty, inequality, unemployment and tensions) nor on the growing marginalization of people in India as well as in other developing countries. The progress in areas like health, education and other social sectors are slowed by the diversion of precious human resources for national security and in combating terrorism and separatist movement. It is also said that the culture of consumerism is the product of globalization. Almost all the consumer items that are being promoted to sustain the economic growth have significant impact on nation and society directly or indirectly. The concept of globalization and the culture of consumerism are antithetical for all that Indian culture stands for. The new information technology and advances in telecommuni-cations have tended to erode the heterogeneity of national life styles, social and economic values and even cultures. This is visible in the standardization of consumer tastes in favour of fast foods (evidenced by the omnipresence of McDonald's and Coca Cola) and American films and soap operas. Consumerism is based on domination, hegemony, exploitation, alienation, concentration of knowledge, wealth and power. On the few top TNCs of the developed nations have inreased their profits manifold, on the one hand, a very significant majority of people around the world are still struggling for their basic needs and existence. The people of Asia, Africa and Latin American regions are still not part of the globalization.

In the present scenario, globalization is irreversible and unstoppable. Most of the countries of the world, willingly or unwillingly, have already accepted it and others may have to accept it. However, it is mostly agreed that globalization should be introduced with humane face for the benefit of the poor and needy. The challenges arising out of globalization require total newness on all fronts—from government to NGOs levels. In this article an attempt has been made to analyse the broad concept of globalization and its effects on people in terms of growth and productivity, poverty and income distribution, as well as employment.

Globalization: A Conceptual Analysis

Globalization means different things to different people according to their ideology and perception. The word globalization is used in two ways. In a positive sense, it is used to describe a process of increasing integration into the world economy. In other words, it means the expansion of economic activities across national boundaries. It is also used to prescribe a strategy of development based on a rapid integration with the world economy and view it as salvation. In other words, globalization is a process associated with increasing economic openness, growing economic interdependence and deepening economic integration in the global economy. In negative sense, it is seen as domination by developed nations over developing nations. In most of the countries, particularly those belonging to the developing world, liberalization policy has not been evolved indigenously. It has been adopted under World Bank—IMF combine conditionality of which internal and external liberalization policies are integral part.

Globalization is not new. Recall the early sixteenth century and the late nineteenth. But this era is different:

New markets—foreign exchange and capital markets are linked globally, operating 24 hours a day, with dealings at a distance in real time.

New tools—Internet links, cellular phones, media networks.

New actors—the world trade organization (WTO) with authority over national governments, the multinational corporations with more economic power than many states, the global networks of non-governmental organizations (NGOs) and other groups that transcend national boundaries.

New rules—multilateral agreements on trade, services and intellectual property, backed by strong enforcement mechanisms and more binding for national governments, reducing the scope for national policy.

According to the World Development Report (2000-01) five actions are necessary:

Promoting global financial stability and opening the markets of rich countries to the agricultural goods, manufactures and services of poor countries.

Bridging the digital and knowledge divides, thus bringing technology and information to people throughout the world.

Providing financial and non-financial resources for international public goods especially medical and agricultural research.

Increasing aid and debt relief to help countries to take actions to end poverty within a comprehensive framework.

Giving a voice to poor countries and poor people in global forums.

The key features of globalization are: (a) Economic features: Growth in Trade; Growth in FDI and Capital Flows; Global Production and consumption; Global competition; Trade and Investment Liberalization Policies; (b) Non-Economic Features: Loss of National Sovereignty; Standardization of values and cultures. In other words, a major feature of globalization is the growing concentration and monopolization of economic resources and power by transnational corporations and by global financing firms and funds and globalization of national policies and policy-making mechanisms. National policies (including in economic, social, cultural and technological areas) that until recently were under the jurisdiction of states and people within a country have increasingly come under the influence of international agencies and processes or of big private corporations and economic/financial players. This led to erosion of national sovereignty and narrowed the ability of governments and people to make choices from options in economic, social and cultural policies. Governments now have to implement policies that are in line with the decisions and rules of these international institutions. The key institutions concerned are the World Bank, the International

Monetary Fund (IMF) and the WTO.

The other fundamental premise of globalization is the relatively unhindered flow of goods and capital (but not people) across national boundaries. There are three economic manifestations of this phenomenon—international trade, international investment and international finance. Globalization requires country's openness to the world economy. There are four elements that are conventionally considered in determining a country's openness to the world economy. There is, most importantly, (i) the proportion of a country's gross domestic product (GDP) that is involved in the international trade of goods and services. Than there is (ii) the related element of the level of tariffs, which speaks to the degree of protection accorded to local production against imports from the world economy. Beyond trade there is (iii) the element of the degree of transnationalisation of production, that is, the extent to which exchange of capital takes place for purposes of production; for the less developed countries, it refers primarily to the import of foreign direct investment (FDI). Transnationalisation of production stands on a different footing from international trade, even though trade is involved prior or subsequent to the production process. Essentially, while in the area of international trade during the era of globalization the relevant actors treat the world as a global market, in the internationalization of production the relevant actors treat the world as a global factory, the different constituent parts or division of which are located in several countries, yet from a single production system. Finally, but not unrelated to the previous elements, in (iv) the extent of state controls on capital movements

It is very common to hear the words privatization, globalization and liberalization. In fact, privatization and globalization are inherent in liberlization. The theoretical foundations for the policy of liberalization including privatization are provided by several interrelated strands of literature mainly contributed by New Right Schools of Thought, Property Rights Literature, the Principal-agent Relationship and Organization and Management Literature. In all there are four New Right Schools of Thought. These are (i) the Chicago School led by Friedman; (ii) the Austrian School led by Hayek; (iii) Public Choice School led by Buchanan, Tullock and Niskanen; and (iv) the supply side Economics School led by Laffer, Gilder and Wanniski. The New Right Schools of thought, inspite of intellectual differences, broadly maintain that state involvement leads to increasing monopoly, increasing budget and suppressing of entrepreneurial behaviour, limiting choice, over production of unwanted services and encouragement to waste and inefficiency. In view of this the New Right has forcefully argued retrieval of the state as a regulator and producer. Therefore, deregulation/ liberalization and privatization are amongst six-point reform agenda of the New Right. The other measures are the reduction of inflation, lower taxation, increasing role of market forces in the provision of public services and institutional and constitutional reforms. The aim of these reforms is to promote competition between rival bureaucracies, reduce the influence of interest groups and corporatist institutions and impose a constitutional upper limit on the public expenditure as a proportion of the gross national product.

The theoretical base of globalization is directly rooted in the principle of comparative advantage, specialization in the production of goods and services based on factor endowment and competition results in benefits to all countries in international trade. In the open economy model (i.e. economy having linkages with global market), international trade leads to factor price equalization and optimum pattern of resource allocation globally.

Globalization is a calculated imperialist design of hegemonization in economic, political, ecological and cultural terrains, threatening loss of economic, self-reliance and political sovereignty, erosion of democratic structures and damaging of plural cultural identities. Not only this, employment of protectionist policies, discriminatory trade conditions, direct intervention in the domestic affairs of LDCs regarding their intellectual property right amount to virtual 'trade war' and destabilization of the fragile economies and strife-ridden politics of the latter. Globalism would remain an idle fancy in the absence of genuine 'internationalism' that is, egalitarian interaction among nations.

As a culmination of the unbridled, unrestrained 'multi-national' capitals, globalization leaves the poorer countries behind in global competition, as the clear objective of capital mobility is profit, prestige and power for its owners and not the well-being of the people at large. This is confirmed by historical and empirical evidence. It is intrinsic to the nature of capital, as articulated by Lenin most vociferously, to move towards exploitable resources. As investments capital has moved and modernized, it has also in the process exploited people and natural resources and often left behind pollution, poverty, inequality, injustice, crime, corrupting and a general degradation of environment—a record not much different from the imperialist history of aggressive capitalism, obsessed with growth.

Globalization is a totalizing process in terms of both hegemonization and homogenization, and extended and subtler American version of European colonial/imperialist ambitions of domination, expropriating and transforming the world in its own image. Ideologically also, it is a derivative of the earlier conceptualizations of 'progress' and 'modernization', premised on the West-centric view of civilization, materialism and economies glorification of the 'invisible hand' of the market, growth-observed industrial industrialism, objectification of nature and an instrumental treatment of humanity.

The spectre of mass resistance and political movements is on the anvil in a majority of third world societies that have set out in the direction of globalization, constantly haunting and scaring to generate chaos and degeneration of whatever little is achieved by these societies. It appears that eventually globalization will prove to be a disaster for the developing societies that will push them into the oblivion of anarchy and instability reminiscent of the Hobbesean state of nature.

The Reality of Globalization

The end of twentieth century witnessed ushering in of an epoch of New World Order in which the idea of globalization found expression and flourished under the auspices and blessings of Breton Wood institutions—notably the World Bank and International Monetary Fund—paving a way for the neo-capitalist hegemony and subjugation in a more vigorous but civilized manner. As a matter of fact globalization is a latest dream selling exercise on the part of U.S. promising a transparent, free and rational world order, which will ultimately culminate into an ideal Global Village.

Liberalization, privatization and globalization are the buzzwords in contemporary world. All goals end here. Privatization worldwide began in 1980s because of rising debt and low commodity prices. Eastern Europe, Russia, Ukraine, Argentina, Brazil, Hungary, Mexico, Poland have already gone through the process. In support of privatization it is said that direct state involvement in commercial activities conflicts with its other roles. The real picture of liberalization, privatization and globalization is quite different and complex.

Uruguay Round agreement brought the WTO into existence. WTO agreements appear to be based on the hypothesis that liberalization is the panacea for all ills in the economy, trade and commerce for the society. The Uruguay Round agreement not only reduced trade barriers—by an average of 40 per cent—but also laid down rules for what kinds of policies governments can make on matters such as intellectual property and investment, making its impact more complex, more expensive to employment and more difficult to predict. It is generally advocated that the free trade would lead to higher rates of economic growth. But the fact is that economic globalization and trade liberalization have concentrated power in the larger entities we know as transnational corporations. It is the TNCs which have benefited the most in the era of globalization. Small farmers are unable to compete in the global economy and are being driven off their lands, leaving the door wide open to the corporations. Free trade has enslaved the hungry rather than freed them. Trade can help to achieve food security, but only if it is democratic and free from corporate control; only if it helps rather than hinders the poor. Further, about one-third of the global trade conducted by the MNCs is instrumental in liquidating national economies. In the political sphere, the nation-states find themselves increasingly constrained, as new enters of power emerge to delimit political sovereignty in terms of foreign aid, IMF loans, deregulation, etc. Growing concentration of economic resources and political power has also aggravated social schisms and conflicts.

The modern world has corporate-managed trade rather than free trade. The trade liberalization has failed the poor and stands in danger of giving trade as a whole a bad name. The poor are going hungry because of the way the trading system is working. Trade liberalization—'free' trade, trade without barriers—is harming, not helping them. The trade liberalization that the WTO oversees appears to be failing the poor, hindering rather than helping them, and handing power to transnational corporations.

India urged that developing countries be allowed greater autonomy in establishing and supporting domestic agricultural policy. A purely market-based approach might not be appropriate for developing countries, it said; for some countries, it might be necessary to adopt a market-plus approach, in which non-trade concerns such as the maintenance of the livelihoods of the agrarian peasantry and the production of sufficient food to meet domestic needs are taken into consideration. While it may not be possible to immediately ensure that developing countries are able to produce at least a minimum percentage of their annual food requirements, this is a goal that has to be pursued.

Globalization has an adverse effect on poor developing countries with an inadequate national capacity. Almost all the countries of the Third World have signed the WTO. While most have gained, the poorest, 800 million hungry people, have lost. Any society, national or international, will ultimately be judged on whether its systems, rules and regulations assist the most needy. By that criterion, the current international trade system is failing. People go hungry because they are too poor to grow enough or to buy enough food. On the other hand, in the late 1990s the world, as a whole, spent more than US $ 500 billion to combat the supposed 'millennium bug'—ten times more than rich countries give to the poor each year in development assistance. By contrast, the amount needed to have world hunger free by 2015—a target agreed at the 1996 World Food Summit—would be US $ 60 billion dollars over 15 years, or US $ 4 billion per year in increased spending, hardly an excessive amount.

Globalization is transforming trade, finance, employment, migration, technology, communications, entertainment, the environment, social systems, values, ways of living, patterns of thinking, cultures and patterns of governance. Unemployment, poverty, inequality and alienation are increasing, partly as a result of globalization. Crime, drugs, terrorism, violence, civil wars, diseases and environmental destruction are becoming globalized. Capital, technology and advanced skills dominate the more reality dispensable factors: unskilled labour and the environment. Cost reductions are carried out and labour and nature suffer. Globalization offers great opportunity for human advance—but only the stronger governance.

The globalization of production is weakening state-centric schemes for implementing economic, social and cultural rights, most dramatically in the wealthier countries of the Northern Hemisphere. It does not however seem to be creating viable alternative mechanisms. Semi-permanent unemployment, attributable in part to the development of increasingly global mechanisms of production and exchange, has already led to a modest shrinking of the welfare state in many countries in Western Europe.

In any case, the impact of globalization on economy, society and polity extends beyond external openness in respect of foreign trade, tariff levels, transnationalisation of production and capital controls. The existing attraction of globalization as well as international pressures, such as from the WTO, encourage domestic policy changes in an effort to bring about greater institutional convergence with the more advanced economies. These policy changes in turn, are likely to have additional impact on economy, society and polity.

Globalization is very uneven process, with unequal distribution of benefits and losses. This imbalance leads to polarization between the few countries and groups that gain, and the many countries and groups in society that lose out or are marginalized. Globalization, polarization, wealth concentration and marginalization are therefore linked through the same process. A World Bank study finds that the poorest 40 per cent of people in developing countries have seen their incomes fall since liberalization began. The evidence is powerful and it discredits the claims of Western government ministers that trade liberalization lessens poverty. The rapid growth of the global economy in recent decades is perhaps most clearly shown by the fact that in 1970 the total number of Transnational Corporations (TNCs) was about 700, but grew by 1998 to at least 53,607 TNCs that were contracted with at least 448,917 foreign subsidiaries. The six largest corporations in the world (Exxon, General Motors, Ford, Mitsu, Daimler-Chrysler, and Mitsubishi) have combined revenues larger than the combined budgets of 64 nations that include 58 per cent of the world's population (including India, Indonesia, Brazil, Russia, Pakistan, Bangladesh, Nigeria, and Mexico). Only seven nations have budgets larger than Ford, Exxon or General Motors: namely France, the United Kingdom, Italy, China, Japan, Germany, and the United States. Size of individual corporations in comparison to nations is impressive. However, their growing influence based on their growing number makes them even more powerful.

The world has become more polarized, with the gulf between the poor and rich of the world widening in recent years. From 1970 to 2000, the share of the poorest 20 per cent rose from 70 per cent to 85 per cent. Uneven globalization is bringing not only integration but also fragmentation, dividing communities and nations. In the aftermath of liberalization, manufacturing by license has given way to competitive manufacturing. Free trade is merely the global manifestation of the division of labour. The forces of global integration and technological advance can and must be harnessed to serve the interests of poor people. In 2000, of the world 6 billion people, 2.8 billion live on less than $ 2 a day and 1.2 billion on less than $ 1 a day. Six infants of every 100 do not see their first birthday, and 8 do not survive to their fifth. Of those who do reach school age, 9 boys in 100 and 14 girls do not go to primary school. These conceal extraordinary diversity and variations.

Globalization has divided the world into several factions that may be called Davos, Seattle, Moscow, Beijing, Tehran and Okinawa factions. The Davos faction includes some 1000 state and corporate elites that annually meet at Davos, Switzerland, to chart the course of globalization. It represents the interests of the Global 1000 largest TNCs and OECD group of rich nations. The Seattle Faction consists of those in the advanced capitalist countries protesting against World Trade Organization in Seattle last year, because their lives have been dislocated by globalization. The Moscow Faction is composed of those countries that by reason of their own failures or discrimination are being left out of the globalization bandwagon. The Beijing faction consists of those countries that have more or less successfully jumped on the bandwagon in the hope of benefiting from its fruits. As a Crossroad of Japanese, Chinese, Southeast Asian, and Western civilizations, the Tehran Faction could be interpreted to include the Islamic militant movement protesting against the economic, political and cultural domination of a western world order. The most eloquent spokesperson for its views happens to be but a secular Christian Palestinian nationalist, Edward said.

Globalization is thus affecting different categories of countries differently. This process can broadly be categorized as follows: growth and expansion in the few leading or fully participating countries; moderate and fluctuating growth in some countries attempting to fit into the globalization/ liberalization framework; and marginalization or deterioration experienced by many countries unable to get out of acute problems such as low commodity prices and debt, unable to benefit from export opportunities. The UNCTAD report also warns of the risks, stating "the process of globalization and liberalization can also give rise to a number of potential negative consequences and challenges to development". It gives details of the following three problems: lose of policy autonomy (the range of policy instruments available to developing countries has narrowed as a result of economic liberalization policies and stringent multilateral disciplines); financial openness and the risk of sentiments of external investor; and the phenomenon of marginalization (in which some developing countries, specially LDCs, are unable to benefit from or meaningfully participate in globalization due to structural supply-side weakness and debt.)

The uneven and unequal nature of the present globalization process is manifested in the fast-growing gap between the world's rich and poor people and between developed and developing countries, and in the large differences among nations in the distribution of gains and losses.

A large number of people in the developed and developing nation have strong reservations about the benefits of globalization to the poor nations and they have shown their resentment through protests on various. In advance of Seattle meeting, more than 1,200 NGOs from nearly a hundred countries—from environmentalists to labour unions, Third World development groups to consumer organizations signed a 'stop the WTO round' petition. The international trading system, said the petitioners, is 'inequitable, un-transparent and in conflict with national and international regimes that promote high environment and development standards'. They proposed a fundamental review of the system, and the development of 'an alternative, humane and sustainable international system of trade and investment relations'. And they urged governments to 'move away from the habit of shaping their international trade policies around offensive interests of large Transnational Corporations'. The recent meeting of WTO in France was also protested by the large number of people.

India and Liberalization

The aim of structural reform programme was to attain a higher rate of growth on sustainable basis through efficiency and productivity originating from relaxation of government controls over production, investment and prices in the domestic economy and progressively opening up of the Indian economy to foreign trade, capital and technology. The structural reform measures constitute the core of the economic liberalization.

Liberalization in India has two dimensions—internal and external. The domestic liberalization policy encompasses all facets of the Indian economy. However, thrust areas are industry, public enterprises, taxation, financial and infrastructure sectors.

The industrial sector has witnessed far-reaching reforms. The New Industrial Policy, 1991 abolished compulsory licensing for all except a few industries. The reform has enabled the taking out of the licensing system for more than 90 per cent of the industrial sector. In case of existing units all major expansions are exempted from licensing. The existing and new units are provided a new broad banding facility with a view to enabling them to produce any article without an additional investment.

In the area of public enterprises five major reforms have been introduced. First, monopoly of the state sector has been drastically reduced from seventeen to four. That is, thirteen industries have been opened to private sector, which was hitherto monopoly of the state sector. This is known as disguised privatization. Within existing public enterprises, sweeping changes favouring increasing role of market forces are in progress. These include performance improvement through a memorandum of understanding (MOU) system, referring of sick enterprises to the Board for Industrial and Financial Reconstruction (BIFR) for the formulation of revival/rehabilitation schemes or closure and enhanced autonomy to select public enterprises for enabling them to become global and domestic players.

Privatization has not been explicitly referred to in the NIP, 1991. Initially the word privatization, it seems has been avoided partly due to political considerations. In the first budget (1991-1992) immediately after the announcement of NIP, 1991, limited selling of government equity under the name of disinvestments policies was mentioned. The selling of government equity below 50 per cent continued till late nineties. It is during October 1999 budget that a full-fledged privatization policy was announced. Under privatization policy, 13 public enterprises and 21 hotels owned by the government have already been privatized.

Based on the recommendations of Chelliah Committee and Raikhi Committee tax reforms comprise of moderate rate of taxation, broadening the tax base, simplification in compliance and extension of modified value added tax (MODVAT) to other areas. Financial sector reforms consist of slashing of Statutory Liquidity Ratio (SLR) and thus increasing the availability of funds with banks, allowing private banks to expand, encouraging new entrants, simplification and rationalization of the interest rate structure. The Government has also opened insurance sector to private sector. The capital market is undergoing similar reforms.

The infrastructure sectors particularly telecommunication, power and roads which were traditionally monopolies have also been opened to the private sector.

External liberalization (i.e. globalization) in India has covered areas such as trade, foreign exchange, capital and technology. The major initiatives include current account convertibility of rupee, allowing exchange rate of rupee to be determined by the market forces in foreign exchange markets, abolition of import through licensing except for consumer goods, drastic reduction in import duties overtime, automatic approval of Reserve Bank of India for foreign equity in select high priority industries, the provision of automatic approval for technology agreements in select high priority industries. In addition Foreign Institutional Investors (FIIs) registered with RBI are permitted to operate in the capital market. Large number of incentives are provided to Non-Resident Indians (NRIs) and Overseas Corporate Bodies (OCB) to invest in India. Indians firms are also allowed to raise capital from International market through Global Depository Receipts (GDRs) and Foreign Currency Convertible Bonds (FCCBs).

Scarcity of income distribution data, obviously, makes it very difficult to arrive at precise assessment of the impact of Globalization on income inequalities, but it is clear that even after nearly one decade of advent of Globalization in India a vast gulf exists between the different income-earners with, as per *World Development Report*, 1999, top 20 per cent of the population accounting for 39.3 per cent of the total income while share of the bottom 20 per cent was only 9.2 per cent.

The point about retailing the foregoing data about persistence of individual-level poverty is that it gives rise to doubts about the positive pay-offs of Globalization as far as the regional inequalities also are concerned. While data sets about income inequalities at individual or percentile and decline levels are relatively scarce, a number of regional or inter-state inequalities data-sets have been generated making it possible to assess the impact of Globalization on real disparities.

According to *Economic Times Research*, the annual data show that over the period 1996 to 2000, 38 per cent of the companies declared losses at the net level in 2000 as compared to 16 per cent in

1996. In the period of economic reforms does the loss making companies whose percentage has increased represent the cost of liberalization.

The cost of economic reforms is also reflected in the number of cases with the Board for Industrial and Financial Reconstruction (BIFR). BIFR till the year 1998 has compiled figures about sick companies on the edge of closure. A total net worth of Rs. 17, 815.56 cr. Has been wiped out two and half times over by accumulated losses amounting to Rs. 7,159.54 cr. Over 2,454 units across 19 industries are affecting around 15 lakh workers. The extent of human disaster is particularly acute in industries like textiles, metallurgy and jute etc.

The various Rounds of Surveys conducted by the National Sample Survey Organization (NSSO) reveal that the average annual growth rate of overall employment (in both the organized and unorganized sectors) was 2.73 per cent per annum in the period 1972-73 to 1977-78 but declined to 1.54 per cent per annum in 1983 to 1987-88 to 1993-94. As per the 55th Round (July 1999-June 2000) of the Survey on employment conducted by the NSSO overall employment grew by about one per cent per annum during 1993-94 to 1999-2000. Employment in absolute numbers has risen from 303 million on 1983 to 374 million in 1994 (2.04 per cent) and to 397 million in 2000 (0.98 per cent). The labour force participation rate deceleration in the growth of the labor force from 2.29 per cent per annum in 1987-88 to 1993-94, to 1.03 per cent per annum in the period 1993-94 to 1999-2000.

A more detailed scrutiny of the inter-state variations in the growth-pattern (UNDP, 1999) shows that two states with high per capita income in 1980-91 viz. Punjab and Haryana lost momentum in the nineties while Maharashtra and Gujarat overshot them indicating that during the Globalization era the Green Revolution lost steam while industry-based growth of Maharashtra and Gujarat was gathering speed. In case (and the probabilities of this being the case are high) economic momentum of Punjab and Haryana declines further the inequalities between the different states of the Indian federal system would certainly be aggravated significantly. In more specific terms, states like Tamilnadu, Kerala, West Bengal, Madhya Pradesh, Andhra Pradesh and Karnataka would continue to stay at their current GNP ranks while Panjab and Haryana would decline and Gujarat and Maharashtra forge ahead while Uttar Pradesh, Bihar and Orissa would continue to remain at the bottom unless those associated with "public governance" address this issue of persisting areal imbalances directly rather than letting the markets (read: MNCs) adopt their basic policy of "Betting upon the strong."

Thus, a worrisome aspect of the impact of Globalization upon the state economies is revealed by the fact there are not only wide-ranging areal differentials in terms of decline of poverty in India but the "Green Revolution" states are finding it difficult to sustain their (low) poverty-shares. While Punjab and Haryana had, till recently taken giant strides in poverty reduction, but, Haryana has already begun to slip with its BPL share in population rising from 0.92 per cent in 1983-84 to 1.83 per cent in 1987-88 and then dipping but still remaining higher at 1.37 per cent in 1993-94 than 1983-84. More recent Planning Commission data updated to 1999-2000 has shown that Haryana has regained its 'quit poverty' momentum but, in a paper prepared as recently as October 2001, Jeffery Sachs, Anupam Bajpai and Annabhi Ramiah have noted that following the Green Revolution high growth occurred in Punjab and Haryana and also, to a lesser extent, in other adjacent states of Rajasthan, Gujarat and Maharashtra, but populous eastern states like U.P. and Bihar failed to take advantage of Green Revolution and this factor can be regarded a cause of "divergence" or enhancement in inter-state inequalities during the Globalization process in India.

One of the most visible manifestations of what one might call a "Globalization failure" pertains to the strategic front of inequalities, a failure which assumes great poignancy in the case of ROI since elimination of inequalities, individual as well as real, was one of the most prominent items on the manifesto of its long "freedom struggle"; the Indian National Congress, which enjoyed pre-eminent dominance for the first four decades of the short ROI history and which is even now in control of as many as 14 states spread in all corners of its vast territory, is also committed to this goal making monitoring of the economic dispersion of the gains (and losses) of Globalization in terms of the territorial contours of the Indian political system an urgent necessity as the political parties which evolve the "correct" policies of public governance on this score is likely to gain better territorial acceptability.

Mr. Manmohan Singh advocated greater interaction with the world and warned that "if our economy is not equipped to absorb, assimilate, and to adopt this technical change which is taking place, all over the world, I think we will be marginalized. Many developing economies are already being marginalized in the new global economic system that has emerged."

If the prevailing political and administrative environment continues, the possibility of recurring crises in the near future is not ruled out. The symptoms have already started appearing. Sluggishness in exports in spite of gradual devaluation of rupee via open market, increasing fiscal deficit, downgrading in international credit rating of India, bearish trend in the stock market, non-preparedness of the Indian people particularly the elite to pay more taxes, etc, are signalling towards another crisis. Liberalization, privatization and globalization policies seem irreversible in India. India should strive to manage these mega trends to the best of its advantages.

Summing up

Human Development Report champions the agenda of the world's weak, those marginalized by globalization, and calls for a much bolder agenda of global and national reforms to achieve globalization with a humane face. It cautions that globalization is too important to be left as unmanaged as it is at present, because it has the capacity to do extraordinary harm as well as good.

Liberalization, privatization and globalization policies have been exercising considerable influence on people and government. In developing countries like India, governance has responded both slowly and unevenly to economic liberalization. It is mainly due to the fact that liberalization policy in India has not evolved indigenously through the participation of political, bureaucratic and other institutions of governance. The liberalization policy is mainly adopted under the influence of World Bank-IMF combine. In case of India the institutions of economic governance have responded very quickly to economic liberalization. The post-liberalization phase has witnessed amendments in many economic laws as well as introduction of economic laws to deal with changed environment.

Supremacy of economic institutions particularly finance ministry accompanied by erosion in the role of planning commission in economic policy making is another outcome of economic liberalization. Setting of new institutions such as Ministry of Disinvestments, Disinvestments Commission, Expenditure commission and regulatory authorities in the field of telecom, power and insurance have increased the jurisdiction of economic administration in the Indian economy. Very fast growth of economic administration in response to liberalization, however, has not succeeded in achieving its goals such as a higher rate of growth on sustainable basis accompanied by improved efficiency and productivity in the Indian economy.

Further, these initiatives have covered mainly those services and areas, which cater to the elite. The areas of social concern such as poverty, unemployment, regional disparities and sectoral imbalance which have borne the brunt of liberalization policy have been kept out of these initiatives. This combination of coverage and neglect, if continued on the one hand would help the elite to consolidate its advantaged position and become partner of the ruling coalition of politicians and bureaucrats. On the other hand it would alienate further the disadvantageous groups, sectors and regions from the mainstream.

Competitive markets may be the best guarantee of efficiency, but not necessarily of equity. Liberalization and privatization can be a step to competitive markets but not a guarantee of them. And markets are neither the first nor the last word in human development. Many activities and goods that are critical to human development are provided outside the market—but these are being squeezed by the pressures of global competition. There is a fiscal squeeze on public goods, at times squeeze on care activities and an incentive squeeze on the environment.

In order to widen their policy options in the future and to strengthen their bargaining power, developing countries have to organize themselves to strive for a more democratic global system.

Greater collaboration among regional institutions of the South (for example, ASEAN, SAARC, SADC, Mercosur, Caricom etc.) especially in sharing of information and coordination of policies and positions, would be beneficial.

The developing countries should have more rights of participation in decision-making processes in the IMF, World Bank and WTO, which should also be made more accountable to the public and to the local and poor communities.

In the twenty-first century, much more focus has to be placed on changing economic policies and behaviour in order that the patterns of consumption and production can be made environmentally sound. What need to be discussed is not only the development model of the

South but much more the economic model of the North and of course to international economic order.

There is also a need to strive for governance at a national level that combines economic development, environmental concern and social justice. In both North and South, the wide disparities in wealth and income within countries have to be narrowed. In a situation of improved equity, it would be more possible to plan and implement strategies of economic adjustment to ecological and social goals.

As globalization becomes the new *mantra* of the powerful on the planet with the unholy Trinity—the IMF, the World Bank, and the WTO—claiming that it will solve all the economic problems of the world (including poverty and deprivation), it is time for the countries of Asia, Africa and South America to pause, take stock and critically appraise the whole process, examining the true and only options available to them.

The developing countries must be provided with a range of options regarding when, how and to what extent they should open their economies. For this, they must press their case in international forums and institutions where decisions on the global economy are made. Failure to do so would mean that they are subjected interminably to policies that further development prospects and options as well.

The developing countries should have more rights of participation in decision-making process in the IMF, World Bank and WTO, which should also be made more accountable to the public and to the local and poor.

There is also a need to strive for governance at a national level that combines economic development, environmental concerns and social justice. In both North and South, the wide disparities in wealth and income within countries have to be narrowed. In a situation of improved equity, it would be more possible to plan and implement strategies of economic adjustment to ecological and social goals.

We are aboard a train, which is gathering speed, racing down a track on which there are an unknown number of switches leading to unknown destinations. No single scientist is in the engine cab and there may be demons at the switch. Most of the societies are in the caboose looking backward.

REFERENCES

Alternative Economic Survey 2000-2001, New Delhi, Alternative Survey Group, 2001.

Babu, B. Ramesh (Ed.), *Globalization and the South Asian State* (Ed.), New Delhi, South Asian Publishers, 1998.

Beyeı, P., *Religion and Globalization*, London, Sage, 1994.

Bhalla, A.S. (Ed.), *Globalization, Growth and Marginalization*, London, Macmillan Press Ltd., 1998.

Bos, Dieter, *Privatisation: A Theoretical Treatment.* Oxford: Clarendon Press, 1991.

David, Dollar, *Globalization, Inequality and Poverty Since 1980,* (Washington D.C. World Bank), Mimeo, 2001.

Eisenstadt, S.N., *Modernization: Protest and Change*, Delhi, Prentice Hall, 1969

Fukuyama, F., *The End of History and the Last Man*, New York, Free Press, 1992.

Hirst, P.Q. & Thompson, G., *Globalization in Question*, London, Cambridge, 1996.

Kishore Adarsh, "Globalization, Living Standards and Equity: Recent Progress and Continuing Challenges: National Experience—India", Paper presented at the Workshop for G-20 Members, Sydney, May 26-28, 2002. Mimeo.

Kurian, N.J. and Ameresh Bagchi, "Regional Inequalities in India—Pre- and Post-Reforms Trends and Challenges for Policy", Mimeo, made available by Dr. Adarsh Kishore, Additional Secretary Ministry of Finance, Government of India, New Delhi, 2002.

Kurian, N.J., "Widening Regional Disparities in India: Some Indicators", *Economic and Political Weekly*, February, 12, 2000, pp. 538-550.

Louis De AIlesi, "The Economics of Property Rights: A Review of the Evidence", *Research in Law and Economics,* Vol. 2, 1980.

Magdoff, Harry, *Globalization: To What End?*, New York, Monthly Review Press, 1992

Nayar, B.R., *Globalization and Nationalism: The Changing Balance in India's Economic Policy, 1950-2000*, New Delhi, Sage Publications, 2001.

Nigel, Ashford, "The Ideas of the New Right", in Jordan and Ashford (ed.), 1993.

Peter, Aucoin, *The New Public Management: Canada in Comparative Perspective,* Montreal, Canada: Institute for Research on Public Policy, 1995.

Prahlad, K. Basu *et al., Governance and Government: Emerging Scenarios in the 21st Century* (Report for FCPC), New Delhi, 1996.

Robert, J. Holton, *Globalization and the Nation-State*, London, Macmillan Press Ltd., 1998.

Rostow, W.W., *The Stages of Economic Growth: A Non-Communist Manifesto*, London, Cambridge University Press, 1960.

Sheth, V.S. (Ed.), *Globalization and Interdependence: Africa and India, Mumbai*, Allied Publishers Ltd., 2000.

"The Economic Performance of The States in The Post-Reform Period". In Rakesh Mohan (Ed.) *Facets of The Indian Economy*. New Delhi, OUP, pp. 215-247.

UNDP, 1999, *Diversity and Disparities in Human Development: Key Challenges for India,* New Delhi.

World Bank, (2001), *World Development Report,* Washington D.C., World Bank.

2

Globalization:

The Nature and its Dynamics

HASSAN RANGRIZ

The recent wave of economic policy reforms in the developing world has been seen as a necessary consequence of a changed world economic system. The key feature of the changed world economy is the element of heightened economic globalization, which provides new external challenges as well as opportunities for development. As globalization has accelerated, it has come to loom large in the perceptions of policy-makers, and adjustment to it in the form of economic liberalization and the shrinking of the state has moved to the forefront of their economic agenda, even when not imposed on them. The phenomenon of economic globalization provides the widest possible context for the examination of economic policy reform. However, as a concept in contemporary social science, it appears in many variants. In one strong version, globalization refers to the presumed emergence of a 'supra-national', borderless global economy with its own laws of motion, encompassing and subordinating the various local economies in a single worldwide division of labour, rendering national governments into municipalities. A softer version of the concept treats globalization less as an end-stage and more as a process in which the 'international' economy becomes more closely integrated, with domestic economic agents increasingly oriented to the global market rather than to particular national economic advancement.[1]

Economic globalization can be said to have originated in the development of a regional international market in Europe as foreign trade increased following the commercialization of agriculture and national specialization in agricultural activities after the Middle Ages[2]. Meanwhile, in a process which can be fairly characterized as imperialism, several European states as they consolidated themselves during the course of the 'long' sixteenth century began bringing other vast geographic regions of the world under their political control and domination. In this manner, many of what had been earlier largely autonomous and self-sufficient economies of these regions were subordinated to the European economies. Thus, the origins of economic globalization lie in the rise of capitalism in Europe and the penetration by capitalism from that economic core into the regional economies of the periphery around the world. The process of penetration across the globe was not accomplished all at once but took place in a succession of expanding concentric circles.

This process was reinforced by the rise of industrialization, which arose as a spontaneous development in Great Britain, though definitely aided directly and indirectly by the state[3]. After having achieved its own industrialization under mercantilist auspices, Britain turned to liberalism in the nineteenth century, for as the most advanced industrial power it now perceived greater economic advantage for itself in the operation of freer trade. However, it has received more credit for its liberalism than was deserved, since in practice its trade policies towards other states were invariably affected by geographical or strategic considerations[4]. More particularly, in relation to the less developed world, while Britain preached the virtues of liberalism, it also insisted, through political and military coercion, on other nations opening their doors to economic penetration by it. Economic globalization thus developed not simply through the operation of some autonomous economic forces, but with military power serving as its necessary midwife. Consequently, its first challenge to economically backward and politically weak areas was invariably a military challenge to their security.

The rise of industrialization in Britain, because of the radical difference it made to the acquisition of wealth and power and, therefore, to economic welfare and military security, forcefully persuaded other European powers and European colonial settlements around the globe to launch their own programmes of industrialization under strongly protectionist or mercantilist policy regimes, intellectually legitimized by Alexander Hamilton in the United States (US) and Friedrich List in Germany. However, this option of economic nationalism was firmly closed for most countries in Asia and Africa because they were overwhelmed militarily by the North Atlantic powers and rendered into colonies or semi-colonies. The only exception during the nineteenth century was Japan, both because of the perspicacity of its leadership and the geopolitical fact that, situated at the northeastern edge of the Eurasian continent, it was far removed as a prey from the industrial powers. Interestingly, the goal of industrialization was integrally linked to the search for national security through military power in Japan's development as it was in that of virtually every major North Atlantic power.

Although economic globalization has thus been under way for long, there is as essential difference nonetheless between the earlier 'extensive' or 'widening' phase of globalization, which linked the entire world economically, and the more contemporary 'intensive' or 'deepening' phase. The extensive phase can be said to have been completed by World War I. The North Atlantic states had been especially active in extending globalization in this phase during the course of the long period between the end of the Napoleonic wars and World War I. The period largely saw internal peace among the North Atlantic powers while they were engaged in the enterprise of extending, forcibly or otherwise, their economic and political sway over the entire world. Indeed, it was Lenin's profound insight that the origins of World War I lay precisely in the completion of the imperialist enterprise of bringing the entire world under the domination of the North Atlantic powers and dividing it up among themselves, at which point they turned—as they were bound to—against each other over the question as to who should preside over the newly created world economy and international system. That question remained unresolved until the end of the World War II, which explains the economic and political turmoil of the inter-war period. The outcome of that war, however, placed most of the world, though not all of it, under the military, political and economic hegemony of the US[5].

It is with the end of World War II that the intensive or deepening phase of globalization began. Until then, the economic integration of the world was largely confined to international trade between national economies, with underdeveloped areas in the periphery tied in a colonial economic relationship, serving as sites for the extraction of natural resources, often as tribute, as kept markets for the manufactures of the North Atlantic powers. Industrial production in the world economy was largely organized in national systems, which were largely though not exclusively responsive to their internal markets. In the post-war period after World War II, the United States as the new hegemony reorganized the world's economic institutions, chiefly in the form of GATT and the Bretton Woods system, to establish what has been characterized as a liberal international economic order, but one that was clearly designed to serve the interests of the advanced industrial powers, more particularly the US.

Under the protective framework of the political and economic hegemony of the US across the world, powerful American corporations, looking for new markets in their search for larger private profits, spearheaded the setting up of production centres in many countries, especially in Europe, organized and coordinated from their headquarters in the US. So vigorous was the new thrust of expansion abroad by them—transformed in the process into multinational corporations (MNCs)—that cries about the spectre of American domination went up in Europe, particularly in France. However, in due course American MNCs were joined by MNCs from among the allies of the US in the OECD, and the expansionary thrust under their joint aegis accelerated from the mid-1970s onwards. While reflecting the heightened globalization, these MNCs, in turn, became the key agents in its intensification. Meanwhile, they grew ever more powerful so that many 'now dwarf some governments in economic power'[6].

Politics and economics as specialized activities for the pursuit of power and wealth, respectively, have been evident in human society since the development of social differentiation in human groups beyond the level of tribes or folk societies. But the unique organizational expressions of these two activities in the modern era—indeed, they are key to the very definition of the era as modern—are states and markets[7]. These two mighty innovations came to define European civilization over the last three centuries or so. Besides, they enabled Europe to overpower physically the rest of the globe, and in turn diffuse the two social institutions across it either by force or by example that process of building states and markets in areas outside Europe, and even in some parts of Europe, is a process that is still going on. Indeed, that is the very heart of the contemporary challenge of development for the less developed world.

The two mighty social innovations of Europe began their development in the sixteenth century. Although some interpretations, as in Marx, see the economy as the primary determinant, with the modern state viewed as an outgrowth of markets, others see the state as prior and determining. In the latter view[8], conflict among kingdoms led to the formation of the modern state, with war activities between states and the consequent need for mobilizing greater economic resources leading to the development of markets. Besides, in line with their prior and determining status, states have always attempted to keep markets subordinate to the higher interests of the state. Given the ambiguity of social facts, the dispute between these two contending views is unlikely to be resolved, but it is sufficient to note that, in the broad sweep of history, states and markets arose about the same time. Their rise was part of the birth of modernity in the world, while it in turn pushed modernity further. Having arisen together, the two social organizations, even they have their separate spheres, are interacting forces, affecting each other. They are dialectically connected, even as they have their separate logics.

The market is a coordination mechanism for the exchange of goods and services on the basis of relative prices. Ideally, it is a self-regulating mechanism that brings together buyers and sellers on a competitive basis. Driven by the motive force of maximizing private gain, the market orders the overall productive system on the basis of demand and supply, determining the allocation of resources among various economic activities. Its key feature of competition between buyers and sellers serves as the driving force behind the noted efficiency of the system. The competition determines which economic actors will survive or flourish on the basis of their efficiency. Survival in competition on the basis of efficiency often rests on innovation in technique, in production and distribution; indeed, technology has become an independent factor in production besides land, labour and capital, and a potent source of economic and political power in the world. The characteristic efficiency of the market system is believed to advance the absolute welfare of society, since everyone gains from it, at least over the long term, even if not in the same measure. This absolute advancement of economic welfare is based on the law of comparative advantage, where everyone contributes on the basis of one's endowment and benefits accordingly. The law, of course, entails a division of labour among economic actors, with specialization based on their capabilities. Absolute gain for all, obtained through the market system resting on a division of labour, implies that there is a basic and ultimate harmony of interests among economic actors, and that the market system should accordingly be allowed to expand since all would gain—eventually even if not immediately. Similarly, it suggests that political boundaries ought not to be allowed to stand in the way of such market expansion, and that different political units ought to be brought within the compass of a single market economic system. That at least has been the liberal creed since Adam Smith, who saw markets, if left alone, to be self-regulating and socially beneficial. In liberalism, absolute gain emergent from the market system has priority (as against relative gain which is critical to states) while political boundaries are seen as an obstacle to the efficiency of markets (as against their being regarded as constituting the very definition of states). Yet, instead of proceeding on the assumption of such absolute harmony in the long run, states have constantly intervened in their external markets or their economic relations with other states. Why that should have been so takes us to the nature of states.

The modern states exists in a world of other states, which are demarcated from each other territorially with defined boundaries, with each state sovereign over its people and claiming exclusive loyalty, monopoly of the legitimate use of violence, and sole responsibility for the protection of its territory and the welfare of its people. The key concerns of the state are fundamentally two: security in relation to other states and legitimacy in relation to its population, at least the important groups within it. Each concern has a critical bearing on markets and the economic system. Here, attention is first directed to national security and the associated need for economic autonomy.

Security is the primal interest of states; it is their very *raison d'etre,* situated as they are in an anarchical inter-state system. Security, in turn, requires power or capabilities, regardless of whether they are sought independently or in alliance. Such a capabilities pertain, in the first instance, to the military arena—the size and preparedness of the armed forces and the size and lethality of their weaponry. But such military power, in the ultimate analysis, rests on economic capabilities[9], succinctly articulates the connection; 'It sounds crudely mercantilist to express it this way, but wealth is usually needed to underpin military power and military power is usually needed to acquire and protect wealth'. There is a caveat, however, for there is a tension between the two elements, which apart from national security, there is, however, another external dimension to the intervention by states in markets to assure both wealth and power, a keener understanding of which requires a little backtracking in history. As states and markets arouse in the sixteenth century, they had somewhat contrary effects on the political and economic organization of the world. States tended to politically fragment the world, organized as they were on the basis of territoriality, legal sovereignty, and exclusive domestic jurisdiction. On the other hand, markets as they expanded tended to encompass several states within a single division of labour. As noted earlier, they further tended to promote integration between several regional economies of the world. Though over a considerable period of time the integration of the world economy took place through physical force, many countries also took part in it willingly as they saw economic advantage in it, in absolute if not relative terms. They continue to participate in it, because there is economic advantage or, put another way, because there is some economic penalty in not participating in it[10].

Even as it may have the potential to advance human welfare, economic globalization also results in the transfer of disturbances from one part of the world economic system to other parts of that system, as abundantly conveyed by the oil shocks of 1973 and 1979 and also by the market crash of 1987. Further, as UNCTAD (1999:v) [11] has pointed out: 'The hambling of the Asian tigers since 1997 has revealed the vulnerability of even the strongest developing economies to the powerful forces unleashed by globalization'. It also generates disturbances in national markets as the entry of economic agents from outside, such as MNCs, affects the fortunes of local economic actors. While the deeper economic integration of the world provides an apparent autonomy to the working of the global economic system, with its own laws of motion, it at the same time exercises an overpowering impact on national economies. National economies are increasingly buffeted by world economic forces which are not always amenable to effective national control. For example, 'financial volatility is a permanent feature of today's globally integrated financial markets' (UNDP 1999: 40) [12]. The consequence can be serious economic dislocations.

Such economic dislocations may eventually make for economic advancement and strengthening of economic capabilities through encouraging entrepreneurship and forcing the pace of innovation, but they can also result in the weakening and erosion of capabilities, marginalization, and de-industrialization. Regardless, they invariably make for gainers and losers. There is, therefore, an inevitable tension between globalization and social cohesion, raising the spectre of social disintegration[13]. Indeed, "international integration can lead to national disintegration. National disintegration may manifest itself growing unemployment, poverty, exclusion or marginalization[14]. In its social impact, globalization can thus let those struggles over shapers in the economic product, which necessarily pull states into them. The struggles are then carried out within and between states. Such struggles necessarily feed into economic nationalism, for states are loath to lose control over their national economies when the consequences can be disruptive for them and their societies. While willing to accommodate globalization for the economic benefits it may bring, all states prefer to maintain a certain level of national autonomy in economic affairs *vis-à-vis* other states.

There is, however, a more structured aspect to the impact of globalization—beyond the cyclical and episodic disruptions that may accompany it—that has implications for economic specialization, which has tended to place countries in a hierarchical order. It has resulted in dividing the economies into 'core' and 'periphery', often through economic and military coercion during the successive stages of an expanding world economic system. Even though the distinction between the two categories may be blurred at the margins, the core economies have been the centres of autonomous growth and expansion, more advanced in technology and research, specialising in capital and skill-intensive manufacturing and producing complex and higher-value goods. The rich economies of the core have thus been the dynamic centres of economic power. In contrast, the poor and marginalized economies of the periphery have stood at the other pole. Largely rendered into a source of raw materials and cheap labour or labour-intensive products as also a market for the higher-value manufactures of the core. The periphery economic were also made dependent on the core, with the core having the ability to transfer its economic disturbances to them or to dominate them politically, and thus to condition their development. Indeed, in some cases, the economic agents of the core—the MNCs in the post-war period—came to exercise dominant control over periphery economies. Globalization, in this perspective, appears then not as neutral universal force exerting itself uniformly around the world, but rather as representing the pressures of the economically advanced part of the world on the less developed part in an asymmetrically interdependent and hierarchically organized international economic system. In this system, the actors in the less developed part lack economic autonomy and are simply the objects of the decisions of the advanced part.

It has been abiding contribution of dependency theory, rising in revolt against modernization theory, to link the location of societies in the hierarchy of the international economy system with the possibilities of national development. Dependency theory was deeply pessimistic about the prospects for development of the periphery as long as it was integrated into the world economic system, which drained its economic surplus. It, therefore, recommended breaking away from the world system in the cause of development. Of course, this radical recommendation masked an *a priori* preference of the theory's proponents, often unstated, for socialism. In its determinative prognosis, dependency theory was subsequently discredited with the rapid industrialization of South Korea and Taiwan and their breaking of the periphery, like Japan earlier in the first couple of decades of the post-war period, deepening their integration with the international economic system by way of a strategy of export propelled growth. However, while dependency theory as a theory is no longer viable, its emphasis on the international system as a factor in national development is enduring. Although dependency theory tended to emphasize the economic aspects of the system, the strategic aspects are no less important in development. It is not without significance that all the three aforementioned countries made their industrial transition under the political and military umbrella of the US, while South Korea and Japan additionally had a substantial physical presence of American armed forces on their soil. Interestingly, China's adoption of an 'open door' economic policy in the post-Mao period was based on *a priori* factor strategic alliance with the US against the Soviet Union and on an understanding over access to the American market. Furthermore, the discrediting of dependency theory does not dissolve the fact of dependence or the lack of national autonomy as a major aspect of existential reality in an asymmetrically divided world.

Economic dependence in a hierarchical world economy has implications for the economic capabilities and well-being of the populations of the periphery states. If the economy is conditioned by outside forces, disturbances that are likely to be transferred to them from the more powerful economic centres would affect local populations adversely, in turn bringing the legitimacy of the wielders of state power into question. Again, dependence within a global system of economic specialization makes periphery countries vulnerable in the world, not only economically but also politically, since to be less advanced and weak economically means to be weak and vulnerable politically in the inter-state system. What matters for states is not simply absolute gain within a world economic system but also relative gain in an inter-state political system—relative gain as between core and periphery. Known as 'political realism' in international politics, this perspective, when translated into the economic sphere, has been referred to as mercantilism, and has historically served as the action framework for countries that are less advanced and, therefore, less autonomous. Against this, the core states, with the advantage of being economically advanced, have often insisted on liberalism as the disciplining framework for the world economic system which they dominate and benefit from. Indeed, one can quite legitimately maintain that liberalism is the economic policy of the strong and is at base the mercantilism of the more advanced economic powers!

From the very dawn of the differentiation between the core and periphery in an increasingly integrating world economy, dependent states have intervened to modify their integration into the world economy and to develop greater economic autonomy so as to advance their national interests, whether in terms of their relative economic and political position in the international system, or the welfare of the local population. They have intervened to replicate, in whole or in part, in their own economies the economic structures of the core countries. Thus was inaugurated in one country after another 'catch-up' industrialization, as if in a ripple effect. As against the core countries which, because of their initial economic head start and therefore economic advantage, believed in free or liberal trade, or 'outward orientation', the late industrializes adopted mercantilist or protectionist policies to foster economic growth and development. In this fashion, they tended to cut down their integration in the world economy, for a shorter or longer period, at times with a view to subsequent re-insertion into the world economy on a more equal basis with the core countries, that is, coordinate with them rather than subordinate to them. In other words, they tried to disengage themselves from the world economy or to disassociate, or to delink from it, that is, they chose an economic strategy of 'inward orientation' or 'self-reliance'. They did this in varying measure and through various techniques-tariffs, quantitative restrictions on imports, and non-tariff barriers. Some carried mercantilism to an extreme so as to set up national autarkic economies, as in the case of the erstwhile Soviet Union and Maoist China. It is nonetheless clear that markets do not exist as creatures given by the forces of nature but are constantly shaped by states in considerable measure because of the very international economic and political order in which they are located.

Justified as excessive inward orientation may be in terms of national security and dependency-reserve or economic autonomy, there are costs to it also. Countries adopting this economic strategy fail to take advantage of the opportunities and advantages that participation in the larger world economy provides. This specific strategy can, moreover, introduce serious economic distortions and therefore inefficiencies and heavy economy costs. For, in attempting to simply replicate the economic structures of the core, it limits taking adequate, if not the fullest, advantage of the particular endowment of the country. One consequence is the setting up of high-cost economies that produce goods of low quality that no one on the outside wants, making for serious balance of payment problems. By the same token, it results in the smuggling in of goods and currency and the setting up of a parallel black economy. States are consequently led to weigh carefully the relative advantages and disadvantages of participation in and withdrawal from the world economic system. The principal issue in economic policy reform for states on the external dimension, therefore, becomes the orientation of the national economy to the world economy. Should the posture be one of inward orientation or outward orientation, disassociation or association, delinkage, 'closed door' or 'open door', or some combination of the two?

This is an issue that cannot have a single answer for all time and for all countries. The answer would depend on the size of the economy, the nature of its endowment, its stage of development, the capacity of its institutions, and its geopolitical location in the inter-state system. Nor can there be a single answer of national scope. The issue would need to be constantly evaluated for various economic sectors in terms of costs and benefits. Perhaps the issue itself should not be either-or, but to what extent. The response would also need to take into account the specific features of the international economy. Here, the stage of intensive globalization seems to raise profound questions both for social science and for the protection of domestic industry.

NOTES

1. Hirst, Paul and Grahame Thompson, *Globalization in Question*, Cambridge, Polity Press, 1996, pp. 7-16.
2. Wallerstein, Immanue, *The Modern World System*, New York, Academic Press, 1974.
3. Gleiss, Linda, *State and Economic Development*, Washington D.C., Institute for International Economics 1990, Chapter 4.
4. Gowa, Jaonne, *Allies Adversaries and International Trade*, Princeton: Princeton University Press, 1994, p. 5.
5. Lenin, V.I., *Imperialism: The Highest State of Capitalism*, New York, International Publishers, 1974.
6. UNDP, Human Development Report, New York, Oxford University Press, 1999.
7. Gilpin, Robert, *The Political and Economy of International Relations*, New York, Basic Books, 1987.
8. Tilly, Charles (ed.), *The Formation of National State in Western Europe*, Princeton: Princeton University Press, 1975.
9. Kennedy, Paul, *The Rise and Fall of Powers*, London, George Allen and Unwin, 1998.
10. Nayar, Baldev Raj, *The Modernization Imperative and Indian Planning*, New Delhi, Vikas, 1997.
11. UNCTAD, Trade and Development Report, New York: United Nations 1999.
12. *Ibid.*
13. Rodrik, Dani, *Has Globalization Gone Too Far*, Washington D.C.: Institute for International Economics, 1997.
14. Bhalla, A.S. (ed.), *Globalization Growth and Marginalization*, Hampshire: Mac Millan, 1998.

3

Contradictions and Challenges of Globalization:

Need for an Alternative

SAROJ MALIK

Globalization is the new buzzword of the last decade of the twentieth century, instrumental in comprehending the changes that have encompassed the socio-cultural and politico-economic spheres of life at local, national and global levels in the recent past and continue even today. Globalization is an idea whose time has come, at least to judge by theway the word is branded about. It is, of course, a controversial and the most widely used and misused term defined in all sorts of ways most nebulous and misunderstood,[1] but still it is popular like an ideology, that currently dominated thinking, policy making and political practice. Its project is global capitalism, or the application of the ideas and institutions of market economy to the world as a whole.[2] Now anyone who dissent globalization is being labelled as backward looking and anti-modern. It reflects the perception that the world is now more interconnected and supposedly more interdependent than it was formerly. It is both a description and a prescription.[2] As a description, Globalization refers to the widening and deepening of the international flow of production, capital, free movement of goods and services, finance, technology management enterprise and consumer tastes. The International and economic order is evolving highly into an electronic network system. Globalization implies the maxim, 'bigger is better'. As a prescription globalization involves the liberalization of national and global markets in the belief that it will produce the best outcome for growth and human welfare.

It evolves the vision of a borderless world dominated by multinationals and financial markets, in the sweep of a homogenised culture shaped by western values on the basis of grand narrative of reason. Perhaps because of the ideological dominance of Neo-Liberal capitalism today, the economic dimension is seen to be the sole idea of globalization. But this is to truncate the process and miss some of its most critical contradictions and crucial challenges. As Giddens pointed out:

> 'Globalization is not only, or primarily, an economic phenomenon, it should not be equated with the emergence of a world system. Globalization is really about the transformation of space and time. I define it as action at distance and relate its intensifying over recent years to the emergence of means of instantaneous global communication and mass transportation.'[3]

But behind this imagined oneness, it presents a picture of paradoxical contrasts, wrapped with number of contradictions and challenges. There is poverty amidst plenty, overproduction *vs* undernourishment, affluence, consumerism and wasteful life in contrast to bare needs and survival, over development *vs* underdevelopment, economic growth *vs* ecological crisis, explosion of knowledge against vast masses of illiterates, universalisation *vs* intense parochialism and homogeneity *vs* heterogeneity. Science and technology instead of being utilised in the service of humankind are used as instruments of domination, exploitation and destruction.[4] Hence given the ambiguities and contradictions involved, it is apparent that globalization is not a single unified phenomenon, but a single syndrome of processes and activities. The illusion of progress turned out to be self-delusion. Due to these contradictions many people all over the world perceive Globalization more as a threat than as a promise. There is now a whole range of interpretation and responses to these phenomena from the sceptics, who exaggerate the consequences for better or worse, to the hyperglobalisers, who doubt both, the intensity of change and usefulness of the concept itself. Somewhere between the two ends of the spectrum, between hyperglobalisers and sceptics are the 'transformationists'. For whom'Globalization is a central driving force behind the rapid social, political, and economic changes that are reshaping modern societies and world orders.'[5] The illusion of progress turned out to be self-delusion. Due to these contradictions many people all over the world and India in particular, perceive globalization more as a threat than as a promise. It is in this backdrop, the need of the hour is to adopt a dictum of 'small is beautiful', where man is the centre of our concern and where development is of the people, for the people and by the people and a holistic attitude is required that covers all human and the whole of humanity. Keeping this view in focus, this chapter is divided into two parts:

1. In the first part an effort is made to highlight the contradictions, drawbacks and discontents of globalization in general and its impact on Indian society in particular.
2. In second part, thrust will be on Gandhian ideas as an alternative to globalization, contradictions, discontentment and challenges.

I

The project of global capitalism is an imperial project. Its area of control is not limited to particular territories, rather it controls the whole world economy and global markets everywhere and all the time.[6] For Anthony Giddens, it means acting and living (together) over distance, across the apparently separate worlds of national states, religions, regions and continents. While A. D. Smith calls it methodological nationalism. According to which the contours of society largely coincide with those of the national state[7]. In other words the unity of national-state and national society comes unstuck; new relations of power and competition, conflict and intersection, take shape between, on the one hand, national states and on the other hand, transnational actors, identities, social spaces, situations and processes. Under globalization, economic development tends to push societies into a common direction, but rather converging, they seem to move along paths shaped by their cultural heritages. The future may look similar, but it won't feel like one. On the contrary the world has become more differentiated, more insecure, more fragmented along with growing gaps in social and economic in equality[8]. Globalization is caught up in the contradictions and discontentment of uneven and combined economic, political and cultural dimensions.

But where lies the roots of this globalised contradictions and discontentment?

The root cause for the current global malaise are following:

1. Massive and reckless industrialisation.
2. De-humanization of science, technology and industry.
3. Ineffectiveness of nation-states.
4. Newfangled consumerism.

Massiveness means mass production leading to mass surpluses, necessitating mass distribution and mass consumption through massive technologicalisation, capitalisation, and monopolization. Though Globalization has achieved stunning achievements in the establishment of a world market of trade and development that is threatened only by increasing environmental pollution, international and intranational inequalities, exclusively regional blocs and the political upheavals that may result from those. It focused on one polity, one form of political organizations best serving the interests of global capitalism. Critics says the process of globalization is lop-sided because it imposes the political and cultural standards of one region of the world namely the west, on all other regions. Globalization is westernization by another name. It undermines the cultural integrity of other cultures and is therefore repressive, exploitative, and harmful to most people in most places.[9] Globalization replaces the image of separate individual societies with one world system in which everything—every society, every government, every company, every culture, every class, every household, every individual must insert and assert itself within a single division of labour. The whole planet operates within this regulatory mechanism of binding and constant division of labour, which we call the capitalist world economy.

Dehumanization implies total concentration of the industries on commercial profit and economic power to a total exclusion of concerns for human health and happiness in terms of physical, intellectual and economic well-being.[10] Capitalist world economy on one hand is governed by the principle of profit maximization and on the another hand the appropriation of surplus labour takes place within a relationship of exploitation not between two classes but among three layers: the central areas or heart lands, the semiperiphery and the peripheral countries and region, which increase the level of conflicts and inequality within the world system. The inner logic of capitalist world system endangers both world integration and world decomposition. The root of problem is how to re-embed the economy in society. Threats create society and global threats create global society. The theory of world risk society, maintains that it is no longer possible to externalize the associated risk conflicts place a question mark over the whole institutional structure. Mainly three kind of risks or threats may be distinguished—First, conflict over the bad or other side of various goods that is ecological destruction and technological industrial dangers caused by affluence. Secondly there are ecological destruction and industrial dangers caused by poverty. Third is danger from weapons of mass destruction. Weapons of mass destruction, available not only to states but also to private organizations (private terrorism) means of existing political threats, will become a new source of danger in world risk society.[11] Advanced industrialism, whether under capitalism, communism or Fascism becomes dehumanized by focusing on productivity and competitiveness, and on power and profit through increased automation and unemployment. The impact of Globalization are evident in the recent post-1991 model of India with its *mantra* of foreign investment is not going to be of much help, and may in fact land us in more difficulties in the near future.[12] Foreign investors and multinational companies have not come to India to create jobs, they have come to make profits. If they create new jobs, it is only for urban masses and elite class and not for common rural masses. Year after year they have been getting rid of the staff in their own countries, in an effort to hike productivity and profits. There is hardly any multinational which is not trimming its labour force.

We do not need more Macdonald's, Pizza hut or Pepsis. They create no wealth only help consume wealth. It is resulting in economic decline and social decay. Impact of globalization are also evident on the village life of India. Due to the irrational mechanization, which was mainly tractorisation relieved village men from arduous jobs of farming and they engaged themselves in playing cards and drinking. The political leadership of the states cleverly look advantage of this situation and exploited these idle people in organising political rallies. Young men instead of engaging themselves in agricultural operations started looking for the white collar jobs. Sometimes these frustrated youths engage themselves in criminal activities.

Globalization in social sciences may be understood and developed as a fruitful dispute. About which basic assumptions and images of society, which units for analysis, can replace the axiomatics of the national-state. The most important political fallout of globalization is the decline of nation-state. David Held, rightly argues that the nation state is being undermined by the forces of globalization. He even foresees its eventual displacement by a world Government.[13] State power is further reduced because transnational grows in scale as well as in number. Wallerstein—one of the first in the seventies to confront the social sciences with the question of Globalization—introduced the concept of a world system and argued that capitalism was the engine of Globalization. Rosenau, Gilpin and Held have concerned themselves more with international politics. They challenge the nation-state orthodoxy by stressing the importance both of technological globalization (the science and information society) and of political-military factors and viewpoints (power politics).[14] In the wake of globalization countries like India, are attempting both, to preserve their national sovereignty and autonomy in global affairs against the dominance of a growing world capitalist system and at the same time opening up selectively, in order to absorb the benefits of the expanding market.[15] The proponents of globalization argue, that liberal democracy is the only suitable form of governance both for managing the modern state and for mediating the forces of rapid economic and cultural exchanges in all societies. Democracy is far liberalization and its development model is part of the larger agenda for globalization. It is a democracy tailored to suit the needs of the market economy, and ignore the traditional value of democracy such as human dignity, freedom equality and justice. Now the focus of the strong state is, in terms of capacity to implement change and not in strengthening participatory democracies.

Kelvin Robins has argued that the development of the world market has far reaching consequences for cultures, identities and life styles. The keyword here has become Macdonaldization. According to this view, there is an ever greater uniformity of lifestyles, cultural symbols and transnational modes of behaviour. In other words it focused upon a single commodity world where local cultures and identities are uprooted and replaced with symbols from the publicity and image departments of multinational corporations. Robertson proposes replacing the concept of cultural globalization with that of Globalization, through a combination of the words 'Global' and 'local'.[16] Culturally globalization has produced contradictory effects. Globalization has opened up the corridor of markets flooded with variety of consumer goods, forcing individuals to earn more, in order to acquire more, yet can never reach a point of contentment. In this consumerist society, the consumption in general and possession and display of certain objects in particular (like designer clothes, expensive cars, labelled shoes and other accessories) are used as recognition props for self-expression and self-gratification, reducing human essence to mere existence[17]. Those who cannot have access to material things envy others. Envy has become a social transformation of aggression, in which self comparisons elicit the desire to have, or snatch or destroy that others have. The significance of man has lost its meaning and purpose and reduced to mere mechanical drudgery. The material progress beyond the requirement of the satisfaction of basic needs and comforts is causing deterioration in the inner self of man. Beneath the surface pleasure of transitory relationship, recognition of self and manipulated consumption, exhibits the underlying malaise from sadness to anxiety and from pathos to panic. The hyper-modernity of our time is destroying the possibility of society, as a unified entity in a universe, that appears to be dominated by money, pleasure and technology.

Is there a way out of this Iron Cage?

There is a need for a great shift and an alternative.

An alternative of a humanistic world view is required which can be a timely corrective to the misplaced priorities of contemporary development based on Globalization model. An alternative mechanism of global, social, economic and political organizations based on certain republican principles: that is the self government of communities in which the public good is at the fore. In the new model there should be only a limited scope for foreign investors, for they cannot be main players in the future scenario, without such model, the mismatch between the nation and its citizens will not disappear. In the new millennium, it is we Indians who have to play the main role, it is we who have to save more, invest more, educate more, plan more and create a new world for those who have been left behind in the development game. All paradigms from globalization to communism have failed to solve the basic problems of poverty, hunger and unemployment, on one hand, and alienation, dehumanization, resource exhaustion, environmental pollution, ecological threat violence, and war on the other hand.

Gandhian Alternative is in fact a reinstatement of the humane that has been displaced by the technicist world view and the infrastructure of the industrial capitalist civilization.[18] The distorted, dismembered and institutionally split self created by globalization can be realigned, reformed and reintegrated with the social in Gandhian schema. Gandhi insisted on self development, offered an alternative life style, alternative world vision and viable set of strategies and peaceful methods for eliminating dehumanized globalization.

II

His philosophy centres around the individual, who through a revolutionary transformation of self, initiates a process of social ordering and helps to create institutions that install and sustain a normal civilization. This requires the cultivation of self in a particular manner and of a particular life style. His development process started at the individual level and is to be attained by educating the masses to a sense of their capacity to regulate and control authority at local, national and global level in ever widening and never ending circles. Gandhi recognises the brute in man and believed that we have become human by a slow process of evolution from the brute. He visualises that 'Satanic' modern civilization',[19] which presents to men all the allurement of material comforts and tempts him to remain a brute.

For realising the self, the first essential thing is the cultivation of a strong moral sense. Morality for him is the acquisition of virtues and selfless service. But acquisition of virtue is not a goal for Gandhi, it is only a beginning for the great spiritual adventure of self-realization. Influenced by the philosophy of *Gita*, he distinguished between the two forms of self—a lower self that is *dehin*, by which man is involved in his worldly activities of *artha*, power, property, security and *kama*. For the proper functioning of the self, it should work within the framework of *dharma*—which is higher self. The Pentagon virtues of Truth, Non-violence, Non-possession, Celibacy and Fearlessness constitutes the basis for an extended self, which in turn manifests itself in compassion and humility. But the global economy of today is creating strong, aggressive, clever and competitive individuals who wish to become rich and powerful.[20]

In his small village Republics, he conceived the relationship between the individual and society as analogous to that between the drops and the ocean. The drops even while they can claim individuality cannot survive without the ocean. So the necessity of remaining in the world arise because on the one hand the world is essential for self-development and on the other world has to be shaped in the image of the freedom and morality that one seeks to attain in one's own life. The search for liberation implies self-development. The process of self-disclosure is thus transformed in the process of co-disclosure. The society which does not fulfil the basic necessity of life and which does not allow to enjoy the fruits of one's labour is not an organic society. For inculcating selfless notions in individual and society, he gave the principle of non-possession. Though complete non-possession is an abstraction. There is a distinction between possession and possessiveness. The evil lies not in possession but possessiveness which is the root cause of conflict. He was of the opinion that there is enough in this world for everyone's need but there is nothing in this world for anyone's greed. For him a social order is a system of elements, inter-related and inter-dependent, which must realise the ideal of a non-competitive, classless, egalitarian society without going through the travail of class war. But under globalization, there would be fierce competition to capture the markets of foreign lands.

For Gandhi each village should be a microcosm of the macrocosm of India—a web of loosely interconnected to give them the status of village Republics. The village community should embody the spirit of home, an extension of family, rather than a collection of competing up individuals. In fact in such a society, State becomes superfluous and undesirable, as every individual in it has attained so much control over himself that he is never a hindrance to his neighbour. For it is a self-regulated society in which there does not remain any need of an external authority to regulate the conduct of individuals. Members of village communities will take care of themselves, their animals, land, forestry and all natural resources for the benefit of present and future generation. It is a society free from exploitation, inequality, class domination, class, conflict, communal disturbance, strikes and any kind of violence.[21] Today in our society there is hierarchy but no community. It has to come from within.

He laid emphasis on Panchayati Raj or democratic decentralization till the last moments of his life, which is the only way out of the devastating effects of concentration and mechanisation of political and economic power. The spirit of democracy cannot be evolved by forcible methods. To him Decentralisation envisions and upholds the cultural and spiritual ideal of simple living and high thinking. He does not hanker after raising merely "the standard of living', he wants to raise the 'standard of life'. Moreover, the important thing for Gandhi was not life itself but 'quality of life'.[22] Moral progress was possible only in a decentralised set-up. He affirms, without decentralisation it is impossible to ensure individual liberty and mental and moral growth of man. Gandhi does not seek, only the decentralization of political power, he rather pleads for decentralization of both economic and political power. The success of political decentralisation depends on economic decentralisation. The essentials of his village Republics were: self-regulation, self republic and self-reliance.

Gandhi's views on economic decentralization stem from his concept of *swadeshi*. In a broad sense, *swadeshi* implies three things, firstly, production, consumption and exchange of goods and services should be locally centred. Secondly it suggests reliance on native polity or indigenous political institutions. Thirdly, it portrays the self reliance as the basic units of society.[23] Gandhi wanted production by the masses in place of mass production. Normally it is known and accepted by one and all that, power flows from top to bottom, rather than the other way around. The village economy has to be diversified to be self sufficient. Gandhi fervently hoped to revitalise the village community in all facets—economic, political and moral.

On political decentralisation, Gandhi stressed that the role of government should be limited to those spheres of activity which cannot be handled by the village panchayats. Gandhi envisions a structure of society, a parallel polity which would exist in the form of an economically self-sufficient, politically self-governing panchayat system as an independent set of institutions from that of parliamentary institutions. Democracy should function with citizens occupying the centre voluntarily. The citizen's centres will bring the citizen to the centre to usher in people's politics in place of party politics.

In the present political context parties have only opportunistic politics. They will join in an alliance with anybody at anytime. All these alliances are not on the basis of any principle but only on the basis of mutual convenience. No doubt dissent is the essence of democracy, but defection is not dissent, rather, it is distortion of democracy. The entire political space is occupied by political parties and people are feeling more and more alienated from the political system. Thus Gandhian decentralisation is a process of limiting the power of the state as well as creation of people's institutions that run parallel to representative centralising institutions and processes. In this way, 'decentralisation is both a means and an end'.[24] Gandhian economic order was not separated as today from the moral and religious order. The experience of mankind testifies to the fact that collective life is more genial, varied and fruitful when it is concentrated in small units and simpler organisations. It is only the small units that have the most intensive life. Collective life itself in vast areas would be wanting in cohesiveness and productiveness. The institution of self sufficient political unit will give training, impart education, provide sustenance and work and above all create consciousness about the need to resist injustice, oppression or aggression. But in the era of globalization, a few clever multinational corporations would win and small companies in most countries would lose. There would be perpetual economic crisis, perpetual unemployment and the world would end up full of discontented human beings.

For Gandhi all activities of man constituted an indivisible whole. But today we dichotomise life into exclusive compartments of politics, economics, society and religion, which are devoid of morality. There is a lack of harmony between man and man, class and class, nation and nation and between man and nature. Consequently our present miseries are mainly due to lack of a holistic approach. When all life is one and whole universe including everybody is the manifestation of God, then why there should be petty conflicts.[25] The entire cosmos is cooperative. When we realise that the world is a mutual, interdependent, cooperative enterprise, then we can build a noble environment. Think globally and act locally in a world that has shrunk metamorphically into a village because of communication technologies and global economies. The root of all actions is in thought. Right action has its roots in right thoughts.

Hence, globalization is not a panacea for the contemporary world crisis, globalization is deepening these crisis. The remedy lies in the deglobalization of the dehumanized trade, investment, and aid schemes. The answer for the twenty-first century lies in the rehumanization of science technology and industry. Having thus clearly visualized dangerous direction in which globalization was pushing the world, Gandhi had worked out a worthwhile alternative for man's peaceful, purposeful and happy existence. In fact, if we want culture of peace and harmony, we must have a technology of peace. Hence, 'small is beautiful' is an answer to 'gigantism mania', which has no rational basis. Gandhian model will bridge the gap between individual and society, city and town, local and global.

NOTES

1. Beck, Ulrich, *What is Globalization*?, Polity Press, U.K., 2000, p. 19.
2. Peters, James and Veltmeyer, Henry, *Globalization Unmasked: Imperialism in the 21st Century*, Madhyan Books, Delhi, 2001, p. 11.
3. Giddens, Anthony, *Beyond Left and Right: The Future Radical Politics*, Polity Press, U.K., 1994, p. 4.
4. Mohanan, B., (ed.), *Gandhi Legacy and a New Human Civilisation*, Gyan Publishing House, New Delhi, p. 72.
5. Heredia, Rudolf C., "Globalization and its Politics: Contradictions and Challenges", *Social Action*, Vol. 52, No.1 Jan.-March 2002, p. 2.
6. Koshy, Ninan, "Political Dimensions of Globalization", *Economic and Political Weekly*, Vol. XXVI, No.18, May 5, 2001, 1514.
7. Beck, Ulrich, *op. cit.*, pp. 20-21.
8. Tehranian, Majid, "Globalism and its discontents: The role of NGO's in the emerging Global Society", *Gandhi Marg*, Vol. 18, No. 4, Jan-March 1977, p. 402.
9. Lechner, Frank J. and Boli, John (ed.), *The Globalization Readers*, Blackwell Pub., U.S.A., 2000, p. 7.
10. Naidu, M.V., "Globalization: Threat or Promise", *Gandhi Marg*, Vol. 21, No.1, April-June 1994, p. 402.
11. Beck, Ulrich, *op. cit.*, pp. 32-39.
12. Dubushi, Jay, "Indian Economy: The Next Fifty Years", *The Tribune*, August 15, 1997.
13. Kaushik, Asha, *Globalization Democracy and Culture: Situating Gandhian Alternatives*, Pointer Pub., Jaipur, 2002, p. 7.
14. Beck, Ulrich, *op. cit.*, p. 31.
15. Jayal, Nirija Gopal and Pai, Sudha, *Democratic Governance in India: Challenges of Poverty, Development and Identity*, Sage Pub., New Delhi, 2001, p. 29.
16. Beck, Ulrich, *op. cit.*, pp. 41-48.
17. Wexler, Philip (ed.), *Critical Theory Now*, Falmer Press, London, 1991, p. 179.
18. Kaushik, Asha, *op. cit.*, p. 12.
19. Gandhi, M.K., *Hind Swaraj or Indian Home Rule*, Navjivan Publishing House, Ahmedabad, 1938, p. 37.
20. Kumar, Satish, "Global Holistic economy only through Bapu's Swadeshi", *Gandhian in Action*, Vol.2, No. 5-6, April-June 1995, pp. 66-69.
21. Sharma, M.L., *Gandhi and Democratic Decentalisation in India*, Deep Pub., New Delhi, 1987, p. 27.
22. Narayan, Shriman, *Principles of Gandhian Planning*, Kitab Mahal, Allahabad, 1960, p. 112.

23. Raghavulu, C.V. and Rao, R. Anand, "Globalization approach to Decentralization and its relevance", *The Indian Journal of Public Administration*, Vol. XXIX, No. 3, July-Sept.1987, p. 710.
24. Sethi, J.D., "Centralization, Decentralization or Parallel Politics", *Gandhi Marg*, Vol. 7, No. 2, May 1985, p. 200.
25. *Harijan*, December 24, 1938.

4

Changing Complexion of Public Administration in the Globalization Era:

Some Emerging Issues

UMA MEDURY

Introduction

Globalization, is ushering far-reaching changes in the political, economic, social, and cultural spheres across the world. Globalization refers to the multiplicity of linkages and interconnections between the states and societies, which make up the present world system. It describes the process by which events, decisions and activities in one part of the world come to have significant consequences for individuals and communities in quite distant parts of the globe. Globalization has two 'distinct phenomena': scope (or stretching) and intensity (or deepening). On the one hand, it defines a set of processes which embrace most of the globe or which operate worldwide. The concept, therefore, has a spatial connection. On the other hand, it also implies an intensification of the levels of interaction, interconnectedness or interdependence between the states and societies which constitute the world community. Accordingly, alongside the stretching, goes a deepening of global processes (McGrew and Lewis, 1992).

Globalization is best thought of as a multi-dimensional phenomenon involving domains of activity and interaction that include the economic, political, technological, military, legal, cultural and environmental (Held, 2000). It implies, from economics perspective, removal of trade barriers, and large-scale entry of multinational enterprises engaged in foreign direct investment. Sociologists perceive it as multi-dimensional, encompassing various processes in the arena of politics, culture, technology, economy and so on. Anthony Giddens defines globalization as 'new' and 'revolutionary' and is mainly due to the 'massive increase' in financial and foreign exchange transactions. This has been facilitated by dramatic improvement in communication technology, especially electronic interchange facilitated by personal computers (Giddens, 1999).

The Organisation for Economic Cooperation and Development (OECD) has defined globalization as a shift from world of distinct, national economies to a global economy in which production is internationalized and financial capital flows freely and instantly among countries (OECD, 1995). Globalization has brought about a formidable global spread of services, goods, technology, ideas and processes. It is also bringing about significant changes in the nature of state, government, and the people as a community. Market forces are asserting a key role over the traditional welfare state. Globalization is having an impact on the public administrative system as it is embedded in the framework of the state. Some analysts have gone so far as to suggest that globalization is "increasingly forcing us to live in an economy rather than a society with shrinking national political power and with government's role in economic affairs now deemed absolute" (Smadja, 2000).

Globalization is ushering in new societal expectations, changing value systems, altering the nature of state and governing systems. This is putting pressures on public administration to respond to the widely fluctuating shifts. It has resulted in major changes in the nature of the state. The information technology revolution has transformed the tasks of administration. There is widespread acceptance of the significant role being assigned to the corporate sector due to the removal of trade barriers. The managerial orientation in governmental operations, and a change in the role of the state from direct provider to regulator, and in provision of an appropriate enabling environment to private sector are assuming increasing proportions. Cerny observes "in a changing globalizing-international and transnational environment, the state has been not only an agent of its own transformation, but also a major source of development of globalization itself" (Cerny, 1994).

Globalization has affected public administration due to impact of pressures generated on it by global institutions, information technology and increasing concern for efficiency and productivity.

The pressures exerted by global institutions are immense. It is defined as the pressure exerted by a formalized institution with a global jurisdiction that has authority and power over individual countries in a given policy area (Welsch and Wong, 1998). The aid conditionalities imposed have wider repercussions as it increases the developing country's financial, military, political dependencies on the West. As Korten (1995) states, the "Bank-approved consultants often rewrite a country's trade policy, fiscal policy, civil service requirements, labour laws, health care arrangements, environmental regulations, energy policy, resettlement requirements, procurement rules and budgetary policies". In many developing countries, people, especially have been devoid of any choice of determining their own priorities, and policy preferences. Structural adjustment policies, pursued by several developing countries have been considered as a negation of local democracy.

The complexion of Public administration in the globalization era is undergoing a transformation. In this chapter, an attempt is made to highlight the impact of globalization with reference to the changing role of state, increasing management orientation in public administration and the civil society emerging as a supplementary democratic model to counteract the effects of globalization. The structural adjustments taking place globally are posing challenges to public administration in redefining the role of the state, making state institutions responsive to the needs of the people, and working towards state-market and state society cooperation. These challenges are discussed in this chapter.

Impact of Globalization on Public Administration

The globalization wave is bringing about an unprecedented expansion of trade, finance, and investment accompanied by unparallelled technological innovations and high levels of consumer demands and expectations. The impact of globalization on the economy is mixed, with benefits accruing due to competition along with economic crisis, weakened state apparatus, propagation of market oriented values, disturbing concentration of wealth leading to increasing levels of poverty, inequality, social crises, with significant repercussions on the development. According to Luke (1992), the new globalised context for public administration incorporates

- Communication, computer technology and a global infostructure;
- Economics and the internationalisation of trade, finance and technology transfer; and
- Natural resource interdependencies in the biosphere.

Globalization is resulting in a transition from centrally planned to market structures and their integration with the global economy world over. This has an impact on the administrative framework, functioning of state machinery along with acquiring new skills, capabilities, change in the mindset of personnel to adjust to the new environment. The nature and processes of public administration have been severely affected by the changing perceptions of the role of state, managerial orientation, market driven approach to development, with increasing advocacy of the complementary roles of government, market and civil society.

Due to globalization, on the one hand, public administration seems to be moving towards protection of citizens' rights, accountability, ethical values, research and training. On the other hand, globalization is also leading to shrinking of public space, violation of human rights and commodification of citizens (Farazmand, 1999).

Globalization propagating economic integration and technological changes is pushing the 'state' towards adhering to certain global standards and behaviours while the internal social and political forces are attempting to assert the role of the state, and its powers in protecting the interests of the governed. Hence, the state is undergoing a new transformative role and as a corollary, the impact on public administration has also been multi-dimensional.

Changing Role of the State

The state has always been the centre-stage of societal governance. Traditionally, many countries embarked on the concept of welfare state—a political system with high degree of responsibility for the welfare of the population. The onset of globalization has resulted in significant changes in the role of the state. The market based approach to public administration is leading to the emergence of a 'competition state' which encourages public choice initiatives, deregulation, privatisation, irrespective of the local political and administrative cultures. Cerny (1997), describes the competition state as one that has been transformed from a primarily hierarchical decommodifying agent into a primarily market-based commodifying agent.

A powerful new paradigm of determining the scope and limits of government action that was dominant in western democracies held the view that government should:

- do less;
- reduce or relinquish their previous overburdening responsibilities;
- privatise public services or their delivery wherever practicable; and
- reform their own operations in accordance with the market concepts of competition and efficiency.

These beliefs in 'government by the market' rest upon the proposition that the market system is inherently a better method of satisfying human wants and aspirations than recourse to government. The first objective of this thinking has been to slim the state and liberate the market forces in a variety of ways such as deregulation as well as through suitable monetary and fiscal policies. The second objective has been to import market concepts and incentives into the operations of the government itself. The third objective is to take measures to reduce the relative size and growth of public expenditure and to cut down the range of functions that the government performs (Self, 1993).

The market theory argues that the government is less efficient than markets over providing services to individuals. The market firms due to competition and profit motive make a more effective use of given resources than the government agencies, which lack similar incentives. Also individuals can choose the services they want from the market, subject to their income, whereas government provision of services leaves them with little or no choice.

This roll back of the state propagated during 1980s and 1990s, especially in the USA and UK, due to influence of neo-liberalism has resulted in deregulation, privatisation and the introduction of market oriented reforms in public services. This has led to a pro-market and anti-state philosophy of 'private good' and 'public bad'. The new political economy of development is based on 'market' and not the state as the central actor, as privatisation is expected to release locked up social initiatives and the developing countries will turn outward to participate in the unfolding process of globalization of the economy.

Focus on Management Orientation in Public Administration

Public administration, traditionally speaking, had the major obligation of promoting public interest. It had to assure representativeness and responsiveness to citizens. The managerial orientation in it is a recent development, which according to one school of thought, was prevalent earlier too but in a varied form and content. The nineteenth century civil service reformers in the USA, promoted managerialism in public service. It had taken the form of emphasising merit and fitness in public service appointments, selection and tenure of public servants to be based on efficiency and performance. This was precisely the reason for the advocacy of politics—administration dichotomy as politics was considered to be the core factor of inefficiency. Later the propagation of scientific management principles by F.W. Taylor wherein organisation has been looked upon in a formal structure, individuals considered as employees, clients, and notions of impersonality etc. indicates that traditionally too, management orientation has been considered necessary to promote efficiency, economy and effectiveness.

The new reform model in public administration, which emerged in 1980s and 1990s as the New Public Management (NPM) has condemned the traditional public administration as a failure. It starts from the premise that the traditional, bureaucratically organized public administration is "broke" and "broken" and consequently the public has lost faith in government (Al Gore, 1993).

The orthodox public administration which remained under attack for many years, has suddenly found a new reform replacement, as Jennings (1995), observes "the major initiatives to reform government processes are built around a shared set of notions. Government should be performance oriented. The management of government has to be deregulated. Public agencies must be entrepreneurial, mission driven, service oriented. Public managers are to be risk takers who welcome participation and reward performance. They themselves are to be judged on their performance. These reform initiatives are targetted at the multiple performance failure of government and the need to build public confidence. They are premised on the belief that traditional bureaucracies have become stumbling blocks to responsiveness, effectiveness and efficiency.

The NPM model is based on certain premises, which include:

- Focusing on achieving results rather than primarily conforming with processes;
- Introducing market principles such as competition, contracting out in the provision of goods and services;
- Making public administration customer driven to enhance service ethic and efficiency;
- Assigning the role of steering activities to the government rather than rowing, relying on third parties such as non-profit organisations, other levels of government in implementation of policies;
- Deregulating the government activities to make it result-oriented;
- Empowering the employees to serve the customers as it promotes teamwork; and
- Changing the overall public administrative culture towards flexibility, innovation, entrepreneurialism, enterprising as 'opposed to' rule-bound, process orientation and focusing on inputs rather than results (Rosenbloom, 2002, *Paraphrased*)

NPM has emerged clearly, as a major manifestation of the competitive state approach. This new paradigm, which has gained wider implementation with a variety of labels reinventing, engineering, quality management, liberation management, focuses basically on changes in the structure and processes of government. Research studies indicate a wider acceptance of NPM model across the world. Kaboolian (1998) identifies three commonalities that appear to support the globalization of NPM thesis:

- the use of the economic market as a model for political and administrative relationships;
- similarity in the 'goals they pursue and the technologies they utilize'; and
- the use of administrative techniques such as customer service, performance-based contracting, competition, market incentives and deregulation.

The western liberal vision, while it correctly captures the importance of market and linkages to the world economy, has underestimated the role of the state in economic transformation in three major ways by failing to perceive

1. the existence of the orthodox paradox that is, that even neoclassical economic reform requires a relatively capable and important state structure;
2. that any state, (i) authoritarian or; (ii) democratic, but especially the latter needs to buffer the socio-political consequences of transformation; and (iii) the liberal vision of economic transformation itself, especially its stress on minimalist states, the exclusive sway of markets and correct policy packages, might not be the only possible path to transformation, or even the most common one (Callaghy, 1993).

In the changing scenario, there emerged a view that individualism, which was embedded in the market and the government guided by market forces is not favourable to any society. Hence, states and markets need to have institutional alternative in the form of non-state actors.

Emergence of Civil Society as a Supplementary Democratic Model

Civil society, which refers to self-organisation of citizens in contrast to the state or government is rooted in western rational decision and political culture. Civil society, comprises the collective of those social organisations that enjoy autonomy from the state, and have as one important goal, among others, to influence the state on behalf of their members. Civil Society organisations are networks of groups formed for pursuing special interests and include all local and externally financed private, charitable, social service, developmental and professional organisations (Blair, 1993).

The development of the civil society organisations is considered as growth of communitarianism. Whether attached to and promoted by the political left or right, communitarianism would emphasise the growth of the third sector meaning non-profit organisations other than those in the public sector, as a solution to many problems of contemporary society (Peters, 1996). The markets being driven by profits, the state organisations due to their inefficiency, and unresponsiveness, the civil society organisations, have gained prominence due to being participatory, flexible, less bureaucratic, cost effective and ability to reach the people.

Diamond (1991) identifies at least six functions of civil society in shaping democracy, these are:

(*a*) Civil society is a reservoir of political, economic, cultural and moral resources to check the process of the state;
(*b*) The diversity of civil society will ensure that the state is not held captive by a few groups;
(*c*) The growth of associational life will supplement the work of political parties in stimulating political participation;
(*d*) Civil society will eventually stabilize the state because citizens will have a deeper stake in social order. Further, while civil society may multiply the demands of the state, it may also multiply the capacity of groups to improve their own welfare;
(*e*) Civil society is a locus for recruiting new political leadership; and
(*f*) Civil society resists authoritarianism.

Civil society provides a single civic identity, which is distinct, and belonging to various groups of citizens, acts as a mediating link between the state and the markets.

Anthony Giddens also in his work *The Third Way: The Renewal of Social Democracy* makes a case for broadening of the democracy with government acting in partnership with agencies in civil society so as to combat civic decline. The established traditions of participative planning and community development can be complemented by experiments in direct democracy. The fostering of civil society is an important task, for the state, with support for the 'bottom-up' politics of community renewal. This implies a greater role for service provision by non-profit organizations; more localized distribution channels; and the public sector should work to develop the capacities of local communities (Ferlie and Fitzgerald, 2002).

The state and market are considered as sources of remote

decisions that might not have much of an impact on the lives of the community. The emergence of communitarian movement, which is a new development, but is gaining momentum, provides a broader perspective to society as comprising new forms of community (local, voluntary, professional etc.) working with the spirit of mutual concern and co-operation. The thinking that has gained coinage is the state delegating more of its functions to partly autonomous local agencies, communities and co-operatives. This is a way of democratic decentralisation.

It is beyond doubt that market techniques such as privatisation, customer orientation, entrepreneuralism, performance orientation are aimed at improving the efficacy of public administration. The clash of private interests with public sector values precipitates the problem. Above all, there is a thing called public interest, which lies at the heart of government operations, and it is irreplaceable by any market philosophy (Bhattacharya, 2000).

Privatisation which is being pursued as a key instrument of globalization has been criticised by Peter Drucker (1999) as "we are learning very fast that the belief that the free market is all it takes to have a functioning society or even a functioning economy—is pure delusion". The transition from a centrally planned to a market economy especially in developing countries, in the last two decades has witnessed doubts being raised about the efficacy of state, its relevance, importance of market forces and ways of striking a balance between state, market forces and the people. Even the western liberal ideas also which earlier downplayed the significance of state, started acknowledging the need to take into cognisance, positive aspects of governance such as effective legal, judicial, regulatory mechanisms, transparency, evolving market friendly forms of state intervention, mobilising social capital in pursuance of public policies and programmes.

Public Administration: Emerging Issues

The globalization pressures on public administration are immense due to which it is undergoing transformation. The emerging global public administration is based on a number of structural adjustments or readjustments that have been taking place around the globe. The readjustments have been in the forms of redefining the scope and boundaries of public and private sectors, of administrative reforms or civil service reforms, of organizational reconfiguration and restructuring and many more (Farazmand, 1994).

The concept of development is gaining a wider connotation. As opposed to its traditional economic orientation, it now implies promotion of all aspects of human life. The Human Development Report (2001) considers 'Human development is about much more than the rise or fall of national incomes. It is about creating an environment in which people can develop their full potential and lead productive and creative lives in accordance with their needs and interests. People are the real wealth of nations. Development is thus about expanding the choices people have, to lead lives that they value. And it is thus about much more than economic growth, which is only a means of a very important one—of enlarging people's choices (*Human Development Report*, 2001).

In furthering development, the earlier minimalist state approach, is giving way to complementary roles of government, market and civil society and their integration. The World Development Report 1999-2000, maintains that in recent decades both experience and intellectual insights have pushed development thinking away from debates over the role of state and markets and the search for a single overarching policy prescription. Hence the state shall not wither away but the structures of government and state will assume a new form. These pose serious challenges for public administration. Some of these include:

Recasting the Role of the State

Globalization, no doubt impacts heavily on the state, its policies, institutions, and personnel. The "Public Sphere" and the space for citizen involvement have been shrinking and the corporate state is making its presence. The biggest challenge for administration is to recast the role of the state. There is a need for evolving a new regulatory state with an expanded agenda. The state needs to be regulatory in nature, providing for mechanisms for ensuring efficiency, setting standards of service, removing market distortions, providing appropriate regulatory/legal framework for players in the market and protecting the interests of consumers, employers, employees and other stake holders.

Osborne and Gaebler (1992) in their work 'Reinventing government' have made a case for government having a key role in towards restructuring of markets through:

1. Setting rules in market place;
2. Facilitating the provision of information;
3. Augmenting demand;
4. Catalysing private sector supplies and new market sectors;
5. Creating market institutions;
6. Risk sharing; and
7. Regulation through application of market-oriented incentives.

Effective economic governance demands the state to make efforts to provide a conducive atmosphere for market institutions to function and at the same time strive to make them socially responsive. For instance, the success of the East Asian economies of Japan, Taiwan, Korea, Hong Kong etc., which were dependent on markets, was to a large extent due to the governed market (GM) paradigm. The essential kernel of the governed market paradigm is state intervention with subsidies, with distortions of relative prices, and with control of credit markets, promoting economic choices and investment and production outcomes that would not have been possible through the ordinary working of the market (Sobhan, 1998). Necessary administrative support is provided towards promoting a competitive climate, and maintaining a stable economy.

In Japan, the government intervened directly in the market to

1. establish sectoral priorities;
2. mobilize resources to hasten their development;
3. protect infant industries;
4. issue guidance on investment levels;
5. organize rationalization and anti-recession cartels;
6. allocate foreign exchange credits;
7. regulate technological flows in and out of Japan;
8. control foreign direct investment;
9. issue "administrative guidance"; and
10. publish white papers on mid- and long-term visions of

Japan's future industrial structure (Okimoto, 1989).

A functioning market economy needs a sound and strong state geared towards evolving a legal and regulatory framework, which ensures predictability, stability, clarity and enforceability. The market-driven processes need to be directed towards achieving economic as well as social development.

Making State Institutions Responsive to Needs of People

The globalising state that is said to threaten the lives of common people, through promotion of elitist policies, can be counteracted by reasserting the role of state institutions in becoming responsive to the needs of people. The World Development Report—2000-2001, '*Attacking Poverty*' asserts public administration to implement policies efficiently, be responsive to the needs of people and redistribute resources for activities that benefit the needy.

The World Development Report 2002 "*Building Institutions for Market*" observed that "weak institutions—tangled laws, corrupt laws, corrupt courts, deeply biased credit systems and elaborate business registration requirement—hurt poor people and hinder development". Countries, which faced such problems, dealt them by creating relevant institutions suited to micro needs that increase income and reduce poverty.

The public institutions can thwart the negative consequences of globalization through suitable interventions. For instance in Korea, the government through employment insurance, public works programme, livelihood protection programmes, provides appropriate social protection by creating a base for a competitive and knowledge based economy.

Similarly in East Asian economies, measures were taken to ensure that different sections of the society economically benefited from the growth strategies. The World Bank (1993) points to several policy measures that have facilitated in providing the benefits of growth to a wide section of the population:

(*a*) provision of universal primary education with increasing access to secondary and higher education;

(*b*) land reform measures in Japan, Korea and Taiwan provided for a more egalitarian ownership of land, assistance to agricultural production both for domestic and export promotion provided increased incomes to a broad group of land holders;

(*c*) promotion of small and medium sized enterprises (most exclusively in Taiwan, to a lesser extent in Japan);

(*d*) in addition, specific welfare measures such as investments in providing housing to low income households (in Hong Kong, Singapore and Indonesia), have also contributed to a lessening of poverty (World Bank, 1993)

The key challenge, to counteract the negative consequences of globalization is to strengthen and revitalise the public institutions in a manner to ensure their legitimacy and effectiveness in protection of public interests. The developing countries need to take concrete measures in this direction.

According to James Wolfensohn, President of the World Bank, (1999) Development requires good governance, meaning open, transparent, accountable public institutions. In a market economy, growth if it is to be lasting, it must be regulated—not over regulated—but guided by public institutions and private professional conduct which establish a foundation of transparency and fairness in economic life .... Effective, accessible public institutions are not just conducive to, but a necessary condition for stable growth.

Establishing State-Market Cooperation

There is a view point regarding creating cooperation between the state and market. Three kinds of interventions have been identified which are functional, institutional and strategic. Functional interventions seek to remedy market failures in so far as prices give the wrong signals. Institutional interventions seek to govern the market by setting the rules of game for players in the market. Strategic interventions seek to guide the market, as these are interlinked across activities or sectors in an attempt to attain broader, longer term objectives of development (Bhaduri and Nayyar, 1996). The state to facilitate market functioning needs to develop the physical infrastructure as well as create indispensable social infrastructure.

In 1994, some economists in India recommended evolving a paradigm of "Socially Responsible Market Economy (SRME)". It seeks to reorient the role of the state and planning through public sector and joint sector, strengthening economic and social service activities through building of human resources, skill development, employment generation and developing infrastructure where private sector and foreign investment are not forthcoming.

The SRME emphasises self-discipline, peer pressure and adherence to codes of conduct by all economic players. These codes are intended to be followed by all concerned sections of the society reflecting their socially responsible economic behaviour in a free market economy. The state is expected to play a balancing role in overseeing the achievement of people's welfare in a market driven economy (Jain, 1996).

This assumes importance as the state is always accountable to the people whereas the market is not. And if there is one thing to be learnt from the unfolding experiences of the post-Soviet reform, it is precisely this. A state which pays little attention to the economic sufferings and marginalisation of a significant proportion of its population, not only discredits itself but also the market process through which such marginalisation occurs (Bhaduri, 2001).

The importance given to market forces in the present scenario might appear to give a reduced role to the state. But the state's role has not diminished, as it has to reconcile the objectives of liberalisation and pursuit of national interests and developmental goals. In the national context, the state must endeavour to create the pre-conditions for a more equitable development, bargain with transnational corporations to improve the distribution of gains from cross-border economic transaction, practice prudence in the macro-management of the economy so as to reduce vulnerability and intervene to minimize the social costs associated with globalization (Nayyar, 2001).

Creating State-Community Synergy

The ultimate goal of development be it pursued by state or the market is to build human capabilities, and enlarge human choices, to create a safe and secure environment where people can live with dignity and equality. Globalization is said to affect communities, their participation in managing their affairs. The biggest challenge to administration lies in not simply strengthening the processes and institutions of government, but also looking at the governed, making them partners in the process of development, strengthening their capacities and empowering them. There is a rapid shift towards, a societal approach to development, with an emphasis on centrality of 'social capital' to development.

Peter Evans (1998) in his analysis of East Asian economies gave a new orientation to the theory of Embedded Autonomy, whereby he emphasises that a significant factor responsible for their economic growth, is the presence of concrete set of social ties that bind these states to their surrounding societies. The State-society interaction, that facilitates gauging the society's response to policies formulated by the state is important. Hence he emphasises the need for a tie-up between state apparatus and its societal constituencies.

A perusal of the structural adjustment policies imposed on the developing countries by the donor agencies indicates that the aid conditionalities, have contributed to social damage in the form of rising inequalities, unemployment, insecurities and so on. Hence to minimise these effects globally efforts are on, towards strengthening local economies through rebuilding of communities. For instance in Britain, there are an enormous range of entities which constitute 'community economic action' wherein nearly one and a half million people participate in it. It takes the form of community enterprises run by local people, credit unions, development trusts working towards economic, environmental and social regeneration of an area, community recycling schemes and so on (Hines, 2000).

In the state of Andhra Pradesh, micro financing has enabled many to rise above the poverty line (ABL). Women form small Self Help Groups (SHGs) avail loans at no or low interest rates to start income generating activities and build a savings corpus. This is the micro financing considered as the viable solution to livelihood where poverty is the overriding factor. The state government is already in the forefront in the micro-financing sector. Activities such as afforestation programmes, multi-crop cultivation, seed-bank, rising of nurseries etc. are being undertaken (*The Hindu*, 2002).

Developing bottom-up participatory processes shall enable the community to have control over their own needs and resources. In Brazil, the involvement of beneficiaries in the process of disbursing development funds has facilitated better interaction with local administration. The Municipal Councils have 80 per cent representatives from the user communities. If they feel that municipal councils treat them unfairly, they can apply for funds directly from the state government (World Development Report, 2000-2001).

Building synergy between state and society needs appropriate strategies to:

- develop, strengthen and sustain collaborative and participative processes;
- foster institutional development that facilitates resource mobilisation, coordination and networking;
- ensure transparency, empowerment, accountability; and
- strengthen human capacities.

Concluding Observations

Globalization has come to stay and as Tony Blair had once commented 'it is irreversible and inevitable'. But at the same time, we need to replace the notion that it is has no other alternative. It is beyond doubt that it has promoted technological advancement, foreign exchange flows, export growth, foreign direct investment, entry of multinational enterprises and so on. But the most important factor that it needs to take cognisance of is to counter the imbalances, isolation, and make it more humanistic. The instability and insecurity it has brought about can be reversed through social cohesion, cooperation which neither the state nor the market can solely provide.

The traditional public administration has undergone a metamorphosis by integrating three critical players i.e. state, market and civil society. The need for a collaborative action amongst the three was reiterated at a Conference in 1998. It recorded the significance of all three sectors in the management of public affairs, with a requirement that there be a 'balance' in state-market relations, 'legitimacy' in the state interactions with the citizens and 'partnerships' between the state and institutions of civil society (Ian, 2000).

In the present administrative scenario, what is needed is not less government, but a better and different government. Public administration needs to gear up to the challenges of

- redefining the respective spheres of state and non-state actors, building mechanisms for better interaction, and cooperation;
- framing suitable laws and regulations that provide necessary stability, confidence, enforcement; and
- building a professionalised civil service possessing necessary competence, skills, public service, participatory, and a pro-citizen ethic.

As Denhardt and Denhardt (2000) suggest, in a democratic society, values such as efficiency and productivity should be placed in the larger context of democracy, community and the public interest. There is need to evolve the concept of a new public service which focuses on serving the citizens than steering, thinking strategically, acting democratically, valuing citizenship and public service above entrepreneurship and ensuring accountability not just to market but to constitutional law, community, citizens interests, and professional standards.

REFERENCES

Bhaduri, Amit and Deepak Nayyar, *The Intelligent Person's Guide to Liberalism*, New Delhi, Penguin Books, 1996.

Bhaduri, Amit, Nationalism and Economic Policy in the Era of Globalization, in *Governing Globalization Issues and Institutions* (ed) Deepak Nayyar, New Delhi, Oxford University Press, 2001, 40.

Bhattacharya, Mohit, *New Horizons of Public Administration*, New Delhi, Jawahar Publication, 2001.

Blair, Harry as quoted in Attur Rahman, Civil Society and Governance in South Asia, in *Governance: South Asian Perspectives* (ed), Hasnat Abdul Hye, New Delhi, Manohar, 1998.

Callaghy, Thomas R., Vision and Politics in the Transformation of the Global Political Economy: Lessons from the Second and Third Worlds, in *Global Transformation and the Third World* (ed), Robert O. Slater *et al.*, London, Lynne Reinner Publisher, 1993, 238.

Cerny, P., "The Dynamics of financial globalization: Technology, market structure and policy response", *Policy Sciences* 24, 4, 1994, 319-342.

Cerny, P., Paradoxes of the Competition State: The Dynamics of Political Globalization' *Government and Opposition*, Vol. 32, No. 2, 1994, 251-274.

Denhardt, Robert B. and Janet Vinzent Denhardt, The New Public Service: Serving Rather than Steering, *Public Administration Review*, Vol. 20, No. 6, 2000, 553-557.

Diamond, Larry (ed), The Democratic Revolution: Struggles for Freedom and Pluralism in the Developing World, Perspectives on Freedom, No. 12, Freedom House, 1991.

Drucker, Peter Quoted in David Korten, The Post-corporate field: Life after Capitalism, West Hart Ford, CT, Kumarian Press, 1999, 151.

Evans, Peter as quoted in Sobhan Rehman (ed), Towards a Theory of Governance and Development, Learning from East Asia, Bangladesh University Press, 1998, 30-34.

Farazmand Ali, "The New World Order and Global Public Administration: A Critical Essay" in Jeanclaude Garcia *et al.* (eds), Public Administration in the Global Village, West Port CT, Praeger, 1994.

Farazmand Ali, "Globalization and Public Administration", *Public Administration Review*, Vol. 59, No. 6, November-December, 1999.

Ferlie, Ewan and Louis Fitzgerald, The Sustainability of the New Public Management in the U.K. in Kate McLaughlin *et al.*, 2002 (eds), *New Public Management Current Trends and Future Prospects*, Routledge.

Giddens, A., *The Third Way: The Renewal of Social Democracy*, Cambridge, Polity Press, 1997.

Giddens, Anthony, Runaway World: How Globalization is 'Reshaping Our Lives', London, Profile Books, 1999, 10.

Held David, The Changing Contours of Political Community: Rethinking Democracy in the Context of Globalization, in Richard V. Ericson *et al.*, *Governing Modern Societies*, University of Toronto Press, Canada, 2000.

Hines Colin, *Localization: A Global Manifesto*, Earthscan Publications, UK, 2000, 39-40.

Ian, Thynne, The State and Governance: Issues and Challenges in Perspective", *International Review of Administrative Sciences*, Vol. 66, 2000, 227-240.

Jain, R.B., Globalization, Market Economy and Human Security in *Indian Journal of Public Administration*, Special Number on Liberalization Policy and Social Concerns, July-September 1996, Vol. XLVI, No. 3, New Delhi, 317.

Jennings Edward T. Jr., "Public Service in an Era of Transformation", *Public Administration Times*, Vol. 18, September, 1995.

Kaboolian L., "The NPM: Challenging the Boundaries of Management *Vs.* Administration Debate, *Public Administration Review*, Vol. 58, No. 3, 1998, 189-193.

Korten David, When Corporations Rule the World, West Hartford CT, Kumarian Press, 1995.

Luke J., "Managing Interconnectedness for Public Managers", in Timmy Bailey M. and Mayer R. (eds), *Public Management in an Interconnected World*, West Port CT, Green Wood Press, 1992.

McGrew A.G. and P.G. Lewis, as quoted in Dunning John H. and Hamdani (eds), *The New Globalism and Developing Countries*, United Nations University Press, Japan, 1997, 12.

Okimoto as quoted in Rehman Sobhan *op. cit.*, 51.

Osborne, David and Ted Gaebler, *Reinventing Government*, Plume Books, New York, 1993.

Peters Guy, *The Future of Governing: Four Emerging Models*, University Press of Kansas, 1996, 58.

Rosenbloom David H. and Robert S. Kravchuk, McGraw Hill International Edition, 2002, 21-22.

Self Peter, *Government by the Market? The Politics of Public Choice*, Macmillan, West Vision Press, 1993, 59.

Smajda, Claude, Time to Learn from Seattle, *Newsweek* (Atlantic Edition), January 17, 2000, 64.

Sobhan Rehman (ed), *op. cit.*, 1998, 46-47.

The Hindu, December 8, 2002.

UNDP, Human Development Report, 2001, Making New Technologies Work for Human Development, Oxford University Press, New York.

Welsch Eric and Wilson Wong, Public Administration in a Global Context: Bridging the Gaps of Theory and Practice between Western and Non-Western Nations, *Public Administration Review*, Vol. 58, No. 1, 1998, 45.

Wolfensohn James, *International Herald Tribune*, 26 February, 1999.

World Development Report, 1999-2000, "Entering the 21st Century", Washington.

World Development Report 2000-2001, "Attacking Poverty", Washington.

World Development Report 2001-2002, "Building Institutions for Markets", Washington.

5

Globalization:
Its Clashes, Contents and Discontents

A.A. SHAIKH

A hundred flowers must be allowed to bloom, creating a rich garden of social action to lend more colour to globalization's humane face.

—*Jagdish Bhagwati*

Globalization today is not working. It is not working for many of the world's poor. It is not working for much of the environment. It is not working for the stability of the global economy……The problem is not with globalization, but with how it has been managed.

—*Josef Stiglitz*

Introduction

Globalization is a process of economic, social, cultural and political integration of the countries of the world. It aims at connectivity, closeness, togetherness and interdependency. It is a phenomenon of unification. Its essence is integrated world with single order. It has been called that it is a *'death of distance'*. The monolith of globalization is unstoppable, we have to accept it and learn to live with it. Its voice is compelling us to be in tune with the new world order. Its pace and range have almost, left no country in isolation and exclusion.

Globalization is neither a new phenomenon nor a newly set process, but it is 200 years old and ongoing with unsmooth trend of inequality. However we have to accept that this growing integration of economies and societies around the world is a complex process that affects many aspects of our lives.

The major constituents of globalization are trade, commerce, technology, science, information, knowledge and culture. There are previews and views on globalization. Opinions on the subject, and the issues it involves are many, some are genuine and some are ingenuine. Studies on the subject are sundry with mixed findings and contradictions. Conflicting views are seen with regard to global sphere and local sphere (variations in policies, and institutional structure). Some find that it has reduced poverty and inequality while other show that it has increased both of them.

Today many passionate debates on various aspects of globalization are continued without being concluded. However a general consensus prevails that the process of globalization is characterized by greater degree of interdependence between the nations through international trade which is one of its positive feature. The volume, direction and the composition of foreign trade of different countries have undergone enormous and dramatic changes in the last 50 years. There are rules governing trade and, therefore, the role of WTO in governance have proliferated accordingly.[1]

However there is a camp that raises doubts for free trade with regard to opportunities, complexities and risks inherent in globalized economy. Some give global warming of globalization emphasizing the high costs of climate change—a global warming, complain that there are no comprehensive studies of the health impact of global warming (impact on health, water quality and human lives).

The other camp that favours and has pro-globalization views shows how the pursuit of social and environmental agendas can be creatively reconciled with the pursuit of free trade.

Thus globalization is an integrated phenomenon which encompasses the kernels of power, culture and environment. It has changed the socio-cultural-ethical value diagram enormously. The main challenge is to combat adverse effects it has generated and evaluate the achievements it has gained. The better future perspective, turns and direction can be attained by these means only.

There is an acute need of guiding the process of globalization with a humane face. However, it is a challenging task, but governments, NGOs, Private Corporations, Think Tanks and the press are involved and interact to get rational outcome. Our insides and far sides preferred may help us to move forward towards a better and safer life for all. The endeavour is to raise standards of living while allowing for the optimal use of the world's resources in accordance with the objective of sustainable development. Uruguay Round Negotiations with respect to trade, money and finance and examining the ways to bring greater coherence to global eco-policy making.

It could be quite appropriate to say that globalization has set a ladder for countries who climb on it, though disproportionately, to achieve its fruits.

In view of given brief outline of the subject, the chief aim of my chapter is threefold; firstly it would deal with analysis of virtues and vices of globalization, secondly, it would focus on some major economic effects. It would take care of anxieties of globalization and would give an agenda for action to combat the issues and omissions involved in globalization. More precisely it would aim at current policy debate on globalization.

Clash of Globalizations: A New Paradigm of Political Thinkers

If one reveals close inspection to the political events of last decade one can clearly see that the dominant tension of the decade was the clash between the fragmentation of states (and the state system) and the progress of economic, cultural and political integration—in other words, globalization. There are two new political thought patterns emerged during 1990s which explain how clash between the fragmentation of states and globalization came to surface. Firstly, Francis Fukuyama's *End of History* which predicted the end of ideological conflicts and the triumph of political and economic liberalism. However he failed to note that nationalism and explosive potential of religious wars remained very much intact.

Secondly, Henry Kissinger's 'realist' orthodoxy proclaimed that a state's military and economic power determines its fate,—international institutions and interdependence are secondary and fragile phenomena; and states' objectives are imposed by the threats to their survival or security. However this model failed to integrate globalization and the rise of non-state actors, international cooperation for challenging the new threats of proliferation of weapons of mass destruction (WMD). Moreover it also ignored, what is called the 'germ of a universal consciousness' the liberal, pro-market-norms that developed states have come to hold in common.

According to some scholars the serious problem with

globalization is that it has reduced the role of a state. State's role now has been limited to social protection, physical protection against aggression or civil war and maintaining the national identity. But to this *New York Times* columnist Thomas Friedman presented contrasting views—barriers with open vistas, obsolescence with modernity, state control with free market. He sees in globalization the light of dawn, the 'golden straight jacket' that will force contentious publics to understand that the logic of globalization is that of peace and democracy.[2]

It has been realized by interdisciplinary thinkers that the course of globalization will not run smooth. There are certain hard realities which it has to face before it can march on to its destination. In a world we have still rivalries among different nations and among great powers. They are not disappeared, they still exist. This rivalry we can see more in the area of nuclear weapons which bear the risk of destruction. We must also bear in mind that if wars between states are becoming less common, wars within them are mounting e.g. Yugoslavia, Iraq, much of Africa and Sri Lanka. The more subtle reality that we must accept that states' foreign policies are shaped not only by realist geo-political factors such as economics and military power but by domestic politics. Even in undemocratic regimes, forces such as xenophobic passions, economic grievances, and transnational ethnic solidarity can make policy making far more complex and less predictable.

The real universe of globalization does not have a single form. As a matter of fact globalization has three forms, each with its own problems. The first is economic globalization, characterized by revolutions in technology, information, trade, foreign investment, and international business. Its main agents are companies, investors, banks private services industries, states and international institutions. This form of globalization poses Marx-Engles dilemma—between efficiency and fairness, inherently alarming that division of labour, specialization and logic of pure competition does not favour social justice. (Herein the discordant tone of the critics is that globalization's ultimate incidence is inequality of income and injustice, however, we shall take this point in detail while discussing the effects of globalization in other section of this chapter. The subject matter is controversial, it all depends on which phase of globalization, which dataset, which time period and which methodology you take for your study).

The second form of globalization pertains to culture. It emphasizes the choice between uniformity and diversity. The challenge comes to uniformity. Diversity is taken as respect and dignity of local culture and language. There comes hate and assaults for Western Culture which is denounced as an arrogant and a mask of a secular, revolutionary ideology and a mask for U.S. Hegemony.

Thirdly, there is political globalization characterized by the preponderance of the United States and its political institutions and by a vast array of international and regional organizations and trans-governmental networks. It is also marked by private institutions that are neither governmental nor purely national. But we must remember that these agencies lack democratic accountability, power scope and authority. It is also true that American legacy is often under the clouds, often faces resistance from other countries and is again affected by America's own dubious position—between the temptation of domination and isolation.

Populist—Fallacious Discontents of Globalization

There are certain arguments against globalization which comes from either by fear, precautions, speculations, political consideration, preserving and protecting pseudo values or self imposed interpretation. We shall examine that they suffer from personal ideology and weak economic logic.

It is true that globalization is beneficial but its optimism rests on very fragile foundations. It is also true that it is neither inevitable nor irresistible. This has been said in the light of some historical background. Globalization is largely an American Creation rooted in the period after World War II and based on U.S. economic might. By extension, then, a deep and protected economic crisis in the United States could have a devastating effect on globalizations as did the great depression. In this argument we see anticipated fear of globalization in the sense that U.S. based globalization might turn like the great depression of thirties. But the symptoms are not seen and in case it turns out to be so then modern state by its fiscal efficiency is capable to operate demand management policies and modern monetary banking institutions and their policies with their post reforms efficiency in participation management, coordination and monitoring are effective and efficient enough to bring adjustment and stability before it comes to any devastating effects on economy.

It is worth to note that we have witness their quick responses and efficiency in overcoming world financial crisis. Before they turn into some fatal economic consequences. Of course, it all depends on how much they are free from ethical crisis, ideological leaning and institutional self interest.

The second discontent is seen in an argument that globalization excludes many poor countries, and the states that it does transform react in different ways. This fact stems from the diversity of economic and social conditions at home as well as from partisan politics. It is also said that at the world level there is absence of perfect integration of markets, services and factors of production. The border issue also paralyze and slow down the integration, but at other times it gives integration the flavours and colours of the dominant state (as in case of the Internet). But enhancement in mobility (though not much true in case of labour) and fall in transportation cost, transaction costs, and communication cost as well as rapid spread of information perhaps gives little space to prevail this argument. Moreover the poor excluded countries, more specially African, Asian and Middle East countries are cooperating and coping up with the globalization. Apart from integrations in different spheres, they are also coming in the realms of globalization preserving and maintaining their diversities.

The third clash is reflected in the argument that international civil society is in the initial state (it has not diffused enough) and globalization presupposes their mature status which hardly exists. Moreover NGOs are politically weak and limited in numbers. They cover a very tiny segment of the populations of their members' state and cannot resist the odds of globalization. Though NGOs are the prime actor in anti-globalization movement but realization is gained and they are coming in the fold of main stream of globalization. NGOs may be less in corroborative for grounding globalization. Globalization is synchronizing and local organizations, institutions and local machineries are coming up to pick up the goals of globalization. They are aware and active with regard to multiple and multi-directional changes and try to adjust with them. Social Safety Net, Movement of decentralization, special development programmes of UNDP have also contributed in lifting the local bodies for the task. Though this much owes to World Bank, IMF, and recently IFC which has proceeded that latest techniques of B-loan lending and initiative of partnerships between the World Bank and IFC. Which will create enormous opportunities for all countries.

The fourth clash of globalization stems from the fact that

globalization can give emancipation to individual but it can't give democratizing regimes. This has been cited with illustration of China. Moreover globalization, through emancipation of individual, does not prevent public institutions like IMF, WB or the WTO from remaining opaque in their activities and often arbitrary and unfair in their rulings. To this we can submit that even in non-democratic regions informal democracy is inherently working which can be consistent to the goals of globalization and after world financial crisis IMF and other international institutions have changed a lot. Recently IMF has declared new testament for international financial crisis and has set new standards which are more loaded with moral accountability. Transparency is also acknowledged and given more weight.

The critics see that globalization has clash with reality that human condition can be improved through the abolition of barriers. This is dubious—they say that globalization is in fact only a sum of techniques such as audio and video cassettes, the Internets, instantaneous communications. These techniques are either with state or private actors. They are not altruistic and their self-interest and ideology drive them. Globalization is with utopian enlightenment which provokes revolt and dissatisfaction. Of course, there is some element of truth in this as has been witnessed in Seattle, Prague, Geneva and Washington. But these protesting group were politically motivated and emotionally charged. This can't damage the cause of globalization. After the above said incidence the international institutions have become morally conscious and they have modified and redesigned their policies of globalization with a humane face. It is worth to note that removal of barriers, though of any kind contribute to efficiency and adjustment. Thus this clash cannot stay permanently.

Another very noteworthy clash that globalization gives a rise, is clash between cooperation and competition. This is very prominent when we have international and transnational matters. It is to be presumed that the nations going for globalization will not mind resultant inequalities, fluctuations and protectionist practices. This is very contrary to the philosophy of globalization which rest on market philosophy and we know that it has inherent characteristics of inequality and instability. Globalization nurses self-interest and competition, while cooperation is altruist and emphasizes selfless togetherness. It has been observed that most rich states will not come at rescue by means of aid or assistance in the time of crisis situations such as the genocide in Rwanda. US did not part with his national interest by not killing non-Americans. This was self-evident during the attack on Afghanistan. As a matter of fact this is hard reality but in present time international appeals and pressures can change the course of destruction and market friendly environment can be generated by social capital.

An Anatomy of Discontents of Globalization

The recent work on discontents of globalization and different themes related to it is so vast to cover and the new literature on it is so fast to keep pace with it that it becomes necessary to follow some formal classification in order to gain clarity of explanation and logical analysis. The views are so diverse that they cannot be brought under one umbrella and the differences are so imperceptible that we cannot make them out. Hence I classify the controversies of discontentments of globalization in the following manner.

1. A Triology of Discontents—Jagdish Bhagwati (2000-2001, 2002).
2. Globalization and its discontents—a pretence of global institutions—IMF, WB, WTO (2002)—Stiglitz's Approach.
3. Open society endangered Soros (1998) Approach.
4. In search of Building an Inclusive World Economy W.B. (2002).

A Triology of Discontents—Jagdish Bhagwati's Approach

As it has been noted by exponents in the fields of international trade and development economics that Bhagwati's innovative and wide ranging contributions to trade theory and development economics have, in Paul Samuelson's words, ushered in 'the age of Bhagwati'. Bhagwati has now become a passionate advocate for righting wrongs in the economic policies of both industrial and developing countries. Bhagwati's writings on this subject have appeared in his seminal works; The Wind of the Hundred Days: How Washington Mismanaged Globalization (2000),[3] 'Free Trade to Day (2000), and 'Coping with Globalization', 'A Triology of Discontents (2002).[4] Bhagwati's work is based on solid logistic—scientific foundations of pure theory of international trade, hence he can convincingly answer the questions raised to globalization and encountering the uproars of its critics.

Bhagwati has identified three discontents of globalization which are focal points in the agenda of those who carry the banners of anti-globalization. These are the capitalism system the process of globalization and the behaviour of corporations. However, it should be understood that all three of these discontents have become interlinked in the minds of many opponents. He says that, 'globalization's enemies see it as the worldwide extension of capitalism. With multinational corporations as its far ranging B-525'.

There are two groups who vehemently come out with some emotions of frustration and misunderstanding regarding capitalist system. The first group is comprising of people of post-war era. Who could not bear the success of capitalism over communism, fascism and socialism and whose alternative development models failed and therefore they started tuning their cry against globalization. The second group is youngsters who lack true education and lost passions for becoming competent see capitalism as a system that cannot meaningfully address questions of social justice, while socialism can address. But we must note that they are unaware of what happened in India during the era of socialist planning. They also do not see the fatal consequences of Soviet socialism. Bhagwati pointed out that markets allow a large number of people to access their targets we must not forget that capitalism gives freedom of choice and initiative that paradoxically, can destroy privilege and open up economic opportunity to many.

The discontent of globalization and capitalism is rooted in misconception and mis-conceivement of education. Today young anti-capitalists carry a confused value diagram of different discipline of education in their mind. They are misled by the idea that social awakenings flow from subjects like literature, sociology. English comparative literature and economics is not one that gives them this. This is indeed peril of education. New literary theory and old Marxist thought have confused the takers of this education, that economics is about values and sociology is about values. It means economics is about self-interest it bothers for means. This has convinced them sociology is a better guide to ethics than is economics. This is not true. Economics is not neutral to ethic. It takes into account concern and consideration. Economics is not a tool for change. Economic analysis helps to enhance development and reduce poverty and provide gainful employment and dignified sustenance. Is this not moral?

Young people also imbibe anti-capitalist attitudes from new technologies that is from cable television and Internet. These technologies have brought image of far-off suffering into watchers' mind, false identification is done and unhappiness is expressed towards capitalist system.

One of the serious discontentment arises for globalization, more specially in the left wing students is the view that globalization will nurse capitalist exploitation of weak nations. Globalization will serve as a vehicle to reach the benefits to capitalism and in the process will harm the innocents living abroad. MNCs will act as a monopolist and exploit nation's resources and manpower, there will be no equal sharing profit maximization and exploitation will dominate. It short MNCs would be damaging the economic fibre of the nation and would let it down. However to this we can submit that the recent empirical work does not support this.[5]

The fragile alliances between young agitators, conventional lobbies, such as the labour movement, new pressure groups such as the environmentalist and human rights crusades, also reflect the successes of anti-globalization movement. "Green and blue alliance herald for labour rights, labour standards; and protection against negative externalities of environment. By this alliance the anti-globalizers have become powerful.

The anti-globalizers believe that globalization has social ills and perhaps it will aggregate the existing social ills. The argument goes like this—while globalization may be economically benign in the sense that it increases over all wealth, it is socially malign in terms of its impact on poverty, literacy, gender equality, cultural autonomy and diversity. By deep thinking and empirically we can assert that globalization is not the enemy of social progress, rather a friend of it. Take corporation: Have they hurt women? Answer is no. Japanese MNCs with their growth and spread, took both men and women together to different places like New York, Paris, London, where the Japanese housewives saw for themselves how women could lead a better life. This experience transformed many of these women into feminist agents of change.

There are empirical evidences pertaining to labour market, wage differentials and employment given by economist Elizabeth Brainerd and Sandra Black have shown, wage differentials against women have decreased faster in industries that compete internationally. In poor countries women have been benefited when gets jobs in global industries. It has been found that their experiences of workers away from home have increased their ability and efficiency and it can experience in liberating one's self. This is indeed nothing but empowering women by globalization.

It is a wrong notion that workers are exploited by MNCs. Ann Harison of Columbia University's school of Business, show that in some developing countries, multinationals pay their workers more than 10 per cent above the going wage, at least in their own factories.

It has been suggested that the comprehensions of social impact of globalization, more specially the increased volatility of employment by imaginative institutional and policy innovations. The World Bank should come forward for accommodating assistance for poor countries who have insufficient resources to meet the situation.

It has been seen that the twenty-first century is characterized by expanding globalization and growing civil society. The important feature that has been seen is that the child labour is prohibited. More children are conversed to school and divorced to work in private firms and factory. This is indeed an improvement in civility. Moreover there are schemes and programmes through which the parents of these children would be compensated for the loss of income incurred by losing income from their children. This is socially hygienic. This will pave the way for enhancing social capital (trust, cooperation, partnership) would lead to further growth.

As it has been seen these days that there is much uproar against corporations which is one of the significant agent of carrying globalization ahead. They do more good to society than harm. Hence they must be defended against ignorant, ideological and strategic assaults. It should be remembered that corporations are by shareholders and ultimately social good is imparted by them. There are many examples at world over which have witnessed that how much and how many ways such corporations are pro-poor. Social good is multidimensional, and different corporations may and must define social responsibility, quite legitimately, in different ways in the global economy.

Open Society Endangered—Soros's Approach

Soros, an authentic financial genius and the greatest living philanthropists has expressed his views on discontents of globalization, though more on the basis of his experiences as a champion in financial market and as a follower of Karl Popper who propounded the concept of Open Society and its Enemies, in his book; *This Crisis of Global—Capitalism, Open Society Endangered* (1998).[6] His basic contention is that globalization has inherent characteristics of capitalism and capitalism is by market fundamentalism which is, today, a greater threat to open society than any totalitarian ideology. Seeing the crisis of global capitalism and by his recent experience Soros reformulated the concept of open society. In Popper's formulation, it stood in contract with closed societies based on totalitarian ideologies, but it could be threatened from the opposite direction as well: from the lack of social cohesion and the absence of government.

Soros was intellectually touched by Russian Melting, 'Latin American Financial Crutch', 'South Asian financial crisis' and IMF's inability to manage these crisis and sought an explanation that why the global capitalist system was unsound and unsustainable. He considered them to be the major factors working for disintegration of the global capitalist system. The greater worry that seized him was breakdown in the global financial system accompanied by a break-down in international free trade.

The capitalist system has inherent tendency of instability in general and the financial markets have this tendency, though often and again in particular. It hardly revert to where it comes from. More precisely instead of acting like a pendulum financial markets have recently acted more like a wreckling ball, knocking over one economy after another. Once the market is unstable we can't impose market discipline and perhaps we do so we impose greater instability. How much instability can society take? The crux of the matter is that market discipline needed to be supplemented by another discipline: maintaining stability in financial markets ought to be the objective of public policy.

It must be admitted that the world monetary institution has to play a very constructive role in such crisis but IMF's programmes did not turn out to be successful and its methods of operation need to be reconsidered. There is a need for additional institution which can work as a subordinate to IMF. Such as one suggested by Soros namely, International Credit Insurance Corporation. Moreover time has come to establish some kind of international supervision over the national supervisory authorities. Apart from this there is also a need for reconsideration about the workings of the international banking system and the functioning of the derivative markets.

The discontentment of globalization lies in the discrepancy between a global economy and a political and social organization that is still basically national in scope. It has been seen that there exists unequal relationship between centre and periphery and the unequal treatment of debtors and creditors. Globalization has generated the germs unhealthy culture in the society with more rampus of capitalism; the unhealthy substitution of monetary values for intrinsic human values. Moral proclamation seems to be not a mission of globalization. Thus Soros has unhesitatingly admitted global capitalism as an incomplete and distorted form of an open society.

What is more dissatisfactory is that we live in a global economy but without adequate political organization of our global society which can act up on to ameliorate the financial market. And if we have not this provision then the global economy can breakdown.

The development of a global economy has not been matched by the development of a global society. The basic unit for political and social life remains the nation-state. International law and international institutions, insofar as they exist, are not strong enough to prevent war or the large-scale abuse of human rights in individual countries. Ecological threats are not adequately dealt with. Global financial markets are largely beyond the control of national or international authorities.

If we go little back in history, we find that Thatcher-Reagan era gave prominence to market fundamentalism and apart from history of capitalism, today, also we see that arrogance of imperial powers, domination of three major currencies such as dollar, mark and yen, and some pseudo shared beliefs and ethical standards are full in cry. As a result we have monetary values and transactional market which can't provide us an adequate basis for social cohesion.

According to Soros the failures of politics are much more dangerous than the failure of market mechanism. The disenchantment with politics has fed market fundamentalism and the rise of market fundamentalism has, in turn, contributed to the failure of politics.

One of the great defects of the global capitalist system is that it has allowed the market mechanism and the profit motive to penetrate into fields of activity where they do not properly belong.

Soros has objected the analogy between economics and physics. The concept of equilibrium has flown from physics in economics in general and financial market in particular. The fundamental difference between the two as it is explained that physical objectives move the way they move irrespective of what anybody thinks but financial market attempt to predict a future that is contingent on decisions people make in the present. Instead of just passively reflecting reality, financial markets are actively creating the reality that they in turn reflect. There is a two-way connection between present decision and future events, which Soros calls reflexivity.

What is interesting in Soros analysis is that this feedback mechanism interferes with all other activities that involve cognizant human participants. Human beings respond to the economic, social, and political forces in their environment, but unlike the inanimate particles of the physical sciences humans have perceptions and attitudes that simultaneously transform the forces activity on them. This two-way reflexive interaction between what participants expect and what actually happens is central to an understanding of all economic, political and social phenomena. It is this concept of reflexivity that Soros brought in the main stream of thinking, to draw some practical conclusions about financial markets; about world economy; and about such broader issues as international politics, social cohesion, and the instability of the global capitalist system as a whole. The fundamental problem is that a stake that failures of the market mechanism pale into insignificance compared to the failure of non-market sector of society—that is the collective interest of the society, the social values that do not find expression in markets.[7]

It is an undeniable truth that politicians, these days, if not always, but often put self interest ahead of public interest and individual economics agents are seen with the attitudes that put success as measured by money and not by intrinsic values like honesty. Thus the tendency of the profit motive and the decline in the effectiveness of the collective decision-making process have reinforced each other in a reflective fashion. The promotion of self-interest to a moral principle has corrupted politics and the failure of politics has become the strongest argument in favour of giving markets an ever-freer region. Here lies the danger, if market is left to its full authority, it produces chaos and ultimately a downfall of global capitalist system. Hence this lead to conclusion that at world over, there must be laws and institutions that are necessary to the preservation of peace, freedom, prosperity and stability and this could be possible by collective—cooperative efforts more specially by United States and its like minded nations—Alliances of this kind for such a noble cause must be formed and encouraged.

Globalization and its Discontents: A Pretence of Global Institutions—Stiglitz's Approach

Stiglitz's book, *Globalization and its Discontents* (2002), has brought reality to surface.[8] He is not anti-globalizer, but reflect himself like a disturbed Hebrew Prophet who is seized within deep agony of seeing how the followers of the path are deviated from their objectives. His objective scientific criticism bounded by respect and dignity of world's grand monetary, trade and development institutions, who stand for globalization and whose programmes and actions which touch almost every one in the world, will help to shape the future of these institutions provided they do not go by any prejudice. He, as a insider, who lived in and worked for, expresses his deep agony that how the armour of ideology and institutional self interest can lead to fatal economic consequences and disturb the world economic order.

Stiglitz argues that the west-acting through the IMF and WTO has seriously mismanaged the process of privatization, liberalization and stabilization, and by following its advice many third world countries and former communist states are actually worse off now than they were before. It is the trade unions, students, environmentalists and ordinary citizens marching in the streets of Prague, Seattle, Washington and Geneva who have put the need for reform on agenda of the developed world. But he does not take a simplistic pro- or anti-globalization stance. Instead he confronts us with the often difficult realities of the world. He states just what he believes the market can be trusted to do and the responsibilities government must hand over to it. To his wit, its solution lies in a substantial shift in the balance of influence between the developed and developing world.

Stiglitz's major thrust is on 'economics of information' which is his lifetime work for which he was awarded Nobel Prize. His main contention is that, information, its nature and its characteristics can explain transparency, disclosure decisions and policy. On this line of thinking his main emphasis is on subjects like bankruptcy, corporate governance and openness of and access to information, are the crucial issues which globalization cannot escape. He opts for gradualism which worked wonders for China and a strong critic of 'shock therapy which miserably failed in Russia'.

The discontentment lies with the fact that IMF's policies failed, not only that they also did not work. Its structural adjustment policies—the policies designed to help a country adjust to crisis as well as to persistent imbalances—led to hunger and riots in many countries. It was neither questioned by many of the people in power in the IMF, nor any developing country could dare to raise objection with the fear that their funding from IMF would be reduced.

IMF's thinking is very unreasonable in the sense that inside the IMF it was simply attended that whatever suffering occurred was a necessary part of the pain countries had to experience on the way to becoming a successful market economy, and that their measures would in fact, reduce the pain the countries would have to face in the long run, but to be true that the level of pain in developing countries created in the process of globalization and development as it has been guided by the IMF and the international economic organizations has been far greater than necessary.

On three counts Stiglitz has shown his discontentment on globalization, firstly, the promoters and the pushers of globalization restrict and discourage open and frank discussion of 'issues and policies, means freedom is restricted or a domain of unfreedom prevails. Secondly the IM's rigidity in accepting the alternative policies. It means 'flexibility' in policy is either not allowed or neglected by some deviceful ways. Thirdly ideology dominates the policy, rationality is either not given space or it is used very niggardly. As a result you have poor results and it seems undemocratic. Terms are dictated to developing countries with the inter ton—'Just do that' or do what we say.

The hypocrisy that IMF works with it is asking developing countries to open up trade and not objecting the protectionism by developed countries. The IMF's policies are dominated by ideology, hypocrisy, and bad economics.

The essence of discontentment shown by Stiglitz is that the market cum government policies are not accepted whole-heartedly. Market and government are complementary. They both are working in partnership and recognize that while markets were at the centre of the economy, there is important, though limited role that government has to play inequality, unemployment and pollution are the issues in which government has to play important role. The initiative must be taken for 'reinventing government'—making it more efficient and more responsive.

The way ahead is to build sound and sustainable international financial architecture and keeping faith in that government can mitigate market failures along with ensuring social justice.

International public institutions for mitigating environmental issues and health issues, good governance, transparency, separating, growth stability approach from poverty reduction approach, no policy contradiction, reform efforts etc. are the requirements of the day. There is an acute need to check capital flows, bankruptcy, exchange rate system, banking policies, improving safety net and response to crisis.

In Search of Building an Inclusive World Economy: How to overcome the anxieties of Globalization (World Bank Policy Research Report 2002)

The World Bank, IMF, IFC, WTO and other international institutions along with professional economists in academia are thinking seriously and working hard to mitigate the situations emerged in the post era of globalization movement. Though there are consensus with contradiction and conflict with confusion but immense efforts have been put for gaining balance, stability and growth. Their pioneering contribution is in creating efficient management for handling the world economic problems. Their major focus is on development, poverty reduction, international financial stability and institutional build up at world level.

'Inclusive world economy' has shown that globalization as a force of total integration of world, specially its third wave, has given a breathing time for poverty and inequality reduction. The trade and development effects are though positive but not sufficient. The report reads, 'developing countries have divided into more globalized ones, where poverty is rapidly diminishing and less globalized ones where poverty is rising. The rapid growth of the new globalizers is generating profound changes in their societies and is challenging rich countries in some markets. The absolute decline of many marginalized countries is a tragedy for both of them and the world. An integrated world can neither tolerate not withstand the exclusion of two billion people from the prospect of prosperity.

The report has classified the anxieties of less globalized, new globalizers, rich countries and global one. The less globalizers are suffering from marginalization and state failure. The new globalizers face the dilemmas of being shut out of markets, subject to the whims of distant investors, uncompetitive, trading good jobs abroad, environmental degradation social dislocation and international imbalances in power. The rich globalized countries face the problems of terrorism, inequality within rich countries loss of manufacturing jobs to low wage countries and homogenization. Lastly the global anxieties are mounting inequality, global warming and the power of government, labour and capital.

The agenda of action of this report is comprising of seven major actions. The first area of action is 'development round' of trade negotiation prime focus on market access. The second area of action is improving the investment climate—focus on incentives. The third area of action is the importance of good delivery of health and education. The fourth area of action is to provide social protection. The fifth one is a greater volume of foreign aid, better managed. The sixth area for action is debt relief and the seventh one is highlighting the importance of tackling green house gases and global warming.

Conclusion

Globalization is welcome, but could it guarantee that it will not bring the whole gamut of Veblen's 'Leisure Class' with conspicuous, consumer Galbraith affluent society though with abundance but with lot of waste, Toffler's 'cultural shock' with human kind like a fast driven dog standing with his tongue out with fast breathing. An imaginary demand excess capacity and sub-optimal state of production. Will it give guarantee that it will not kill social conscience? Will it definitely appear with human face or the world would seize within ruthless self-interest? These are the serious questions it poses and we must not only think on them but thinking well must be revealed.

NOTES

1. Stanley Hoffmann's new political paradigm explains this fact that during last decade, many countries especially those born of decolonization, remarked themselves to be no more than pseudostates without solid institutions, internal cohesion or national consciousness. The end of communist region revealed long hidden ethnic tensions. Oppressed minorities demanded independence. In some Middle East and South Asian countries rulers waged open warfare against their subjects. These wars increased the importance of humanitarian interventions, which came at the expense of the hallowed principles of national sovereignty and non-intervention. Moreover the sudden and surprised attack of 11 September 2001 showed that for all its accomplishments, globalization makes an awful form of violence easily accessible to hopeless fanatics which gives witness to the fact that terrorism is the bloody link between inter-state relations and global society. As countless individuals and groups are becoming global actors along with states, insecurity and vulnerability are rising.
2. See *Clash of Globalizations* by Stanley Hoffmann for further discussion on this, foreign affair, July/August 2002.
3. See the review of Bhagwati's book, *The Wind of th^ Hundred Days: How Washington Mismanaged Globalization* by Deena Khatkhate in Finance and Development, Sept. 2001, Vol. 38, No. 3, p. 57.
4. See, *Coping with Anti-Globalization—A Triology of Discontents* by Jagdish Bhagwati, Foreign Affairs, Jan-Feb. 2002, p. 2.
5. Jacques, Derrida, a French Philosopher has espoused 'Deconstructionism and with its advocacy of an 'endless horizon of meanings' left the typical student of literature without anchor. Derrida's technique is to deconstruct every political ideology, including Marxism. Typically, however, it is capitalism that becomes the focus of these efforts, not Marxism after the collapse of Soviet system, open society with its emphasis on freedom, democracy, and the rule of law, lost much of its appeal as an organizing principle and global capitalism emerged triumphant. Capitalism with its exclusive reliance on market forces poses a different kind of danger to open society and market economy are closely linked and market fundamentalism can be regarded as merely a distortion of the idea of the open society. That does not make it any less dangerous. Market fundamentalism, endangers the open society inadvertently by misinterpreting how markets work and giving them an unduly large role tc play.
6. Soros has linked politics with market mechanism and as a logical corollary with globalization to explain his discontentment for globalization—for detail discussion on this point see p. xxii, of *The Crisis of Globalization* by Soros.
7. Reflectivity means a two-way feedback mechanism between thinking and reality which is borrowed from Newtonian physics namely equilibrium.
8. For more elaboration and detail discussion see Stiglitz (2002) 'Globalization and its Discontents'.

REFERENCES

Bimal, Johan, *India's Economy in the New Millennium—Selected Essays*, New Delhi, UBSPD Pvt. Ltd.

Diana, Tussie (ed.), *The Environment and International Trade Negotiations Developing Country*, Stake (2002), Palgrane, Macmillan, in association with International Development Research Centre, 2002.

Douglas, A. Irwin, *Free Trade Under Fire*, Princeton in Press, 2002.

Frans, J. Schuurman (ed.), Globalization and Development Studies: Challenges for the 21st Century, New Delhi, Vistaar Publications.

Globalization: Policies, Strategies and Partnerships—Commonwealth Business Forum 2002 (ed. papers).

Jagdish Bhagwati, *A Stream of Windows' Unsettling Reflections on Trade, Immigration and Democracy*—Oxford in Press, 1999.

Jagdish Bhagwati, *Free Trade Today*, Princeton University Press, 2002.

James D. Malcolm, *Financial Globalization and the Opening of the Japanese Economy*, Curzon Press, Richmond, Surrey, (332.4 M2F4), 2001.

Jagdish Bhagwati, *The Wind of the Hundred Days: How Washington Mismanaged Globalization*, Cambridge, Mass, MIT Press, 2000.

Jean Dreze and Amartya Sen, *India: Development and Participation*, Oxford University Press, 2002.

Jeffrey Harrod and Robert O'Brien (ed.), *Global Unions? Theory and Strategies of Organized Labour in Global Political Economy*, Routledge, London, N.Y., 2002.

Joseph E. Stiglitz *et al.* (ed.), *The Economic Role of the State*.

Maximine Dalton, Chris Ernst, Jennifer Deal and Jean Lesli, Success for new Global Manager, what you need to know to work across distances, countries and cultures centre for creative leadership Jossey—Bass A Wiley Company, San Francisco, 2002.

Naresh Kumar, *Globalization and the Quality of Foreign Direct Investment*, Oxford University Press, 2002.

Olson, Mancur, 'Dictatorship, Democracy and Development', *American Political Science Review,* 1993.

Peter L. Berger and Samuel P. Huntington (eds.) *Many Globalizations: Cultural Diversity in the Contemporary World*, Oxford University Press, 2002.

Raj Kapila and Uma Kapila (ed.), India's Economy in the 21st Century, a collection of selected articles—Academic formulation, 2002.

Reinicke, Wolfgang H., Global Public Policy: Governing without Government? Washington D.C., Booking Institute, 1998.

Ronald W. Jones, 'Globalization and the Theory of Input Trade, MIT Press, Cambridge, Massachusetts, London, 2000.

Samiha Fawzy (ed.), 'Globalization and firm competitiveness; in the Middle East and North Africa Region. The World Bank Washington, D.C. The Mediterranean Development Forum-3, 2002.

Stiglitz, J.E., 'Distinguished Lecture on Economics in Government: The Private Uses of Public Interests: Incentives and Institutions', *Journal of Economic Perspectives*, 12(2), 1998, 3-32.

Stiglitz, J.E., 'On Liberty, the right to know and public discourse: The Role of Transparency in Public Life', paper prepared for the Oxford Amnesty Lecture, Jan. 27, 1999.

Soros G., *The Alchemy of Finance, Reading the Mind of the Market*, A Touchstone Book, published by Simon and Schuster Inc. N.Y. London, Little Brown & Company, 1987.

Stiglitz Joseph, *Globalization and its Discontents*, Allen Lane, Penguin Press, 2002.

The Economist, Globalization, Making sense of an integrating world'. The Economist Pocket Asia, 2002.

The World Bank (Middle East and North Africa Region) Orientation in Development Series. "Reducing Vulnerability and Increasing Opportunity; Social Protection in the ME and N. Africa, 2002.

Y.V. Reddy, 'Lectures on Economic and Financial Sector Reforms in India', Oxford University Press, 2002.

Part II

ISSUES AND IMPACT

6

India Under Globalization:
Facing an Unequal World

PUSHPA BISHT

> Globalization is not a trend, it is not an affair, it is not an intended game, but it is actually the international system that replaced the cold war system and like the cold war system globalization has its own rules, logics, pressures, incentives, gears and moving parts that will and do affect everyone's country, everyone's company and everyone's community, either directly or indirectly.
>
> —*Thomas Friedman*

It is indeed a paradox that while in terms of political history globalization is yet in its infancy, at the same time it is a surge that has overtaken the world and that now determines the design for a new world order. As far as nomenclature goes, globalization is perhaps the most commonly and variedly used political and economic terminology today. While a comprehensive definition of globalization would include political, economic and social aspects and would imply the process of progressive integration of the world driven by larger concerns for survival yet increasingly the term is used to refer to liberal capitalism. In fact the terms liberalisation, privatisation and globalization (LPG) are used almost as synonyms and are intermixed with ease. The reason for this is not difficult to trace as the most visible form of globalization does appear to be economic liberalisation that has presided over the integration of diverse societies into a world market with the advanced countries like the United States, UK, Germany and Canada emerging as major players.

Globalization is a modern day phenomenon that transcends boundaries and borders. While it would be too simplistic to describe globalization as liberal capitalism, at the same time this is how it is often described. To understand why this intermixing has taken place, we have to go to the background of globalization. Although the terminology is new, the phenomenon is new, the concept is not new and one cannot really argue that globalization has suddenly descended on the world. In fact this concept dates back at least a century. The liberal capitalism of nineteenth century is often referred to as global economy. International trade, the prevalence of free markets and a relatively unfettered price mechanism were either consciously or implicitly accepted by sovereign states. The four decades spanning 1870 to1914 were characterised by *laissez faire* and there was virtually no restriction on the movement of goods, capital and labour across national boundaries. This concept can also be traced to the writings of economists John Maynard Keynes. In his *Economic Consequences of the Peace*, Keynes mentions that, sitting in London one could order by telephone product of the whole world or invest in wealth in any quarter of the world (Keynes, 1921). Keynes believed that international economic integration in this period contributed to positive economic growth. However, World War I ravaged the economies and forced country after country into protectionism. The collapse of the gold standard, the Great Depression that pushed free trade firmly onto the backburner, the surfacing of narrow economic nationalism and the pursuit of 'beggar your neighbour' policies were all deglobalising trends. Political pessimism surfaced as countries retreated into a shell. It took the Second World War and more than a quarter of a century to reverse the trends. It was only after World War II ended that serious efforts were made to promote greater integration of the economies the world over.

This trend of post-war years was a move towards the establishment of an international economic order not a world economic regime. True, markets opened in many parts of the world and policies were liberalised. But it would be a mistake to sum up and dismiss globalization as economic liberalisation. However, liberalisation is an important aspect of globalization. It is also the embryonic form in which the phenomenon has originated. As of now it is also the most visible form of globalization. While a faithful interpretation of globalization should defy such a categorisation, as globalization should not be categorised in terms of geography, content and intent, yet it is a harsh reality that key players have emerged in globalization principle among these being the United States of America. It is also a reality that economic interests determine and many times outbid political interest and trade and economic activity are becoming increasingly influential in world politics. With the economic sector being the only sector that has succeeded in becoming truly global as country after country leaves behind autarky in favour of free market economy, much of the definitions of globalization revolve round or refer to the expansion of economic activities across political boundaries of nation-states. They refer to deepening economic integration, increasing economic openness and growing economic interdependence between countries in the world economy. This has been propelled by technological change and information revolution that has brought the world closer. It has been facilitated by the dynamics of post cold war world politics that has catapulted multilateral economic institutions like the World Bank, the IMF and the World Trade Organisation into the forefront as a complex interdependence binding the economic and the political interest of states ensures a dramatic change in global political environment.

India: Awakening to a Globalised World

The origins of globalization in India need to be analysed in terms of economic changes brought about in the country in the last decade of the twentieth century. It is true that ever since independence India has been battling enclaves in the economy. By the 1980s it had become evident that the paradigm of developmental planning adopted in India wherein the state played a predominant role, was neither balanced nor sustainable. The 1980s saw some deregulation of the industry and lifting of trade restrictions. However, these changes were hesitant, piecemeal and tentative. The definitive move towards economic globalization came in the summer of 1991 when the country found itself in the midst of a serious balance of payment crisis and was bailed out by the IMF and the World Bank that offered programmes of stabilisation and structural adjustment which India was hardly in a position to refuse. The liberalisation and globalization of the Indian economy are the key components of the package of reforms adopted and implemented following the 1991 crisis. As has been wont with many developing countries, India's awakening into the globalised world has been a rude one.

In the changed context of the New Economic Policy (NEP), there has also been a significant change in the perception of the role of the state. Seen as a radical departure from the earlier inward-oriented policy, the reaction to liberalisation has been almost wholly dichotomic and has been besieged by apprehensions of state minimalism. While the market forces have been instrumental in propelling the process of economic globalization, the question that arises is what happens to the conscious decision of governments? Does the nation-state become redundant under globalization? Neo-classical economists argue that the intervention of governments in markets is unnecessary. Thus the state should be rolled back and given a minimal role. They accept markets with their self-corrective mechanism as a preferred alternative to the state and free market economy as imperative for economic prosperity. However, if one is to take into account the consequences of the economic integration of the nineteenth century, it will be seen that economic globalization has a history of asymmetry and the results of *laissez faire* were far from equitable. No doubt the imperial countries gained from this integration, as did the new lands of USA and Canada. However the third world countries—Asia, Africa and Latin America lagged much behind. In fact countries like India, China and Indonesia experienced severe underdevelopment despite their open door policies.

Since the world now as was then is made up of unequal partners, to contemplate of a global order where countries are equal *per se* would be incurably utopian. There will always be a certain degree of contradiction and conflict. It would be wrong to conclude that globalization is going to pave the way for the world to become one big conglomerate. The disturbing questions that now arise in the present scenario are—where does power get located? Who gets privileged and whom does one marginalize? Whom do we deny?

While globalization tends to benefit liberal capitalist countries like the USA and Canada, much of the world viz. Africa, Latin America, the Middle East and much of Asia has been left out so far. Linda Weiss has pointed out that since 1967 the concentration of foreign investment in the United States followed by U.K., Germany and Canada has gone up by 12 per cent (Weiss, 1998). Thus managing the process in such a way as to ensure equitable development and avoid marginalisation of the weak and vulnerable has become a major challenge especially so as the benefits of globalization have not spread evenly among nations. In fact they have not spread evenly even within countries. As key players move centre-stage in the globalised world, principally the USA, Canada and the European Union, and eager contenders like China wait in the wings, what will be the future of India?

India's man of destiny Jawaharlal Nehru's contention that India was destined to emerge as the fourth major power after the USA, the Soviet Union and China was both optimistic and quixotic (Nehru, 1961). In 1989 Henry Kissinger included India in the group of great economic, political and military powers (Nye, 1990) and later optimistically as a centre of power. In 1995 Paul Dibb identified India as a future major power in Asia (Dibb, 1995). The seventh largest country in the world with an area of 3.367 million square kilometres. India's territorial size, manpower and natural resources should have ensured for her a position of reckoning, but this has not happened. As far as Nehru's predictions go they may prove true to a point as China prepares to make its debut as the next candidate for great power but beyond that it falls short. India's unenviable economic position has made it slip several notches and it has great ground to cover if it is to gain a position of some advantage in the globalised world.

That giantism is not a demographic identification is obvious from the fact that a country like Canada ranks much higher than India in terms of both political and economic respect. Although it does have a surface area of 9.971 million square kilometres, Canada has a population of only 31.1 million as against India's one billion. Like India, Canada has had to deal with a multi-cultural and a multi-racial environment. The language issue endangers its political solidarity and the independence movement of Quebec is a threat to the historical mould of the country. On the economic front, Canada is a commodities driven economy which could be susceptible to booms and busts. Yet it has risen successfully from a small client economy to become one of the top contenders in the global economy. It boasts of a GDP of 580.6 billion US dollars and has comparative advantage in industries ranging from fibre optics to aerospace. It is both a member of the economically powerful G-8 countries as well as one of the richest developing countries in the world. Among the G-8 countries too it has the lowest cost of living.

Canada along with the U.S., Germany and Switzerland removed restrictions on capital movement in 1973. Since 1988, the US investment into Canada has increased five-fold and since 1994 it has benefited a great deal from the NAFTA. Canada enjoys this position of comparative advantage not only because its proximity to the U.S. makes it a prime location for foreign investors but also because its advanced technology and immense technological potential makes it a keen contender in today's knowledge based global economy. In fact the Canadian and U.S. economy are similarly advanced and already partially integrated and these two countries that constitute North America enjoy a third of the world's annually created wealth.

Although India cannot be written off as even with its low per capita income, it has the fifth largest GDP in terms of purchasing power parity, yet weak economic capabilities is the reason for its dependence on Western Powers. At present the country faces an unequal equation. It comes in the bracket of those powers which not only do not have necessary leverage to influence the course of the globalised world but also cannot necessarily buy for themselves a position of advantage. In fact, though a giant in demographic terms India remains yet a middle Asian power and a minor world power. This is so because today the identification of giants in the global arena is not demographic but economic in nature. India's ambiguous position is not to be envied. According to Lyon (Lyon, 1968) the leading question is whether India is simply the last as well as the least in the enumeration of great powers or whether she is a power in the big league in the Asian context. The very fact that this ambiguity exists points to India's doubtful credentials as far as her power position goes. She definitely does not belong to the group of great powers nor does she have sufficient clout in South Asia or in regional organisations like SAARC. Holding three quarters of the territory and population within its geo-political region, a position that should have accrued to her naturally has evaded her. Thus India's internal problems preclude an international role for the country. An improvement of India's economic capabilities will undoubtedly give her some clout and will lay the foundation for encouraging regional economic cooperation in the subcontinent and beyond and will equip her better to face the globalized world.

That a dynamic economy is the undergrid to political power in this globalised world has been amply proved by the emerging importance of China. In 1989 Frances Fukuyama had predicted that all states would become liberal democracies (Fukuyama, 1989). More recently Michael Doyle has projected that this would take place between the mid twenty-first and before the beginning of the twenty-second century (Doyle, 1997). However, a fast emerging China belies such predictions. The growing importance of communist China which, although it went for market reforms as far back as 1978, is still very much an authoritarian and regimented state, is a pointer. The US's obvious acceptance of China's communist dictatorship and its comparative lack of appreciation of India's political democracy makes it clear that in the power driven globalised system there are no ideological brothers and the prospects tip favourably for the economically empowered. China's ability to successfully woo and engage the US is a direct outcome of the smart moves it has made in the economic arena and its credible performance therewith. If this was not the case what would explain the US's augmentation of China's nuclear missile capabilities through technology transfer or the growing collaboration between the western-liberal giant and the epitome of communist regimentation. How is it that India, an ideological ally of the US continues to be sidelined even more than a decade after the dissolution of the USSR. It is India's visibly disadvantaged economic position that allows a comparatively advantaged China to score over it in the world fora. It is also the reason why India continues to be equated with a much smaller and politically weaker Pakistan rather than to be treated at par with China. The USA's determination of its policy towards India through the prism of Pakistan which has a history of military rule, and which, had it not been for its geo-political advantage, would have been anathema to the US, is a clear indicator of India's present position. Moreover while the cold war was a state based power structure with states balancing states, confronting them or aligning them, the balancing is very much there in globalization. Thus a US must balance a China, Japan balance Korea, India balance Pakistan or China and so on. The difference is that the balancing now has strong economic overtones with markets becoming important geo-political actors.

Wither Indian State?

With India's foray into globalization there have emerged two extreme views—one that believes that the process must be countered and the other that says 'go with the flow'. Both are faulty, as reforms have to be tested on the touchstone of pragmatism and national interest. Just as globalization is a fact not an option so also liberalisation in India is a fact not an option. No country, certainly not India can divorce itself from the change in the world environment that has thrown up globalization as a pervasive dynamic phenomenon. It has also made concepts like autarky, isolationism and state intervention more or less redundant. It has brought into focus terms like integration and liberalisation and like all nations India today faces accelerated global challenges. The question that arises is what happens to the state?

While the case for the state may have been repeatedly overstated, it suffers because it has hardly been judiciously stated. Whatever the political or economic environment, there is definitely a responsible role for the state both nationally and internationally. In fact Keynes, a key figure in the fashioning of post-war multilateral institutions had ironically put forward a strong argument in favour of national policies. Keynesian theory holds that governments could stabilise the economy through a combination of fiscal and monetary policies directed at controlling the level of aggregate demand. This would flatten or eliminate business cycles that otherwise may lead to economic depression (Janda, *et al.*, 1992). The great liberal thinker, John Stuart Mill too admitted that an industrial society, left to itself, harboured inequalities and denied individuals the fruits of their labour while rewarding property owners (Mill, 1965). As such it would be a mistake to assume that markets *per se* are an answer to the developing world's problems. In the economic globalization as seen by the world today, there are two major sets of players, viz. transnational corporations which dominate investment production and trade and international banks or financial intermediaries which control the world of finance. These have succeeded in eroding the old fashioned autonomy that states enjoyed. However, it would not only be naïve but also dangerous to write off the state. India's fate and destiny in the globalised world will be directly affected by her ability to overcome problems that have been internalised and without the solving of which it cannot have much of a *locus standi*. Therefore it is important for India to approach and handle the changes with maturity and not to slip into the quagmire of state or market acrimony.

Liberalisation in India undoubtedly portends far-reaching implications. The reforms in their all-embracing sweep tend to affect time-tested institutions. They raise doubts about the developmental planning adopted by India and also reflect the failure of the state mechanism run on the axle of socialism. Notwithstanding the fact that liberalisation pulled the country from the precipice of economic disaster, the reforms have generated a great deal of scepticism. Although in the aftermath of the crisis of 1991 intellectual conversions did take place and there emerged a school of thought that supported this alternate strategy of development, yet at the same time liberalisation also generated a great deal of resistance. Viewed as a state reducing and market expanding doctrine, it has not had a warm reception among the votaries of Indian socialism. There is concern that liberalisation amounts to a direct attack on the normative and institutional foundations of India's traditional social, economic and political legacy. There is also a great deal of doubt whether the reforms will contribute to the sustainable economic growth that will ultimately make a huge difference to our war on poverty.

Of course, this state *versus* market debate is not new. Historically it can be traced to Adam Smith (Smith, 1937). The classical and later the neo-classical economist guided by the Smithian vision of the 'invisible hand' tried to establish the superiority and indispensability of free market economy as against state control. Even in countries like United States and Japan there are globalisers and there are protectionists, there are votaries and there are opponents of liberalisation. However this debate assumes importance in India as, given the circumstances under which liberalisation was adopted, it has little contextual validity. The reforms having come as a conditionality imposed by the World Bank and the IMF as the basis for giving financial assistance to India to tide over the balance of payment crisis, it makes little sense to espouse a 'pro-state' or 'pro-market' view. Moreover, it must be understood that the liberalisation of an economy is an extremely difficult process to reverse. Whether adopted out of conviction or compulsion liberalisation is here to stay. Hence it is important to move beyond the state-market dichotomy.

In his 'Wealth of Nations' Smith has advocated free competition and lesser role for the state. However, in a problem fraught economy like India, such an approach will create several imbalances and if *laissez faire* is to be the general rule the economic majority will stand to suffer even more. *Laissez fairism* and liberalisation thus cannot be adopted theoretically and the western model in a straitjacket is definitely not suited for India. It is a fact that countries differ from each other geographically, politically and culturally and each has different sets of factors working on them. Thus each needs its own set of economic reforms and factors that may be right for one country may not work with another. It is therefore imperative to take liberalisation out from its classical and neo-classical western mode and adapt it to suit the realities of the Indian economy. India must explode the neo-liberal myth that liberalisation can only be carried out in the environs of *laissez faire* and must put an end once and for all to the state *versus* market debate.

Combating State Minimalism

The policy of liberalisation in its basic conceptual form involves a significant change in the nature, role and importance of the state. It seeks a reduced role for the state, shrinks the sphere of state activity, reduces governmental functioning and divests the state of its political power in the economic field. The buzzword is 'market' and the feeling is 'roll back' the state. This lesser role for the state has serious implications at all levels—political, economic, social, cultural and environmental. Since such an attitude is anathema to the Indian economic and social culture, it becomes important to analyse the paradigmatic shift in the nature and role of the state under the sweeping impact of liberalisation and globalization.

Economic globalization ushers in a greater reliance on the market mechanism and indicates deregulation and a reduction of governmental controls. This in itself signifies a break from the established conventions of Indian planning and policy formation. The deep involvement of the government in the economic affair of the country is largely a post-independence development in India. The policy of planning and the interventionist state were adopted keeping in mind the need for social and economic welfare and justice to the people. The ideology of socialism enshrined in Indian Constitution visualised ascendancy of the state apparatus. The state was regarded as the major agent of development and the commanding heights of the economy were in its control. Under liberalisation there is a demand for the state to be rolled back and many tasks to be handed to the markets (World Development Report, 1996). However, is a lesser role for the state really warranted in India? Liberalisation poses the moot question—is a reduction in controls the automatic answer to India's ills?

The economic success of China after the initiation of reforms is a lesson to India that state control and effective planning are not dispensable concepts. Despite China's drastic shift of gear from the confines of communist ideology to market reform, totalitarian planning in China covers the economy as a whole. Although rigorous control and supervision on the Chinese model is not advocated for India—and there is really no danger of this in a democracy—yet a degree of control is imperative. China's success in market reforms has undoubtedly been engineered by the state. Even in the first three decades of over-centralised planning, China had made impressive all round development. Successful groundwork had been done in population control, literacy and effective agricultural reforms had been introduced. Although authoritarianism is not the ultimate for economic success, a study of reforms in China would certainly make it appear that the development prospects of an economy are to a great extent conditioned by the degree of state intervention and a definite role for the state.

The economic development of countries like Japan, South Korea, Taiwan and Singapore can also be credited to strategic state intervention in areas like credit availability and provision of industrial and export infrastructure. This has gone a long way in boosting the economic growth rate of these countries. Thus the fastest growing economies of South East Asia, while relying on market mechanism to maximise economic efficiency also have corrective intervention by government in the areas of public goods and externalities. The Asian Tigers demonstrate that the state must play a substantially important role and it is in fact the dynamics of state action rather than the invisible hand of the market that ensures accelerated economic development. While integrating with the world market, it must be realised that they cannot perform the function of governments. National policies account for many international economic developments. In fact in today's world, with free market forces getting increasingly mingled with protectionist tendencies and the developed world indulging in unfair consular practices, tight controls and draconian immigration laws, India will need extremely prudent diplomacy and extremely smart national policies to capture opportunities in the global world. Moreover the nation-states of the industrial world are enhancing their political clout and using it cleverly through transnational corporations, international banks or financial intermediaries. These countries are also responsible for creating international regimes of economic and political discipline that seem to thrive on selectivity. The normative and prescriptive view of globalization thus tending to harbour a dualistic structure, the state can hardly afford to abdicate. On the contrary it has an added responsibility of ensuring a greater voice for the poorer countries in the institutions of global order.

There are many areas that cannot be left to the market like infrastructural development, defence, maintenance of law and order, provision of health goods, investment of human capital, protection of natural resources and environment. The role of the state becomes extremely crucial in India, especially since it has undertaken the onus of ushering in the egalitarian credo. Since theoretically liberalisation tends to attack the state apparatus, it is important to guard against the impending danger of state minimalism. While the strategic withdrawal of the state from a number of areas may be a good thing it can hardly be presupposed that one can radically ensure uniformity of conditions and opportunities for all countries by easing the world over with markets.

The threat perception to the state under the Structural Adjustment Programme (SAP) makes it necessary to work out a solution wherein liberalisation and statism can be correctly balanced. Since the state is itself instrumental in pushing through liberalisation, it would be absurd to expect the state to roll back or to suggest liberalisation as an alternative to the state. Since the IMF, World Bank touted state minimalism is not for India, what is needed is a new role and agenda for the state. Markets are not infallible; besides market mechanism creates unequal and unfavourable terms. Asymmetries like free movement of capital and unfree movement of labour or access to markets in developing countries without a corresponding access to technology have to be corrected among others The market can be a good servant when it is intelligently utilised but a bad master when it is allowed to have free play (Rao, 1994). Markets function on profit basis. They are given to monopolistic tendencies which may result in imperfect competition. Besides they are not concerned with social infrastructure. When markets fall short of long-term objectives, the state must step in. State intervention in a variety of ways is needed to ensure that the 320 million not benefiting directly from the market mechanism can still find jobs and seek a better living.

It is true that the hegemonic role of the state promoted in the Nehru era has its days numbered and rightly so, but the marginalisation of the state should certainly not be the precondition of liberalisation. The state should not be sacrificed on the altar of free market economy. On the contrary, there is need to make it an organised and a coherent force. The issue now is not state *versus* market but a justifiable partnership between the two and the compatibility and coordination of both in the larger interest of the nation.

Recognizing Goals

In the light of the above argument it becomes important that the goals of social and economic justice be focussed on. Thus the need arises for strengthening India's socialist framework. Socialism is more than a sentimental attachment for India. Its relevance is clear from the fact that liberalisation or no liberalisation the poor still look towards the state for the availability of health care, food and other essential affordables. According to Gunnar Myrdal state planning and control of the economy are necessary not only to enhance capital formation and ensure productive investment but also to enable investment in social and economic overheads, eliminate monopolistic practices and to ensure that private profit motive and inequalities do not overshadow the economy (Myrdal, 1968). There is justified concern that under the NEP socialism will stand to suffer as liberalisation questions the country's socialist credentials. While it is painfully true that so far socialism and the welfare concept of the state have failed to deliver the goods, yet it would be a grave mistake to equate this failure with the failure of the ideology itself. On the contrary, the ideology cannot be faulted rather it is the failure of proper interpretation and implementation of the ideology. Socialism does not suffer from basic conceptual fault but contradiction between goal and strategy. That it has become a victim at the hands of Indian politics is obvious. There is imperative need to re-examine socialism and to bring it to its true form and content.

The need to strengthen the socialist fabric of the state is self-explanatory considering the fact that unlike liberalisation whose very concept, nature and manner of adoption were very sudden, socialism for India has been the result of studied effort and analysis of the Indian eco-politico culture. Hence liberalisation should not be allowed to endanger it. Moreover, while liberalisation is extractive, socialism is sustainable. Liberalisation *per se* cannot be expected to ameliorate the condition of the poor, the unemployed, the uneducated and the undernourished. The pattern of economic development it envisages may result in jobless growth and employment of skilled labour leaving the poor and unskilled to fend for themselves. An equitable partnership between capital and labour can only thrive within the state. In fact this has been proven by the German model of 'social partnership'. This model shows a comprehensive framework of partnership between major interest groups including banks, government employees associations and unions (Turner, 1998). Strong institutions are at the core of German social market economy.

Simply proclaiming to be democratic and socialist is not enough. Socialism gains meaning only when it becomes an asserted movement for social and economic justice. It demarcates a positive and substantial role for the state. It is in fact a blueprint for the state to work positively. The solution lies not in abandoning socialism in favour of liberalisation but in evolving a paradigmatic shift in development thinking without losing sight of socialist goals. There is need to deeply analyse the basic postulates of liberalisation and their contextual validity *vis-a-vis* socialism and social concern.

Resolving Paradoxes

Reforms in India are here to stay as India can ill afford to slip into its trial and error method at this juncture. With the need to adapt the reforms arises the need to resolve several paradoxes that liberalisation brings with it. India under liberalisation attempts to juxtapose the traditional with the modern, pits planning against free market, seeks long term changes from short term governments and tries to resolve market behaviour with the goal of greater social justice.

The most acute among these paradoxes is whether planning and liberalisation can go hand in hand as traditionally the latter has always been viewed as an adversary of the former. Although at the outset the juxtapositioning of the two may appear not just curious but visibly awkward yet the completion of two plans and initiation of the Tenth Five Year Plan in the era of liberalisation belies such contentions. India's adherence to planning cannot be dismissed simply as the inability of a nation wracked by chronic poverty and unemployment to move away from the shelter of the state even while embracing liberalisation. It underscores the importance and responsibility of governments to direct the reforms logically and to contain them wherever necessary. The Ninth Five Year Plan (1997-2002) emphasises the need to recognise the complementarity of the State and private sector initiatives in the development process. In fact this Plan has been developed in the context of four important dimensions of state policy viz. the quality of life of the citizen, generation of productive employment, regional balance and self-reliance. These are very much dependent upon the state for their attainment. The Tenth Five Year Plan sets an ambitious eight per cent growth target for the plan period 2002-2007. In fact FDI is the key component of this Plan and 11 per cent of the government's support to the Plan comes from disinvestments. Using the occasion of the finalisation of this Plan, Prime Minister Atal Bihari Vajpayee has clearly reiterated that the reforms will be actively pursued.

Liberalisation as adopted in India does not imply the total abdication of planning. Rather it implies purposive planning and not totalitarian planning resulting in the regimentation of the economy. The onus of suggesting policy framework for promoting sustainable development in key sectors of agriculture, industry, infrastructure and social services lies with the government. What is needed are forward looking policies that are calculated to command the confidence of both domestic and international investors. In fact foresighted state policies can surely improve upon the outcome of free and unfettered market forces.

The second paradox that needs to be resolved is the importance of regulations in liberalisation. That the open general license has replaced the license permit system is a welcome step. The open general license has considerably liberalised trade and there is significant dropping of tariff rates. Production controls have been dismantled giving the Indian firms the freedom to decide how much, where and what to produce. The budget of February 1999 saw simplification of excise rates. Liberalisation in the financial sector has led to partial freeing of interest rates and private entry into banking. No doubt under the reforms, the financial market has become more efficient and the cost of capital is significantly reduced enhancing its productive uses. Liberalisation may mean easing of controls but it should not mean total removal of regulations. In fact regulation need to be more judicious in the absence of controls. Thus rules of the game have to be prescribed and liberalisation cannot be allowed to proceed in an unbridled manner but must necessarily abide to the rule. The case for regulations both protective as well as promotional can hardly be overstated given the fact that liberalisation has pushed India into a ruthlessly competitive world. Competition without competitiveness can be a nation's undoing. Simply ensuring free competition does not ensure competitiveness. Many factors ranging from macro economic policies to micro policies on a multi-level basis must augment the ability of the nation to compete successfully (Rao, 1998). Regulations need to be intelligently devised and it is essential to recognise and to do away with counter productive regulations. In the end it is the efficiency of the regulations that determines a country's economic success. Any economy that wants to run efficiently, whether it is free market or socialist needs a lot of regulations. Not only are the total number of restrictions in all likelihood more in the US than in India but these regulations are also effective in a way they are not in India (Basu, 2002).

Another unenviable paradox is the need for long term planning in the face of short-term governments. While sound economic policies are necessary, they are not sufficient to ensure progress. They must be rooted in good governance. It is disturbing to note that one decade of reforms has seen six governments and four Prime Ministers. It is important to recognise the fatal dangers of economic and political populism that unstable governments may give in to (Sen Gupta, 1995). Such governments have negative impact. In their bid to remain in power they pursue policies that are not effective in the long run. Governments that come and go do not augur well for policies that are necessarily long term. The shorter the duration of the government the more populist the policies and the more populist the policies the greater the damage to the economy and the more difficult the task for successive governments. Besides, minority governments held to ransom by coalition partners are faced with similar predicament. Although it is some consolation to note that the BJP that had earlier viewed the reforms in India with suspicion has long since changed its stand and the second phase of reforms, which is seen as the most difficult phase has come at a time when the BJP led National Democratic Alliance, is in power. However hardliners within and outside the party focussing aggressively on *swadeshi* platform continue to attack the reforms in one way or the other. The recent standoff within the ranks of the government with respect to the government's disinvestments policy simply brought out into the open the lack of consensus within. The debate that was sparked off within the BJP led NDA government in the September of 2002 with the move to privatise two public sector oil giants, viz., Bharat Petroleum Corporation Limited (BPCL) and Hindustan Petroleum Corporation Limited (HPCL) soon escalated into a dispute on privatisation and reforms *per se* stalling the disinvestments of both these companies for the next four months. Although the government claims that its 'broad plan' to break the deadlock has been successful as is reflected in the Cabinet Committee on Disinvestment's decision on January 26, 2003, to put up HPCL for bidding by strategic investor and to disinvest government equity in BPCL through a public issue, yet the fact is that the differences between the Disinvestment Ministry on the one hand and the *swadeshi* lobby on the other hand persist. While the Swadeshi Jagran Manch has in the past accused the BJP of selling out to foreign investors, the Bhartiya Majdoor Sangh has attacked the government's proposal of liberal labour laws. With its own partners and allies bent on derailing the reforms, the union finance minister is hard pressed to garner a consensus to pass 23 finance bills, many of which are crucial to the second generation of reforms. Once the Lok Sabha is dissolved for the 2004 elections, all pending legislations will automatically lapse. Thus the task before the present governments and successive governments is tedious and fraught with difficulties. As rhetoric swings between liberalisation and planning, there remains the ever-present danger that the new economic policy will become the victim of a slanging match between the Ministry and rabble-rousers within the government. Thus it is important to guard against political instability, populist policies and political rhetoric.

Perhaps the most important challenge that India faces under the new economic globalization is to make markets—that thrive on profit motive and believe in the survival of the fittest—socially responsive. It is but acceptable that in the era of reforms the state has been compelled to let go of a notable degree of its former attitude and action. This may not be such a bad thing. The important question is under the changed context which bodies will be responsible for safeguarding the interest of the common people and which are the areas where the state needs to reconceptualise itself. In order to re-establish its credibility the state has to come up with a meaningful role. It must minimise the conflict between growth and equity, as this cannot be left to private organisations or institutions, which may discriminate between cause, context, region and even gender. This is doubly important because equity is not just a socialist sentiment but makes economic sense. It is an important contributor to growth as it makes the process of growth more meaningful. The class that stands to benefit is also inspired to contribute. The state must correct gross inequalities, eliminate monopolistic practices and regulate wisely the supply of capital so that liberalisation does not end up contributing to a 'jobless, voiceless, rootless, ruthless and futureless growth' (UNDP, 1996). Free market economy must never be allowed to promote individualism, rampant consumerism and marketisation of politics. The state must ensure that markets adhere to a code of conduct and adopt a socially responsible economic behaviour (Wadhwa, 1994). The principle of organised greed, commodification of life and monopolies must be guarded against. Adam Smith's contention that common good is paradoxically best served when an individual pursues his self-interest is difficult to accept in the Indian context, as is the trickle down theory of neo-liberals. The state must provide the development dynamics that will ultimately percolate the benefits of economic growth to the poor and the disadvantaged.

Although there is no mathematical calculus for economic engineering and for determining the exact parameters of state intervention, certain factors do have a telling impact. Proper allocation and mobilisation of natural resources according to their scarcity or abundance; controlling rates of population growth and breaking the vicious cycle of high birth rate and low per capita growth; ensuring greater level of education and literacy; promotion of health and nutrition; social security and agricultural reforms are what will contribute to sustainable growth. Employment should be the central objective and not merely a corollary of such growth. The development prospects of India will be largely conditioned by policies that will have a direct bearing on these. Without addressing these problems no government can hope to even make a dent into the monolithic problem of unemployment and poverty (Dreze and Sen, 1995).

Given the fact that the state continues to remain a repository of hope for the poor and underprivileged who form India's vast majority, it must ensure for itself a strategic economic and political role notwithstanding the theoretical trappings of liberalisation and globalization. The enduring path to a country's success lies in economic insight accompanied by political vision. At the India Today International Conclave held in New Delhi in January 2002, Yashwant Sinha, India's former Finance Minister said—India has to be ready for tomorrow for tomorrow will come. The threatening asymmetry that India faces in the world fora desperately calls for effective and efficient governments that can ensure for India bargaining power and empower it to capture opportunities in both local and global arenas. Thus even while underscoring the importance of market competitiveness, it becomes equally important to ensure the same degree of competitiveness for governments.

The UNDP calls for globalization with ethics—less violation of human rights, not more; equity—less disparity within and between countries, not more; inclusion—less marginalisation of people and countries, not more; human security—less instability of societies and less vulnerability of people, not more; sustainability—less environmental destruction, not more; development—less poverty and deprivation, not more (UNDP, 1999). Sound governance and strong domestic institutions are required to ensure that liberalisation in India conforms to these demands of greater social justice. The state must see to it that the open door policy does not work for the profits of a chosen few. Free market economy must not end up creating islands of prosperity surrounded by sea of destitution. In today's world with globalization being a reality that cannot be denied, it is time to shed parochial blinkers. The answer lies in re-examining the traditional, evaluating the modern and determining the acceptable contours between the two.

REFERENCES

Basu, Kaushik, *Times of India*, January 16, Ahmedabad, 2002.

Dibb, Paul, Towards a New Balance of Power in Asia, Adelphi Paper 295, International Institute for Strategic Studies, London, 1995.

Doyle, Michael, *Ways of War and Peace: Realism, Liberalism and Socialism*, W.W. Norton, New York, 1997, pp. 480-81.

Dreze, Jean and Sen, Amartya, *India: Economic Development and Social Opportunity*, Delhi, Oxford University Press, 1995.

Fukuyama, F., *The End of History*, National Interest, Vol. 16, 1989, pp. 3-18.

Janda, K.; Berry, J.M.; Goldman, J., *The Challenge of Democracy*: Government in America, Boston, Houghton Mifflin Company, 1992, pp. 648-52.

Keynes, J.M., *The Economic Consequences of the Peace*, London, Macmillan, 1921.

Mill, J. S., *Principle of Political Economy*, ed. Sir W. J. Ashley, Ashley M. Kelley, New York, Book II, Chapter I, 1965, pp. 199-211.

Myrdal, Gunnar, *Asian Drama*, Vol. II, London, Penguin Press, 1968.

Nehru, Jawaharlal, *India's Foreign Policy: Selected Speeches*, September 1946—April 1961, Publication Division, New Delhi, 1961, p. 305.

Nye, Joseph S., Jr., *Bound To Lead: The Changing Nature of American Power*, Basic Books, New York, 1990, p. 235.

Rao, C.H. Hanumantha, Changing Roles of Planning and Markets: The Emerging Pattern in India, *Mainstream*, Annual, 1994.

Rao, S.L., Towards a National Competition Policy for India, *Economic and Political Weekly*, Vol. 33(9), 1998.

Sen Gupta, Arindam, Politics Makes Good Business Sense Too, *The Economic Times*, August 2, New Delhi, 1995.

Smith, Adam, An Enquiry into the Nature and Causes of The Wealth of Nations, *Modern Library*, New York, 1937.

Turner, L., *Fighting for Partnership*, Cornell University Press, Ithaca, 1998.

UNDP (1996), Human Development Report, Oxford University Press, New York.

UNDP (1999), *Human Development Report*, UNDP Programme, New York.

Wadhwa, Charan D., *Economic Reforms in India and the Market Economy*, Allied Publishers, New Delhi, 1994.

Weiss, L., *The Myth of the Powerless State: Governing the Economy in a Global Era*, Polity Press, Cambridge, U.K, 1998, p. 186.

World Bank, World Development Report, From Plan to Market, New York, Oxford University Press, 1996.

7

Role of Civil Society Organizations in the Era of Globalization

ALKA DHAMEJA

Introduction

The role of civil society and its institutions has become very important in the present globalization context as many socio-economic areas that hitherto belonged to the state are opening up to non-state sectors. Keeping pace with the neo-liberal and new-right perspectives, the globalization debate has once again raised the vociferous chant of rolling back the state. The state is being projected as a facilitator and coordinator of the private and non-government sectors. Many new developments have given rise to different forms of civil society associations that are beginning to influence policy decisions. These include a fundamental change in the state's commitment to welfare, reduction of social security provisions, disenchantment of people with government policies, global accent on state minimalism, predominant role of multiple actors in governance; and success of voluntary initiatives as well as corporate ventures etc. As a result, the civic sector or civil society sector is emerging as a viable proposition to supplement or refine the functions of the state and market.

Civil society is not a new concept, a term widely analyzed in the eighteenth and nineteenth centuries, it seems to have re-emerged in the twenty-first century with conformist, reformist and many a time radical agendas. The earlier forms of governance structures appeared in the shape of societal mechanisms based on cooperation, mutuality and consensus between different groups of individuals. The society comprised private and public interests of its people and was a precursor to the state. In fact, the earlier thinkers do not make a distinction between society, civil society, political society and market state. Gradually, when societal strength came to be analyzed in associational and organizational terms, the concept of civil society was born.

The contemporary meaning of civil society, as an integral part of society and a kind of sphere outside and distinct from the political or market sphere is, however, emerging slowly in the globalization context. Society has come to be comprised of three distinct components: state sector, market sector and civic sector. The relationship between these three constituents has been a matter of debate all through the evolution of the concept of civil society. Problem is with the meaning of civil society, which is sometimes contrasted with the state and the market, but sometimes the state itself is seen as comprising the civil society. The term 'civil society' is generally defined as a particular group of society with a clearly demarcated purpose, functions, organization and means in pursuit of its agenda. It is though a broad concept that is hard to outline. The debate continues about what civil society means and this spills over into its relationship with the other sectors.

The civil society actors have come to be known as the civil society organizations or the institutions of civil society. They could be considered as a country's 'social capital', which refers to the norms and networks that enable people to coordinate collective action. Other terms used to describe them are 'civic institutions', 'social movements', 'non-governmental organizations', 'non-profit organizations', 'third party sector', 'private voluntary organizations', and 'independent advocacy groups'.

The civil society, generally refers to those groups, networks and relationships that are not organized or managed by the state. It is expected to identify major problems in society, articulate current issues, empower the disadvantaged, serve as an independent voice in strategic debates and provide a constructive forum for exchange of ideas and information between key actors in policy process. Civil society encompasses enormous diversity. In terms of membership and constituents, it includes just about all types of associations, for example, academic institutes, community based organizations, consumer protection bodies, environmental campaigns, human rights advocates, labour unions, relief organizations, professional bodies, religious institutions, women's networks, youth campaigns and sometimes even business associations. The viewpoints on the composition of civil society are varied and contestable in the absence of a consensus on its nature and scope.

The meaning of civil society organizations can thus be best understood in the light of the relationship of civil society with the state as well as the market. In the present context, both state and the market determine the complexion of civil society. This chapter aims at defining the term civil society by bringing out the key phases in its evolution and the influence of different perspectives on its growth. It tries to address issues pertaining to the role and domain of civil society organizations in the globalization context. It also throws light on the problems and constraints in conceptualizing and analyzing the role of the institutions of civil society in the global scenario.

Evolution of Civil Society

The discourse in globalization and its various manifestations is now finding a voice through various community based efforts, which do not rely on the state itself. The globalization trend is forging communitarian solutions to all problems. The idea of civil society is, however, as old as the Greek City States. Right from Aristotle and Cicero, until the time of John Locke in the seventeenth century, the term civil society was used interchangeably with political society and the state. The self-conscious and self-confident bourgeoisie class was known as civil society. To these classical philosophers, "to be a member of a civil society was to be a citizen—a member of the state" (Karlson, 2002). Originally, civil society is a European phenomenon. The earliest development of civil society as a non-political identity is associated with complex social and economic forces at work in the eighteenth century, as power devolved from monarchs to popular assemblies. The idea of civil society was first articulated by the philosophers of the Scottish Enlightenment (Baker, 2002).

Hegel was the first philosopher to develop a recognizably modern notion of civil society in his philosophy of rights (Beteilli, 2000). He sought to resolve the contradictions that existed in civil society as a result of its peculiarity by reference to the universal state. It is only at this point that the state and civil society came to be regarded as separate spheres (Baker, *op. cit*). To Hegel, however, civil society was identical with the private and the particularistic, and characterized by the conflicting and avaricious striving of individuals and classes for largely materialistic ends, while the state was seen as the embodiment of universal ethical values and rational civilization (Karlson, *op. cit.*).

It was Antonio Gramsci, who isolated civil society as a category of importance in its own right. Gramsci characterized civil society as the realm of culture and ideology, or more concretely as the associational realm (Baker, *op. cit*). Gramsci rejected the dichotomous view in which the state is counterposed to civil society and in which the latter embraces all non-state and non-public relations. For Gramsci, civil society exists as a kind of intermediary, linked both with the economic structure and with the state (Urry, 1981).

Various schools of thought have added to the understanding of the concept of civil society. The Relative Autonomy approach of Neo-Marxists has underlined the limitations of state-centric theory that has led to a definitive shift from state to civil society. The other influences have come from Pluralists and neo-pluralists. Robert Putnam's social capital approach, which we will discuss later, and the New Communitarian perspective have added extensively to the vast literature on civil society discourse. The New Communitarians seek to restore the ailing institutions by changing people's values, and thus their attitudes and behaviour, thereby rendering major structural reforms less necessary (Barber, 1996).

The evolution of the concept of civil society and its various perspectives have tried to define its meaning and scope. Therefore, any discussion on civil society without an analysis of the role of the state and market and their relationship with civil society is fraught with problems. They all define, limit and complement each other. The historical growth of the concept of civil society, as we have seen, has outlined the functions of civil society institutions in terms of its association with the state and private associations. The modern meaning of civil society has to take off from here and locate itself broadly within the relationship between the state, market and civil society in the globalization context.

Relationship between the State, Market and Civil Society

The contemporary relationship between state and civil society originates from classical liberalism. Liberal theory considers civil society to be a necessary condition for democratic states. Central to liberalism is the distinction between the public and the private spheres. The public sphere is based on representative government and the rule of law. The private sphere is that of individual action, contract, and market exchange, protected by and yet independent of the state (Barber, *op. cit.*).

A highly articulated civil society with cross-cutting cleavages, overlapping membership of groups, and social mobility is the presupposition for a stable democratic polity, a guarantee against permanent domination by any one group and against the emergence of fundamentalist mass movements and anti-democratic ideologies. The state is hemmed in—indeed transformed—by these internal forces, just as it is by international forces. But society is also transformed by the state. Social organizations, and the structure of society as a whole, are moulded by the opportunities and impediments that the state presents, just as they are affected by other social organizations and by the openings and limitations posed by the world economy (Migdal, 2001).

It has been observed that the site at which society enters into a relationship with the state can be defined as civil society. It is accordingly conceptualized as a space or public sphere where people can pursue self-defined ends in an associational area of common concerns. A space, which nurtures and sustains its inhabitants rather than control them and their relationships. A space that exists outside officially prescribed channels of communication provided by the state, where 'free' public discussion and debate can take place. The inhabitants of this space are linked together by social bonds created out of new identities and new institutions (Chandhoke, 1995).

Civil society has thus been described as the locus of the "light side" of collective action of social movements. It comprises the social realm in which the creation of norms, identities, institutions, and social relations of domination and resistance are located (Cohen and Arato, 1994). The contemporary collective endeavours, however, are more in tune with the state. Even the concept of civil society generated by new social movements, as has been rightly observed, does not necessarily deny or undermine the validity of modern state apparatuses. The new social movements have no desire to question the legitimacy of the state or directly take over the state (Gupta, 1999).

What is noticeable about civil society, in today's context, is its supposed interchangeability with NGOs. Even though the NGOs are the major constituents of civil society, thcy still do not form the entire gambit of civil society organizations. As NGOs constitute a major part of civil society organizations, their structure needs to be looked into. Julie Fisher (1998) talks of two major types of NGOs: (i) locally based grassroots organizations (GROs), and (ii) nationally or regionally based development assistance organizations called grassroots support organizations (GRSOs). GRSOs are usually staffed by professionals who channel international funds to GROs and help communities other than their own to develop.

In addition to these vertical connections between GROs and GRSOs, there are two other types of NGOs in the Third World defined by their horizontal connections with each other—GRO networks linking local communities to one another, and networks of GRSOs. Although NGOs have traditional roots, the GRO networks and GRSOs, have emerged in the latter part of the nineteenth century. The two most common types of GROs are local development associations, such as village councils or neighbourhood associations that represent an entire community and interest associations that represent particular groups within a community. A third type of GRO, include borrowers' groups, pre-cooperatives and cooperatives, which may make profits (*ibid.*).

Coming to the relationship between the market and civil society, in the globalization context, one of the pertinent questions relates to what exactly should civil society constitute. Should markets be included in the notion of civil society? Classic liberals tend to regard markets as crucial institutions of civil society, and contemporary liberals see productive and commercial associations and networks as part of civil society. By contrast, the Left emphasizes equality and democratic control over the market economy. Many of them are wary of the dangers of markets and therefore separate them from civil society in their tripartite model, which incorporates civil society, the state and the economy or the market sector. As a corollary, it is also debatable whether multinational firms can be regarded as part of the emerging global civil society (Baogang He, 2000).

Sometimes, civil society is referred to as the "third sector". The third sector concept has been developed to distinguish non-profit NGOs from the state sector and private profit sector or to characterize what has been described as "that space that is neither government nor business, occupied by citizens who take actions responsive to their needs" (Weaver and McGann, 2000). Based on freedom of association, civil society provides a check on and a balance to the other two sectors (government and the market) via citizen societies, non-governmental organizations (NGOs), and other associations (Callahan, 2002).

Clearly, the precise boundaries of non-governmental activity are a matter of debate. Nevertheless, it is generally agreed that civil society lies outside the public sector of official governance. Second, civil society is not the market, it is a non-commercial realm. No doubt, there are borderline cases, but it is generally agreed that civil society lies outside the private sector of market economy. But again anything that is non-governmental or non-commercial cannot be called civil society (Scholte, 2000).

There is thus no agreement on the constitution of civil society. In the globalization era, its domain still remains blurred. The present day civil society has to be different from its earlier counterparts as it does into have to deal just with national and regional problems, but has to adjust itself to the global influences that do not always come in the form of choices. The overlapping of market, state and civil society boundaries may conflate the purpose of civil society, which appears to have re-emerged with a defined agenda of an enabler rather than a transformer.

Re-emergence of Civil Society in the Globalization Context

The contemporary meaning of civil society, as we have seen, regards it as a non-commercial sphere that works in tandem with the market and the state. Its aim is not to dislodge the state or the market, but better their functioning through applying pressure on the state and market in the form of protests, participation, mediation and information. The current meaning of civil society is more in consonance with the cosmopolitan rather than the pluralist or elitist view of democracy that does not curb the state or restrict the civil society. In fact, it talks of enhancement of non-state, non-market solutions in the organization of civil society and the increasing role of global civil society.

The recent re-emergence of civil society has been more of a response to excessive statism in East European nations. The social movements in Poland were characterized as the rise of 'civil society against the state'. The Polish movement was defined as the 'rebirth of civil society'. It is being seen as the salvation of both socialist and capitalist societies suffering from an overdose of bureaucratic rationality (Chandhoke, *op. cit.*). The concept of reconstruction of civil society has also been revived in the West. In the former West Germany, the welfare state is seen as a mechanism by which to repoliticize the economy and dissolve the sharp boundaries between state and society. In France, there has been a totalitarian expansion of capitalism, which engulfs all spheres of social activity under single dimension of economic activity (Baogang, He, *op. cit.*).

The idea of civil society re-emerged when theorists began to insist that a social community is capable of organizing itself independently of the specific direction of state power. The concept of social refers to the capacity of states or societies to establish a sense of community, which leads a significant proportion of the society in voicing their concerns and seeking active involvement in the affairs of community, and in sharing in the benefits of community action (Rahman, *et al.*, 2000).

Robert Putnam's 'Social Capital' (1993) has brought the age-old issue of civil society to the forefront. Putnam attacks the social science tradition that views "the actors of the state and society locked in a zero-sum game and argues that highly active civic associations are strongly associated with effective public institutions. Norms and networks of civic engagement have actually promoted economic growth instead of inhibiting it" (Sobhan, 1998). Putnam shows that the regions of Italy that have both flourished economically and suffered less corruption are those that have fostered social capital formation. These are regions where citizens are more trusting to one another in civil society (Brathwaite and Strang, 2001).

Putnam's approach is essentially society-centred. The nature of distribution of power in the society and the quality of civicness will determine whether a vicious or virtuous circle dominates the governance structure. The role of the state is seen as a dependent variable. Putnam emphasizes a symbiotic relationship between the state and the community. The state's action or policy contributes to the development of trust and networks of civic engagement among members of the community and they in turn become sources of discipline and information for the public agencies as well as dependable agencies for implementation of public projects. (Sobhan, *op. cit.*)

There are many other reasons for the renewed interest in civil society. The civil society has become a theme of compelling interest throughout the world, as citizens' activism and democratization encounter post-Cold War realignment of religious fundamentalism, economic development and other forces. Public fatigue with tired party systems has sparked interest in civil society as a means of social renewal. Especially in the developing world, privatization and other market reforms offer civil society the chance to step in at places where the governments have retracted their reach. Finally, the information and technology revolution has provided new tools for forging connections and empowering citizens (Callahan, 2002).

The growing role of NGOs and global civil society has also

characterized the re-emergence of civil society. Bilateral and multilateral aid donors have switched significant fractions of their budgets from national governments to NGOs (Pearce, 2000). The 1990s has seen a surge in civil society as well as global civil society organizations (GCSOs). The proliferation of NGOs throughout the world has spurred interest in what has been called "the space of uncoerced human association" (Fisher, *op. cit.*). In recent years, NGOs have begun to look beyond their local and regional roles and have become increasingly adept at bonding together in common purpose. By pooling resources and coordinating their actions, they have even strengthened their presence in international deliberations on a range of global issues. Thus, we can witness an emerging international or global civil society.

The concept of global civil society is hardly new, although the term has come into widespread circulation recently. Over the past few years, efforts to strengthen cross-border links among NGOs have run parallel to the far more visible crusade to create International Government Organizations (IGOs) that could bring the rule of law to global affairs. The early 1990s have produced attempts to institutionalize global civil society, especially in the United States and Europe (Callahan, 1999).

Globalization, it is presumed, has contributed to the weakening of the governance abilities of the states and intergovernmental organizations, especially in the economic sphere, while strengthening civil society in many countries in the world and planting the seeds for an evolving global civil society. (Schechter, 1999). The democratizing function of civil society has assumed a higher profile, and NGOs have been identified as a possible point of contact with its building blocks, namely civic associations. Coupled with these changes has been an increasing awareness among NGOs of their own potential role in the wider development picture.

The process has been spurred on by the United Nations, which has moved to the fore in promoting civil society as a development issue. United Nations Development Programme (UNDP) and United Nations Children Emergency Fund (UNICEF) have introduced procedures to provide voluntary associations with greater access to their systems. Assumptions about the nature of NGOs have allowed the issue of 'access' by the voluntary sector to dominate discussions about civil society within the UN (Whaites, 2000). In recent years, the social capital concept also appears to have been caught on with the influential global institutions such as the International Monetary Fund and the World Bank.

The idea of civil society has now taken on a political dimension as some donors have become preoccupied with 'good governance'. This tendency has acquired an economic as well as moral rationale with the 1991 World Development Report, in which democracy has been projected as not only ethically desirable but also more efficient (*ibid.*). The World Bank recognizes that civil society plays a critical role in helping to accentuate the voices of the poorest people in the decisions that affect their lives, improve development effectiveness and sustainability, and hold governments and policymakers publicly accountable. The success stories of the sustained voluntary efforts need to be taken note of in order to strengthen the civil society.

Civil Society Organizations: Pressures and Constraints

The growing importance of civil society has also brought with it a variety of constraints and pressures. In reiteration of some of the maladies that have inflicted civil society, it can be pointed out that the civil society has not been conceptualized tightly. This is the reason why varied perspectives on its meaning, nature and composition have come to obscure its very essence. It has been observed that just as the attention paid to the state has failed to account for civil society, the focus on civil society fails to comprehend its complex relationship with the state. For instance, in India, civil society is seen by most theorists as a volatile association of social groupings, which are based on caste and kinship linkages, or on religious mobilization as much as on voluntary social associations. The problem with this kind of formulation is that it fails to distinguish between counter-civil society movements. Society, in this perspective, is collapsed into civil society. The civil society is thus being treated as a residual category, as a veritable collection of everything that is not state. It has become a conceptual ragbag, consisting of households, religious denominations, and each and every activity, which is unconnected with the state (Chandhoke, *op. cit.*).

Community identities, as has been put forth, have always been fluid in India. This fluidity gives considerable scope for political entrepreneurs to reshape the boundary and the concerns of the identity of a community. It recent years, the process of modernization and particularly politics as well as access to media and other technological devices have actually increased the mobilization potential and sharpened the self-image of splinter ethnic groups and sub-national identities, quite contrary to homogenizing efforts of modernizing elite (Bardhan, 1999).

When civil society is seen as tradition, the internal contradictions between communities and within communities are completely overlooked. It has been argued that the well-being of modern institutions can be guaranteed only if civil societies are understood as comprising truly autonomous bodies. There is a need to be wary of giving in to traditional solidarities and associations as they are inimical to the modern institutions (Gupta, *op. cit.*).

Civil society by itself, therefore, has no teleological virtue, unless it is accompanied by an interrogation of what constitutes its sphere itself. In the same way, a call for rolling back the state, has no particular virtue, unless it is accompanied by a determination that the oppressions of civil society will be dismantled. The ability of civil society to prevent the state from exercising absolute control is an essential but not a sufficient condition for democracy. The existence of civil society as a sphere of participation, deliberation, dialogue and contestations is no indication of the capacities of individuals to participate in all these activities (Chandhoke, *op. cit.*).

Critics have even pointed out the various limitations of the idea of social capital in explaining state-society interactions in the context of developing countries. It has been averred that there are a few potential problems associated with the development of civil society institutions that would nurture social capital. Looking at the state-civil society institutions develop in an authoritarian environment and what the state can do in enabling the growth and expansion of those institutions, the emphasis is on the 'recursive cycles of interaction between state and civil society actors'. Putnam's work is derived from the historical experience of Italy that suggests that a country's stock of social capital is inherited. Social capital with Putnam's framework thus cannot be accumulated (Sobhan, *op. cit.*).

The tendency to equate civil society organizations with NGOs, as we have seen, limits our understanding of a broad process of interaction among different types of organizations. The concept of civil society has been 'grabbed' by NGOs as one relating closely to their own natural strengths. On the surface, civil society is intimately connected with the role of local community associations or groups, and with the indigenous NGO sector. Among donors, interest in civil society has been associated with the evolution of the conditionality of aid in the 1980s. Donors have begun to reappraise the role of civil society in providing a foundation for sustainable democracy. The combination of donor, NGO and UN interest provides the background to the civil society 'grab' (Whaites, *op. cit.*).

The states are adopting new strategies, using NGOs for their own purposes. (Baogang He, *op. cit.*). Some analysis see the recent quests for community control as little more than a state-orchestrated managerial reform to take over institutions. Other critics view it as an interpretation between state and community spheres that is more than genuine community control. Still others portray it as an attempt to redress profound crises now confronting capitalist classes (Breathwaite and Strang, *op. cit.*). Both state-centred and society-centred approaches are now proving problematic and inadequate. Importantly, it is believed that the civil society approach is itself problematic if it does not take account of global civil society. It seems that the idea of global civil society combines elements of both anti-state and anti-nation positions (Baogang He, *op. cit.*).

The growing size, sophistication, and influence of the GCSOs, have been facilitated and actively encouraged by one main factor—the Neo-liberal consensus that emerges from the power centres in the West. Among other things, the consensus dictates: (a) the state in particularly third world countries should withdraw from the social sector, (b) the market should be freed from all constraints, and (c) communities in civil society should organize their own social and economic reproduction and well-being. The state has thus been liberated from its traditional responsibilities of providing the conditions of human flourishing (Chandhoke, 2002).

The vision of civil society *sans* well-defined role of the state is thus replete with serious consequences, which not only weakens civil society, but also jeopardizes the future of GCSOs. It has been pointed out that by drastically reducing the importance of proximity, the new technologies change people's perceptions of community. The potential for building global civil society might come at the expense of weakened identity with one's state and with the civil society within the country in which one has one's primary abode. In the absence of a global public space and an opportunity for dialogue, robust global community may remain a distant dream (Schechter, *op. cit.*)

Francis Fukuyama in his original essay *The End of History* (1989) offered a vision of a world purged of ideology, in which history has come to an end because there are no alternatives to the institutions of the present, representative democracy and the market, The future would, therefore, be the endless repetition of more of the same, with politics centred in bureaucratic problem-solving, limited social engineering and liberal compromise (Hirst, 1994).

This indeed is a very pessimistic projection of the socio-economic and political reality. Alternatives to absolute state or market control over production and provision of goods seem elusive. Democratic decentralization, participative decision-making, and community management of resources through different civil society organizations can solve the problem to some extent. Voluntarism and associationalism have been part of the culture in the developing countries, their pertinence needs to be harnessed, more so, in the globalization context. The very fact that the number of community organizations, voluntary agencies, self-help groups, non-public, and non-market associations has grown tremendously and that too with more systematic agendas is a step in the right direction.

A Futuristic Perspective of Civil Society Organizations

The reappearance of civil society institutions has historically heralded the advent of democracy. In fact, to a large extent, how we conceptualize and evaluate civil society depends on how we visualize democracy, the converse also holds true. Democratic political theory privileges civil society because it assumes that the existence of democracy is inextricably bound up with that of civil society (Cohen and Arato, *op. cit.*).

The increasing labelling of civil society as NGOs and vice versa in the present globalization scenario, needs to be looked into. For some NGOs, the labelling of all potential partner groups as 'civil society organizations' reflects the continued acceptance of a universalistic view of civil society. As has been observed, when civil society is referred to as 'sphere of public debate', its meaning transcends the synonymous treatment with NGOs that it receives. For instance, newspaper readership is used by Robert Putnam as one of the indicators for contrasting the strength of civil society in Northern Italy with its weakness in the South (Fisher, *op. cit.*). Questions that need to be taken up are: how do NGOs separate beneficial from non-beneficial civil society, how do they maintain autonomy and accountability, what type of self-regulation do they follow and how do they weave a strategy for nurturing civil society into a strategy for nurturing civil society into a strategy for building the capacity of the state (Eade, *op. cit. emphasis added*).

Given the importance that donors and NGOs attach to the concept of civil society, it matters a great deal that NGOs do not slip into the divide over the meaning of civil society, particularly where societies are heterogeneous and divided. The says in which NGOs perceive civil society, and consequently plan projects to facilitate the work of civic associations, can have a significant effect on the extent of devolution of civil society in the countries in which they work. The NGOs should try fully to explore the theoretical implications of civil society and clearly articulate their own interpretations of its nuances (Whaites, *op. cit.*).

Recent decades have brought general retreat from centralized governance with trends toward devolution, regionalization and globalization. Governance has shifted from a unidimensionality of statism to a multidimensionality of local, national, regional and global layers of regulation. Although large-scale globalization has not dissolved nation-states, this form of collective identity has lost its previous position of overwhelming primacy. In the late twentieth century, world politics is also being deeply shaped by sub-state solidarities like ethno-nations and by non-territorial, trans-border communities based on class, gender, race and religion (Scholte, *op. cit.*).

There is a strong emphasis on community not as a social or geographical construct, but as a virtual space of shared cultural and moral affinities that express the ethics of self-governance. The focus is on a fair, practical and right-based shaping of daily institutional practices in each sphere of individual life. Informal community initiatives are now being organized all over South Asia, with or without government help and they have often succeeded in serving those most vulnerable sections of society that governments find difficult to reach. By opening spaces for civic engagement, CSOs, households, businesses and the media can contribute to governance processes for human development in general and an improvement in the lives of local communities in particular. The emergence of the self-instituted civil society as an independent social partner alongside formal political and economic structures, will thoroughly modify governance systems (Human Development in South Asia, 1999).

In July 2002, the World Civil Society Forum met in Geneva to discuss that would help in strengthening international co-operation between civil society and international organizations (Callahan, 2002).

The implications of the global civil society are hazy, yet tantalizing. Some ponderables could be: will huge networks and coalitions of citizen activists come to rival international governmental organizations (IGOs) in the next century as leading vehicles of transnational cooperation, will new democratic processes arise at the worldwide level that can offset the clout of global capital, and will national public policy debates increasingly be influenced by social and economic norms that hold sway globally (Callahan, 1999). These key concerns need to be addressed.

NGOs and social movements must keep in mind that their influence on the process of global governance will remain quite limited unless they succeed in effectively channelling the action of national governments and influencing the allocation of resources mobilized by governments and multilateral institutions (Zoninsein, 1999). The new trends in globalization cannot be a remedy for all ills. Socio-economic development has to be indigenous, contextual and innovative. Especially in the developing countries, where community plays a pertinent role in production of goods and services, more so, at the micro-level, the solution lies in 'globalization'. There is a need for more research in the areas of community building democracy, citizenship, role of GCSOs and collaborative networking among the NGOs. It has been pointed out that Village Councils in which women and *dalits* have a central police will be a genuine institutional innovation. They can give a new lease of life to democracy in India (Beteile, 2002).

To be usable today, the category of civil society must be reconstructed. "Reconstruction", could be defined in the non-systematic sense, as "taking a theory apart and putting it back together again in a new form in order to attain more fully the goal it has set itself." (Cohen and Arato, *op. cit.*). The "resurrection of civil society" that pushes the democratization process forward is possible in either case, with or without surviving forms of recognized association, with or without memories of earlier mass mobilization. What is needed is a civil society, which is seriously engaged in self-reflection, is preoccupied with the means used to accomplish its tasks, and which brings about slow and incremental but substantial changes in the state. A civil society that is accessible and responsive to the subalterns, marginal and the radical (Chandhoke, 1995, *op. cit.*)

There is an urgent need for the government, civil society and private sector to work as partners in crucial areas of participatory development. Without a civil society to nourish engaged citizens, it has been observed, politicians turn into 'professionals', out of touch with their constituencies; while citizens are reduced to mere antagonists or turn into ungrateful clients of government services they readily consume without being willing to pay for (Barber, *op. cit.*).

Market-state endeavours have overwhelmed the economy in the recent past with many public sector enterprises divesting and opening up to private entrepreneurs. There have been successful ventures between state and civil society, especially in the areas of information technology and resource management. It has to be seen how the market can fruitfully associate with state as well as civil society in the future. The convergence between NGOs and informal profit-oriented enterprises, it has been observed, offers some promise for building a different model of society, since profits generated within this new non-profit for profit nexus are invested in public as well as private goods and services (Fisher, *op. cit.*).

It has been argued that democracy needs to be broadened and deepened, with government acting in partnership with agencies in civil society so as to combat civic decline. The retention of high levels of autonomy and self-organization will be important if these agencies are not to be swamped by distorting state power. Established traditions of participative planning and community development can be complemented by experience in direct democracy (McLaughlin, *et al.*, 2002).

Successful civil society institutions, as we have seen, is a world-wide phenomenon, Micro-credit societies in Bangladesh, Bonding Associations in Panama. Women's Groups in Kenya and Local Credit Networks in Guatemala are some instances that can be cited. Some examples of civil society initiatives from India include Pani Panchayats, Sangharsh Samitis, Fodder Banks, Grain Banks, Citizens' Forums. Bhagidhari Associations, the Chipko Movement, Narmada Bachao Andolan, Tehri Dam Movement and so on. The Panchayati Raj Institutions through their Gram Sabhas have been quite successful in bringing the civil society closer to the government to some extent.

New Delhi Television Channel covered a very successful endeavour of the village people on running a grain bank in Chattisgarh some time back. Ramkothi Block in District Durg had set up a grain bank ten years ago. It is now reaping benefits by providing excess grains at subsidized prices to the poor farmers to withstand drought conditions. It is also running a High School with the available funds. It has been pointed out that the Bal Manchs, which are presently existing in eight districts of Rajasthan, have been set up by the help of UNICEF. These are emerging as civil society initiatives that are shaping the agenda for children in panchayats, schools and ultimately at all levels of administration. In Ajmer, these panchayats have successfully taken up issues like prevention of child marriages, counselling against drug addiction, and promotion of school enrolment (*The Hindu*, December 14, 2002).

At the Asian Social Forum held in Hyderabad in January 2003, people from all over the world expressed that they did not want to privatize essential services such as water supply, but at the same time did not want the state either. An opinion voiced by a member of the water supply organization of the citizens in Bolivia has a profound implication. He stated that private enterprises are for rich people and state enterprises are basically private enterprises of the political party. What is needed is an enterprise based on four pillars of management namely transparency, efficiency, participation and social justice (*The Hindu*, January 9, 2003).

It is heartening to note that it is possible today to have World Social Forum or the Asian Social Forum that can weave together a range of different movements and activists. The Asian Social Forum did bring together more than 15,000 people from the continent. And the World Social Forum had more than 60,000 people raising their voice against all forms of violence, discrimination and oppression (*The Hindu,* March 9, 2003).

In wanting to open up new democratic terrain, the core justificatory principle is that major arenas of social, economic and political power—power over people's lives and power that shapes the life of society itself—should be harnessed to a doctrine of democratic responsibility. This is a responsibility that acknowledges a framework of obligations and accountability, recognizes a range of legitimate stakeholders and seeks ways in which these stakeholders can have an effective voice. An approach of this kind will not be impressed by attempts to construct iron walls between 'public' and 'private' centres of power, but will instead want to apply the doctrine of responsibility to both (Barber, *op. cit.*).

The civil society, in the globalization context, has assumed entrepreneur like characteristics. This new thinking should not be seen as a shift in power from the state to civil society, but rather as the natural evolution of the relationship between those who govern and those who are governed. Couched in positive terms, governments are learning to govern better through heeding the popular voice; and citizens are learning to be better citizens through exposure to the regular rules and disciplined practices of associations of civil society. The private sector has a large stake in the expansion of civil society because civil order fosters economic growth. The synergies arising out of the emerging relations between the state, private sector, and civil society must thus be put to practical use (Rahman, *et al., op. cit.*).

Community endeavours have become more pertinent with the receding of the state from certain areas and the influx of market associations at the national and international levels. To understand the transformative role of the civil society, its undertones have to go beyond its interlinkages with NGOs and other Community Based Organizations. Other indicators of civility have to be sought. A well-informed and well-informing media could bring in the necessary change. All institutions in society cannot be called civil society organizations. They must have a specific purpose, a clear-cut agenda, an organized *modus operandi*, an autonomous functioning mechanism and a self-reflective evaluation capacity.

Civil society, it is being put forth by many, reflects the change in the global aspect of the society more than any other component. What needs to be seen is that the civil society organizations do not assume anti-democratic, fundamentalist and oppressive proportions. A clarity on their boundaries, access, role and functions is a precondition for their success. A country rooted in strong civil society traditions could ensure the observance of all the prerequisites of good governance namely transparency, efficiency, accountability, participation and responsiveness. This is, however, possible only if conditions for a mutually advantageous existence of state, market and community are nurtured and sustained in the globalization context.

REFERENCES

Baker, Gideon, *Civil Society and Democratic Theory: Alternative Voices*, Routledge, London, 2002, 4-5.

Baogang He, "Civil Society and Democracy" in April Carter and Geoffrey Stokes (Eds.), *Democratic Theory Today*, Polity, Cambridge, 2002, 204-219.

Barber, R., "Three Challenges to Reinventing Democracy" in Paul Hirst and Sunil Khilnani (Eds.), *Reinventing Democracy*, Blackwell, U.K., 1996, 98.

Bardhan, Pranab, "The State Against Society: The Great Divide in Indian Social Science Discourse" in Sugata Bose and Ayesha Jalal (Eds), *Nationalism, Democracy and Development: State and Politics in India*, Oxford University Press, New Delhi, 1999,.

Beteille, Andre, *Antinomies of Society: Essays on Ideologies and Institutions*, Oxford University Press, New Delhi, 2000,.

Beteille, Andre, "Village Republics", *The Hindu*, September 3, 2002.

Brathwaite, John and Heather Strange, "Introduction: Restorative Justice and Civil Society" in Heather Strang and John Brathwaite (Eds.), *Restorative Justice and Civil Society,* Cambridge, U.K., 2001, 2.

Cahoone, Lawrence, E., *Civil Society: The Conservative Meaning of Liberal Politics*, Blackwell, U.S., 2002, 204.

Callahan, David, "What is Global Civil Society", *Features*, Vol. 3, No. 1, January-February, 1998,.

Callahan, James J., *Article and Web Alert*, The American Centre, New Delhi, 2002, 1-9.

Chandhoke, Neera, *State and Civil Society: Explorations in Political Theory*, Sage, New Delhi, 1995,.

Chandhoke, Neera, "Civil Society Hijacked", *The Hindu*, January 16, 2002,.

Cohen, Jean L. and Andrew Arato, *Civil Society and Political Theory*, MIT Press, London, 1994, 74-75 and 515.

Drucker, Peter, "Age of Social Transformaton", *The Atlantic Monthly*, Vol. 274, No. 5, Nov., 1994.

Eade, Deborah, "The Discourse of Civil Society" in Deborah Eade (Series Editor), *Development NGOs and Civil Society*, Oxfam, London, 2000, 23-24, 135-137.

Ferlie, Ewan and Louise Fitzgerald, "The Sustainability of the New Public Management of the U.K." in Kate McLaghlin, Stephen P. Osborne and Ewan Ferlie (Eds.), *New Public Management: Current Trends and Future Prospects,* Routledge, London, 2002.

Fisher, Julie, *Non-Governments: NGOs and Political Development of the Third World,* Kumarian, USA, 1998, 4-17, 30, 76-77, 165-173.

Gupta, Dipankar, "Civil Society or the State: What Happened to Citizenship" in Ramachandra Guha and Jonathan Parry (Eds.), *Institutions and Inequalities: Essays in Honour of Andre Beteille*, Oxford University Press, New Delhi, 1999.

Hindess, Barry, Nikolas Rose and Claus Offe, "Modern Regimes of Governance" in Richard V. Ericson and Nico Stehr, (Eds.), *Governing Modern Societies*, University of Toronto Press, Canada, 2000.

Hirst, Paul, *Associative Democracy: New Forms of Economic and Social Governance*, Polity Press, Cambridge, 1994.

Human Development in South Asia, *The Crisis of Governance,* Oxford University Press, New Delhi, 1999, 128.

Karlson, Nils, *The State of State: Invisible Hands in Politics and Civil Society*, Transaction, USA, 2002.

Kaufman, Michael, "Community Power and Grassroots Democracy: The Transformation of Social Life" in Michael Kaufman and Haraldo Dilla (Eds.), *Community Power and Grassroots Democracy: The Transformation of Social Life*, Zed Books, London, 1997.

Migdal, Joel S., *State in Society: Studying how States and Societies Transform and Constitute one Another*, Cambridge, U.K., 2001, 4-5, 56-57.

Pearce, Jenny, "Introduction" in Deborah Eade, *op. cit.,* 2000.

Rahman, Atiur, Sayed Naimul Wadood and Mohammed Abu Eusuf, "Civil Society and Governance" in Hasrat Abdul Hye (Ed.), *Governance: South Asian Perspectives*, Manohar, New Delhi, 2000, 428-457.

Schechter, Michael G., "Globalization and Civil Society" in Michael G. Schechter, (Ed.), *The Revival of Civil Society: Global and Comparative Perspective*, (International Political Economy Series), Macmillan, London, 1999, 67 and 80.

Scholte, Jan Aart, "Global Civil Society" in Ngaire Woods, (Ed.), *The Political Economy of Globalization*, Palgrave, New York, 2000, 174-180.

Self, Peter, *Political Theories of Modern Government: Its Role and Reform,* George Allen and Unwin, London, 1985,.

Sobhan, Rehman, "State, Society and Economic Performance" in Rehman Sobhan (Ed.), *Towards a Theory of Governance and Development: Learning from East Asia*, University Press Ltd., Bangladesh, 1998, 39-40.

Sobhan, Rehman, "Towards a Theory of Governance and Development" in Rehman Sobhan (Ed.), *ibid.*

Subramanian, A.K. Venkat, "Towards People's Politics", *The Hindu*, May 8, 2001.

The Hindu, August 6, 2002.

The Hindu, December 14, 2002.

The Hindu, January 9, 2003.

Urry, John, *The Anatomy of Capitalist Societies: The Economy, Civil Society and the State*, Macmillan, London, 1981, 18-22 and 66.

Viswanath, Kalpana, "Despair and Hope", *The Hindu*, March 9, 2003.

Weaver, R. Kent and James G. McGann, "Think Tanks—Civil Society in a Time of Change" in James G. McGann, and R. Kent Weaver, (Eds.), *Think Tanks and Civil Societies: Catalysts for Ideas and Action*, Transaction, U.K., 2000.

Whaites, Alan, "Let's get Civil Society Straight: NGOs, the State and Political Theory" in Deborah Eade, *op. cit*, 2000, 125-127.

Zoninsein, Jones, "Global Civil Society and Theories of International Political Economy" in Michael G. Schechter, (Ed.), *op. cit*, 1999, 11 and 51.

Website Reference

http://www.undp.org.lb/partners/civil.html

8

Globalization, Sovereignty and Human Rights: A Perspective

ARUN KUMAR SINGH

Globalization is a global lexicon today. It is the ideology of the present century—more powerful and pervasive than any other. Its reach is global and universal. There is no society, today, that has escaped its influence and impact. It is all encompassing. Its impact can be seen, felt and realized on economic, social, cultural and political life of the people all over. No other ideology in the human history had such an appeal and application. It has transcended all the barriers—territorial, ideological, economic, social, political, ethnic, racial and religious. It is a gender-neutral word in a gender divided world.

Today, only one ideology has come to exist and that is the 'globalist ideology'. It has become a *mantra* for all the policy planners, corporate world, academics and activists. It is the hotly debated concept of the new century. 'In this realm, globalisation today is where internationalism once was'. Though, the word 'globalization' is hated by many, the reality is that there is no alternative to it. Either we learn to exist with it or be ready to be doomed. The UK government's White Paper on globalization of December 2000—*Making Globalization Work for the Poor* exemplifies the 'TINA' school of thought that 'there is no alternative' to globalization and we must learn to live with it. The worldwide anti-globalization protests only substantiate its universality.

The contour of world economic and political order is, today, different from what it was about a decade ago. The UNDP Human Development Report, under the caption—*The world has changed*—observes:

> Over the past decade dramatic events have changed the global political order—the end of the cold war unleashed a wave of global political integration. The fall of the Berlin Wall in 1989 and the end of the cold war removed political and economic barriers—bringing more than 400 million people in Eastern Europe and Commonwealth of the Independent States (CIS) and almost 1.3 billion people in China and Viet Nam into the world of global contacts and communications. Ideas and information began to flow freely as countries lifted censorship, travel restrictions and prohibitions on political parties and civil society organizations. And foreign investment poured into China, Viet Nam, Poland and Russian Federation—as did McDonald's, Hollywood movies and CNN real-time global news.

The disintegration of the Soviet Union was acclaimed in the west and America and celebrated as the 'end of history' and the triumph of liberal democracy. In fact, it was the triumph of capitalism over communism. "The New World Order" as Peter Harris puts it, "is based upon 'progressive internationalism', which promotes new global partnerships, crossing old ideological frontiers and buying old enemies". The twenty-first century is witnessing the unprecedented and unstoppable march of the forces of globalization reinforced primarily by the capitalism propelled market forces. Is there anybody in any region of the world who is not affected by this new *avatar* called globalization?

But, what is globalization? Is it a new concept or just an old wine in a new bottle? What impact does it have on the life of the people? How has it affected the nation-states and what forces govern them? Does it go well with human rights? And, more importantly, have all the societies been affected equally? These are some of the vital questions, which need to be addressed and analyzed.

Globalization as a Concept

The term globalization is defined differently in different context. According to Robert McCorquodale "globalization is a contested term and there is no one accepted definition of it". In a broader sense it includes two things—integration of the world and interdependence of the sovereign nation-states. The term is all encompassing is defined and understood in both 'economic and non-economic contexts which broadly include socio-cultural, historical and political'.

As Harriss observes:

> Globalization is of course a controversial term, defined in all sorts of different ways. That it has come into use in the last 10 years or so is an indication that something has been happening out there in the 'real world' to which it refers—the world is more interconnected and supposedly more interdependent than it was formerly, as a result of changes in the global economy—notably rapid movements of large volumes of money and the increased volumes of trade—as well as changes in communications and information technology".

It includes cultural and political changes. To some it means 'de-territorialization'. The idea that globalization is characterized by de-territorialization is advanced by Jan Aart Scholte in his book *Globalization: A Critical Introduction*, Macmillan, London, 2000.

As S.T. Akindele says:

> Globalization refers to the process of the intensification of economic, political, social and cultural relations across international boundaries. It is principally aimed at the transcendental homogenization of political and socio-economic theory across the globe. It is equaliy aimed at 'making global being present worldwide at the world stage or global arena" [S.T. Akindele: 2002:12]

It deals with the ' increasing breakdown of trade barriers and the increasing integration of world market'.

Globalization is further seen in the context of ascendancy and dominance of capitalism; market forces and liberal democracy particularly in the aftermath of the collapse of the Eastern bloc in the late 80s and 90s. "Globalization" as quoted in S.T. Akindele means the "broadening and deepening linkages of national economies into a worldwide market for goods and services, especially capital". It aims at "removing all national barriers to the free movement of international capital" reinforced by the "supersonic transformation in information technology. It is principally aimed at the universal homogenization of ideas, cultures, values, and even life styles as well as at the de-territorialization and villagization of the world".

The UNDP Human Development Report clearly spells out that the events of the 1980s and the 1990s that took place in the Eastern Europe and in the former Soviet Union *'sped the pace of globalization and deepened the interactions among the people. They have also defined the character of global integration, giving rise to new markets, new actors, new rules and new tools. And they have created an era of globalization that is intensifying contacts—not just between countries but between people*'. Globalization, in sum, means connecting people, connecting places, connecting cultures and connecting values. As one commentator points out:

> the last quarter of the twentieth century witnessed an upsurge in the process of globalization. The world has noted increasing integration of international markets for goods, services, technology and finance. Such an upsurge in international economic activity, which is now being referred to as globalization, has been interpreted by most social analysts, public officials and mass media alike as marking the dawn of a new era. The new era, with the breakdown of national boundaries, has been acclaimed as an era of "critical transformation" bringing about an "end of geography/ history", in a "new global village". The "new village" reflects the universal acceptance of the western arrangements and "management" of societal problems in a post communist world. It also increasingly shares a "world culture" dominated by the affluent west.

The current phase of globalization has three characteristic features. First, shrinking space, which means 'peoples lives—their jobs, incomes and health—are affected by events on the other side of the globe, often by events they do not know about'. Secondly, 'shrinking time, which is seen in the speed with which markets and technologies are changing. And more importantly, disappearing borders. National borders are breaking down, not only for trade, capital and information but also for ideas, norms, cultures and values. Peoples lives around the globe are linked more deeply, more intensely, more immediately than ever'. Globalization is also seen in terms of free movement of goods, services, capital and technology but not capital.

Globalization as Paul Streeten remarks has two important

indicators—integration and interdependence. Today international integration is taking place at a rapid space due to the 'increased flow of trade, capital, money, technology, people, information and ideas across national boundaries'. Similarly, interdependence between the nations has increased primarily due to increase in the volume of trade. "Between 1820 and 1992 world population increased five-fold, income per head eight-fold, world income 40-fold, and world trade 540-fold". The process of economic integration and interdependence has been accelerated since the 1990s due to the breakdown of the ideological barriers between the nations and group of nations after the fall of the Berlin Wall in 1989.

The concept of globalization has also been examined in terms of "universalization of particularism and particularization of universalism", that is, what is local is global and what is global is local. This two-fold process has many aspects. "Clearly it is a political, social, and cultural process, but it is foremost an economic process".

Some scholars view globalization as the march and spread of American capitalism. As *John Harris* puts it:

> globalization is to great extent a euphemism for American imperialism. The power of capital is not only expressed through the financial flows that no one actually 'plans', but also in the very deliberately constructed policy networks linking government, corporate sector and *inter alia* universities, that operate behind barriers of official secrecy".

It is in this context that certain popular terminologies such as Disneyfication, McDonaldization, and Coca-Colonization are placed. But, does globalization mean Americanization? There are some who argue that it does as we see the world being dominated by the American corporate houses, American financial institutions, American technology and military, and American popular culture—American food, American films, American songs, American television, and American print and satellite media. In other words what is global is American.

There are others like John Micklethwait and Adrian Wooldridge who holds the view that globalization 'not necessarily' means Americanization. Liberal virtues such as accountability, transparency, and individual rights that are associated with globalization are no doubt often deemed to be American but the United States has no monopoly on them. Classical liberal thinkers—John Locke, David Hume, and Adam Smith were British thinkers and the popular terminology—*laissez faire*—a French phrase. Similarly, the EU's Constitution like that of the American upholds the values of democratic representation and individual rights. They also point out that:

> Nor does globalization necessarily mean the Americanization of popular culture. True American films can be seen almost all over the world, the Big Mac is the closest thing we have to a universal food, and Britney Spears is hard to avoid, even if you are in Tibet. But cultural trade is a two way process. If you look at popular musicals (Andrew Lloyd Webber's) or the bestseller lists (the *Harry Potter* series), Britain continues to exercise a powerful influence on the United States.

If globalization is all about Americanization or Europeanization, then where do we place and locate the cultures of others? These two commentators argue that *'globalization does mean the triumph of a particular nationality. The essence of globalization is that it increases choice' (ibid).* But who has choice in the market driven globalized world? Definitely, it could not be the poor men (and women). Can one imagine a sight where a hungry man/woman looks helplessly at the American food outlets—McDonald and Pizza Hut?

Stanley Hoffmann illustrates various features of globalization. First, it is multidimensional. It has three basic dimensions—economic, cultural and political. Each dimension has its advantage and disadvantage. Economic globalization is the product of "recent revolutions in technology, information, trade, foreign investment, and international business. The main actors are companies, investors, banks, and private services industries, as well as states and international organizations". The prime mover is capitalism. The 'present form of capitalism poses a central dilemma between efficiency and fairness, wealth and social justice'. He argues that 'specialization and integration of firms make it possible to increase aggregate wealth, but the logic of pure capitalism does not favour social justice. Economic globalization has thus become a formidable cause of inequality among and within states'.

As regards the cultural dimension of globalization, Hoffmann notes:

It stems from the technological revolution and economic globalization, which together foster the flow of cultural goods. Here the key choice is between uniformization (often termed "Americanization") and diversity. The result is both a "disenchantment of the world" and reaction against uniformity. The latter takes form in a renaissance of local cultures and languages as well as assaults against western culture, which is denounced as an arrogant bearer of a secular, revolutionary ideology and a mask for U.S. hegemony'.

Political globalization is the product of both—the economic as well as the cultural globalization. To quote Stanley Hoffmann, political globalization is 'characterized by the preponderance of the United States and its political institutions and by vast array of international and regional organizations and transgovernmental networks (specializing in areas such as policing or migration or justice). It is also marked by private institutions that are neither governmental nor purely national--say, Doctors Without Borders or Amnesty International'. Stanley Hoffmann argues that the fate of American hegemony is uncertain as it 'faces significant resistance abroad and is affected by America's own oscillation between the temptations of dominance and isolation'.

Second, the benefits of globalization, though undeniable, are limited as well as uneven. Hoffmann argues that globalization is 'largely an American creation, rooted in the period after World War II and based on U.S. economic might. A deep and protracted economic crisis in the United States could have as devastating an effect on globalization as did the 'Great Depression'. Moreover, the 'reach of globalization remains limited as it excludes many poor countries'. This is partly because 'the world is far away from a perfect integration of markets, services, and factors of production'.

Third, one of the main features, rather the effect of globalization, has been the rise of social movements in the form of civil society. But this 'international civil society remains embryonic'. Besides, many non-governmental organizations constitute only a tiny segment of the population of their members' states. They largely represent only modernized countries. Also, the NGOs have little independence from governments.

Fourth, it is also doubtful that globalization leads to ensuring 'individual freedom' and 'succeed in democratizing regimes as one can see today in China'. Hoffmann also argues that democratization or emancipation does not prevent institutions such as the International Monetary Fund, or the World Bank from 'remaining opaque in their activities and often arbitrary and unfair in their rulings'.

Fifth, Hoffmann also questions the capacity of globalization in 'improving the human condition through the abolition of barriers'. He points out that 'Globalization is in fact a sum of techniques (audio and video cassettes, the Internet, instantaneous communications) that are at the disposal of states or private sectors. Self-interest and ideology, not humanitarian reasons, are what drive these actors'. He further argues:

> behaviour of these actors 'is quite different from the vision of globalization as an Enlightenment-based utopia that is simultaneously scientific, rational, and universal. For many reasons—misery, injustice, humiliation, attachment to traditions, aspiration to more than just a better standard of living—this "Enlightenment" stereotype of globalization thus provokes revolt and dissatisfaction'.

Sixth, globalization suffers from contradiction in the sense that:

> On the one hand, international and transnational cooperation is necessary to ensure that globalization will not be undermined by the inequalities resulting from market fluctuations, weak state-sponsored protections, and the incapacity of many states to improve their fates by themselves. On the other hand, cooperation presupposes that many states and rich private players operate altruistically—which is certainly not the essence of international relations—or practice a remarkably generous conception of their long-term interests. But the fact remains that most rich states still refuse to provide sufficient aid or intervene in crisis situations such as the genocide in Rwanda.

This is in contrast with ' the American enthusiasm to pursue the fight against Al Qaeda and the Taliban'.

Stanley Hoffmann further examines the effects of globalization on international politics and sovereignty, the impact of globalization on national citizenship, and the relationship between globalization and violence with particular reference to terrorism. First, globalization has resulted in emergence of "global society" since 'no state can do everything by itself'. This has ensured peace between the states. This 'seeks to ensure fairness in the world market and create international regulatory regimes in such areas as trade, communications, human rights, migration, and refugees'. But, this process is inhibited by 'the reluctance of states to accept global directives that might constrain the market or further reduce their sovereignty. Thus the UN's powers remain limited'. It is the market ' which has been the main beneficiary of the state's retreat' and 'not global governance'.

Economic globalization has affected state's sovereignty as 'it deprives many states of independent monetary and fiscal policies, or it obliges them to make cruel choices between economic competitiveness and preservation of social safety nets'. At the same time, as Hoffmann remarks:

> The United States displays an increasing impatience toward institutions that weigh on American freedom of action. Movement toward a world state looks increasingly unlikely. The more state sovereignty crumbles under the blows of globalization or such recent developments as humanitarian intervention and the fight against terrorism, the more states cling to what is left to them.

Second, while analyzing the impact of globalization on the nature of citizenship, Stanley Hoffmann points out that the national character of citizenship remains intact despite the global integration of the economic life of the people. There is a 'strong resistance to cultural homogenization'. It is primarily because of the preponderant nature and reach of the nation-states. As Hoffmann observes 'over the centuries, increasingly centralized states have expanded their functions and tried to forge a sense of common identity for their subjects'. He cites the example of the European Union where 'a single currency and advanced economic coordination have not yet resulted in creating a sense of post-national citizenship'. This explains the limit of the world economy, which is very partially unified by technology, in 'engendering a sense of world citizenship'.

Third, Hoffmann is of the opinion that there exists a ' relationship between globalization and violence'. The traditional nature of war and conflict is still a reality. The 'distrust' among the nations 'who prefer to try to preserve their security alone or through traditional alliances prevents a more satisfactory institutionalization of world politics—for example an increase of the UN's power'. He thus argues that:

> Globalization, far from spreading peace, thus seems to foster conflicts and resentments. The lowering barriers—makes it possible for the most deprived and oppressed to compare their fate with that of the free and well-off. These disposed then ask for help from others with common resentments, ethnic origin, or religious faith. Insofar as globalization enriches some and uproots many, those who are both poor and uprooted may seek revenge and self-esteem in terrorism.

Hoffmann also reflects on globalization and terrorism. There are several forces behind the root of terrorism. According to him ' It (terrorism) can also been seen as a product of globalization. Transnational terrorism is made possible by the vast array of communication tools'. He argues that "*Islamic terrorism*" should be viewed not only in the context 'of support for Palestinian struggle and opposition to an invasive American presence. It is also fuelled by *a ' resistance to "unjust" economic globalization and to a Western culture deemed threatening to local religions and cultures'*.

He points out that as 'globalization facilitates terrorist violence, the fight against this war without borders is potentially disastrous for both economic development and globalization'. The fight against terrorism would ' restrict mobility and financial flows' and anti terrorist measures could generate 'antiglobalist reaction comparable to the chauvinistic paroxysms of the 1930s'.

According to him, both terrorism and fight against it violate sovereignty particularly of ' those states accused of encouraging terror'. Moreover, the fight against terror has allowed the states 'to tighten their controls on their own people, products, and money'. This situation has provided 'reasons (for the states) to violate individual rights in the name of common defense against insecurity'. As Hoffmann remarks, (thus) '*terrorism is a global phenomenon that ultimately reinforces the enemy—the state—at the same time as it tries to destroy it*'. In this way terrorism and globalization are interlinked in the sense that the one draws sustenance from another.

Finally, Hoffmann argues that the United States in order to retain and maintain its supremacy in the globalized world needs to shun its 'temptation of unilateralism, and arrogant demonstrations of contempt for other views'. As he observes, *'a hegemon concerned with prolonging its rule should be especially interested in using internationalist methods and institutions, for the gain in influence far exceeds the loss in freedom of action'.*

Further, for the "globalized society" to succeed, the US must make 'resources available for economic development' to poorer countries and refrain from '*the right-leaning tendencies (of the American system and diplomacy) towards excessive reliance on America's greatest asset—military strength—as well as an excessive reliance on market capitalism and a "sovereigntism" that offends and alienates. That the mighty United States is so afraid of the world's imposing its "inferior" values on Americans is often a source of ridicule and indignation abroad'.*

Whatever may be the arguments provided by Hoffmann no one can deny that globalization to a great extent means triumph of American giant companies, American values and, American culture. Fukuyama's concept of end of history was basically to celebrate the victory and dominance of American political and economic system in the aftermath of the disintegration of the USSR. Globalization in true sense of the term is ascendancy of American capitalism, and, for many, American imperialism. In the post Cold War period the direction of the US foreign policy has been guided by the economic interest of the American business and corporate houses. This is very much evident in its foreign policy postures over Kyoto Protocol, global terrorism, or vis-à-vis China and Iraq. Today, American capitalism is being promoted and protected by its unmatched military and political might. Who can deny the fact that we are living in the Mac World?

Globalization, Sovereignty and Nation-States

The phenomenon of globalization has seriously challenged the identity and sovereignty as well as the working of the nation-states. If globalization means emergence of borderless states then the very existence of the nation-state is questioned. Who controls the territory, population as well as the government in the globalized world? Not certainly the nation-states. Deterritorialization of the nation-states is taking place. Products and capital are moving with the least possible hindrance. As Human Development Repot remarks '*national borders are also breaking down in economic policy—as multilateral agreements and the pressures of staying competitive in global markets constrain the options for national policy, and as multinational corporations and global crime syndicates integrate their operations globally.*

The states are in no capacity to take economic decisions such as what to produce, how to produce and, for whom and how much to produce. The process of liberalization and privatization has seriously weakened the control and functioning of the bureaucracy considered to be the backbone of the states. What we are witnessing, today, is the emergence of "contracted and atrophied states".

As more and more countries belonging particularly to the "Third World" are taking recourse to free trade, the national and international economic policies are being taken not by the national governments but by powerful international economic and financial institutions like the International Monetary Fund, the World Bank and, the World Trade Organization. These institutions are being ably supported by a new class of the people, called technocrats, who have taken over the role of the traditional bureaucrats. This process has gathered momentum in countries of Eastern Europe and the CIS where a dramatic transition from centrally planned economic system to market democracies has taken place. This is equally true in case of the so-called socialist countries like China, Mongolia and Viet Nam.

While commenting on the nature of 'global governance', the HDR points out that (a) 'intergovernmental policy-making in today's global economy is in the hands of the major industrial powers and the international institutions they control—the World Bank, the International Monetary Fund, the Bank for International Settlement', (b) 'ad hoc and self selected policy' groups such as G-7 are making *de facto* global economic policy in which developing countries and G-15 have the least say, and (c) there is little participation of the poor countries in ' the formulation and implementation of the new rules that govern markets'. This was very much obvious during the Uruguay round of GATT negotiations and this is equally apparent in case of WTO negotiations where the poor countries have little capacity and skill to bargain with the rich countries. Their weakness in the negotiating capacity has further been compounded due to the breakup of the common "South" position on global trade issues.

This highly skewed system and arrangement of global governance has adversely affected the notion of sovereign equality as propounded by the UNO. As HDR remarks 'the rapidly increasing multilateral agreements—the new rules—are highly binding on the national governments and constrain domestic policy choices'. The 'unbalanced'

Trade Related Aspects of Intellectual Property Rights (TRIPS) has further eroded the sovereign decision making power of the poor countries as almost all knowledge-based production is now subject to tight intellectual property protection. Moreover the TRIPS agreement '*provides an enabling environment for multinationals, tightening their dominant ownership of technology, impeding and increasing the cost of transfer to developing countries*'. In sum we can say that in the age of globalization the internal and the external behaviour of the nation-states is conditioned and governed by the multinational corporations as well as the multilateral institutions like the IMF, the World Bank and the WTO. Sovereignty belongs to those who are strong and powerful.

The 'establishment of globalized economic institutions' like the IMF, the World Bank and the WTO has, on the one hand, been 'a symptom of and a stimulus for globalization' and, on the other, it 'indicates the trend away from the dominance of the state as the exclusive unit of analysis in international affairs'.

The World Bank report observes that the 'global events and international agreements are putting constraints on state's arbitrary action and are increasingly affecting its choices' (World Bank Repot: 1997:12, as cited in *ibid*). Besides, as McCorquodale puts it states no longer enjoy '*exclusive control over their economic, legal, political and sovereign affairs. Moreover, the current trend of globalization differs from past transnational influences on state sovereignty in the scale and speed of its operation*'.

The transnational flow of goods, capital, people, and ideas has equally affected the sovereign identity of the nation-states and so have the transnational corporations and intergovernmental institutions. The rise in popular participation at the grassroots level, emergence of civil-societies and the enhancement of non-governmental organizations have also influenced and limited the activities of the nation-states. As one commentator points out:

> (the) globalization process has led to a corresponding decline in the role of the modern nation-state in regulating the nature of the growth of the political economy at the national level, as the multinational corporations driven by market forces have taken over. Economic reforms are being forced upon the nation-states so that national economies can be 'restructured' in accordance with the external changes taking place at the level of the global economy.

Globalization has also forced the nation-states to "retreat" from their welfare activities and become the promoter of the interests of the global capital/capitalist class. The people are being left to the discipline and dictate of the market forces more and more brutally. As Aijaz Ahmad observes:

> (it) is the state that is dismantling welfare and implementing liberalization in all the countries across the globe. In other words, the nation-state has become weaker in relation to capital, whose will it must implement most savagely, and weak in relation to labour, whom it treats with hateful contempt. In other words, the state is now not even pretending to be anything but the managing committee of the whole bourgeoisie—and this time, not the *whole* but also the *transnational* bourgeoisie. In the Third World, the state no longer even pretends to represent the people *against* imperialism. It represents imperial interest to the people.

Moreover, the 'retreat of the state from the realm of the popular entitlements, health, education, employment, preservation of natural resources, and so on' has enabled the NGOs and social movements, to fill the 'vacuum'. But the sad part of it is that they are 'always narrow and local in focus and frequently dependent on foreign funding agencies'. Besides, in the name of performing the social responsibility of the state, they appear to supplant such 'historic forms of mass organization as the trade union and the political party' and, are 'funded from the imperial centres and have channels to such things as World Bank'.

They, thus, represent the interest of the imperial power and agencies instead of fulfilling the aspirations of the 'third world' masses. However, in advanced countries, who hate the concept of 'too much government', such retreat of the state is celebrated as the triumph of 'neo-liberal ideology' in the name of the 'end of history'. The 'retreat of state', in other words, has signalled the doom for socialism and triumph of capitalism.

But, does all this mean that the state has become irrelevant and purposeless in the age of globalization? The answer is big ' NO'. Only its nature and character has changed, particularly in the developing countries where the welfare function of the state has declined. As Aijaz Ahmad points out ' the mythology of globalization includes the sizeable myth that the nation-state is on way out. In reality, imperialism itself needs not the abolition of nation-states in the Third World but the strengthening of them for its own purposes'.

First, a strong nation-state is required for the secure movement of capital. The US is the main capital exporting country, today, for the reason that ' the bearers of its capital could rely on the support, including the crucial military support, that their nation-state could provide them, anywhere in the world'.

Second, a strong nation-state is required as it creates space for the deep penetration of capital. Imperialism, capitalism and nation-state are interrelated and (they) reinforce each other.

Third, ' *far from destroying the nation-state in its march toward globalization, capital indeed needs the state for the enforcement of the contract law, internationalized legal systems and other instruments that are necessary to insure linkages between national and transnational market forces* '. The US is not averse to the Chinese communism as it protects the interest of its big corporate houses.

Fourth, a strong nation-state is required to protect the interest of the bourgeoisie from the 'jungle aspects of economic globalization', particularly in the wake of the rising trends of anti-globalization movements and the phenomenon of terrorism.

Globalization and Human Rights

The widespread anti-globalization movements from Seattle to Genoa and the cry for 'globalization with humane face' indicate that everything that globalization does is not uniformly good and acceptable. While globalization has worked well for a few, it has marginalized, dispossessed, deprived and, destroyed many. While the rich and the powerful have benefited, the poor and the weak have been excluded and subjugated. Globalization in this sense is not an inclusive phenomenon but an exclusive one. There are many, particularly in the Third World, who are questioning the impact of globalization not only on the nation-states but primarily on the human beings. Globalization has resulted in loss of jobs, cultural identity, democratic rights, clean air and water (John Micklethwait and Adrian Wooldridge: 16). It has not only created social and cultural divide but also economic, technological, and digital divide between and within nations.

Studies are being conducted to find out the impact of globalization and its agents particularly that of MNCs and WTO on economic, environmental and developmental rights of the people. As Professor Jagdish Bhagwati has remarked:

> globalization—a focal point of hostile passions and sometimes—violent protests—has become a phenomenon doomed to unending controversy. Advocates cite its virtues and its inevitability. Central to many of the protests against it is the trilogy of discontents about the idea of capitalism, the process of globalization, and the behaviour of corporations. And all three of these discontents have become interlinked in the minds of the many protesters. Globalization's enemies see it as the worldwide extension of capitalism, with multinational corporations as its far ranging B-52s.

It is in this perspective that discourse on relationship between globalization and human rights becomes important and inevitable. Today, there is no divergence of opinion that globalization has resulted in widespread social and economic inequality. It has increased the incidence of poverty, hunger, and disease. As Vandana Shiva has pointed out 'starvation is the inevitable result of policies of globalization which are transforming food from a basic need, to which everyone has a right, to a globally traded-commodity'. The denial of right to food is the most important violation of human rights.

The Human Development Report, 1999, had observed that '*gaps in income between the poorest and the richest people and countries have continued to widen. In 1960 the 20 per cent of the world's people in the richest countries had 30 times the income of the poorest 20 per cent—in 1997, 74 times as much*' (HDR: 36). The HDR, 1999, further observed that economic disparities in terms of per capita income has sharply increased in Sub-Saharan Africa and other least developed countries. Moreover, as the HDR remarked

> 'the transition economies of Eastern Europe and the CIS have experienced the fastest rise in inequality ever. Russia now has the greatest inequality. Income inequalities also grew markedly in China, Indonesia, Thailand and other East Asian countries that had achieved high growth in earlier decades. Recent studies show inequality rising in most OECD countries during the 1980s and early 1990s'.

Economic inequality and income disparities between and within the nations have contributed to rise in social strife and ethnic conflicts at an unprecedented scale, particularly in Asia and Africa. As HDR, 1999, observes '*uneven globalization is not only bringing integration but also fragmentation—dividing communities, nations and regions into those that are included and those that are excluded*'. The extreme inequality between the marginal and the powerful are 'igniting' social tensions and conflicts. The 'retreat of state' from social and welfare responsibilities has deepened the problem of economic inequality and human insecurity. The "horizontal inequalities" between groups—whether ethnic, religious or social—are major cause of the current wave of civil conflicts. The shrinking job and economic opportunities has further compounded the problem.

Ethnic Conflicts and 'Humanitarian' Intervention

The rise in civil strife and ethnic conflicts has contributed to violation of human rights at an unprecedented scale. The conflict between the communities has invited strong intervention both from the state and outside forces. The intervention in the internal jurisdiction of the nation-state in the name of humanitarian crisis and human rights violation has become a dominant aspect of the post-cold war world politics.

The sole superpower—the USA—has emerged as a global policeman. In the name of humanitarian crisis it sends its military, backed by NATO and UNO, at its will. The examples are galore, from Somalia to Kosovo and from Iraq to Afghanistan. Such military interventions, both from within as well as the outside have resulted in death and displacement of civilians, particularly women and children. Such interventions are being done and thought about primarily to protect its (the US) global economic interest as well as that of its allies.

Today, poverty is the single most factor responsible for human rights violation. Now it is a known fact that globalization instead of reducing poverty has increased it. Globalization has also contributed to hunger and destitution as the result of withdrawal of the state from economic activities. Privatization and commercialization of farm sector have contributed to fall in food production. This is further compounded by the intervention of the WTO to reduce farm subsidies.

Globalization, Human Insecurity and Human Rights

Human security and human rights are interrelated concepts. The linkage between human rights and human development was clearly established by the Human Development Report, 2000. The HDR, 1999, while quoting the Report of 1994, defines human security in terms of safety from such chronic threats as hunger, disease and depression. It also means protection from sudden and hurtful disruptions in the patterns of daily life whether in homes, in jobs or in communities.

The Report lists seven categories of threats to human security such as economic insecurity, food insecurity, health insecurity, personal insecurity, environmental insecurity, community and cultural insecurity and political insecurity. The Report further illustrates the types of threat to global insecurity as the result of famines, ethnic conflicts, social disintegration, terrorism, pollution and drug trafficking. The process of globalization has resulted in emergence of such threats to human security having profound bearing on human rights violations.

Moreover, Globalization has led to 'sudden disruption in the patterns of daily life—in jobs and livelihoods, in health and personal safety, in the social and cultural cohesion of the countries'. Threats to human security have emerged due to collapse of financial markets, increasing corporate mergers and bankruptcies. The rise in the incidence of AIDS/HIV, global warming and global crime has further threatened human security. The mechanism of TRIPS under the dictates of the WTO has made medicines, particularly the life-saving drugs, costlier and put them beyond the reach of the common masses. It has seriously threatened the people right to health.

Besides, globalization has contributed to heavy job losses and worsening employment conditions in both poor and rich countries resulting in severe economic and income insecurities. It is primarily due to the restructuring of the economic and social sectors at the behest of the IMF, World Bank, WTO and other economic and financial institutions. The pressure for increasing efficiency and cost reduction has brought in newer technologies that on the one hand displace labour and on the other demand highly skilled labour force. This favours some while excludes many. The digital divide between and within the nations has further compounded the problem. It has excluded many from the job market.

Globalization, MNCs and Human Rights

It is a matter of debate whether there is a positive or negative correlation between the multinational corporations and human rights.

There are some who argue that MNCs promotes human rights as they have 'provided new roads and communication, clean water, health and sanitation services, housing and educational facilities to the workers and improved corporate law through increased transparency in negotiations and contracts'. Therefore, 'the impact of MNCs on human rights is beneficial'. Spar cites the example of certain MNCs like the Gap, Reebok and Starbucks that took steps to reduce child labour and exported cleaner, greener technology to their plants in Mexico.

The MNCs also protect human rights as they observe WTO and other international human rights standards on child labour and environmental protection. MNCs are also promoting a culture of philanthropy. The recent example of Microsoft king, Bill Gates, donating about $ 2 million for AIDS fighting is the case in point. Bit compared to its huge investment, about $ 400 million, this amount is just a peanut. In fact his philanthropy and slogan of 'localization' are efforts aimed at earning the legitimacy in the Third World.

Meyer also cites the examples where MNCs have been responsible for violation of human rights, particularly in the Third World countries. In India Union Carbide was responsible for over 7,000 deaths and 65,000 injuries. People continue to suffer from the long-term effects of the 1984 disaster. Besides, the concerned US Company has failed to perform its social and ethical responsibilities in the aftermath of the human tragedy of such magnitude. Similarly, in Mexico, environmental destruction and union busting have been standard operating procedures for many MNCs. He also cites the example of human rights violations by the major oil companies, which have been responsible for environmental disaster due to mining and oil spillage.

Another argument in favour of globalization vis-à-vis human rights is that it is making people conscious of their culture and identity. Today, what is local is global and what is global is local. The term ethnic has become a *chic*-ethnic food, ethnic dress and ethnic songs and music. In other words, globalization has created space for those who were not heard and cared for. Globalization has also created a strong sense of assertion on the part of the hitherto marginalized, dispossessed and oppressed. This can be seen in the rise of the social movements from below and interaction of hitherto 'dormant cultures' with dominant centres of power. In place of the earlier 'think global, act local' slogan there is now a shift to 'think local and act global'.

Moreover, anti-globalization movements have helped in raising issues related to various aspects of human rights—be it cultural, economic, developmental and environmental rights. It has galvanized various sections of the masses that were marginalized and excluded in the globalization process. It can be seen in consolidation of workers' movement, strengthening of the green-peace movement and rise in consciousness among the people about the effects of globalization. The anti-globalization protests from Seattle onwards are viewed as movement towards the 'step-by-step globalization of welfare standards', in response to the 'attacks from capital. It is seen as a desirable step in securing the rights of human beings anywhere'.

The anti-globalization protests, by bringing together protesters from different countries at a single location helped by the global networks of the new information and communication technologies have created a new kind of protest space, 'a transnational public sphere', earlier monopolized by the MNCs and international financial institutions. It has strengthened the 'global civic alliances' with focus on gender, environment, social development and racism. And called for a 'global New Deal' or a 'global social contract' against the unrestrained movement of capital.

Another dimension of globalization is that it promotes consumerism and that has a bearing on the rights of the dispossessed and marginalized, particularly the women and children. Today, 'female prostitution, traffic of women (*specially child prostitution)*, poverty and the countries economic policies are all closely related subjects'. Globalization on the one hand has adversely affected the economic and financial condition of the vulnerable sectors of the society, mainly the women and children particularly in the Third World countries and on the other it has created a consumer culture where women have become a commodity. As Tammy Quintanilla remarks:

> the sex trade has flourished and reached considerable proportions at various levels. The more marked conception of the assumption that "sex sells" can be seen at all levels, from sexist advertising to the traffic of people, through pornography, erotic phone calls, call-girls and hostesses, sexually provocative shows, mail order brides, street prostitution, sexual tourism and other forms of trade in sex. Sexual exploitation of the girls, boys and adolescents can be seen in each of these forms mentioned.

Consumerism has also contributed to the distortion in consumption pattern of the poor as many in the Third World are transferring their limited income from productive to wasteful expenditure such as on MNCs food, films, shoes and clothes.

Conclusion

But, despite all the problems it generates, globalization is a force that does not allow the luxury of saying 'stop, I want to get off'. It is impossible to stop the Internet, satellite television and telecommunications, impossible to ban air travel or pop culture, the global mobility of trade, investment and currency flows. Globalization a fact of life and the real question is altogether different: What sort of globalization do we want and how can we get it? As Jagdish Bhagwati has put it '*A hundred flowers must be allowed to bloom, creating a rich garden of social action to lend more colour to globalization's humane face*'. Globalization is the only ideology of the present world order.

REFERENCES

Ahmad, Aijaz, 'Globalization: A Society of Aliens?', *Frontline*, October 13, 2000, pp. 49-52.

Ahmad, Aijaz, 'Globalization and the Nation-State', *Seminar*, 437, January, 1996 pp. 43-52.

Bhagwati, Jagdish, 'Coping with Antiglobalization: A Trilogy of Discontents', *Foreign Affairs*, Vol 81(1), 2002, pp. 2-7.

DN, 'Globalization of Protest', *Economic and Political Weekly,* XXXVI, No 40, 2001, pp. 3818-3819.

Hain, Peter, ' For Progressive Internationalism', *Frontline*, March 15, 2002, pp. 63-66.

Harriss, John, 'Globalization and World's Poor: Institutions, Inequality and Justice', *Economic and Political Weekly*, XXXVII, No. 23, 2001, pp. 2034-2037.

Hoffmann, Stanley, 'Clash of Globalizations', *Foreign Affairs*, July/August, 2002, pp. 104-115.

Human Development Report (2000): Human Rights and Human Development, OUP.

Human Development Report (1999): Globalization with Human Face, OUP.

Human Development Report (1994): Human Development and Human Security. OUP.

Imle, John, 'Multinationals and the New World of Energy Development', *Journal of International Affairs*, 53 (1), 1999, as cited in Meyer.

Knight Foster, 'NAFTA Promises Payoff in Environmental Benefits', Forum for Applied Research and Public Policy, Summer, 1995, as cited in Meyer.

Kothari, Rajni, 'Globalization and Revival of Tradition: Dual Attack on Model of Nation Building', *Economic and Political Weekly,* XXX, No. 12, 1995, pp. 625-633.

Kumar, Ashutosh, 'Globalization and After', *Economic and Political Weekly*, Vol XXXVII, No 4, 2002, pp. 309-312.

McCorquodale, Robert, 'Globalization and Human Rights', *Human Rights Quarterly*, Vol. 21, 1999, pp. 735-766.

Meyer, William H., 'Human Rights and MNCs: Theory Versus Quantitative Analysis', *Human Rights Quarterly*, Vol. 18, 1996, p. 368.

Meyer, William H., MNCs, 'Globalization and Human Rights', 1999, http://hypatia.ss.uci.edu/brysk/Meyer html.

Muralidharan, Sukumar, 'Monopoly in the Dock', *Frontline*, December 6, 2002, pp. 31-33.

Quintanilla,Tammy, 'Globalization of Sex Trade', 1997, http://www.socwatch.org.uy/1997/globalization.

Sengupta, Chandan, 'Conceptualizing Globalization: Issues and Implications' *Economic and Political Weekly*, XXXVII, No. 33, 2001, pp. 3137-3143.

Shiva, Vandana, 'Profits Over People', *Frontline*, July 5, 2002, pp. 118-120.

Spar, Deborah L., 'The Spotlight and the Bottom line: How MNCs Export Human Rights', *Foreign Affairs*, 77 (1), 1998, as cited in Meyer.

9

Economic Prospects and Environmental Problems of Globalization

T.V. MURALIVALLABHAN

Introduction

Globalization is taking place at a very rapid rate throughout the world. Both in the developed and developing nations, the impacts of globalization are obvious at the political, economic, social and environmental levels. When the economic activities like capital investment flows, technological transfers and lobour mobility take place, the consequences are still debatable. International trade is one of the major means of bringing the triad of globalization, liberalization and privatization. The most vulnerable area of increased economic activity is the environment. This article is an attempt to throw light on the emerging environmental problems as a result of the globalization process and the steps taken to solve them through international organizations like the WTO.

Globalization means expanding the activities from a local, regional, and national levels to a global or international level. Activities are mainly economic, technological or political. But Bruno Amoroso has defined it in another way. "By the term globalization is meant new forms taken on by the process of accumulation in the world of triadic capitalism (USA, Japan and EU). In its current form, globalization is the means being used to control the market and available resources so as to increase world wide profit"[1]. The chances of accumulating profits have gone up in the recent years. The impact of globalization also has increased both in quality and quantity.

The impacts of Globalization are determined generally by four parameters:

1. Reduction of trade barriers so as to permit free flow of goods across national frontiers,
2. Creation of an environment in which freeflow of capital can take place among nation-states,
3. Creating a conducive environment for the free flow of technology, and
4. Bringing a suitable atmosphere for the free mobility of labour among different countries.

Hence the factors of economic activities namely capital, technology, and labour are directly linked in the process of globalization. Therefore, when the process of liberalization and privatization which are considered as the follow up actions of globalization take place; the economic activities will be fully covered under the umbrella of globalization.

A Brief History

The inner socio-economic and political spirit of globalization could be traced in the old classical principle of the '*laissez faire*' policy which demands least government intervention and most freedom to the people in their activities. During the nineteenth century, the enthusiasm for the free trade policy vanished, thanks to the increased degree of exploitation that came along with the increased role of capitalism. But the last quarter of the twentieth century saw the decline of the socialist empire in the world and politically the world has come under a unipolar system under the umbrella of the United States. This phenomenon further activated the process of the search for new markets in the developing countries in order to increase the profit and capital accumulation. Many third world countries including India faced a political and economic instability during this period and the International economic institutions like the World Bank and IMF got directly involved in the escape (?) techniques adopted by these nations. Hence the triad of economic transformation (Globalization, Liberalisation and Privatization) was brought about by the triad of international economic institutions (World Bank, IMF, and WTO) with the remote control of triadic capitalism (USA, Japan, and European Union).

International Institutions and Globalization

The decade of 1990s marks two defining characteristics—one, the continuation and strengthening of economic globalization and two, the growth of Foreign Direct Investment (FDI) flows which are more than the growth of international trade flows. These two peculiarities reveal the fact that the economies of nation-states over the globe are becoming integrated at a high pace. A large share of FDI inflows to developing countries consists of cross border mergers and acquisitions rather than the setting up of new plant by a Trans National Corporation (TNC).

The International Bank for Reconstruction and Development (IBRD) also known as the World Bank, the International Monetary Fund (IMF), and the World Trade Organization (WTO) are the three international organizations involved in the promotion of globalization. Ninety per cent of the world trade is taking place among the members of the WTO and hence WTO plays a significant role in determining the degree and direction of globalization in the world.

The World Trade Organization (WTO) is the only international body dealing with the rules of trade between nations. The WTO believes that liberal trade policies—policies that allow the unrestricted flow of goods and services—multiply the rewards that result from producing the best products with the best design, at the best price.

WTO Globalization and Environment

While helping the integration of nation-states by activating the process of golablizaiton, the WTO is very much concerned about the state of environment. The brochure 'Trading into Future' published on behalf of WTO says that there are many provisions in the agreement to deal with the environmental concerns of the world. The objectives of sustainable development and environmental protection are stated in the preamble to the agreement establishing the WTO. The 'Green Provisions' in the WTO agreements dealing with environmental issues are the following:

- GATT Article 20: Policies affecting trade in goods for protecting human, animal or plant life or health are exempt from normal GATT disciplines under certain conditions.
- Technical barriers to Trade (*i.e.*, product and industrial standards) and sanitary and phytosanitary measures (animal

and plant health and hygiene): Explicit recognition of environmental objectives.

- Agriculture: environmental programmes exempt from cuts and subsidies.
- Subsidies and Countervails: allows subsidies, up to 20 per cent of firm's costs, for adapting new environmental laws.
- Intellectual property: governments can refuse to issue patents that threaten human, animal or plant life or health, or risk serious damage to the environments (TRIPS Article 27).
- GATS Article 14: Policies affecting trade in services for protecting human, animal or plant life or health are exempt from normal GATS disciplines under certain conditions.

About 20 of the 200 international agreements (outside WTO) dealing with various environmental issues currently deal directly with trade. WTO believes that when the international environmental issues, like global warming and loss of biodiversity, could be addressed only by an international understanding and international co-operation, that could be extended only through an international body like WTO, which promotes the globalization process.

Eco-labelling of environmental friendly proudcts is an important environmental policy instrument adopted by WTO in the trade, so that, each nation will be forced to produce and exchange only goods produced in an environmental friendly manner. The provision of as much information as possible about environmental policies adopted by countries is another step taken by WTO and this step helps the passing of information regarding domestic environmental protection. Another important step is the prohibition of the transportation of dangerous toxic chemicals between countries, which could have otherwise increased the dumping. The committee on Trade and environment further sees the increase in the benefit of the trading partners, when the trade liberalization and globalization take place. They believe that sustainable development promotion is possible with the globalization process.

World Bank and IMF

The World Bank is the largest global agency to fund projects of developments especially in developing countries. The projects connected with tropical, rainforests, building roads, dams and extractive industries are the areas in which the WB is pumping money. In the late eighties and early nineties the World Bank began to take environmental issues more seriously. As a result in 1992 the world bank came out with a world development report emphasising the interrelationship between environmental protection and development promotion. From 1993 to 1997, the major focus areas of the World Development Reports were state versus market. But the World Development Report (WDR) 2003, stresses the importance of human, natural and environmental capital, as well as, social cohesion and social stability. The report titled 'Sustainable Development in a dynamic World: Transforming Institutions Growth and Quality of Life' is a useful directive for attaining sustainable development in the age of globalization.

The International Monetary Fund is another financial institution that lends huge amounts to its member countries based on certain conditionalities. Conditions have been attached to IMF lending since the mid 1950s, emphasising monetary, fiscal and exchange rate policies of a country. But the number and severity of conditions increased during the 1980s when the IMF made a paradigm shift from project lending to programme lending. Programme lending became a major issue when the trends of globalization set in. Instead of one project, the coverage of a loan extended itself over many programmes that may help to form an easy way to globlization. The overall quality and capacity of the macro economic policy of a country for economic growth became a major factor in the conditions.

The broadened concept of conditionality is based on five assumptions; (*The Hindu*, 20-12-2001):

(*i*) balance of payments deficits are evidence of domestic economic mismanagement;

(*ii*) markets are superior allocators of resources;

(*iii*) economic agents respond positively to removal of restrictions;

(*iv*) growth and development are private sector led; and

(*v*) all these are facilitated by a liberalised policy environment.

From these assumptions it is clear that the ultimate purpose of lending, which is expected to be fulfilled through the conditionalities, is to promote liberalization and globalization. By solving the domestic economic mismanagement, through the market forces and by removing restrictions the domination of private sector is being established. Hence the role of IMF and World Bank is being redefined in the sense that they have reoriented their policies with emphasis on creating conducive conditions for Globalization Liberalization and Privatization. The structural reforms demanded by the IMF, from the recepients also aim the same.

Globalization and Economic Impacts*

The waves of globalization are striking the coastal areas of both the rich and poor nations. The poor nations, also have now their say in international platforms. "For the first time, poor countries have been able to harness the potential of their abundant labour to break into global markets for manufactured goods and services. Manufactures rose from less than a quarter of developing country exports in 1980 to more than 80 per cent by 1998. Countries that strongly increased their participation in global trade and investment include Brazil, China, Hungary, India and Mexico."

The more globalised developing countries could increase their per capita growth rate by only 1 per cent in 1960s, but, 3 per cent in 1970s, 4 per cent in1980s and to 5 per cent in 1990s. This growth rate is now more than that of their developed counterparts. The experience is that now trade goes hand-in-hand with faster growth. As a result of the opening up of Chinese economy in the mid 1980s and the consequent integration of that economy with the rest of the world, the number of rural poor in China declined from 250 million in 1978 to just 34 million in 1999. India and Uganda also could reduce poverty as a result of the integration with World Economy.

The Report of World Bank is optimistic about the present trend of globalization which is considered as the 'Third Wave' of globalization. This trend may result in the reduction of poverty and inequality all over the world.

Divergent View

At the end of the Third United Nations Conference on Least Developed Countries in 2001, the members were concerned about the increase in the number of Least Developed Countries (LDCs) from 25 to 49 since the category was created by UN in 1971. They were worried about the increasing wealth gap seperating the rich and poor nations. The concern

---

* World Bank Report on 'Globalisation Growth and Poverty'.

of the planners in the poor countries is that how the globalization process is going to solve this problem.

Some development experts say that there are no win-win perspectives in globalization as some in the developed countries would say. Only stronger growth can reduce global poverty. The multidimensional impact of globalization driven by market forces consists of economic, political, cultural and social effects. The huge inflow of funds in the form of loans advanced by international financial institutions is not being fruitfully utilized since the developing societies are affected with widespread corruption and bad governance. Moreover it is feared that the cultural diversity of many recipient countries is adversely affected by the cultural invasion of the West. In a world-wide mobile population the chances of spreading diseases like AIDS, SARS etc. are very high, particularly when the health standards of least developed countries are very poor. Also, rise of terrorism, cyber crime and transnational crimes are at the increase as a result of the dynamics of globalization.

It is under these above mentioned circumstances that we have to see with a difference the vow of the leaders of the world's richest nations (G-8, 2001) to make globalization work for everyone including the poorest countries. The leaders said they would seek 'enhanced co-operation and solidarity with developing countries, based on a mutual responsibility for combating poverty and promoting sustainable development'. They also decided to form a new global fund to fight AIDS, TB, Malaria etc in developing countries.

Apart from the economic, political and social impacts, the impacts on environment is also very significant. There are many environmental issues which are to be tackled both at the international and local levels. Here, we should remember that globalization of both prospects and problems are taking place. The problems have to be solved and prospects are to be promoted. Only effective international co-operation is possible to bring a uniform pattern of sustainable development through globalization.

Environmental Impacts of Globalization

The claims of development occurred in the North, and South are not at zero costs. We have to remember that "the Earth is not a system in the sense of a political, philosophical, or mathematical system. It is much closer to digestive systems, heating systems and plumbing systems".[3]

Hence while undertaking the dynamics of mechanistic economics to function as the system of the planet, we should be doubly cautious. Economic, environmental and social aspects of development are very much interested. "Economists maintain that trade helps the natural environment, as rich countries can better afford to protect their unspoiled areas. Environmentalists counter that the pursuit of national wealth drives global environment degradation and that freetrade accelerates this process".[4]

Environmental degradation is a more common and serious problem than the economic problems like rapid inflation, excessive foreign debt as economic stagnation. "Never before have regions as geographically separate as South East Asia, Africa and Latin America been simultaneously and similar—that is global forms of environmental degradation".[5]

The trinity of Globalization (policy) liberalization (technique) and privatization (target) that is going on all over the world with the ultimate objective of profit maximization has done enough damage to the environmental balance of the planet. The state of the planet 2002 is in very poor condition inspite of the three decades of talks, premises and proposals and over 300 environmental treaties.[6] The delicate position of the planet is made clear by the following facts—

- By 2000, CO_2 emissions had risen 18.1 per cent above 1990 levels in the US, by 10.7 per cent in Japan, 12.8 per cent in Canada and 28.8 per cent in Australia.
- Weather-related disasters (such as droughts, windstorms and floods) have increased by 160 per cent between 1975-2001, killing 440,000 people. 1990s were the warmest decade since written records began.
- Every 160,000 km^2 forests are being depleted. If the present rate of depletion is continued, 50 to 90 per cent of the species that live in forests will be lost by the middle of the twenty-first century.
- In 2002 alone, water shortages killed over 7 million people.
- Above 2 billion hectares of soil, equivalent to 15 per cent of the Earth's land area, have been degraded by human intervention.
- 50-100 species are vanishing everyday—10,000 times faster than natural extinction rates, faster than at anytime in the last 65 million years.

The vital signs, 2002-03 also says about the dismal picture of the condition of the planet.[7]

- Food born illness is of the most widespread health problems. In 2001, WHO estimated that 450 million people worldwide had a mental or neurological disorders. Mental illness is universal, affecting people in all nations from every background.[8] More than 120 million people are affected by depression (12%), Nearly 1 million people end their lives each year and an estimated 10-20 million people try to kill themselves.

From the nineteenth century to the late 1980s the terms 'internationa-lization' and 'transnationalization' were used instead of globalization. The role of transnational and multinational corporations cannot be underestimated in the pursuit of globålization. Over consumption of natural resources for over production in order to satisfy the greed of a consumerist society with the ultimate objective of a high-level profit squeeze has resulted in the problems mentioned above. The need of the hour is to formulate and implement right policies for protecting environment. In this respect, what we need is a new form of global governance with the participation of every nation.

The Triadic Forces of Globalization

"Since 1970, the world economic power is concentrated in the three nations of the world—USA, Japan and European Union. This triad had 37,000 transnational corporations (TNCs) that controlled over 200,000 affiliates throughout the world. Two-thirds of these

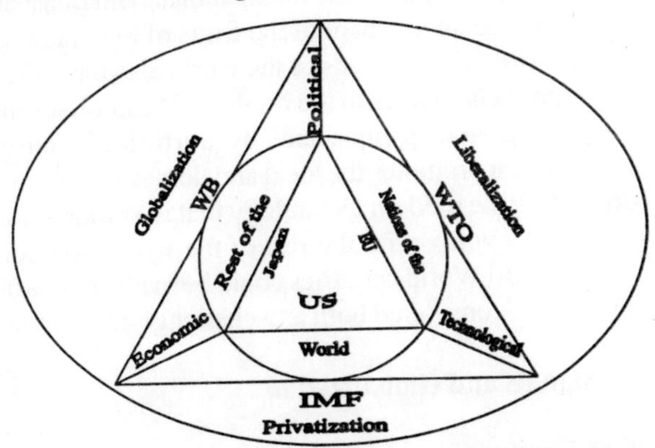

The Triad of Techniques, Institutions and Countries

transnationals (26,000) came from 14 of the most industrialized countries. World's leading 100 TNCs ranked by foreign assets held US $ 3.4 trillion in global assets in 1992, of which about 40 per cent were assets located outside their home countries. The top 100 control about one-third of the world FDI stock."[2]

The US, Japan and EU, have a remote control over the economic, political and technological changes taking place all over the world. The major policies of IMF, WB and WTO are guided by these countries. The financial help is given to poor countries by the IMF, the developmental assistance in the form of institutional and technological advice is given by WB and the social, environmental and political strengths of the countries are reflected through the WTO agreements. As a result of this Triadic influence of countries, techniques and institutions, the biggest TNCs have sales, which exceed the aggregate output of many developing countries. Indicators of globalization are Foreign Direct Investment, world trade employment level etc. UN studies reveal that TNCs have concentrated on those countries that have already crossed the border of development and have done nothing to the world's poorest 50 countries.

The US, Japan and European Union have direct as well as indirect control over the economic, political and technological changes taking place all over the world. The major policies of IMF, World Bank and WTO are to a very great extent guided by these nations. The triadic superpowers of the world are exerting their influence on the triadic international economic institutions for accelerating the paces of globalization, liberalization and privatization in the rest of the world. As already seen, the vast empire of the multinationals and transnationals will be taking away the major share of the fruits of the opening up of economy. But the rest of the nations of the world also have their own opportunities to pose challenges to the products of multinationals.

By forming regionai groups, and by nurturing a culture of consumption style that promotes the local and domestic commodities, and by incorporating the modern technology that is available from the integration of the economy with the rest of the world, the domestic economies of the Third World countries could be made more efficient. Here globalization is considered both as a challenge and opportunity.

The 'Green' Signals and Globalization

In the 1970s and 1980s some major environment development related changes in the domain of policies, politics and ideologies took place. Again the spread of Green Parties and NGOs all around the world and the awareness that is disseminated by these groups have succeeded in checking the invasion of the production super powers on natural resources. As a result, "economic processes of production and consumption are increasingly analyzed and judged as well as designed and organized from both an economic and ecological point of view. Some profound institutional changes in the economic domain of production and consumption have become discernible from the late 1980s. Among, these changes were the widespread emergence of environmental management systems, the introduction of an economic valuation of environmental goods via the introduction of ecolakes, among other things, the emergence of environment inspired liability and issuance arrangements, the increasing importance attached to environmental goals such as natural resources saving an recycling among public and private utility enterprises and the articulation of environmental consideration in economic supply and demand."[9]

The economic and environmental colonialism should give way to ecological modernization. For that, global environmental restructuring based on the policies discussed above should occur. A green philosophy of development, green policies, green technology, green products and green markets, green benches in courts and afterall a green education can contribute a lot in protecting the environment while promoting economic development. The economic and political globalization should be accompanied by globalization of the concerns for environment. Then only the dark clouds of modern mechanistic development which hovers above the world could be changed into a heavy downpour of sustainable development.

NOTES

1. Bruno Amoroso: *On Globalization, Capitalization in the 21st Century*, St. Martyrs Press, New York, Chapter 3, 1998, p. 52.
2. UNCED: World Investment Report 1994.
3. Henrich D. Holland and Ulrich Peterson: *Living Dangerously*, Princetar University Press, 1995, p. 4.
4. Corey L. Lofdahl: *Environmental Impacts of Globalization and Trade*: MIT Press, Cambridge 2002, Preface.
5. Servaas Storm: CWM Naastepad (Ed) *Globalization and Economic Development* (2001), Edward Elgas.

6. *The Ecologist Asia*, Vol 10, No.3 July/September 2002, pp. 4-8.
7. Vital Signs 2002-03 World Water Institute, *Earthscan*, London 2002, p. 16.
8. *Ibid*, p. 144.
9. Arthus, P.J. Mol, *Globalization and Environmental Reforms*, The MIT Press, London, Chapter 3, p. 60.

10

Globalization and Gender Issues in India

SWETA MISHRA

Globalization, the concept of the late 1990s, remains dominant even in contemporary times. It means different things to different people. The term, which is used to describe the shape of the changed world economy, has become fashionable but its meaning and implications, particularly for the third world countries, are far from clear. Globalising is transforming trade, finance, employment, migration, technology, communications, the environment, social systems, ways of living, cultures and patterns of governance. All this is bound to have serious implications for women.

The process of globalization has been accelerated by economic reforms and the liberalisation of trade and investment policies, undertaken even by developing countries. Most developing countries have replaced the old import substitution policies by export promotion and openness. Besides economic transformation, globalization involves changes in the social and political structures and status of societies as also has cultural implications at the individual, the country and the global level.

Globalization: Conceptual Paradigm

Globalization, the most fashionable word of the 1990s, means the victory of capitalism over socialism because the economic values of globalization are in line with those of capitalism and contrary to the values of socialist central planning. Since, the economic determines the political, globalization implies the eventual elimination of socialist authoritarian regimes.[1]

Globalization inevitably means that the nation-state will lose most of its powers to the rising might of the MNCs. The emerging global order is no longer shaped by nation-states but it 'is spearheaded by a few hundred corporate giants, many of them bigger than most sovereign nations.'[2] At the national level, the power of these corporations is so strong that they have 'to a larger extent emasculated state control over national economies and societies.'[3]

Globalization is a long, multifaceted process, with diverse, at times conflicting effects, with an assured future but whose future form is not possible to predict. According to Giddens, globalization can be defined as the intensification of worldwide social relations which link distant localities in such a way that local happenings are shaped by events occurring many miles away and vice-versa.[4] Similarly, for Robertson, globalization refers both to the compression of the world and the intensification of consciousness of the world as a whole.[5] Robertson wants to draw attention to political and cultural ideas such as human rights, global environmental responsibility and cosmopolitanism, which, in their various ways, project a sense of single humanity. He emphasizes the meaningful and interpretative aspects of social life, including the world images in which globalization is represented.

In its radical sense, globalization means the development of a new conjunctural change toward greater international trade and investment within an existing set of economic relations.[6] It can be defined, simply, as the expansion of economic activities across political boundaries of nation-states. It refers to a process of increasing economic openness, growing economic interdependence and deepening economic integration between countries in the world economy.[7]

Holm and Sorensen has provided a working definition of the term globalization. According to them, globalization is defined as 'the intensification of economic, political, social and cultural relations across borders'.[8] From this definition, it becomes clear that globalization is not simply an economic phenomenon. Immanuel Wallerstein defines globalization as the triumph of a capitalist world economy tied together by a global division of labour.[9] Martin Albrow agrees to the definition given by Holm and Sorensen and defines globalization as 'all those processes by which the peoples of the world are incorporated into a single world society,' a society in which 'humanity' becomes for the first time a 'collective actor'.[10]

Globalization is viewed as a process by some writers. According to them, this process had led to the latest stage of capitalism that is global capitalism or globalization. According to Sivanandan, 'If imperialism is the latest stage of capitalism, globalism is the latest stage of imperialism'.[11] A similar definition is provided by Wilkin, who, defines globalization as a process of transformation in the capitalist world system, one that intensifies an array of structural and ideological tendencies as all aspects of the world system come increasingly into the orbit of what we can see as a single and continuous circulation of ideas, commodities, social relations and, most important, sites of conflict.[12]

From the above discussion, it becomes clear that globalization is unavoidable and is not a condition but a set of interrelated process that encompasses all aspects of life i.e., economic, political, social, cultural, military and so on. As a process, it coexists with other processes and forces that operate on a local, national or regional level.[13] It involves both quantitative and qualitative changes with the result that globalization cannot be measured by statistical indicators alone.

The Gender Issues

Since the last decade of the twentieth century, it has been realized that women hold the key to sustainable development. In fact, an appreciation of the critical role that women can play arose from the contribution of women in struggles against colonialism and in national wars of independence. After World War II, the concept of equality of the sexes as one of the basic principles on which a community should be based was incorporated in UN Charter. Since then, there have been a number of conferences and conventions on the theme of Women in Development. The adverse impact of Structural Adjustment Programme[SAP] on women's livelihoods, employment, education, health, social welfare and political participation have all simultaneously brought out the indomitable determination of women to save themselves, their families and their children through strategies of survival and struggle against the depredations of both domestic and foreign elite.

A large number of gender issues continued to determine the nature and shape of Indian society, like most traditional societies where women are treated unequally and do not/cannot enjoy, an average quality of life equal to that of men in terms of life expectancy, health, morality, access to education, access to employment, access to lawful freedoms, and the meaningful exercise of civil and political rights. Although this is true of women globally, their task in developing society like India is doubly difficult. They have to break loose from the bonds imposed upon them by their traditional societies, as also avoid the trap presented by development and modernizing process in which new forms of exploitation and new problems are embedded.[14]

Even after fifty-five years of independence, we see that women received only a small share of developmental opportunities and were often excluded from education, from better jobs, from participation in political systems and from adequate healthcare. Aspects of a general bias against women, which is well documented in the literature, has dwelt on the prevailing economic inequities with low share of jobs and low wages paid to women as compared to those enjoyed by men.[15] We are struggling to find out wages and means to wriggle out of the acute problems entangling the process of development. Yet, the fact remains that we are facing acute problems of human development. Besides, we also see that the participation of women and consumption is exceedingly low in the entire dynamics of the development process. It is surprising that over the years we have tried to find scapegoats in various interrelated issues i.e., population, poverty, propaganda and plurality for all the ills that the country has been through, but we could never see our problems in the light of gender perspective.

Globalization and Gender Issues

The process of globalization has made these problems more complex, by setting in newer trends of the market. Besides other consequences, it has put extreme pressures on the poor men and women. It has resulted in adverse consequences for women, manifested in the increased physical violence against them on a global scale.[16] They have been marginalized not only economically but politically as well as socially. Many of them have been rendered jobless both in the organized as well as unorganized sector.

Apart from the negative impact, there is a positive side also. As a result of globalization, women's educational prospects have improved, contraception has been made more widely available, a more egalitarian set of gender relationships has been popularized and there is a reduction of gender inequalities.[17]

Thus, it can be seen that globalization has a mixed impact on women. It is positive as well as negative. It depends on us to decide whether the impact is positive or negative. On the basis of the experiences of the last few years, we can safely say that the gender inequalities are less severe today than it used to be half a century ago. The following paragraphs will examine the effects of globalization on a number of key inter-related gender issues like education, health, employment, empowerment, violence, etc.

Education and Gender

Education is the key to human advancement and also a way of reducing gender inequalities. Globalization has contributed to narrowing the literacy gap and the school enrolment gap between the genders. Globalization has influenced women's education both in a positive as well as negative way.

The positive developments include—undermining the traditional cultural belief that women's education is not important since they are confined to the four walls. Though this attitude still persists, but due to globalization its strength has weakened and the education of girls has been made more possible. Secondly, women's education has become necessary today for purely labour market reasons. The employers prefer to employ women because they are more adaptable to the demands of a flexible labour market.[18] Thirdly, as a result of globalization, the number of professional, technical and managerial jobs have increased and the gender bias in professional careers have reduced. The global mass media has promoted the images of successful career women. Finally, the international bodies—part of globalization process—have assisted the cause of women's education. As a part of this, the UNICEF Girl's Education Programme has stimulated gender sensitivity and encourages the enrolment of girls in schools.[19]

Negatively, the reductions in public expenditure can reduce education budgets and may also increase the cost of education. This will have a direct impact on women's education, especially in the third world countries, because education for girls is not considered necessary as it is for boys. As a result, the gender gap in education still persists in these countries.

Health and Gender

Health is essential for the satisfaction of basic human needs and to improve the quality of life as also a fundamental human right and a worldwide social goal.[20] Health care and nutritious diet remain distant dreams for women and continues to be an issue of serious concern in developing countries, especially India, where men outnumber women in total population. Globalization has in some ways reduced the problem by providing employment for women, by raising education standards and by changing social attitudes concerning the status of women in society. 'By educating women, the vicious multigenerational cycle of poor child health, low educational performance, low income, high fertility, and poor child health has been broken'.[21] It has contributed to the rise of life expectancy—slightly more for women than for men. It has also contributed to the reduction of infant mortality—slightly more for baby girls than for baby boys. It has made contraception more widely available thereby reducing hazards for women. Local, national and international campaigns on women's health, either on their own or with the support of inetrnational bodies such as the WHO, have had some effect in highlighting women's health issues and in improving services.[22]

Despite these improvements, globalisation has increased the health risks for women in third world countries. The SAP too has affected the women. The SAP has led to reductions in the state health care provisions. As a result, women are the sufferers. Another negative effect is that it has encouraged freer sexual attitudes and hence higher rates of family breakdown with the women usually left to care for the children. It has encouraged the growth of sex tourism on a large scale.[23] Consequently, young girls have started working in brothels and massage parlours thereby endargering their health.

Empowerment

Women's empowerment is a must because it means "equipping them to be economically independent, self-reliant, have a positive self-esteem to enable them to face any difficult situation and they should be able to participate in developmental activities and in the process of decision-making".[24] In the field of empowerment, globalization has made a positive but modest contribution. Their entry into the labour market gives them more freedom as well as more power, as they have income of their own. The advances which the women have achieved as a result of education, has also contributed to their empowerment enabling them to have a greater say in decision-making even in the most traditional societies. The spread of democratic forms of government, spurred on by globalization, has been another factor that has contributed to the rise of women's power. Now almost every country provides the right to vote and the right to be elected to both men and women. Globalization has not greatly assisted the representation of women in the national assemblies of their countries even though it has encouraged the spread of democratic forms of government.[25]

On the negative side, globalization's effect on women's empowerment is that women are no more tolerating even a slightest injustice done to them. As a result of empowerment, they no longer want to stay at home and do the household chores. They think they have become equal partners and are contributing to their homes in the same way as the men. Due to this, their expectations from their husbands has increased which is not tolerated by them especially in the third world countries. Consequently, it leads to confrontation and finally to the breakdown of marriage. This is not a good sign for any society and it needs to be checked immediately.

Employment and Gender

The status of women and its contribution to social and economic development largely depends on the availability of employment opportunities for women. Globalization has influenced both the quantity and quality of work available for women. It has increased the number of jobs available and at the same time, has altered the nature of jobs. The technological changes in the recent years has led to a decline in the traditional manufacturing and other heavy jobs and a rise of the service sector where women have been able to compete very effectively with men.[26] The foreign direct investment by MNC's in several developing countries had led to the creation of Export Processing Zones where women provide up to eighty per cent of the labour force.[27] Besides these, women, especially in the developing countries, have gained an advance over men in the light manufacturing sector, such as textiles, clothing and footwear. Occupational segregation has declined slightly but it is still a feature of labour markets.

On the other hand, though the gender gap in labour force participation has narrowed significantly over the years, still women are facing lots of problems as a result of globalization. They are still the minority in the paid labour force in the world. Their pay is lower than men's[28] even though pay differentials have narrowed slightly in many countries. Data for earnings in manufacturing for eighteen developing countries show that women's earnings vary from 45 per cent of men's (South Korea) to 89 per cent (Burma). This differential arises from women being proportionately more concentrated in industries which pay low wages, in less skilled occupations within each industry, and also in being paid less than men when doing the same job.[29]

Globalization has encouraged the growth of 'feminized' employment, that is, low-paid, insecure, part-time or contract work. The quality of these jobs in terms is not as good as it is in the traditional 'standard' work model. Despite recent improvements, women's rate of unemployment is higher than men's in most countries. It has not equalized women's position in the labour market vis-a vis that of men. This has rightly been pointed out by Persons and Gonas. They are of the view that gender inequalities in employment may have narrowed at the general level but 'when employment categories are examined in more detail—in terms of status, degree of security and actual hours worked—then it becomes clear that gender inequalities remain'.[30]

Gender Violence

Violence against women is primarily a gender issue. It is not limited to domestic violence. Women are exposed to abuse, mental and sexual harassment and even rape. According to a study conducted by WHO, every 54 minutes a woman is raped in India.[31]The National Crime Reports Bureau study found that the frequency of rape cases have almost doubled from 7,289 to 13,754 during the decade 1985-1995[32] and subsequently every year it is increasing. According to NCRB, the number of rape cases in India increased from 15,468 in 1999 to 64,496 in 2000, a jump of 6.6 per cent.[33]

Globalization also has its impact on gender violence. Globalization has been undermining the cultural tradition through its employment, technological and cultural effects. The media, especially in the wake of globalization, has glamourised the women resulting in more exposure which ultimately leads to violence against women. Globalization has encouraged the growth of sex tourism. Young girls are entering into prostitution business which again is a violence against them. Medical advances, which can ascertain the gender of the foetus, have resulted in more abortions of baby girls in recent years resulting in violence against them even before birth.

On the positive side, globalization has created social awareness about violence against women to a great extent. In the recent years, due to the publicity given by media, women have become more aware about the violence against them. This means that more cases of violence against women, including rape, are being reported; more public discussion of the problem takes place; and it is beginning to be seen as a gender problem rather than a problem of general lawlessness.[34] It has made contraception more widely available thereby increasing their autonomy and choices.

Summing Up

The discussion on globalization and gender issues in the preceding pages clearly shows that the effects of globalization on gender equality have been mixed. It has strengthened rather than weakened those forces and processes which advance gender equality. Positively, globalization has contributed to the increase in women's participation in the labour market and has narrowed the gender gap in employment rates. It has increased the need for caring in society. It has contributed to narrowing the illiteracy gap and the school enrolment gap between the genders and in many countries, school attendance and school performance by girls has exceeded than that of boys in recent years. There is a rise of life expectancy for women and reduction of infant mortality slightly more for baby girls than for baby boys. The technological and international aspects of globalization have facilitated the growth of women's social movement across the globe. Finally, the advances in education achieved by women in recent decades has contributed immensely to their empowerment. In all these ways globalization has contributed to the reduction of gender inequalities.

On the other hand, there are some negative impact too which has undermined the welfare of women. Globalization has encouraged the spread of western culture to all parts of India which has definitely improved the status of women in the society. But the biggest drawback is that it has undermined local cultures which has resulted in large numbers of divorce, one-parent families and rise of sex tourism. Globalization has encouraged the growth of 'feminized' employment, that is low-paid, insecure, part-time or contract work. The progress in political empowerment as well as in reducing legal discrimination against women has been slow. Though they have a right to vote still they hold a disproportionately low proportion of senior government positions.

Thus, it can be said that globalization has helped in removing gender inequalities to some extent. But a great deal remains to be done. The gender issues are yet to be solved. The gender issues of yesterday are replaced with the concerns of tomorrow and are going to be as new as tomorrow itself. The effort should be to go beyond the *status quo* to create structures and norms that do not merely adapt to existing conditions

NOTES

1. George, Vic and Wilding, Paul, *Globalization and Human Welfare*, Palgrave, New York, 2002, p. 5.
2. Barnet, R.J. and Cavanagh, J., *Global Dreams*, Simon and Schuster, New York, 1994, p. 14.
3. Strange, S., "The Limits of Politics", in *Government and Opposition*, Vol. 30, p. 298.
4. Giddens, A., *The Consequences of Modernity*, Polity Press, Cambridge, 1990, p. 64.
5. Robertson, R., *Globalization: Social Theory and Global Culture*, Sage, London, 1992, p. 8.
6. Hirst, Paul and Thompson, Grahame, *Globalization in Question*, Polity Press, Cambridge, 1996, p. 7.
7. Nayyar, Deepak, "Globalization: The Game, the Players and the Rules", in Gupta, Satya Dev (ed.), *The Political Economy of Globalization*, Kluwer Academic Publishers, Boston, 1997, p. 13.
8. Holm, H. H. and Sorensen, G., *Whose World Order: Uneven Globalization and the End of the Cold War*, Westview Press, Boulder, 1995, p. 1.
9. Holton, Robert J., *Globalization and the Nation-State*, Macmillan, London, 1998, p. 11.
10. Albrow, Martin, 'Introduction', in Albrow, Martin and King, E (eds.), *Globalization, Knowledge and Society*, Sage, London, 1990, p. 8.
11. Sivanandan, A., "Globalism and the Left", in *Race and Class*, Vol. 40, Nos. 2-3, 1998-1999, p. 5.
12. Wilkin, P., "New myths for the South: Globalization and the conflict between Private Power and Freedom", in *Third World Quaterly*, Vol. 17, No. 2, 1996, p. 228.
13. George, Vic and Wilding, Paul, *op. cit.*, p. 19.
14. Yadav, Sushma and Mishra, Anil Dutta, *Gender Issues in India Some Reflections*, Radha Publications, New Delhi, 2003, p. 1.
15. Sen, Sunanda, "Structural Adjustments and Gender Issues in Developing Countries", in Rajput, Pam and Swarup, Hem Lata (eds.), *Women and Globalization Reflections, Options and Strategies*, Ashish Publishing House, New Delhi, 1994, pp. 55-56.
16. Yadav, Sushma and Mishra, Anil Dutta, *op. cit.*, p. 120.
17. George, Vic and Wilding, Paul, *op. cit.*, p. 113.
18. *Ibid.*, p. 122.

19. Bellamy, C., *The State of the World's Children 1998*, UNICEF, New York, 1999, p. 56.
20. Mishra, Sweta, "Health of Working Women: India and Canada", *Paper presented at a Seminar on Women at Work Place: India and Canada*, March 21-22, 2003, organized by Centre for Canadian Studies, H.P. University, Shimla.
21. Todaro, M. P., *Economic Development*, 7th edn., Pearson Education, Harlow, 2000, p. 348.
22. Doyal, L., "The Politics of Women's Health: Setting a Global Agenda", in *International Journal of Health Services*, Vol. 26, No. 1, 1996, p. 48.
23. George, Vic and Wilding, Paul, *op. cit.*, pp.127-128.
24. Chauhan, S.S.S., and Bansal, Gaurav, "Various Dimensions of Women's Empowerment", in *Social Welfare*, Vol. 49, No. 5, August, 2002, p.10.
25. George, Vic and Wilking, Paul, *op. cit.*, pp.132-133.
26. *Ibid.*, p.114.
27. International Labour Organisation, *World Development Report, 1998-99*, ILO, Geneva, 1998, p. 142.
28. Elder, S. and Johnson, L.J., "Sex-specific Labour Market Indicators: What they Show", in *International Labour Review*, Vol. 138, No. 4, 1999, p. 458.
29. Stewart, Frances, "Can Adjustment Programmes Incorporate the Interests of Women?", in Afshar, Haleh and Dennis, Carolyne (eds.), *Women and Adjustment Policies in the Third World*, Macmillan, London, 1992, p. 22.
30. Perrons, D. and Gonas, L., "Perspectives on Gender Inequality in European Employment", in *European Urban and Regional Studies*, Vol. 5, No.1, 1998, p. 9.
31. Yadav, Sushma and Mishra, Anil Dutta, *op. cit.*, p. 3.
32. Parasher, Utpal, "Beware of Delhi, Study Warns Women", in *The Hindustan Times*, February 1, 1998.
33. Yadav, Sushma and Mishra, Anil Dutta, *op. cit.*, p. 3.
34. George, Vic and Wilking, Paul, *op. cit.*, p. 128.

11

Globalization and Child Labour

SUSHMA YADAV

Globalization is a fact of twenty-first century which cannot be overlooked. It is a process by which an increasing share of world production is traded internationally, and the productive systems of different countries become more and more interdependent. Given that globalization is unlikely to stop, it seems reasonable and desirable to understand the consequences and various dimensions of globalization. There must be gainers and losers from the process of globalization. Who are they? Are children among the latter or among the former? Is further liberalisation and privatisation likely to raise the number of children engaged in labour? Is there a direct link between exposure to international trade and child labour? However it must be remembered that globalization is different from internationalisation. While the latter refers to economic and social interactions that occur across national boundaries, the former denotes the expanding scale, growing magnitude, speeding up and deepening impact of inter-regional flows and patterns of social interaction (Held & Anthony 2001). Globalization process in not limited to economic dimension, it also involves a number of key non-economic forms of social interactions relating to culture and governance.

Moreover, globalization has also changed the traditional economic thinking that countries with a relative abundance of labour i.e. the developing countries will export labour intensive products, while countries with a relative abundance of capital—the developed countries will export capital-intensive products. Since, within each country, an increase in trade raises the price of the abundant factor relative to that of the scarce one, an implication of this thinking would be that 'globalization', will make workers worse-off relative to capitalists in the developed world. This vision of the world has undergone a change over the last few decades. while the traditional theory equated economic growth with the accumulation of physical capital (buildings and machinery) per head of population, modern theory attaches much greater importance to the accumulation of human capital (knowledge and personal skills). The human capital is embodied in skilled workers. Further, globalization does not simply mean more international trade in final goods. It also means more trade in intermediate goods. Falling transportation costs and advances in linkages and information technology facilitating the co-ordination of dispersed production activities, are in fact favouring the segmentation of production process as also the location of different segments of the same process in different countries. Although the immediate beneficiary of this intra-industry trade expansion are the developed industrial countries, the potential implications of such process for developing countries, in general, and for child labour in particular, cannot be overlooked.

There is cross-country evidence to suggest that exposure to international competition may result in more children going to school, rather than to work in developing countries. This is because a necessary condition for a country opening itself to international competition is that it should have a sufficiently large share of educated workers. The developing countries can turn globalization into an opportunity to reduce child labour by investing more on educational subsidies, more schools and maintenance grants for school children as well as public health facilities so as to enhance mortality and reduce fertility.

Child labour has become a significant topic on campaign and research agenda at the beginning of the twenty-first century. Trade union, NGOs, the ILO, UNICEF and a number of social movements are actively involved in campaigns against the continuing exploitation of child workers across the globe. The problem is substantial as studies show that there are more then 400 million child workers in the world (UNICEF, 1997) and at least one in four children between the ages of 10 and 14 work in the Third World (Bowel, 1994), the worst part is that most of these children work in terrible conditions—unhealthy and inhumanely cruel. On another level, child labour drives down wages and replaces adults. The practice perpetuates poverty. The impact of globalization on child labour in India becomes crucial because India is the home to the world's largest population of children. India, as a nation, has always proclaimed to follow a proactive policy in the matter of elimination of child labour. This is sought to be achieved through constitutional and statutory provisions combined with a range of development measures and policies. The strategy of the Government has been to eliminate child labour sequentially beginning with the most hazardous forms and subsequently moving towards the less hazardous forms. Since the Global Report on Child Labour, 2002, prepared by the ILO highlighted the close interlink between poverty and child lobour, India is also trying to address the issue through the implementation of its national poverty eradication programmes and simultaneous sustained efforts at providing primary education to the children. Education for all children in the age-group of 6-14 years has been made a Fundamental Right by the 93rd Amendment Bill to the Constitution passed in May 2002 (86th Amendment Act).

Besides being a founder member of the ILO, India has ratified 39 ILO conventions. Out of which 20 are core conventions.

The ratification by India of the UN Convention on Rights of the Child (CRC) in 1992 has set in motion a process of greater state initiative and public accountability. It has imposed a legal obligation upon the state to "undertake all appropriate legislative, administrative and other measures for the implementation of the rights recognised in the convention as well as its responsibility to submit to the committee on rights of the child periodical reports on the measures that they have adopted which give effect to the rights recognised and the progress made on the enjoyment of those rights.

The Constitution of India lays down that child labour in factories, mines and any other hazardous occupations should be prohibited (Art. 24), and that children below the age of 14 years should get free and compulsory primary education (Art. 45); because the tender age of children should not be abused and that they are not forced to enter avocations unsuited to their age and strength (Art. 39-C). The Constitution also states children be given opportunities and facilities to develop in a healthy manner and in conditions of freedom and dignity and that childhood be protected against moral and material abandonment (Art. 39-f). Read together, the above constitutional provisions have a potential for laying down very comprehensive guidelines for a total elimination of child labour.

Legislation pertaining to child labour has existed in India for over a hundred years. The enactment of the Factories Act, 1881, and the Mines Act, 1901, was, to some extent, influenced by the ratification of I.L.O. Conventions by British India. From the time of independence, India has committed itself against child labour. Guided by the provisions of Art. 24, Art. 39, and Art. 45 of the Constitution of India, India has sought to take care of its children and ensure the safety of workers. Bonded labour was sought to end by the Bonded Labour System Act of 1976 while the Child Labour Act, 1986 'prohibits the employment of children who have not completed their 14th year in specified hazardous occupations and processes'. However, the act does not fulfil the suggestion of ILO Convention No. 138 that the minimum age for employment should not be less than fifteen years. In 1994, the Elimination of Child Labour Programme was announced which pledged to end child labour for two million children in hazardous industries as defined in the Act of 1986 by the year 2000. But only about 4 per cent of the five year estimated cost of eight and a half billion dollars was allocated for child labour elimination programmes in 1995-96.

The passage of Constitution (86th Amendment) Act in May 2002 to make education for all children in the age group 6-14 years a Fundamental Right can surely be a milestone. Specially in view of the fact that Myron Weiner attributed the prevalence of child labour in India largely to the failure of educational system.

Child labour can be measured by the figures in the Development Indicators of the participation rate of individuals aged 10 to 14. But the limitation of this measure is that it does not count children working at younger ages i.e., aged 6 to 10 and also children engaged in unofficial, especially if illegal, work activities. It thus does not include the most undesirable form of child work. In addition to this, we can consider the primary school non-attendance/drop out rate. Although, children not attending school may not necessarily be working in the home or elsewhere, they tend to be more exposed to the worst form of abuse (from hazardous or very hard work to prostitution).

The main cause of child labour is assumed to be poverty. Indeed, data reveal a negative association between income and child labour. Similarly, higher primary enrolment is associated with lower labour participation among children. The correlation cannot be perfect partly because work in informal or illegal labour markets is usually underreported, and partly also because a sizeable proportion of children combines, in some countries, work with school attendance.

It is important to keep in mind the fact that children do not normally choose to work. Mostly, the decisions are thrust upon them by their parents. Even in the case of the child who is expelled, or runs away from home, the reason for his or her working can be traced back to parental actions that made it impossible for the child to remain in the home. The only exception are children who are abducted, or who get lost or are separated from their families due to war, or some natural disaster. A cross-national study edited by on Giovanni Andree Cornia on *Harnessing Globalization for Children: A Report to Unicef* shows that exposure to international trade does not appear to encourage child labour. On the contrary, higher foreign trade appears to be associated with a lower incidence of child labour. However, the existence of considerable national differences in the exposure to international trade and the incidence of child labour seems to indicate that the type of policies a country pursues shifts the relationship between child labour and globalization.

The study also concludes on the basis of data surveyed that there is no *prima facie* evidence that globalization will necessarily result in more child labour. Rather, it finds signs that suggest that international trade and economic integration offer governments the opportunity to reduce child labour. Since trade promotes economic growth, the opportunity could come in the form of higher income. Or it could be that the relative wage changes brought about by international trade are conducive to less child labour. An important role is also played by the capital market and educational policy. If there is an increase in the remuneration of skilled, or just literate, adult workers and the opportunity-cost of time spent in education falls, it would reduce the labour force participation of each school-age child.

Studies reveal that there is no empirical evidence that globalization increases child labour. But it has been found that in a country that has a large uneducated workforce globalization raises the wage rate of uneducated workers. Therefore, unless the government takes steps to counter the reduction in the incentive to educate children, the net effect of globalization is likely to be an increase in child labour. However, in developing countries that have a larger number of workers with at least a basic education, globalization raises the wage rate of educated workers. Thus, developing countries can turn globalization into an opportunity to reduce child labour by spending more on education and public health.

However, there may be/are demographic pressures that are generated or compounded by the globalization process that shape the demand for and supply of child labour as well as child labour standards. Suppose that globalization raises the wage rate of uneducated unskilled labour. This means that not only unskilled adult workers, but also child workers, are paid more per unit of time. As the opportunity-cost of time spent in education goes up due to globalised markets, the marginal cost of education also rises. At the same time, as the remuneration gap between educated and uneducated labour becomes smaller, the return to education will decrease. Both these changes will reduce the incentive for parents to invest in their children's education. If simultaneously, there is an increase in the unskilled wage rate, the child labour will increase.

A critical demographic aspect of globalization was a rapid increase in the rate of population growth in the developing countries like India and many others in Asia, Africa and Latin America. The population-explosion in these regions could be seen as an aspect of globalization because despite the fact that the leaders of these states tended to be anti-globalists, they were willing to join some of the new global institutions established at the end of the second world war like the U.N.O. and its many sub-agencies like I.L.O., W.H.O., F.A.O., UNICEF etc. This was a development of major demographic significance because one of the key goals of these organisations and agencies was to promote the global diffusion of knowledge and technologies needed to ensure that all people gained access to basic health facilities and nutrition. The availability of such knowledge and the life-saving opportunities induced a dramatic drop in the mortality rate in the developing countries while the subsequent reduction in the rate of fertility tended to lag or continue. Consequently, the proportion of child population (0-14) years in Asia, Africa and Latin America during the period 1950-2000 were much above those of Europe during the same period. This size of population provides the pool of which child labour is a sub-set. If rise in population is controlled, the supply of potential child-workers could fall in the long run. There is cross-country evidence to suggest that policies aimed at lowering mortality are likely to reduce child labour.

The growing population in the developing countries generated pressures on global good-supply which resulted in famines or near famines during the 1960s in India as well as China and Indonesia—the three largest newly independent states. The response of these states was to initiate food expansion and also fertility containment programmes. Both the responses programmes were a function of globalization in that their diffusion and development were greatly assisted by UN agencies and involved global diffusion of new technologies. These can surely be seen as welcome trends that hold promise for the struggle to end the worst forms of child labour in the near future.

An indication/evidence of this trend is available in the data on economically active population 1950-2010 available with ILO (1997). The calculation of the incidence of child labour in the age group of 10 to 14 years on the basis of ILO (1997) data for countries in Asia, indicates that the incidence of child labour in the age group of 5-9 years has empirically been found to be small, for example for India in 1993-94, it was less than 2.5 per cent. Similarly for the children in the age group of 10-14 years, the activity rate declined from 35.43 per cent in 1950 to 14.38 per cent in 1995. (Chaudhri 1997). However, it is important to note that these data cannot identify the illegal or hazardous forms of child labour.

Although the demographic data discussed above indicates that the incidence of child labour will fall significantly in the near future, there is the other side too. The data also indicates that between 1995 and 2025, the labour force of the low-income countries will grow from 1.4 to 2.2 billion. A 57 per cent increase in the size of the labour market, over a twenty years period, does not bode well for the bargaining power and well-being of labour in the developing states even if these nations manage to sustain high rates of growth. What can happen if the social dimension of the globalization process is poorly managed is particularly patent in the case of Indonesia where mass poverty, the incidence of child labour, and political instability have greatly increased as a consequence of the financial crisis. Therefore, to the extent that the globalization limits the capacity and willingness of nations to directing resources to those areas that can assist human development, the trend is and should be a cause of great concern to those who wish to see the elimination of the phenomenon of child labour and especially its worst forms. The ILO's studies should be read as a warning and a message that strengthening education, social security, labour law and industrial relations can go a long way in ensuring that the globalization process is managed effectively and used to eliminate child labour.

There seems to be a correlation between globalization and trade expansion on the one hand and trade expansion and child labour on the other. The question relevant here is why do countries trade. The classic answer handed down by Recardo to this question is of comparative advantage. A country can increase its wealth and welfare if, instead of directly producing all the goods its members wish to consume, it specialises in the production of those goods that it can produce at relatively lower cost than other countries, and exchanges the surplus for the goods it does not produce. The cost of a good depends on the prices of factors used for its production. Since the prices of traded inputs are the same everywhere, differences in the relative costs of traded goods reflect differences in the relative prices of non-traded goods used as factors of production. Standard trade theory predicts that countries specialise in the production of traded goods that make more intensive use of the non-traded factors of which they have relatively greater abundance. Labour and capital are acknowledged non-traded factors. It is natural that with an increase in trade, countries with a relative abundance of labour i.e. the developing countries will thus export labour-intensive products while countries with relative abundance of capital, will export capital-intensive products. Since, within each country, an increase in trade raises the price of the abundant factor, an implication of globalization and trade-expansion is that globalization will make workers better-off in the developing countries.

This has important implications for child labour. According to the restructured trade theory (Adrian Wood 1994), countries export the products which make greater use of the relatively more abundant type of labour. Thus, within each trading country, the benefit of increased world trade accrues to members of the relatively larger skill group i.e. illiterate, literate or skilled. In developed countries, globalization widens the gap between skilled and unskilled wage rates because there are comparatively more skilled than literate workers, and the number of illiterates is insignificant. But in developing countries with a relative abundance of literate workers, what widens is the wage gap between literate and illiterate workers, while the wage gap between skilled and just literate workers becomes narrower. By definition, working children in fact, fall in the "illiterate workers" category. As globalization leads to an increase in gap between literate end illiterate wage-rates in developing countries, it is bound to give parents an incentive to produce fewer but better educated children. If it translates into actual school enrolments of children from poorer families, where child labour is mainly concentrated, this ultimately, would help reduce child labour.

Thus, there are studies that forecast that if properly harnessed, globalization should spur growth and economic development leading to social progress and a system where child labour is eliminated. However, this is yet to happen in the developing countries. There is evidence to show that with globalization, child labour is increasing—mainly in export industries due to greed, connivance and complacency. Child labour is a result of the above three. The greed is of those who employ children at a cost only one-sixth to one-third of the adult wage. The connivance is of government who turn a blind eye to the practice by not applying concerned labour laws. And the complacency of all of us who continue to want cheaper consumer products regardless of the exploitation involved in production. It means that strong legislation with effective enforcement mechanisms on the part of the government and increased public awareness are essentially needed if we want to make any progress in eliminating child labour. The trade policies of big businesses must also reflect a commitment to core labour standards and basic human rights.

It is feared that in the developing countries, globalization and liberalisation would also result in casualisation of workers which would further add to the already large workforce in the informal sector in countries like India which have more than 90 per cent of their work-force in the informal sector. Therefore, employment generation and decent working conditions in the informal sector have to be our primary concern besides very strong anti-poverty programmes.

Consumer campaigns to insist that governments add a label clearly stating that child labour has not been used in the making of the goods being sold can go a long way in solving the problem of child labour and can make globalization a boon for the deprived and exploited children. It should be noted that till now, there are few organised boycotts of such products, however spontaneous action by consumers is forcing change. Therefore, the international community urgently needs to take the initiative to enforce labour standards around the world because it has been seen that in no single case has child labour been eliminated voluntarily.

What needs to be done is clear. Statistics reveal that countries with a predominance of fast and shared economic growth accompanied by a rising Human Development Index (HDI) and Gender Development Index (GDI) and falling Human Poverty Index (HPI) are bound to experience decline in child labour. In India, Kerala's elimination of child labour in contrast with Uttar Pradesh and Bihar's continuing problems is attributable to the Human Development Index and Gender Development Index or the lack of it (Chaudhri 1997; Mishra 2000).

Thus, the fears that globalization will increase the incidence of child labour do not seem to be realistic given the decline that is being induced by the falling proportion of children in the vast majority of states. (ILO 1997) However, the need to continue the pressure on national governments, multinational corporations, and domestic companies through civil society can be hardly over-emphasised. The role of the I.L.O. in this context becomes far more significant in the era of globalization in that it should use all opportunities to elicit commitments from the nation-states, MNCs and other stake-holders for enhanced commitment to family planning, child development, and the elimination of child labour.

REFERENCES

Anker, Richard and H. Melkas, *Economic Incentives for Children and Families to Eliminate or Reduce Child Labour,* ILO, Geneva, 1996.

Aghion P. and Williamson, J.G., *Growth, Inequality and Globalization, Theory, History and Policy,* Cambridge University Press, UK, 1998.

Boserup, E., *Population and Technology,* Basil Blackwell, Oxford, 1981.

Boyden, Jo, "The Relationship Between Education and Child Work", *Occasional Papers Child Rights Series No. 9, UNICEF,* International Child Development Centre, Florence, 1994.

Burra, Neera, *Born to Work: Child Labour in India*, O.U.P., New Delhi, 1995.

Centre for Media Studies, Poverty and Child Labour: The Impact of Poverty Alleviation Programmes on the Incidence of Child Labour: A Study, Child Labour Action and Support Project, ILO, New Delhi, 1996.

Chandrasekhar, C.P., "The Economic Consequences of the Abolition of Child Labour: An Indian Case Study", *The Journal of Peasant Studies,* Vol. 24, No. 3, April, 1997, pp. 137-39.

Chaudhri, D.P., *Dynamic Profile of Child Labour in India,* 1951-1991, CLASP, ILO, New Delhi, 1996.

Chaudhri, D.P., "A Policy Perspective on Child Labour in India with Pervasive Gender and Urban Bias in School Education", *The Indian Journal of Labour Economics,* Vol. 40, No. 4, 1997, pp. 789-808.

Cigno, A., *Economics of the Family,* New York, Clarendon Press, 1991.

Cigno, A. and F.C. Rosati, *Why Do Indian Children Work, and is it Bad for Them?* IZA DPN 115, Bonn, 2000.

Cigno, A., Rosati F.C. and Z. Tzannatos, *Handbook of Child Labour,* The World Bank, Washington, D.C., 2001.

Duranton, G., *Globalization, Productive Systems and Inequalities,* Centre for Economic Performance, London, 1998.

Easterlin, R.A., "The Globalization of Human Development", *Annals of the American Academy of Political and Social Sciences,* Vol. 570, 2000, pp. 32-48.

Grootaert, C. and R. Kanbur, "Child Labour: An Economic Perspective", *International Labour Review*, 134, 1995, pp. 187-203.

Held David and Anthony McGraw, "The Great Globalization Debate: An Introduction" in David Held and A. McGraw (Eds.) *The Global Transformation Reader,* Polity Press, Oxford, 2001.

Hilowitz, Janet, *Labelling Child Labour Products: A Preliminary Study,* ILO/IPEC, Geneva, 1997.

ILO (2002), *A Future Without Child Labour,* Global Report Under the Follow up to the ILO Declaration on Fundamental Principles and Rights at Work, Geneva.

Mishra, L., *Child Labour in India,* O.U.P., New Delhi, 2000.

UNICEF, The State of the World's Children, 1997: Focus on Child Labour, O.U.P., New York, 1997.

Weiner, Myron, *The Child and the State in India,* O.U.P., New Delhi, 1991.

12

Globalization and Consumerism:
A Study of its Impact

MANOJ SINHA

Introduction

Globalization is a new contemporary stage of development of capitalism all over the world. It is a process of social change in which geographical and cultural barriers are reduced. This breakdown of barriers is the result of transportation, communication and electronic communication. It also involves a process by which economies of different countries are oriented to a global market and are controlled by multinational and global financial institutions. It is not merely an economic process, it is also a cultural process. It creates, by the help of media, a monoculture—a culture of rich and powerful. It is no longer a theoretical concept; it is a glaring reality, impinging upon almost every aspect of human existence—economic, political, environmental, and cultural and the like.

Globalization has a long history as a political and cultural reality and as a religious and cultural movement. The first stage of the globalization process started with the early Egyptian, Babylonian, Greek and Roman Empires, which united the world of their time. The second stage traced later part of 1400s when European explorers voyaged out of Europe to "discover" new lands. Trade expanded between Europe and the new worlds. Gradually, the process of colonisation started. The third stage of globalization started in the nineteenth century along with the expansion of colonial empires and trade. The globalization intensified with the advent of the industrial revolution in Europe as different countries in Europe sought raw materials and markets for its products. This period ended with the

World War II, but its ideological, economic and cultural consequences continue to influence till today. With the rejection and failure of socialism as an alternative, the whole world is thrown open to market economy, liberal democracy and the powerful march of Western cultural values all over the globe with the help of power tools of information technologies. Today we live in a new stage of globalization.

I have listed the characteristics of globalization and its consequences in order to lay down some markers:

(*a*) deregulated capital markets with the possibility of speedy transfer of capital;

(*b*) communications and information technology which makes possible action at a distance in real time which can be very short;

(*c*) active forex markets with supporting financial markets with new products (*e.g.* derivatives, options) which allows speculators to take positions in any currency around the world where there are potential profit opportunities;

(*d*) greater geographical spread and increased mobility of fixed, i.e. direct, investment;

(*e*) rapid and linked reactions as between different financial markets which work round the world round the clock, as well as between financial markets and forex markets;

(*f*) the emergence of a global media network linked with a global communications network;

(*g*) the fashioning a of a global consumer culture and a global music/film/TV culture benefiting from all the above, especially (b) and (f);

(*h*) increased but as yet imperfect and legally impeded mobility of labour;

(*i*) greater awareness, though, as yet, not very effective redress of human rights violations, ecological disasters, famines and refugee problems, benefiting from (b) and (f);

(*j*) speeding up of technological change leading to increased concentration of capital via mergers and takeovers but at the same time increased competition between the surviving large companies.

Consequences of Globalization

1. reduced control of the nation-state over its macro economic affairs especially in the matter of budgetary policy and monetary policy;
2. increased volatility of forex and financial markets;
3. displacement of manufacturing industry from its old locations in the North to selected locations—Asia, Latin America—in the South;
4. a dematerialisation of the industrial products (the weightless economy);
5. a feeling of increased job insecurity in the North as well as the South;
6. increasing feminisation of the labour force;
7. rapid spread of new technology embodied in new investment in the favoured locations of foreign direct investment;
8. rapid industrialisation, despite some recent setbacks, of Asian economies;
9. increased marginalisation of economies previously reliant on intergovernmental aid who are unable to attract capital, especially in Sub Saharan Africa.

The Central Question

The issue is whether globalization is benevolent or malevolent. Or perhaps is it benevolent to the powerful North to which belongs Canada and malevolent to the poor South where India forms a part. Is it just a continuation of the imperialist system of the nineteenth and early twentieth century under a new glossy facade of liberal democracy and free markets? The answer to this crucial question has to be multi-layered. We need to distinguish as between North and South and according to the historical phases outlined above. It will also be different according to whether we take a mechanistic or an organicist view. Let us begin with the dominant paradigm in the social sciences, which is mechanistic. In this view, if we begin with the North then capitalism was benevolent in its Keynesian phase while full employment prevailed. Contrasted with those golden years, globalization has brought job insecurity, financial volatility, weak state and an erosion (threatened rather than actual) of welfare benefits. Flexible labour markets (in

Anglo Saxon economies at least) have weakened trade unions and through them social democratic parties. Income inequality has increased markedly rewarding highly educated people who are in demand in the new technological enterprises relative to blue-collar workers large sums as compensation. Big corporations merging and retrenching are seen as villains of the piece. They are relocating abroad, outsourcing, downsizing, flattening the hierarchy, imposing insecure and demanding job contracts etc. There was, for a while, in the mid 1990s real concern that work will shrink or disappear though the rising employment record in the Anglo Saxon economies, at least, has disproved that prediction.

The critique of large global or transnational corporations also extends to the ecological damage done by the growth of production. The migration of capital to the South is criticised for employing cheap labour, which lacks the healthy working conditions of labour in the North. International trade, which has steadily liberalised and took a big upward jump, with the negotiation of the treaty establishing the WTO, is then characterised as a transmission belt of all the evils of globalization. Radical groups in the South echo this critique. They see the flow of global capital as a reestablishment of hegemony, with the end of self-sufficiency as an ideal for the autonomous development of the South. They join their Northern counterparts in pointing out the ecological damage. Since the self-sufficiency ideal was built on a denial of free trade as a beneficial arrangement, they too see the WTO as the problem.

At the start of the recent World Trade Organization (WTO) conference in Seattle, director-general Mike Moore stated the conference was doomed to succeed. His exercise in sloganeering failed as dramatically as the conference. There can be no doubt that a radical rethink in how the WTO positions itself with the public is necessary. Forget economic arguments and claims of being the one true path to prosperity, the WTO needs some old-fashioned warm-and-fuzzy hype. The WTO needs a little Santa Claus magic to fix the public relations nightmare of the Seattle conference.

As conferences go, Seattle could not have turned out any worse for the WTO—the 135 members failed to reach an agreement on the main issues; Bill Clinton rode into town and made it clear that, like every other world organization, the WTO would have to play by America's rules if it wanted to survive; and, the enduring image of the WTO's millennial conference will be police clad in black riot-gear putting the boots to protesters.

The image may be reassuring for those corporate and government types who like nothing better than a good dose of law and order to ensure that mobs, peaceful or unruly, do not interfere with the righteous progress of globalization. Fortunately for them, there was just enough unruliness that the mainstream media could dismiss all the protesters in Seattle as antisocial, violence-hungry rioters.

For the less ideologically sound, the pictures from Seattle were disturbingly reminiscent of images from around the world of law and order run amok. It was another blow to the WTO's efforts to convince the unconverted of the never-ending wonders of free trade. Now, the organization faces a serious public relations conundrum. How does a faceless international organization responsible only to the governments of its members and dogged by effective protests create a positive public image?

The WTO is not the first organization to face such insurmountable obstacles, and the advertising world has a solution for the WTO's problems. It simply has to find a celebrity spokesperson that can dispel those visions of jackbooted police officers, and reinforce the idea that capitalism, trade, globalization and consumerism are inherently good for all of us.

Positive Aspects

There are many potentially positive aspects of globalization, if it is pursued for the common good, not just for the benefit of a few. Today globalization has led to the opening up of the national boundaries to international trade and global competition. Developments linked with globalization have opened up boundless possibilities for human development, enormous new opportunities and enhanced the quality of life for many people in the third world countries. For example, the production of goods for consumption on a massive scale has brought not only a better and more varied goods available to every citizen, but also has brought enormous change in people's value system. Those who have and are able to buy the goods have attained greater comfort, speedier communication and faster travel. Information technology has converted the world into a "global village". The events of far-off lands are easily accessible in our living rooms. This process has promoted exchange of ideas and customs between peoples of different countries. Today our ways of thinking and behaving are now challenged beyond accepted traditional patterns. The horizon of our perspectives has suddenly embraced 'the global village' beyond the confines of our homes. And this has been reciprocally beneficial. In addition, live communication of facts makes us partake instantaneously in the events of history. It also creates and promotes global concern. We now have the possibility of immediate worldwide attention to global issues, particularly to people in emergency situations. For this reason, it is irrational on our part to reject it outright; an uncritical attitude towards it is unwise. We need to affirm the positive side of this development and make use of the many opportunities it offers for our development.

Negative Aspects

While some economists and politicians approve these developments, many people look at this process with much apprehension. They look at the global village as an order or mechanism for greater economic exploitation and political oppression. Globalization has many dimensions: economic, technological, political, cultural, social, environmental, ideological, etc. Each of them affects the local either positively or negatively. Let us see some of its negative aspects:

(a) *Economic Aspect*

The world market has emerged as the dominant economic force. While some nations have tremendous economic advantages, others have become more and more dependent. The main players in the present process of globalization are the governments of powerful nations (in particular the G7), transnational cooperation, the IMF, the World Bank and the WTO. The development of all third world countries has to be related to the world market. This is so because the overall control of the global economy is in the hands of the G7 countries. They control the monetary system and international trade. The multinationals and other institutions with the help of the state control all development processes. The foreign debt works as an instrument to control the development process in these countries. Terms and conditions on the loans are imposed on them, which make them almost impossible to develop on their own terms. The role of developing countries is simply to provide cheap labour to attract investors and to provide raw materials, which are at the mercy of fluctuating prices. They are to meet the needs of others as cheaply as possible. This unfettered growth of the multinationals and the emphasis on foreign trade are not conducive to a development pattern that is oriented to the basic needs of the people. The market forces often determine the production needs and patterns. It is unfortunate that they seldom take into consideration the basic needs of the people. The production of the goods for export or for the conspicuous consumption of the rich becomes the market force today. In the globalised free market, the only people who count are those who have goods to sell and those who have the money to buy. This in turn drives many to the margins of the economic life. The small entrepreneurs have very little chance of survival in this system. Only the stronger and successful competitors survive and thereby widening the gap between the rich and poor, both between countries and within country. One cannot deny that there has been a worldwide growth in poverty, inequality and the human misery. Social injustice is becoming an accepted reality. It is said that the top 20 per cent has access to 82.7 per cent, while the bottom 20 per cent struggle to survive on 1.4 per cent. The weak, the poor and the inexperienced ones are pushed to the outer rims of the society. Globalization works for the benefits of the rich while the poor become commodities since they are used as cheap labours. It is very clear that the present economic pattern no longer serves the interest of the majority of the people. It rather destroys the lives of many people due to its unjust distribution of wealth, exploitation and deprivation of basic needs. Indeed, it has created a situation of marginalisation, exclusion and social disintegration. India currently faces all these economic realities squarely.

(b) *Political Aspect*

The development of the third world countries with the help of industrialized countries has many political implications. The process of globalization from the beginning was fraught with competition, conflict, domination and exploitation. The opening up of the national boundaries for free market has led to a neo-colonialism allowing not only economic domination, but also political domination over the poor nations. For example, the policies of liberalisation and withdrawal of subsidies, which are the conditions imposed by the IMF and the World Bank, have resulted in the curtailing of the state's power. Today, globalization is creating a government more committed to the protection of foreign investments and less to the protection of the citizens of the country. Many third world countries like India are forced to abandon its social responsibilities. This makes many people to ask whether the present process of globalization is compatible with democracy, social justice and the social welfare state. While the state is rendered relatively powerless, it has become a mere tool of the rich and the powerful. Its sole function is to suppress any organized resistance by oppressed people of the unjust system.

(c) *Social Aspect*

The market ideology of globalization gives a notion that people who cannot afford goods and live in rural areas are considered uncivilized and backward. They feel isolated from the privileged groups. This wrong notion creates an inferiority complex among the poor rural masses that urges them to migrate to the cities and towns in search of employment and better living. It encourages migration not only within a country, but also encourages people to migrate to other countries. It is estimated that there are seventy million workers around the world. The migrant workers are the most exploited people. They suffer from insecurity and social exclusion. This social exclusion is deeper than the economic level and begs for attention especially in the developed countries.

An ever-increasing economic pattern and the expansionary character of globalization leads to lowering of labour costs and wages. In the struggle to be more competitive, labour costs and wages are being driven down. Companies go in for 'restructuring' and 'downsizing', which creates redundancies. Permanent employment and skilled workforce is being replaced by the casual and part-time employment creating immense insecurity among the workers. While wages are being lowered, but working hours have been increased. Yet it is almost impossible for a poor worker to rebel against the company that employs him or her. Powerlessness is one of the consequences of globalization for so many people in the lower brackets of society. All these lead the poor worker to involve in all sorts of anti-social activities.

The profit-oriented free market has also let loose the present day social realities. Consumerism and materialism have overwhelmed modern society affecting every aspect of life. Society has become impersonal, mechanical and inhumane. The present society and its penchant for unprincipled living, selfishness, corruption, opportunism, and violence are the product of consumerism and materialism.

(d) *Cultural Aspect*

Globalization means the export and import of cultures. Globalization involves cultural invasion. Technology is power. It becomes the carrier to those systems and ideologies (values and cultures) within which it has been nurtured. The whole idea of progress and development is decisively shaped by western life-style, worldview and its structures of which Canada forms a part. A monoculture is fast emerging. When we say, "mono-culture", it means the undermining of economic, cultural and ecological diversity and the acceptance of a technological culture developed in the West and the adoption of its inherent values. The tendency is to accept the efficiency with productivity without any concern for compassion or justice. In traditional societies, people maintained a very strong practice of community ownership of land and property. The accumulation of wealth by individual was not encouraged, but today wealth is increasingly regarded as belonging to individuals and not to the community. The slow erosion of traditional cultural values leads to lack of cohesion in societies. The indigenous culture and its potential to save human development and the earth from destruction are vastly ignored, a problem being faced not only in Indian society but also in more developed societies, the one glaring example being the indigenous Cree population of Canada.

(e) *Impact upon Indigenous People*

With the accelerating deterioration of the global economic and political situation, the indigenous people face further marginalisation and graver threats of continuity and sustainability. In many parts of the world, the indigenous people have become the victims of big reservoirs, mega projects, wild life sanctuaries, mines, industries, etc. An indigenous writer from Pacific region writes his experience as follows:

> The advertisement on our local TV demonstrates this concept very clearly. The ad begins with people living happily in a joyous environment where there is fun, plenty of food in the garden and an abundance of fish in the sea. Then the big ships came with big money, which they gave to the chiefs for the forests. The result is total displacement, impoverishment and ecological destabilisation.

In the name of development, people are forcefully evicted from their ancestral land and the abode of the various spirits they worship using repressive measures and often without proper compensation. They are simply ignored, silenced and despised. For example, in India, 100,000 people are going to be displaced by the Sardar Sarovar Project in Gujarat, 60-70 per cent of whom are indigenous people. Around 130,000 are expected to be displaced by the Narmada Sagar Project in Madhya Pradesh of whom 65-70 per cent are indigenous people. James Bay Hydro-electric complex in Canada makes a parallel case for investigations in this regard. Likewise, in the name of development, the indigenous people who are already powerless and exploited are further reduced to powerlessness and bondage. It is disheartening to see that indigenous people are made environmental prisoners in their own land.

(f) *Ecological Aspect*

Globalization involves environmental degradation and pollution. The pattern of development that we uphold today is capital-intensive. An ever-increasing economic pattern and the expansionary character of mechanisation and massive industrialisation of the economic world-order are reducing the non-human segments of creation to mere status of object without any intrinsic value. People simply analyse nature from the viewpoint of its usefulness to humans and they are all set to be exploited according to human's wishes. Forest and fishing resources are depleted for quick profits. Mining companies rape resources with little regard to the environmental and social costs. The sustaining power of the earth for nurturing life is being destroyed. The whole planet is at threat. Thus, the ecological catastrophe today is the direct product of modern industrial and technological growth, and the modern lifestyle.

13

Consumer in the Globalized World

JAI NARAIN SHARMA

"The market needs a place, and the market needs to be kept in its place."

—*Anon*

It is popular these days to say, "We are nation of economic illiterates." We probably are especially when it comes to our role as consumers. In fact, some people who have been working in the consumer movement for decades claim that on the whole we have less consumer savvy than our grandparents. There are many reasons for this. For the last two or three decades we have been living in a society that says, "If it doesn't work or if it falls apart, just throw it away and get another one." Products and services these days are far more complex than ever before—few of us can understand the workings of today's automobiles as our grandfather understood his mechanically simple Model and we are blitzed now, more than ever, by advertisers hawking. "Trust me," "This is god for you," "It will make you popular," "You need this."

If indeed we are illiterates when it comes to consumer issues, the schools, colleges, and universities must accept much of the blame. Educating young people to be savvy consumers has never, enjoyed a high priority in these institution. Instead, they have been more concerned with teaching people how to producers—doctors, lawyers, teachers, bookkeepers, secretaries, and so on.

Another institution that must accept much blame is the one that, in the final analysis, is the best of all vehicles for adult education—the news media. While there has been a vogue of consumer reporting in recent years, most newspapers and radio and TV stations have done a poor job of alerting people to a host of questionable marketplace practices. (Ironically, the press does a reasonably good job of the telling people about the fly-by-night rip-offs. The fly-by-nights do not, advertise. The supermarkets, retailers, and bankers do, and that may explain why the media carry so few reports about the tricks of these institutions.)

In spite of the fact that the school and the news media have done a poor job of educating consumers, more and more consumers are asking for such education. At the college level this expressed need is being translated into a growing demand for courses in consumer's economics.

Nevertheless, one should not overlook the reality that such courses can generate more problems for administrators and boards of trustees than virtually anything else in the curricula. Much the same as a newspaper must pay the price of cancelled advertising for good consumer reporting, a college or university undoubtedly courts the possibility of unhappiness among its supporters in the business community when it offers consumer of commerce often get worked up over the notion that students from such courses will show up in stores, clipboards in hand to do price-comparison surveys that, in the chamber's of view, will only disrupt local business.

But for more worrisome than the local controversies that consumer courses can generate are the efforts by large businesses and their trade associations to mould and shape the content of the consumer courses as much as they can. When effective, these efforts are tantamount to having the funeral directors association write the chapter in the text on purchasing funerals, the insurance industry on banks, and so on. In some instances such influence on the consumer courses by vested economic interests has seriously distorted the courses.

In spite of recent advances in pro-consumer legislation of an increased level of education and more discretionary time to stop and compare, consumers continue to be misled, misinformed, and duped in the marketplace. They are sold, for example, sweaters guaranteed to be "100 per cent virgin acrylic," but the 'able is meaningless since virtually all acrylic fibres are new ("virgin"), not reprocessed.

Consumers are sold motor oil with guarantee percent pure Max oil" but there is no evidence that Max motor oil is any better than fifty other kinds made elsewhere. They are sold Anacin with "23 per cent more of the leading pain reliever," but they are not told that ingredient is common aspirin. They are sold Alka-Seltzer to relieve upset stomach, yet Alka-Seltzer contains aspirin which is not advisable for stomach distress because "It could cause bleeding in already existing ulcers and could eventually lead ulcers."

Consumers are also sold cars with promises of appeal and "a touch of class" when, in fact, the product can be expected to start rusting out within two years. There is not much sex appeal in a two-year-old car which is full of "body cancer", even if it has tinted glass, denim-covered bucket seat, and orange rallye stripes down both sides. The automobile is a particularly good example of an expensive commodity about which most consumers know very little. Its technical specification (e.g., a comparison of drum and disc brakes, 6 cylinders and 8 cylinders, electronic and breaker-point ignition systems, etc.) and the economic costs of owning and operating it are hidden beneath a pile of advertising garbage.

"Look at those sleek rectangular headlights," hawks the salesman, but he does not tell you they cost three times as conventional round ones which serves the same purpose.

"I'm sure you'll want the racing package," but he fails to say that the shock absorbers, the spring, and the steering linkage remain the same as those on a conventional sedan.

"Now those raised white letters on the tires really make this car sharply' he says, but he is unable to give you any information on the quality of the tires compared to alternative brands. No car salesman or television commercial ever presents rupees estimates of automobile depreciation. Yet depreciation is the single most expensive factor in owning a typical car. It costs the consumer of a new car, kept three to four years, upwards of Rs. 10,000 each year in the lowest resale value due to technical and market obsolescence. Even though depreciation estimates are readily available (and indeed are published monthly), they are carefully concealed from the average consumer. Instead, a large dose of automobile advertisement is devoted to meaningless statements on "ride engineering" and "crafted elegance."

II

The marketplace is full of "germs." Consumers are constantly exposed to false and misleading claims. No consumer is immune. Children are bombarded each year by over thousands television ads, which infect them with an insatiable demand for snacks, sweets, drinks, toys, and pills. College students get hooked on life insurance policies, which they rarely need and which they could most often have purchased for thousands of dollars less had they only known the market. Millions of other consumers also become financially sick when they require medical services not covered by health insurance companies who promised "to pay when the going got rough."

The consumers' natural resistance is further broken down by horse traders, car dealers, and real estate agents who stretch limited budgets until they scream. In trying to regain financial health, many susceptible consumers seek charlatan advice from tax magicians, finance companies, and legal wizards. Even after death, disease is rampant in the necromarkets for funerals, markers and memorials.

It is not easy to be a rational economic consumer. There are many definitions of "rational". But to an economist "rational" means the striving to equate the marginal utility per dollar spent on every good or service in the consumer's portfolio. It requires a lot work and thought to get the most utility satisfaction from each additional dollar spent. The task is made considerably more difficult—if not impossible—when the consumer buys under pressure or buys on impulse. Both of these phenomena distort the consumer's ability to weigh costs and benefits, and as a result, lead him to purchase goods and services which give less than optimal satisfaction.

It is virtually impossible not be influenced by meaningless, misleading, and deceptive advertisement. Even the staunchest consumer advocates must, as Dylan said, "sometimes have to stand naked." In front of the bathroom mirror they, too, wonder if that secret new toothpaste will really make their teeth "whiter than white", if that secret formula will restore "natural colour to their hair and leave only a touch of gray." But for most part, consumerists have learned to discount advertisements by treating them with a healthy dose of skepticism. They develop and cultivate a keen recognition sales bait and the hooks which it most often conceals.

Unless the consumer is reading a catalogue which only lists product, its specifications, and price, he can usually find the easily. Some are small and some are large, but all are designed to catch the consumer and pull him into a purchase he would otherwise not have made.

Claims such as "selling elsewhere for," "should sell for," "list priced at," and "suggested retail price" are small-barbed hooks. So are the statements of "verified value," "certified value," "confidential price list," and "below cost." They catch greedy consumer who think they are going to get more than that for which they pay.

Guarantees and warranties are hooks if they fail to state exact nature and duration of the guarantee. (2) the manner in the guarantor will respond, and (3) the name and address of the guarantor. The phrases "double guarantee—lifetime guarantee," and "absolutely guaranteed" are meaningless and deceptive not supported by these three pieces of information.

Even if a guarantee provides these three pieces of information, it may still be meaningless. One ad guaranteed that the consumer of Rs. 200, "patented" diet would lose weight. It was a lifetime guarantee, promising a full refund of the Rs. 200 and stating the name and address of the guarantor. The advertisement included the catchy statement "We wouldn't say it , if it were not true!" But the truth was patented diet turned out to be a simple printed instruction:

"Eat nothing and drink 6 glasses of water each day for four days a week. Substitute willpower for calories."

Obviously, the guarantee was both meaningless and deceptive, although it was true in a strict sense.

III

The market situation for the consumer has changed dramatically in the past ten years, especially in the last five years with India's new approach to economic reforms which has revolutionized thinking and caught the imagination of one and all. With the ushering in of the regime of liberalization, the consumer is in a position to pick and choose the product of his liking from a multiplicity of bands and varieties. Considering the volume of our middle class buyers with money power, which in terms of sheer numbers is more than the total population of several advanced countries put together, business firms have realized the huge potential of the market to be tapped. No wonder many global players are keen to set up shop in India, either by way of direct investment to tie-ups with the Indian partners. A few years ago, it was common to see everyone coming from the Gulf walking in at the arrival lounge with TVs, two-in-one cassette players or even refrigerators. But things have changed now. Now bringing "white goods" or electronic goods into the country from abroad is no longer an attractive proposition. That's because many international brands are available locally at a competitive price. That is not all. Evan some of the domestic brands have established a reputation for themselves in international markets.

With such a multi-choice marketplace the decision to buy should be easier. Strange as it may sound, that 'choice' which the Indian consumer had been waiting for, is now becoming more and more difficult! Reason—the consumer is confused with too many brands, all of which seem to be similar with hardly any price difference. Given the level of sophistication of product/services, an average consumer just seems lost in a welter of new terminology. Now the market speaks a new language of E-Commerce, ECS, DEMAT, ATM, e-Mail, internet Networking, Quadra Focus, Dolby, Golden Eye which sounds Greek and Latin to a common man. But no dealer or retailer can take a customer for a ride as long as he is equipped with some knowledge of the terminology of the globalised era or at least makes a pretence of it.

The consumer of today and tomorrow needs the right kind of help and support when it comes to making a choice. But dealers/retailers, who are more concerned about their own commissions with each brand they sell, may not be particularly open about the demerits of the brand they are selling. The dealer may even go to the extent of persuading the buyer to take the brand for which he gets a better commission, by listing the demerits, real or imaginary of the particular brand the customer is interested in and overrating the brand he is interested in selling. This is where the government and the NGOs should step in to help the consumer in decision-making, by periodically issuing reports of comparative ratings in the performance/quality/price of each and every household item of goods/services available in the market. This is where the consumers of the advanced countries have an advantage as they have access to the kind of information which helps them to make a wise choice. In the absence of such objective rating reports, the Indian consumer is guided more by his personal experiences and that of his friends and relatives.

Though we may not match the consumerism of the advanced countries, we have come a long way from the days of shortages and captive markets. The 'billion' mark in our population, makes a great deal of difference making the market highly profitable with great potential for growth. Thus many global players are making a beeline to our shores so as not to miss a share of the pie. Companies to stay competitive will focus on "customer driven quality". Each customer will be, hopefully, treated as an individual, not a mere number in the statistics of buyers. As Mr. John A. Young, President of Hewelett-Packard, remarked some time back: "Satisfying customers is the only reason we are in business". A few companies keep customer satisfaction as a measure of their success. This only means there will be more products/goods of all types/services of good quality being made available in the country. To be a world-class quality company it is essential to be a world-class customer. This is the most important reason why in a nation where production of "duplicate" stuff is lucrative business, the consumer has to be on his guard.

One thing which is a certainly is that tomorrow's products will have more sophistication and more features than they have at present, that give added value for money. It does not mean that the products which are time tested will become obsolete but the newer products will be more attractive for the consumers because of additional built-in features and also give him a feeling that he is getting his money's worth. For instance, a portable radio, will be able to receive AM/FM stations, will have built-in clock, and a tape-recorder. A standard bicycle may be lighter but sturdier, fitted with more gears to make riding easier. The market researchers and designers will work closely and interact with consumers to find out what consumers are looking for. We have come a long way from the days of the gramophone record to the more sophisticated audio/video cassettes and compact discs which have revolutionized the music scene. The ubiquitous cassette player has made music a part of the everyday life of the common man, from the street hawker to an office manager. Innovations will be the order of the day with companies spending millions of rupees in bringing out ever new models into the market to capture the imagination of the people who are all potential consumers. This is likely to be the trend in the twenty-first century where muscle/entertainment/leisure activities/food will be big business. Those with vision, the capacity to innovate and imagine are the ones who will rake in the profits.

Availability of 'white goods' will improve dramatically and the goods will come with more and more sophisticated features. For example, already most of the TVs come with remote control and multi-channels. TVs with bigger and flatter screens and additional features like PIP (Picture-in-Picture) will be offered to consumers. A TV screen will be the "work station" of a future home with "Cable TV" containing not only entertainment channels, news, features but Internet will become a reality. We will thus have a "wired home" from where the consumer can enjoy a programme of his choice round the clock, read newspapers and magazines of one's choice (not only from India but worldwide) and hunt for bargains in products, travel, finance and so on. So it is imperative that the consumer of the twenty-first century becomes computer-savvy to prepare for a society geared to information technology depending more and more on Internet, E-Commerce and E Mail. some may bemoan the fact that the good old art of letter-writing is almost a thing of the past, thanks to the E Mail but that is the price one pays for progress. It does not mean, however, that E-Mail has completely over-ridden the epistolary form of writing. There are still some die-hard letter writers who would love to feel the pages of a letter written by a loved one between their fingers. The personal touch is what matters to them.

"Network Society" → Revolution in information → Quicker → Availability at the click of a mouse

Consumers should be prepared for a "revolution" in finance management. Electronic Clearing Service (ECS) will become commonplace with little or no paper work. We are moving towards "paperless transactions and paperless offices" where computers will play an important role in data storing and data retrieval. Plastic money in the shape of credit cards will be more the rule than an exception, at least in the urban centres. ATMs will mushroom all over towns within easy reach of everyone., 24 hours of the day. A bank may no longer be a place to just deposit money and withdraw it when you want. It will be a "single windows" for doing many things—pay your LIC premium, water, electricity, telephone etc. bills in time, sell stock invest and other instruments for investing stocks/shares, assist in investment decisions, transfer money from one place to another, provide easy credit, guide in travel related matters, and so on. Your banker will thus become your friend, guide and philosopher. But a wary customer will make it a point to check his accounts status regularly to see that no wrong payments or delayed payments are made due to either oversight or tardy work by the bank employees. It is wise to remember that we are dealing with human beings. Computers do no mistakes but humans do.

The sense of happiness that has crept into the psychic of even the educate consumer who think the process of liberalization and globalization has done wonders to consumerism and the fact that many goods and services are there at a competitive price should not lull consumers into a sense of complacency. No doubt a host of quality products and services, unprecedented in the consumer history of our country are coming in and such trend will continue whether one likes it or not. It looks as though the process of liberalization and globalization is irreversible and we have to accept it. However, we should keep in mind that for any business or industry, the driving force is profit making and not commitment to the welfare of the consumers. It is said, "Managing only for profit is like playing tennis with your eye on the scoreboard and not on the ball." But, unfortunately, that is what we are witnessing today and perhaps will see more of it in the days to come, given the fact that the field is getting more and more crowded with more and more players. Consumers must therefore not let down their guard and expose themselves to the hazards of unquality products, and there is no dearth of pedlars of such stuff. Moreover, they should think carefully about product features, for example, whether they need features like 'powered-windows' for their cars which is luxury (and sometimes a risk when the switch is activated inadvertently) they can live without. Such fixtures are redundant and do not add anything or improve the enjoyment of a product/service while wasting precious scare resources.

There is an inherent unfairness in the growing tendency to compare our consumerism with that of the advanced countries. Our teeming masses, having just crossed the billion mark (second biggest population in the world) have just come out of the suppression of colonial occupation. Fifty odd years in a nation's history does not count for much when compared with the head-start a few advanced countries had in industrial activities. Mere availability of a certain class of goods should not mislead us to think that we have reached the level of consumerism of the advanced countries. In the USA, General Motors and Ford auto giants bring out new models every year with each leap in technology, to suit the changing tastes of the consumers. Compared to such a phenomenon we are way behind, as far as introduction of new models is concerned. But the question is—do we really need new models every year, given the fact that less than five per cent of those who have the capacity to buy automobiles go in for such model changes regularly and that too only because they get a tax benefit? As things stand now, most car users find it difficult to go in for a newer model even after ten years of using one car, let alone after one year. And that is not because they love the old model but because of other constraints. But this state of affairs is definitely going to change in the coming days with easy access to funds and added to it the technological advances in methods of recycling the used Models. In such a context, the recent proposal to import used cars from overseas is ridiculous, and sounds suspiciously like a ploy to cheat not only the country but the consumers. On the contrary, we should be exporting more cars to earn foreign exchange.

When we come to the scene of environmental concerns, the pathetic state of our neglected eco-system is a sad reflection on the total lack of concern for the environment whether it is governmental agencies or the industries, or business houses. In the corridors of power, the development lobby is powerful but there are few who champion the cause of the fragile environment. That is because environment does not have a vote while people have the power of the vote! Those who oppose mega projects are branded as retrograde and reactionary.

It is said, "Technology is like a steam-roller. If you are not on the steam-roller then you are destined to become part of the road." That is why consumers of tomorrow should perforce be aware of the newer developments so that they can make meaningful choices. They should treat technology as a friend rather than as an adversary. For example, the very people who a few years ago were apprehensive about computers and Information Technology and opposed them, are welcoming them now because of their awareness of the benefits of these innovations designed to speed up transactions and help the consumers.

Customer is like king! If that is not to remain a mere slogan consumers will have to organise and assert themselves and show who the king is. They have a powerful tool in their hands—the money in their pockets which no one can touch. They must reject cheap and sub-standard stuff. The market learns fast provided it is taught in time where it really stands, by the consumers. Competition will force companies to adapt to the rapidly changing dynamics of the market in which they are operating. Highly successful companies are very pro-active when it comes to customer expectations.

Quality should receive top priority in any purchasing decision by a consumer. They have a right to quality goods/services of their choice and thus right they must exercise with care. If, for example, more consumers are "seconds" and "export rejects", a wrong signal is sent to the pedlars of such stuff. In such a case, the sellers have cheap stuff which will be lapped up by consumers. As long as they are making handsome profits without taking any trouble to improve quality, the human tendency—is to enjoy the profits without having to work hard for it. If the consumers compromise on quality they have only themselves to blame for the sub-standard goods they have to put up with.

We tend to ape the advanced countries in matters of dress and food preferences. But this aping does not to areas which really matter. Like for instance, when it comes to matters of safety and self-protection, we exhibit a curious lack of the most elementary concern. For example, in foreign countries even a cyclist believes in protecting his head against injuries by wearing a helmet, even though traffic is very orderly and disciplined and accidents are few. In India drivers of two wheelers think that helmets are for policemen, workers and miners and zoom around like maniacs, carrying two or three additional people, including infants and small children on the pillow, in front or wherever space is available. They throw not only their own safety to the winds but are exposing others to risks. Unless forced by law, few take the trouble to wear helmets. The new motor cars come with seat belts which few driver and passengers wear, as if it is some piece of decoration for the car! Indulgent parents keep small children on their laps while driving and even allow them to do the steering—an astonishing violation of safety norms indeed. In the advanced countries such violations meet with immediate punishment and hence people never violate safety norms. It is also mandatory for small children to be secured in car seats while travelling in cars, even if it is within the town for short distances. Thus it is imperative to educate consumers with regard to safety and other aspects, so that these norms are observed as a matter of rule. Mere provision of safety features without strict enforcement of safety norms becomes a meaningless exercise.

Many consumers purchase goods using credit which they pay off in instalments. Frequently, the buyer signs an agreement with the creditor for only part of the purchase price, the rest of the price he pays immediately to the seller as a down payment. The seller will give the consumer the good, but is likely to give the title (or certificate showing evidence of ownership) to the creditor in exchange for the balance of his money.

Credit, or the ability to pay later for goods and services received now, would be an unequivocal benefit to the consumer if it costs nothing. Unfortunately, that is not the case, even if the advertisements crying "By Now! Charge it! Pay Later! Relax, you have Master Card!" make the cost seem not to matter. The credit industry earns from 10 per cent on some automobile loans at credit unions, to 36 per cent on some other types of instalment credit at finance companies, to even higher rates from loansharks and other illegal creditors. If the average rate were 13 per cent on all credit, then the average household pays over $ 350 a year in finance charges. It is little wonder that the industry spends so much to advertise that "credit is chic."

What the industry fails to say is that "debt is a drag". Consumers pay dearly for the ability to have goods now, instead of saving and buying when they can afford to pay for them. Personal bankruptcies are rising sharply, resulting millions of dollars in losses which are passed on to creditors and noncreditors alike.

When Anil Ambani asked Tim Sebastain why he does what he does, he replied coolly, "Mortgage".

The BBC anchor may, or may to, have been serious in the recent promotional interview, but his answer clearly touched a chord with millions who follow a peculiar modern *mantra*: Buy now, pay later.

Long a fact of life in the west, mortgages now account for 50 per cent of all retail finance in India. But houses, two wheelers and other essentials are only part of the credit story. Today, a growing number of city-slickers blithely run up huge Nokia 7650 bills, rock every night at Athena or Djinns, keep time with Espirit…and achieve all this with a seamless swipe of plastic. They then borrow tom pay back their loans.

So, is India—traditionally, a society of savers—now going to succumb to that maddening American syndrome, where people go to counsellors for 'debt-therapy' and join 'Borrowers Anonymous' to discuss how they can blame their shopaholicism on prenatal influences?

In the final analysis the bottom line for consumers of the twenty-first century—the true measure of consumerism is improved quality of life through better quality of products and services at competitive prices.

In conclusion: "Where there is no vision, people perish."—Proverb.

REFERENCES

Dunning, John, *Multinational Enterprises in a Global Economy*, Workingham; Addison-Wesley, 1993.

Galbraith, John Kenneth, *The New Industrial State*, Boston, Houghton Mifflin Co., 1967.

George, Susan, *How The Other Half Dies: The Real Reason For World Hunger*, London: Penguin, 1976.

Global Report to the President of United States, Washington, D. C, United States Government, 1980.

Mishra, A.D., *Gandhism After Gandhi*, New Delhi, Mittal Publications, 2002.

Murthy, D.B.N., *Consumer and Quality*, New Delhi, New Age International Pvt. Ltd., 2001.

Schumacher, E.F. *Small is Beautiful: A Study of Economics as if People Mattered*, New York: Abacus, 1989.

Sharma, J.N. *Alternative Economics*, New Delhi, Deep and Deep Publications, 2003.

Sharma, Rashmi, *Gandhian Economics A Humane Approach*, New Delhi, Deep and Deep Publications, 2003.

Wilson, S. Brain, *On Third World Legs*, New York, Prager Publishers, 1995.

14

The Female Consumer in the Globalised World

ASHU PASRICHA

Today, although there is a general understanding about the meaning of the term "globalization," there is still some confusion because, due to its complex nature, globalization can be viewed from different perspectives. Regardless, there is still a consensus that we are increasingly connected and that sovereignty restrictions are being reduced. As a result, there are more and more supra-state and extra-boundary forces; these have been accompanied by an increase in global problems.

The globalization of the market economy enables us to advance from an age of international trade to an age of international production. There are now global telecom networks connecting all the countries of the world. In addition, the movement of populations, production, science and technology, and culture is increasing. The number of international organizations and transactional corporations is indicative of the degree of organized connections throughout the world. These connections are not only political, economic, and cultural, but also diplomatic and military. The increasing integration of regional organizations is a manifestation of the increasing trend towards global integration. The United Nations, whatever its role, has for the last fifty years brought together all the nations of world.

It can be said that there is no society today that is isolated from outside world, and global relations between states, societies and nations will be drawn closer and closer together in future. Although it will take a long time to achieve a complete integration of the world, this developing trend cannot be denied. "Globalization" and "integration" can be described as the process of the increasing closeness of global human interconnections.

Today, "globalization" is fundamentally driven by economic forces. It is the progress of science and technology, as well as the development of the forces of production, which promotes this process. The acceleration of this model of development undoubtedly is a process that began in the last twenty years, but if we look back at world history, globalization actually began in the late Middle Ages with the advent of capitalism; the founding of the New World can be considered a starting-point, from which time capitalism became more and more cosmopolitan.

The development of capitalism was not purely an economic process. The opening of the world markets, especially in earlier periods, was often achieved by force. The forerunners of globalization engaged in bloody wars in order to export commodities, seize colonies, steal gold and riches, and to engage in slave trade. Backward countries, including large parts of the Americas, Africa, and Asia were victims of the development of this mode of cosmopolitanism. The history of the worldwide development of capitalism is a history of the humiliation of such countries. From the point of view of the countries of the East, we cannot forget how the forerunners of capitalism invaded, robbed, and engaged in war with colonies and semi-colonies in the East. It is important to recognize this aspect of the historical process.

Women are not economically powerless. They own wealth in their own right, they are important investors, shareholders, trust and capital holders. They contribute directly to the work-force and two-thirds of the archetypal female consumers work in and out of the home. Yet, in these areas men still predominate, and the female contribution while considerable is still subordinate to that of man, and will be for a little while yet.

In the woman's function as consumer, however, se is indomitable and it is indisputable that the phenomenon of female consumption in Western society is marked by two overriding principles: first that it is massive and second, that it is both frequent and extensive.

In the first case, we must note that expenditures which she controls directly make up the largest sectors in consumer expenditure indices. Just over 70 per cent of the gross national product at factor cost. Of this expenditure two of the largest categories carry 28 per cent of the total, food and clothing and footwear bought almost entirely by women.

Apart from these sectors women were also responsible for the purchase of most household and chemist goods, and were largely responsible for the actual decision to buy most goods in the consumer durable section. In fact, taking the first five categories of consumer expenditure by sex would be, female to male, at least 54-45 per cent.

All these estimates of expenditure are, however, in money/value terms and in order to do justice to the second principle of female consumption, its frequency and extent, it is important to note the number of individual purchasing decisions quite apart from simple value. One durable item, for example, which may represent a male or female purchase represents one purchase decision. Yet, several thousand food purchase decisions would be required to make up the same financial value of a durable item and in these decisions, women predominate.

In fact, taking this angle rather than purchase value, it is estimated that women in Canada and America decide 75-90 per cent of consumer sales. Yet, in addition to the two principles underlying female consumption which we have just observed, there is one other factor which must be noted. Parallel to these two principles but, in a sense, more pervasive, there is the fact that female consumption, for all that it is massive, rhythmic and essential and despite the fact that without it the consumer marketing industry would disintegrate with startling rapidity, is a phenomenon which is so taken for granted that it is, in effect, denied.

This denial is demonstrated by the myriad marketing text books, manuals and reports which forbear to make one mention of the woman buyer, although the entire thesis of their work may revolve around hers.

It is demonstrated by all advertisers and makers who persist in observing the female consumer through their, usually male, eyes and often smug and ignorant preconceptions; who insist on portraying her and communicating to her in their terms, instead of hers.

It is denied by the lectures, the business consultants, the trade magazines, the researchers, the managing directors and the data clerks, who play around with the mechanics of the marketing organization and forget that the starting handle does not lie with them but in a shopping basket held firmly and capably by a woman; the female consumer of whom they really know little and of whose real welfare they care less, if at all.

Yet, because this is a sortie into what could be termed an institution it does not, by means, suggest a bland reiteration of the obvious. The aim is not just a reformulation of the old, old story, a dusting round the edges of the standard stereotype. It is a description of the female consumer with a difference in that it sees her function through the emphasis of her vantage point and *en route*, it is to a large extent a criticism and reformulation of many of the assumptions and principles which the advertising and marketing industry has held about the woman buyer for far too long. These conventions will be challenged, evidence shaken out and reformulated, new principles contended, old information represented *in toto* and some basic criticisms made.

It is a moot point whether a female consumer could be definitive at a time when women generally, let alone women as buyers, are undergoing what is only the tip of a major change which few fully comprehend and the final effects of which we can only begin to speculate on.

While the investigation of women as buyer has been relatively catholic, it is by no means exhaustive. It would have been possible to cover the same proportion of ground again but with other data, other angles, other facts. What have been covered are those areas, which the author considered to be ripe for summary or carrying out for criticism.

Nevertheless, no matter how we observe the women buyer, we must note that the relationship between her and the marketing industry is certain to undergo some fundamental and exciting changes. We must also note, unfortunately, that the timing of these changes will probably depend to a large extent on the resistance of the marketing industry than the potential for change in women which, on political and historical analyses, is largely inexorable.

'Shopping' and 'Consuming' should not be regarded as synonymous for the same process. Shopping is usually considered to be the physical process of purchasing goods which may last minutes or months and often ends long after the purchase of one article, usually by reappearing as experience in the purchase of another. Consuming subsumes the whole complex of social and psychological factors which surrounds the shopping process, and often the fact of it. The buying or purchase of goods is merely the culmination of the long and intertwined shopping and consuming process and involves a simple financial or credit transaction.

The shared values of large groups of people influence the means used to satisfy human needs. These values vary substantially among groups. For example, the people of Lincoln, Nebraska, would probably not satisfy their hunger with pickled octopus or fried snake, but some people in the world do. The French consider corn-on-the-cob as a food most appropriate for animal consumption. Whereas the colour to be worn at funerals in the United States, is ordinarily black, it is white in Japan and purple in Latin American countries.

These, influences are observable in the products made and consumed by various groups of people. The importance of this kind of group influence is widely accepted in marketing today and has been referred to as culturalogical to differentiate it from a psychological orientation that has essentially concentrated on the individual.

The very essence of marketing focuses on culture and society because they perceive marketing as the delivery of a standard of living. Certainly those who characterize marketing in this way must be very interested in consumer behaviour. It is only through studying the consumer's interests and decision-making process that appropriate goods and services can be delivered to him or her.

Women are faced with a real, personal and important problem in relation to their capacity to make use of family resources. They experiment until they establish the mode or organization which is felt to be reasonable for their personal abilities and suitable for their family. Like commercial firms they do not maximize their situations.

The family may be viewed as an agent that influences the behaviour of its individual members. This involves an awareness of the effect that various beliefs, life-styles, socioeconomic status, and patterns of interaction among members have on an individual member's market behaviour. The family is, therefore, seen as a reference group.

Because of the nature of man, a young person must be cared for and nurtured both physically and psychologically, most often this is handled in a family environment. Parsons and Bales contend that no society has found an effective substitute arrangement for the family. Even in the kibbutz where a community-oriented structure exists, the basic socialization responsibilities remain with the parents, that is, the family continues to exist as a distinct unit. Because the socialization process begins at birth, the family's influence on the behaviour of the individual member can be substantial.

The other perspective on the family is a unique entity. The family is viewed as a unit that has specific identifiable characteristics and an existence beyond a simple summation of the behaviour or outlook of its individual members. The uniqueness of the consumption patterns of the family entity is, often a product of the intimacy of shared concerns and priorities.

The family shapes its members' personality characteristics, attitudes, and evaluative criteria, that is, the way its members look at the world and how they relate to it. To a large extent this influence is informal and exerted on the individual over an extended period of time. Part of this influence includes the acquiring of a consumer outlook. As Boyd and Levy have contended, "people are born with apparently insatiable needs and desires. From their first moment they are learning what specific things to consume and the ways to consume them, and, quite as important, what not to consume."

In describing similar circumstances, Riesman and Roseborough stated that what children learn from their parents is a kind of basic set of domestic arrangements, for instance, a view of furniture as specific functional items to acquire rather than as a stylistic concept and, consequently, the need for home furnishings such as ranges, refrigerators, and television sets. The same individuals are likely to learn styles and moods of consumption L-from their peers.

The amount of influence the family has will vary at different periods of its members' lives. For example, a very young child may have relatively little contact outside its immediate family environment until the age of four or five years. Typically, the number of socializing agents increases substantially upon entering school with the regular non family contact with teachers and schoolmates.

The family's consumption patterns change over time as family composition changes. For example, the bachelor stage is characterized by significant spending on entertainment, food away from home, vacations, etc. while the newly married couple either spends or causes to be spent (by their friends and family) substantial amounts on sterling flatware stereo equipment, etc.

The housewife controls a substantial part of her husband's economic resources and the adequacy with which she manages them, in combination with her own where she works as well, has a significant impact on the mental and physical health of several people. In a way, she is a junior manager whose administrative responsibilities often exceed those of her husband. In addition, her work and the satisfactory completion of it is often as important to her in her perception of role as her husband's success in his work is to him.

Corporate Globalization

Corporate globalization stands for the worldwide domination of mega corporations over nations and their people. It is a New World Order where governments become subservient to the wealthy elites who control these megacorps. In the article, *The Making of the New World Order*, Richard K. Moore traces the rise of the megacorps to the machinations of the United States to establish collective imperialism, a bold new global scheme that came about at the end of World War II. With the control of all the sea lanes by US military presence, a "Pax Americana" protected the interests of large corporations in the so-called "free world" or "elite controlled zone." The "free" population of the countries designated as Third World was likewise held in check by military dictatorships that served the interests of big business.

In addition, an international economic infrastructure was put in place with the creation of UN bodies such as the IMF, World Bank, World Trade-Organizations. The investment environment of liberalization, deregulation, free flow of trade without territorial restrictions, etc. set the stage for reaping windfalls of profits that made mega corporations a powerful entity. The power was not only economic but political as well. The elites, although non-elected, have dominated commissions that set policies for the world's economy. Thus came about a megacorp governed world.

Half a century later, these megacorporations have well entrenched themselves in this planet. They have succeeded in making governments be their proxies and represent their interests rather than the good of their nations and peoples. Now we have an association of economies rather than of states. The Asia-Pacific Economic Corporation (APEC) is a case in point. It is cooperation indeed but cooperation for exploitation. The shift from simple trade cooperation to the designation a free trade bloc in the Pacific-rim took place in 1993. Economic cooperation without free trade means something else. Freedom is liberating when you talk of equals. Among freedom becomes dominating.

Governments have abdicated their duty to protect human and natural resources. Protectionism is contrary to free trade. Environmental protection under government hands is superseded by ownership of resources giving the private business sector power to exploit these resources.

Obviously this is the age of neo-liberal economics. There is no such thing as a "free market" because the market is controlled by cartels. The rule of thumb of these monopolies is super profits that benefit a few and enslave the teeming masses. That is the kind of corporate globalization that APEC espouses.

Other trade agreements include the North American Free Trade

Agreement (NAFTA), waiting to be widened into Free Trade Area of the Americas (FTAA), and the Multilateral Agreement on Investment (MAI) which makes of big business "corporate citizens" with the right to sue governments, individuals, and organizations that do not carry out its agenda. Master control of global capitalist economic trade policies is in the hands of the World Trade Organization (WTO). Together with the International Monetary Fund (IMF) and the World Bank (WB), WTO completes the triad that ensures the reign of a capitalist international economic order.

Women's Enslavement

Peoples of the world, particularly the poor, oppressed and downtrodden, pay the price of corporate globalization. They pay the price of having their minds controlled and fed with programmes in the mass media, the information highway, the school curricula, etc. that rationalize neo-liberalism. If the state's ideological apparatus does not work and prevent people from questioning and protesting, they pay the price of suffering repression from the state. The political apparatus strikes its fangs and peoples' rights are curtailed and violated.

Those who become an obstacle to corporate needs (e.g., union leaders) are isolated in prisons that have become concentration camps of the neo-liberal regime. Among the urban and rural poor, workers, farmers, fisherfolks, indigenous people, the most vulnerable are women and children in all sectors. Women's rights and children rights are rampantly violated.

In the restructuring of agricultural production, farmers are reduced to agricultural workers, contract growers who lose their farms to crop conversion with no produce for subsistence and local consumption. In this process, peasant women suffer a heavy toll. Most of them get displaced. Although they perform 40 to 60 per cent of the farm activities, they do not get compensated. And if they are hired as agricultural workers, they are paid less than the men.

The incursion of transnational corporations in agribusiness has introduced chemical products harmful to women. The vulnerability is due to the natural openings in a woman's body; allowing the entry of pesticides, insecticides, fertilizers, etc.

The very agrarian structure that favours large landowners perpetuates feudal relations of indebtedness and female bondage. Added to this is current industrialization at the expense of agriculture. The interests of small farmers, tenants, and settlers are disregarded whenever policies are promulgated to keep farm prices down and favour purchasing the power of urban inhabitants. Because women hold the purse strings in some societies, theirs is the headache of making both ends meet, the nightmare of feeding their families keeping them alive.

Then too there is the expropriation of the land of indigenous people in the name of "development" to service the needs of big companies with the establishment of hydroelectric plants and the exploitation of forests, oil, and mineral resources. With militarization that usually accompanies land expropriation, the women, especially the young girls, face the danger of being molested and raped. Indeed, a climate of fear and uncontrolled forms of violence are established by the large companies and the landowning elite.

Again in the name of globalization, prime agricultural lands get converted into industrial estates and tourism development projects. Deprived of their source of income, families end up migrating and seeking greener pastures in cities or abroad.

In the industrial sector, economic violence has been institutionalized in the industrial sector. Industrialization, yellow unionism, and cooperative dispute management disregard workers' rights and are hostile to all workers. Women in particular are prevented from joining unions.

The market-oriented hiring schemes reduce wages, remove job security, and undermine unions through temporary hiring, job-sharing, contractualization, and labour-contracting. To avoid giving benefits, companies hire workers for five months and then get new ones for another five months. Very few are given permanent status. Pregnancy tests are imposed on women to be sure that the companies do not have to pay maternity leave.

Subcontracting involves take-home work paid on a piecerate basis making the women work longer and harder. The rate of exploitation is tremendously high. For a garment that sells at $15 in US department stores, a sewer gets only 10 cents! Labour markets and skills training do not guarantee the welfare of workers and are geared to serve the interest of big business. With current economic crisis, many firms have closed and a good number of women have been retrenched. The gender division of labour has not been very fair towards women.

In the service sector, most women in search of employment land in the service sector. Domestic service has been globalized. Literally this is modern slavery with the women working deep into the night, abused physically and even sexually. The quickest way to be employed is to join the entertainment industry. Working in bars, climbing ships, servicing men in brothels, this is the sex trade today. The globalization of the sex industry using high tech like the Internet has led to widespread sex trafficking, pornography, prostitution, paedophilia. Super profits are raked at the expense of women and children.

Only through solidarity can we put an end to the feminization of poverty and lift the multi-burden of class, sex, race, ethnicity, age, health, religion. Only through solidarity can we counter the corporate cooperation to treat humans as pawns in the phenomenon of labour mobility and tackle the feminization of migration with its special features of greater and graver violence against women migrant workers. Only through solidarity can we ever hope to create alternatives to corporate globalization!

To conclude, however, we must note that the female consumer is an enigma we know 'not wisely, but too well'. The problem is, the time has run out when we could get away with doing so.

REFERENCES

Blackwell, and Kollat, *Consumer Behaviour*, Winston, Holt Rienhart, 1968.

Boyd, H.W. Jr. and S.J. Levy, *Promotion, A Behaviour View*, Englewood Cliffs, New Jersey: Prentice-Hall, Inc, 1967.

Chesler, Phyllis, *Women and Madness*, Allen Lane, Penguin Books, 1972.

Frank, Ronald, E., William F. Massaey and Donald G. Morrison, 'The Determinants of Innovative Behaviour with Respect to a Branded, Frequently Purchased Food Product', in L. George Smith (ed.) *Reflections on Progress in Marketing*, Chicago, American Marketing Association, 1964.

Grubb, Edward, L., "Consumer Perception of "self concept" and its Relation to Brand Choice of Selected Product Types', in P.D. Bennett (ed.), *Marketing and Economic Development*, Chicago, American Marketing Association, 1965.

Haines, George, 'A Study of Why people Purchase New Products', in R.H. Haas (ed.) *Science, Technology and Marketing Association*, Chicago, Chicago Press, 1966.

Katz Elihu and Paul F. Lazerfield, *Personal Influence*, New York, The Free Press of Glencoe, 1955.

Kotler, Philip, *Marketing Management: Analysis, Planning and Control*, New York, Prentice Hall, 1972.

Parsons, T. and R.F. Bales, *Family Socialization and Interaction Process*, New York: The Free Press, 1955.

Riesman, D. and H. Roseborough, "Careers and Consumer Behaviour", in *Consumer Behaviour. The Life Cycle and Consumer Behaviour*, Vol. II, L. Clark, ed., New York, New York University Press, 1955.

Scott, Rosemary, *The Female Consumer*, London: Associated Business Programmes, 1976.

Wattenberg, B.J., "The Forming-Families: The Spark in the Tinder, 1975-1985," in 1974 Combined Proceedings—New Marketing for Social and Economic Progress and Marketing's Contributions to the Firm and to the Society, R.C. Curhan, ed., Chicago, American Marketing Association, 1975.

Part III

COMPARATIVE PERSPECTIVE

15

Globalizing Tribal Economy

PRIYANKA PRIYADARSHINI and M.C. BEHERA

Introduction

All the countries in the world experience the process of globalization. The term 'globalization' has become an all inclusive, virtually all-purpose explanatory device for social analysis as reflected in its use in two broad senses. In a narrow sense, globalization is a process of "increasing economic integration and growing economic interdependence between countries in the world economy... driven by the lure of profit and the threat of competition in the market"(Nayyar, 1995:3). In this sense, it includes discussions on multinational corporations, unregulated flows of international capital, multinational free trade areas and economic role of the state (see Bryan: 1995; Hirst and Thompson: 1996; Amin: 1997 and Amoroso: 1998). In its broad sense, it embraces into its folds a much more political and cultural dimension, and is understood in terms of interdependence of economic and cultural process (*ibid.* Jameson: 2000). What is more imposing and apparent in the process of globalization is the process of economic integration through MNC investment in countries world over and aid assistance by international agencies to developing countries.

It is to be noted that international discourse on development is associated with the process of globalization, which, precisely, aims at participatory sustainable development. Understandably, it refers to development with distributive justice in that it seeks participation of people whom development is meant for.

MNC investment and consequent globalization of financial markets through inflow of global capital from the capital rich to the capital poor regions has resulted in economic crisis in many developing countries. What Koreans call 'IMF suicides' is simply the fallouts of a development process sustained not principally by domestic savings and investment but by huge infusion of foreign capital. The Mexican financial collapse of 1994 and the East-Asia crisis are viewed to be the consequence of the characteristic failure of global capitalism to ensure a smooth and reliable flow of global capital to sustain development process (Bello: 1999; Sachs and Baja: 1998). And that failure is most acute, which can be empirically verified, in fast growing economies. Stiglitz (2002) has highlighted such issues in his study of the impact of IMF financial aid to development countries. He terms IMF as a 'part of Treasury Turf' 'reflecting the interest and ideology of the western financial community,(Quoted in Ghosh: 2002) Stiglitz blames IMF policy for sickening poverty in many developing countries, sharp inequalities in income and wealth distribution, accentuating as time goes on, the surging tide of joblessness...'(*ibid.*, 3980-81) India, however, could avoid economic turmoil of East-Asia type because it is not as fast growing and it is not as dependent on foreign capital as crisis experiencing countries did. From the very beginning, Indian economists were aware of grave dangers of unquestioning reliance on foreign capital and free market forces in a developing country (Kumar: 1992, 1997; Bhaduri and Nayyar: 1996).

Empirical evidence with reference to the above countries show that a developing country cannot ensure economic growth with sustainability by integrating its economy to more vigorous economic forces and thereby depending on foreign capital and free market forces. Further generalization of the effects of economic development in backward regions would reveal different levels of economic achievements among various heterogeneous groups out of same economic programmes within an economy. The elite class set the development agenda for the nation as a whole after independence. This could not realize plan objectives because their perception of development was not same as that of others (Kumar: 1997). There emerged an economic gap between two sections. The then idea about development of people by developing an area through large-scale industrialization has been a failure with Bihar and present Jharkhand as case to the point. Because, this was an elite perception of development meant for the other section. The futility of rural development exercises by 'outsiders' comes to limelight in these years when various studies are conducted applying Participatory Rural Appraisal (PRA) techniques (Chambers: 1983).

Development of less developed region and its people by integrating its development exercises to the inflow of foreign capital and free market forces or of weaker sections of a society through development policies formulated by the 'other' section has been proved futile. There is a difference between perceptions of priorities and interests between two sections and inability of backward region and weaker section to gain from development exercises. The inability can be viewed in terms of difference in 'entitlements' (Sen: 1981), which exist or are created in the development process.

The task of economic development in less developed region and of less developed people does not depend only on the facilities offered; by well functioning markets and beneficial exchanges, but also on the fundamental role of human capabilities and their reliance on basic education, health services, ownership patterns, social stratification, gender relations and the opportunity of social cooperation as well as political protest and opposition. Difference in social opportunities not only leads to diverse achievements in the quality of life, but also influences economic performances, and in particular, the extent to which the facilities offered by functioning markets can be used by citizens in general (Dreze and Sen: 1998).

In the *Assessing Aid* report of World Bank (1998), it is found that aid effectiveness has been inversely related to the quality of economic policies and the strength of institutions. This relationship is established through an empirical analysis of the impact of aid in relation to economic policies and the institutional environment in the recipient country (Hansen and Tarp, 2000).

Aid agencies put forward conditions for the effectiveness of development aid. It is but natural to think that conditions like good governance, and strong institutions could not be developed in a time period during which the aid is meant to achieve its targetted objective. On the other hand, where the conditions exist, the aid is effectively utilized and hence, at the end of the 1990s, the donor community moved from conditionality to selectivity (Hermesand Lensink, 2001:11). One of the conditions is good governance. The political conditions that amount to the understanding of good governance are reflections of donors' view on process of democratic status and reduction of state involvement in the economy. The concept is heavily influenced by the western view of what should constitute good governance. Doornbos (2001), however, questions the universality of the concept, for, he argues, prescriptions of good governance are different for different cultural contexts.

It is further to be noted that the development paradigm in the context of globalization, in other words, the international development discourse falls into core-periphery debate. Ideas originate in the cores, in the offices of the ILO, IMF, UNDP, World Bank to mention a few, but are imposed upon the peripheries, such as in Third World countries and in their rural areas. Ideologies embody a planners core, centre-outwards, top-down view of rural development. The conditionalities prescribed by aid agencies for rural development are clearly indicative of top-down flow of ideas. In fact, at ideological level, those who are concerned with the development of rural people, the 'others', "start with economies, not people; with the macro not the micro; with the view from the office, not the view from the field"(Chambers, 1993:). Further ideas of rural development learnt in the universities of the West are transplanted in Third World countries (Chambers, *ibid.*,5), by the people who studied outside (Farida, personal communication). Of course, some apparent modifications are made for better understanding of the people of the country, but the 'core' idea remains.

In the national context bureaucracy involves in the development process at various levels and bureaucratic misunderstanding (Barnard, 1998) of peripheral issues affects the process itself. Liberalization prescribes state interventions at selected sectors to correct market irregularities that create and widen existing social inequalities. Bureaucracy requires an understanding not only of the functioning of market under liberalization but of peripheral issues of the nation in relation to developed countries and within these countries. A balance has to be sought in perspectives of development at three levels, international development perspectives, national perspectives and perspectives of people at peripheral level. Government has its own agenda, perspectives and priorities, compulsions and constraints and programmes (Chambers *op. cit.* 69-110) and above all a bureaucracy as functional machinery. Bureaucracy, however, functions within a professional frame and bureaucrats have their mind set (Chambers, 1983) in appreciating the development perspectives. Obviously, there remains a gap; put simply, a misunderstanding by bureaucracy of development perspectives of the people that differ greatly from national and international perspectives and from their own professional understanding. Because of bureaucracy and their professionalism, ideologies of the core always dominate that of the periphery. The strength of professionalism is specialization, simplification, assimilation remains dominant "through training and rewards, conservative and well-defined and therefore is stable" (Chambers, *op. cit.*6). This stability makes the new requirements, which are associated with new development paradigms, instable and weak, and thus render development plans and policies ineffective.

With this backdrop, an attempt is made in this chapter to examine if MNC investment could benefit the tribal people of Arunachal Pradesh in general. This chapter is based on empirical analysis of data pertaining to employment issue in the state. The study is a preliminary enquiry of empirical data that draw on both primary and secondary sources. Primary source data draws on observation during field study in connection with other project works over a period of twenty years in different places of the state, discussion with subject experts and local scholars and on internal government records. Secondary source comprises relevant works on the topic.

The gamut of discussions is accommodated in three sections. The first section highlights the prevailing condition on employment from in the process of state-sponsored development exercises. The second section deals with implications of MNCs investing in Arunachal Pradesh mainly on infrastructure and tourism. The third is the concluding section.

SECTION I

Economic development in Arunachal Pradesh is an exercise of the state after independence within the framework of tribal development. The paradigm of tribal development has assumed a distinction of its own because of Nehru's *Tribal Panchashila* (Elwin: 1959: xiii) and special constitutional and administrative safeguards (see Srivastava: 2002, Mohanty: 2002 and Sankaran: 2002), which are in the nature of positive discrimination. According to the policy framework, the development has to be 'in the line of their own genius' with due respect to 'tribal rights in land and forests' and without overwhelming them 'with multiplicity of schemes' and without 'introducing too many outsiders into tribal territory' (Elwin; *op. cit.*).

In spite of theoretical soundness of tribal development philosophy and plan programmes introduced in this regard, there is neither uniform level of development[1] nor there is achievement in terms of objective realization in the sense of developing tribals in the line of *Tribal Panchshila* (Behera: 1994). At present, after a period fifty years of development efforts, the following trend has emerged in employment front:

There is a decline in the percentage of Arunachalee population (Table 15.1) implying that the inflow of non-Arunachalee population has increased over the years as economic activities have been diversified and intensified with increase in plan expenditures from Rs. 201 lakhs during First Five Year Plan to Rs. 1,29,853 lakhs during Eighth Five Year Plan. The increase in non-Arunachalee population could be accounted to the declining percentage of Arunachalee workforce (Table 15.2) to total workforce. It also transpires from Table 15.3 that percentage variation of Arunachalee population during 1981-91 over 1971-81 is more as compared to non-Arunachalee population. Contrary to it, the percentage variation of non-Arunachalee workforce is positive and quite significant while it is negative for Arunachalee workforce during the period of reference. Obviously, the inflow of non-Arunachalee population to the territory is to add to the workforce requirement.

Table 15.1: Percentage of Arunachalee Population to Total Population

Year	*Persons*	*Male*	*Female*
1961	88.67	NA	NA
1971	79.02	72.27	85.69
1981	69.82	64.85	75.59
1991	63.66	59.22	68.82

Source: Census of India, 1991, 1981, 1971 and 1961

With reference to this trend and on the basis of observations the following discussion emerges on employment front and related issues:

1. The emerging elite class—mostly 'contractor-breed-politicians' and bureaucrats—has been involved either directly or indirectly[2] in various State-sponsored development activities by employing non-Arunachalee workforce. In construction work in private sector, no Arunachalee worker is found as wage earner except a few in interior villages who take road construction work on sub-contract basis and engage themselves temporarily when outside workforce is not available. In government sector, especially in engineering departments, however, a few of them are found working as mason or as work supervisor or a wage labour. It is, therefore evident from Annexure 15.1 that only 2.54 per cent of Arunachalee main workers are engaged in construction works. Percentage-wise participation stands at 2.32 per cent in rural areas and 8.49 per cent in urban areas respectively. In terms of total figure it is recorded at 5,539 persons in rural areas and 730 in urban areas.

Table 15.2: Percentage of Arunachalee Workforce to Total Workforce

Year	*Persons*	*Male*	*Female*
1961	NA	NA	NA
1971	78.14	67.47	93.39
1981	70.92	59.92	87.31
1991	63.12	52.44	80.94

Source: Same as Table 1.

2. Due to relaxation in educational qualification and reservation regime, a large chunk of educated population has entered into government jobs. They have better access to information about development schemes of the government than those unemployed and living in villages. Moreover, these employees mostly absent themselves away from their works, and take advantage of their position in government jobs in availing of development schemes which are otherwise not meant for them. They execute works under these schemes with non-Arunachalee workforce [3].
3. A non-Arunachalee is not allowed to undertake any economic activity in his name. Licenses are issued only to Arunachalees in the name of Arunachalees.
4. In government undertaking like Nigmoi Fruit Processing Unit (AHPIL), Along and PCL, Tezu no Arunachalee was found working in grades other than IV grade. These employees also did not attend their duties regularly. Because of their absence along with some other managerial problems (see Ete: 1998-99 for discussion on AHPIL) the units are now defunct. (Presently, AHPIL has started functioning by private initiative.) In NEEPCO Hydel Project, Yazuli, however, some IV and III grade employees are Arunachalees. In Nafra circle, Miji people are engaged as wage earners[4] in NAFRA Chemicals in resin collection. Presently, there are some instances of local people running their own shops [5]. In general, tribals of Arunachal Pradesh do not prefer to work as wage earners. Even in tea plantations all the workers (manual) are non-Arunachalees. In forest based industries, a few Arunachalees involved (0.67% of total Arunachalee main workers are recorded under livestock, forestry, fishing hunting, plantation and allied activities) in either as Licence holders or as timber contractors or as owners of elephants or transport

vehicles. Arunchalee employers also do not prefer Arunachalee workers [6].

5. In agriculture, a bulk of workforce comes from non-Arunachalee populations [7](Roy and Kuri: 1997). Percentage wise it is 1.20 per cent but it is significant in terms of total persons engaged in agriculture.
6. Wage-employment programmes for poverty alleviation—such as JRY—are executed either by non-Arunachalee workforce or by machine power (Mantaw: 1997: ch-8).
7. Even after fifty years of development exercise the industrial sector has not made any significant headway. About 67.44 per cent of main workers are engaged in primary sector activities, 8.66 per cent in secondary sector activities and 23.90 per cent in tertiary sector activities. The participation rate among the Arunachalees in the above activities is 87.16 per cent, 2.98 per cent and 9.86 per cent respectively. A very negligible percentage (0.45%) of Arunachalee main works is recorded in manufacturing, processing, servicing and repairs (Census 1991; paper I of 1993). It transpires from Annexure-1.1 that only 21.78 per cent of total workers in secondary sector belong to Arunachalees.

Table 15.3: Decadal Variation of Population and Workers in Arunachal Pradesh

Population Category	*% Variation during 1981-91 over 1971-81*	
	Population	*Workers*
Total		
Persons	41.62	6.69
Male	42.67	26.54
Female	40.40	(-) 28.62
Arunachalee		
Persons	52.15	(-) 34.74
Male	53.88	(-) 2.44
Female	50.42	(-) 64.88
Non-Arunachalee		
Persons	33.45	34.38
Male	34.94	39.09
Female	31.54	20.61

Source: Estmated from Census of India, 1971, 1981, 1991.

8. Conspicuous consumption discourages saving habit and thus investment. Lack of investible surplus in private sector deters employment-generating capacity of the economy.

9. The genesis of development in a region is its population as economic reproduction requires production of the means of material existence and production of labour force (see Engles: 1997: 6). In a directed economy like Arunachal Pradesh, the production of material means is an exercise of planned directives. But the conditions for reproduction labour forces within the economy do not exist over a short span. Hence, there is demand for labour outside the economy. There is a lack of capacity building in Arunachal economy in terms of reproduction of labour force. A section of main workers because of traditional skill endowment and altitude are not available to undertake works under various development schemes. The other section, being the product of present system, prefers white-collar jobs or employment avenues (8.25 per cent of Arunachalee workers are recorded in 'other services') promising easy money. The desire to earn more so as to keep up with the Joneses has upset work discipline and has exposed work system to corrupt practices. Potential Arunachalee workers do not prefer to engage themselves as wage earners under various schemes rather they prefer to benefit from various schemes by engaging non-Arunachalee workers.

With regarden to the peculiarity about the condition of labour supply in Arunachal Pradesh, development schemes become relatively abundant as compared with willing Arunachalee workforce to work in them. Consequently, there is a demand for workforce from outside the economy.

SECTION II

When this is the overall situation in employment front, the state government is making efforts to solicit foreign investments. It has proposal to invite MNCs to explore the possibility of investment in various sectors. As market directs the MNC investment, there is little chance of MNC investment in manufacturing sector in view of inadequate infrastructure (Barthakur: 1995; Shukla: 1997). Of course, there is a talk about the investment in infrastructure and tourism.

With a very poor industrial base (secondary sector contributing only about eight per cent to the State Domestic Product, the potential consumers of infrastructure would be household and government sector. When majority of the Arunachalees still live in villages (5.8 per cent of them live in urban centres), when *jhum* cultivation is still predominant (77.7 per cent of operational area comes under *jhum* according to 1985-86 Agricultural Census), majority of Arunachalees will lack purchasing power to consume infrastructure (such goods will not be subsidized, see the discussion that follows) directly or other goods produced using the infrastructure because price will be determined by market forces. The cost of production will go up because of global specialization of labour and technology and prevalent geo-environmental factors.

Because of the general backwardness of the territory, the government would grant special concessions like tax holidays, supply of power, etc. at subsidized rates to attract investors. About more than 85 per cent (Table 15.4) of the state revenue comes from central grants, as the state has virtually no source of its own. As the centre suffers from revenue deficit, it may not meet any extra revenue grant required consequent upon special concessions to MNCs. Again considering general backwardness of people and lack of purchasing power with them along with constitutional obligations for their uplift, the government has to provide subsidy for the consumption of infrastructure. The only possible way to do so is to cut back investment on social sectors which are more labour intensive and which bear long term significance in terms of capacity building of the economy.

Table 15.4: Revenue Receipts in Arunachal Pradesh (Rs. in Lakhs)

Year	*Total Revenue Receipt*	*Transfer from Centre*	*% of Transfer from Centre to Total Revenue Receipts*
1990-91	35822	31172	87.02
1991-92	44573	38875	87.22
1992-93	50317	44091	87.63
1993-94	54442	45147	82.93
1994-95	60584	51346	84.75
1995-96	75377	64622	85.73
1996-97	50044	70391	87.94
1997-98	82720	72676	87.86
1998-99	92734	82928	89.43
1999-2000	102139	89222	87.35

Source: Annual Budget Review, Directorate of Economics and Statistics, Government of Arunachal Pradesh, Itanagar.

When the government cuts down social sector expenditures full cost pricing is recommended so as to eliminate subsidies. These areas then become profitable for private investment. The real wage rate in the economy would fall resulting from full cost pricing of output unless there is a corresponding wage hike. Moreover, consequent upon the cut down of government expenditure on social sectors, Arunachalees employed in various capacities at various levels therein either would lose the job or be shifted to other similar works in the tertiary sector which is already over expanded. Hence, horizontal mobility of labour even holds little possibility. MNC investments are usually capital intensive and thereby promise less scope for labour absorption. Integrating the market with global economy would amount to the free play of market forces, contrary to development philosophy for tribals, where less or no skilled Arunachalee workforce stands little chance to compete, in case MNCs employ labour intensive technology. The scope for vertical mobility of labour is not possible given the skill endowment concomitant to their existing economic life at large (Behera: 1998-99). As a matter of fact, however, the elite section would like to invest on human resource development keeping an eye on employment in MNCs. But the commoners would not have their own resources for the purpose. Consequently, there will be a wide gap of inequality among wage earners concomitant to variations in the level of human resource development (*cf.* Acharyya and Marjit: 2000). An attempt to reduction of inequality in wages would suggest for government support, as a matter of Constitutional obligation for positive discrimination, to those who cannot invest in human resource development. But the government support in this direction would again amount to more subsidy and cutting down of government expenditure in some other sectors and thereby affecting the employment level.

In Arunachal Pradesh, resource base is clan/community owned at least in principle except reserved forests. Majority of people still look to forests as a means of livelihood and forest provides employment to a fairly large chunk of workforce. Activities of MNCs, no doubt, would exert pressure on forest resources thereby depriving many of their employment. Distribution of pay offs for the use of community resources would be asymmetric in view of community's distinct stratification in elite and traditional bound groups[9].

In case of investment of tourism, the distribution of payoffs and the employment of the Arunachalees will go in the above line. Linkage effects like transportation, etc. would benefit elite class more than the other section of people.

SECTION III

Tribals in general and Arunachalee tribals in particular enjoy compensatory concessions under state protection. The development process has stratified the society into neo-elites and others (Misra: 1993). Elites have various capabilities in view of their access to available economic social opportunities and political power. The tradition bound group has capabilities quite different from what are required in the process of economic development through MNC investment. Hence, MNC investments will promise least employment opportunities to Arunachalees and fail in ensuring economic growth with distributive justice and sustainability.

With 80 per cent reservation of jobs for Arunachalees and the other 20 per cent being open to all, there is the scope of Arunachalees of getting absorbed into activities other than agricultural activities when earlier non-Arunachalee employees would go on retirement. Government jobs have more security and stability and flexibility in terms of work discipline as compared to jobs in private sectors. Agriculture sector also has great potentiality (98.80 per cent of total agricultural workers are Arunachalees) to release labour to other activities if agriculture is modernized using capital intensive technology. This being the nature of the economy; predominantly agricultural with insignificant industrial sector and a saturated tertiary sector (*cf.* student-teacher ratio, doctor-patient ratio, people : administrative headquarters ratio; see various issues of Statistical Abstract, government of Arunachal Pradesh), the promise for the future development with inflow of foreign capital through investment by MNCs carries little promises for the development of the people of Arunachal Pradesh in that the human resource is not so developed (considering their large percentage of participation in agriculture and low participation in other activities, especially in industrial sector) to meet the labour requirement of the MNCs with a specific level of skill endowment. Presently, the revenue transfers from the Central government ploughs back because the state depends on outside production and on raw material supplies of major products to a greater extent. Given the present socio-economic condition (*cf.* Behera: 1998-99), the benefit from MNC investment will be concentrated around elites and will be ploughed back (*cf.* Stiglitz: 2002—much of the money given to save Indonesia found its way to its source) to other parts without percolating down to the grassroots. MNC investment may develop the territory but the least to its people at least in near future unless the internal dynamics of the skill endowment improve to the extent to accept the challenges of MNC investment.

Moreover, new technologies applied to the production system at this level of development in Arunachal Pradesh through MNC investment would further divide the society, in which already an elite class has emerged. 'New technologies make full employment policies of the traditional sort unworkable. It is throwing social division of labour into a flux. A combination of this increasing stream of new technologies, unfettered market competition, and weak and fractured social institutions is generating an anarchic environment of disorganized global capitalism.'(see Ghosh; *op. cit*: 3981).

The gap of inequality would further be widened in the society where politicians and bureaucrats are at decision-making position (*cf.* Behera: 2002a) and are at a level quite different from the commoners in terms of command over and access to resources and information (*cf.* Sharma: 1995). This has been the experience with IMF's policy of economic development and global concern for gender equality. "IMF's policy gets congenial allies in the political and business establishments in every country. Blame should go to ruling political class and their accomplices''(Stiglitz: 2002 quoted by Ghosh: 2002:3981). The hold of tradition (*cf* Behera: 2002) and gender equality efforts in the traditional social set-up are found to be stumbling blocks in ensuring gender equality (See Ghosh; *ibid*.; Vyasulu and Vyasulu: 1999; Kandiyoti: 1998; Burdon: 2000; Cornwall: 2000; Whitehead and Lockwood: 1999) in its real sense. The same argument also holds good when development efforts through vigorous economic forces operate on traditional bound stratified societies (*cf.* Behera: 1998-99). Experience shows that, "globalization of trade, investments and banking can only mean further dictation and domination of the developed countries and further indebtedness and impoverished of the underdeveloped or developing countries" (Naidu: 1999).

However in this era of globalization Arunachal Pradesh cannot be kept isolated for long. And inviting global forces is not likely to benefit its people. Obviously, inflow of foreign capital could not be directed to achieve desired objectives effectively in tribal areas because of market irregularities and lack of pre-conditions. Moreover, MNC investment is driven by the lure of profit motive through market forces, but tribal development depends more on considerations other than market forces. It is, therefore, suggested for human resource development in both quantitative and qualitative terms so that tribal people benefit from the process of globalization. It is further suggested to fulfil, conditionality like engendering participation in the process of development, transparency and good governance, etc. as pre-requisite towards realization of sustainable economic growth with distributive justice.

ANNEXURE 15.1
Per cent Distribution of Industrial Categories of Arunachalee Main Workers According to 1991 Census

Category	*Persons*	*Male*	*Female*
Mainworkers*	44.93	47.36	42.49
Rural	46.05	48.05	44.06
Urban	26.77	36.71	15.88
PRIMARY SECTOR	87.16[96.25]	80.15	94.99
Rural	89.50	83.32	96.22
Urban	22.21	16.31	37.18
a. Cultivators	85.01[98.80]	77.48	93.43
Rural	87.44	80.73	94.74
Urban	17.61	12.00	31.84
b. Agril. Labours	1.41	1.42	1.40
Rural	1.39	1.42	1.35
Urban	2.00	1.26	3.86
c. Livestock,forestry,fishing hunting and plantation and allied activities	0.67[23.80]	1.12	0.15
Rural	0.60	1.03	0.13
Urban	2.60	3.05	1.48
d. Mining & quarrying	0.07[24.29]	0.13	neg.
Rural	0.07	0.14	neg.
Urban	0.00	0.00	0.00
SECONDARY SECTOR	2.98[21.78]	4.91	0.83
Rural	2.72	4.53	0.74
Urban	10.37	12.50	4.97
a. Manufacturing, processing and repairs in household and other than household industry	0.45[10.55]	0.51	0.38
Rural	0.39	0.46	0.33
Urban	1.88	1.49	2.88
b. Constructions	2.54[26.80]	4.40	0.45
Rural	2.32	4.07	0.42
Urban	8.49	11.01	2.10
TERTIARY SECTOR	9.86[26.09]	14.94	4.18
Rural	7.78	12.15	3.04
Urban	67.41	71.19	57.85
a. Trade and commerce	0.87[16.56]	1.23	0.46
Rural	0.74	1.05	0.40
Urban	4.39	4.86	3.20
b. Transport, storage and communication	0.47[26.44]	0.87	0.03
Rural	0.40	0.75	0.02
Urban	2.45	3.32	0.25
c. Other services	8.52[27.68]	12.84	3.69
Rural	6.65	10.35	2.62
Urban	60.57	63.00	54.40

* Estimated with reference to total Arunachalee population.

Note: Figures in the brackets show % of Arunachalee workforce to total workforce in each category.

Source: Census of India 1991, Union Primary Census Abstract for SCs & STs, Paper-1 of 1993.

NOTES

1. People in interior villages still pursue their earlier means of livelihoods. Since no study is available quantifying various levels of development among Arunachalees, the fact of statement is made on the basis of observation.
2. Bureaucrats are found enjoying the benefit from various development packages in the name of their family members and other relatives.
3. The ethic of responsibility and accountability is lacking. Absence from work is not officially reported nor recorded because of various local considerations.
4. Mijis of West Kameng district are engaged as wage workers by NAFRA Chemicals which extracts resin from pine trees in the area. Even technical works like cutting the tree is done by skilled labour form outside the state. Mijis simply collect the resin and carry them to the collection centre.
5. There are some tribes like the Apatani among whom eldest son inherits ancestral landed property. Middle sons in many cases are landless and they are in search of job opportunities. They are very much receptive to various development measures.
6. There is a love for easy money and absence of work discipline at this stage. Besides, a tribal abhors working as wage earner with fellow tribal. Employers are aware of this fact.
7. (a) Customary law that 'he who clears the forest first owns the land for his needs' prevails among many tribal groups. Presently, elite households engage non-Arunachalee labour to clear the forests, which become their individual property. Non-Arunachalee workers use such land either as tenants or as sharecroppers. The availability of such workforce and elite households' manipulative capacity to manage government subsidies also contributes to land occupation in the name of horticulture gardens.
   (b) In villages, there is a shortage of family labour for agriculture because of school going children and migration of elites to urban centres. The shortage is more acute in villages where there is expansion of agricultural land. Because of economic diversification and decline in the practice of communal appropriation of labour on cooperative basis, there is a heavy demand for non-Arunachalee workers.
8. The Administration had adopted a policy of introducing consumption of exotic goods in the name of People's Presents (see Behera: 1994: Ch-3) which in course of time has resulted in conspicuous consumption without any motive for saving and investment. Goods consumed in the economy are made available because of the integration of Arunachal economy to the market economy. Use of consumer durables has also been taken as a status symbol by Arunachalee elites.
   At the early stage of development, marginal propensity to consume (MPC) is very high. This is more so among the tribals because of their attitude towards pleasure pursuits.

9. Individual families may not share the compensation by themselves, which they receive for allowing their lands to developmental uses. The village community shares by way of feasting. Some unscrupulous individuals also swindle away money in between. The glaring example is the compensation sharing on transfer of land to Arunachal University. The Village Head told the villagers that the land was given on donation. Only recently they came to know about the money received by him on behalf of the village community. Sometimes, village community demand a share on individual compensation, on the plea that after transferring the land, individual families will make use of village land thereby delimiting the area of use by village community.

REFERENCES

Acharyya, R. and Marjit, S., 'Globalization and Inequality, An Analytical Perspective', *EPW*, Vol. XXXV, No. 39, 2000, pp. 3503-3510.

Agricultural Census (1985-86): Directorate of Agriculture, Government of Arunachal Pradesh, Naharlagun.

Amin, S., *Capitalism in the Age of Globalization: The Management of Contemporary Society*, Zed Books, London, 1997.

Amoroso, B., *On Globalization: Capitalism in the 21st Century*, St. Martin's Press, New York, 1998.

Barnard, A., 'Hunter-gatherers and bureaucrats: Reconciling opposing worldviews', Quoted in Barnard, A., 'The Foraging Mode of Thought', in Henry Stewart, Alan Barnard and Keiichi Omura (eds), *Self-and-Other Images of Hunter Gatherers,* Senri Ethnological Studies-60, National Museum of Ethnology, Osaka, 1998.

Barthakur, I. K., The Report of the group on Industrial development of the North-East Region including Sikkim and Andaman and Nicobar Islands, *Ministry of Finance, Department of Economic Affairs*, New Delhi, 1995.

Behera, M.C., *Planning and Socio-Economic development of the Tribals*, Commonwealth Publishers, New Delhi, 1994.

Behera, M.C. (1998-99): 'Impact of Orange Cultivation on Traditional role of Galo women' Report of Minor Research Project of UGC, Unpublished.

Behera, M.C. (1999-2000): 'Identification and Enhancement of Cultural Heritage', Report on Village India (Arunachal Pradesh Chapter) of UNESCO-IGNCA, New Delhi, Unpublished.

Bello, Walden, 'Asia heads back into Underdevelopment?' *The North-East Daily*, January 2, 1999.

Bhaduri, A. and Nayyar, D., *The Intelligent Person's Guide to Liberalization*, Penguin Books India (P) Ltd., New Delhi, 1996.

Bryan, D., *The Chase Across the Globe: International Accumulation and the Contradictions for Nation States,* Westview Press, Boulder, 1995.

Burdon, T., *Links,* November, Oxford, Oxfam, 2000.

Census of India, Union Primary Census Abstract for Scheduled Castes and Scheduled Tribes, 1991.

Chambers, R., *Rural Development: Putting the Last First*, Longman & Scientific Technical New York, 1983.

Chambers, R., *Challenging the Professions, Frontiers for Rural Development,* Intermediate Technology Publications, Southampton Row, London, 1993.

Cornwall, A., 'Making a difference?: Gender and participatory development', *IDS Discussion Paper, 378,* Institute of Development Studies, Brighton, 2000.

Doornbos, Martin, 'Good Governance': The Rise and Decline of a Police Metaphor', *The Journal of Development Studies*, Vol. 37 (6), 2001, pp. 93-108.

Doran, C. and Jose, J., 'Globalization, the Patriarchal State and Women's Resistance in Singapore', *Gender and Technology and Development, 6*(2), 2002, pp. 215-232.

Drize, J. & Sen, A., *Economic Development and Social Opportunity*, OUP, New Delhi, 1998.

Economic Review, Directorate of Statistics and Economic Affairs, Government of Arunachal Pradesh, Itanagar, 1996.

Elwin, V., *A Philosophy for NEFA*, 2nd Edition, Shillong, 1959.

Engels, F. 1948, *The Origin of the Family, Private Property and the State*, Progress Publishers, Moscow, 1985.

Ete, Minto (1998-99): Problems and Prospects of Fruit Processing Industry in Arunachal Pradesh (A Case Study of AHPIL, Nigmoi), *M. Phil Dissertation of Arunachal University,* Unpublished.

Farida Akhter, Personal communication, 2003.

Ghosh, D. N., 'Globalization, the IMF and Governance', *EPW*, Vol. XXXVII, No. 29., 2002, pp. 3980-3982.

Government of Arunachal Pradesh, *Statistical Abstract,* Directorate of Statistics and Economic Affairs, Itanagar, 1996.

Government of Arunachal Pradesh: Ninth Five Year Plan (1997-2002) and Annual Plan (1997-98), *Planning and Development Department*, Itanagar.

Hansen, H. & Tarp, F., 'Aid Effectiveness Disputed', *Journal of International Development*, Vol. 12(3), 2000, pp. 375-398.

Hermes, N. & Lensink, R., 'Changing the Conditions for Development Aid: A New Paradigm?", *The Journal of Development Studies*, Vol. 37 (6), 2001, pp. 3-16.

Hirst, P. and Thompson, G., *Globalization in Question: The International Economy and the Possibilities of Governance*, Polity Press, Cambridge, 1996.

Jameson, F., 'Globalization and Political Strategy', *New Left Review 2nd Series, 4,* 2000, pp.49-68.

Kandiyoti, D., 'Gender, power, and contestation: rethinking bargaining with patriarchy' in C. Jackson and R. Pearson (eds.) *Feminist Visions of Development*, Routledge, London, 1998.

Kumar, A., 'Unemployment and the structural adjustment Policies—Worsening Crisis due to Loss of Sovereignty', *Janata*, March 8, 1992, New Delhi, 1992.

Kumar, A., 'Fifty Years of Freedom from the perspective of the Poor', VJJR-61, Raj Niwas Marg, Delhi, 1997.

Mantaw, H., Poverty Alleviation Programmes and Tribal Development, M.Phil dissertation of Arunachal University, *Unpublished,* 1997.

Misra, K.K. 1993, *Tribal Elites and Social Transformation*, Inter-India Publications, New Delhi, 1994.

Mohanty, P.K., Development of Scheduled Castes and Scheduled Tribes in Independent India, *Journal of Rural Development, 19(4)*, 2000, pp. 535-571.

Naidu, M.V., 'Globalization: Threat or Promise', *Gandhi Marg*, Vol. 21, No. 1, 1999, pp. 21-25.

Roy, N.C. and Kuri, P.K., 'A Study of Institutional Changes of Land ownership and the need for Land Reform in Arunachal Pradesh', *Report of Minor Research Project of UGC*, Unpublished, 1997.

Sachs, J.D. & Bajpai, N., 'Money Order', *The Telegraph*, December 21, 1998.

Sankaran, S.R., 'Welfare of Scheduled Castes and Scheduled Tribes in Independent India—An Overview of State Policies and Programmes', *Journal of Rural Development,* 19(4), 2000, pp. 507-534.

Sen, A., *Poverty and Famines—An Essay on Entitlement and Deprivation,* OUP, Delhi, 1981.

Sharma, B.D., *Globalization: The Tribal Encounter*, Har Ananda Publications, New Delhi, 1995

Shukla. S.P., Transforming the North-East, High Level Commission Report to the Prime Minister, *Planning Commission,* New Delhi, 1997.

Srivastava, B.N., 'Working of the Constitutional Safeguards and Protective Measures for the Scheduled Castes and Scheduled Tribes, *Journal of Rural Development,* 19(4), 2000, pp. 573-602.

Stiglitz, Joseph, E., *Globalization and Its Discontents*, W. W. Norton and Company, New York, 2002.

Vyasulu, P. and Vyasulu,V., 'Women in Panchayati Raj: Grassroots Democracy in India, Experience from Malgudi', *Background Paper 4, UNDF, Meeting of Women and Political Participation: 21st Century Challenges*, March 24-26, 1999, New Delhi, Unpublished.

Whitehead, A. and Lockwood, M., 'Gender in the World Bank's poverty assessments: six case studies from Sub-Saharan Africa' *Discussion Paper No 99,* United Nations Research Institute for Social Development, Geneva, 1999

World Bank, *Assessing Aid: What Works, What Doesn't and Why, The* World Bank, Washington DC, 1998.

16

Current Trends in Canadian Economy in the Era of Globalization:

A Third Millennium Perspective

B. RAHAMATHULLA

One of the important functions of Canadian foreign policy is to accelerate the economic growth and development by stimulating and attracting investment both from domestic and international investors and to expand the free trade with the intention to integrate with the global economy. Department of Foreign Affairs and International Trade of Canada has taken a number of initiative to promote International Free Trade. For instance, Foreign Direct Investment (FDI) has grown from \$ 96.1 billion in 1986 to \$ 180.4 billion in 1996. This constitutes roughly 10 per cent of total investment. FDI increased by nearly \$ 35 billion from 1993 to 1996. The United States of America was the main foreign investor with more than \$ 118 billion followed by the United Kingdom \$ 16.5 billion, Japan \$ 6.7 billion, France \$ 5.29 billion and Germany \$ 4.97 billion. The main objective of welcoming Foreign Direct Investment in Canada is to create new jobs and to expand international trade. 40 per cent of Canada's domestic product flows from international trade, \$ 1 billion of Canada's exports sustain 11,000 jobs and every \$ 1 billion in foreign investment helps to create an estimate 45,000 new jobs over a period of five years in Canada[1].

The following table indicates that Canada is becoming a more open economy.

Trends in Foreign Trade

		1976	1999
1.	$\frac{X+M}{GDP}$	37.8%	72.0%

2. Capital Inflow and Outflow/GDP 1945-80 1999
87% 171%

A. Exports and Imports

	By Countries %			
Country	1971	1981	1991	1999
Exports				
US	67.8	66.2	72.3	83.6
EEC	14.1	10.3	08.5	04.9
Other OECD	08.4	03.1	01.8	01.9
Others	08.9	14.3	10.8	04.4
Imports				
US	70.0	68.1	69.3	74.3
EEC	12.0	11.0	10.3	08.6
Japan	06.2	05.2	06.2	03.3
Other OECD	03.4.	02.3	03.2	03.9
Others	09.2	15.1	10.8	07.6

Source: Statistics Canada (All in Canadian Dollars).

Canada's outward investment has also grown fastly from $ 64.7 billion in 1986 to $ 170.8 billion in 1996. This has strengthened Canada's growth in export, creation of jobs and facilitated R&D activities. The trade among the three NAFTA (North American Free Trade Agreement) countries—Canada, United States and Mexico has risen to $ 462 billion in 1997 from $ 269 billion in 1993 and thus an increase of 72 per cent. Canada is pursuing trade and investment liberalisation both at the regional and multilateral levels. For instance, a Free Trade Area of the America's (FTAA), a trade liberalisation initiative within the Asia-Pacific and free trade agreement with the countries of European Union indeed are accelerating the Canadian economy and is growing at 8-9 per cent annually[2].

The private companies are acquiring outward investment through partnership, joint venture, acquisitions, mergers etc., for penetration into new markets, for strengthening their operation and this strategy would fetch Canada abundant growth and export opportunities besides creation of a number of jobs.

The following table indicates Canada's Exports and Imports from 1971 to 1999.

By Categories

(In percentage)

	1971	*1981*	*1991*	*1999*
Exports—				
Agri. and Fish Products	13.4	12.7	09.2	06.9
Energy Products	07.4	14.3	09.9	08.2
Forestry Products	16.6	15.5	13.1	10.5
Industrial Goods	26.3	24.8	21.9	15.4
Machines and Equipment	11.5	14.9	20.6	22.9
Automotive Products	23.3	16.2	22.8	26.0
Consumer Goods	01.6	01.7	02.4	03.7
Imports—				
Agri. and Fish Products	08.6	07.6	06.9	05.3
Energy Products	05.9	12.5	05.1	03.2
Forestry Products	01.1	00.9	00.9	00.8
Industrial Goods	21.2	19.9	18.8	18.6
Machines and Equipment	26.7	29.1	32.7	32.5
Automotive Products	26.1	20.3	23.6	22.8
Consumer Goods	10.5	09.9	12.1	11.1

Source: Statistics Canada.

The Multilateral Agreement on Investment

In 1995, Canada and other countries within the 29-member Organization for Economic Co-operation and Development (OECD) launched negotiations toward a Multilateral Agreement on Investment (MAI).

These negotiations are taking place at a time when global investment is growing at phenomenal rates. Since 1980, foreign direct investment in Canada has nearly tripled to $188 billion and Canadian investment abroad grew almost seven fold to $194 billion.

Canada benefits from both inward and outward investment. Foreign direct investment in Canada helps generate economic growth and it is responsible for one out of ten jobs in Canada. Canadian companies investing abroad become more competitive. They gain access to new technologies and increase research and development activity at home.

The principal aim of the MAI negotiations is to establish a broad framework of agreed principles and commitments governing the treatment of foreign investment. To ensure better and secured access for Canadian goods, services and investments, Canada has long been a strong advocate of clear, equitable and transparent rules governing international trade and investment.

Two principles form the basis of the MAI negotiations: non-discrimination and fair protection for investors and their investments. Non-discrimination means that governments treat foreign and domestic investors the same way.

A satisfactory MAI would:

— secure commitments and standards of treatment for Canadian investors and investments from MAI countries that Canada now enjoys with the U.S. and Mexico;
— consolidate Canada's status as an attractive place for foreign investment;
— provide Canadian investors abroad with greater protection and more certainty regarding potential arbitrary or discriminatory treatment of their investment; and
— establish an effective dispute settlement mechanism that would provide Canada and Canadian investors a means of legal redress in the face of discriminatory actions by foreign government.

Canada will accept only an MAI that:

— completely preserves our freedom to act in key areas such as culture, health care, education, social programmes, the environment, labour standards, programmes for Aboriginal peoples, programmes for minority groups and management of natural resources;
— fully maintains our ability to preserve and promote Canadian culture;
— preserves legislative or regulatory action by government in the public interest;
— preserves Canada's ability to maintain current investment measures and foreign ownership measures. and
— since the outset of negotiations, the Government has consulted extensively with provincial governments, non-governmental organizations, business and labour to ensure that the interests of all Canadians are properly reflected in negotiating position.

A sub-committee of the All-party House of Commons Standing

Committee on Foreign Affairs ad International Trade conducted public hearings on the MAI at the request of the Minister for International Trade. The Government tabled a formal response that replied positively to all of the Committee's recommendations and reiterated Canada's position.

Such an agreement would also represent an important first step towards the negotiation of truly multilateral investment rules at the World Trade Organization (WTO), whose membership comprises 132 countries from around the globe.

The next meeting of the MAI Negotiating Group is scheduled for October 1998[3].

Structural Changes in the Canadian Economy (1971-1999)

	1971		*1981*		*1991*		*1999*	
Sectors	*$b*	*%*	*$b*	*%*	*$b*	*%*	*$b*	*%*
Agriculture	9.8	3.2	9.2	1.9	11.4	1.9	13.6	1.8
Fishing etc.	4.4	1.3	5.0	0.8	5.0	0.7	5.4	0.7
Mining etc.	18.0	5.3	17.0	3.5	22.4	3.7	26.8	2.6
Manufacturing	61.9	18.2	84.0	17.2	94.9	15.8	136.8	18.2
Construction	24.9	7.3	37.9	7.8	40.1	6.7	41.7	5.6
Transformation	15.3	4.5	20.6	4.4	24.7	4.2	35.0	4.7
Communication	4.5	1.3	11.5	2.4	19.0	3.2	26.5	3.5
Finance, Insurance	53.5	15.7	71.7	14.7	95.6	15.9	120.7	16.6
Community Services	78.4	23.1	125.5	25.8	155.0	25.8	180.4	24.0
Trade	31.0	9.1	48.7	10.0	64.4	10.7	92.4	12.3
Utilities	10.3	3.0	18.5	3.8	23.0	3.8	25.3	3.4
Govt. Services	27.8	8.2	37.3	7.7	44.9	7.5	45.5	6.1
Total	339.8		486.9		600.4		749.9	

Source: Statistics Canada. All in Canadian Dollars.

The Free Trade Area of the Americas

The 1994 Miami Summit of the Americas created a broad blueprint for great economic, political and social co-operation among the nations of the Americas. An integral part of this blueprint was the Free Trade Area of the Americas (FTAA).

In April 1998, Prime Minister Chretien and leaders from 33 other countries launched negotiations on the FTAA at the second Summit of the Americas in Santiago, Chile. Canada will chair these negotiations for the first 18 months.

From 1991 through 1997, Canadian exports to Latin America and the Caribbean more than doubled, from $ 2.8 billion to $ 6.4 billion.

Canada now exports more to Latin America and the Caribbean than to Germany and France combined.

The economies of Latin America and the Caribbean have come of age, and the Americas is now a market of more than 700 million people. Canada can't afford to self itself shore in this important new market.

The FTAA would result in common rules across the Hemisphere, making it easier and less bureaucratic to do business and discouraging corruption. It would also protect substantial Canadian investments and open new markets to Canadian goods by lowering or eliminating high tariffs or other barriers now applied to them.

In particular, the FTAA would open up the dynamic, fast-growing economies of the Americas to small and medium-size Canadian firms—the source of most new jobs in Canada.

The FTAA would also help all countries of the region to reap the social benefits of free trade. Unlocking the potential of the region will generate more prosperity, and can help governments fund their social agenda—education, health, alleviation of poverty.

Negotiations on the FTAA are slated to begin in September 1998 and are expected to last seven years. The negotiating committee met for the first time in mid-June in Argentina.

Canada will be a leader in consulting its citizens on how the FTAA should evolve with the help of Parliament and will only sign a good deal that has the support of the Canadian public.

Canada will safeguard its vital interests in such areas as culture, health care, education, social programmes, the environment, labour standards, programmes for Aboriginal people, programmes for minority groups and management of natural resources.

The FTAA will co-exist with the NAFTA, the Canada-Chile Free Trade Agreement, and other regional or bilateral agreements[4].

Early Voluntary Sectoral Liberalization in APEC

The Asia-Pacific region is an important market for Canadian export—over half of Canadian exports to destinations outside the United States are to this region.

New Trends

1. Deficit Elimination
2. Tax Reduction
3. Debt Repayment
4. Smaller Govt./Privatization

Current Fiscal Position

Federal Govt.	$ 10.9b	(Surplus)
Alberta	$ 1.4b	(Surplus)
B.C.	$ 1.3b	(Deficit)
Manitoba	$ 1.0b	(Surplus)
Newbrunswick	$ 2.1b	(Surplus)
New foundland	$ -3.4	(Deficit)
Nova Scotia	$ -2.6	(Deficit)
Ontario	Balanced	
Quebec	Balanced	
Saskatchewan	$ 0.9b	(Surplus)

Source: Statistic Canada. All in Canadian Dollars.

In 1997, when Canada hosted the Asia-Pacific Economic Cooperation (APEC) forum, APEC leaders committed to an ambitious initiative to advance early voluntary sectoral liberalization (EVSL) for a package of 15 sectors.

The nine priority sectors identified are environmental goods and services, fish and fish products, forest products, energy, toys, medical equipment and instruments, chemicals, gems and jewellery, and telecommunications. There is also broad interest in six other sectors: oilseeds, civil aircraft, rubber, fertilizers, automotive and food.

The EVSL process aims to reduce trade barriers in certain sectors and identify opportunities for economic and technical co-operation that will help to grow markets.

Canada is front and centre in moving this sectoral initiative forward. Of the priority sectors, Canada is chair of the APEC sectoral working groups on environmental goods and services and on fish products, and is a co-spensor of forest products. Canada is also leading the process in the civil aircraft and fertilizer sectors and is co-lead on oil seeds.

The Benefits of EVSL

The introduction of EVSL would have a positive impact on trade, investment and economic growth for individual APEC members and in the APEC region as a whole. The successful competition of a sectoral agreement—particularly in sectors in which Canada has assumed a leadership role, such as fish, forst and environmental products and services—would mean important economic benefits for Canadians.

Fish and Fish Products

Trade liberalization in the fish and fish products sector will result in significant benefits for Canada's fishing industry, particularly in British Columbia. It would help the industry upgrade its catches to higher-value products for Asian markets.

Open markets would help arrest the decline in fisheries-related jobs, support more secure incomes for fishers, and favour employment in the higher value-added processing sector.

Consumers will benefit from greater selection at more competitive prices.

Forestry

Canada is the world's largest exporter of forest products and would be a major beneficiary of liberalized trade in wood, pulp, paper and paper products.

Japan is Canada's single largest offshore market for wood products, second only to the United States. By removing tariffs that hinder our trade with Japan in this sector, Canada will be well positioned to increase trade and diversity sales, thereby helping to mitigate the recent negative impact of the Asian financial crisis on Canada's forest sector.

As an international leader in sustainable forest management, Canada intends to encourage its APEC neighbours to move toward the goal of sustainable forest management.

Environmental Goods and Services

Canadian firms have developed globally competitive technologies and have carved out expertise in a variety of niche areas including water and waste water treatment, hazardous waste management, resource protection and air quality management.

APEC economies accounting for 65 per cent of the global market for environmental goods and services. Liberalization will translate into new opportunities for Canadian companies to break into emerging markets in the region.

As developing Asian countries experience and industrialization and modernization, environmental technologies will be more widely available at decreased costs[5].

The Minister for International Trade Pierre S. Pettigrew was optimistic of growing Canadian economy as he remarked that:

> "I am pleased to present the year 2000 edition of Opening Doors to the World: Canada's International Market Access Priorities and to report on the continuing success that Canada is enjoying in the international marketplace. Last year's edition noted that Canadian exports of goods and services had reached a record level in 1998 for the seventh year in a row. I am delighted to report that the trend has continued in 1999, with the new record $ 410 billion, an increase of 11.3 per cent over last year. It is important for the Canadian economy and for generating jobs in Canada that continue to build on this success in the years ahead."

> "Trade is important to every Canadian. From the self-employed entrepreneur to the factory workers from small business owner to corporate executive and from child to pensioner, we as Canadians all have a state in ensuring, that products and service flow smoothly over international borders. Most importantly, we rely on clear and predictable rule to govern this trade"[6].

CHANGES IN INCOME DISTRIBUTION

A. Real Income ($ 1996)

FAMILIES			
		1980	*1996*
Lowest	20%	9,729	7,721
Next	20%	31,722	25,484
Middle	20%	47,948	43,375
Fourth	20%	64,366	63,272
Top	20%	1,03,1723	1,10,091

B. Measure of Inequality: Gini Coefficient

FAMILIES		
1971	*1984*	*1996*
0.386	0.408	0.431

C. Role of Government in Redistributing Income: Share of Income

FAMILIES					
		% 1987 Before T&T	*% After*	*% 1996 Before T&T*	*% After*
Bottom	20%	2.8	7.6	2.1	7.4
Next	20%	11.1	13.4	10.0	13.1
Middle	20%	18.0	18.2	17.5	18.0
Fourth	20%	25.3	23.6	25.6	23.8
Top	20%	42.7	37.2	44.8	37.6

International Corporations

Ratio of Top 20% to Bottom 20%				
USA	Australia	New Zealand	Canada	Japan
15	9	8	6.5	4

Canadian exports of goods and services reached $ 409.8 billion, or 43.2 per cent of GDP, in 1999. This continued the dynamic performance of the past half decade, which saw trade grow by 9.1 per cent on average. This trade performance was accompanied by solid growth and outstanding job creation, especially in the most recent period.

Although much of the attention in discussion about trade is focused on exports, the increased flow of imports actually facilitates export production. Producers benefit from lower prices from foreign suppliers and a greater variety of goods and services than are available in the domestic market. Not only are a wider variety and improved quality of goods directly beneficial to consumers, they also may enhance the efficiency of production to the extent that the variety and/or quality of intermediate goods contribute to productivity. In Canada,1999 import of goods and services totalled $ 385.2 billion, an increase of $ 26.2 billion, or 7.4 per cent over 1998.

Canada's two-way trade in services was valued at $ 104.9 billion in 1999, an increase of $ 6.2 billion over 1998. The increasing share of trade in services relative to GDP indicates its growing importance to the overall economy. Exports of service as a share of Canadian GDP was up from 4.3 per cent in 1994 to 5.2 per cent in 199, while the share of service imports to GDP was up from 5.8 per cent in 1994 to 5.9 per cent in 1999[7].

"While the United States is Canada's single largest trading partner for services, its share of Canada's service trade is less than its share of merchandise trade. Between 1994 and 1999, the importance of the United States as a supplier of services to Canada has increased slightly from 60.6 per cent to 61.5 per cent. The EU, on the other hand, has maintained a stronger market share in services than it has in goods"[8]. Predictably the Canadian economy would dominate in the New Millennium and further strengthen its foreign policy objectives of pragmatic internationalism.

NOTES

1. See for details Canada's state policy, Department of Foreign Affairs and International Trade, May 1998.
2. *Ibid.*
3. *Ibid.*
4. See for details Canada's state policy, Department of Foreign Affairs and International Trade, May 1998.
5. *Ibid.*
6. Opening doors to the world: Canada's International Market Access 2000.
7. *Ibid*, p. 2.
8. *Ibid.*

17

Globalization and Foreign Direct Investment: India and Canada

GOVIND PRASAD

Introduction

Globalization is misunderstood to be a new concept. The fact is that it was known to the world even more than four centuries ago. New technologies and means of transport have incredibly shrunk distances, demolished national borders, brought human societies with all their productive and creative capacities together and made the whole world as a very small place. The world is now considered as a global village. During the last few decades of the Twentieth century, the term globalization is very commonly used. Globalization has picked up several enemies and has lost few good friends in recent years. There is hardly any economic, social or political forum where people do not talk about globalization. Today this word is being used with business, trade, culture, village, terrorism, etc, and we very often hear 'global village', 'global warming', 'global trade', 'global terrorism', etc.

Diverse views have been expressed with regard to the meaning of the term globalization. The fact is that it has different meaning for people of different nations. Europeans think globalization brings refugees and genetically engineered foods. They would like to ban both. In the Third World globalization is seen different but equally fearsome animal. For people in Western countries it means cultural and economic imperialism. To a lot of young men in the Middle East, the two—Gulf Wars were the part of the globalization. To a lot of Americans, globalization means not just free trade but also terrorism. It does not just imply free flow of merchandise and capital, but also SARS, the deadly respiratory virus from China. If they could, they would like to insulate themselves from these risks of living in a small indivisible world. In this chapter, we have taken globalization as a process which opens up the economies for the free flow of goods, technology, capital and manpower and allows free flow of goods and services, capital, technologies, and human capital from one country to other country.

The supporters of globalization have strongly advocated for the adoption of globalization by the developing countries. The reasons were that it would eliminate poverty, reduce inequality of income and that there would be faster economic growth of the developing economies. A new economic policy (NEP) of 1991 based on liberalisation and privatisation and globalization (LPG) replaced the socialist model of economic development. As a part of this new economic policy several economic reforms have taken place. The private sector is being encouraged to take up all production and commercial activities, role of government and government aided sector is getting restricted to core activities. This has been done by most of the other countries of the world particularly in Asia Pacific countries.[1] All these steps have, perhaps, been taken by developing nations for the purposes as mentioned above.

Foreign direct investment flows (inflows and outflows) have occupied a prominent place in the global economy. It is an important avenue through which investment takes place in any country. "The importance of FDI extends beyond the financial capital that flows into the country. In addition, FDI can be a tool for bringing knowledge and integration into global production chains, which are the foundation of a successful exports strategy."[2]. It is also said that the FDI flows are vital for accelerating desired degree of growth and development. One of the objectives of introducing globalization was that it would attract foreign direct investment which will generate employment, reduce income inequality and poverty. Further, it would allow free flow of human capital from one country to other. More than a decade has passed since India and other developing nations have introduced various reforms under the process of LPG.

In this chapter, an attempt has been made to highlight the position of FDI flows in the World, in general, and India and Canada, in particular. Further, this chapter also examines whether Canada has been successful in exploiting the opportunities of investment in India during Post-Globalization period.

FDI in the Globalised World

The past few decades have witnessed a dramatic increase in the World FDI. The position of inflows and outflows of FDI is given in Table 17.1.

Table 17.1: Value and Annual Growth of FDI during 1982-2001 (Billions of Dollars and Percentage)

Items	*Value at Current Prices (Billions of Dollars)*			*Annual Growth Rate (Percentage)*					
	1982	*1990*	*2001*	*1986-1990*	*1991-1995*	*1996-2000*	*1999*	*2000*	*2001*
FDI Inflows	59	203	735	23.6	20.0	40.1	56.3	37.1	(-)50.7
FDI Outflows	28	233	621	24.3	15.8	36.7	52.3	32.4	(-)55.0

Source: World Investment Report, 2002, p. 4.

It is clear that inflows and outflows of FDI in absolute terms showed an increasing trend in 1990 and 2001 as compared to 1982. Further, the annual growth rate of both inflows and outflows declined during 1991-1995 as compared to 1986-1990. However, the period 1996-2000 has been good for FDI inflows and outflows. There was decline in 2000 in inflows and outflows of FDI. As shown in Table 17.1, World FDI inflows and outflows in 2001 amounted to $ 735 billion and $ 621 billion respectively, a drop of 51 per cent in the former and 55 per cent in the latter. This was the first drop in inflows since 1991 and in outflows since 1992. This is true in the case of both developed and developing nations. FDI inflows to developed countries fell by about half, from $1 trillion in 2000 to $ 5.03 billion in 2001. Inflows to developing nations decreased by much less—14%—from $ 238 billion to $ 205 billion. Trends in FDI outflows were very similar: Outward investment from developed countries declined from $ 1.4 trillion in 2000 to $ 0.6 trillion while that from developing countries also declined but by much less. It is strange to notice that the sharp decline of global flows in FDI has been marked in spite of the fact that there were about 208 changes, as shown in Table 17.2, in FDI laws were made by about 71 countries in 2001. This maximum number of changes were made by the Asian and Pacific Region.

Table17.2: National Regulatory Changes, 1991-2001

Year	*No of countries that introduced Changes in their investment*	*No of Regulatory Changes of which*		
		More Favourable	*Less Favourable*	*Total*
1991	35	80	2	82
1992	43	79	-	79
1993	57	101	1	102
1994	49	108	2	110
1995	64	106	6	112
1996	65	98	16	114
1997	76	135	16	151
1998	60	136	9	145
1999	63	131	9	140
2000	69	147	3	150
2001	71	194	14	208

Source: World Investment Report, 2002, p. 7.

It is evident that out of 208 changes made in 2001, 194 or about 93 per cent created a more favourable investment climate in an effort to attract more FDI. We do not have data for 2002. But as per the prediction of the United Nations Conference on Trade and Development the picture of FDI flows in 2002 was gloomy. It is said that for some developed countries the inflows and outflows have declined in 2002, while in some cases only one might have been declined. The picture has been similar for developing nations too.

The data relating to FDI inflows, in absolute terms, in developed and developing countries and some of Asian and other countries for the period 1996-2000 are given in Table 17.3.

Table 17.3: Foreign Direct Investment Inflows (*In bn $*)

Countries	*Year*					
	1996	*1997*	*1998*	*1999*	*2000*	*Total*
India	2.6	3.6	2.6	2.2	2.3	13.3
Malaysia	7.3	6.5	2.7	3.5	5.5	25.5
Korea (Rep of)	2.3	2.8	5.4	10.6	10.2	31.3
Argentina	6.9	9.2	7.3	24.1	11.2	58.7
Mexico	9.9	13.8	11.6	11.9	13.2	60.4
Brazil	10.5	18.7	28.5	31.4	33.5	122.6
China (mainland)	40.2	44.2	43.8	40.3	40.8	209.3
Developing countries	152.5	187.4	188.4	222.0	240.2	990.5
Developed countries	219.7	271.4	483.2	829.8	1005.2	2809.3

Source: World Investment Report, 2001 Promoting Linkages, UNCTAD

It is clear from Table 17.3 that the developed nations have attracted more FDI inflows as compared to that of developing countries. Table 17.4 shows distribution of FDI inflow during 1985-2001. It is evident that more than three-fifths share of FDI in the world goes to developed nations. In some years, it is even four-fifths.

Table 17.4: Distribution of World FDI inflows during 1985-2001

(Percentage)

Region	*Year*				
	1986-1990	*1991-92*	*1993-98*	*1999-2000*	*2001*
Developed countries	82.4	66.5	61.2	80.0	68.4
Western Europe	38.4	46.0	33.7	51.9	45.7
European Union	36.2	45.3	32.1	50.2	43.9
Japan	0.2	1.2	0.3	0.8	0.8
United States	34.6	12.7	21.7	22.6	16.9
Developing countries	17.5	31.2	35.3	17.9	27.9
Africa	1.8	2.2	1.8	0.8	2.3
Latin America and The Caribbean	5.0	11.7	12.3	7.9	11.6
Asia and the South Pacific	10.6	17.4	21.2	9.2	13.9
Central & Eastern Europe	0.1	2.2	3.5	2.0	3.7
Least Developed Countries	0.4	1.1	0.6	0.4	0.5

Source: UNCTAD, FDI/TNC database.

Table 17.5: FDI inflows In Selected Asian Developing Countries in the Year 2001

(Billion US $)

Serial No.	*Country*	*FDI*	*Percentage Share to World Total*
1.	China	46.8	6.4
2.	Hong Kong	22.8	3.1
3.	India	3.4	0.5
4.	Indonesia	-3.3	-0.4
5.	Korea	3.2	0.4
6.	Malaysia	0.6	0.1
7.	Philippines	1.8	0.2
8.	Singapore	8.6	1.2
9.	Sri Lanka	0.2	0.0
10.	Thailand	3.8	0.5
Developing Economies		204.8	27.9
World		735.1	

Source: (1) World Investment Report, 2002, UNCTAD.
(2) International Financial Statistics, January 2003.
(3) Economic Survey, 2002-2003, p.133.

Though developing nations became important host to attract FDI during post globalizations period the increase of FDI in developing nations is not so pronounced as we find in the case of developed nations. The surge in FDI has for the most part been centered around the US, the European Union and Japan. The figures relating to FDI inflow in selected Asian countries, as given in Table 17.5, shows that these countries received merely 27.9 per cent in the year 2001 of the total FDI inflow of the world.

This may further be noted that there has been a pronounced change in the composition of FDI from the resource and manufacturing sector to services and technology in intensive production.

The ranks and the amount of FDI attracted by different countries in 1999 are given in Table 17.6.

Table 17.6: Rank and Amount of FDI In Different Countries in 1998-99

Rank	*Country*	*Rs. in Million*
1.	USA	4,26,550.31
2.	Mauritius	1,89,061.00
3.	U.K.	1,33,718.16
4.	Korea (South)	91,261.81
5.	Japan	78,576.06
6.	Germany	67,770.40
7.	Australia	59,064.32
8.	Malaysia	54,509.80
9.	Israel	42270.15
10.	Netherlands	40,751.01
11.	Belgium	39,048.33
12.	Cayman Island	36,227.10
13.	France	35,987.00
14.	Singapore	33,429.34
15.	Italy	28,524.72
16.	Thailand	24,586.21
17.	Switzerland	24526.14
18.	Canada	23501.45

Source: SIA News Letter, February 1999.

It is evident that the US which allocates $ 450 billion per year to military spending for bombing Somalia, Afghanistan and Iraq and allocates merely $ 12 billion per year to development assistance for poor countries is the biggest beneficiary in respect of FDI and stands first in rank for FDI. The rank of Canada for FDI inflow was 18 in 1998-99. The other developed nations including G-8 nations, where the citizens enjoy good average life of above 80 years or so with average income of $ 25,000 or more per person are also fortunate to attract more FDI inflow. India attracted merely $ 13.3 billion out of total of $ 3799.8 billion (merely 0.35%). During 1996-2000 The developing nations including India, on the contrary, have not been favourites for investment. It is sad that world's two billion people living in Sub Saharan Africa, the Andean region, Central Asia and other parts of the world are devoid of medical aid, clean water, basic sanitation and education, etc., and are fighting for survival. The FDI could play a vital role for removing the poverty of these people. It may be noted that even the corporate America, the most vocal advocate of globalization, seems to be shying away from investment in developing nations. One way of finding out the corporate sector's commitment towards globalization is by checking out whether they are still investing abroad. According to a recent study by Deloite Consulting, investment by US manufacturing companies abroad has fallen by 60 per cent in the last two years. In 2000, the US manufacturing companies invested $ 58 billion abroad whereas two years later their direct foreign investment had fallen to $ 23 billion which is less that half of what was invested in 2000. Part of the decline is, of course, explained by the global economic recession. Another reason could be that multinational corporations are learning from past experience. They have cut down investment in most Southeast Asian and Latin American countries after the financial crises in these countries. For instance, foreign investment in ASEAN countries fell by half during 1996-2001. Multinational corporations are also shifting focus of their investment from low-wage developing economies to European markets that have skilled workers, better infrastructure and more reliable economic institutions. For instance, in 2001, American manufacturer directed 94 per cent of their foreign direct investment to high wage countries. This was merely 87 per cent in 2000. After September 11, 2001, US based multinational corporations are also faced with security concerns. It seems that the trend of decline in direct foreign investment may grow in the short term."[3]

During the last three years the leaders of the world promised concrete action to cut global poverty by one half by the year 2015 in a series of commitments known as the Millennium Development Goals. The US took only baby steps by granting, perhaps, $ 4 billion per year as foreign aid as against $ 150 billion per year as military spending. It is perhaps, first time in the history, that the rich are so rich and poor are so poor, that even the little diversion of funds from rich to poor countries would save the millions of people from death.

The position of FDI inflows in Canada from various countries is given in Table 17.7. It is evident that FDI inflows in Canada are on the rise in absolute term. The maximum FDI inflows in Canada are from U.S.A. followed by Europe. The contribution of FDI inflows from Asian countries is at the third place. Among Asian countries, Japan's contribution is the maximum and that of Hong Kong comes at the second place.

Table 17.7: FDI in Canada (Stocks)

(Millions of Canadian Dollar)

Year	*1990*	*1996*	*1997*	*1998*	*1999*	*2000*	*2001*	*2002*
Asia-Total	8463	13715	15319	14758	14228	13949	15287	
Australia	758	661	847	1135	1419	1593	1628	
China	NA	206	235	226	214	194	203	
Hong Kong	1374	3022	2971	2957	2278	3374	4266	
Japan	5222	7873	7990	8393	8206	7897	8285	
Malaysia	25	124	166	133	71	97	96	
New Zealand	NA	NA	NA	NA	NA	101	98	
Other Asia/Oceania	7	35	29	22	25	31	NA	
Other Pacific Rim	427	1169	2424	1338	1259	-19	NA	
Philippines	NA	NA	NA	NA	NA	2	2	
Singapore	88	278	273	195	175	133	132	
South Korea	312	112	132	142	168	184	185	
Taiwan	19	114	153	107	115	96	98	
United States	84089	121943	128978	146893	172802	191017	214960	
South & Central Africa	281	247	372	441	404	703	719	
Europe	36400	43722	47207	54392	57967	93361	86983	
Middle East	252	120	99	99	100	770	NA	
Africa	6	36	77	80	61	145	100	
Total FDI in Canada	130932	182126	194277	219389	248618	302299	320931	

Source: Statistics Canada Catalogue #67-202

Table 17.8: Canadian Direct Investment Abroad

(In Million of C $)

Year	*India*	*Asia*	*USA*	*Total*
1990	94	7,636	60,049	98,402
1996	128	17,407	93,939	181,238
1997	122	19,383	110,707	218.607
1998	169	22,278	133,267	262,909
1999	247	23,179	143,612	283,228
2000	123	25151	164,526	340,366
2001	147	28,811	198,404	389,486

It is evident that United States of America is the favourite destination for Canada to invest. About 50 per cent of Canada's investment is in USA

FDI in India

India, which according to the UNDP Human Development Report, 2003, has slipped from the rank of 124 in 2002 to 127 in 2003 and which has the impressive performance in improving economic growth and reducing poverty and yet is the home for the largest number of hungry people at 233 million while 40 million children, more than one third of the world's total, are not in primary school. This is a country where there are vast regional disparities, as the benefits have not reached in several areas and to several people. The indicators in respect of people living below $ 1.00 per day, undernourished people, under 5 mortality rate, etc., are given in Table 17.9.

Table 17.9: Indicators of People Living Below $ 1 Per Day, Undernourishment People, etc., in India, China and Pakistan in 2003

Indicators	*Country*		
	India	*Pakistan*	*China*
Population Living below $ 1 Per Day (%)	34.7	13.4	16.1
Unnourished People (%)	24.0	19.0	9.0
Literate Females per 100 Literate Males	82.0	60.0	98.0
Under 5 Mortality Rate (Per 1000 Live Births)	93.0	109.0	39.0
TB Related Mortality (Per 100,000)	42.0	45.0	21.0
Land and Cell Phone Access (Per 100 People)	4.4	2.9	24.8
Population access to Medicine	Very Low	Low	Medium

Source: *Times of India*, July 9, 2003.

The need for inflow of FDI in India is clear from the above mentioned indicators. The position of availability of food, water, medicines, and education, etc., to millions of Indian people in 1991, when the new economic policy was adopted, was not better. The idea was that the new economic policy would attract large amount of FDI inflow and it would help the poor and needy. The real position of inflow of FDI during 1990-91 to 2002-2003 is given in Table 17.10. The Table shows the rising trend of inflows of FDI in India.

Table 17.10: FDI Flows in India during 1990-91 to 2002-2003

(*US Million $*).

Year	*Foreign Direct Investments*	*Portfolio Investment*	*Total*
1990-91	97	6	103
1991-92	129	4	133
1992-93	315	244	559
1993-94	586	3567	4153
1994-95	1314	3824	5138
1995-96	2144	2748	4892
1996-97	2821	3312	6133
1997-98	3557	1812	5369
1998-99	2462	-61	2401
1999-2000	2155	3026	5181
2000-2001	2339	2760	5099
2001-2002	3904	2021	5925
2002-2003	2256	386	2642

Source: Reserve Bank of India, Bulletin, March 2003, p. S 251.

Table 17.11: Number of FDI Approvals, Amount Approved and Actual Amount of Inflows of FDI In India during 1991-2002

(*Rs. in Crores*)

Year	*No. of FDI Approvals*	*Amount Approved of FDI*	*Actual Inflows of FDI*
1991	289	534	351
1992	692	3888	675
1993	785	8859	1787
1994	1062	14187	3289
1995	1355	32072	6820
1996	1559	36147	10,389
1997	1685	54891	16425
1998	1191	30814	13340
1999	1726	28367	16868
2000	1726	37039	19342
2001	1982	26875	19265
2002	1966	11140	21286 (Jan-August)
Total	15998	2,84,812	1,29.868

Source: (1) SIA (FDI Data Cell), Department of Industrial Policy & Promotion, Ministry of Commerce & Industry.
(2) Economic Survey, 2002-2003, p. 134

The inflow of FDI was more pronounced in some of the sectors. "The most important sectors to attract FDI in India during 2002-2003 are power (27.4%) telecommunications (19.9%) electrical equipment including computer software (9.8%) and the transportation industry (7.4%). These four sectors accounted for roughly 50 per cent of FDI inflows. Electrical equipment including computer software and electronics are the sectors which have attracted highest approval technology transfer".[4]

Another noticeable feature of FDI in India is that the actual inflow of FDI in India is much less than the amount of approved FDI. This is clear from Table 7.11.

According to one study FDI averaged a pitiful $ 250 million a year during 1985-90. A close perusal of data given in Table 17.3 shows that after liberalization of 1991 FDI inflow increased substantially to a peak of $ 3.6 billion in 1997 and then declined thereafter to only $ 2.3 billion in 2000. Even in the peak year of 1997 the Table shows that FDI into India accounted for just two per cent of all FDI inflows to developing countries. By 2000 India's share had fallen to less than one per cent. And if we include developed countries, India's share in 2000 was a miserable 0.2 per cent of all FDI inflows. Our record also compares badly with either developing country. As against total of $ 13 billion received by India during 1996-2000, China (Mainland) received $ 209 billion, Brazil $ 213 billion and even little Malaysia got almost $25.5 billion, or double what India got. It may be observed from Table 17.5 that in 2001 India has been on third place in respect of FDI and China and Hong Kong had been ahead of India. It is a fact that, for various reasons, India is facing tough competition even from China, Hong Kong and some other Asian countries in attracting FDI. Some of the reasons for being behind other Asian countries are as under:

1. In several developing countries including China and other East Asian countrics a lot of FDI has gone into export oriented manufacturing industries which supply global markets. India has failed to attract this kind of FDI despite of our huge pool of unskilled and semi-skilled labour. The reasons include the anti-export bias of our foreign trade policies, the unusual rigidity of our labour laws, the weakness of our infrastructure especially power, ports, roads and railways and slow and cumbersome administrative procedures, etc.

2. Infrastructure including energy has been a major sectoral destination for FDI in countries that have successfully attracted large inflows of FDI. Here too India has had only limited success. Our weak regulatory-cum-policy framework especially for pricing and investment decisions to infrastructure sectors, has discouraged FDI. Our electric power sector provides the classic example. No one would like to invest when a large proportion of the users does not pay. It is clear from the Enron/Dabhol case that a network of government guarantee is no substitute for payment by the users of electricity. Further, unlike many developing countries, India has faltered in privatization of its infrastructure utilities through strategic sales to foreign companies. Just compare our record in airlines and telecom to little Sri Lanka. They successfully sold management control of their national airline and telecom utility to foreign transnational companies several years ago. In contrast, India has made little progress with our government owned airline (A-I, I A) and telecom companies Actually in telecom India has made significant headway in attracting FDI in new ventures after a somewhat torturous process of evolving a workable regulatory-cum-policy framework.
3. In certain sectors our policies actively discouraged FDI by setting caps on foreign equity holding. This is true for telecom, airline, banking and insurance sectors amongst others.
4. FDI inflows have been discouraged by the apparent lack of governmental commitment and creditability in a number of high profile cases which misfired including Tata Singapore Airlines venture, the little Bangalore International Airport and, of course, Dabhol Fifth. According to many reports, the 'high transactions costs' of doing business in India deter many foreign investors.
5. Finally, there are all the other reasons, which have damped growth of domestic investment, including the slowdown in the pace of economic reforms rising fiscal deficits, uncertainties of coalition politics, weak infrastructure and the global slowdown since late 2000. These also affect FDI negatively.

At the time of introduction of globalization it was emphasized that it would be for the well-being of the people of the developing nations and other parts of the world. "Globalization, in the ultimate analysis, is to be seen as only a means to enhance people's wellbeing. All policies and programmes must focus on people."[5]

The welfare of the people is possible only when the FDI inflow enhances the pace of growth and development, creates more employment opportunities and reduces poverty. It will not be out of place to examine the position of these aspects.

The growth rates of GDP and of different sectors in India are given in Table 17.12.

Table 17.12: Growth Rates in Value Added Over Different Periods Estimated Simultaneously

(% Per Annum)

Period	*Sectors*			
	Agriculture	*Industry*	*Services*	*GDP*
1951-79	2.24	5.18	4.55	3.50
1980-91	3.42	5.32	6.18	5.04
1992-2000	3.26	6.78	7.78	6.11

Source: Manoj Panda (Chapter-2)

Table 17.13: Estimates of Employment in Organized Public and Private Sectors during 1990-2001

(Lakh Person as on 31 March)

Years	*Public and Private Sectors Total*		
	Male	*Female*	*Total*
1990	227.0	36.44	263.53
1991	229.52	37.81	267.33
1992	231.48	39.08	270.56
1993	231.51	40.26	271.77
1994	232.21	41.54	273.75
1995	232.97	42.28	275.25
1996	235.14	44.26	279.41
1997	236.08	46.37	282.45
1998	233.92	47.74	281.66
1999	232.84	48.29	281.13
2000	230.37	49.23	279.60
2001	228.40	49.49	277.89

Source: (1) Ministry of Labour, (DGE&T).
(2) Economic Survey, 2002-2003, p. S-50.

"The reform measures undertaken since 1991 have placed the economy on a higher growth path of above 6 per cent during 1992-2000. Though still below the long-term performance of some of the newly industrialized countries of East Asia, the GDP growth rate during the 1990s translates to a respectable growth rate of above 4 per cent in per capita terms"[6.] It is estimated that the GDP growth rate in the near future would be 8 per cent.

The employment scenario in India in organized public and private sectors during Post-Globalization period are given in Table 17.13.

There is slight rise in employment till1997. The period after 1997 witnessed decline in number of employment both for male and female. There is move by the developed nations to capture the service market particularly legal and accountancy in India. In fact, Cardiff Law School, Cardiff University, U.K., in association with Welch Development Agency and the British Council, has prepared an annual programme to send professors to train at least 8 Indian law teachers. The argument in support of this advanced by Prof. Phil Thomas of the School is that the programme would make Indian lawyers capable of meeting global challenges. "With overseas investors and joint ventures seeking new opportunities in India, there is a need for an appropriate service infrastructure in order to make these investments happen in an efficient, cost effective and legally proper manner. This infrastructure includes legal services."[7.] The fear among Indian lawyers is that the programme will adversely affect them. It is clear that the FDI inflow is going to affect the profession of Indian advocates and Chartered Accountants in India.

The foregoing facts show that the GDP has increased during 1992-2000 but the employment in organized public and private sectors has improved during 1990-1996. The level of poverty in India is a matter of concern. The poverty ratios, estimated on the basis of 30 day recall period, and the number of poor people in India are given in Table 17.14.

Table 17.14: Estimates of Poverty in India

Year	*Poverty Ratio*			*Number of Poor (Million)*		
	Rural	*Urban*	*Combined*	*Rural*	*Urban*	*Combined*
1987-88	39.1	38.2	38.9	231.9	75.2	307.1
1993-94	37.3	32.4	36.0	244.0	76.3	320.3
1999-2000	27.1	23.6	26.1	193.2	67.1	260.3
2007*	21.1	15.1	19.3	170.5	49.6	220.1

*Poverty Projection for 2007.

Source: (1)Tenth Five Year Plan, Vol.1, Planning Commission.
(2) Economic Survey, 2002-2003, p. 213.

The poverty ratio has declined from 36 per cent in 1993-94 to 26.1 per cent in 1999-2000. "The poverty reduction target set by the Planning Commission for the Tenth Five Year Plan aims at achieving a poverty ratio of 19.3 per cent for the country as a whole, 21.1 per cent for rural areas and 15.1 per cent for urban areas."[8]. In absolute terms, "the number of poor people has come down from 320.3 million in 1993-94 to 260.3 million in 1999-2000 and it may further be reduced to 220.1 million in 2007. The decline in poverty ratio and number of poor people is more marked in rural areas as compared to that of urban areas. The findings of other researchers in respect of poverty in India show that the poverty ratio and number of poor people are much more than what is stated above. Further, 260.3 million poor people is enough to indicate the level of poverty in India." The economic growth and human development must move together, otherwise neither growth nor human development can be sustained. This requires much more investment in human development, particularly universal quality basic education as well as higher levels of education and skill training to enable the countries to compete in the global marketplace. In order for economic growth to be job-led, focus should be on labour-intensive as well as knowledge-intensive patterns of production."[9] The picture given by UNDP Report, 2001 shows the human poverty in India. This is given in Table 17.15.

Table 17.15: Human Poverty in India

Deprivation	*Value*
1. Survival deprivation People not expected to survive till age 40 (%) 1995-2000	16.7
2. Deprivation in education and knowledge Adult illiteracy rate (%) 1999	43.5
3. Deprivation in a decent standard of living	32.5
3.1 Population not using improved water resources (%) 1999	12.0
3.2 Underweight children under age five (%) 1995-2000	53.0
Human Poverty Index Value	34.3

Source: Human Development Report 2001, (New York, 2001). Table 4, pp. 150-1.

The picture of poverty level in India, as presented by the UNDP Report, 2003 is not very encouraging. According to the report still 24 per cent people are unnourished, 34.7 per cent of the population live even at below $ 1 per day and access to medicine in India is very low. This is clear from Table 17.9.

'It is high time that for better inflow of FDI, prescriptions have to follow diagnosis. The correction of above mentioned negative factors would boost FDI. The position of FDI in India would be improved by reform of labour laws, the removal of SSI reservation, systematic reductions in customs duties, sustained success in privatization (especially of public utilities), decisive reforms in the power sector, removal of sectoral caps of FDI, reductions of fiscal deficits and a result based commitment of government's political and administrative resources to solving the problems encountered by FDI in India. It is encouraging that much of this is on the government's policy agenda. The sooner the agenda is successfully implemented the sooner we can expect positive results. The converse is also true'[10]

Globalization and Indo-Canadian Economic Partnership

The comparative picture of India and Canada in terms of imports and exports as percentage of GDP and life expectancy, education, GDP per capita, etc., are given in Table 17.16 and Table 17.17.

Table 17.16: Imports and Exports as Percentage of GDP

Country	*Imports of Goods & Services*		*Exports of Goods & Services*	
	1990	*2000*	*1990*	*2000*
India	10	17	7	14
Canada	26	41	26	44

Source: World Development Report, 2002, pp.198 and 200.

Table 17.17: Life Expectancy, Combined Primary, Secondary and Tertiary Education, GDP Per Capita, etc., In India and Canada

Country	*Life-expectancy at birth in yrs (2002)*	*Combined Primary Secondary & Tertiary Enrolment Ratio (%) (1999)*	*GDP Per Capita (PPP US$) (2000)*	*Life Expectency Index*	*Educa-tion Index*	*GDP Index*	*HDI Value (2000)*	*GDP per Capita (PPP US$) Rank minus HDI Rank*
Canada	78,8	97	27,840	0.90	0.98	0.94	0.940	4
India	63,3	55	2,358	0.64	0.57	0.53	0.577	-1

Source: UNDP Report, 2002, pp. 149 and 151

Economic ties between India and Canada, for various reasons, is more than a century old. Globalization had created a lot of interest of entrepreneurs from Canada and other countries. It is a well-known fact that Indians went to Canada as unskilled and semi-skilled workers at the end of nineteenth century. They contributed a lot in the Canadian economy by taking up jobs in factories and agricultural fields. Today their position has changed and they are in Canada as skilled workers, technicians, engineers, doctors, businessmen, politicians, etc. They occupy important positions in the socio-political and economic life of Canada. At present, Canada has become second home for Indians. The economic partnership between India and Canada, during pre-globalization period, were mostly related to trade particularly to merchandise and manpower. The position of trade between India and Canada during post-globalization period is given in Table 17.18.

Table 17.18: India and Canada Trade during 1990-91-2001-2002

(*In US $ Million*)

Year	*Imports*	*Export*	*Total Trade*	*Balance of Trade*
1990-91	311.70	156.60	468.30	-155.10
1991-92	280.10	188.60	468.70	-91.50
1992-93	405.27	191.15	596.42	-214.12
1993-94	232.69	226.09	458.78	- 6.60
1994-95	261.79	266.33	528.12	4.54
1995-96	379.20	309.98	689.18	-69.22
1996-97	290.05	325.02	615.07	34.07
1997-98	391.07	402.43	793.50	11.36
1998-99	371.40	477.54	848.54	106.14
1999-2000	383.4	582.57	966.02	199.12
2000-2001	392.01	661.03	1053.04	269.02
2001-2002	531.2	586.8	1118.0	55.6
2002-2003	567.7	692.5	1260.2	124.8

Source: 1. Directorate General of Commercial Intelligence & Statistics.
2. Monthly Review of the Indian Economy, CMIE, Centre for Monetary Indian Economy, July, 2003, pp. 94-95.

Several items were imported from India by Canada whereas several items were exported to India. In most of the years the balance of trade was in favour of Canada. It was in 1994-1995, for the first time, that the balance of trade became in favour of India. And again after the gap of 1995-96, the balance of trade has always been in favour of India.

The post-globalization era has offered new areas of economic partnership. Canada showed more economic interest in India to take advantage of partnership. The first major effort was made in January 1996, when the then Prime Minister Jean Chretien visited India with *Team Canada*. The Team Canada consisted of Canadian entrepreneurs, companies of every size, in every sector, and from every region of Canada. Team Canada signed several business deals worth several million dollars in Mumbai and Delhi. The Prime Minister said, "Today's signing signals loud and clear that Canada is back in India—and we are here to stay. Today we have injected new life into the relationship between Canada and India. And the deals signed will mean thousands of jobs and new economic growth in both our countries."[11]. In addition, five new agreements between Canada and India were also signed in order to strengthen the bilateral co-operation. The five agreements included: (a) an agreement on double taxation; (b) Two memoranda of understanding between the Alberta Research Council and Oil India and Oil and Natural Gas Corporation, Ltd. of India; (c) A memorandum of understanding between the Ontario Ministry of Transportation and the Indian Ministry of Surface Transport; (d) A memorandum of understanding on co-operation in telecommunications; and (e) A declaration of intent to negotiate an agreement on the transfer of offenders.

The remarks of the Canadian Prime Minister were, "These agreements are part of our major effort to raise relations between two countries to a new level of relevance and importance. Along with the unprecedented size and prominence of the Team Canada delegation, and the trade and investment deals that Canadian businesses are signing here, they signal to the world that the Canada-India partnership is back in business."[12]

In 1999 the Canada India Business Council led a Mission organized in partnership with Canadian Indian Business Councils, FICCI, CII. The Mission was coordinated by the Canadian High Commission and supported by the Department of Foreign Affairs and International Trade. The Mission was organized for Canadian executives in traditional sectors such as a power, oil and gas, environment, telecommunications, and agri-food, and emerging sectors such as transportation, automotive, financial and insurance services, building products and insurance services, building products, construction, urban development. The mission visited Delhi on 26th October 1999 for 11th Business Council. Meeting with Federation of Indian Chamber of Commerce and CII.

A full programme of seminars and meeting were arranged and Canadian companies were allowed to show their products, services and capabilities to expand their business in India or explore the potential for collaborations. Thus, continuous efforts have been made by both the countries for Canadian business and investment in India. It is high time to examine how far Canada has been successful in exploiting opportunities for investment in India during post-globalization period. Table 17.8 shows the Canadian investment in India and other countries. As stated earlier, the bulk share of Canadian investment is in U.S.A. Asian countries get merely 7 per cent of Canadian investment. India received only 0.095 per cent in 1990 which came down to 0.035 per cent in 2001. The data collected by India-Canada Joint Business Council, as given in Table 17.19, also reveal the same picture of Canadian investment in India during post-globalization period.

Table 17.19: India Canada Investment and Collaboration

(Rs. in Million)

Year	*Canadian Investment in India*	*Total Foreign Direct Investment in India*	*Canadian Investment in India as %age of Total FDI in India*
1991	48.60	5341.10	0.91
1992	7.80	38875.40	0.02
1993	272.80	88593.30	0.31
1994	420.80	141871.90	0.29
1995	13735.60	320717.20	0.28
1996	1965.42	361468.05	0.54
1997	3842.64	548913.47	0.70
1998	3156.79	308135.05	1.02
1999 (till April '99)	51.00	78459.94	0.07
2000			
To be added later on			
2001			
2002			
2003			
Total (Jan '91 to April '99)	23501.45	1892375.39	1.24

Source: Indian Investment Centre (IIC) and Secretariat for Industrial Assistance (SIA).

This indicates that, for various reasons, India has failed to attract Canadian investment and Canada has failed to take advantage of the investment opportunities in India during Post-Globalization period.

"The Government of India is making continuous efforts to make India an attractive destination for FDI in the region by providing an internationally competitive investment climate in terms of policy framework, factors and institutions. The FDI policy is reviewed continuously to make it more investor friendly in order to increase FDI. The Government has permitted route for FDI up to 100 per cent in most activities"[13]. FDI inflow under the process of globalization in India should be for the happiness and prosperity of Indian people. Speaking at the inauguration of the 15th Indian Economic Summit jointly organized by CII and the World Economic Forum in New Delhi, the present Prime Minister of India said, "our goal is clear. We will globalize to India's advantage. In the process, we will, ensure that the fruits of productivity and gains of growth bring about a qualitative change in the life of our people."

Canada has to take initiatives so that she is the front and centre in the dynamic theatre of the Asia Pacific Region and India. In the Canadian Pacific personality goes beyond trade and investment. It is also about people. It is a well known fact that in Canada more than 50 per cent of the people came from Asia and have worked in ships, factories, mines and on agriculture and have contributed towards the economic development of Canada. In Focus India it was stated "India represents one of the most exciting emerging economies with the potential to evolve into an economic "Tiger" in the next century. India is now at a crucial juncture in its development. It is imperative that Canada be well positioned to capitalise on opportunities in this dynamic environment"

Conclusion

Direct foreign investment plays a vital role in reducing poverty, creating job opportunities and development of any country. Foreign direct investment in the world showed increasing trend during last two decades or so. The rising trend of FDI was more in developed nations compared to that of developing nations. However, the opposite trend of FDI was marked in the year 2001 though several countries made many favourable laws for attracting FDI in their countries. Further, the developed nations were the recipients of bulk of total FDI of the world. More than 60 per cent and in some years even more than 80 per cent of FDI was received by the developed nations whereas the requirement of the developing nations for FDI was more due to poverty, hunger, lack of facilities for education and health, etc.

The inflow of FDI in Canada also showed a rising trend during post-globalization period. However, the rank of Canada in attracting FDI was below several countries.

For various reasons, the major portion of FDI came to Canada from USA. European countries were second and very small portion of FDI was invested in Canada by Asian countries. In return the destination of bulk of Canadian investment was USA. Rising trend of inflow of FDI during Post-Globalization period in India has been witnessed but the position of FDI is much below expectation. India is behind several Asian countries in attracting FDI. There are several factors responsible for this state of affairs of FDI inflows in India. Canada showed its interest for increasing trade and investment in India.

So far several efforts have been made by these two countries in this direction. India has been able to export more to Canada than its imports from Canada and turned its balance of trade in its favour from 1996-97 onwards. However, India has miserably failed to attract Canadian investment. It is high time to make sincere effort at the earliest so as to remove the bottlenecks for encouraging foreign investors for the growth and development of the country.

NOTES

1. Pacific Region is defined as made by history and interest as by latitude and longitude. Asia Pacific countries include all the countries in the Pacific. These include Japan, Hong Kong, China, Malaysia, Philippines, Singapore, Mexico, Taiwan, South Korea, Thailand, Brunei, Australia, New Zealand, Vietnam, Laos, Cambodia and other islands.
2. *Economic Survey*, Government of India, 2002-2003, p.132.
3. *Economic Times*, 13th May, 2003.
4. *Economic Survey*, Government of India, 2002-2003, p.133
5. Human Development in South Asia Report, 2001, Mahbubul Haque Human Development Centre, p.1.
6. ADB Key Indicators, 2002, Population & Human Resource Trends & Challenges, pp. 5-6
7. *Economic Times*, 1st August, 2003.
8. *Economic Survey*, 2002-2003, p. 214
9. Human Development in South Asia Report, 2001, Mahbubul Haque Human Development Centre, pp. 1.
10. *Economic Times*, 4th October, 2003.
11. Team Canada's Release, January, 10, 1996, p. 1.
12. Team Canada's Release, January, 11, 1996, p. 1.
13. *Monthly News Letter*, Vol. XXXIX No., August 25, 2002, Indian Investment Centre,
14. Department of Economic Affairs, Ministry of Finance, Government of India, p.15.

18

Impact of Globalization:
India and Canada

NAINA SHAIK MOHAMED

Introduction

Canada had a golden age economic growth until seventies. It made Canada as a land of foreign investment. But the two global forces—globalization and decline in aggregate productivity initiated reform measures in the early 80s. India, second largest country in terms of population, initiated her reforms in 1991 and has achieved some satisfactory results so far. If India can replicate Canada in terms of economic growth and development, not only Indians benefit from the rise in the living standards, but also, like Canada, India will become a sought after market.

Canada has had a remarkable open economy. Being fully integrated into the global system, Canada was the eighth largest trading nation amongst the industrialised market economics. About 30 per cent of its GDP came from trade, mostly with United States which was by far the country's biggest market, taking 80.3 per cent of Canada's merchandise exports in 1993 and supplying 73 per cent of its merchandise exports. Over 55 per cent of its manufacturing products were exported.

The realities of the new global environment touched virtually every aspect of Canadian life. The country faced enormous challenges and changing opportunities emanating from the new global competitive environment. Its economy has been experiencing profound structural changes related to such domestic and international development. These pressures made the Canadian economy to restriction. In a half-hearted and halting manner, the process of liberalisation of the Indian economy began in the 1980s or even before. Impact quotas were replaced by tariffs, personal income tax rates were substantially reduced and licensing for private investment was partially deregulated.

As against Canada, economic reforms in India followed a gradualist approach, but had essentially been crisis driven. The year 1991-92 witnessed a stabilisation-induced recession, but growth soon picked up thereafter. The authorities in India recognised the fact that in order to achieve rapid growth, efficient use of resources was essential and competition both domestic and foreign was the best means of ensuring efficiency.

This chapter is organised as follows: in the first section initial conditions and then reform strategies of the two countries are compared and further reforms required in both countries are discussed.

Initial Conditions

Canada

The Canada and India began reform measures for differing reasons while the Indian reforms were undoubtedly crisis driven; the Canadian reforms began for a variety of reasons. Two globalization forces—globalization and a persistent slow down in aggregate productivity growth—had dominated the economic development of the industrial Canada.

Globalization was the increasing integration of the international economy. In some respects it was a new situation; in other it was old, a return to pattern of international economic independence that was accepted as normal before World War I. At that time, it was of pattern of international economic independence that provided pre-World War I Canada with a golden age of economic growth.

The second force, a large slow down in productivity growth struck the entire industrial world in the mid-1970s. This included Canada as well as Australia, Japan, etc. This slowdown had continued through the present and promised to continue into the indefinite future.

There were additional factors, less important yet worth noting that has also greatly changed the Canadian economy. Canada's resource-extraction industries would be among the most affected by the debate over the world's ecology. Furthermore Canada's population and wild life were among those at most risk. What the future of the world economy will generate for Canada a resource-rich, highly open, wealthy and industrialised country with a strong social democratic tradition—is unknown.

India

Statistic bear testimony to the fact that the genesis of the economic crises in India, which surfaced in 1991, lies in the large and persistent macro economic imbalances that developed over the 1980s. A detailed examination of the government expenditures over the 1980s suggests that the root cause of the crisis was the large and growing fiscal imbalances.

The balance of payments came under severe strain from one liquidity crisis experienced in mid-January to another in late June 1991. On both those situations, foreign exchange dropped significantly and the government had to resort to measures, such as using its stock of gold to obtain foreign exchange, utilisation of special facilities of the IMF. Having resorted to these measures the government was about to avoid a default in terms of meeting its debt service obligations and financing of exports. Subsequently, the government embraced upon a comprehensive programme of economic reforms.

Impact of Globalization

Canada

A first consequence was a sharp decline in the stability of governments to control their own macro economic destinies. In early 1980s things had been different. The failure of Mitterrand's policies eroded the ability to pursue idiosyncretic policies. Access to the international capital markets on a large scale essentially transformed the deficits of the 1980s from an economic catastrophe to an economic policy problem. Canada's standard of living had been significantly increased by its ability to trade its resource-based and manufacturing products for those of other economies. But as seen, the benefits of economic integration did not come without a price.

A second predictable consequence of globalization was the renewal of large-scale capital flows across the world economy. Canada participated as a net recipient of international capital flows to finance private and public debt. The share of net issues of Canadian securities purchased by foreigners rose from 10 per cent in the 1960s to 60 per cent in the 1990s. Capital markets that were largely closed were very open. Conversely, Canada had to lose the confidence of domestic investors and domestic economy was at substantial one.

A third consequence of globalization was the diminishing effectiveness of national union movements. For the Canadian economy, the consequences of the labour movement were brought closer in time by the rise of anti-union sentiment in the US and by the NAFTA. Labour movements induced restriction of output below the competitive level and thus diminish productive efficiency. Another issue from the labour movement was a threat to the premium wages bargained by unions which compressed the wage distribution over the century.

India

India's economic reform programmed since the 1990s has evolved two basic sets of policy measures. The first set aimed to achieve macroeconomic stabilisation by reducing both fiscal and the balance of payments deficits. The second set economic measures introduced to alter the production structure by increasing the role of markets through domestic deregulation and by trade liberalisation. Further measures of liberalisation were carried out in recent years in public sector enterprises, financial and banking systems, capital markets and energy sector.

Great importance was placed on savings and investment to economic development. Gross national savings had been slowly increasing from 16 per cent in 1972 to 21 per cent in 1992 and then 28 per cent in 1998. Despite such increase, there was still a huge savings gap; both in private and public sectors. Good governance no doubt would generate more domestic savings in India. However, capital shortages are likely to continue in India in foreseeable future. To overcome such shortages, India will need to create an investment, which is acceptable to foreign investors also.

Another important effect of globalization was tackling the problem of over-population. The Indian economy was ill placed to support a current population growth of 2 per cent per annum. The over population coupled with such current growth rate of population would put intolerable burden on the future growth capacity of the economy and condemned the poorer sections of the community. Per capita income was around US $ 340 (1995). Assuming a GDP growth rate of 7 per cent and annual population growth rate of 2 per cent per capita income would increase by 5 per cent only. But unfortunately in Indian economic programme, the focus on the demographic factor has been lost.

Closely related to population question, another area in which the economic reform programme in India made little impact was the labour market. At present, the Indian labour market was characterised by huge unorganised sector than the fortunate organised sector. There were about 270-300 million people in the unorganised sector whose minimum wages could not be fixed on a meaningful basis. Thus, it was left behind the more fortunate workers in the organised sector. However, even in the organised sector of labour market, there was serious problem of disguised unemployment. The National Renewal Fund, which was established to manage the redundancy in the labour market, had disappointed so far. Thus, proper legislative measures were required to strengthen the position of labour in India.

Future Scenario: Canada and India

The future might bring any of the outlined scenarios. However, the following trends could be expected: Canadian government would lose their residual ability to manage Canada's macro economy in their own or in the countries interest. Large scale international capital flows would make it possible for countries following product economic policies to attract investment and grow rapidly. Large scale international capital flows would also make it next to impossible for governments of countries like Canada to follow policies that did not have the confidence of international community of financial speculations. Slow productivity growth would mean the end of the expansion of the social welfare system.

In the first phase of economic reforms, beginning from 1991, significant measures were taken by the Government of India to liberalise the investment and trade engines. However, challenges lying ahead are fomidable. There are major areas of the economy, which need to be radically changed in the next phase of economic reforms. Supply of safe water and interrupted supplies of power especially for industry have to be the top priority. Some major reforms are also needed in the agricultural sector. To achieve this, it is necessary to encourage domestic savings and investments, more so by way of involvement of the private sector. An image of a clean and transparent administration in India is also a precondition for attracting higher levels of foreign investment.

REFERENCES

Asian Development Bank (1995), *Key Indicators of Developing Asian and Pacific Countries*, Vol. XXVI.

Bhagwati, J.N. and Desai, P., *India: Planning for Industrialisation*, Oxford University Press, London, 1970.

Bajpai, Nirupam, *Economic Crisis, Structural Reforms and the Prospects of Growth in India*, Development Discussion Paper No. 530, Harvard Institute for International Development, 1996.

Coulombe, S. and Bernstein, J.I., *R & D Productivity Growth in Canadian Communications Equipments and Manufacturing*, Carleton University and NBER, Industry, Canada, 1996.

Gera, Surendra and Make Philippe, *Employment Performance in the Knowledge-based Economy*, Human Resource Development, Canada, 1996.

Lee, C. Franc, *Implications of Technology and Imports on Employment and Wages in Canada*, Industry Canada, 1996.

McFetridge, D.G., *Competitiveness and Measures*, Department of Economics, Carleton University, 1995.

Rao, Someshwar, P. *et al.*, *Canadian Based Multinationals: An Analysis of Activities and Performance,* Industry Canada, 1994.

Rao, Someshwar, P., *Governance Structures, Corporate Decision-making and Firm Performance in North America*, Micro Economic Policy Analysis, Industry Canada, 1996.

World Bank, *Economic Developments in India—Achievements and Challenges*, A World Bank Country Study, Washington, D.C., 1995

19

Rhyme, Retham:

Cultural Globalization in India and Canada

I. FRANCIS GNANA SEKAR

Introduction

Heaven is defined as an American salary, a Chinese cook, an English house, and a Japanese wife. Similarly, a hell is defined as a Chinese salary, an English cook, a Japanese house and an American wife. Thus, for heaven, the continents such as America, Europe and Asia are combined and their special features are amalgamated. On the other hand, for hell, the same continents but their limitations are absorbed.

Globalization—Meaning

The term "Globalization" is practically defined by their common usages of their merits and limitations. Asian Development outlook report 2001 defines globalization as the ongoing economic, technological, social and political integration of the world that began after the Second World War.

Globalization refers primarily to integration of various nations of the world at the economic level. However, even if the primary thrust of globalization is economic integration. It also includes as a significant component cultural extension and emergence of a cosmopolitan culture through creation of new habits of thoughts and feelings, new behaviour patterns and attitude, which are supposed to be in broad.

Globalization refers to the process of reducing barriers between countries and encouraging closer economic, political and social interaction. Globalization is also projected to increase vastly the ability of people everywhere to improve their standards of living by sharing knowledge and the fruits of human labour across the globe (Teachers of the world, 2002).

Globalization has many impacts on culture. The Cultural eruption took place in the continents. Culture and multi-culture become the order of the day.

Culture—Meaning

Culture refers to the complex of values, idea, attitudes and other meaningful symbols, that serve human race to communicate, interpret and evaluate as member of society. Culture includes both abstract and material elements. The abstract elements include values, attitudes, ideas, personality types and summary constructs such as religion. Material components include books, computers, tools, buildings and the many products offered by marketing organization. Primarily culture is passed from one generation to the next generation by institutions such as the family, religion and schools. (Engel. *et al.*, 1986).

According to Michael *et al.*, culture is defined as an "integrated system of learned behaviour patterns that are characteristic of the members of any given society, culture is learned, shared and transmitted from one generation to the next. Culture is primarily passed on from parents to their children but also transmitted by social organization special interest groups, government, schools and church.

Globalization and Culture

Globalization is Americanisation. The attraction of the American way of life and culture is so powerful. Throughout the world that the US has drawn the criticism of other governments who perceive it as a threat to their own cultures as noted in global learning experience. In another development the ministerial meeting of the WTO in Seattle, early in December 1999, precipitated large-scale public demonstrations by a number of organizations who were concerned about some aspect of world trade and/or the WTO itself. Globalization and its impact on the homogenizing of global cultures and values (Michael, 2001).

Globalization leads to cultural invasion. In olden days, India was an attractive place for those who wish to trade in India. Trade follows the flag.

The English, the Dutch, the French traders, merchants and business men try to conduct India by discovering sea routes. Vasco da Gama who landed in Kapaud, in Kerala, India. The East Indian Corporation came to India just to trade. Thus, through trade across the boundaries cultural eruption took place.

Cultural transmission is inevitable whenever there is a chance in one country's economic policy. Due to globalization, a major economic eruption took over throughout the world, indeed. There must be some effect on cultural situation. Mahatma Gandhi, the Father of the Nation has also accepted this consequence of cultural transmission and explosion. Gandhiji said, "I don't want my house to be walled in on all sides and my windows to be stuffed. I want the cultures of all lands to be blown about my house as freely as possible. But I refuse to be blown off my feet by any".

As rightly pointed out by our Father of the Nation, we are possible provided that the cultural heritage of India should not be disturbed at any cost.

In the early part of Indian History ambassadors had visited India and wrote many valuable information about many dynasties. For example, Megasthenes the ambassador of Selucas, who had described the palace of Chandra Guptha Maurya in glowing terms. Yavan Suvang, the great ambassador who came from China had made glorifying memories of Indian cultures.

But due to changes in political and economic policies, the cultural heritage of the country has totally lost its originality and value. During the year 1991, globalization was introduced. As a consequence, we can visualize many changes in culture, life style of the Indians during the past thirteen years.

Indians are very rich and traditional with reference to cultural heritage and habitual matters. Indians are very much believers of religious activities and ceremonies. Their epics like *Purana* and *Kapiya* insisted them very much. The rituals leads to make them a good life. All other religions, which had birthplace of India, like Buddhism, Jainism, Hinduism, Sikhism.

Koichiro Matsuura, Director-General of UNESCO said, "Every culture springs from an intermingling encounters and clashes. In contrast, it is isolation that kills civilizations."

In fact, every culture is the corollary of multiple factors, the result of influences through expansion and exchange. And although some cultures were able, at some time in history, to spread their influence extensively throughout the world, let us remember that they drew their force from the links that they forged with other cultures and were thus enriched, transformed and shaped.

Indian Household—Income, Expenditure Habits

Number of people added to India's population between 1991 and 2001, is 181 millions, change in the absolute number of people below poverty line of $1 a day in India since 1990 was +40 millions. Changes that a household in Delhi is a super rich household have the following. One, which owns colour TV, refrigerator, washing machine, and car and has an average monthly income of more than Rs. 32,000. One in two persons is a super rich household—one that owns, colour TV, refrigerator, washing machine, car and has an average monthly income of more than Rs. 32,000. One in five person's proportion of India's super rich households concentrated in Mumbai, Delhi, Ahmedabad, Bangalore, Chennai and Pune (Humanscape.com).

How a consumer demand a product or service. The consumer used to take buying decisions based on his habit or desire. In other words, consumers used to buy goods and services based on their habit or desire. The consumers are accustomed to do their purchase.

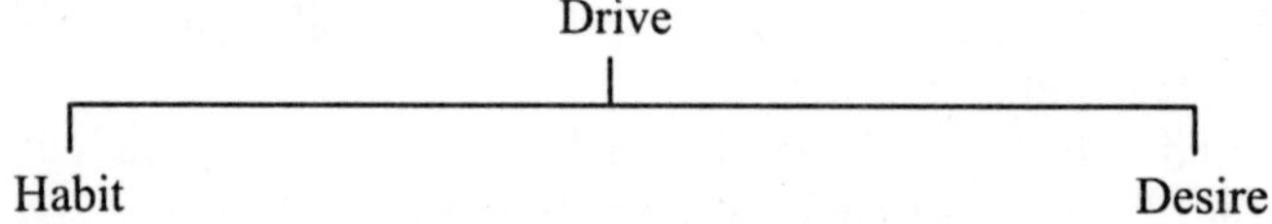

Under monopolistic competitive market situation we have many large number of big firms and they are willing to spend more money on selling cost for their identification and unique selling propositions (USPS). Usually, consumers are habitual buyers. Though there are many goods which are flooded in the market, the consumers recognise their loyal brand by their habitual behaviour. These habits are based on social and cultural values. The following cases will illustrate how people are traditional to cultural base.

For cleaning the teeth, people are traditionally used herbals like neem stick, baniyan stick, ash, and powder. For breakfast people used to take idli, dhosai. People used to drink milk, curdwater, tea, and coffee. People used to wash their floors with cow dung. People used to take rest and sleep by using mat made up of Korai. But, these habits have been changed. What people believed and have traditional and habitual values have been changed? People are now desire drive. Consumers are very informed about certain products through advertising. As a consequence, habit drive consumer is now under the preview of desire drive consumers, now-a-days, consumers are aware about time. They are much time conscious. Then, it is prestige for the consumer to use a product. Time and prestige leads to conspicuous consumption. Globalization changes all habits to desires. There is a deviation from nature to artificial.

For cleaning the teeth nylon brushes and chemical toothpastes are flooded in the market. People like to consume bread and omelette, instant cooks, pizza with coke or Pepsi as their breakfast. Different types of tiles and marbles have been used for flooring purpose in houses. People are civilized to sleep only on mattress. Thus, natural habitual consumption has been changed into artificial desire consumption. Even today the mineral water (Where there is no mineral added) is banned by the government in the recent days.

Packaged/Mineral Water

A study conducted by the Centre for Science and Environment (CSE) says that most of the brands of packaged / mineral water available in India contain pesticides. Several of them banned due to the pesticide content which is significantly higher than permissible limits. This can cause serious physical impairment ranging from damage to the central nervous system to lung cancer. The study reveals that the packaged water brands in Delhi have 36.4 times higher total pesticide content than the permissible limits; Mumbai brands have 7.2 times the standard content. Evianbrand, which is imported from France and not bottled in India, is the only brand in which no traces of pesticides were found.

The European Economic Commission directs that the maximum residue limit for total pesticides is 0.0005 mg per litre and 0.0001mg per litre for a single pesticide. The pesticides, which were tested for, include organochlorines, Organophosphorus, Chlorpyrifos, Malathion and DDT. The CSE lists contain the country's leading packaged / mineral water brands but most of them are MNCs. The CSE list contains the country's leading packaged/mineral water brands. Ramesh Chahan's Bisleri, the market leader, ranks 15th amongst 17 water brands studied in Delhi with the total pesticide content being 79 times more than the prescribed limits and seventh amongst 13 brands studied in Mumbai. Coca-Cola's Kinley has been ranked 8th in Delhi with 14.6 times more than the prescribed limits of pesticides, while it is on the 15th spot in the Mumbai list (Business Standard, 2003).

Thus, globalization changes the habit of the consumers. The consequences are at the cost of common man's innocent health. Globalization is required to start capital-intensive industries with their capital and advanced technology. But MNCs involved in consumer durable goods like cool drinks, chips, packaged water and so on. The local indegenous entrepreneurs with the local resources can do these. A multigiant need not try to compute with tiny units.

Canadian Household—Income and Expenditure

Consumption expenditures per household have trended upwards but have done so in a highly cyclical fashion. Consumer spending is very sensitive to the business cycle and the business cycle is not dead. The recessions of the early 1980s and early 1990s both caused average household expenditures to drop by similar percentages of just over 9 per cent.

Table 19.1: Distribution and Trend of Expenditures by Income Group

(*Percentage*)

Particulars	*Poorest 20% of Households**			*Richest 20% of households**		
	1969	*1996*	*Charge***	*1969*	*1996*	*Charge***
Food	27.2	18.5	-8.7	14.8	9.6	-5.2
Shelter	23.3	31.8	8.5	12.8	13.2	0.4
Household Operation	5.1	6.6	1.5	3.8	4.0	0.2
Furniture and equipment	3.9	2.5	-1.4	4.8	2.6	-2.2
Clothing	6.9	4.0	-2.9	8.3	4.4	-3.9
Transportation	9.5	10.6	1.1	13.1	11.6	-1.5
Medical & Health care	5.3	2.9	-2.4	2.7	1.6	-1.1
Personal care	2.3	2.3	0.0	1.9	1.4	-0.5
Recreation	2.4	4.5	2.1	3.9	5.5	1.6
Reading & Education	1.5	1.9	0.4	1.6	1.7	0.1
Tobacco & Alcohol	4.0	3.6	-0.4	3.3	1.7	-1.6
Miscellaneous	1.7	2.8	1.1	1.4	2.8	-1.4
Total current consumption	93.3	91.9	-1.4	72.4	60.2	-12.2
Personal Taxes	2.1	2.8	0.7	19.6	30.4	10.8
Security	1.3	1.6	0.3	5.2	5.9	0.7
Gifts & contributions	3.3	3.7	0.4	2.8	3.4	0.6
Total expenditures	100.0	100.0		100.0	100.0	

* Households include both families and unattached individuals.

** Change in percentage points.

Source: People Patterns Consulting based on Statistics Canada, Family Expenditure in Canada.

Expenditures per household averaged just above $ 34,000 in the late 1960s and then jumped quickly to reach $ 40,000 by 1979. The recession of the early 1980s caused expenditures to dip by 9.5 per cent. The subsequent recovery helped establish a new peak of $ 41,600 by 1989. Again, the early 1990s recession caused a dip of 9 per cent. By 1997, average expenditures per household were still 3.5 per cent below the 1989 peak and only 0.5 per cent above the 1979 peak. The swings in average expenditures have been more volatile than the swings in average family incomes.

Savings Habit—Indian Situation

Indians are very much strong and staunch believers in savings. Indian middle class income people are the much targetted for globalization. The multinational companies are aimed at the Indian middle class income people. The young yuppies and Double income but no kid (DINK) group is also another target for multinationals to open their market and catch these targetted people for developing their market share. The English and American culture regarding savings are quite different from our Indian culture. The English and American work hard for the entire weak and spend their whole income during the weak end. They never save for themselves and for their legal heirs. They used to spend lavishly.

But Indians are very sentiments and have more attachment to their forefathers as well to their young generations. These strong sentiments and attachments have been perturbed and disturbed due to globalization. There is distress in savings habits. Indians are afraid of debt. But, now the culture due to globalization has been changed. Conspicuous consumption rules the people. Now-a-days, debt culture emerges. So, traditional Indians, a society of savers, now going to succumb to that maddening American syndrome where people go to counsellor for "debt-therapy" and join "Borrowers Anonymous" to discuss how they can blame their shopaholicism on pre-natal influences? A recent survey by JD Power Asia Pacific 2002, India Consumer Financing Satisfaction Study revealed that 82 per cent of car buyers finance their purchases, a jump from 74 per cent two years ago. The average age of the borrower has also fallen, heralding the entry of a brash new buyer who has a greater appetite for risk. City bank recently launched a teen credit card. According to Bank sources, roughly 43 per cent of the total urban population has taken loans in one form or the other, and 22 per cent of the population would like to. Only a third of the population is not interested in borrowing at all.

India has nearly six million credit card holders with an annual card spend of Rs. 8,100 crore. A large chunk of this amount is spent on leisure and entertainment, pubbing, clubbing and jelling out. Holidays on instalment and personal loans for vacation have become common (*Sunday Times*, 2002).

Thus, traditional culture has been destroyed by globalization. With the aim of conspicuous consumption savings for future doctrine has been totally vanished. The Government has gone to one more step to add fuel to the fire for lavish spending. The Government appointed Kelkar committee for personal taxation. The Kelkar's final report suggested to cancel standard deduction, tax rebate under section 88 and deduction under section 80L of the Income Tax Act 1961. If the Government implements the above, then the habit of savings may be discouraged. As a consequence, totally traditional savings habits are discouraged and royal spendings are quite encouraged. This again led to conspicuous consumption.

Savings Habit—Canadian Situation

The changing distribution of incomes, expenditure, savings and debt remains a significant issue. The distribution question goes far beyond a simple comparison of the rich and the poor but also addresses age

Table 19.2: "Household Specific Savings Rate"* as Percentage of Disposable Income

Particulars	*1969*	*1978*	*1982*	*1986*	*1992*	*1996*
All households	2.0	7.5	10.0	5.1	4.5	8.8
2 adults, no children	5.7	10.7	13.8	7.8	7.0	11.3
All tenants	0.0	Na	4.3	-0.5	-1.1	1.4
Owners without mortgage	3.2	Na	16.9	12.4	10.1	12.0
Owners with mortgage	3.7	Na	7.9	3.2	3.3	8.9
Poorest 20% of households	-20.6	-8.6	-5.2	-8.7	-15.8	-13.1
Richest 20% of households	10.1	13.0	17.8	14.0	14.0	18.4
All families of 2 or more	2.3	7.6	10.2	5.4	4.9	9.3
2 adults, 2 children**	0.6	4.1	8.5	5.1	4.9	9.7
Female lone-parent	Na	Na	Na	-4.0	-5.6	1.3

* Net changes during the survey year in the value of transacted assets and liabilities.

** Average of 1.8 in 1996.

Source: People Patterns Consulting based on Statistics Canada, Family Expenditure in Canada.

differences and different types of families. The long-tern trends suggest that the rich (the top 40%) have indeed been getting a slightly bigger piece of the pie relative to all the groups below them on the income scale. The longer-term trends also suggest that young families have been losing out. Single-earner families and single-parent families have lost the most ground in the 1990s.

Conclusion

The term globalization is universally accepted as an integration of various nations of the world at the economic level. It tries to change the roots of culture. The habitual drives are influenced by desire drives. In India the middle class income people are the main target. Their cultural savings habits are slowly vanished. The new middle-class *mantra*: *Dil Chahta hai*. Instantly, buy now pay later.

In Canada the changing distribution of incomes, expenditure, savings and debt remains a significant issue. The distribution question goes far beyond a simple comparison of the rich and the poor but also addresses age differences and different types of families. The long-term trends suggest that the rich (the top 40%) have indeed been getting a slightly bigger piece of the pie relative to all the groups below them on the income scale. The longer-term trends also suggest that young families have been losing out. Single-earner families and single-parent families have lost the most ground in the 1990s.

Heaven is defined as an American salary, a Chinese cook, an English house, and a Japanese wife. Similarly, a hell is defined as a Chinese salary, an English cook, a Japanese house and an American wife. Thus, for heaven, the continents such as America, Europe and Asia are combined and their special features are amalgamated. On the other hand, for hell, the same continents but their limitations are absorbed.

To recall the words of our Father of the Nation, Mahatma Gandhi in this regard is worth. So, we want the cultures of all lands to be blown about our country as freely as possible. But we refusing to be blown off for feet by any.

REFERENCES

Asia Development Outlook 2001, Oxford University Press, New York, 2001.

Business Standard, February 5th, 2003.

Humanscape.com.

James F. Engel, Rozer D. Black Well, Paul W. Miniard, *Consumer Behaviour*, CBS College Publishing, The Dryden Press, Japan, 1986.

Michael R. Czinkota, Iikka A. Ronkainen, Michael H. Moffett, E uzeneo Moynihan, *Global Business*, 3rd Edition, Harcourt Collete Publishers, USA, 2001, p. 28.

Sunday Times of India, December 1st, 2002.

Teacher of the World—2(4)2002.

20

Globalization and Advertising:

A Comparative Study of Television Advertising and their Effect on Children in India, United States, Japan and China

NEERU KAPOOR

'The end of geography', 'The borderless world', these are two of the more provocative phrases used to describe the process of globalization which underpins the world economy. John F. Kennedy once said, 'Our most basic common link is that we all inhabit this planet. We all breathe the same air. We all cherish our children's future. And we are all mortal', what was true thirty years ago is even more so today. Put another way, as it is in a West African proverb, 'Rain does not fall on one roof alone'. What happens to our neighbours is increasingly of direct relevance to us, and these days what we might call our 'virtual' neighbours may be half a world away. It has been suggested that we are entering an age where political or security schisms are no longer definable in geographic terms but rather are international phenomena based on increased discord between societies and civilizations. At worst, this could lead not to a global village but rather to a number of global villages each shallowly interconnected but deeply separated by resurgent nationalism and cultural and economic chauvinism. But at best the trend is towards integration and the convergence of government policies for mutual benefit. Increased communication technologies, travel and contact present new opportunities for many seeking emancipation or positive change. A first core aspect of globalization is the transformation of global economic activity.

Technological change and government deregulation have permitted the establishment of transnational networks in production and marketing of goods and services. The new 'production' network describes firms and multinational enterprises (MNEs), who use advanced means of communication, and new flexible techniques of production so as to spread their activities across the globe. The global advertising is used to communicate and influence buying behaviour among existing and potential customers all over the world. The ability to transfer a successful campaign world-wide is a critical advantage to a global company.

The potential for effective global advertising is increasing as new concepts such as product cultures are emerging. Today, bounding is based on global geography—youth culture, for example—rather than ethnic or national culture. As an example, clothing products can be targetted to males 18 to 25 years old, throughout the world to a worldwide segment. William Roedy, director of MTV Europe, sees clear implications of such product culture for advertising. 'Eighteen-year-olds in Paris have more in common with eighteen-year-olds in New York than with their own parents. They buy the same products, go to the same movies, listen to the same music, sip the same colas. Global advertising merely works on that premise', he says. Human wants and desires are very similar if presented within recognizable experience situations—people everywhere get hungry, want value, quality, the latest technology made available and affordable, wants to be loved and respected.

The Global Children's Market

The global children's market holds tremendous potential. Even though American children constitute only a small fraction of the global market, according to Competitive Media Reporting, U.S. advertisers spent $ 894 million on children's television in 1996, an increase of 11 per cent over the 1995 expenditure (Crowe 1997). Children five to fourteen years of age in Japan, South Korea, and the People's Republic of China alone represent a total market of 223,327,000 people (McNeal 1992). By the year 2001, 21.6 per cent of the total Indian population was in the age group of 4 to 14 years. The reason why this segment has become so powerful is that children market is growing immensely in size. Further, many Asians purchase high-priced clothing and toys for their children. Japanese families spend more than 3.1 billion U.S. dollars a year on children's shoes and clothing (Abdoolcarim 1994). Chinese children's overall index of influence on family spending on 25 items is around 68 per cent (McNeal and Yeh 1997). Overall, the global children's market holds tremendous potential, and marketers all over the world have attempted to influence the consumer socialisation of the children by advertising heavily on television.

Previous international research has examined parental responses to purchase request (Ward *et al.* 1986) and advertising induced family conflict in the United States, Britain and Japan (Robertson *et al.* 1989). However, research has not related family communication patterns to attitudes toward television advertising in general or examined advertising-related parental practices in a cross-cultural context. Extending family communication research to a cross-cultural setting should increase our understanding of family processes in other nations. Family communication patterns are a potentially valuable tool for segmenting families across international borders and assessing the degree of parental concern about and mediation of children's advertising exposure. Our study examined family communication patterns and general attitude toward television advertising among parents of children three to fourteen years of age in India. The perceptions of Indian parents were compared with the parental beliefs in United States, Japan and China on this issue. Our study concentrated on television advertising because it is the most prevalent and controversial form of children's advertising (McNeal 1992). We first discuss general attitude toward television advertising. Then, as theoretic background, we discuss the concept of children's consumer socialisation and parent-child interaction. After discussing our study methods, we report our results. A review of the studies conducted in the United States, Japan and China on the issue is made and their findings are compared with our results. Finally, we consider the implications of our findings.

Attitude toward Television Advertising

Attitude toward television advertising has been studied primarily in the United States. Numerous studies have shown an economic and a social dimension of attitude toward advertising in general. The social dimension includes the detrimental or social consequences of television advertising. Typical criticisms are that television advertising makes false and misleading claims, promotes undesirable values, including materialism, and exploits vulnerable and disadvantaged groups. All of those claims are practically relevant to advertising directed to children. They are an important, but controversial target for advertising.

"Advertisers are taking advantage of their childishness", says Lars Maren, senior advisor to the Swedish Culture Ministry. In India, children are considered vulnerable and susceptible to the influence of television advertising since parents' believe that they do not have the skills and experience required to process advertising messages in the context of their reality and needs. This gives advertisers an unfair advantage in persuading children to buy various products.

The economic dimension, in contrast, includes favourable beliefs about television advertising, such as, beliefs that advertising provides information or raises the standard of living (Andrews 1989). Apart from providing useful product information, it provides a child the opportunity to evaluate the attributes of different product offerings and teaches him/her the effective buying skills. Generally, Americans hold a somewhat negative overall attitude toward television advertising (Pollay and Mittal 1993). Senator Hillary Clinton wanted to introduce a bill empowering America's Federal Trade Commission to stop unfair marketing to children, especially to under-fives. In Europe, legislation to curb marketing to children is spreading.

Thus the effects of television advertising on children, is a matter of controversy and debate at both national and international levels. As the critics as well as the advertisers have differing view-points, an attempt has been made in the study to identify the harmful as well as the beneficial effects of TV ads on children. The intent is to help marketers exploit their potential and prevent the possible damage they can do the growth and development of children's healthy consumer learning by evolving appropriate advertising strategies. Moreover, despite the attention this topic has received to date, much needs to be learnt about the development of children's consumer socialisation in the period from early childhood to early adolescence. Thus an attempt has been made to establish the role of TV ads in children's consumer socialisation and how the parent-child interaction helps to strengthen this process.

Children's Consumer Socialisation

Children's consumer socialisation, according to Scotward, *et al.*, refers to the "process by which young people acquire skills, knowledge and attitudes relevant to their functioning as consumers in the marketplace". It is based upon three components—background factors, socialisation agents and the learning mechanism. The background factors include the socio-economic status, social class and religious background of the family, the stage of cognitive development of the child and the sex of the child. The socialisation agents are those individuals who are directly involved with the child and have influence on them because of their frequency of contact and importance. These agents include the parents, siblings, peers, teachers, the media and media personalities such as sports stars and famous television or movie stars. The learning mechanism emphasises on modelling and reinforcement, which implies that certain aspects of consumption behaviour are transmitted from the parents to the child and those aspects that are learnt early in life tend to persist into adulthood.

The study attempts to investigate the impact of the background factors, socialisation agents, childhood consumption experiences and training on children's buying response. Even though there are various socialisation agents, the study focuses on the influence of television advertising and of parents and other family members. The background factors include the cognitive development of the child, sex of the child, and the family income. The process is depicted in Figure 19.1.

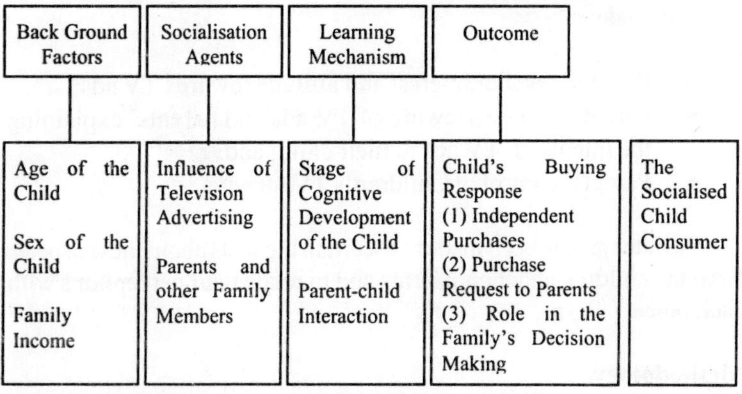

Figure 19.1: Child's Consumer Socialisation Process

Parent-Child Interaction and Influence of Television Advertising

Television advertising has an impact on parent-child interaction. The impact can be positive as well as negative. Action for Children's Television (of the USA) summarized the negative concerns, thus: "In the case of children's advertising, the purpose is to use the child as a surrogate salesman to pressure the parents into buying the product. This is unfair to the child and to the parent, and can be damaging to the parent-child relationship". Some members of the marketing community, however, hold a contrary view, claiming that advertising can result in a positive interaction between the parents and the child teaching the latter intelligent habits of purchase and consumption. They can teach them price and quality relationship, including experiences with the use of money and ways to shop for quality products. They can even influence the child's brand preference and help to distinguish fact from exaggeration in TV ads. Banks suggested that the exchange between the parents and child "may actually facilitate the child's ability to cope with the realities of independent living".

But whether children learn positive or negative consumer values from TV ads depends, to a large extent, on the amount and the nature of the parental communication. Generally, parents expect the child to learn consumer skills through imitation, but the present study seeks to ascertain the amount of the parent-child interaction, taking place in various households with regard to the influence of TV ads on the children. For this purpose, a number of variables were considered. These include:

- Parents' level of interest and attitude towards TV ads;
- Parent-child co-viewing of TV ads and parents' explaining the intents of TV ads to their child; and
- Parents' control of Children's TV viewing.

An attempt has been made to ascertain the facts about these aspects from the children and their parents and to relate their perceptions with each other.

Methodology

The data for the study were collected mainly from primary sources. Two non-disguised, structured questionnaires were designed, one for the child and the other for his/her parents. A survey was conducted in the National Capital Territory (NCT) of Delhi and a sample of 500 children was drawn. The multi-stage sampling technique was used in selecting the respondents from the five different zones of the NCT of Delhi. The presence of a television set at home was one of the pre-conditions for the selection of a respondent.

Child-Respondents

The child-respondents were selected keeping in view their age and sex. 98 (19.6 per cent) respondents belonged to the 3 to 6 years age group, 207 (41.4 per cent) to the 6 to 12 years age group and 195 (39.0 per cent) to the 12 to 14 years age group. The sample of 500 children consisted of 243 (48.6 per cent) males and 257 (51.4 per cent) females.

Parent-Respondents

A sample of 500 parents were interviewed for the study and their responses gathered.

Data Analysis

After collecting the responses from 500 children and their parents, an attempt was made to gather information about the various aspects by relating the children's perception about the influence of TV ads to that of the parents. The chi-square analysis was conducted between various sets of variables, in order to determine whether or not those variables were related. Pearson's correlation coefficient was used to identify the degree of association between various sets of responses in order to ascertain whether they were positively or negatively related to each other.

Findings of the Study

The results of the study revealed that television advertising has emerged as a powerful medium for teaching children skills, knowledge and attitudes relevant to their buying response in India. TV ads offer advertisers an opportunity to extend their influence and set visual standards, which the child imbibes and imitates. In India, families are going distinctively 'nuclear', smaller in size and highly interactive with their children. Children are granted 'franchise rights' in buying decisions in their families earlier than ever before. They not only buy products for their own use, but also considerably influence the purchase behaviour of their parents.

Children's Cognitive Development and Consumer Socialisation

In conformity with the Piget's work, stages of cognitive development were found to play an important role in children's consumer socialisation. The study has revealed that children of all age groups, of both sexes, and from all income-groups, were regular TV-viewers. Young children (under eight years of age) were found more attracted towards TV ads. With increase in their age, children's interest in TV ads, however, declined. The study further revealed that the amount of interest the parents evinced in TV ads was found to contribute significantly towards the interest children took in such ads. Parents who were interested in TV ads helped in building their children's interest in a positive manner.

Children's Perception of TV Ads

Children were found to evaluate TV ads on two main criteria: First, did the TV ad entertain second, did it provide the product information needed for making the purchase decision. A dramatic shift has been noticed in children's perception of TV ads, as they moved from early childhood to early adolescence. For most children under the age of eight, the entertainment aspect of TV ad was most important. Music, jingles and the attractiveness of the models used in TV ads had great influence on them. However, children above the age of eight were quick to identify the informative and persuasive role of TV ads. They got impressed by ads, which were comparative in nature, gave needed product information and whose photography was good.

Children's overall affective response, their trust and believability in TV ads declined with the age. They were able to detect specific instances of deception and misrepresentation in such ads. It was also found that children became better-informed consumers with age, using information gathered from TV ads to evaluate the product offerings.

Children's Buying Response

The study has revealed that children above 12 years of age enjoyed purchasing power and purchase independence, while the majority of the young children did not enjoy much of it. Children's buying response got reflected in their making purchase request to their parents for the products meant for them as well as for the family.

Children's Purchase Request Influenced by TV Ads

Both the parents and the children felt the impact of TV ads on children's purchase request to some extent. With the increase in the age of the child, parents' perception of children's purchase request being influenced by TV ads was found to decrease. The sex of the child and the family income did not play any significant role in influencing children's purchase request.

It has also been noticed that the number of hours children watched TV, their interest in TV ads, the attractiveness of the model used in the ad and the comparative features of the ads contribute significantly towards children's purchase request.

Role of Children in Family's Purchase Decision

Even though children's role as buyer has not emerged as very effective but their role as decider, influencer and information-gatherer for household durables and automobiles, which were high-priced and high-involvement products, was appreciated by the majority of the parents. Thus the children's role in the family's purchase decision has significantly increased.

Children's Sex as a Determinant of Family's Purchase Decision

Children from both the sexes were found to be playing an important role in the family's purchase decision. However, the girls were found to be more interested in personal products, consumables and toiletries while boys preferred playing role in case of the household durables and automobiles. One of the significant findings of the study is that in the traditional male-child-dominated families, an increased importance is given to the female child. Their role has been felt equally important to that of the boy, specially, among the educated middle-income families. It is a healthy movement towards the children's consumer-orientation. Thus, from the marketer's point-of-view, the role of child's sex cannot be ignored.

Parent-Child Interaction as a Determinant of Children's Buying Response

Although television advertising may have initially stimulated interest in a particular item, the parent-child interaction was found to have played a significant role in influencing children's buying response. Parents who resorted to more of co-viewing, explaining and teaching children about TV ads could help them to regulate their buying response within the family's norms. It was also noticed that children from families characterized by a high level of parent-child interaction had more knowledge about consumer-related matters. They were better able to filter puffery in TV ads, were better informed about products and their characteristics and knew how to manage within the family budget. These children showed a higher regard for their parents' opinion.

Parent-Child Interaction and Influence of Audio-Visual Techniques

How far the various audio-visual techniques in TV ads played a role in influencing children's purchase request depended to a large extent on the parents' co-viewing and teaching. Children, whose parents resorted to more of explaining what was real and what was artificially created in TV ads, looked for substance in such ads. They got influenced by ads, which provided them with product information and helped them in knowing the distinguishing features of the various products. For them music and jingle did not play an important role. They were more interested in the cognitive aspects of TV ads and learning from them. Their buying response was more influenced by the product information from such ads.

Low Level of Parent-Child Interaction

One of the findings of the study, which is rather disappointing is that the number of parents resorting to co-viewing and explaining children as to what was real and what was artificially created in TV ads was dismally small. Whatever little restraint, was exercised by the parents, was in the form of restricting the number of hours children watched TV. Very few parents regulated the TV programme to be seen by the child. A small amount of co-viewing and children's consumer education was found to have taken place among the lower and upper middle income-group parents with higher level of education and holding high degree of interest in TV ads. They were more likely to restrict their children's TV-viewing to ensure that they were exposed only to quality TV programmes. Those parents did not criticize the TV ads but spent time with their children teaching them the positive as well as the negative attributes of such ads and to extract useful information out of them.

Parents' Perception of Influence of TV Ads on Children

An overwhelming majority of the parents felt that TV ads had a positive influence on their child as they provided him with necessary product information. Most of them admitted that advertising was a useful informative tool and an essential stimulus in educating a child about the standards for product evaluation. Apart from teaching basic purchase consideration, involving comparison of quality and value for money, advertising was also seen to provide an opportunity for establishing within the privacy of the home, certain restrictions with respect to the family's economic situation. It was also considered important for defining the acceptability of different product categories, from the parents' viewpoint. Perhaps more important was the whole-hearted endorsement by parents of the instructive potential of TV ads. Parents stressed the importance of continued utilization of advertising time to educate child about health, hygiene and safety matters.

A few parents appeared to be concerned and to have some complaints about TV ads. But for most of them, this concern was not so intense as to favour banning ads altogether rather they were of the opinion that ads should be restricted. There should be a strict regulatory framework to curb the misrepresentation and manipulation of facts in them. An effort has also been made to review the research conducted by the researchers abroad on the related issues.

Television Advertising and Children's Consumer Socialisation in the United States, Japan and China

Efforts have been made by the researchers in the United States, Japan and China to measure the extent of the children's consumer socialisation being effected by television advertising and the role of parent-child interaction in that process.

A study by Reid (1979), titled "The Impact of Family Group Interaction on Children's Understanding of Television Advertising," investigated the influence of the family on the ability of children to comprehend the advertising directed towards them. Reid observed nine families, over a three-month period, and each family was given a high, moderate or low ranking based on its consumer teaching orientation. The results indicated that even the pre-school children had the potential to understand TV advertising and were affected by the consumer teaching orientation of the family.

Moschis (1985), in the study, titled "The Role of Family Communication in Consumer Socialisation of Children and Adolescents," provided an example of how family communication pattern affected children's and adolescents' preferences for several sources of information, including, parents, peers and the mass media. Four types of family communication patterns were studied. These included *laissez faire*, protective, pluralistic and consensual families. *Laissez faire* families were characterised by little parent-child communication, while protective families stressed obedience and social harmony, with little consideration given to developing the child's own opinions. Pluralistic families encouraged the child to develop new ideas and promoted open communication without insisting on obedience to authority while consensual families combined the idea of children developing their own views with the need for social harmony and family cohesiveness.

Moschis found that children and adolescents from pluralistic families preferred information from a variety of sources, with a higher preference for parents' advice rather than children from other families. In contrast, adolescents from protective families were highly receptive to peers and, to a lesser extent, television advertising. *Laissez faire* children, too, relied less on parents' advice, but were more likely to rely on peers implicating the use of fewer information sources.

In a similar study entitled, "Mothers' Communication Orientation and Consumer-Socialisation Tendencies," by Carlson, Grossbart and Ann Walsh (1990), examined the maternal view of parent-child communications with younger children (grades K-6). The theory suggested that *laissez faire* mothers might have yielded to requests, but they were not proactive consumer-socialisation agents, as evidenced by their lower scores on co-viewing, co-shopping and considering children's opinions in buying decisions. In contrast, protective mothers seem to emphasise their own, not children's views of marketing/media influences on children's consumption choices and their role in determining children's consumption experiences. The theory further indicated that pluralistic mothers did more to encourage children's exploration and understanding of the marketplace and development as consumers. This was reflected by more consumer goals, co-viewing, discussion of ads and responsiveness to requests. Finally, according to family-communication theory, consensual mothers like pluralistics, emphasised on children's learning about marketing/media experiences with children and allowed them to exercise considerable independence as consumers. Thus, the results indicated that differences in socialisation behaviour were related to mothers' communication orientation.

Using consumer socialisation as a theoretical foundation, Rose, Bush and Kahle (1998), in their study, titled "The influence of Family Communication Patterns on Parental Reactions toward Advertising: A Cross-National Examination," examined family communication patterns and general attitudes towards television advertising among mothers of children three to eight years of age, in the United States and Japan. A four-category typology, based on concept and socio-orientation, was used to classify mothers of both nationalities. *Laissez faire* (low socio, low concept-orientation) mothers had the most positive attitude towards and the lowest mediation of their children's exposure to television advertising. Pluralistic (low socio, high concept-orientation) and concensual (high on both dimensions) mothers had the highest mediation and most negative attitude towards advertising. The responses of protective mothers (high socio, low concept-orientation) were between these extremes. Overall, American mothers were distributed relatively equally across categories, whereas Japanese mothers were classified primarily as either *laissez faire* or protective.

In another study, titled "Chinese Children as Consumers: An Analysis of their New Product Information Sources," Santa Barbara (1999) sought to determine where from Chinese children as consumers learn information about new products and their attitudes toward different sources of information. Barbara found that Chinese children utilized a wide variety of information sources to learn about new products, including parents, retail outlets and the mass media, and that they considered the television, to be the most important of all media. The effect of gender, age and family occupation was also considered.

Her findings were in conformity with those of James U. McNeal and Mindy F. Ji (1996), in their study, titled, "Children's Influence on Chinese Families Now found Leisure Time and its Marketing Implications". Where the latter had observed that children had "pester power" and influenced their parents' purchases of products and services. They also observed that rather than replacing the significance of family as an information source, television supplemented that relationship by providing a wider base of information.

A Composite View of the Influence of Television Advertising on Children's Consumer Socialisation

The results of the study revealed that the United States and Japan traditionally have led the world in television viewing and advertising expenditures. The Japanese spend more time watching TV than any other Asian people, approximately 2.5 hours a day (Lin 1993). In the United States, however, children 2 to 11 years of age watch an average of 2.7 hours of television a day (Nielson Media Research 1997). Children's advertising is strictly controlled in the United States through a series of government regulations and voluntary restrictions. Federal limitations limit advertising on children's programming to 10.5 minutes an hour on weekends and 12 minutes an hour on weekdays (Belch and Belch 1998). Advertising to children is pre-approved by the networks and monitored by the Children's Advertising Review Unit of the Better Business Bureau. Together those organizations provide a comprehensive set of restrictive and self-regulatory guidelines for the types of appeals, product claims and techniques that companies can use when advertising to children (Belch and Belch 1998).

Children's advertising in Japan is generally less regulated than that in the United States. Though the Japanese government officially allows only 6 commercial minutes per length program (Rowley 1996), broadcasters have circumvented the restriction by airing shorter programmes (Romaprasad and Hasgowa 1990). No special restrictions are imposed on the number of advertisements during children's peak viewing times, broadcasters do not pre-clear advertising directed to children, and Japan has no equivalent to the detailed self-regulatory guidelines of the CARU of the Better Business Bureau (Ward, Wackman, and Wartella 1987).

There are no strict controls regarding children's advertising in India. There are no specific time limits regulating advertising on children's programming as are there in United States and Japan. However, in order to develop and promote healthy advertising practices in Doordarshan and other TV channels, Code for Commercial Advertising, Doordarshan and TV Advertising Standards Council of India is there. It provides a comprehensive and exhaustive list of the standards of conduct. Responsibility for the observance of the rules rests equally upon the advertiser and the advertising agency. Even though, code of professional ethics and self-regulation in television advertising have been devised, the various provisions of both these regulatory bodies are either being completely ignored or being loosely interpreted as to leave the door wide open for any manner of promotion or any kind of product.

Family Communication and Attitude toward Advertising

Children's consumer socialisation is considered very important in USA where children are routinely introduced to consumption process before they can talk or walk (McNeal and Yeh 1993). It has been shown for years in research among US children that the family is probably most instrumental in teaching young people basic rational aspects of consumption such as satisfying basic consumer needs in the marketplace (Riesman *et al.*, 1956), understanding price-quality relationships (Moore and Stephens, 1975), and shopping for differing qualities among products (Ward *et al.*, 1977). Evidence suggests that family communication processes modify the effects of other socialisation agents, in particular television (McLeod *et al.*, 1982).

Carlson and Grossbart 1988, in their research suggested that parents who are anxiously, emotionally involved in child-rearing 'tend to be most concerned about other socialisation agents' and have the most negative attitudes toward advertising. Parents who are preoccupied with their children's maturation and development tend to be the most distrustful of institutions, such as the mass media, that may interfere with their efforts to actively shape their children's consumer experiences.

International research has found that Japanese children watch less television, display less independence, and exhibit lower levels of verbal communication than their American counterparts. American mothers, as a group, emphasize independence and individualism more than Japanese mothers, who emphasize interpersonal harmony and group goals. Parents' in the United States emphasize open idea-oriented communication, promote autonomy, advocate individual achievement, and begin consumer training when children are very young. Japanese parents believe that children mature slowly. They indulge and tolerate young children, and emphasize manners, consideration for others and respect for authority. They protect their children from outside influences.

Overall, the American mothers hold negative attitudes toward television advertising and exhibit family communication patterns that are particularly likely to convey negative attitudes toward advertising. Hence, American families may transmit a sense of skepticism toward advertising whereas Japanese children may not have the same degree of skepticism instilled into their emerging cognitive construction of advertising. Japanese mothers, in contrast, appeared to have a more optimistic view of advertising and place fewer controls over their children's viewing habits.

While analysis of consumer socialisation of children has received much attention in the USA and in other Western nations, scant attention has been paid to it in the nation with the world's largest population—China. McNeal and Yeh (1997) examined Chinese children's income, spending, saving and their influence on their parents' spending. As only children, Chinese children act like "little emperors/empresses" exerting great influence on the spending of their families as well as spending a substantial amount of their money on their own needs and wants. The authors found that although, Chinese parents are viewed by their children as much less important than television as a new product information source, they do provide a major role in assisting their children to grow as consumers by providing them information about certain new products. Two models of the two-step flow of communication were found to exist in Chinese families: (1) media to children and children to parents'; and (2) media to parents' and parents' to children. Hence, domestic and international marketers who rely on these findings for strategic guidance should consider targetting the children of China as consumers.

Children's Growing Maturity and Parent-Child Interaction

In response to the controversy prevailing with regard to the influence of television advertising on young children all over the world, the study has revealed that Indian children are not as easy a target, as advertisers and critics believe. They are able to analyse TV ads and develop a realistic approach towards them. It has been further noticed that children as young as six years, could understand the purpose of TV ads and distinguish them from TV programmes. Armed with the knowledge about the advertiser's persuasive intent and skepticism about the truthfulness of advertising claims, children above the age of eight years were found to have the ability to respond to TV ads in a mature and informed manner. Although the children were found to play an important role in the family's purchase decision and made frequent purchase request to their parents they were not solely guided by TV ads. A substantial number of the elder children reported product attributes as one of the basic reasons for their purchase. Thus, an important fact to be considered is that today's children have grown up with television and have learnt to cope up with this medium to some extent.

Finally, in conformity with the findings of the studies conducted by the researchers in the United States, Japan and China, the results of the present study also show that the TV ads contribute significantly towards the Indian children's consumer socialisation. Majority of the Indian parents accept and appreciate the TV ads that teach their children good consumer values. They admit that these ads contribute to a broader understanding of the market place and help in developing effective consumer skills among Indian children. However, it was also found that early parent-child interaction was a key element if parents did not want their child to be effected adversely by TV ads. Parents have a responsibility to teach their child about the realities of the commercial world, just as they teach him how to cross a road safely. They play a crucial role in determining what their child learns from TV ads as they supplement the information provided in them. The final lesson that a child extracts from the viewing of TV ads may be a joint product of what was shown on the screen and what was taught by the parents.

Implications of the Study

For advertising practitioners, our findings have several implications for examination of global markets. First, international advertising managers need to consider differences in the distribution of communication patterns across nations. Since it has already been observed that parents in different countries hold different attitudes about the influence of television adverting on children, hence family communication patterns are an important means of describing, characterizing and classifying parents' across nations. Second, information gained from examining family communication types could be used to segment markets internationally and formulate effective positioning strategies. For example, advertising managers and media planners could use such categorization to target international advertising campaigns. Perhaps television may not be the most efficient medium to reach children in the families where parents tend to emphasize vertical relationships, obedience, social harmony and limit their children's exposure to outside information such as television advertising. Third, the question of who should be the target of an advertisement—parents or the children—could be addressed by such categorization. Fourth, parent-child interaction could also predict the type of programmes children are allowed to view and the type of products they are allowed to use. But marketers are expected to resort to self-regulation. They should always take into account the level of knowledge, sophistication and maturity of the audience to which their messages are directed. Since young children have a limited capability for evaluating the credibility of what they watch, a special responsibility lies upon marketers to protect them from susceptibilities.

The study also has certain important implications for the parents and the policy-makers all over the world. First, family, as a social unit, needs to play a more important role in mediating the influence of TV ads on their children. Parents should critically evaluate what their child watches on TV, resort to more of co-viewing of TV ads and teaching children how to become discerning viewers, better able to protect themselves from the negative influences of TV ads. Second, television should be included in the school curriculum in a positive way. Teachers might explain children about TV ads and how to extract the relevant information from them. Third, parents and teachers should publicly voice their concern over what they consider harmful TV advertisements, especially during prime time or when children are the principal users of television. Fourth, since heavy TV-viewers were found to be highly influenced by TV ads, efforts should be made by the parents to encourage their children to take active part in educational and sports activities, so that their growing dependence on TV can be reduced resulting in their reduced exposure to TV ads. Fifth, the governments all over the world should articulate well-defined and comprehensive policies on television advertising and children.

REFERENCES

Action for Children's Television, *Testimony before the Federal Trade Commission*, November 1971.

Belch, Raymond A. and Stephen A. Greyser, "*Advertising and Promotion:An Integrated Marketing Communications Perspective*," 4th Ed., Boston, Irwin/McGraw Hill, 1998.

Bill Crowe, "Advertisers See Big Guys in Little Eyes," *Broadcasting and Cable*, July 28 1997, pp. 47.

Carlson, Lee and Sanford Grossbart, "Parental Styles and Consumer Socialisation of Children," *Journal of Consumer Research*, June 15, 1988, pp. 77-94.

George, P. Moschis, "The Role of Family Communication in Consumer Socialisation of Children and Adolescents," *Journal of Consumer Research*, Vol. 11, March 1985, pp. 893-913.

Gregory M. Rose, Victoria D. Bush and Lynn Kahle, "The Influence of Family Communication Patterns on Parental Reactions toward Advertising: A Cross-National Examination," *Journal of Advertising*, Vol. 27 (Winter 1998), pp. 72-84.

James U. McNeal, *Kids as Customers*, Lexington: Lexington Books, 1992.

James U. McNeal and Mindy F. Ji, "Children's Influence on Chinese Families Newfound Leisure Time and its Marketing Implications," *Asia Pacific Journal of Marketing and Logistics*, Vol. 8, 1996, pp. 32-57.

Ken Wells, "Selling to the World: Global Ad Campaigns, After Many Missteps, Finally Pay Dividends," *The Wall Street Journal*, August 27, 1992, pp. A1.

Leonard N. Reid, "The Impact of Family Group Interaction on Children's Understanding of Television Advertising," *Journal of Advertising*, Vol. 8, March 1979, pp. 13-19.

Les Carlson, Sanford Grossbart and Ann Walsh, "Mothers' Communication Orientation and Consumer-Socialisation Tendencies," *Journal of Advertising*, Vol. 19, No. 3, 1990, pp. 27-38.

M. Vijayanunni, *Census Atlas, India,* New Delhi, Registrar General and Census Commissioner, 2001, pp. 11.

Nielson Media Research, *National Audience Demographic Report*, September 1997, New York.

Pollay, Richard W. and Banwari Mittal, "Here's the Beef: Factors, Determinants, and Segments in Consumer Criticism of Advertising," *Journal of Marketing*, July 1993, pp. 99-114.

"Pressure Growing to Ban Ads Aimed at Children", *The Times of India,* New Delhi, January 17, 2001, pp. 6.

Rose, Gregory M., "Consumer Socialisation in the United States and Japan," *Working Paper*, University of Mississippi.

Santa Barbara, "Chinese Children as Consumers: an Analysis of their New Product Information Sources," *The Journal of Consumer Marketing,* Vol. 16, No. 4, 1999, pp. 345-365.

Scotward Wackman, D. B. Ronald, and Lesser Gerald, *Effects of Television Advertising on Consumer Socialisation*, Working Paper, Marketing Science Institute, Cambridge, Mass, 1974).

Seymour Banks, *Summary of Research on Child Development and the Effects of Mass Media on Television Advertising on Children* (Chicago: Leo Burnett Co., 1971).

Zoher Abdoolcarim, "Consumer Kids Get Star Billing," *Asian Business*, October, 1994, pp. 22-26.

21

Globalization and Consumerism:
A Comparative Study of India and Canada

G.Y. SHITOLE

Introduction

Consumerism is as old as man, who did not know how to produce, but was endowed with plenty of mother nature to discover, use and consume. Therefore the ancient consumer moved from place to place to hunt for food. Today man has evolved into a seasoned producer and consumer of a large number of goods and services. At the same time the consumers constitute the largest unorganized public body in the country. Globalization is the process of internationalization and in the recent past most of the countries in the world have undertaken various steps towards globalization which has led to a change in the nation's environmental and cultural conditions. In view of this, an attempt is made in this chapter to study and analyze the comparison in India and Canada in the context of globalization.

The term consumerism involves the action of individuals and organizations in response to consumer's dissatisfaction arising from exchange relationships which is an attempt to preserve the free enterprise economy by making the market work better. It basically covers the areas of *consumer guidance, protection, education* and *representation*. The consumers constitute the largest segment of the society and they are unorganized. Therefore, protection of their interests and rights is vital to the general welfare of the people, which is the major goal of any modern welfare state. This calls for a well regulated mechanism to oversee that the consumer gets satisfaction for their spending and do not suffer. Thus consumerism is a social and legal force that aims at protecting the general interest of the consumers. The introduction of modern technology and development of large scale enterprises, emergence of professionals, mass production and distribution have contributed to make all our transactions more competitive and highly complex. Unfair trade practices, adulteration and spurious products have added to the misery of consumers. Thus consumerism has now become a movement by consumers designed to ensure fair and ethical practices towards consumers by manufacturers, retailers, dealers and others. Consumerism is a convenient word for the sum total of consumer consciousness, awareness about consumers rights, annoyance with rising practices and poor performance of consumer goods and concern at the deteriorating conditions in the environment.

Objectives of the Study

1. To study various aspects of consumerism.
2. To study consumerism in India and Canada with comparison.
3. To study the impact of globalization on consumerism.

Customer and Consumer

The word customer is used as a single unit which makes purchases may be by individual or by groups of people who are involved in the decision making process. It refers to the purchaser of a product or service and they may or may not be the ultimate consumer. Whereas the term consumer refers to the end user of a product or service. They may or may not be the customer.

Consumer Behaviour

Consumer behaviour means the study of consumer's decision and approach while they spend their available resources such as time, money, efforts etc. on various consumption related items. It is related to the decision making process of consumers.

Importance of studying consumer behaviour:

- It helps to understand purchase behaviour and their preferences.

- It helps in market segmentation.
- It helps while preparing market strategies.
- It helps to understand the latest consumer trends and tastes.
- It helps in preparing promotional strategies.
- It helps for product development.
- It helps to learn how to maximize satisfaction and customer loyalty.

Features of Consumers in India and Canada

The consumers in India are very heterogeneous in composition, following different religions, speaking different languages, using very different products and services and adhering closely to their varied traditions. They are also largely poor, illiterate, ignorant and apathetic, therefore, they remain at the receiving end.

On the other hand the Canadian consumers are realistic and practical in nature. They are slow in decision making and also they have firm determination about their choice. They are not hasty or thoughtless while deciding about the product brand. The Canadian people in general are not mad about something new as Indians are and at the same time they are not influenced by advertising and exaggeration. The literacy level is much higher as compared to India, so the expectations and standard of living is higher. The Canadian consumers purchase branded products only. The Canadian population is migratory in nature and people from different nations have migrated to Canada. Thus the cross-country population purchases different products and services to adhere to their varied needs. The internal texture of India is varied due to age-old traditions prevalent in every region. In spite of the multi cultural texture of the Canadian community, there is homogeneity in terms of consumption due to the rapid spread of super markets and exposure to media in Canada.

Consumerism and Globalization

Globalization is the process of internationalization and the Indian economy accepted this process in the real sense from 1991. This has a big impact on consumer market in India because of entry of multinationals in a big way and increase in competition in the consumer products. At present some of the products from China are available in Indian market at very low cost as compared to the Indian goods and the customers have switched over to these goods. It was due to the craze among Indian customers to buy foreign goods and the process of globalization gave further opportunity to them to buy foreign goods in every product line. Several authors as under have defined the process of globalization:

According to Paul Bairoch "Basically globalization concerns an economic phenomenon implicating a strong international interconnection. It is a situation wherein industrial and commercial companies as well as financial institutions increasingly operate trans-nationally, in other words, beyond national borders. This goes hand-in-hand with an increase in mergers and acquisitions of industrial, commercial and financial companies, leading to an increase in the global role of large multi national companies and to the lessening of the role of nation-states.

According to John W. Meyer the term globalization has a number of dimensions as below:

(*a*) Globalization means the increased political and military interdependence of a set of sovereign nation-states and the expanded and strengthened set of organizations involved here, states are the main actors conceptualized.

(*b*) Globalization means the increased economic interdependencies of a set of national or substantial economies and the relevant multilateral and international public and private organizations here, states and firms are the main originating actors.

(*c*) Globalization means an expanded flow of individual persons among societies through socio-economic migration, travel and political expulsion, here states and individuals are the main actors discussed.

(*d*) Globalization means the expanded interdependence of expressive culture through intensified global communication. Themes from music to ethnic revival spread like fads through the world society and the organizational structures arise to spread them. All types of actors from individuals to organizations to national states are involved.

(*e*) Globalization means the expanded flow of instrumental culture around the world put simply, common models of social order become authoritative in many different settings.

India accepted the policy of globalization since 1991. There has been greater impact on the consumer market as a result of this policy and all multi-national companies products are being sold in the Indian market. This has created competition with brand marketing. On the other hand Canada globalised much earlier than India and the market mechanism existing in Canada has travelled to the spirit of globalization almost in a natural manner. There are market players from other countries like China and south-east nations. In Canada there is hardly anything like local or regional products. The country depends more on the products imported than on the products within the country which are limited in number. So they depend on other countries like Japan, Taiwan, Mexico and other countries so much as to go for brand names habitually.

Consumer Education

The term education means an attempt to improve the literacy level of citizens in respect of consumerism. This also includes emphasis on formal and informal education creating awareness and building confidence in the minds of people to fight for their rights. This may be possible by increased number of educational institutions in the society. Consumer education can be defined in the following ways:

- Consumer education means developing individual skills, concepts and understanding required for every day living, to achieve within the framework of one's values, maximum utilization of and satisfaction from one's resources.
- Consumer education is a vehicle by which an individual can gain understanding of changes in the economy, clarify personal goals, values and attitudes, identify alternatives and make decisions that will result in maximum satisfaction and benefits.
- Consumer education is a continuous process of learning concerned with the quality of life as influenced by choice in the market place.
- Consumer education is consumer information, consumer awareness and appropriate decision making for the individual.
- Consumer education is a process of making consumer aware of their fundamental rights as consumers and to motivate them to realize their rights.

- Consumer education is a process of gaining knowledge and skills needed in managing consumer resources and taking action to influence the factors that affect consumer decisions.

Objectives of Consumer Education

1. To develop consumer skills i.e. writing letters of complaint.
2. To gain knowledge.
3. To develop understanding.
4. To produce informed consumers.

Aspects of Consumer Education

1. *Economic Aspects*—price/cost and quality etc.
2. *Health and Safety Aspects*—contents of product, effects of their use, warnings etc.
3. *Socio-Cultural Aspects*—learning habits, setting trends etc.
4. *Environmental Aspects*—effects of consumption of product, pollution, scarce resources etc.
5. *Legal Aspects*—mandatory requirements of labelling, packing etc., provision of replacements, compensation etc.

Consumer Education Methods

1. Participatory lectures
2. Demonstration
3. Field Activities
4. Learning by experience
5. Role playing and games
6. Project work
7. Project testing and evaluation

Contents of Consumer Education

1. Resource management
2. Decision making
3. Sound purchasing habits
4. Learning skills
5. Health and safety

6. Conservation
7. Environment protection

Resources of Consumer Education

1. Newspapers
2. Magazines
3. Leaflets of products provided by the producers
4. Radio and television
5. Labels and packages
6. Government handouts
7. Environmental protection groups and consumer organizations

Consumers need education in India. They are educated by demonstration, field activities, learning by experiences etc. There are specialized bodies, social organization, universities, colleges etc. providing consumer education. However in Canada, consumer education is a part of social responsibility of business and the business conductors provide consumer education to induct the consumers into the new varied products and their effective usage.

Consumer Guidance

The term consumer guidance means providing information to the consumers about various products in respect of quality, price, handling instructions, after sales service etc. It is a part of consumer movement because it includes informing about various consumer laws and creating awareness among them about their rights. The consumers are to be protected from dangers to their life and informed of the safety measures to be followed while using the products.

Consumers in India need information about various products in respect of quality, price, handling instructions, after sales service etc. In Canada, the consumer guidance becomes a part of the promotion of the product and services itself. The advertising and publicity campaign in Canada largely takes care of consumer guidance with reference to the product quality, price, handling instructions, after sales service etc. They also have consumer guidance cells to independently give justice to the customers. In short, the legal system takes care of consumer guidance. The consumer products' details are always printed on the package by which they get brand names in Canada. Most of the

Canadians go for the products of brand names as they are educated by the products itself.

Consumer Protection

Consumer protection means protecting the interest of consumers which includes protection of consumers health, safety, economic interests etc. The following aspects of consumer protection are important:

(*a*) *Consumer Legislation*: It refers to the laws of the country passed to meet the specific requirement of the people and protecting the interests of people. *e.g.* Consumer Protection Act 1986.

(*b*) *Consumer Aids*:
   1. Product safety measures
   2. Education
   3. Information
   4. Service
   5. Protection

(*c*) *Redressal*: Relief available to the consumers
   1. Removal of defects from goods.
   2. Replacement of the goods.
   3. Refund of the price paid.
   4. Award of the compensation for the loss suffered or injury sustained.

(*d*) *Redressal Machinery*:
   1. District Forum—claims up to Rs. 1 lakh
   2. State Commission—claims more than Rs. 1 lakh and less than Rs. 10 lakhs
   3. National Commission—claims above Rs. 10 lakhs
   4. Supreme Court—apex authority

Consumer protection in India is protecting consumer's health, safety, economic interests etc. In this connection different laws are passed like Consumer's Protection Act 1986 etc. Many times it is observed that the consumer is expected to ask for justice, defend his stand and wait for the redressal. However in Canada most of the business houses consider that consumer protection is inherent duty of the business itself and for consumer it is inherent right to get safe and economic product or services.

The consumer redressal is very fast and deterrent in Canada as compared to India. The loss of compensation given by quantifying the intangible loss is almost absent in India but it is very strong in Canada. This system in Canada is found very easy for consumers and difficult for suppliers. The local print media takes cognizance of consumer protection which is very strong.

Consumer Problems

The following problems of consumers in India are noticed due to the existing market mechanism and loosely sold products:

(*i*) Dishonest vending
(*ii*) Adulteration
(*iii*) Excess Prices
(*iv*) Sub-standard quality
(*v*) Incorrect weights and measures

However in Canada almost all the products are well packed and branded with label on the package giving standard weight, quantity, brand, price etc. The marketing philosophy is altogether different in Canada and, therefore, the consumer problems are minimum.

Consumer Expectations from the Market

In most of the countries the consumer expectations are concerned with various dimensions of quality due to the impact of the international market. The consumers generally expect the following things from the product:

1. Safety
2. Durability
3. Efficiency
4. Value for money
5. Economy
6. Flexibility
7. Continuity
8. Guarantee
9. Warranty

In Canada the trend is for value addition to consumers for which the business has to constantly practice better and better quality at lower and lower cost.

Factors Influencing Consumer Decisions

Generally the following factors influence the consumer chöice in addition to the purchasing power which is the most common factor:

1. Age
2. Sex
3. Family Size
4. Social Status
5. Occupation
6. Employment status
7. Mobility
8. Habits
9. Environment
10. Educational level
11. Exposure to media
12. Peer group pressures

In India the consumers decisions are mainly taken by the parents jointly in case of consumable goods as well as durables and luxury goods. In Canada patriarchal power structure is shaken tremendously due to women's freedom movement. The country has also been moving towards the formation of classlessness on the basis of equality. Therefore, the terms like 'the head of the family, guardian and husband' as more powerful than others are rejected. The children are brought up in such a way that they make decisions to exercise their freedom. Hence in Canada each member of the family is independent and their individual choice is very important. Most of the times the choice of the product depends as per the opinion of the person who is paying for such product.

Rights of Consumers

As per different Acts protecting consumers' interest, the following various rights of consumers which have been internationally accepted:

1. The right to safety
2. The right to choose
3. The right to be heard
4. The right to information
5. The right to healthy environment
6. The right to consumer education
7. The right to redressal
8. The right to boycott

The above rights of consumers are found to be almost the same in both the countries.

Conclusions

1. Canada is the country which is globalized much before India and there are market players from different countries in the world like China, Taiwan, Japan etc. On the other hand the Indian market has globalized recently and different aspects of consumerism are changing accordingly.
2. The consumerism is dependent on business ethics which we find less in India as compared with Canada. This has reduced consumer problems in Canada.
3. In Canada the legal framework is perfectly healthy for the consumers which takes care of their problems.
4. Local print media is very powerful in Canada, for which the market players give importance and due to this the consumer grievances are minimum.
5. Indian consumers are facing many problems due to loose product sales and hardly few products are found branded and sold in standard packets. On the other hand in Canada most of the products are sold with branded packets on which weight, price etc. is printed which minimizes the consumer problems.
6. Consumer education in Canada is a part of the social responsibility of business. The business conductors provide the consumer education.
7. Consumer protection, consumer problems, consumer expectations from the market, factors influencing consumer decisions and rights of consumers these things are almost the same in India and Canada.

8. Due to globalization in India and Canada there is excessive buying or buying not out of need alone but out of attraction for a new item and the lifestyle is found demanding expensive living. This has resulted in saving less and spending more.

REFERENCES

Canadian Social Trends, Volume 3, Thompson Educational Publishing Inc., Canada, 1999.

Gorden R. Foxall & Ronald E. Goldsmith, *Consumer Psychology for Marketing*, Rutledge Publishers, London, 1994.

Henri Wai & Chung Yeung, Economic Globalization, Crisis and the Emergence of Chinese Business Communities in Southeast Asia, *International Sociology*, June 2000, Seige Publications, New Delhi.

International Times, An Economic Times Report on Canada, 15th July 2002, Mumbai.

John Mancy, Indo-Canadian Business—Yet to realize true potential—*Trade Links*, July 2002.

Kearney A.T., Your Consumer—Your Boss, *The Economic Times*, 10th May 2002, Mumbai.

Nair Suja R., *Consumer Behaviour in Indian Perspective*, Himalaya Publishing House, Mumbai, 2001.

Paul Bairoch, The Constituent Economic Principles of Globalization in Historical Perspective, *International Sociology*, Volume 15, Number 2, June 2000, Sage Publications, New Delhi.

Ramachander S., Consumer Behaviour and Marketing Towards an Indian Approach?, *Economic and Political Weekly*, Vol. XXIII, No. 9, Feb. 1998.

Rao S.L., India's Rapidly Changing Consumer Markets, *Economic and Political Weekly*, Vol. XXXV, No. 40, Sept.30-Oct. 6, 2000.

Sethi Mohini & Sitaraman Premavathi, *Consumerism A Growing Concept*, Phonix Publishing House, Mumbai, 1994.

Sherlekar S.A., *Trade Practices and Consumerism*, Himalaya Publishing House, Mumbai, 1997.

22

Gender Inequity of the Job Market in a Globalization Era:

A Comparative Study of Jobs for Women on Canadian and Indian Job Sites on the Internet

SONIA KHAN

Introduction

Globalization has been identified as the tool for restructuring the global societies, economically, politically and socially. The term describes the extension of the traditional patterns of international economic activity to high levels and to new areas: technology, trade, production, finance, investment, and information. Emphasizing economic and gender equity, the goal of globalization is to create a 'New World Order' of integration and homogenization of diverse nations through encouragement of 'free trade, single market formation, liberalization and creation of advancement opportunities for all (i.e. men and women)'. This trend has no doubt been a catalyst in attempting to bring about some standardization in terms of removing global differences, especially in the economic aspect. But, the process has not yet achieved one of its important objectives of eradicating the gender inequity within the workforce that forms the edifice of the world economic structure. The blind movement propagating worldly benefits has consumed both the developing and developed nations and unfortunately has somewhere in the run become oblivious of the very ill effects it has stemmed or strengthened throughout the world. A noteworthy observation is that globalization, however ideal it may be considered has not yet proved to be very supportive of gender equity.

On one end globalization has opened up a plethora of opportunities for the workforce, regardless of gender, but on the other end this process has overlooked the intricacies of gender biases that dominate the minds of employers, thereby strengthening gender segregation of employment opportunities in certain economies of the world.

This chapter addresses the gender inequity issue in the job market, highlighting the case of jobs for women, through a comparison between the developed and strong economy of Canada with that of the developing economy of India. The study intends to find out the extent to which gender segregated jobs still exist in a globalizing world. It is an attempt to identify if at all the Canadian and Indian job markets are offering gender segregated jobs to be apt for females alone and how these particular job openings indirectly signify the perception of women and status accorded to them in these two countries. The study is an attempt to examine if the globalization phenomenon is attaining one of its major objective of removing all gender inequities in the job market, and identify if it is the developed or developing nations that are benefiting more from the globalization process, in terms of bridging the gender inequities prevalent in the job market.

In view of the effects of globalization on gender role in the economy, it is imperative to review the concept of gender and gender inequity in the job market.

Concept of Gender

The term Gender Studies has often been confused with the study of female gender alone. It is, therefore, important to clarify the meaning of Gender. Many sociologists have explained the term gender.

A few meanings of gender are reviewed here. Anderson (1993)[1] states that gender can be referred to as socially learned behaviours and expectations that are associated with the two sexes. Kathy Davis (1991)[2], reports that gender is investigated in terms of the individual (how men and women behave, their beliefs and attitudes, gender identity), in terms of social structure (gender divisions in the social activities or labour of men and women) and in terms of symbolic orders (gender symbolism, how we think about 'masculinity' and 'femininity'). Ferree (1990)[3], believes that gender is a hierarchical structure of opportunity and oppression. Chodorow (1997)[4], has attempted to study gender differences on the basis of a psychoanalytic approach to define how the emergence of gender identities takes place.

This makes one understand that gender is not a physical, but a societal construct. Gender is something that emerges with the social roles associated with either males or females in a particular society. The developed and the developing societies show striking differences between the ways in which they favour or marginalize a particular gender.

The developed world has in a short span of time recognized the importance of according near equal status to both genders in all areas of life, but the developing world has yet a long way to go in terms of equating men and women as equals. Lindsey (1994)[5], mentions in her study that as quoted by Miller and Swift, George Orwell might have put it this way "all men are equal but men are more equal than women". Ever since the birth of civilization, men have been perceived to be physically strong, confident and aggressive and women considered as fragile, subdued, and nurturing. This perception has become a manifestation of either gender even in the contemporary societies. Such gender perceptions while tinctured in all spheres of our personal identities even spill over to the professional spheres and tend to reinforce profession based gender stereotypes. Gender relations play an important role in the division of labour, the distribution of work, income, wealth and productive inputs with important macroeconomic implications. It implies that even economic behaviour is gendered and may have serious implications towards the global economy in a globalization culture. As the Globalization Website[6] cites that many critics fear that globalization, in the sense of integration of a country into world society, will exacerbate gender inequality. Globalization may be having many liberating consequences for women but in many countries women remain at a significant disadvantage, the precise role of globalization in causing or perpetuating that condition is in dispute reinforcing gender segregation and gender-typing of occupations. The need is, therefore, to touch upon the significance of gender inequity being promoted in the job markets with view of jobs being offered for males or females.

Gender Inequity in the Job Market

Gender Gap /Inequity as explained by Young, Fort and Danner is the "departure from parity in the representation of men and women in key dimensions of social life". Over the years many gender stereotypes have been shed on account of progress and achievements being made by women at par with men but gender inequities still exist in many societies. This is so because many societies still consider men and women to be worlds apart and can never assign women an equal status to that of men. The extent of progressive outlook and development of a society determines the degree of gender gap that may exist between men and women in a particular country / society.

Gender aspects like employment, careers, education, exploitation, have been addressed both in Sociology and Women Studies. The studies of these dimensions of gender help to provide an insight into the status accorded to women in different countries. Prime Minister Jawahar Lal Nehru has rightly said "You can tell the condition of a nation by looking at the status of its women". Especially in male dominated and patriarchal societies, the status of women is quite low compared to men. Women are relegated the second status to that of men. Fox (1992)[7], believes that some women are rendered invisible, particularly women who are not European-American (among others). It is believed that women of developed societies are less subject to gender biases than women in developing societies.

Speaking of Globalization being an eradicator of gender biases, Bifani-Richard (1999)[8] report that besides furthering opportunities for women in professions, the process may have a crucial negative effect of strengthening 'gender stereotyping of employment', and such a negative effect should not be overlooked. For the purpose of this study focusing on female jobs, the perceptions held by employers in the job market, regarding appropriate jobs for women need to be reviewed.

General Perception of Jobs for Women

Throughout ages the unexamined myth has existed, that men are adept at certain jobs while women are adept at others. But no scientific study has been conducted to ascertain what gender may be appropriate to what job. Gender stereotypes even in the professional world are built due to traits associated with being a male or a female. While intelligence, technical bent and toughness of body and mind is considered to be the mark of a man, subjugation, tenderness and home making skills are associated with women. While beauty is said to be a major virtue of a woman, brains are supposed to be the possession of men. Though such misconceptions have changed over time, it is yet a mammoth task to make it acceptable to the global society that women can be ascribed a status equal to men, of possessing 'beauty with brains'. Taking the perception of women in view, Wadia (1995)[9] voices his apprehensions that 'for ages beauty used to be the forte of womanhood; at present it is the intellect that is coming uppermost, although it is questionable whether continuing what it has been for centuries, the intellect of women will ever succeed in completely ousting the supremacy of her beauty'.

Many studies have been conducted on attempting to understand the kind of professions / jobs considered suitable for women and the kind of fields women opt for in consonance with their gender. Ginzberg *et al.* (1966)[10] in their research on the lives and careers of educated women report that women predominate in fields like nursing, social work and library science. In an open job market women usually hold the positions of teachers, secretaries, nurses or are in administration if better. Ahmad (1986)[11] while discussing women in professions in India, notices that throughout the history of women in professions, these are the traditional jobs that have always been considered ideal and sought after by women. But with the growth and importance of education for women, it is interesting to note that women have ventured into the 'non-traditional', 'male dominated professions' too and are emerging as great achievers.

Such gender related job associations consciously or unconsciously lead to the creation of gender based job segregation in the job market. Women are marginalized to jobs that identify with their traditional gender roles. Employers too have a misconception/pre conceived notion that women make poor supervisors, men do not like reporting to women, women become emotional under stress, they are unable to be absent from home (mentally and physically). These factors that can also hold true for men are overlooked when hiring men. It is seen that stereotypes operate in subtle ways to limit employment opportunities for women.

Considering these existing realities of gender based job segregation even in a glcbalizing world, the following objectives have been designed to try to compare the gender based job divisions in the job market. This study has taken up a comparative case of Canada and India in order to identify gender inequities present in the job market. The following objectives are addressed:

Objectives

— To identify if at all there are any Canadian or Indian job sites on the internet exclusively offering 'Jobs for Women'

— To identify and compare the kinds of jobs advertised on the Canadian and Indian job sites for 'Females', i.e. 'female required'.
— Identify the management level of jobs (top, middle or lower level of management), advertised for women in Canada and India in view of globalization.
— To analyze the advertising text / language of the advertised jobs for women in order to reflect the status accorded to women in Canada and India.

The objectives attempt to investigate if at all globalization is having any positive effects in encouraging the increase of the female workforce of the compared economies through provision of gender neutral opportunities in the job market.

Methodology

The research paper is based on primary and secondary data. Logging on to the Internet and browsing the Job sites has enabled the collection of the primary data. Initially using search engines like Google com, Alta Vista and Yahoo, Canadian and Indian Job sites have been located on the net. For the purpose of convenience, only those sites have been selected where a member registration user is not required. Further, the sites for the purpose of this chapter are selected from the Top Job sites featuring in Canada and India.

All the job categories present on each site have been searched for in order to return all kinds of available jobs for women. From the search results, the the first 20 jobs on each site have been taken into consideration. To further get an insight into any exclusive jobs advertised for women, through search option on the sites, 'female'search parameter has been entered to return jobs for females alone.

The study is based on the following sample.

(5 Job Sites)

— 1 international Job site:
Monster.com (20 Jobs in Canada, 20 in India) = 40 Jobs
(jobsearch.monster.ca & monsterindia.com)

— 2 National Job sites each:

For Canada: 1. Workopolis.com = 20 jobs
2. WorkInfonet.ca = 20 jobs
For India: 1. Naukri.com = 20 jobs
2. JobsAhead.com = 20 jobs

Total Sample = 120 job ads
(60 Job ads from the Canadian Job market)
(60 Job ads from the Indian Job market)

Secondary data has been collected through consulting books on Gender from the library.

The data analysis has been done using mathematical methods and content analysis.

Findings and Interpretation

For the facilitation of recording results and their interpretation, the results have been divided into various heads as per objective and discussed thereby.

All job categories like Administrative, Banking, Care Giving, Forestry, Engineering, Government, Health Care, Manufacturing, Marketing, Public Relations, Social Service, Teaching, Hospitality, Tourism, Transport and others have been included to search for the jobs for 'female' required. The attempt has been to take a total of 60 jobs for women in Canada and 60 for India. Though for the Indian sites, 20 jobs each for women have been provided at each site, for the Canadian site search results for women, the sites have not returned 60 jobs but only 32 jobs labelled as female jobs. Therefore, the percentage category of jobs has been calculated from the overall total jobs returned from the Indian (60 jobs) and Canadian (32 jobs) job sites respectively. This is the first striking indication that there are not many jobs labelled exclusively for 'women/ females' in Canada, signifying that perhaps there is less gender bias for jobs in a developed and progressive country like Canada.

Job Sites exclusively for Women

Using search engines like Google, Altavista and Yahoo for the search parameter 'Indian job sites for women' and 'Canadian job sites for women', an attempt has been made to identify if at all there are any sites in Canada and India that are exclusively catering to providing jobs for women alone. The returned result shows that for Canada, there is such one site viz—www.harbour.sfu.ca/scwist/jobs— hosted by the women organization—Society of Canadian Women in Science and Technology (SCWIST)'. This site offers jobs for Canadian women in fields like science and information technology. The site provides links to further sites like Careerwoman.com and Advancingwomen.com. SCWIST's is a non profit voluntary organization and its mission is to promote and empower Canadian women in science and technology. It promotes equal opportunities for women in scientific, technological and engineering careers. It even aims at improving social attitudes on the stereotyping of careers in science and educates the public about careers in science and technology. Another organization, viz. 'Human Resource Development Canada (HRDC)' too offers its site—www.hrdc-drhc.gc.ca—that lists job opportunities especially for women. The HRDC has its various branched out links for jobs for women in the various provinces for Canada.

In the case of Indian sites for jobs for women, no particular site has been returned through search. The results are an indication that organizations offering jobs for women are providing job sites for prospective female employees in Canada. But, in India, though there are many organizations addressing the issues of women, they haven't yet hosted any jobsite exclusively for women.

Nature of Jobs Advertised for Women

All categories of jobs offered on sites including have been used to search the job openings for females. A keyword search using the word 'female' has been used to return the jobs that have been advertised strictly featuring the word female wanted/required, regardless of the job. The percentage result for each category of job is given in Table 22.1.

The results show that in the Indian job market, there is a lot of demand for females for 'secretarial' and 'marketing executive' jobs i.e. 17 per cent each. Other than this, it is also desired to have females to manage and look after the 'front office/ front desk/ reception' of any organization (15%). This may be linked to the fact that women are inherently more pleasant and welcoming. They help provide the first contact agents for outsiders and instrumental in building the first impression/ image of the organization. They make soft-spoken image builders and are patience listeners/ query handlers. These very traits

Table 22.1: Jobs for Women

Sr. No.	*Job Category*	*India (% jobs)*	*Canada (% jobs)*
1.	Secretarial	17	0.0
2.	Marketing executive	17	12.5
3.	Front Office / Reception	15	12.5
4.	Co-ordinator	13	6.0
5.	Customer Care	12	0.0
6.	Public/Guest Relations	5	0.0
7.	Managerial	3	3.0
8.	Telephone Operator	3	0.0
9.	Expert in fields	15	12.0
10.	Domestic help	0	10.0
11.	Cleaner	0	10.0
12.	Social service	0	6.0
13.	Restaurant Service	0	6.0
14.	Care Giver / Personal care	0	22.0
	TOTAL	100	100.0

also open up the fields of 'customer support' (12%) and 'public / guest relation' jobs (5%), where women are considered more desirable than men. The high demand for women in the above jobs highlights the fact that more women are still associated with lower cadre jobs requiring a good degree of interpersonal interaction skills.

It is seen that for 'managerial jobs' only 3 per cent openings have been marked strictly for females, both in India and Canada. This is relatively lower to the demand for women in blue-collar jobs. This is also a reflection that globalization has yet been reluctant in offering managerial cadre opportunities for women.

In India, nine independent jobs for females as experts in various fields have been reported out of the 60 jobs. These are jobs requiring female 'Gynecologist', 'OB2 Developer', 'Linguist Expert', 'Finance Accountant', 'Creative multimedia artist', 'Boutique Incharge' and 'Beautician/Therapist'. This finding is interesting to note, as it is a reflection that the status of females has risen in India too on account of education. The more educated, ambitious and intelligent ones are competing and excelling in all fields, from information technology to finance and accounting which were fields, earlier considered to be mastered by males alone.

For the Canadian Jobs it is noted that many jobs advertised are in the social sphere aspect of 'care-giving', (22%), 'domestic help' (10%) and 'social service'(6%). None such job is found on the Indian sites.

This implies that in Indian context these are still considered menial and lowly jobs for women, not a respectable profession/job to be advertised. The nature of these jobs for women is in consonance with the "Ethic Of Care" that is inherent in women. Their caring, nurturing and providing role for the family and society is also used in the job market for the creation of jobs like 'personal care', 'house attendant', and 'cleaners'.

There are 12 per cent Canadian jobs requiring 'Expert' in "Technical Support', 'Physiotherapy' and 'Teaching'. For the other front office and marketing jobs, the tally is close in job markets of India and Canada.

Level of Job (Top, middle or lower level management) advertised for Females

In earlier times the words man and manager were supposed to go well together but woman and manager were considered incompatible. Though the gender related stereotypes of women in managerial and executive positions have started fading, it has not been a very easy climb upwards for females. Table 22.2, compares and identifies what management level jobs are advertised more for female candidates.

Table 22.2: Management Level of Jobs for Women

Sr. No.	*Job Category*	*India (%)*	*Canada (%)*
1.	Top Management	15	15.0
2.	Middle Management	25	44.0
3.	Lower Management	60	41.0
	TOTAL	100	100.0

The job results show that for Top Level Management positions many companies do not specify gender requirement but offer an open and fair competition for the competent candidates in order to be gender neutral. The global economy in this case definitely supports the educated women and provides her equal opportunities to that of men for competing for top level positions in the job market regardless of the field/profession.

Though on both Indian and Canadian sites the jobs for women in top management are only 15 per cent in comparison for middle and lower level jobs, it is a good sign that women have reached neck to neck in capability, on the ladder of management to seek top level positions. Top-level management jobs for 'females' have been reported, requiring female 'Doctors', 'Public Relations Manager', 'Administrative Manager' and 'Technical Officers'. The gender division of labour in paid work takes the form of horizontal and vertical occupational segregation, with women confined to particular types of work and at lower levels. These findings can be supported by the research of Mitra (1997)[12] who believes that discrimination against educated women has reduced to a considerable extent. She says, "it is all too easy to follow the path of the past but the past is not the present and women's aspirations have changed". This signifies that educated women no longer underestimate themselves and offer their male counterparts a challenge in all top-level openings in the job market. The globalization process is encouraging in offering jobs to educated women regardless of the job market being of a developed or developing country.

In Canada, mid management jobs featured are a significant 44 per cent with less number in lower level management i.e. 41 per cent.

In India, females are still most demanded in the lower level management jobs, i.e. blue collar jobs, like 'receptionists', 'office attendants', 'customer support executives', 'cleaners', 'housekeepers' etc., which are low paying jobs requiring bare minimum skills. The job market is conspicuous in having the requirement of a female for the lower level care-taking jobs. Middle management level jobs offer 15 per cent openings for women in India. This reflects that due to the slow but steady progress of women, more education, awareness, demand for equal rights and economic and social independence, a growing force of women are now visible in middle management jobs. These jobs require both a reasonable level of education and skills, like jobs of 'marketing', 'sales', 'office coordinators', 'public relations', 'human resource management', etc.

It is interesting to note that the meaning of lower level job differs from country to country. *e.g.* the jobs for domestic help, home support worker, cleaner, personal care attendant, stewardess and waitress in restaurants, are considered lower level jobs in India but are thought of as respectable professions in a country like Canada. The stereotypes and taboos attached with each job for women are a direct reflection of the progressive level of a particular social milieu. It seems that the global job market has not yet been able to evolve standard and universally acceptable definitions of top, middle and lower level jobs. Perhaps even if these definitions are coined, it would be a mammoth task to convince the world societies with diverse biases and prejudices, to adopt the same and discard the taboos associated with working in a particular field/profession.

The Advertising Text used in Job Advertisements for Females

As regards requirements for jobs advertised for women, in both Canada and India, the basic requirement of education seems to feature in 90 per cent jobs. Even most of the lower level jobs have demanded the requirement of 'graduation' or 'Bachelor Degree'. Depending upon the position being offered, there are jobs that have specified a minimum of 1-2 years previous experience or no experience. This highlights, that be it Canadian or Indian job market, in the contemporary times education is a basic requirement and this requirement has changed the views of female education, which is now in equal priority to male education. High level jobs, technical jobs and those of secretarial level, demand knowledge of computers, but as reported by Haffkin and Taggart[13], particularly in IT jobs women are required for work related to word processing or data entry, comprising only small percentages of managerial, maintenance, operating systems, or software development. As found in the results, lower level jobs as that of cleaners and domestic help have not specified any skills or fundamental requirements. It is believed that such jobs are open for semi skilled and unskilled women too.

In the Indian job market higher number of jobs for females are for secretarial, reception and marketing positions. One important finding is that, besides the basic requirement of education, 'personal skills' like that of communication are a requirement featuring in almost all the advertisements. The requirement of having 'pleasant personality' and 'excellent/good communication skills', features dominantly. The use of such words reinforces the stereotypes attached to gender projecting the fair looks, tenderness and femininity of women. Other noteworthy observations of text like. 'dynamic female', 'smart female' 'positively groomed' also features in some advertisements. This indicates that jobs which require first person interaction with the companies clients, are more open for females and further require the female to be 'presentable/good looking', soft spoken and a good communicator. This is so because she is to be largely responsible for creating the first impression and image of the company / organization. This goes in consistency with the belief that women are good at building public relations. An indirect indication of the use of the above words in advertising jobs for women shows that in India the female gender is still considered to recognized and weighed in worth of the female virtues a woman may possess. Even if the economic and social standard of a female is high, the femininity is given due credence and is never overlooked.

Such does not appear to be the case of text used in Canadian jobs for women. The words specified above as requirements are virtually absent from all the jobs advertised. The job ads do not show any gender specific language used for requirements. Rather, there is emphasis only on gender neutral language specifying basic qualifications and general requirements of being 'self motivated' having 'willingness to learn' and someone being 'professional in manner'. This signifies that in Canada, it is the working ability of a woman that is perhaps given more weightage than the physical attributes she may possess.

Analysis of Gender Equity/Inequity in the Canadian and Indian Job Market

A noteworthy result of this study is that comparing the case on Canada and India, it is seen that job labelling for women is more evident in case of the jobs figured on the Indian sites where all 60 and even more jobs specifying 'female' requirement are found. But in the case of female jobs returned from the Canadian sites taken for the study, only about half the number i.e. 32 jobs have been returned. This is an indirect indication of the fact that there is definitely more gender segregation of jobs in the Indian job market. This may be a result of the gender inequities, male dominance, taboos, prejudices and stereotypes attached to women that are still deeply inherent in the Indian society. Though globalization can be credited for creation of an alarming rate of professional avenues for absorption of women in the Indian economic workforce, the process has had near negligent effect in elevating the status of the majority of Indian women or allay their fears of confidently entering the paid-work domain, however professionally capable they may be. The early discrimination against the girl child and the worthlessness attached to the education of the girls, especially in rural India further significantly effects the strength of females in the workforce. The UNDP[14] Report on India highlights that 'only 37.7 per cent women are literate as compared to 65.5 per cent men, and far fewer girls than boys go to school. Even when girls are enrolled in schools, fewer girls than boys manage to stay in school for a full ten years'. The reason of illiteracy and lack of education is the main cause, which further reinforces the low status accorded to women, and puts doubts on their professional capabilities. In the Indian society there are still preconceived ideas of what women are capable of and stereotypes of what is considered women's work. These beliefs spill over into the subconscious minds of the employers too and are actually reflected in the nature in which various jobs are advertised.

For the Canadian job market, the results show that Gender Inequity does not feature much in the job market, as most of the jobs advertised for any position are gender neutral. This further suggests that globalization in terms of job opportunity creation, overlooks the gender biases in the developed societies and has benefited the case of women. In the developing and traditional societies, on the other hand, globalization is still struggling to shed gender segregated jobs, and is complying with and even at times strengthening the gender stereotyping of women in the job market.

Conclusion

The study reveals that whether it is the case of Indian or Canadian Job market in a globalizing process the descrimination against 'educated women' has decreased considerably. Globalization has been a boon for educated women in the job market, regardless of the country they belong to. For top-level positions in any filed or organization, the jobs offered are gender neutral and based strictly on competency and ability of the candidate. For such positions the job market refrains from labelling any specific gender requirements. This reflects that there is fair competition. The urban job markets of any country are more gender neutral and are reaping the positive effects of globalization.

It is further concluded that developed societies are definitely moving on a faster pace in shedding gender stereotypes but the developing and under developed societies will take time to get rid of the gender inequities prevalent in all spheres of life which includes the professional sphere too. The strength and progress of any nation depends on its human force/resource, i.e. population (which comprises both genders). It is, therefore, important for the all institutions (social, educational, political and legal) in a nation to realize the importance of equal treatment of both genders and provide equal opportunities to all in order to achieve the desired national growth. The study shows that the developed countries are benefiting more from globalization in terms of bridging gender inequity of the job markets than the developing and traditional countries like India, where such inequity is still deep rooted and the female gender is considered apt only for certain occupations.

The low participation rate of women in jobs/workforce in any country, does not reflect that there is a lack of ability or interest, rather, indicates that women face obstacles in education, discrimination in career advancement, and social pressures. These factors are reflected through the job market, which offers women relatively lesser career options and further strengthens gender stereotypes by segregating jobs on the basis of gender and discouraging women from entering 'non-traditional' careers.

Brown and Pechman (1987)[15] report in their study that none of the accounts of occupational segregation yet give total satisfactory explanations of why women are over represented in secondary markets, how particular occupations become male or female, why this differs between different societies and in the same society over time, how and why shifts occur, and the effects of technological change, despite many excellent case studies. Globalization is the significant revolution of the contemporary time sweeping the globe. It is the buzzword of the vocabulary of all nations, but before embarking on the same, its pros and cons need to be weighed to evaluate the justification of its objectives of providing gender equity among others. Tiwari (2001)[16] quotes Pt. Jawahar Lal Nehru as saying 'We talk of revolutions, political and economic. And yet the greatest revolution in a country is the one that affects the status and the living condition of its women.' As women and economy are closely associated, it should therefore be the task of the researchers to further investigate the traits of job market in order to identify and address issues, specially related to women employment, which can encourage the eradication of the still pervasive conscious and subconscious gender biases inherent in the psyche of the employers to achieve the job related gender equity objective of globalization.

NOTES

1. Anderson, M.L., *Thinking about Women: Sociological Perspectives on Sex and Gender* (3rd edition), Macmillan Publishing Company, New York, 1993, p. 59.
2. Davis, K., Critical sociology and Gender Relations" In Davis, K. and Oldersma, M.N. (Eds), *The Gender of Power*, Sage Publications, New Delhi, 1991, p. 65.
3. Ferree, M.M., Beyond Separate Spheres: Feminism and Family Research. In *Journal of Marriage and the Family*, 1990, p. 52.
4. Chodorow N.J., Gender, Relations and Difference in Psychoanalytic Perspective In Meyers D.T New York *Feminist Social Thought—A Reader*, Routledge, New York, 1997, pp. 7-18.
5. Lindsey, Linda, L., *Gender Roles—A Sociological Perspective* (2nd edition), Prentice Hall Inc. New Jersey, 1994, p. 68.
6. The Globalization Website: http://www.emory.edu/SOC/globalization/issues02.html.
7. Fox, K., Choreographing differences in the Dance of Leisure: the Potential of Feminist Thought. In *Journal of Leisure Research*, 1992, 24(4).
8. Bifani-Richard, P., Notes on Trade, Sustainable Development and Gender In UNCTAD's *Trade, Sustainable Development and Gender*, 1999.
9. Wadia, A.R., Women and the Professions In Sharma, U, Sharma, B.M. (Eds) *Women and Professions*, Commonwealth Publications, New Delhi, 1995, p. 50.
10. Ginzberg *et al.*, *Life Styles of Educated Women*, Columbia University Press, New York, 1966.
11. Ahmad, K., The Trishankus: Women in Professions in India. In *Sociological Bulletin*, Vol. 33, (1& 2), 1979.
12. Mitra (ed.), *Women and Society: Equality and Empowerment*, Kanishka Publishers, New Delhi, 1997.
13. Hafkin, N. & Taggart, N. The Impact of IT and Globalization on Women's Work. In *Gender, Information Technology and Developing Countries*: An Analytical Study.
14. UNDP Report. (http://www.undp.org.in/Report/Gstrat/strat-3.htm)
15. Brown, C; and Joseph Pechman, (eds), Gender in the Workplace, 1987.
16. Tiwari, R.S., Feminism and Globalizations vs Indian Women Empowerment. In Avasthi, A. & Srivastava A.K. (eds) *Modernity, Feminism and Women Empowerment*. Rawat Publications, New Delhi, 2001.

23

Globalization and the Changing Dynamics of Indo-Canadian Relations

C. VINODAN

Globalization is a term that has become fashionable since 1980s when it began to replace the words like '*internationalisation*' and *transnationalisation*' as a suitable term to denote the ever intensifying networks of cross border interaction in all areas of human activity: social, political, cultural, financial and economic[1]. The concept covers an enormous variety of contemporary social change and the connections between which are not yet clear. The process of globalization has played a major role in the growth and dynamism of global politics after the Cold War. Globalization at present is being viewed as an ongoing process. India and Canada are the countries which has been tremendously influenced by the phenomenon of globalization.

The world is in a period of unprecedented transformation in which many long held values, beliefs and concepts of social order as being discarded as states, nation, ethic groups redefine their relationship with each other. It is too simple to claim that the pulls and pressures of globalization turned the world upside down. The September 11 terror attack on the United States further redefined the contours international relations. The roots of the present era of change ran much deeper than the demise of the Soviet empire. I would argue that the forces of globalization and the growing menace of international terrorism are the two variables which have the potential to redraft the relations between nations. The information revolution within the ambit of globalization has the dynamics to change the international system. So any bilateral relations in the twenty-first century should be looked at through the prism of this new dynamics.

The process of transition is not yet complete and even the full scope of change remains nuclear, it is impossible to predict the future. This leaves Canada and many other countries facing the problem of making domestic and foreign policy against a backdrop of policy process is further complicated by the active involvement of special interest groups whose narrow agendas invariably make it difficult to look at any issue in its broarder context. As a result policy making is often a confrontational rather than consensual process. It is more evident in the case of two strongest democracies of the World—India and Canada. In this context this chapter is an attempt to analyse the emerging frontiers of the Indo-Canadian relations especially in the context of globalization and different growth trends in India. It also examines the effectiveness of Indian and Canadian diplomatic tools in facing the new realities.

Canadian Foreign Policy in a Globalised World

Canada has pursued a value based foreign policy and always acted as a responsible democratic and peace loving nation in the international system. In its long history of international relations Canada did not adopt military option for achieving its foreign policy goals.[2] The Canadians were strongly motivated by humanitarian instincts, whether through contributions to humanitarian aid, human development, peace keeping, the environment and the creation of an equitable rules based international system. Canadians sought progress towards an ideal in international governance: democratisation and the disinterested peaceful resolution of disputes have always been important goals for Canada. Canada's special relationship with the United States had profound influence in its post-War foreign policy priorities but Canada never moved away from its value based foreign policy either to support American coercive diplomacy or to further its own economic and political interests.[3] Canada has clearly set out its foreign policy agenda for the twenty-first century. Some of the major foreign policy goals are:

- To reinforce Canadian Unity on the international stage;
- To maximise and protect Canadian access to the USA market;
- To promote rules based systems governing trade, financial markets, energy and the environment and to prevent the collapse of existing regimes;

- To engage China, Russia and India in the international system and to prevent the emergence of a hostile hegemonic power in Asia or Europe;
- To promote international regimes that protect Canada's ecosystems and so prevent uncontrolled environmental change;
- To deter and prevent the threat of nuclear, chemical or biological attack on Canada or on the United States;
- And finally to fight against the menace of global terrorism.

These developments of a hierarchy of interests, including the identification of vital interests, is the first step in defining Canada's role in the new century. But any such identification should be looked at through the capabilities for furthering these interests. The Canadian government's statement, Canada in the World claimed that the Canadian international role benefited from the following capabilities.

- Canada is an open, advanced society;
- Canada's geographic location favours in the new international context, providing Canada a window on Asia/Pacific, the new Europe, Latin America and direct access to the Algophone and Francophone Worlds and to the homelands of Canadians originating from every part of the globe, making up its multicultural personality;
- Canada has active membership in the clubs that matter, including the G7;
- Canada is a non-colonial power, whose constructive multilateralism appeals to those nations seeking to build a new and better order.

Impact of Globalization

Globalization has observed a new chapter in international relations. Globalization is a process of growing interdependence between people of all nations. According to the International Monetary Fund, *Globalization is characterised by increases in flows of trade, capital and information, as well as mobility of individuals, across borders.* It is fashionable to claim that the greatest challenge facing Canada in the twenty-first century is globalization. By globalization we mean the increasingly integrated nature of economic systems made possible by the spread of technology and the information it carries. It is essential that one of the necessary by-products of globalization is increasing income disparity and the marginalisation of a self-perpetuating under class, both within advanced industrial societies and geographically in Sub-Saharan Africa and elsewhere. Further more, globalization may come up against resistance even in the developing world.[4] The Canadian policy makers are well aware of the dynamism of globalization process in the evolving international system.

It is indisputable that the individual leaders and not states decides a nation's role in the international system. Therefore, Canada's place in a globalised world will be a function of the course its political leaders set. In this respect, the option lie between two extremes: isolationalism and internationalism. Over the years, Canada has followed both courses. But the challenges of globalization has forced the Canadian policy makers to adopt itnernationalism through economic and strategic engagement across the globe. Asia-Pacific in general and India in particular assumed high place in Canadian foreign policy. India has completed a decade of economic growth and has emerged as a nuclear armed country. It is estimated that India may well emerge in the next two decades as a significant power in the broader Asian environment and on a global scale. India's economic development is a powerful driver of India's overall situation. High growth encourages greater stability of its government and stronger relations with major global powers.

In the past few years, India's foreign policy has moved away from its ideologically grounded Nehruvian roots and sought to broaden its ties with the rest of the world. Economic issues loom larger, reflecting India's faster growth and reliance on global market based economic linkages. India's fastest growing knowledge economy has attracted international attention to the South Asian region.

Canada has emerged as India's major extra regional partner in the twenty-first century. The emergence of WTO and the process of globalization has offered many common challenges to India and Canada. Economic ties-growing trade and investment and especially the intricate linkages between Indian and the Canadian Information Technology industries are the foundations of the new relationship. The challenges thrown open by the menace of global terrorism has further strengthened this new relationship. But inspite of all these factors Canadian trade with India is only one-tenth of its trade with China which itself indicates a huge potential ahead. It was a major oversight on the part of Canada not to have seriously engaged with India in the past.

Indo-Canadian Relations: A Brief Review

India and Canada share a lot of things in common. Both the countries are multicultural and multiethnic societies: their roots in the constitutional law and political structure are very much the same: both are federal states and are governed by a parliamentary system of governance: both of them has been classified as Middle Powers: both of them have general traditions of liberalism: and both as key centres of their regions have special responsibility towards their respective regions.

Canadian ties with India reach back to the late 1940s and extend across many dimensions of international relations.[6] In the early years there was a fundamental convergence in the approach to international affairs between New Delhi and Ottawa, on such issues as the Commonwealth, the United Nations and the situation in Asia.[7] Leaders of both countries saw themselves as representatives of Middle Powers who were interested in influencing international affairs in a constructive manner. They shared an identity of perceptions on the need to enhance relations between Asia and the West to promote multilateral organizations and to foster Third World development. Canada's relationship with India intensifies because of common Middle Power perspective which led the two nations to co-operate in the Common Wealth of Nations. The 1950s and 1960s was the period of intense Canadian involvement in South Asia, especially in the economic sphere.

Canada's Official Development Assistance (ODA) effort was launched in India as early as 1950. Since then India has ranked among the largest recipients of Canadian ODA, with a total flow of assistance over the decades reaching nearly $ 2 billion.[8] The subsequent years witnessed the formation of an intensive relation between Canada and India, based on a diplomatic discourse buttressed by development co-operation, immigration to Canada and the establishment of educational, cultural and scientific linkages. But the lack of congruency which surfaced over issues like Korea, Indo-China and Hungary transformed as once special relationship between India and Canada into one characterised by ambivalence.[9] India's nuclear explosion of May 1974 further damaged the earlier closeness between India and Canada. The diplomatic fallout exacerbated certain other irritants affecting the Indo-

Canadian relationship and precipitated a distancing in their foreign policy positions.

The political breach widened during the later 1970s and 1980s as the two countries adopted increasingly divergent positions with regard to many of the principal global and regional issues in international politics, international trade and investment and international development. One result of this widening political distance was a steady diminution of India's significance in Canadian foreign policy, in favour of other Asian countries and geographic regions and a parallel decline in India's relative claim on Canadian aid resources. The reduced profile for India in Canada's international relations became apparent in the Liberal Government's foreign policy statement, *Canada in the World: Government Statement*[10] (hereafter the Government Statement) February 1995, which conspicuously avoided any reference to that country (or indeed, to South Asia as a whole). Although other regions of Asia and the developing world were highlighted among the declared goals of Canadian foreign policy, there was no mention of India, not even in the statement on international assistance. This particular omission seems all the more curious given the magnitude of the Canadian aid effort in India up till now, and the mounting concern that Canada is lagging behind other countries in linking up with the accelerated growth performance of India's developing economy.

The foreign policy framework set out in the Government Statement emphasised the three primary goals of Canadian international relations, notably the pursuit of prosperity, the search for global security and the international articulation of Canadian values and culture. The prosperity objective in Canadian foreign policy focuses on the promotion of international economic relations, bilaterally and through the regional and global initiatives, most notably the North American Free Trade Agreement (NAFTA), Asia-Pacific Economic Co-operation (APEC) and the World Trade Organization (WTO). Although absent from the Government Statement, India had been identified as a priority market for the purposes of Canada's International Business Strategy. In June 1995, the Canadian Department of Foreign Affairs and International Trade (DFAIT) introduced its Focus India[11] initiative, a launching point for the building of Canada's trade and economic strategy for India.

The Focus India scheme sought to integrate the combined efforts of the federal and provincial governments and incorporated inputs from the private sector to identify opportunities and help promote Canadian economic interests in India. The aim was to encourage Canadian firms to capitalize on the burgeoning business opportunities in the new India; to elicit interest in the formation of strategic commercial partnerships designed to access the wider market potential of South Asian region; and to contribute to India's economic prosperity and sustainable development. Focus India targetted three sectors in particular energy (including oil, gas and electric power), telecommunications and environmental products and services; and it encouraged Canadian business to enter into collaborative arrangements with Indian counterparts in these industries through direct investment, joint ventures and technology transfers. Through this integrated approach, Ottawa seeks to reach out and mobilize all available resources in Canada to help intensify Canadian private sector involvement in India, and thus contribute to India's economic growth and sustainable development.

At the provincial level of government, Canadian provinces (except for Quebec) have participated actively in the Team Canada approach to Asian market development. Most provinces (except for Quebec and Saskatchewan) were involved in the Team Canada mission to India. Several provincial governments, most notably Alberta and British Columbia, are themselves actively engaged in the promotion of their respective economic interests in Asian trade, especially in telecommunications and high-technology industries, agriculture and natural resources.

The trade promotion initiative has been matched by a rising level of CIDA Industrial Cooperation Program (CIDA-INC) supported business actively in India. Since 1989, CIDA-INC disbursements in India have reached around $ 2.5 million a year. CIDA-INC also supports two key business linkages between Canada and India; one between the Canadian Manufactures Association and (Indian) Confederation of Engineering Industries, the other between the Canada-India Business Council and the Federation of Indian Chambers of Commerce and Industry. In comparison with other international competitors, Canadian business seems to have been generally reluctant to invest in joint ventures, transfers of technology, or the establishment of subsidiaries in India. For their part, Indian industries generally do not look to Canada as a source of advanced technology, management skills, or financial capital. Out of more than 5000 industrial agreements concluded by Indian companies between 1981 and 1990 a mere 52 were with Canada. To be sure, a few Canadian multinational enterprise, like Bata Industries and Alcan Aluminium, have operated in India for many years.

Despite recurrent attempts to promote trade and business linkage with India, the Canadian commercial presence in that economy remains paltry. The Canadian private sector has been slow to respond to expanding market opportunities in India, due in part to persistent barriers to international trade and investment embedded in India's economic policy regime. The bulk of Canadian exports to India in recent years consisted of commodities, most notably grains and oilseeds, mineral and mineral products, chemicals and wood products. Indeed, Canada's share of India's imports has diminished over the past decade and more. Total merchandise exports from Canada to India peaked at $ 489 million in 1985, and slipped in subsequent years before rebounding to $ 391 million in 1988. By 1994-95 Canada had fallen to 24th place among India's trading partners, trailing behind all other G7 countries.[12]

The Indo-Canadian relations are strengthened by a wide network of cultural, educational and scientific linkages. Prominent among these is the Shastri Indo-Canadian Institute for Educational Exchanges. Academic exchanges between the two countries are organised for a long time. There are exchanges between Canadian Universities and Indian Universities and there are visits by scholars and scientists between the two countries. The popularity of Canadian studies in India is increasing. The activities of the Indian Association for Canadian Studies (IACS) is a laudable example in this regard.

Canadian Non-Governmental Organizations (NGOs) historically have been active in development work in India in co-operation with Indian counterparts. The broader Canadian public attitude to India seems to be especially attuned to issues of poverty alleviation, human rights and environmental concerns. Besides, India has been a major source of immigration to Canada for a decade. The flow of migrants has resulted in the growth of relatively large communities with an aggregate population of approximately 400,000 centered mainly in British Columbia and Toronto. The Indian ethnic presence contributes to Canada's multicultural mosaic and helps cement social and cultural bonds with India, while also providing a stimulus to tourism, trade and investment and to small and medium scale industries co-operation. Some East Indian Ethnic organisations and prominent individuals have emerged as visible articulators of community interests and concerns regarding Canadian foreign policy towards India. In this respect, the Information Technology Community is very powerful for lobbying Indian interests. This social connection is now becoming more politicised. Ottawa's interest in South Asia stems from the fact that the Indian subcontinent is Canada's leading source of immigrants. The Indo-Canadian population offers a basis for contacts between the two countries and if Canada maintains a reasonable open immigration policy, the exchange increase further. In the twenty-first century South Asian people with their large number will have greater impact on the country with the smaller population.

Canadian Aid Transfers to India

Bilateral ODA is direct aid to recipient country from Canada with the majority of programmes being administered by CIDA. Globally bilateral ODA accounts for almost 70 per cent of total Canadian ODA; multilateral aid comprises about 30 per cent. In Asia as a whole levels the bilateral and multilateral aid are not as extensive, however, there is considerable variation in country to country. The flow of Canadian ODA to India, on a country to country basis totalled nearly 17.4 per cent in 1999-2000, the latest year for which official data are available (see Table 23.1).

Table 23.1: Distribution of Canadian ODA by Type of Aid 1999-2000

(Per cent)

	Bilateral	*Partnership*	*Est. Multilateral*
Asia Regional	90.1	0.0	9.9
ASEAN	100.0	0.0	0.0
Bangladesh	64.1	4.8	31.1
Cambodia	44.2	10.6	45.2
China	55.0	10.7	34.2
India	17.4	16.8	65.8
Indonesia	86.1	10.4	3.5
Laos	11.8	25.3	62.9
Malaysia	35.5	42.5	22.0
Nepal	43.9	15.1	41.0
Pakistan	53.3	2.4	44.3
Papua New Guinea	0.0	29.0	71.0
Philippines	63.2	25.4	11.4
Sri Lanka	24.9	14.7	60.4
Thailand	41.6	52.6	5.9
Vietnam	33.7	12.1	54.1
Other Asia*	19.8	7.6	72.6
Other Oceania**	53.4	0.9	45.7
TOTAL ODA TO ASIA	54.2	10.8	36.7

Source: Statistical Report on Official Development Assistance, 1999-2000.

Table 23.1 shows that India is poorly placed in Canadian aid and other assistance. The lower profile for India among Canada's aid recipients reflected, in good measure, the cumulative legacy of past impediment to aid programme implementation in India, the discordant positions adopted by India and Canada on global economic questions, and the increasing attention devoted by CIDA to new programming strategies for China and South East Asia.

Canada considers itself a comparatively small scale aid donor to contemporary India, notwithstanding the shared experience in high-level development corporation in the past. Canada ranks eleventh among bilateral donors to India, and there is a substantial disparity between Canadian aid volumes and those of the leading donors, Japan, Germany, the United States, the United Kingdom and the Netherlands. Paradoxically, Canada's aid effort seems to have acquired a more pronounced public awareness, and perhaps greater goodwill for Canada in India, than the dollar value of the transfers themselves might warrant. In reality, however, Canadian aid transfers tend to be too small and too diffuse to acquire significant policy leverage, or impact on India's development efforts. Recent cutbacks to Canada's aid budget, and the continued shift in geographic emphasis in favour of other countries and regions, imply that the Canadian donor profile in India is destined to decline still further.

India's Economic Transition and Canadian Business Interests

The Indian economy has become one of the fastest growing in the world since 1991, when India began a structural adjustment programme after balance of payment crisis. It created accelerated growth and a new class of economic powerhouse. The dizzying rise of India's information technology industry, in particular raised great hopes for future sustained growth rates. High growth also fosters outward looking politics and is particularly beneficial to Indo-Canadian ties. The reform process has been accompanied by a greater openness toward foreign direct investment and technology transfers, despite certain restrictions. Private capital flows to India began to surge in the early 1990s, reaching US $ 4.5 billion in 1993-94, of which US $ 273 represented direct foreign investment.[13] Among the leading sources of private investment were the United States, Great Britain, Japan, Germany and Singapore. The trends in the 1990s in Asian trade and finance reveal a close connection between flows of investment, technology transfers and joint ventures and expanding international economic activity. Compared to others in the Asia-Pacific Rim, the Canadian private sector has lagged behind in adapting to this emerging pattern of investment related intra industry trade. Canada does not figure prominently as a source of foreign direct investment preserve impedes Canadian commercial access to the dynamic domestic markets of Asia and further more inhibits Canadian participation in the expansion of intra-industry trade across Asia and the Pacific. The apparent disinterest on the part of the Canadian private sector has had the effect of limiting the transfer of economic and technological resources and skills that flow along with investment and which can often exceed the benefits derived from equivalent flows of aid.[14] In an efforts to stimulate commercial activity and build interest in Canada—India business potential, the government of Canada embarked a series of high profile trade missions to India in the 1990s. The most notable one was the *Team Canada Mission* to India in January 1996. This visit created a conducive atmosphere for bilateral relations. After that visits from both sides of high-powered official and non-official delegations strengthened the economic ties.

India has been attracting an increasing amount of Canadian attention in recent years. The political leadership in both countries are determined to boost their economic ties and exploit the benefits of globalization in the new century. Although exhibiting a considerable amount of variability from one year to the next, Canadian exports to India appear to have established an upward trend (see Table 23.2).

Table 23.2: Canadian Trade with India

	Canada's Trade with India (C$ '000s)			
	January-December		*January-August*	
	2000	*2001*	*2001*	*2002*
Exports	541,025	646,866	456,849	412,561
Imports	1,232,112	1,154,662	795,148	891,698
Trade	1,773,137	1,801,528	1,251,997	1,304,259

Source: Trade Data online. Industry Canada. 9 July 2002 and 1 November 2002.

While the Canadian top exports feature many traditional items like dried peas, newsprint, wood pulp and fertilizers, the last couple of years have seen Canadian wireline and optical telecommunications equipment jump to the top of the merchandise export list. Inward trade flows have grown more consistently, and much more robustly, expanding about fourfold since 1992. Indeed, 2001 was the first year in over a decade in which Canadian imports from India declined, albeit quite modestly. The import list is dominated by clothing and textile items, but Canada also purchase significant amounts of diamonds and seafood (especially shrimps and prawns) from India (see Table 23.3).

Table 23.3: Canada's Merchandise Trade with India, 2001

S. No.	*Canadian Imports from India*		*Canadian Exports to India*	
	Merchandise classification	*%*	*Merchandise classification*	*%*
1.	Knitted or crocheted apparel	18.2	Edible vegetables, roots and tubers	30.6
2.	Apparel not knitted or crocheted	13.6	Paper and paperboard	12.8
3.	Organic chemicals etc.	7.9	Wood pulp and other pulp	9.7
4.	Pearls, precious stones/ metals etc.	6.1	Optical/photographic equipment etc.	9.4
5.	Cotton	4.8	Electrical machinery and parts	9.4
6.	Other textile articles	4.2	Fertilisers	6.7
7.	Leather articles	3.2	Salt, sulphur, lime, earth, stone etc.	4.7
8.	Boilers, mechanical appliances etc.	3.1	Boilers, mechanical appliances etc.	4.3
9.	Articles of iron or steel	3.1	Ores, slag and ash	3.2
10.	Carpets, other textile floor coverings	3.0	Iron and steel	1.9
	Top 10 as % of Total from India	67.2	Top 10 as % of Total to India	92.7
	Indian Imports as % of Cdn Total	0.34	Indian Exports as % of Cdn Total	0.17

Source: Trade Data Online. Industry Canada. 4 November, 2002.

Conclusion

India's emergence out of the nuclear shadow in 1998 changed its strategic status in the region and its role in the eyes of the world. At the same time India's rapid economic growth and expanding military strength during the past decade point toward an increasingly prominent role for India in the overall Asian scene. India's foreign policy rests on a strong consensus that India must remain an autonomous actor and that it prefers a multipolar world political and security structure. India's economic, political, foreign and security evolution in the next few years will determine its domestic and international policy agenda, as well as its relationship with the United States, Canada and other major powers. India's economic liberalisation has created opportunities for Canada to invest and to expand trade in India. Within South Asia, India is Canada's leading trading partner. But within Asia India's position is very low. Canadian trade with India is only one-tenth of its trade with China which itself indicates a huge potential ahead. India's growing middle class population provides a stable foundation on which to build a larger market for Canadian products and services in the twenty-first century.

The long term case for commercial co-operation is based upon the existence of support and complementaries in the economies of the two countries to make them mutually gaining partners in trade and trade related activities. Canadian industry is very much interested in infrastructures like communications, power and roads and all those spheres that India need to mobilize in order to attract foreign investment to develop industries so that they could be co-operative in the globalised world. Canada can use India as a production procurement and trading base for capturing the growing markets of South Asian countries. Canada is now looking to diversifying its international business beyond the Untied States. This is where India fits in appropriately. India is an open, democratic and safe country with clean record of honouring her international commitments. The advantage offered by the Indian market include a stable democracy with an independent judiciary, a large pool of entrepreneurial management, engineering and scientific expertise and huge and developing market. The advantage offered by the Indian market outweighs the disadvantages. The potential for Canadian involvement in India is enormous. While increased opportunities for investment will receive Canada's interest in India, a more stable political environment will be required if improved ties are to be sustained. Even though India has a tremendous potential to attract Canadian investment, converting it into reality is a challenging process. What is required is a firm determination and will on both sides. The need of the hour is to restructure policy options in vital areas of co-operation which are bound to increase in the coming years.

NOTES

1. Joseph S. Nye Jr. and John D. Donahue eds. *Governance in a Globalizing World*, Brookings Institution Press, Washington DC, 2000.

2. John and Norman Hillmer, eds., *Making a Difference?: Canada's Foreign Policy in a Changing World Order*, Toronto, Lester Publishing, 1992.
3. Robert Bothwell, *Canada and the United States: The Politics of Partnership*, Toronto, University of Toronto Press, 1992.
4. Marc Ferranti, *Globalization Tidal Wave, Info World*, 27 November, 2000, 36—37.
5. Nossal Kim Richard, *The Politics of Canadian Foreign Policy*, 3rd ed., Prentice Hall, Canada, 1997.
6. For an account of Canada-India relations in the past, see Arthur Rubinoff, *Diplomatic Overview;* Ashok Kapur, *South Asia: The Diplomatic and Strategic Setting*, and Kim Nossal *Canadian Strategic Interest in South Asia*, 1947-1987; all in A.G. Rubrinoff, ed., Canada and South Asia: Issues and Opportunities, Centre for South Asian Studies, University of Toronto, 1988. See also W.M. Dobell, *Canada and India: The Mulroney Years, Journal of Asian and African Studies, 1990.*
7. See Reid Escert, *Envoy to Nehru*, Oxford, New Delhi, 1981.
8. For an analysis of Canadian aid to India in the context of Canada's wider development co-operation effort in Asia, See Martin Rudner, *Canadian Development Assistance to Asia: Programs, Objectives and Future Policy Directions: Canadian Foreign Policy,* Vol. 1. No. 3, Fall 1993.
9. Ashok Kapur, *Canada and India in Ruberioff* ed., *Canada and South Asia: Political and Strategic Relations.*
10. Canada, *Canada in the World: Government Statement*, Ottawa, Canada Communication Group, 1995.
11. *Focus India*, Ottawa, Department of Foreign Affairs and International Trade, 1995.
12. *The Globe and Mail*, March 20, 1995.
13. World Bank, *Global Prospects and the Developing Countries*, Washington D.C., The World Bank, 1995.
14. Alexander Yeats, *Development Assistance: Trade versus Aid and the Relative Performance of Industrial Countries, World Development, 1982*, 863-9.

24

Globalization of Equity Market:
The Challenges to Asia Pacific and Indian Stock Exchanges

P.M. MEERA MOHIADEEN

Introduction

Very recently the major stock exchanges like NYSE and NASDAQ have felt the need for developing a Global Equity Market. This is because of several large companies from Japan, Canada, India and Europe has started listing on major stock exchanges like NYSE or NASDAQ outside their original countries. Investors in these countries are having a freedom to invest in any part of the world. They trade in a given stock listed in different countries with different time zones. Investment banks and brokers would save on multiple exchange memberships, companies on multiple listings and compliance costs, and investors on duplicate fees to local and foreign brokers. Merging the clearinghouses could produce big savings. Active institutional investors want to take advantage of the price discovery process as it unfolds on different stock exchanges operating in varying time zones. Global exchanges where trading never stops.

Taken into account the above mentioned advantages, the major stock exchanges fear that if they can't make global trading easier and cheaper, their customers will join or create private electronic market. Already some attempts were made by the Morgan Stanley, Swiss Stock Exchange and Merrill Lynch to form a private electronic trading; Jiway, Virt-x and MLX Market Edge respectively. Further, the Tokyo, Toronto, Sydney, Sao Paulo, Hong Kong and Mexico stock exchange try to establish a link with NYSE, German stock exchange with London Stock Exchange and French, Belgian and Dutch stock exchanges merged and form a EURONEXT. Therefore, it is not only the major stock exchanges like LSE, NYSE and NASDAQ have felt the need for developing a global equity market but also the Indian and Asia Pacific countries too.

Asia-Pacific economies have recorded the highest rates of domestic savings in the world, with governmental policies and fiscal incentives contributing to this. Real interest rates were positive and from an international perspective, high, and the government sector also made direct contributions to saving particularly in South Korea, Taiwan and China. High savings rates were one factor contributing to strong investment performance, external capital was another. Several Asia-Pacific economies kept a firm grip on their financial markets and forced

Table 24.1: FDI Outflows from major Economies (BoP figures)

(US $ million)

Country Name	*1991*	*1992*	*1993*	*1994*	*1995*	*1996*	*1997*
U S A	31380	42660	77950	75210	96650	81070	121840
Canada	5837	3547	5711	9303	11656	11632	14044
E U	106113	108975	97088	120787	159124	151962	203237
U K	16310	18990	26580	33800	44090	35160	61440
France	23930	31270	20600	14440	15820	30350	35480
Germany	23720	19670	15260	17260	38840	29520	33130
Netherlands	13567	14409	12036	17355	19626	23094	20369
Sweden	7262	419	1471	6685	11399	5112	11465
Italy	6928	6502	9271	5628	6925	6049	10225
Spain	4422	2192	2652	3831	3650	5208	10042
Belgium	6271	11407	4904	1371	11603	8044	7899
Switzerland	6541	6057	8764	10763	12170	11599	14503
Latin America	.453	1376	2827	5194	2346	2270	9097
Mexico	167	655	609	2006	.482	.319	1037
Brazil	1014	137	491	1037	1384	.467	1042
Australia	1662	6033	2500	2473	3842	5854	5832
Japan	31620	17390	13830	18090	22510	23440	26060
Asian NIEs	4070	4446	6103	9109	10972	12659	13641
S. Korea	1489	1162	1340	2461	3552	4640	4449
Taiwan	2055	1967	2611	2640	2983	3843	5222
Singapore	526	1317	2162	4008	4437	4146	3970
Thailand	167	147	233	493	886	961	532
China	913	4000	4400	2000	2000	2114	2563
World	198143	200800	240900	284261	322514	333629	423666
Industrialised Countries	189782	179984	205810	241481	306465	283476	359236
Developing Countries	8324	20714	34929	42512	45642	49161	61138

them to serve the needs of the industrial sector. Table 24.1 shows the Foreign Direct Investment Flows (FDI) from major economies and Asia-Pacific Economies.

A large proportion of the worldwide FDI outflows (about 85 per cent in 1997) originate from the industrialised countries. (Table 24.1) The dominance of industrialised economies as sources of FDI outflows is another expression of the dominance of firms from those economies in many segments of global industry. However from the early 1990s developing countries have been increasing their share in the total outward FDI flows. In 1995, they accounted for about US $ 48 billion or 15 per cent of the total FDI outflows. This increase in FDI outflows from the developing countries has been led by the emergence of substantial outward FDI activity by the newly emerging Asian economies. In 1995, for instance, outward FDI from Hong Kong, Taiwan, China, South Korea, Singapore and Malaysia accounted for about $ 42 billion or 90 per cent of the outward FDI flows from the developing countries (UNCTAD 1996). All these developments necessitated the Asia-Pacific countries businessmen to invest their funds to the foreign countries through equity or bond. Further, some of the Asia-Pacific countries also got FDI from the industrialised nations. Table 24.2 shows the FDI inflow of some of the Asia-Pacific countries and India during 1995-1999.

Table 24.2: Amount Raised through Euro Issues

(*Amount in US Dollar in Millions*)

Year	*GDRs/EDRs*		*ECBs*		*Others*		*Total*	
	No.	*US$*	*No.*	*US$*	*No.*	*US$*	*No.*	*US$*
1992-93	2	240	–	–	–	–	2	240
1993-94	17	1586	9	1020	–	–	26	2606
1994-95	30	2113	2	65	1	77	33	2256
1995-96	7	616	–	–	6	870	13	1466
1996-97	8	1438	–	–	15	1512	23	2950
1997-98	2	418	–	–	15	2005	17	2423
1998-99	1	186	–	–	1	70	2	255

Source: The Prime Directory, 1999, p. 38.

Indian companies like Satyam Online, Reliance etc. have been tapping the resources through Global Depository Receipts and External Commercial Borrowings in the international markets. Table 24.3 shows the amount raised by the Indian companies through Euro issues. The entry of the Indian companies in to the global equity market has forced the Indian stock market to thrive on challenges and become internationally competitive by upgrading quality of their services. Hence, the Indian Capital Market has also felt the impact of the globalization seriously. Therefore, this chapter focuses the area in which the Asia Pacific and Indian Capital Market is focusing their attention to meet requirements of the emerging global equity market as well as challenges in the years to come.

Table 24.3: FDI Inflows in India and Some Asia-Pacific Countries during 1995-1999.

(US $ Millions)

Country Name	*1995*	*1996*	*1997*	*1998*	*1999*
India	2144	2426	3351	2258	2168
Indonesia	4346	6194	4673	.356	3270
Malaysia	4178	5078	5106	3727	3532
China	35849	40180	44236	45460	40400
Singapore	7206	7854	9710	7218	6984

Source: IBA Bulletin, October 2001, p. 4.

Challenges to Stock Exchanges

Demutualised the Stock Exchange

To transform Indian and Asia-Pacific capital market into a global equity market it would require the infusion of a large quantum of resources. But at present the stock exchanges are not in a position to inject additional capital due to the depressed primary market throughout the world and unable to push even established corporate bodies to raise the money in the international capital market. However there is a way out is to form a demutualised stock exchange. In USA and London, stock exchanges are discovering the advantages of the demutualised stock exchange. Under this concept, a demutualised stock exchange is one, which is a corporate body, whose shares need not necessarily be owned by the stockbrokers. As far as India is concerned the authorities already permit to open the demutualised stock exchanges. In this way the stock exchanges Asia-Pacific countries can enhance the quantum of resources.

Development of Derivative Products

The increased penetration of Internet, rising purchasing power and availability of wider variety of financial products are contributing to rapidly evolving investors' expectations and value perceptions. Over the last few years, there is an emergence of global investor, who demanded identical products and services of a global nature anywhere in the world. Therefore, they are expecting many derivative products. It is the duty of stock exchanges to look into the development of new product in the existing product and generating revenues from the global investors. The investors would like that the stock exchanges should provide facilities for trading in all financial products, both cash and future products given the close links among all financial markets and products. Indian Capital market and some of the Asia-Pacific countries therefore, can meet the global investors' as well as their own investors' demand through providing cash and future products to the investors.

Make Use of Latest Information Technology

The major challenges to the stock exchanges in India and Asia-Pacific today is how to managing and utilising the information due to the technical nature of the subject. The essential pre-requisite for the stock exchanges is to participate in global operations is the introduction of technologies and systems in tune with the international market standards. The information technology pervades all the areas of financial services through variety of equipments such as foreign exchange and money market dealing systems, depository maintenance, stock broking, clearing and market information delivery system. Asia-Pacific countries like Indonesia, Thailand, Philippines, the level of technology is relatively low for a variety of reasons such as adverse stand on brokers, poor telecommunications infrastructure, and limited choice of banking and financial service packages. But in India the National Stock Exchange (NSE) happens to be the first stock exchange in the World to use satellite communication for security trading. Apart from the trading through satellite, now NSE is in the process of setting up a terrestrial communication link for all its members so that, in case of possible mishap with the satellite communication system, National Stock Exchange (NSE) members should be able to trade without any interruption. Similar arrangements can be made by the other Asia-Pacific countries for the enhancement of the Information Technology.

Train the Employees and Brokers

The key elements that shall provide a competitive edge to stock exchanges of the twenty-first century will not be physical assets but knowledge assets and information. Therefore, the stock exchanges must give the opportunities to the existing brokers and staff of stock exchanges to develop the latest technical knowledge in the securities dealings. At present the stock exchanges have the inadequate staff strength and also dearth of latest information technology knowledge. For instance, the Securities and Exchange Board of India (SEBI) has 200 officers and 150 staff members. On the other hand the US Securities and Exchange Commission (SEC) have 3000 staff members. Hence, stock exchanges are going to train the existing staffs and as well as recruit the technical persons to meet the present as well as the future challenges.

Reducing the Risk through STP

At present the Asia-Pacific stock exchanges are unable to track each broker's exposure to the entire market as also in different stock on a real time basis. Once the stock exchanges are able to ensure that the safest Straight Trough Processing (STP) are brought into use for connecting the broker offices with the banks and depository participants (DP) on real time basis, the risk will be reduced to greater extent. For monitoring member's exposure, NSE has been the first stock exchange in the World, which introduced the system of exposure monitoring on real time basis. NSE has developed unique software for this purpose. Hence, the stock exchanges in the Asia-Pacific countries can make use of the software brought out by the NSE or make arrangement on their own and try to reduce the risk in securities dealings.

Rolling Settlement

World over, Electronic Fund Transfer (EFT) and credit facilities on stock have been a prerequisite for the success of the rolling settlement. In India the Reserve Bank of India and SEBI recently decided to allow banks to finance the brokers for margin trading in shares. But there are some practical plight to avail these facilities in India. Asia-Pacific countries like Indonesia, Thailand, and Singapore etc. are lacking this type of facilities. Hence, the authorities should consider the demands of the capital market participants and take speedy measures to provide credit facilities to all the scrip and announce the EFT.

Forward Trading

The removal of the forward trading (*Badla*) in India has been dramatically reduced the investor's ability to participate in the market.

Badla has been around for over 100 years and has successfully coped with many changes. According to a FICCI study, it is actually a product that should have been exported to global markets rather than abandoned. What is worse, says FICCI, it has been thrown out without any reasonable alternative being in place. Hence, this is looked into new dimension and takes necessary steps to design the product in trouble free manner and try the product to attract the Indian investors at large. Therefore, to foresee the future challenges to the stock exchanges, the efficient functioning of the forward trading are imperative.

Capital Adequacy

Indian stock exchanges did not attach much importance to capital adequacy requirements by way of minimum net-worth until NSE set standards in this area before a broker can commence business. China, Indonesia, Malaysia and Taiwan are also not given much importance to the capital adequacy. Therefore, every stock exchange should aim at improving and monitoring its broker's capital adequacy level. The financial institutions in this aspect should follow the increasingly stringent capital adequacy norms that apply internationally. World over, capital adequacy is based on capital plus reserves, which makes up the net worth. But in the Indian context, the stock exchanges and SEBI redefined it and added the borrowed component. Hence it should be adjusted to the existing world standard and that will increase the number of brokers in the field.

Strategic Alliances

Except Japan and Hong Kong stock exchanges, there has been very little effort on the part of the stock exchanges in other Asia-Pacific countries to broaden their operation and expertise knowledge to the entire world. This can be done through the strategic alliance with the foreign stock exchanges in the international level. Already, there are two Asia-Pacific stock exchanges which are establishing the relationship with the NYSE. Therefore, the remaining stock exchanges are going to take up necessary measures to have a strategic alliance with the NYSE. The major stock exchanges like NYSE, LSE and NASDAQ have felt the need for developing a global equity market to form an alliance with other country's stock exchanges for trading purposes.

Transparency

Earlier investors did not have access to correct information about what is happening in the trading ring of the stock exchanges. The NYSE has tried to solve this problem by making it mandatory to disclose trade information as soon as trades are executed. The brokers have to pass on the information in less than 90 seconds after the trade is executed. But as of today the common investor has no access to information about the order book position in different stock on real time basis even on the NYSE. For making markets more efficient it is desirable that both the buy and sell order books including the order depth in each stock are made available to the entire market on a real time basis. But in India NSE has been doing the above right from its inception. Therefore, the other Asia-Pacific countries' stock exchanges make the technological changes in the existing trading system and made available the information in a transparent manner.

Harmonising Securities Laws

The creation of the Global Equity Market there should be unification of the securities law and regulation of the various countries. It requires amendment of the existing corporate laws of the member country. Otherwise the dream of the global equity market will not come true. For instance, The Australian Stock Exchange and its much smaller New Zealand counterpart have merger plans in the works, but the process has slowed because there has been little progress in the two countries' efforts to harmonize their corporate laws and securities laws. Many Asia-Pacific countries still have the age-old stock market regulations. These regulations should be updated and it will suit to the present requirements.

Unification of Settlement

Another major requirement for the success of the Global equity trading is the unification of the settlement. The common currency for all the member countries is not possible. Hence, there should be a proper settlement system. Otherwise the global equity market idea will not be carried out smoothly. The uniform taxes and a uniform takeover codes also essential for the global equity trading. Therefore Indian and Asia-Pacific countries unify the settlement procedure for making the global equity trade.

Formation of Global Capital Market Organisation

The global exchanges may not remain under the regulatory purview of any national regulator. For instance the European Union may have to consider a multinational regulatory body for the purpose. If companies start getting listed on international exchanges, the regulatory problems are existed. This problem cannot be easily resolved by having bilateral Memorandum of Understandings between any national regulators. The problem being complex in nature and more multinational approaches may become necessary. For maintaining "law and order" in global capital market it is imperative to establish an international organisation like the WTO.

Conclusions

To meet the demands of the global investor Indian and Asia-Pacific stock exchanges needs larger resources and it can be mobilised only through demutualising of stock exchange. Further, stock exchange uses the latest information technology to redefine the business and should upgrade the existing level of information technology to increase the competitiveness. The Indian and Asia-Pacific stock exchanges should follow the stringent capital adequacy norms that applied by the International stock exchanges. The stock exchanges try to reduce the risk in security dealings through the STP. The authorities of Asia-Pacific and Indian have considered the brokers demands and make speedy measures to provide loan facilities on stock and announce the EFT. Another welcoming measures to be taken by the stock exchanges to make the strategic alliance with the NYSE, LSE and NASDAQ. Finally, it is highly essential to disclose the information about the securities dealing in a transparent manner to survive the security industry.

NOTES

The Financial Express, September 25, 2001, p.7.

The Hindu Business Line, September 19, 2001, p.1.

Patil, R.H. "The Capital Market in 21st Century", *The Economic and Political Weekly*, November 18-24, 2000, pp. 4097-4102.

The Prime Directory, 1999, pp. 3, 38.

The Economic and Political Weekly, Nov. 25, 2000, pp. 4234-35.

The Economic and Political Weekly, Nov. 18, 2000, pp. 4100.

Garnaut, R., (1988) *Asia's Giant*, Adelaide: University of Adelaide.

Asian Development Bank (1971) Southeast Asia's Economy in 1970s, London, Longman.

Business Week, Asian Edition, January 15, 2001, pp. 48-50.

25

Demand for Regional Autonomy in an Era of Globalization:

A Comparison of India and Canada

A.N. PANDA

The present age can be referred to as an age of globalization. Though there had been a desire in the minds of some thinkers and statesmen to amalgamate the whole world into a single entity and several efforts have been made in the past to bring the people of different countries closer, globalization has actually started dominating the world since the nineties of the last century. Globalization has emerged as an irreversible process with far reaching consequences. It has inspired the human beings to ignore the division of mankind into different nations on geographical considerations and to undermine the sovereign power of the nation-states.

Rapid expansion of mass media and mass communication has not only brought the people of different parts of a big country closer but also it has brought the people of different nations nearer by ensuring a better understanding among one another through an easy exchange of ideas, knowledge and experiences. Development in science and technology has globalised economy, provided a better transport system and widened the choice of the consumer by enabling him to select from a wide range of products. Globalization has expanded the market and lessened the control of national governments in the affairs of individual's economic consumptions.

Globalization is "reduction of transaction costs for transborder movement of capital and goods, thus of factors of production and goods"[1]. It envisages a world order in which the economies of different countries are interlinked to satisfy the material needs of their people. It emphasises on the creation of a single international market and reduction of the authority of the nation-state. Thus the meaning of globalization is basically a restrictive and economic one[2]. Beyond its economic implications, globalization has encouraged the world not to remain only as an international society of independent sovereign states rather it has changed the world into an interconnected global order where free exchanges take place in all areas of human activities[3]. Globalization assumes free flow of trade, finance, technology and information. In the present day world no nation can remain isolated and aloof to the happenings in other parts of the globe. Today we live in a global society.

Regionalism in an Era of Globalization

But though the forces of globalization propose a global community by reducing the importance of geographical limitations and try to free mankind from the clutches of sovereign authority of the nation-states by transforming the citizens of a country into the citizens of the world there is also a totally opposite trend noticed throughout the world which negates the spirit of globalization. In spite of the realisation that mutual dependence and cooperation bring maximum benefits and remaining isolated is detrimental to one's own interests, the people of different regions still nurture a sense of parochial feelings. They shape their ideas and orientation on the basis of their narrow and limited interests. They consider themselves neglected by the system and blame others for their unsolved problems. They are becoming more conscious of their actual or/perceived deprivation and differences and consequently there has been a growth of regionalism within the boundaries of the nation-states.

The free flow of information across the national boundaries accentuates the feeling of regionalism and alienation by making the people more aware of their own privation. "Whether in the form of ethnic nationalisms, demand for minority or people's rights or sessionism, local struggles and movements have been shaped by global discourses on governance, development and structural adjustment programmes, as much as by human rights discourses which increasingly acknowledge if not emphasise cultural diversity"[4]. As "the state is itself both a resource and a distributor of resource"[5] the people of every region strive for a control over the state and failure to have such a control ends in resentment and germinates a feeling of being isolated and overlooked.

"The term regionalism represents the regional idea in action as an ideology, as a social movement or as the territorial basis for regional planning, it is also applied to the scientific task of delimiting and analysing regions as entities lacking formal boundaries"[6]. People living in a definite geographical area develop an attachment towards it and seek an identity on the basis of that region. Religion, language, culture, common tradition etc. often help in creating a strong bond among the people of a region.

The people of a region, to assert themselves, seek a separate identity. "Human beings are identity seeking animals, both as individuals and as collectivities"[7]. Thus regionalism and failure of regional aspirations give rise to desire for identity formation.

The movement for identity formation does not stop with the formal recognition of a distinct identity of the people of a region and their rights by the political structures of the country. Sometimes it leads to a struggle for less control from the main centre of power and ends in a demand for autonomy or self rule. The demand for autonomy is one of the many manifestations of regionalism.

"Today most of the world's states are multi ethnic societies and most of them include ethnic minorities which account more than 20 per cent of their populations. Such multi-ethnic societies tend to be politically divided in their domestic affairs and if their populations are also stratified, the rise of violent confrontation is imminent"[8]. "Movements for regional autonomy or actual independence have continued to grow in political importance even in what might be seen as the historical leaders in nationhood as well as being major problems for many new states......"[9].

In all plural societies cleavages do occur at political, cultural and economic levels. Regional imbalance becomes an established fact in all big nations. All these result in creating resentment and dissatisfaction among the people of a region which in turn give rise to regionalism. As the people of a region consider that more power generally brings more opportunities to override regional imbalances and fulfil regional aspirations they desire for more power or autonomy from the central government. Therefore, the governments of the peripheries demand more power from the central government to take independent decisions concerning their own region. This trend is marked in all countries, more particularly in big countries having large population with numerous differences.

Both India and Canada are plural societies with many ethnic and minority groups living in them. Both the countries have adopted a centralised federal form of government. As there are many cleavages in the civil societies of both the nations they face many similar problems. One of the common problems these two countries are confronted with is the feeling of resentment of the regional governments against the centre. As a result the demand for more power or autonomy by the governments of different regions is voiced in both the countries. This demand is rooted in the constitutional division of power between the central governments of the peripheries in both India and Canada.

Distribution of Powers between the Central Government and Government of the States in India

Though the Constitution of India has described India as a 'Union of States'[10] like all other federations it has created two levels of government, the central government and governments of the units and divided powers between them. It has allocated specific powers to both of them. However, the method of distribution of powers by the Indian Constitution is a unique one. There are three lists of power, i.e., (i) Union list, (ii) state list, and (iii) concurrent list. In the union list there are 97 items which are of all India importance, such as Defence, Foreign relations, Currency and Coinage, Railways, Post and Telegraph, Airways etc. and these subjects are put under the jurisdiction of the Central Government. These state governments exercise power over the subjects of state list which contains 66 items such as public order, Local self government, Agriculture, State industries, offences against state law etc. As the list suggests these are of the local importance and managed by the governments of the respective regions. In the concurrent list 47 items are included over which both the Central government and State governments have control and both can make law on these items, but pre-eminence is given to central law in case of a conflict between the central law and state law. Criminal law, marriage and divorce, Forests, Economic and Social planning, Labour welfare, Weights and measures, Price control etc. are the subjects of concurrent list. The residual powers are vested in the centre.

The powers and position of the Centre and the States in financial field are also very complicated. From Article 264 to Article 300 of the Constitution deal with the financial relation between the Centre and the States. The state list covers 19 financial items such as land revenue, sales tax, entertainment tax, Tolls etc. while the central list has only 12 items such as customs, income tax, corporation tax etc. But as the centre has jurisdiction over the whole of India the financial potentialities of the central items are much more. As a result the centre has more financial capability than the states.

Another factor, which is an extra constitutional development in India has effected the fiscal relation between the centre and the states. Two extra constitutional bodies have come into existence to regulate the development and planning in India and they have a say in the overall planning process in the country. The Planning Commission and the National Development Council both of which have the Prime Minister of the country as their chairman have control over the states in fiscal matters because the state plannings are liable to be approved by these bodies.

The strong position of the centre vis-à-vis the states in financial field follows its power in legislative and administrative relations with the states.

Along with these constitutional and extra-constitutional provisions granting a pre-eminent position to the centre vis-à-vis the states constitution has also made the centre more powerful by providing it with power to tackle exigencies in a part or whole of India. The constitution has given some emergency powers to the centre to deal with external aggression or internal armed rebellion, failure of constitutional machinery in any state of India and financial instability in India or any part of the territory thereof under the provisions of Articles 352, 356 and 360 respectively.

Whenever there is an emergency of any kind the power of the centre increases manifold. Though no emergency under Article 360 has been declared in India till now, the other two articles have been used in India several times. Often their use has been subject to many criticisms; particularly the use of Article 356 in several occasions has invited criticisms from different quarters, because the centre has used them against the state governments which were controlled by the political parties other than the party at the centre. Mrs. Indira Gandhi had used it 48 times during the period from 1966 to 1977 and from 1980 to 1984 and the Janata Party had used it 16 times during three years, from 1977 to 1980[11]. Thus it is considered against the federal spirit of the constitution[12]. Therefore, the Chief Ministers of Andhra Pradesh, Tamil Nadu, Kerala, and Jammu and Kashmir had demanded the deletion of Article 356[13].

Another arrangement provided by the Constitution, though it is not directly related to the division of powers between the states and the centre, has remifications on the functioning of the Indian federation and enjoyment powers by the Centre and the States in their respective fields. The provisions with regard to the appointment and powers and functions of the constitutional heads of states, the governors are such that the powers of the centre increases vis-à-vis the states. The governors are appointed by the centre's constitutional head and continue in their office during his pleasure. Though normally the governor functions as the constitutional head during the time when a popular government functions in the state sometimes he exercises his discretionary power over-riding the advice of the popular government of the state and recommends measures to the centre which may not be liked by government of the state. For example, he can reserve certain bills passed by the state legislature for presidential assents or he can recommend the declaration of state emergency under Article 356 and even the dissolution of the State Assembly. Therefore, very often he is criticised as an agent of the centre and sometimes the political parties, other than the parties in power at the centre demand the recall of some governors, and such demands are generally ignored by the centre. The provisions related to the office of the governor in the constitution reflect the centralised character of the Indian federation and sometimes the abolition of that office is demanded[14].

Thus, in the distribution of powers, a clear dominating position is given to the centre and it has control over all important subjects as well as the over-riding power over state laws on the subjects mentioned in the concurrent list. Along with these provisions, even on subjects of state list, the centre can legislate in some special situations and centre's directives are to be respected by state governments. This arrangement by the Indian Constitution has led scholars to say that India is "a unitary state with subsidiary federal features" [15] and "Indian Constitution is definitely unfederal" [16].

A federation is a multi-tiered decision making system in which each level has its own powers and functions and manages its own affairs. Both the centre and the states are recognised by the Constitution. "Though there are agencies and devices for Union control over the states in many matters subjects to such exceptions, the states are autonomous within their own spheres as allotted by the Constitution and both the Union and the States are equally subject to the limitations imposed by the Constitution, say, for instance, the exercise of legislative powers being limited by Fundamental Rights"[17]. Therefore, it can be said that India is a federal state with a unitary spirit.

Demand for More Power by the Regions in India

In a composite society like India which consists of various groups with separate identities based on ethnic, linguistic, cultural, religious and other factors there bound to be tension in the political system. When economic and developmental interests are added to the identity issue, problem of regionalism becomes more complex and the sub-national forces become more active. As a result regionalism has been manifested very often in violent form either demanding greater autonomy and power or secession from the Indian federation. This trend has become an integral part of the political process in India since its inception as an independent nation and all parts of India are affected by this malady.

The over-riding of the centre is often resented by the state governments and more so when the governments of the states are formed by political parties other than the party at the centre. So long as there was one party dominance in India and the Congress Party controlled both the Centre and most of the State governments there were less friction. Differences between the centre and the states were sorted out at the party level. But when many regional parties were formed in different states and they came to power in their respective states they developed a fear-psychosis and demanded more autonomy and less control from the central government. Thus the DMK in Tamil Nadu, Akali Dal in Punjab, Siv Sena in Maharashtra, Telugu Desam in Andhra Pradesh, National Conference in Jammu and Kashmir and such other parties in other states are vocal in autonomy demand.

"Changing the federal balance in favour of states has been a major issue in Indian politics from time to time"[18]. But with the emergency of coalition era at the National level and growing importance of regional parties and regional leaders the assertion for more power for states has become louder. At the political level states desire more autonomy and less interference from the Centre.

But the real issue of demanding more power for the states is in the financial field; states have acquired more responsibilities over the years but they lack resources to meet these expenses. "The only meaningful autonomies are financial autonomy and that of being able to maintain law and order effectively"[19]. The increasing dependence of the regions on the centre is the result of distribution of powers in financial matters and the ever expanding responsibilities of the states in other matters as provided by the Constitution.

At the same time regional disparities in financial field are increasing due to the effects of liberalisation and privatisation. The Central investment in poor areas earlier helped them to better their economic condition. But due to disinvestment the poor states are deprived of public sector investment[20].

The states' demand for more powers from the Centre in mobilising financial resources should be analysed in the light of this development. The states believe that independence in financial relations with the Centre will enable them to fulfil the regional aspirations of their people in a more effective way. They can plan their own development schemes taking into account the local needs and without any interference from the Centre.

Distribution of Powers between the Centre and the Provinces in Canada

The Constitution of Canada declares Canada not a federation but one dominion[21]. But scholars like Ronald L. Watts regard it as "a highly centralised federation"[22]. The Constitution gives power to the central legislature over more important subjects like regulation of trade and commerce, postal service, currency and coinage, Naturalisation and aliens, navigation and shipping etc.[23] and the provinces are given powers on amendment of provincial constitution, direct taxation within the province, municipal institution in the province, solemnization of marriage in the province, Property and Civil rights in the province etc.[24]

"All the important responsibilities of government and unlimited financial powers were assigned to the Central government. The Provinces were assigned relatively minor authority over mainly local matters and were made dependent on the Central government for funds. The subordinate position of the Provinces was further emphasised by the assignment of residual power to the Central government, by the provision for reservation and disallowance of Provincial statutes and by the declaratory power enabling the central government to legislate in particular circumstances in areas normally within the provincial jurisdiction"[25].

"The provinces in Canada were assigned exclusive jurisdiction on subjects enumerated in Section 92 of the Act and the Dominion had jurisdiction over the rest and for 'greater certainty' Section 91 of the Act enumerated 29 subjects which were assigned to the Dominion (Federal) Parliament. The enumerated subjects assigned to the Provinces were just 16 in number and they were essentially of a local nature. Section 91 also empowered the Federal Parliament 'to make law for the peace order and good government of Canada in relation to all matters not coming within the classes of subjects by this Act assigned exclusively to the legislatures of the Provinces'. This is an all embracing provision which enables the Federal Parliament to make laws on subjects which are within the exclusive jurisdiction of the Provinces on the plea that they affected the peace, order and good government of Canada. At the top of this, the Federal Government was given power to disallow any law passed by a Provincial legislature within a year of its enactment"[26].

"During the First World War the federal Parliament enacted the War Measures Act which came into force in the issue by the federal government of a proclamation that war, invasion or insurrection, real or apprehended exists. The Act empowers the federal government to make regulations on almost any conceivable subject. The War Measures Act was proclaimed into force for both world wars and during both wars the federal government embarked an extensive economic and other controls in regulations made under the Act"[27]. "Apart from the two world wars, the War Measures Act has been proclaimed, in force on only one other occasion and that was the 'October crisis of October 1970, when the Front de Liberation du Quebec, a violent Quebec separatist group had kidnapped a British diplomat and a Quebec Cabinet Minister (who was later killed by his captors) and had made various demands as the condition for their release"[28].

However, "the evolution of Canadian federalism is frequently described in terms of alternations between periods of centralisation and decentralisation"[29]. At the time of crisis the centre dominates, at other times the Provinces enjoy their power. Though resentments are voiced sometimes serious friction normally do not take place in Canada.

But the concentration of minority groups in Canada has become one of the important factors to determine the relation between the Central government and Provincial government. "The concentration of francophones in Quebec has enabled them to look more to the Provincial government in Quebec city than to the federal government in Ottawa to maintain and promote their interests. Consequently, since confederation Quebec has been an aggressive champion of Provincial autonomy"[30].

"Canadian federalism was originally established with a strong central government and limited provincial authority, but the system has become quite decentralised. The national and Provincial governments have co-implemented various policies but the latter have exercised many important fiscal, financial and Constitutional responsibilities. First ministers meetings have emerged in the past three decades as prominent opportunities for conducting inter-governmental relations and voicing Provincial discontent with federal arrangement[31].

If a comparison is made between India and Canada with regard to power sharing between the Central government and the governments of the Provinces it would appear that the arrangements in both the countries are similar. Both the countries have a federal form of government with a strong Central bias. But the operation of federal model in both the countries differ due to the nature of party system, socio-economic conditions, and size of population and territory. As a consequence the nature of demand of regions from the centre differ in both the countries and the autonomy demand also differs. In India though identity factor plays its role in the demand for more autonomy by the states, economic factor plays a more important role, whereas in Canada identity is considered more important by the states to require their assertion, because Canada is already a developed country.

Secondly, the movement for more autonomy is very often associated with violence in India. Sometimes the centre has to apply repressive measures to suppress such movements as these movements become militant. But in Canada negotiation can be used as an effective means to deal with a demand of the Provincial government.

Thirdly, the reason for less friction between the Centre and States in Canada is the manner in which minority problem was managed in Canada at the time of confederation formation. "Confederation confirmed the minority status of French Canadians but in return gave them real powers with the creation of the Province of Quebec, their main territory, where government would be dominated by French speaking people. Provinces were then granted exclusive powers over such matters as property and Civil Law, Education, Social services and Local works.[32] But in India the problem of minorities did not end with the formation of the federation. Even after the implementation of the Constitution several efforts have been made to solve minority problems by reorganising the federation and creating some new states. But new minorities have been coming up in the new Provinces to put forward their demand of being neglected by the respective state governments. The oppressed minority of the past becomes the oppressor majority of the present and this process continues to give rise new demands. Unless an all-round development takes place to fulfil the needs of all, the problem will not cease in India and minority problem cannot be solved by peaceful methods.

NOTES

1. Gill, Stephen, "Globalization Market Civilisation and Disciplinary Neoliberalism" *Millennium*, Vol. 24(3), 1995, pp. 399-423.
2. Elsenhans, Hartmut, "Political Economy or Economic Politics? Prospects of Civil Society in Era of Globalization", *The Indian Journal of Public Administration*, October-December 2000, Vol. XLVI, No. 4, p. 568.
3. Held, David *et al.*, *Global Transformation: Politics Economics and Culture*, Polity Press, Cambridge, 1999, p. 49.
4. Pfaff-Czarnecka, Joanna; Raja Singham-Senanayake, Darini, "Inventing Ethnicity in some South and South-East Asian States and the Global Ecumene" in Pfaff-Czarnecka, Joanna; Rajasingham-Senanayake, Darini; Nandi, Ashish; Gomez, Edmund Terence; *Ethnic Futures: the State and Identity Politics in Asia*, Sage Publication of India (P) Ltd., New Delhi, 1999, p. 10.
5. Brass, Paul ed., *Ethnic Groups and the State*, Barnes and Noble Books, Totowa, New Jersey, 1985, p. 26.
6. *Encyclopaedia of Social Sciences*, Vol. 13, 1968, p. 378.
7. Oommen, T.K., *Citizenship, Nationality and Ethnicity*, Polity Press, Cambridge, 1997, p. 20.
8. Morris-Hale, Walter, *Conflict and Harmony in Multi-ethnic Societies: An International Perspective*, New York, Peter Lang Publishing Inc., 1997, p. 332.
9. Robertson, David, *Dictionary of Politics* (Second Edition) Penguin Books, London 1993, p. 332.
10. Constitution of India, Art-1.
11. *Times of India*, New Delhi, 6.10.98, p. 8.
12. Karunanidhi, New Delhi, *Times of India,* 29.8.98, p. 98, p. 12.
13. *Times of India*, New Delhi, 17.10.96, p. 8.
14. Nayanar, E.K., demanded the abolition of governor, *Times of India*, New Delhi, 7.11.96, p. 12
15. Wheare, K.C., *Federal Government*, London, Oxford University Press, 1971, p. 28.
16. Mukherji, K.P., "Is India a Federation"? *Indian Journal of Political Science*, July-September 1954, Vol. XV, No. 4, p. 177.
17. Basu, D.D., *Introduction to the Constitution of India* (12th Edition), New Delhi, Prentice-Hall of India Pvt. Ltd., 1989, p. 285.

18. Baruah, Sanjib, "Autonomy for all States", New Delhi, *The Times of India*, 26.7.2000, p. 8.
19. Subrahmanyam, K., "A Dependency Syndrome", *The Times of India*, New Delhi, 25.7.2000, p. 14.
20. Kurien, N.J., "Widening Regional Disparities in India", *Economic and Political Weekly*, February 12, 2000.
21. Section 3 of the BNA Acts 1967-1976 as quoted in Hogg, Peter W., *Constitutional Law of Canada*, Toronto, Canada, The Carswell Company Limited, 1977, p. 448.
22. Watts, Ronald L., "The American Constitution in Comparative Perspective: A Comparison of Federalism in the United States and Canada", *Journal of American History*, Vol. 74, Issue 3, December 1987, p. 771.
23. Section 91 of the BNA Acts 1967-1976 as quoted in Hogg, Peter W., *Constitutional Law of Canada*, Toronto, Canada, The Carswell Company Limited, 1977, pp. 459-461.
24. Section 92, *Ibid*., pp. 462-463.
25. Watts, Ronald, L., "The American Constitution in Comparative Perspective: A Comparison of Federalism in the United States and Canada", *Journal of American History*, Vol. 74, Issue 3, December 1987, pp. 771-772.
26. Kapur, A.C. *Select Constitutions*, New Delhi, S. Chand & Company Limited, 1983, p. 404.
27. Hogg, P.W., *Constitutional Law of Canada*, Toronto, Canada, The Carswell Company Ltd., 1977, p. 252.
28. *Ibid*, p. 253.
29. Cairns, Alan C., "The other Crisis of Canadian Federalism", *Canadian Public Administration*, Vol. 22, No. 2, Summer, 1979, p. 176.
30. Watts, Ronald L., "The American Constitution in Comparative Perspective: A Comparison of Federalism in the United States and Canada", *Journal of American History*, Vol. 174, Issue 3, December 1987, p. 778.
31. Stewart, Marianne C.; Kornberge, Allan; Clarke, Harold D.; Acock, Allan; "Arena and Attitudes: A Note on Political Efficacy in a Federal System", *Journal of Politics*, February 1992, Vol. 54, Issue No. 1, p. 181.
32. Narang, A.S., *Ethnic Identities and Federalism*, Indian Institute of Advanced Study, Shimla, 1995, p. 102.

26

Globalization Poses New Challenges to South-South Solidarity

PRAMOD MISHRA

Introduction

Today Globalization has become a way of life for most of the nations of the world. If the peoples across different continents want to escape the adverse effect of globalization, they find it rather challenging. The developing nations of the world have willingly been trapped in its net in their long-term strategy of getting rich by hook or by crook, getting oüt of the devastating and multiplying debt trap. Now-a-days, whether one likes it or not, in any discourse on national or international political or social order, an overt or covert impact of globalization is clearly visible. Perhaps, the fastest and unthinkable growth in communication technology has facilitated the global networking of peoples and ideas even in the remotest part of the world.

The purpose of this chapter is to link these questions. First, why is globalization so important today in the lives of people all over the world? Second, can any social science debate in the present-day world be free from the draconian impact of globalization? Third, can one identify some operational indices of globalization rather than getting bugged by its economic orientation? Fourth, how have the global community in general and the common people and intelligentsia of the developing in particular respond to several multiplier effect of globalization, especially in reorienting their socio-cultural and political lives? Last but not the least, can there be a panacea for the nations of the South to somehow absorb the dehumanizing effect of globalization and continue to forge meaningful linkages among themselves at least to minimize the harmful effects?

The Nomenclature of Globalization

Globalization emerged as a buzz word in the 1990s. Without going into the major jargons, let me highlight some of its major operational indices. At the present juncture, the most frequent use of globalization is in relation to transformations in the international political economy, and particularly within the organization of capitalism. The most popular terms for characterizing these changes is the economic globalization or the globalized capitalism.[1] The main thesis of economic globalization is that the capacity of sovereign nation-states to protect their domestic economies and citizens is diminished by global economy. Instead of wealth being created by national governments through financial investment, production, distribution and marketing—it is now created at the global level, outside the control of national governments and domestic public policies. Since the 1970s changes in production, labour and financc have been dramatic. Production is now delocalized. In the past, goods and services were produced by workers within a national territory for local consumption and later for international markets. Today workers in the developing countries provide the cheap labour and they produce components to be assembled worldwide for a global market. Thus, one can say, instead of workers say of Mexico, Nigeria or Bangladesh being part of a national economy, they are increasingly integrated into the global economy. Thus, globalization has brought profound changes in labour practices. Workers located in different countries are now increasingly integrated into a global factory and a new international division of labour. With the emergence of Brettonwoods system in the post-war period and the development of world and IMF in 1973, technological developments have enabled financial transactions to move across multiple national borders at the speed of lightning thereby inhibiting effective state control. Thus the globalizing economy being increasingly non-territorial, involves integrated production and services and is shaped by global actors like the MNCs whose views on global competitiveness and interests cannot be reduced to the interests of specific national actors.

There is however another dimension of globalization, which one can categorize under cultural and political. We all know that throughout recorded history men and women have travelled long distance in pursuit of trade, of empire, of converts and of shaping of spiritual culture of many places in different regions of the world. Ideas, objects and people "outside" are now more and more obviously present than they have ever been. These can be regarded as cultural and political dimension of globalization.[2]

Positive and Negative Aspects of Globalization

At present there are two competing and contradictory views about the significance of globalization in cultural and political terms. The first view focuses on clashes and tensions, the other on the emergence of a global, multicultural and cosmopolitan civilization. The first one is represented by Samuel Huntington, Fukuyama and Benjamin Barber. Huntington suggests that the post-cold war period is characterized by a "clash of civilization". Civilizations are broadest forms of culture and identity. To him in the foreseeable future, there is a possibility of the conflict of cultural values between the "west and the rest". Thus western liberal values are juxtaposed against so-called orthodox civilizations, which include Islam, Confucianism, Hinduism and Buddhism. Fukuyama in his paper, *The End of History* associates the post cold war period with the world-wide hegemony of western liberalism and forms of governance. Benjamin maps a conflictual situation between two competing tendencies: homogenizing values of "Mcworld"—the internationalization of American consumer culture—that sees every one wearing a Michael Jackson T-shirt, watching CNN and Hollywood movies, eating at the McDonalds, using Microsoft and talking of "Jihad *vs* "Mcworld", the fragmenting tendencies of ethnic and cultural nationalism that led to genocide and ethnic cleansing in Bosnia.

The other dominant view of culture and politics, is the complex interconnection and social ties leading to a new global infrastructure which links individuals, families and associations across nation-state boundaries into the "reality of world society". Several scholars have developed upon this hypothesis. For instance, Perlmutter, talks of the gradual emergence of a global civilization based on more transparency, religious pluralism and a holistic culture[5]. Rosenau highlights on the shared values of globalism or cosmopolitanism which points to aspirations for a state of affairs where values are shared by all the world's five billion plus population. It also connotes a conception of political identity and ideology that is worldwide[6]. Thus, the cultural focus of globalization tends to be on a worldwide phenomena that includes "interconnections, interchanges and movement of people, images, commodities" across national territorial frontiers.

Susan strange highlights that there has been a transformation from national consciousness to what might be called "global consciousness" which involves changes in perceptions, beliefs, ideas and taste. What this basically means is that while cultural differences persists, the sensibilities and susceptibilities of individual human beings are increasingly modified by the process of global homogenization[7] such a notion also matches the utopian dream of a "global village"[8] which was first coined by Marshall McLuhan in 1964. He conceived of a world as one community. A modest effort of experimenting with such a novel idea has been given a fair trial in Auroville of Pondicherry in India.

Anthony Giddens gives yet another interpretation of globalization by treating it as the intensification of worldwide social relations which links distant localities in such a way that local happenings are shaped by events occurring many miles away and vice versa.

Such intensification is possible in ecological, economic, strategic and ethical spheres[8]. For instance, ecologically speaking, there is a worldwide recognition of global climatic change, deforestation and desertification. In the economic sphere, there is the awareness of the low wages of labour in the global factory located mostly in a developing country. Strategically speaking, the uses of nuclear weapons, IBMs and spy satellites have made the world into one strategic sphere. Ethically speaking, one can notice a worldwide discourse on democracy, human rights, poverty and cultural values. Speaking on a similar tone, Edward Soja treats globalization as a new political-cultural governing order[9] such a new order embraces an emergent global economy characterized by changes in production labour and finance. However, it also includes notions of global governance, global civil society and the idea of an emergent global civilization.

As regards identifying some common responses to globalization, Frederic Jameson identifies four of them. First, globalization is dismissed as nothing more than "globaloney". Second, he claims, globalization is nothing new, as it even existed in the neolithic age. When cultural artifacts were exchanged across trade routes well before the emergence of nation-states. A third response relates globalization to the changes in the world market and capitalist networks. It maintains that capitalism has always been globalising. Finally, he would like to regard it as a third stage of capitalism or multi-national capitalism[10].

Contradictions of Globalization

The prevalent metaphors of globalization sound elusive and the global processes are fundamentally contradictory. On the one hand, it can be seen as a universalizing tendency that is producing a world that is borderless, seamless, integrative and convergent, on the other hand, it can be argued that that globalization is a particularising tendency that is creating a world characterized by fragmentation, disintegration, divergence, balkanization and tribalism. Globalization in the present millennium will continue to be shaped by complexity and contradictions. Some major contradictions are: (1) inclusion and exclusion; (2) wealth and impoverishment; (3) economy and environment; (4) modernity and post modernity; and (5) national citizen and global citizen. We can briefly highlight each one of them.

Inclusion and Exclusion

Globalization clearly differentiates between classes, genders, nationalities and regions and irrationally pursues the policy of "pick and exclude". One can illustrate from the practices of the European Community (EC) which has been reinforcing unequal relations and privileges between citizens of the member-states and "other residents". Besides, these days the policy of exclusion is followed by many states on matters of trade, finance and investment. For instance, during the last two decades, we can notice a deepening of economic relations within a "triad" (EC, Japan, Southeast Asia and NAFTA). Thus a large number of developing nations from Asia, Africa and Latin America are not included in the global economic and financial relations. Globalization is a structural relations in which some people and states are irrelevant. Even within the developed North, the poor, homeless, refugees and immigrants experience economic and social exclusion and thus do not enter global civilization on an equal footing.

Growing Wealth and Impoverishment

In the 1970s and 1980s modernisation theory promised that developing countries would "take off" if they opened their economies to free trade, that wealth will trickle down from rich to the poor. With the dawn of the new millennia, ironically enough, the rich are getting richer and the poor getting poorer within the North and the South and between the North and the South. In 1960, the poorest 20 per cent of the world's population accounted for 2.3 per cent of the world's income; by 1997, this number has declined to 1.1 per cent. As highlighted by a revealing study by Bradshaw and Wallace, at the present juncture, more than 35000 children die daily (mostly in the developing countries) from preventable diseases. The glaring inequality between the rich and poor countries is also reflected in the average annual income. Whereas in case of the rich countries (like Canada, US, Australia, Japan and Germany) the average annual income is $ 21174(US), by contrast, the poorest 42 states mostly in Sub Saharan Africa, a large part of South Asia, Nicaragua and Haiti, the average income is less than a single US dollar a day. In case of a large number of developing countries, the state's ability to cope with emergencies and natural disasters is very low, thus leading to thousands of deaths and millions of dollars of damage. This uneven effect of globalization is further aggravated by a host of political, economic and political problems associated with the development in the post-colonial states.

The Economy and the Environment

Rapid economic growth in several parts of the world has left a spillover effect on environment. Large-scale migration and urbanization has exacerbated that process. These days, deforestation, desertification, pollution, the depletion of ozone layer and resource depletion are not confined within the territorial borders of the national state. But obviously the developing countries are the worst hit. Ironically, where there has been the political will to develop transterritorial regulations for trade, finance and investment, there has been no comparable commitment for environment. Urbanisation also causes strains on the global ecosystem. It is estimated that by 2025, sixty-one per cent of the world's population in some of the mega cities in Latin America and Asia and the absence of clean water and sanitation for a large majority of the slum population, one notices a perpetual spread of fatal diseases.

Modernity and Post Modernity

Today, globalization indicates a modern integrated economy on the one hand, but a post-modern fragmented political sphere on the other. Fundamental to the project of modernity was the idea of progress—

human societies were on a continuous path towards the good society. The post-modern perspective rejects the idea of progress and remains skeptical towards the idea of a good society. Besides, paradoxically, post-modernism rejects all grand narratives—basically theories that purport to explain all human relations. In some respects, globalization discourse is a current example of a grand narrative of "all embrasive market overriding all other logics, whether that of state, civil society, democracy or principle of justice. While globalization seems to fulfil the economic vision of modernity the political and cultural projects remain underdeveloped.

National Citizen and Global Citizen

Now-a-days, the idea of a democratic citizen, an invention of the modern nation-state sounds paradoxical. On the one hand, it assumes membership in a nation-state, equal civil belonging in a political community and cultural belonging in a national community. However, in reality, the notion of equal belonging in a political community is contradicted by history of discrimination on the basis of race, ethnicity, gender, sexuality and religion. Throughout human history, the process of nation formation have entailed brutal conquest incorporation and colonialism. Recently a French historian, Ernest Renan (1992) has emphasized that nation formation in different parts of the world also involves long processes of "forgetting difference". He cites a burning example of the way the settler societies such as Canada, USA and Australia imagined themselves by forgetting the differences of the aboriginals/indigenous peoples.

International migration is giving rise to ethno-cultural communities in old societies that previously had imagined themselves as homogeneous. In societies as diverse as India, Canada and South Africa, the persistence of ethnic and cultural minorities is leading to two contradictory dynamics; one notices individuals celebrating their multiple and conflicting (or transcultural) identities, while the other witnesses ethnic tensions, conflict and violence. In either case, the modern notion of individuals belonging to a single political and cultural community is obsolete. Most states today are multiethnic and multi cultural and will be increasingly so in the next millennium. Such a scenario has raised the idea of global citizenship, but it is in an underdeveloped stage due to the lack of global governance. Today the call for global citizenship is more a matter of necessity than choice. It is mainly due to two developments. The first relates to transformation of nation-states, including the erosion of state sovereignty and the states' growing inability to protect its citizens from the vagaries of globalization. The second focuses on the complex and contradictory forces of globalization, which cannot be subjected to control by a single nation-state. These two developments suggests the need to strengthen the role of supranational institutions to curb the excesses of global economy, minimize social marginalization and exclusion, amiliorate growing inequality and impoverishment and confront global environmental problems. Although it sounds like a "peddling utopia",[12] it is also recognised that in order for a global citizenship to emerge, supra national institutions will have to be open, accessible, democratically accountable and reflective of the needs and aspirations of world's citizens. Till now the institutions of global governance whether OECD, WTO or APEC have suffered from a democratic deficit with much of their deliberations clouded in secrecy and with few or no mechanism for inputs by individuals, groups and/or movements within the civil society. The paradox now is between the diminished national citizenship and an underdeveloped global citizenship.

New Challenges to the Developing World from Globalization

As regards the impact of globalization on the developing world in general there seems to be no consensus. Let me begin with a poem by Wistawa Szymbarky, the Polish Nobel laureate for literature in 1996. The caption is; "The Century's Decline". He writes:

> Our twentieth century was going to improve on the others
> it will never prove it now
> its gait is shaky
> its breath is short
> Too many things have happened
> that were not supposed to happen
> and what was supposed to come about, has not
> happiness and spring among other things
> Were supposed to be getting closer
> A couple of problems were not going
> to come any more
> Hunger for example
> And war and so forth

...Any one who planned to enjoy the world
is now faced
With a hopeless task
......
God was finally going to believe
In a man both good and strong
But good and strong
Are still two different men
......

The world has changed dramatically in the last 50 years, but its institutional grid has not. Less than a quarter of the members of IMF and world were present when the institutional structures were crafted under the Brettonwoods system. Developing nations joined gradually over the years, but did so as rule takers, not rule makers. There are now nearly 200 countries in the international system and their packing order has shifted. The advent of regional alliances and union have prompted a realignment of positions and interests across the globe. With the passage of time, the mismatch between the antiquated structure of multinational institutions and their larger global environment has increased and so have tensions.

The institutional mechanism of global decision-making appear glaringly inadequate if you judge to the extent to which they truly represent the countries and the peoples of the world. For instance, the nations that are least represented in multilateral leadership positions relating to their size are, China and India which account for 37 per cent of global population. The group of seven industrialized countries (G7)—Canada, France, Germany, Italy, Japan, UK and USA-plus the rest of EU represent a mere 14 per cent of the world's population, yet they control 56 per cent of the votes in the IMF executive board. As in all clubs, the rules of multinational institutions reflect the preferences of the founders. For instance, Bank of International Settlements (BIS) was an exclusive club for 50 years—a forum for central bankers from advanced economies to cooperate and help promote international financial stability. Although the ambit if BIS has rapidly expanded to include banking supervision and financial market monitoring, its governance structure still remains closed to major developing countries, in a move to broaden the base of IMF's powerful international monetary and financial committee, USA spearheaded the creation in 1999 of the group of 20 (G20)—a new forum for consultation on matters relating to the global financial system, which includes larger developing countries. But the group still leaves the poorest countries voiceless.

The global environment within which multinational institutions operate has changed the way that make these institutions and their leaders more important. Mounting frustrations at the mismatch between the widening agendas of international organisations and the narrow base of their governance were manifest in their ugly battles that erupted over the selection of the Director-General of the WTO in 1999. Its predecessor, the GATT had limited powers; consequently disputes over its leadership were muted. The WTO however refers to a much larger game and has substantial sanctioning authority. Developing countries resented what they considered stacked rules of the game coming out of GATTs Uruguay Rounds of trade negotiations, so the selection of a new WTO Director-General in 1999 became even more critical.

Some critics advance the argument that globalization is likely to adversely affect the growth of state sovereignty. At present, all government organs, including the regional and local ones will have to listen to the dictates of the World Bank, IMF and WTO as these organisations send their representatives to all these bodies. These global bodies can have a major say not only in funding the leading projects, but also in laying down labour standards and environmental safeguards. As many of the national level projects are totally controlled by the World Bank or MNCs in terms of state sovereignty on economic and financial matters, most of the developing countries have lost grounds.

Yet another argument is advanced by the critics that due to globalization of capital and investment, the solidarity of the labour class in the developing countries is totally broken. The working class in these nations is fragmented. Several stringent immigration laws prevent workers to emigrate on a large scale. On the other hand, in the name so-called "global factory", poor workers have been paid low wages by sub-contractors and often subjected to harsher rule of hire and fire. Many of these workers being women have been easily victimised and often "niked".[14]

However, the intermediate layer—the middle class in these countries has taken up the opportunity. The professionals, the employers and the managers of these countries may bargain and strike a deal with any MNC. For instance, these people can set up a factory in India or Mexico and send the products to USA or Canada. Thus, one notices globalization of middle class and elites in these countries. Today the middle classes in these countries are in a state of dillemmas and their loyalties are dependent upon technology, market and money (which have been already globalized). Today the national affiliation of middle class say in India is replaced by a sort of corporate citizenship and to them now the Indian state is no good. Thus the erosion of the middle class from national affiliation is a big issue. Similarly the few big families in the developing world have put their money in the banks of Switzerland, UK or USA. Thus, the governments in these countries are left with only poor workers. As a result the quality of governance in these countries has already gone down. The state is now both a mechanism of development and corruption. One can cite several illustrations from these countries to substantiate these points. For instance, in Ghana, cocoa and aluminum production has been taken over by Kaiger, a German company and supported by the World Bank. In that process, the top elites in these countries, have got a lot of money but the people at large remain impoverishment. South Korea is another case of development and corruption. Borrowing heavily from the American companies, it was successfully manipulated by the ruling elites in order to bring a very high rate of growth for several years in the 1970s and in 1980s but globalization has changed the picture. South Korea no longer enjoys the protection of the United States. Because several Korean companies borrowed so immensely they had to face the deregulation of the market forces and several reverses since 1987 East Asian economic crisis. Now sooner or later, several Korean companies will have to be sold to the American companies.

Another major impact of globalization on the developing world can be seen in the area of civil societies which have become less effective now in controlling their respective national government.

Besides, one can trace the imprint of neo-colonialism in the way the voice of the south has been suppressed or minimised by WTO dominated by the North. In the North dominated global trade, the developing states have hardly any voice. Even on patenting and intellectual property rights, a badly divided South has at best a muted voice. The role of middle powers like India and Brazil are now minimized on the global transactions. TNCs now play an overwhelming role in all spheres of life in the developing countries. Even in the remotest part of the world, one can notice the cultural invasion of neo-imperialism in the form of Microsoft, McDonalds and Michael Jackson euphoria.

Today as to the status of power relations among the nation-states. It is really lamented if it is reduced to the imprint of structural adjustment in Asia, Africa or in Latin America. Now as a result of the dominant representation of the World Bank and IMF in several decision-making bodies of the southern states, their people are really in a state of dilemma. Today the situation has come to such a level that South-South cooperation has practically been reduced to a minimum. Now the capacity of the hitherto powerful southern states has been reduced as result of dependency syndrome and the logical conclusion of a trap. However, there is a silver lining for a state like India, which because of its highly skilled IT professionals has made its presence felt in the Silicon Valley, the nerve centre of major world business. Some of these professionals are one of the most highly paid individuals in the world. That is in contrast to other kinds of cheap jobs going to the South, where one can find the displacement of subsistence and development of the working class concept slowly emerging. The role of fibre optics has empowered the civil societies in India and these phenomena simply cannot be explained in terms of North-South dichotomy and exploitation.

On a final note on the adverse impact of globalization, let me briefly recapitulate the inspiring talk by the well-known Canadian diplomat, Stephen Lewis on January 29, 2001 at the international week celebration of the university of Alberta, Edmonton. He lamented the fact that as an after effect of globalization, millions of people in the developing world not only face starvation, but also are victims of AIDS and merciless deaths. In his opinion, especially the most vulnerable sections of in several countries of Asia, Latin America and Africa are the women, minor girls and children. In such an appalling situation, Lewis was highly critical of the role of the G-7 countries and their presenting compliments to one another at the economic summit held in Davos recently. He specially appealed to the youth to join as worthy global citizens in large number worthwhile civil society movements thereby playing a positive role for the empowerment of the most vulnerable sections of the society in any parts of the world.

Some Positive Developments

Some scholars in a recent book prescribe some positive preconditions for a better functioning of globalization.[15] They are hopeful that can work to lift overall prosperity and reduce poverty, if its scope is broadened and to include liberty and democracy... When the anti-globalization crowd demonstrated in Seattle and Washington during 1999, the demonstrators mostly comprised of white middle class workers. Jagdish Bhagwati, a noted economist from Columbia University makes a succinct observation on this development. He writes: "to say that globalization need a human face. This implies of course that it lacks one"[16]. In his observation, on the qualitative responses of both the North and the South he adds, "Rich politicians embraced globalization in the decades following world war second forging the international economic order. By contrast, the poor countries walked away from it, treating it as a peril rather than an opportunity. But today the mainstream policy makers in poor countries are busily abandoning autarkic attitudes while rich countries lobbies and responsive politicians are reinventing for themselves the very fears that the old chastened policy makers in poor countries consider to have been disastrous for their well-being."

Some other analysts have taken recourse to a discourse of "there is no alternative" (TINA) whereby the faceless beast of globalization has robbed individuals and collectivities of their powers of self-determination. Some economists have highlighted that the developing nations with the most open economies—the nations that thoroughly plugged into the global market system—grow the fastest. The most stubbornly poor nations, it seems are so poor because they are unglobalized.[17]. This theory helps us to explain as to why East Asia with its embrace of global markets has massively reduced poverty while sub-Saharan Africa, featuring more statist economies and unappetizing political environment for foreign investment, has been less successful. Fernando Henrique Cardoso, President of Brazil indicates a note of cautious optimism about globalization when he says: "In the international arena challenges are arising that threaten the existence of democratic global citizenship...and the growing global importance of the global economy has yet to be matched by a proportional improvement in international governance structure"[18]. He also believes that markets are subject to "manias, panics and crashes"...Markets offer very fewer solutions when problems are related to fundamental and ethical values, such as the idea that all human beings are created equal. He agrees with sociologist, Manuel Castells to usher in an era of citizenship and equal opportunity.

Way Out for South-South Solidarity

Today, the nation-state in South is a broker for the World Bank, IMF and TNCs. It is also a prison guard of its own people, so that they do not move out of the country. At present, there is hardly any scope for further emigration to Europe, which has a 40 per cent unemployment or underemployment. Even the situation in north America is not very rosy for the prospective emigrant workers with the exception of the highly skilled IT professionals. The South must seize this opportunity to improve more intra-regional trade through regional trading blocs. The success story of infrastructural linkages and joint collaboration in new technology as initiated by ASEAN, should be emulated by other regional grouping of the south nations.

The nations of the South can also forge meaningful linkages in the area of social security, especially on the empowerment of women, child labour and environ control. All these nations can work as pressure groups to lobby with the TNCs in order to improve standards in these areas. Already these nations have left their marked imprints at the Unsponsored Environment summit (RIO), Women summit (Beijing), and population summit (Cairo). At the G77 level all these nations will have to go to the original visions of the Bandung Summit (1955). They will have to focus on the marginalized and disenfranchised people. The future for South-South cooperation will have to be fundamentally anti-TNCs. Recently they have achieved another success at the UN in the safeguarding of the interests of the indigenous peoples all over the world. They have also raised their dissenting voice at Amsterdam on the global mismanagement of environment. They have really taken a rallying point to protect nature and people's livelihood.

NOTES

1. Don Marshal, "Understanding late twentieth century Capitalism", *Government and Opposition*, 31, 2, Spring, 1996.
2. For details see Saskia Sason, *Globalization and its Discontents*, New York, New Press, 1998.
3. Samuel Huntington, 1996, *The Clash of Civilization and the remaking of the World Order* (Simon), Fukuyama, 1992, *The End of History*, and Benjamin Barber, 1998, Democracy at Risk: American Culture in a Global Culture, *World Policy Journal,* 15, 2, Summer
4. Barber, *Jihad vs. Mcworld*, New York, Times Books, 1995.

5. Hv Perlmutter, "On the Rocky Road the First Global Civilization", *Human Relations*, 44, 9, 1991, 897-1010.
6. James N. Rosenau, *Turbulence in World Politics,* Princeton, Princeton University Press, 1990.
7. Strange Susan, "The Errosion of The State", *Current History*, November, 1997, 365.
8. Anthony Giddens, *The Consequences of Modernity: Se and Society in the Late Modern Age,* Cambridge, Polity Press, 1990.
9. Edward Soja, *Postmodern Geography*, London, Versa Books, 1989.
10. Frederic Jameson, "Preface, in F. Jameson and M. Miyosh (Eds), *Cultures of Globalization,* NC, Duke University Press, 1998.
11. York Bradshaw and Michael Wallace, *Global Inequalities*, Pineforge Press, Sage, 1997.
12. Stephen Castles, "Globalization and Migration: Some Pressing Contradictions", *International Social Science Journal*, 50, 2, 1998, 179-87.
13. "Naming a New Era", 2000, *Foreign Policy*, Summer.
14. Giles Mohan, "Dislocating Globalization: Power, Politics and Global Change", *Geography*, 2000, 125-27.
15. John Micklethwait and Andrian Woolridge, *Future Perfect: The Challenge and Hidden Promise of Globalisation*, New York, Crown Business, 2000.
16. Jagdish Bhagwati, "Globalization in Your Face, A New Book Humanizes Global Capitalism", *Foreign Affairs,* July/August, 2000, 134-38.
17. Robert Wright, "Will Globalization Make You Happy?", *Foreign Policy*, 2000, 54, 56-64.
18. Fernando Enrique Cardoso, "An Age of Citizenship in Naming a New Era", *Foreign Policy*, Summer, 2000.

27

Globalization and Regionalism in the Asia Pacific Region

SUNIL SONDHI

Introduction

In recent years, dramatic international changes have ushered in transformations in the economic, political and socio-cultural arrangements of forces and structures. These events revolutionised the economic and trade relations, production and communications. They also reshaped relationships between capitalist powers, and shifted ideological paradigms. World systems scholars starting from Polanyi, Wallerstein, Keohane, and Robertson, just to name a few, argued that globalization dates as far back as the onset of modernisation although recent breakthroughs in the communication and information technology have succeeded in bringing it in the realm of culture and consciousness. Today's complex interdependence has redefined the notion of hegemonic power considering the new character of its influence over sovereignty, autonomy and accountability of states (Keohane and Nye 1989).

The early part of the 90s saw a pattern of a tri-polar political-economic structure defined by trade competition and cooperation. The increased wealth and influence of Pacific Asia as well as the emerging relationships among major capitalist powers in Northern America and Western Europe introduced a new geo-economic perspective called regionalism. The movement started with the European decision to integrate their economies after the German reunification. The long stalemate in the General Agreement on Tariffs and Trade (GATT) negotiations and the US' need to reposition itself to address the increasing economic strength of Asia and Europe prompted the formation of the North American Free Trade Area (NAFTA). The ascent of Pacific Asia as a new epicentre of capital accumulation, the growth of inter-regional trade which started in the 80s and Japan's move to increase trade relations and mechanisms of influence to other Asian countries encouraged a form of regional cooperation.

The conceptual and theoretical implications of the occurrence of at first seemingly incompatible processes of wealth accumulation ignited debates regarding the eventual twenty-first century world system. Considering the inference associated with the General Agreement on Tariffs and Trade (GATT) and the eventual establishment of the World Trade Organisation (WTO) regime in the early 90s, macrostructural debates over whether what will prevail will be a multilateral, interdependent system with close cooperation among capitalist powers, or a regional bloc scenario consisting of trade and investment blocs in North America, Europe and Asia occupied the attention of policy makers and scholars. Now that things are moving on, it is becoming clear that the two tendencies are not mutually exclusive, since nation-states in their bid to retain critical participation in the global economy are now adopting a mixture of domestically oriented, regionally directed and globally aligned industries. In Asia, the different regional economic integration efforts however were affected by the financial crisis that hit the region starting in 1997. Current talks among stakeholders are taking on a different tune at the beginning of the new century.

For those seeking for alternatives to the current development model, socialism's lost of appeal and the many difficulties being experienced now by countries which adopted the model has brought to the fore the need for a new alternative vision that could address the multiplying negative effects of the new world order. For civil society organisations, besides following closely the unfolding developments on economic and international relations, an equally important concern which they have to put more attention to is on how to protect and strengthen the normative and ethical alternatives that were already established by past state-society engagements. Specifically in Asia, how could the democratic space obtained by social movements through their long and hard fought struggles against colonialism and dictatorship be expanded and reach a cross-border dimension so as to challenge the negative implications of the processes of globalization and regionalism? In the seemingly overwhelming measures by dominant economies against their poorer trade partners, how could the marginalising consequences of unregulated market operations be addressed and poverty alleviation realised?

As nation-states lose their power to protect their national economy, economic decisions were transferred to transnational structures which operate under the baton of a global, complexly organised and exclusionary logic of the market. The "reterritorialised" political and economic relations of states (de Sousa Santos 1995) transferred control of decision-making processes concerning wealth creation and distribution beyond national borders. For civil society, the enhanced power wielded by capital, firms and information networks poses more difficult problems, since work in these three domains needs more capacity building efforts from their part. Because the traditional focus of civil society in the past has been its engagement with the state in the struggle to democratise control over national and local resources, the "transnationalisation of state" (Cox 1987) and the seemingly irreversible drive toward economic interdependence determined by internationally mobile capital have redefined the arena of struggle. This change requires a new set of political and socio-economic strategies on the part of the new social movements and non-governmental development organisations which this chapter refers to in its discussions about civil society.

Gill's synthesis of Cox and Braudel's understanding of the world order involves an investigation of relatively persistent pattern of ideas, institutions and material forces which form historical structures which dominates particular societies or civilisational forms in both space and time. Reproduction of reality rests on the understanding of the dialectics of social structures. Space and time must be understood in relation to value and power. As the earlier proponents of the approach like Gramsci and Polanyi effectively showed, understanding the contradictions of social structures provide social actors with instruments to transform society.

In the book *Empire and Emancipation*, Nederveen Pieterse discussed that the dialectic of resistance in opposing domination, calls upon resources that are or appear to be the opposite of the dominant imperial ones... yet, if the emancipatory movement is to succeed in its objectives, it must also, to an extent, bring itself to the level of its opponent. It necessitates measures which he further proposed like the appropriation of the opponent's technology, and selective emulation of its mode of organisation and strategy. These justify the now common call in the movements for alternative to "talk the talk and walk the walk".

Also, Pieterse mentioned that together, domination and emancipation, empire and liberation constitute a force field in which they increasingly interpenetrate one another, and in the course of this backstage negotiation the actual process of humanisation of social relations takes shape. This approach challenges civil society to come up with a cohesive counter-hegemonic plan that could equip it with viable mechanisms in its engagement with the emerging more complex geopolitical and geoeconomic struggle that necessitates what Gramsci called "war of position" (Forgacs 1988) in the local, national and global levels.

The Pacific Century and the Asian Crisis

The modernisation of Asia is one of the most important and dynamic developments in the last three decades of the twentieth century. Two factors contributed to this: first is the spectacular economic performance of Japan, the tiger economies in East Asia and key members of the ASEAN (Association of South East Asian Nations), which is largely attributed to the NIC (newly industrialised country) model of development and the structural power of the internationally mobile capital during the last twenty years; second is the transition to a market economy by China and Indochina.

The dialectical process between the reconstruction of a regional identity and strengthening of links (see Gamble and Payne 1996), as well as the demand for openness of national economies to the global economy pushed for the different efforts of building regional economic integration. Recent trends in both investment and trade flows are strengthening this push making regional trade bloc formation inevitable. A regional trading bloc can be defined as an association of states that reduces intraregional barriers to trade, investment and human capital (Bergsten and Noland 1995).

Regionalism should be viewed in relation to the question of hegemony. In what is emerging to be a post-hegemonic world order, the Gramscian concept of equating hegemony with the foundation and establishment of a system with relatively universal appeal, with mechanisms which permit the institutionalisation of conflict and the weighting of subordinate interests in a transnational political settlement is still very much valid. As shown by the different Asian regional initiatives namely the ASEAN Free Trade Area (AFTA), the East Asia Economic Group, and the Asia Pacific Economic Cooperation (APEC), the hegemony over regional politics and economic arrangement along a specific line is a struggle between state strategies which are seeking to define the regional project.

The economic expansion of Asia as Arrighi (1996) and Frank (1994) argued, should be viewed as a return to a world system that saw an important role of Asia in what they call Sinocentric tribute-trade system. Today, Asia's emerging political, economic and cultural influence is based on foundations which are different from the dominant Anglo-American model. In East Asia, strong states engineered the shape of their economies (Chowdhury and Islam, 1993). The development strategies and the adoption of the NIC development model of the neighbouring countries are factors that shape the flows of trade and investment in the region and this redefined the development context for the rest of developing countries. After the financial crisis, the framework for Regionalism suffered a conundrum and became a problem-solving exercise that failed to generate a sound solution. Growth, chartered through the "Asian way of capitalism" characterised by state intervention and protectionism, was put into review and became a launching pad for critiques against corruption.

The interregnum between the old and the new, dynamic Asia is connected by the lingering stories of poverty in peripheral areas found both in the developed and developing economies. The 1998 Poverty Report of the UNDP estimated that Asia and the Pacific region has 83 per cent of its people in the international poverty line or having an income of $1 per day. More than ever, it is still relevant to raise questions whether or not development is taking place, what kind of development, and towards what direction is it leading. The growing list of the underprivileged that is being sacrificed in the altar of economic growth is steadily increasing. Cheap labour continues to be the major attraction for investors, low wages and the denial of workers' rights for security and welfare (CETRI 1982, Thomas 1995) are still prevalent. Mobile capital is undermining the habitat of indigenous people and their communities, causing their displacement to make way for mines and factories leading to environmental pillage that strip and destroys sources of livelihoods. Between 1981 and 1990, more than 3 million hectares of tropical forest were lost in South East Asia and the Pacific (UNDP 1995:25).

Effects of export-led strategies and Structural Adjustment Programmes (SAPs) in poor countries in Asia as in the rest of the developing world, brought about crisis in social reproduction and an intensified commodification of the everyday life. The transfer of power to private capital effect reforms that caused the diminished redistributive capacity of the state resulting to decreased allotment to public expenditures. These transferred the burden of providing basic needs to the family which in turn gives extra load to women who do two-thirds of all the work in Third World societies (Gill 1995:92). The gains achieved by women in the transformed gender relations were eroded by the impact of adjustment and transition because they then have to work harder to fulfil their multiple roles as mothers, household managers, community workers and producer of goods and services (UNDP 1995:41), reinforcing the inequality between gender. This could be highly observed in Asia's poor enclaves.

Regional Integration and the Japanese Dominance in Asia

Though market oriented, Asian capitalism is influenced by the Japanese development model which is deeply rooted on a tradition where social and political institutions are governed by the principles of hierarchy, authority and long-term commitments (Yun-han 1995). To understand the current differences in Asian regionalisms, it is important to examine Japan's role in the region and how the NIEs (Newly Industrialized Economies) and ASEAN economies reacted to that role. The enigma of Japanese international policies and its paradoxical image as an economic giant—political dwarf (Mendl 1995) could be attributed to the many checks and balances within its system, its chequered history and its close association with the United States. With its $ 4.3 trillion economy, a vital market and huge capital which is financing international structures like the UN and even the US budget deficit, Japan as a 'major league' player in global politics is maintaining a dual role. The first is that of an Asian hegemony with strategic role in Asian economic, political and security dimensions, and on the other hand, a part of the western alliance.

Suspicions concerning the Japanese intent to establish a yen-bloc in Asia could be traced back to its earlier militarist attempt under the Asia Co-prosperity Sphere project. At present, its ever-increasing post cold war involvement in international affairs shows its desire to expand its role in the shaping of the New World order. In APEC, Japan's manoeuvres perennially faced a head-on collision with its long time ally, the US. It is rhetorically endorsing the goal of free trade in the Asia-Pacific region in APEC, and at first explicitly refused to endorse the East Asia Economic Caucus proposed by Malaysian Prime Minister

Mohammed Mahathir as an alternative economic grouping, which would exclude the United States. Japan, in Washington's view was the main engineer of the 1995 Osaka Declaration, which deferred the conversion of APEC into a free trade area by diluting its focus on trade liberalisation through its successful lobby for the principle that liberalisation must be flexible, voluntary, and non-binding. This moved APEC away from the US's earlier victory in the Bogor Summit of 1994.

Japan's vehement objection against the adoption of the free trade principle in APEC is motivated by several reasons. One is to protect Japanese agriculture and domestic businesses. Japan knows that the US is trying to achieve what it failed to accomplish during the Uruguay round of the GATT, which is to gain a foothold in Japan and the Asian NIEs' agricultural market. Concerning regional economic integration, domestic popular political pressures (ex. farmers groups' campaign) to protect the country's food supply to external forces is a consideration in Japan's international positioning. Another reason is Japan's recognition of the US' free trade agenda which is beyond reduction of tariffs and restrictions, it extend to the so-called "structural factors" or non-tariff barriers like non-transparency, discriminatory standards and exclusionary business practices (Bello 1996). The view is shared by Korea who also fear the institutionalisation of expansive definition of trade barriers in APEC.

Lastly, Japan's manoeuvring in APEC stems from its interest to protect its *de facto* trade and investment integration of the region which it has achieved through informal economic processes. The amount of Japanese capital which swirled around low cost labour sites in Asia during the first half of the 90s alone was at $ 51 billion (Bello, 1996:2). Japanese manufacturing facilities producing component parts now dotted the region.

With the current entrenched position of Japanese investment in Asia it can be said that Japan have realised regionalisation of its economy, taking advantage of cheap labour cost and access to the regional market without any need for a free trade agreement. Inter-Asian trade increased from 47 per cent in 1990 to 53 per cent in 1995 (1996 IMF Report) showing the fortification of Asian economies and securing its geoeconomic competitive advantage in relation to the economies in the western side of the Pacific. The proliferation of Japanese joint venture arrangements with other Asian firms do not include transfer of technology, making the partners dependent both on Japanese capital and know-how.

The successful promotion of the Japanese model of development which most analysts now call the "flying geese" model (Kennedy 1994, Hutton 1995), is making regional economic integration a *de facto* reality, with dependent economies serving as Japan's appendage. The alliance supporting Japan's position in APEC could be defined as a way of upholding the "Asian way of capitalism" against the Anglo-Saxon way, while critics in the region call it the "JapaNIEsation" of Asia. With the exception of Singapore, Hong Kong and the Philippines who are supporting the US agenda, most Asian governments are backing the Japanese counterstrategy of preserving the current terms of relation in APEC and preserve the NIEs' policies of using state intervention in their economic affairs.

The US Influence in the Pacific

Most Asian economies including Japan and the NIEs have a love and hate relationship with the US. With $ 6.7 trillion economy and strong trade relations with Asia's tigers and would-be tigers, the US remains to be the Pacific's Goliath. Since its hosting of the APEC Summit in Seattle, the US hold the staunchest lobby for the realization of a free trade bloc in the region. Seventy five per cent or $ 120.2 billion of the total US trade deficit of $ 159.6 billion in 1995 is with APEC's ten Asian economies (Bello 1996).

To understand the US' motive in its push to institutionalise APEC as a free trade area, it is imperative to trace its unilateralist strategy from the cold war period and today's transition toward a multi-polar world order. The growth of Asia's robust economies should not only be attributed to the successful implementation of state-assisted capitalism. Asia's tiger economies were "allowed" to practice some deviation from the free market method of trade and investment as well as accrue trade surpluses because their development was used as an instrument to contain the spread of communism in the region during the cold war. Now that communism have lost its appeal and there is yet an alternative path that could challenge neo-liberalism, the US' policy shifted towards translating its trade deficit in Asia to trade surplus.

After the honeymoon and when former allies became targets, the US' bombarded the NIEs with its trade weapons. Walden Bello's Dark Victory: The United States, Structural Adjustment and Global Poverty discusses the US crusade to resubordinate the NIEs. The offensives include: anti-dumping measures and voluntary exports restraints to prevent exporting countries like Korea to amass further trade surplus; withdrawal of the General System of Preferences status (GSP) or preferential tariffs which assisted the development of Taiwan, Korea, Hong Kong, Singapore and Malaysia in the past; massive forced revaluation of Japan, Korea and Taiwan's currencies in relation to the US dollar following the Plaza Accord in 1985 to make their goods non-competitive with US products; and the infamous Super 301 and Special 301 clauses of the US Trade Act of 1988 which is being used as a threat to countries like China, Japan, Korea, Indonesia, the Philippines and Thailand who are in the top list of countries found to be violating the intellectual property rights (IPRs) of US corporations. The hardest to be hit by the US retaliatory measures is Korea which is now the only tiger economy where the US enjoy a trade account surplus.

The US is complementing its unilateralist measures with multilateralist tactics and regional approach. The GATT negotiation and later on the World Trade Organisation (WTO) are the initial field, trade concessions which failed in GATT was renegotiated in NAFTA and in APEC. With massive overproduction resulting from high agricultural subsidies in the US, pressure to open up Asian markets for US products is mounting. Again, Korea is a prime example for this case with its heavy dependency on US foodstuffs resulting from the erosion of its agricultural base due to previous trade agreements with the US. The US sees the Asia Pacific as a key element of US trade strategy. The APEC, therefore, could be more destructive than GATT because it will fast track the implementation of trade related reforms agreed upon in GATT. APEC will also serve as the US' means to regain control over East Asian markets which are getting more and more fastened within Japan's orbit and at the same time prevent the possibility of an exclusive "Asia-only" regional bloc as proposed by Mahathir. APEC is also seen as a way to dismantle state control in economic affairs in Asia.

Asia-Pacific Regionalisms: Bubbles gone Burst

The buzz in various international political economic circles in early 1990s was that the twenty-first century would be the Pacific century. Asia being the most dynamic and major destination of important foreign direct investments, as well as a market not to be missed, started the scramble for other economic power to gain a foothold to its markets through regional integration schemes. It is still the most dynamic and exciting market now but much has changed because of the crisis. The aspiring economic tigers lost their fangs while the economic model was stripped of its lustre. Among the crisis' fatal victims are the various projects of regional formation, most of which are now grasping for breath.

The ASEAN Free Trade Area

The ASEAN Free Trade Area (AFTA), compared to the other projects, is still the most cohesive among the various regional projects but it was now being described as a sunset organisation by no less than the Singaporean Foreign Minister S. Jayakumar in his talks in the international circles. AFTA is an accelerated formation of the Association of South East Asian Nations or ASEAN. ASEAN is now composed of the six original members (Brunei, Darussalam, Indonesia, Malaysia, the Philippines, Singapore and Thailand), plus Vietnam, Laos, Cambodia and Myanmar which joined the formation before the closing of the twentieth century. The original ASEAN is a regional organisation established by Southeast Asia's pre-democracy autocrats following the end of the Vietnam War. It played an important role for the region's political cooperation since its establishment in 1967.

As originally envisioned, ASEAN would have been the vehicle to accomplish limited trade liberalisation through coordinated regional industrial import substitution (Mendl 1995:106). Several building blocs were established to build up the region's industrial capacities, among which include: the Preferential Trading Agreement (PTA), the ASEAN Industrial Projects (AIP), the ASEAN Industrial Complementation Scheme (AIC), and the ASEAN Industrial Venture (AIV). These projects were not implemented as planned because ASEAN focused on regional political issues and instead became a US-backed political alliance against the expansion of communism in the region during the Cold War.

ASEAN's second birth as AFTA was in 1992, it adopted then a more decisive resolve to accomplish its original agenda, which is to create a free-trade zone with a stronger sub-regional focus. As a direct response to APEC which showed a strong potential to become a rival formation, AFTA was further revitalised in 1996 through fastracking of former targets. However, because of the 1997 financial crisis and the failure to put flesh at efforts of currency stabilisation, the AFTA is now falling apart. There are a number of stakes casted at its heart and it includes the following.

For the six founding members of ASEAN, free trade was intended to be fully effective by 2002, with Vietnam achieving the same status by 2006, Laos and Myanmar in 2008, and Cambodia by 2010. Developments following this year's Ministerial Conference though negated possibilities that the six founding members will be able to meet their schedule. The crisis which severely affected three of ASEAN's key member countries (Indonesia, Philippines, and Thailand) made the members inclined to protect their domestic economies more than furthering regional cooperation. Malaysia's refusal to liberalise its auto industry triggered this. When the other AFTA members agreed to let Malaysia maintain its high tariffs on car imports until 2005, a domino effect followed as other countries have pushed to extend their deadlines up to year 2010 on sensitive products citing their difficulties experienced following the crisis.

By the year 2003 a Common Effective Preferential Tariff scheme, which applies to all manufactured goods and processed agricultural products, is supposed to be accomplished but member countries are passing what is now jokingly called a "mile-list" of products to be exempted. The year 2003 target is an acceleration from the original target date of 2008. Using a simultaneous internal trade liberalisation and external trade discrimination, a wider market with a reduced tariffs of between 0-5 per cent level is projected, which according to free trade promoters will provide the economies of scale that will induce capital and technology intensive industries. The AFTA free trade is seen by its architects as a way to break the long standing barrier to economic cooperation caused by the relatively low degree of complementarity in economic structures among ASEAN members (Kwan 1994).

By creating an integrated ASEAN market and production base, AFTA projected more competitive regionally based industries using foreign multinationals and ASEAN based firms. A horizontal division of labour in industrial goods is expected to occur as well as increased flow of foreign direct investment resulting from the creation of a common market for a population of more than 400 million people which is larger than the EU's 372 million or NAFTA's 387 million. AFTA trade now totals $ 250 billion and about 20 per cent of which is within the region (ASEAN update, see www.Asean.org/).

Failure at integration could also be attributed to the fact that different governments have different visions of regional free trade. Free market pushers like the Philippines and Singapore views the regional reduction of tariffs as a precondition to eventual integration into a global free trade system. On the other hand Indonesia and to some extent Malaysia, saw regional preferential trade as a step towards a large, protected regional market that would stimulate regional industrialisation via import substitution. The different members are also at different levels of economic capacity (original six compared to new members except perhaps Vietnam) and it is hard to balance the differences. Lastly, but not the least important aspect, the earlier race for regional integration projects was much reduced now. When APEC was rendered as a trade bloc, the necessity for AFTA to push ahead diminished.

The Asia Pacific Economic Cooperation

APEC started essentially as an inclusionary framework for multilateral dialogue and policy co-ordination as well as a market led expression of a regional identity. Beyond being an annual meeting with a photo of twenty-one economic leaders (all males) representing a Trans-Pacific cooperation, the Asia Pacific Economic Cooperation (APEC) have lost much of its steam. It failed to rise above its inertia after years of debating about its final model, it achieved very little progress to institute effective regional trade liberalisation, and, it failed to do anything during the Asian crisis and had thus forever lost its opportunity to become an essential vehicle for economic integration.

APEC is a ministerial forum composed of twenty-one countries and territories which are officially referred to as "member economies". Stretching from Asia to Australia, across the Pacific to North and Latin America, its member countries include: Aotearoa (New Zealand), Australia, Brunei, Canada, China, Chile, Hong Kong, Indonesia, Japan, Mexico, Malaysia, Papua New Guinea, Peru, the Philippines, Russia, Singapore, South Korea, Taiwan, Thailand, the United States and Vietnam.

APEC's member economies are composed of a diverse group of small, middle and major economic powers with conflicting domestic concerns and international alliances and interests. In terms of population, trade, investments and economic wealth, it collectively represents a combined Gross Domestic Product of over US $ 16 trillion

(1998), 57 per cent of global trade and 40 per cent of the world's population (APEC Introduction, www.apecweb.org). It could play a central role in realising global free trade by ensuring the creation of a free trade area in the Pacific Rim. A ministerial level meeting is held every year attended by head of states of member economies. Aside from a small secretariat in Singapore, APEC has hardly any bureaucratic infrastructure.

About 80 per cent of APEC's combined GNP comes from its two biggest economies—Japan and the US. According to its "2020 Plan", member economies have pledged to liberalise trade on a "complete non-discriminatory" basis, promote investments among members and achieve an "open regionalism" which is characterised by a borderless trade within the Asia Pacific region by the year 2020.

From Canberra to Auckland

Since its beginning in 1989, APEC members do not have a consensus on what it really stands for. Key players within APEC manoeuvred and pressed to define the nature which the cooperation will finally take. Since its inception, the Asian lobby (Malaysia, Thailand and Japan) would like APEC to remain as a consultative group where technical cooperation on economic matters among governments could be facilitated (Bello, 1996). The Anglo-Saxon group (United States and Australia) on the other hand contests that APEC should be a formation that will eventually lead to a regional free trade area. To understand its dynamics, it is important to look at how it developed and the underlying context behind the move of key players within it.

APEC started as a cautious initiative suggested in the late 1980s by the Japanese Ministry of Trade and Industry (MITI) chief Hajime Tamura. The original idea was to form a forum for technical cooperation on economic issues, along the lines of the Organisation for Economic Cooperation and Development (DAGA 1996). Because the proposal failed to draw US' attention which at that time is preoccupied with GATT and NAFTA, Australia made the breakthrough by hosting the first Ministerial Meeting in Canberra in November 1989. Realising at that time that Australia's survival and future in the new international economic order depends on strengthening its position in Asia, the Labour government of then Prime Minister Bob Hawke proposed the strengthening of economic cooperation in the Pacific basin (Motoyama, 1995). Hawke planted the seed to the idea that the grouping would serve as the basis for a future free-trade area which was later on pursued by his successor (Paul Keating). APEC was officially established as an "informal economic dialogue" to help coordinate views on trade and economic issues. Australia's integration with Asian economy stems from the fact that its agricultural, energy and raw material exports are becoming increasingly dependent specially to Indonesia which is its gateway to the Asian market.

The original 12 members (Malaysia, Singapore, Thailand, Philippines, Indonesia, Brunei, South Korea, Japan, New Zealand, Australia, Canada and the United States) agreed to establish a ministerial forum to discuss Asia-Pacific economic issues which is to be coordinated through senior officials' consultations. An unwritten rule that there would be an equal number of ASEAN and non-ASEAN countries was first adopted during the said meeting but was later dropped when membership expanded (Motoyama 1993:2002).

The second meeting was held in Singapore in November 1990. Japan up to that point was still in the "wait and see" mode while at the same time keeping a pragmatic political strategy of being at the core of competing projects to reshape relations around the regional identities of East Asia and Asia Pacific (Gamble and Payne 1996). Until 1992, nothing much was achieved due to APEC's preoccupation with sorting out its membership. Being an artificial construct, with no natural geographical boundaries, no common historical, cultural or social base, no coherent identity of its own, APEC found it hard to set parameters for membership (Bello, 1995).

China, Taiwan and Hong Kong were accepted as new members during the third summit held in Seoul, Korea in November 1991. It was also during this summit when APEC finally achieved its first sense of focus through the "Seoul Declaration of APEC Ministers". The Seoul Declaration, highlights that economic growth will be the basis for regional interdependence and strong common interests which in turn will produce a healthy and balanced development. This economic growth, it was agreed, was built on a spirit of partnership and commitment to the free flow of goods and capital (Kelsey, 1995).

The fourth summit was held in Bangkok, Thailand a year after. Mexico and Papua New Guinea were accepted as new members. During this summit, Japan's proposal to establish a small Secretariat in Singapore to strengthen the functions of APEC was accepted. It was also during this summit when APEC Ministers created an Eminent Persons Group "to enunciate a vision for trade in the Asia Pacific

Region" (EPG, 1992). The EPG was composed of conservative free traders from throughout the region, headed by economist C. Fred Bergsten, director of the Institute of International Economics. The IIE is a think tank financed by US corporate lobby. The EPG was dissolved later on during the Osaka Summit. During its existence, the EPG played an influential role in lobbying for APEC's institutionalisation and its strategic relationship with GATT.

In November 1993 the US, under the Clinton administration replaced Australia as the leader of the free trade lobby in APEC. The reason for the heightened US interest was the agenda to secure a fallback to GATT (General Agreement on Tariff and Trade) which was experiencing rough sailing at that point. An Asia-Pacific regional free trade area that would supplement NAFTA in the event GATT fell through was seen as crucial for the US interest. One reason for such GATT apprehension is the fact that the GATT consensus rule is complicated.

The fifth summit was held in Blake Island, Seattle where the guiding vision of open regionalism was developed. In the November 1994 summit, member economies committed themselves to more open trade and investment and application of free market principles while assuring that GATT will be passed at home. The vision of an Asia Pacific "community of free trading nations" was also established. Malaysian Prime Minister Mohamad Mahathir's boycott of the meeting, and a general feeling by the Asians that they have to make more economic adjustments while the US will have more competitive gain than them, prevented the formal declaration of a free trade area as APEC's end goal.

The Committee on Trade and Investment (CTI) was created to simplify and harmonise customs procedures and standards, identify barriers to trade, implement a set of non-binding investment principles, and work to harmonise GATT-Uruguay Round implementation among APEC members (Spero, 1995). Other support bodies are also created, they were: Economic Committee, Budget and Administrative Committee, Eminent Persons Group (EPG), and the Asia-Pacific Business Forum.

During the sixth summit in Bogor, Indonesia, APEC announced a moratorium on new members until 1996 after the acceptance of Chile as 18th member. The Bogor summit gave flesh to the Blake Island free market vision through the signing and issuance of the "Declaration of Common Resolve" on 15 November 1994. The declaration gave full and active support to WTO, and gave birth to the "2020 Plan". Intense lobbying from Washington, Canberra, and the EPG encouraged Indonesian President Suharto to board the free trade bandwagon. Suharto endorsed the EPG's 2020 Plan despite strong opposition from some sectors of the Indonesian economic bureaucracy. Pressure from the host government led to the signing of the Bogor Declaration by Malaysia and Thailand though the two governments viewed it as non-binding, China supported the view (Bello 1996).

In the Declaration of Common Resolve, the leaders announced their governments' commitment to complete the achievement of free and open trade and investment not later than 2010 for industrialised economies, 2015 for NICs, and 2020 for developing economies. The Declaration further stated the following:

We wish to emphasize our strong opposition to the creation of an inward-looking trading bloc that would divert from the pursuit of global free trade. We are determined to pursue free and open trade and investment in the Asia-Pacific in a manner that will encourage and strengthen trade and investment liberalisation in the world as a whole.

The city of Osaka, Japan hosted the seventh ministerial summit. During this summit the US actively supported and effected the establishment of the Business Advisory Council to encourage the engagement of business in APEC processes. This summit came out with an "Action Agenda" for free trade. The Eminent Persons Group was disbanded due to Asian governments' lobby which was based on a commonly held view that the EPG was being used as an instrument by the US and Australia to push their free trade agenda.

The Osaka Summit made highly apparent Japan and US' contesting agenda. Japan expressed that there was too much emphasis on trade liberalisation. The then Foreign Minister Yohei Kono suggested to stress trade facilitation measures like harmonising customs procedures throughout the region, and on economic cooperation in the form of aid to the less developed APEC member countries. Accelerated aid to the less developed APEC countries was necessary, Kono asserted, because trade liberalisation in an uneven playing field would merely accentuate inequalities within the region (FOCUS 1995).

Japan tried to exempt agriculture from any liberalisation plan, the move was backed openly by South Korea, China, Taiwan, and informally by Malaysia and Indonesia. The move prompted the US to remind Japan of the substance of the Bogor Declaration (Motoyama 1995) which covers agricultural products. The US has targetted the

Asia-Pacific countries as a dumping ground for its huge grain surpluses. Prior to the summit, the US have launched punitive unilateral trade moves against key APEC trade countries on grounds under the 301 provisions of the US Trade Act of 1988.

The Action Agenda reaffirmed previous goals of regional trade liberalisation and highlighted APEC's determination to explore joint initiatives under the WTO to ensure APEC's consistency with the WTO Agreement (APEC 1995). The Japanese and Asian views prevailed in Osaka. The Action Agenda recognised the three pillars of APEC: trade liberalisation, economic cooperation and trade facilitation as well as affirmed Malaysia and Thailand's position in Bogor that liberalisation should be voluntary, flexible and non-binding.

The then 18-member economies submitted their individual liberalisation plans for collective review and was approved in the Manila Summit as the Manila Action Plan for APEC (MAPA). It was adopted on 25 November 1996. It includes the individual and collective action plans and progress reports on joint activities of all APEC economies to achieve the Bogor objectives of free and open trade and investment in the APEC region by 2010 and 2020, and joint activities among members under Part II of the Osaka Action Agenda. Besides that, nothing much was achieved though as the Summit was at the heels of the Osaka summit where much of the debate occurred. Manila was actually an anti-climax after the Japanese agenda prevailed the year before.

As for the Vancouver Summit, it could be best remembered as the summit when Clinton lectured upon the humbled Asians who are reeling from the crisis then on how to save their economies by following the bitter pill diagnosed by the IMF and endorsed by the body. The policies did not solve the crisis and made the problem deeper than necessary. The Vancouver Framework for Enhanced Public-Private Partnership for Infrastructure Development was also approved together with the Blueprint for APEC Customs' Modernisation which targetted year 2002 for full implementation.

The Kuala Lumpur summit of 1998 failed as well to give an alternative package to the battered economies. The Japanese rejected an APEC expansionary programme for which the Japanese offer of $ 30 billion was to be used. Much attention was focused on how the host country handled the Anwar affair and accusations of human rights violations. The Ministers signed the Kuala Lumpur Action Programme on Skills Development. The Early Voluntary Sectoral Liberalisation agreement with non-APEC members at the World Trade Organisation, which was earlier discussed in Vancouver, was adopted.

Much of the energy for the 1999 Auckland summit was in preparation for the WTO Round in Seattle. The leaders reaffirmed their commitment to the Bogor Goals of free and open trade and investment by 2010/2020, endorsed a new APEC Principles to Enhance Competition and Regulatory Reform, and agreed that priority would be given to trade facilitation in 2000.

Despite new agreements and documents that each summit produced, the process of developing APEC principles (open regionalism, etc.); its role in realising global free trade; and its target and general timetable (2020 plan) all lose its significance after APEC failed to provide help during the crisis. The competing interests and integration projects in APEC further intensify. The shooting down of Japan's proposed Asian Monetary Fund by the US during the crises added to the feeling among Asian elites that a regional formation without Anglo-Saxons would be better.

The campaign to push APEC to adopt organisational coherence is a dead issue after the Osaka meeting. Prior to the Seattle meeting of the WTO in 1999, some campaigns in Asia is sympathetic to the view of just to bury APEC. APEC and the other regional trade blocs serves as WTO's implementing mechanisms. Just as the IMF and the WB need governments and instruments to implement policies and actualise Structural Adjustment Programmes (SAPs), the WTO needs governments and regional trade blocs to push forward global free trade (ALARM 1996). Regional liberalisation therefore is a way of ensuring global liberalisation in an easier to negotiate step-by-step manner.

Both AFTA and APEC are projects of Asia's elite and excluded civil society from participating in any of the processes. It is not surprising that unlike the EU, the common people do not feel their presence despite the costly hosting and much publicised Summits. When both eventually folds up, no ordinary folk would even miss them in the newspaper headlines.

Regional Civil Society's Initiatives on APEC

A counter consensus from the progressive blocs on free trade and trade liberalisation were already audible during the height of the GATT debates in the region. People's movements in the Philippines, Korea, Japan and Canada have already articulated their strong apprehension about the massive environmental and social costs of economic openness amidst governments' projection of a coming economic paradise. The expansive opposition to the GATT and the furtherance of economic liberalisation which have already created havoc on the lives and rights of those belonging to vulnerable sectors of society in APEC aroused progressive groups in the region to mobilise and monitor APEC processes.

Opposition to APEC, like the contention in GATT generated different views from Asia Pacific civil society spectrum. On one side, some networks think that to address the APEC and to seek participation in its deliberations is to legitimise an essentially anti-people initiative. They have raised reservations to engage the APEC because of what they deem as inherently limited chances for civil society to contribute meaningful influence in the processes. On the other, a broad network of NGOs and social movements feel the urgency to assert civil society's right to intervene in APEC processes due to its expected impact on millions of poor people in the region. They hold what might best be called "a pragmatic view" that it is not easy to transform APEC into a pro-people forum, but it is an important venue where specific policy reforms can be advocated and won. APEC's seemingly formidable threat to workers, consumers, farmers and small entrepreneurs is daunting but these latter groups believe that there are spaces within it where people's concerns could be raised as well as in parallel international agreements however few and narrow.

According to documents from the Kyoto People's NGO Forum on APEC which was held parallel to the Osaka Summit, these small openings in a seemingly exclusionary process include: the recognition of sustainable growth, equitable development and national stability as the three pillars of APEC in the Bogor Declaration (1994 APEC Summit); and the commitments made by APEC member countries in UN Summits. It is viewed as crucial to remind the signatory countries to these UN summits that are part of APEC to uphold the gains of those summits.

A strategic engagement in APEC by civil society networks and groups who favoured such move could be traced in a document issued by the Host Committee for the Manila People's Forum on APEC 1996. The initiatives started in Seattle when labour, human rights and environmental coalitions gathered and discussed in a forum titled "The Hidden Cost of Free Trade" which was held parallel to the 1993 APEC meeting. A year after, despite restrictive measures employed by the

Indonesian government, regional NGOs met in Bogor to monitor the APEC processes and raised issues of common concern on the liberalisation agenda at the summit. In 1994, a broad network of NGOs and social movements gathered in Kyoto and arrived at a strong consensus to formally oppose APEC and its neoliberal agenda notwithstanding the participants' minimum level of unity regarding the form of intervention. The forum stressed the need to delegitimise APEC and prevent it from consolidating. The Kyoto Declaration expressed:

we fully support cooperation among countries and their peoples ... but unanimously reject the basic philosophy, framework and assumptions of the model of free market and trade liberalisation embraced by the APEC agenda.

and asserts that,

genuine development must be centred on the needs of people and nature, and deliver real social and economic justice... Genuine development must also affirm the fundamental civil, political, economic, social and cultural rights of individuals and peoples, and the obligations of states to promote and protect such rights.

The alternative regional networks in the region believe that there should be another option beside those being presented by Japan, the United States and global institutions of capital. The sufferings inflicted by free trade, neoliberalist policies and structural adjustments to the poor are fierce enough, there should be another choice. Regionalism and globalization is beyond trade and economics, it is connected to the everyday lives and future survival of those being squeezed out from the trade race. It is, therefore, crucial for people's discourses to be heard above the limited range of voices coming from those who compose the APEC Business Advisory Group.

The essential point of criticism is the lack of political accountability on the side of government representatives who are attending the process. Alternative groups deems it important to remind each representatives that they have responsibilities to their constituents who elected them as head of states, which enables them to attend APEC meetings as "economic leaders" of the "member economies". Governments of member economies are obliged to abide by the decisions, plan and policies agreed upon in the forum, yet as economic leaders performing the requisites of their involvement in APEC, head of states are not doing an official act of government and, therefore, cannot be taken to task for their decisions. It is also becoming observable that the interests being advanced in APEC are limited to those of the business sector and multinationals, much of the affected citizenry are excluded from the processes. Lastly, civil society in the last nine years of APEC's existence have time and again protested about the lack of space for participation and transparency in APEC decision making processes. Decisions arrived at in APEC do not go through formal democratic processes and institutions of the member economies. There are also no venues where people could get balanced information which could enable them to challenge and influence those decisions.

The different sectors of civil society in the region bewail the fact that their governments are signatories to all the UN World Summits which have produced volumes upon volumes of reports and materials confirming the connection between poverty and policies generated by liberalisation and neoliberalism. Ironically, the same governments adopt the 2020 Plan and free trade agenda of APEC, which will perpetuate the vicious cycle of poverty resulting from the policies assailed in the UN World Summit statements.

In the sectoral level, the international labour movement created a regional initiative around APEC. This was born during the People's Summit on APEC in Vancouver. This showed an increased labour movement and NGO collaboration in building a counter consensus around APEC. The Asia Pacific Regional Organisation (APRO) serves as the major labour organisation focusing on APEC. The International Congress of Free Trade Union affiliates in the region constitutes it. Meetings organised for APEC discussions led to the formation of the Asia Pacific Labour Network (APLN) which have members in Chile, Mexico, USA, Canada, New Zealand, Australia, Papua New Guinea, Singapore, Malaysia, Philippines, Thailand, Hong Kong, Taiwan, South Korea and Japan.

During the Manila People's Summit of 1996, APLN issued a statement called "A Trade Union Vision for APEC". The statement summarises the labour sector's agenda of promoting the improvement of working conditions and people's welfare as a necessary component of the internationalisation of market. This statement and all concurrent resolutions were upheld in Vancouver. The issue concerning the Labour Clause generated opposing positions, which were not reconciled.

The development of regional groupings that monitors and face the challenges given by geo-economic formations and the expansion of experiences in the parallel forums to important global economic meetings like APEC, WTO, UNCTAD, etc. contributed to the formation of transnational initiatives that has achieved a level of coordination which was seen in Seattle in 1999 and Washington this year. Though it never went beyond organising a parallel forum to each summit, the APEC People's Forum contributed in the exercise of collective resistance to a seemingly unstoppable process of globalization. This opposition gave impetus to multiplicators on how to enhance and retool for the new era of opposition.

The East Asia Economic Group (EAEG) and the Asia Europe Meeting (ASEM)

Proposed and advocated in 1991 by Malaysian Prime Minister Mohammad Mahathir as a response to the formation of regional blocs in Europe and North America and to APEC's evolution in this direction, the EAEG advanced a form of closed regionalism or an exclusive intra-Asian economic bloc and excluding countries on the other side of the Pacific. It is an expression of resistance to the US' pressure to fast-track trade liberalisation in the region, and at the same time a measure to preserve the operative system of state-assisted capitalism inherent to the NIC model of development which the bloc adheres to. The bloc covers China, Laos, Cambodia, Vietnam, Japan and the NIEs. The EAEG was accommodated as a caucus within APEC in 1990.

All EAEG countries are dependent to the US market as an absorber of their products. Malaysia's offer of a leadership to Japan in the EAEG prompted Japan to seriously consider which identity it will prefer, a major Asia Pacific player or East Asian leader. The formation of Asia-Europe Meeting or ASEM, in Bangkok in late February of 1996, provided a major landmark for EAEG. ASEM brought together ten Asian governments which were precisely those targetted by Malaysian Prime Minister Mahathir for inclusion in EAEG, and fifteen heads of state from the European Union. ASEM signify the formal establishment of EAEG and formalised East Asia as a macro-region.

ASEM, in many aspects came about because of APEC. It is a geoeconomic and geopolitical wildcard pulled by the ten Asian countries to put a balance between the three main economic centres of the world today. It was envisioned to place Asia in a strategic position of being in the middle of the two firmly established economic powers of Europe and the US. ASEM could provide the Asian economies a counter pressure to the trade aggression of the US. The EAEG was viewed by the US as the greatest threat to APEC. The integration of East Asia and ASEAN as a production base and its own biggest market would liberate them from the US economic and political dominance. The combined growth of intra-Asian trade and steps toward the direction of EAEG consolidation so worried the US that it threatened to withdraw its security presence in Asia Pacific if the covered countries will continue to economically exclude the US in the region.

After the ASEM takeoff in Bangkok in February 1996, follow up actions took place that year which include the Customs Cooperation Meeting (CCM), the formation of the Working Group on Investment (WGI), a Senior Officials Meeting on Trade and Investment (SOMTI), and, the setting up of a Business Forum. Meetings of these working groups occurred throughout 1997 to further consolidate their structures in preparation to the second ASEM Summit held in London on April 1998. Other areas of cooperation were also formed like the Asia-Europe Environmental Technology Centre (AETC) and the Asia-Europe Foundation (ASEF).

The Asian crisis which altered the earlier perspective of a Pacific century made European attitude take a quick turn around in the second ASEM held in London in 1998. That is, from Asia as an opportunity not to be missed towards Asia as a problem to solve. The Asian financial crisis dominated the discussion. Very obvious as well is the fact that the former regard to developmentalist states in Asia as an equal partner to the Europeans was diminished and instead replaced by a triumphalist attitude of Western superiority to the East (Noor, 1998). This shift of being defensive to the Asian advance to that of having a problem solver role gave impetus for the EU in its bid for governance on the neoliberal lines already articulated and promoted by the US government. The London ASEM was used by the EU to persuade Asian leaders that stability and restoration of confidence in Asian economies and financial markets would return if the stricken countries pursue their IMF reform programmes.

The London ASEM achieved the acceptance of World Bank assistance in relation to the restructuring of financial sectors, and to social measures to address poverty, and adherence to WTO rules in order to preserve an open trading system. It also clinched full and rapid implementation by all ASEM partners of the Trade Facilitation

Action Plan in order to further open up trade and expand investment between Asia and Europe.

Compared to APEC, ASEM has a twin advantage: First, it has a developed policy coordination through legal and operational integration within Western Europe through the EU. This is something lacking in APEC and in fact what it tried to address in its formation. Second, compared to APEC, ASEM's concerns are broader as it covers cooperation in political, economic, and other fields.

The problem-solving event couched under the title "A Shared Interest in Restoring Stability" was a disappointment for the Asians as it failed to produce solutions. After all the talks, the Asian leaders heard the same formula shoved upon them earlier in the APEC summits of 1997 and 1998. Asian leaders felt that instead of helping the problematic economies, the crisis was seen as an opportunity to lecture them about the mistakes embedded in the 'Asian way" of managing economies. An ASEM Trust Fund was created and entrusted to the World Bank later but was also viewed as too little too late, and will not answer the long-term effect of the crisis. The third ASEM summit will be held this coming October at Seoul.

The various processes of regional formations if viewed broadly and beyond the issue of inter-regional dialogue, are completing the requirements of capital accumulation on the global scale, and states as its instruments defines and guarantees the constitutional effects of international treaties.

The ASEM NGO working group started with an easier experience of getting an audience with the European Union considering the level of access currently available to the European networks in the European Council. It is doubtful if that can be replicated in Asia considering the manner accorded to NGOs by authoritarian governments in Asian countries. All the ASEM Civil Society Forum held so far shows how NGOs are treated in the process. Conferences which were supposedly organised for civil society were not even publicly announced. The events were held in among the most expensive hotels in host countries, the "disruptive" or "uncivil" sections of civil society were not invited. The notion of "people to people dialogue" being held by organisers is still limited to the elite section of the populace and quite far from what the civil society organisations understood it to be. It is an enigma then how the formation's recognition of civil society's role in governance and global partnership will be realised.

The ASEM NGO Working Group

Following the developments in People's APEC Forum and the recognition to establish a similar structure to monitor the processes as well as seek participation in ASEM, the ASEM NGO working group was established in 1996 to prepare for the parallel conference in Bangkok. However, the groups within ASEM having learned from their experiences in the APEC campaign and faced with a different character of ASEM organised their efforts in a more structured way. The group served as a point of convergence for ASEM I and II and is continuing its consolidation in preparing their strategies for ASEM III.

The broad networks which form the organising group of the Bangkok ASEM NGO Forum included PARC (Pacific Asia Regional Coalition), ARENA (Asian Regional Network for Alternatives), and ACFOD (Asian Cultural Forum on Development) just to name a few from ASIA; and the CIIR (Catholic Institute for International Relations), TNI (Transnational Institute) and Asia House from Europe. In the ASEM II, One World Action, TNI, CIIR, Asian House, and Focus for the Global South coordinated the civil society conferences. These networks have interlocking constituencies as well as long histories of bilateral and multi-lateral partnerships since the 80s. The UN Economic and Social Council (ECOSOC), United Nations Children's Funds (UNICEF), Food and Agriculture Organisation (FAO) and the UN World Summits also recognize these groups. Apart from their achievements as networks, member organizations and national groups have their respective share of international advocacy work. The ASEM III host committee in Seoul is turning out to be a very well organised group composed of almost 50 vibrant civil society organisations in South Korea.

NGO inputs to ASEM, will be built on the already ongoing alternative development policy and programme dialogue between concerned European and Asian NGOs (TNI 1995). Grassroots inputs to the dialogue are provided by the NGOs who have grassroots membership, *e.g.* Forum of the Poor in Thailand, People's Solidarity for Participatory Democracy in South Korea, etc, as well as NGOs who have PO partners, *e.g.* Pacific Asia Research Centre in Japan, Institute for Popular Democracy in the Philippines, ERA Consumer in Malaysia, etc.

Since the ASEM and the NGO Working Group on ASEM are still evolving, it is still too early to measure how NGOs could create impact to the formal process. In the coming meeting in Seoul, the alternative forum would lobby for the formation of the Civic Forum as a venue where civil society could engage in the formal processes at all levels. In a few consultations organised by the EU, NGOs who were active in the alternative forum were already invited to participate. Information tours, which were held both in Europe and Asia, were received by Parliaments and important development agencies of the visited countries. It is still a lingering problem though that despite the increasing recognition of civil society's importance in development processes, many policy makers could not yet comprehend the essence of civil society and the contribution of their participation in policy processes.

Civil society organisations have achieved a new level of activism following the success of lobbies in the MAI and the effect of mobilisation to the outcome of the WTO discussions in Seattle in 1999. In many national-level experiences, civil society organisations have already proven their mettle in enhancing policies and making project implementation more efficient as in the case for example of engagements in UN projects on environment.

The EC Directorate covering South and Southeast Asia also expressed openness to further develop partnership and exchange with the NGOs in post ASEM III activities. If the Civic Forum will be adopted, it is expected that the level of cooperation and participation would reach a new landmark.

The State of Civil Society in Asia

The theoretical matrix provided by the work of M. Nerfin (1986) and the partnership works of Cohen and Arato (1992), as well as by de Oliviera and Tandon (1994), shows conscious use of the category of civil society. Their works discussed the triadic paradigm of state, economy and society, emphasising the close relationship of the public and private realm. They traced civil society from Hegel's ethical ideal. The term has already been associated with various definitions and interests and had been subjected to diverse debates in the past. Israel Batista of the World Council of Churches in a PP21 conference gave it a more pulsating definition, for him it is not merely a concept. It is the attempt to reconnect the theory of civil with political thought analysis and social actions. In his article on Asian Action he gave the following considerations of civil society as a concrete action and reflection processes:

- civil society as a "space" from which organised people address the issues which are generated within society.
- civil society as a strategy of "social transformation", (quoting Fritz Erich Anhelm's emphasis on community building from below).
- civil society as a "laboratory" for experiencing people's participation and interactions in building comprehensive and participatory democratic society.
- civil society as a "classroom" for learning and training in the struggle.

While interest in civil society is broadening and slowly claiming a space in the unfolding politico-economic mosaic in the region, the challenges confronting it are also increasing. One of the most formidable threats that it has to address is the growing resignation of governments to the increasing hegemony of neo-liberalism. Most organised groups within civil society for a time was overwhelmed by the transformations brought about by the altered geo-economic and geopolitical situation and were confused regarding how to explain it and arrive at appropriate actions to engage in it and maintain relevance.

Now that energies are being spent to sharpen organisational positions and measures are being made to matter in what Ohmae termed as "region states" (1995), civil society actors have recognised two complementary tasks as requisites of an effective political strategy. These are: (a) The multiple levels of intervention and engagement in the struggle for defining social development, and (b) Networking among movements for alternative development. It is also widely accepted that finding coherent unity between theories and practices of alternative development is a must in order to be included in the overall development debate.

The term civil society itself is still vaguely defined in many regional documents which have spearheaded efforts at gathering Asian social movement leaders towards the creation of alternative views to the post-NIC development model. Although breakthroughs are being made at different levels in sketching a vision of a regional future that will promote economic dynamism and sense of community in the region, a long and difficult struggle is seen and understood before it could be realised. Many gaps are still to be filled to further current efforts of deconstructing concepts, elaboration of classical formulations and tools of analysis as well as explore other multidimensional approaches for alternative development work. In the painstaking venture, the role of the intellectuals, and the people's subjective consciousness in the new arena of struggle should be further expounded.

The region offers a rich tapestry of culture, spirituality and religion. Combinations of which lends colour and texture to the institutions of civil societies that flourished notwithstanding colonisation and political turmoil brought about by totalitarian regimes, military dictatorships as well as civil wars. These differences are oftentimes highlighted by conflicts resulting from the national agenda of organisations. Notwithstanding the differences, a slow movement to build processes for transnational participatory democracy is taking place. PP21 defined it as the accumulation of power from below to represent the diversity of citizens' responses to globalization and attempts toward the formation of more horizontal processes of decision making. The seed of this initiative comes from the realisation that the NIC model of development may have created the dragons, but the dragons are now facing a great problem considering the harm done to society and environment by its growth ethos (Bello, 1991).

With the advent of global communications and leaps made by communication technology, ideas and goods tear their way beyond borders penetrating the everyday lives of different peoples, gradually dissolving cultural and geographical boundaries. The preponderant role of the media has aided the trend being pursued by corporations toward globalization. Likewise, the progress in technology made contributions for the rapid dissemination of information concerning civil society efforts from different countries known to many.

The emerging conflict of knowledges resulting from the prevalence of indigenous knowledge systems in some areas, the influence of Western practices and concepts brought about by modernization, as well as colonial histories and other factors coexist and animate Asian social movements, bringing about the need for new abstractions. For this purpose loose networks of intellectuals like ARENA (Asian Regional Exchange for New Alternatives), and Focus on the Global South, for example, came into being. The needs of the present emphasises a more pro-active role for experts, and their involvement in the ongoing redefinition of social movements in the light of new socio-cultural arrangements and categories which is being infused in the emerging communitarian voluntary actions (ARENA, 1994).

What remained central and particular to civil society's strength is the agenda of people's organised participation in development. This strength continues to give it potentials, initiatives, imagination and versatility. People's participation is now meandering at two complementary levels: from above and below. From above, civil society is now engaging in regional and national policy making and being recognised by governments and institutions like the UNDP and the Asian Development Bank.

In April 1996, an Asia Pacific Regional World Bank NGO Policy Meeting was held in Manila. During that meeting, the World Bank admitted the existence of some adverse effects of Structural Adjustment Programmes to the economies of poor countries in the region. An agreement was forged for NGO participation in future World Bank projects. An example of such partnership include a consultative status gained by the Freedom from Debt Coalition (the broadest Philippines network on economic and development issues) in the World Bank formulation of the strategy to fight poverty in the Philippines.

Democratisation from below is taking various forms and scale. It is spearheaded by communities who are asserting their own power and self management, preservation and development of the diversity of culture, life forms and knowledge systems, as well as pursuance of alternative development and human scale economies (or economies of communities). Such community initiatives are scattered in Thailand, Sri Lanka, Bangladesh, India, and the Philippines (see Serrano, 1994, IADEA Workshop Report 1997). The assertion of identity must be complemented by the familiarity with the whys and hows of disempowerment. In the Philippines, the popular education circle is now arguing for the redefinition of "people" towards "actually existing people", not limiting it to NGOs and other terms of objective categories (de la Torre, 1992). "People" then will not only refer to the left's previous notion, but closer to Jurgen Habermas' idea of communicative power relevant to those who are seeking for alternative paradigm, the real actors in the life world. Dealing with the local language and the treatment of subjective consciousness like spirituality, identity, etc., is what the new form of struggle is all about: the meshing of the language of reform and everyday politics.

Community Development work involves a plethora of innovations and resourcefulness. Many initiatives, which started as home-grown projects, are now being shared and adopted with appropriate adjustments from source countries to other countries within the region. Detailed accounts of how citizens take on the responsibilities of providing basic services and goods as well as people to people sharing of alternative development approaches can be read from the works of Richard Holloway (1986), David Korten (1986 and 1990), and Isagani Serrano (1994).

Current discourses on civil society in the region have broadened the practical horizon of most political activists and have facilitated a lot of regional advocacy efforts in preparation to UN Summits which started in Rio de Janeiro. It also inspired processes toward the formation of ambitious projects like the Asia Pacific Civil Society Forum. The competing regionalist projects (APEC, and ASEM) prompted regional responses to parallel the emerging structures.

Recently, debates concerning the role of civil society in politics came to the fore considering the involvement of many national voluntary organisations in elections. Civil society's crucial role in legitimising governance in the political transition of many Asian countries during the 80s expanded the arena for manoeuvrability of many social movements and enhanced state-society relationships (Alagappa 1995). Specifically in South Korea and the Philippines, civil society's mediating role in politics is indispensable. The operating rule of thumb at the moment is the recognition that social movements should have a state agenda which is within the boundaries of influence generation over political-administrative and economic processes and unconstrained discussion in the cultural sphere (Serrano, 1993).

Another arena of engagement where civil society is experiencing a paradigm shift concerns the market. Relationships between the non-profit sector and the profit-making corporations are experiencing changes. For all practical purposes, a more pro-active engagement with the market and its institutions are taking shape in Japan, South Korea, Sri Lanka and the Philippines (Asia Pacific Civil Society Forum, 1995 and CIVICUS, 1999). In these countries, a broadening section of civil society are cognisant of the fact that though the market cannot be expected to be concerned with equity and fair competition, it has brought about concrete and much wanted improvements in the quality of life of many people. A few influential actors within civil society in the region are looking at possibilities for a pro-active engagement with the market society, although the initiatives are being met with scepticism by many of their colleagues.

These shifts in methodology and advocacy strategies do not make civil organisations adopting these innovations less radical, less critical, and less liberative. The traditional idea of revolution which used to inspire many conscious efforts in the past was characterised by rejection of any possible engagement with liberal democracy. Unfortunately, all revolutionary projects failed to deliver their promised utopia. It is now common to hear within alternative movements' discussions, the idea of exploring multiple levels, forms and arena of struggle and at the same time address the opponent in a language that it will understand most.

Global policy advocacy and networking through holding parallel regional conferences to state sponsored conferences and UN Summits became integral part of many national level organisations and served as their contributions to the regional level networks they are affiliated with. Starting from the UNCED Process where environmental NGOs organised and mobilised themselves to gain access and actually influenced both the UNCED negotiations and evolution of the global NGO community (see Princen and Finger's Environmental NGOs in World Politics, 1995), national governments like in the Philippines from then on held processes of local to national consultations for every UN Summits. Repeatedly, regional initiatives hammered down the message of genuine development centred on the needs of people and nature as well as the delivery of real social and economic justice as primary concern and basis of state, market and civil society efforts. Economic growth and promotion of trade must serve the people, and should not become ends themselves.

In preparation for the demands required by international advocacy and networking, big NGOs and social movements professionalised the training to arm their representatives for such tasks. Such efforts include for example the People's Diplomacy Training Course rendered regularly at the University of New South Wales in Australia. The course was initiated in 1989 by the 1996 Nobel Peace Prize recipient Jose Ramos Horta. The project trained a good number of international lobbyist in the region ranging from representatives from movements for self determination to development NGOs. The different women's networks are also effective in training women to do lobby work in the UN and other international venues. Training workshops were also held in preparation for UN Summit lobby work since the UN Conference on Environment and Development.

Walden Bello see transnational democracy as the wave of the future, where the popular sector will serve as an equal part of the triad together with the state and business, and as a dominant part later on in this triad (1994). Considering this view, Edicio de la Torre challenged

Asian civil society leaders who attended a preparatory meeting for the World Summit on Social Development held in Manila in 1994 to ponder the following questions: "How do we construct? After criticising hierarchical, authoritarian, and vertical structures, how do we construct horizontal, participative and democratic structures, which will be effective?".

Regional Civil Society: More than a Dream?

The different sectors of Asian civil society are cognisant of the comprehensiveness and multidimensionality of the present development processes and the lack of space for participation and manoeuvre in the new trade regimes and geo-economic formations. As the world condition approach a "high or radicalised modernity", there is also an increasing possibility and necessity for the development of a global civil society which is offering complex and interdependent global alternatives (Waterman 1996). This new phenomenon is also called by Richard Falk as "globalization from below". The initiatives' strength lies on the movements' advocacy for the inclusion of ethical and normative dimensions like democracy, equity and environmental protection to counterbalance the negative effects of regionalism and globalization.

Apart from posing a critique to the formal initiatives, mechanisms and processes are taking place and converging toward the formulation of alternatives to the development path offered by the dominant neo-liberal consensus. Initiatives include researches and studies on development being done by non-governmental organisations (NGOs) and independent development think tanks, forging of linkages between indigenous peoples, women's groups, environmental networks, etc., as well as a reorientation towards new internationalism and solidarity being discussed in labour and workers groups.

As the phenomenon of regionalism continue to cast its influence to the dominant forces which are shaping the present and the future of Asia, one of the most dynamic inclination of civil society in the region is to build a corresponding response. However, the current regionalisation of people's initiatives and the direction they are heading are both controversial and challenging developments for observers and activists within the different sections of Asian civil society. Between honesty and hope, is a regional civil society which will spur what proponents in the region call transnational participatory democracy possible? Are current initiatives of forging sectoral, issue based, and multi-dimensional networks effective enough as building blocs towards that dream? Are the proposed alternatives of these alliances viable?

To examine whether or not Asian civil society initiatives of engaging the different state-market nexus efforts of regional economic integration are effective enough, it is important to analyse the strength of the currently existing regional networks and their relationship with grassroots civil society, the alternatives that they are proposing, and its contribution in the policy process. Criticizing formal processes and offering alternatives are not enough, what is crucial and urgent is to be heard in the processes, ensure that the proposed alternatives will be adopted and included in the implementation, while continuing with the alternative development programmes in the grassroots.

The networks discussed in this chapter are accomplishing their alternative development actions in two parallel ways: engaging governments both in the regional and national levels in development debate, and carrying out their autonomous development projects through local/national members. They are showing a new way of doing politics or what Seabrook called "politics of hope" (1992), which is about fighting and claiming the present, the here and now, and not only a dream and faraway future.

It is noteworthy that many of today's regional networks are approaching advocacy work in ways which are considered as departures from their old traditions. Many actors within these movements know that it is not valid to reject liberal democracy, what is more important is how to radicalise liberal democracy through the use of the institutional and symbolic resources of liberal democracy itself.

Civil Society's Alternative Regionalism

The different efforts of engaging regionalism are based on the common view that APEC, ASEM or any of the mainstream regional formation serves the interest of the poor. This is because of the economic development model that guides mainstream regionalisms, which is the free market model. The APEC People's Forum and the emerging formation around ASEM in many respects are not just echoing hollow rhetoric despite the many limitations that they have to hurdle in bringing their messages across governments, business firms and the Asian people at large. Each is a network of networks as well as networks of national organisations with solid local constituencies and NGOs with partner local groups. Each member organisation has its own record of engagement with national and global decision making bodies. The position being carried by these formations regarding the official regional initiatives are result of painstaking processes of consultation and crystallisation of previous stands of member organisations concerning free trade and trade liberalisation.

The alternative conferences that they hold parallel to official regional conferences also goes through processes of consensus building, coalition and strategy formulation. They offer a paradigm that carry different assumptions from those being espoused by AFTA, APEC and ASEM. In the book titled *Challenging the Mainstream* (1995:67), Walden Bello lined up the core of key ideas of the emerging paradigm as discussed by civil society groups from Thailand, the Philippines, Korea and Taiwan. It has its core in the sustainable development perspective, and the major components of which are already featured in many constructive dialogues between civil society and governments. The dialogues in turn have resulted to the creation of common grounds for partnerships.

In the same book, the following are enumerated as the terms of an alternative structure for regional integration:

(*a*) limitation of the members of the bloc to the newly industrialising economies and the developing countries of the Western Pacific;
(*b*) development of regional environmental and labour codes that would regulate the behaviour of corporations in the region;
(*c*) the coordination of technology transfer, research and development strategies, with the emphasis on developing alternatives to unhealthy and environmentally destructive technologies; and
(*d*) the development of trading relationships that enhance rather than diminish the capacities of communities in the region.

In terms of assessing how civil society in Asia mesh the optimism of the will and the art of engaging in decisive action for reform, judgement is based in terms presented by Nederveen Pieterse's arguments on globalization and politics (1997) where he discussed the new contours of the politics of resistance for the coming century. Following Nederveen Pieterse's first argument, it can be said that most of the currently existing regional networks in Asia have long graduated from the "opposition to proposition" question. In the national and regional level, the big networks were already locked in intense negotiations with government officials, and international financial institutions to advance proposals that will give a more humane face to the new national and regional policies. What remains to be fleshed out and negotiated further are specific measures that could address the effects of blanket and rapid liberalisation on environmental, social and human rights issues; specific policy initiatives on structural adjustment programmes which is now being linked to regional agreements; and, establishment of concrete safety nets to balance the effects of economic deregulation with state and corporate accountability.

Engagement with states and international bodies however is still a risky business, since part of the openness still emanates from the desire to coopt civil society in the projects. Some organisation fall to this risk specially if there is a lack of unity caused by differences in positions which is quite common within the NGO community everywhere. As exemplified by events leading to the 1996 APEC Summit held in Manila, multiple positions adopted by different organised network caused the presence of four parallel NGO conferences. It was replicated in Vancouver the following year when there were two parallel people's summits. In the Philippines itself, disunity was highlighted by bitter debates emanating from a coalition's role in the government process of chartering the Individual Action Plan of the Philippines government in APEC. Events like those, which transpired in Manila in 1996, and which was unfortunately repeated in Vancouver in the 1997 APEC Summit should be avoided in future civil initiatives.

The appreciation of the role of the market and the growing efforts to engage in economic activities are positive developments. Such engagements may result in partnerships where civil society could use the capacity of the market mechanisms to inject vitality and dynamism to society in general. After all, it is now proven how demanding consumers could determine the flow of goods and services as well as spur innovation. The power of organised demand, which was proven by Consumer's International in previous campaigns, have unlocked new doors which civil society in general should further explore. In Malaysia, the consumers groups bridged people from all walks of life in pushing companies to be more friendly to sustainable growth, taking advantage of the market's readiness to take risks and promote innovations if gains could come in exchange. Consumers' demands are now being heard on how production should be done, making them partners in production (or prosumers), although the activism does not cover Malaysian transnational firms operating in countries like the Philippines or Indonesia.

Current NGO economic agenda is not comparable to the scale and level of the state-market nexus which are being challenged. It can indeed be said that most of the economic engagements are modified Mondragon type programmes which may have limits, but, they are teaching people how to define the meaning of the word possible and unleashing new energies to create new and bigger alternatives. These could be the pillars for the redefinition of international political economy and a seed for radical political economy. The combination of efforts aligned with popular economics (cooperatives, people to people trade, etc.) and high level advocacy to global financial institutions are formerly uncharted terrains that are now being mastered by civil society. At this early stage of treading these waters, prospects are becoming visible showing that there is no limit to imagination and commitment to change. Projects like the people to people trade and autonomous currency initiatives shows that a community could engage in trade and create a "shadow" society shaped by the member's real perceived needs and dreams.

Current Regional Networks: How Representative and Effective?

In terms of building a united front however, there are many fundamental characteristics that could be viewed as flaws in all the current regional networks. Generally, members of Asian progressive movements recognise the many limiting factors which hinder efforts of building a regional civil society. The primary factor is the distinct geographical and cultural features of Asia. Due to the great distances between countries, language differences, poverty, the prohibitive cost of travelling and the underdeveloped communication facilities in most peripheral parts of the region, there is still a people to people communication and interaction. Differences in language, culture, and religion are immense. Histories of colonialism contributed as well to such divergence, making Asian national social movements isolated from the rest and to have country-centric perspectives, priorities and programmes. NGOs also have great differences in work standards and capacity.

Besides from the geographical, cultural and historical factors there are seemingly intractable weaknesses of regional networking. Foremost of which is the fact that north-south alliances is still stronger than regional people to people linkages. This tendency is stronger in the case of NGOs given the circumstances related to funding. Because of NGOs' dependency to northern donors and support groups, what is still operative is "south-north-south" relations, with the north facilitating the connections.

Secondly, the establishment of a regional people's movement even on specific issues is still an aspiration, no single regional network could claim to represent Asian civil society. The problem of representation even (or specially) among the groups which identify themselves to be from the left of the political spectrum is rooted on the national dynamics where these movements are coming from. The nuances between the different groups are given and has strong ideological and historical reasons. It is always a tricky task for organisers to identify groups that could represent civil society from each country. This lead to a connected question concerning the process of inclusion within networks. So far, in terms of preparing for regional meetings and organising a network, the operative measure normally adopted is to have a broad convenor or host group to ensure that the range of participants will also be broad.

Thirdly, in terms of the character of representativeness in the broad initiatives, organisers of APEC People's Forum, ASEM NGO Working Group and PP21 admit that NGOs and big networks outnumber the organic or grassroots based organisations. The imbalance could be attributed to the fact that it takes huge amount of resources to shuttle from one international conference to another and at the same time monitor regional processes. The language used in the different official processes also requires a higher level of education and expertise for those who wish to intervene in the respective processes. In terms of human resources, the "diplomatic veterans" or experts in the field of international work can be found largely in the ranks of NGOs, especially bigger, regional and international ones who have more resources. The people at the base are minimally involved in the regional process though they are present in national meetings in preparation for regional ones. This gave rise to remarks that what is currently present is emerging alternative regionalism from the middle.

A positive development in recent years is the emerging gender balance in representation. "NGO and social movement advocacy and public relations" positions are now evenly balanced between women and men, even if in most cases organisational leadership in the strong sectors (labour and peasant) are still dominated by men. In terms of managing Secretariats, women still do the less prestigious but crucial staff work like administration, communication and information facilitation as well as conference preparations.

In regional and global fora, representativeness is still biased even within social movements. Most likely it will be those based in the national offices or headquarters of organisations that will get to attend international fora if they decide at all to engage in such exercises. Another factor is that international and regional solidarity remains a secondary agenda to many country groups and social movements (ARENA, 1999). Issues of survival like food security, rights and welfare are still the primary concern, and justifiably so, of grassroots organisations.

Since there is a lack of horizontal distribution in terms of professional skills and material resources between NGOs and grassroots organisations, measures are needed to alter this situation. Most NGOs have to reflect more and instil measures like sponsoring an organic activist in every international gathering that they will participate in. Demands for gender consciousness, grassroots participation, empowerment, pluralism, accountability and solidarity are since a long time part of the resolutions of conferences and plans of action—it is time to make them real. The use of and democratic access to modern technologies is another aspect of networking and advocacy work that has long been discussed. Still, an intensified crusade to make resources available to the grassroots is urgently needed.

The tasks ahead for regional networks are indeed daunting. Indeed, transnational advocacy have made a distinct position in the repertoire of movements' actions and the new trade regimes already tasted its power as experienced in Seattle in 1999 and earlier by the OECD during the campaign against MAI. Financial institutions however are hardening its position against further "disruptions" by protesters and lobbyists, security measures and rights violation to free speech and assembly were outrightly violated in recent events.

Developmental language and rhetoric is also getting more tricky and misleading. There is much talk about poverty reduction for example but new set of global rule for investment which will expose weak economies to further afflictions were also firmly set and these will create serious implications to the plight of the poor. The foreseeable aggravation of the exploitation by transnational corporations of workers, women and the environment resulting from the governments' renunciation of their role to impose regulations will make all the gains achieved by NGOs in all recently held UN Summits practically eliminated.

Since free trade agreements are already operational, there is no use for NGOs and lobby groups to think that it could be reversed. The remaining option is to stall events, which are speeding up liberalisation and to continue in exerting efforts on how they could be influenced and humanised. The rapid establishment of trade structures is making civil society organisations operating in the national and global levels simply overwhelmed by all occurring formations, reducing their initiatives to scattered and reactive activities. It is also alarming that in some post-transition democracies like the Philippines and South Korea, there is a rolling back to intense police handling of protests.

There is a need, therefore, to come up with a cohesive way of engaging in the different state-market formations. There are several assumptions that need reconstruction as well. For effective approaches to be designed, it should be clear to civil society formations that all existing geo-economic formations are established to create markets and not to control it. In the emerging century it is the activities of states, which are, being restricted and what is being broadened are the activities of corporations. This reality cannot be approached using the old sweeping way like working for a general social clause in free trade agreements. The needs of specific countries are nuanced thereby creating the need to consider the differences in goals, conditions, and social contexts.

Initiatives should be exerted in studying trade and investment flows. Lobby activities should be refocused. Instead of simply opposing foreign investments, groups should recognise that there are several good effects, which could be gained from foreign investments and to look at ways on how to make these kinds of investments beneficial to the majority. Considering the currency crisis, which created a long lasting effect in the economies of the region, lobby groups should work together to demand for the establishment of international institution that will control and discipline capital.

It is becoming increasingly fashionable to talk about parallel formations and transborder civil society networks. It is indeed logical that the current state-market nexus be met by corresponding regional and global civil society organisations. However, it is still important to link international efforts with national and local level initiatives.

Progressive groups should continue to exert efforts in pushing governments to be more democratic and to support the interest of the poor.

It is disturbing to observe that the similarity between government summits and the "people's summits" which are aspiring to challenge the former is being limited to the token parallel conference from the side of civil society. Aside from coming up with a common reading about the negative implications of increasing globalization of trade and production, concrete counter-measures are not yet coherently formed. Membership is still a lingering dilemma. Organising who is supposed to be talking to whom (and in some occasions who could stand whom politically) at which meeting already requires huge amounts of networking skills. It is a given that the left is experiencing maybe its most serious dilemma in terms of unity, in most instances this disunity is backfiring to each individual initiatives. It is no longer a question of representativeness but a question of how each formation claiming to represent the majority could come together to form a cohesive challenge to a perceived common enemy.

Continuity is another Waterloo. While governments are building on previous efforts (with bottleneck issues notwithstanding), networks seems to be perpetually trapped with the amazing ability to start from base one in every international conference. The People's Summit on APEC held in Vancouver (which followed the Manila experience) is a very glaring example on how not to move forward. The debates in various workshops emanated from the lack of the necessary clarification and information of previous discussions. What made experiences like these disheartening is the fact that the building blocs for parallel NGO and labour networks already took a huge amount of energy to put in place. From the gathering of environmental and labour councils in Seattle in 1993 to the formal Kyoto and Manila People's Summit, discussions and debates have moved inch by painstaking inch until a common reading of the current global political economy was achieved.

Conclusion

Sections of civil society in the region however divided concerning positions on how to address the emerging regional integration shares the same aspiration of seeking possibilities to articulate the contention of those who are feeling the adverse impact of the triumph of neo-liberalism. The initiatives exerted in the last five years shows growing maturity and competence to address the needs of the time. The continuing efforts of civil society to be heard amidst the din of contending capitalist agenda signify that there are opposing views that are seeking to formulate viable alternatives to the development path being offered by the emerging arrangements.

In terms of civil society's contribution to the transnationalisation of democracy in the region, it can be said that the openings achieved by strong civil society in some countries like the Philippines, Thailand, Korea, and Japan are encouraging efforts to organise and strengthen groups and organisations in other countries where the spaces are narrower. The continuing repression of people's rights to organise and oppose government policies in countries like Indonesia, Burma, and to some extent Malaysia and the Philippines are posing serious threat that might affect the gains achieved before. The growth of regionalism and the development of closer links of region states (growth triangles like Singapore-Malaysia-Indonesia, Hong Kong and adjacent parts of Mainland China for example) could change the way people will relate to each other in those areas. Sentiments of Asianess (brotherhood and sisterhood among Asians) are beginning to be stirred with the closer links made possible by revolutions in communication technology and regional events. It is a challenge to transform the sentiment towards finding a way on how to bring people's interests and welfare as primary goal in whatever forms of regional economic integration, which will eventually dominate in the region.

The biggest challenge is how to make the "actually existing people" identify with the alternatives, see them as a vehicle for the realisation of their hope and put a stake on the alternative agenda. Therefore, the process of programme, priority setting, and building of advocacy position should remain close to what the alternatives claim to serve. Lastly, it should be understood that all these initiatives is for changing and reclaiming the present (the here and now), as well as building the future. Therefore, the need for understanding what is happening, and the mobilisation to change it are urgent and necessary responsibility of everyone.

REFERENCES

Alagappa, M., *Political Legitimacy in Southeast Asia. The Quest for Moral Authority* (Stanford, Stanford University Press), 1995.

ASEAN, 2000, AFTA Update, www.seasec.org

APEC, A Vision for APEC, Report of the Eminent Persons Group to APEC Ministers, Bangkok, Asian Cultural Forum on Development, 1992.

APEC, Declaration of Common Resolve, Bogor, APEC, 1994.

APEC, Osaka Action Agenda (text printed in The Jakarta Post, Tuesday, Nov. 21, 1995.

APEC Secretariat, APEC Updates and Brunei Priorities 2000, www.apec.org/

APEC Labor Rights Monitor, APEC and Free Trade, ALARM Update, July-August, Hong Kong, ALARM, 1996.

Arrighi, G., The Rise of East Asia and the Withering Away of the Interstate System, Binghamton University, New York, 1996.

ARENA, (2000) Movements Directory, www.asianexchange.org/.

ARENA, Engaging the Asian Development Bank, Voices from NGOs, *Asian Exchange*, Vol.12, No.1, October 1996, Hong Kong, 1996.

ARENA, New Directions, Paradigms and Perspectives, Hong Kong, *ARENA*, 1994.

Asia Pacific Civil Society Forum, Civil Society Country Reports. Documents from the conference with the same title, Seoul, Korea Coalition for Citizens' Movements, 1995.

ASEM Briefing Papers, Part of ASEM Documents provided by the DG1B Directorate-General for External Relations (South and South East Asia) of the European Commission, 1996.

Batista, I., Civil Society: A Paradigm or A New Slogan? *Asian Action* July-September Issue, Bangkok, Asian Cultural Forum on Development, 1993.

Bello, W., *Dragons in Distress: Asia's Miracle Economies in Crisis*, London, Pluto Press, 1992.

Bello, W., *Dark Victory: The United States, Structural Adjustment and Global Poverty*, London, Pluto Press, Food First and Transnational Institute, 1994.

Bello, W., *Clash of Development Models in Asia and the Pacific*, Hong Kong, ARENA, 1994.

Bello, W., APEC and the Conflict of Capitalism, Challenging the Mainstream: APEC and the Asia Pacific Development Debate, Hong Kong, Asian Regional Network for Alternatives-ARENA, 1995.

Bello, W., APEC's Unauthorised History, Bangkok, Forum on the Global South FOCUS, 1996.

Bergsten, C.F. and Noland, M., Pacific Dynamism and the International Economic System, Washington D.C., Institute for International Economics, 1993.

Centre Tricontinental, Free Trade Zones and Transnational Corporations in Malaysia, The Philippines and Sri Lanka, Louvain, CETRI, 1982.

Chowdhury, A. and Islam, I., *The Newly Industrializing Countries of East Asia*, London, Routledge, 1993.

Cox, R., *Production, Power, and World Order: Social Forces in the Making of History*, New York, Columbia University Press, 1987.

de la Torre, E., Responsive Governance and People's Participation. Paper presented to the Asian NGO meeting for the World Summit on Social Development, 1995

De Oliviera and Tandon R., An Emerging Civil Society, PRIA, New Delhi, 1994.

De Sousa Santos, B., *Toward a New Common Sense: Law, Science and Politics in theParadigmatic Transition*, Routledge, New York, 1995.

DAGA, What is APEC? (part of email conference-discussion in preparation for the APEC People's Forum in Manila on November 1996).

Finger, M. and Princen, T., *Environmental NGOs in World Politics. Linking the Local to the Global*, London and New York, Routledge, 1995.

Focus on the Global South—FOCUS, The APEC Summit in Japan: The Other Side, Bangkok, Development Policy Research and Practice—Chulalongkorn University, 1995.

Forgacs, D. (ed), *An Antonio Gramsci Reader*, (New York, Schocken Books).

Gamble A., and Payne, A. (ed.), *Regionalism and World Order*, London, Macmillan Press, 1996.

Gill, S., (ed.), *Gramsci, Historical Materialism and International Relations*, Cambridge, Cambridge University Press, 1993.

Gill, S., (ed.), Theorising the Interregnum: The Double Movement and Global Politics in the 1990s, *International Political Economy: Understanding Global Disorder*, (Hettne ed.), Halifax Fernwood Publishing, 1995.

Hamelink, C., Trends in World Communication. On Disempowerment and Self Empowerment, Penang, Southbound and Third World Network, 1994.

Held, D., *Democracy and the Global Order. From Modern State to Cosmopolitan Governance,* Cambridge, Polity Press, 1995.

Hettne, B. (ed), *International Political Economy, Understanding Global Disorder,* Halifax, Fernwood Publishing, 1995.

Hogan, T., *A Guide to Central Thinkers and Social Theory*, (Beilhars ed.) Sydney, Allen and Levin, 1992.

Holloway, R., Civil Society—the Non Profit Private Sector: Trying to Categorize it in Bangladesh. Paper presented to UNICEF, Dhaka, Bangladesh, 1993.

Hutton, W., The State We're In, *The Political Economy of the World's Capitalisms,* London, Jonathan Cape.

International Monetary Fund, Inter-regional Trade Report, from the ISS database, 1996.

JETRO, Japanese Outward FDI Declined while Inward FDI Increases. Japanese External Trade Organization 1998 Report, 1998.

Kelsey, J., Economic Fundamentalism, Kyoto, APEC NGO Forum Papers, 1995.

Kennedy, P., *Preparing for the 21st Century,* New York, Vintage Books, 1994.

Keohane, R.O. and Nye, J.S., *Power and Interdependence*, 2nd Edition, Boston, Little, Brown, 1989

Korten, D., *Community Management: Asian Experience and Perspectives,* Connecticut, Kumarian Press, 1986.

Korten, D., *Getting to the 21st Century,* Connecticut, Kumarian Press, 1990.

Krugman, P., *Geography and Trade,* Massachusetts, MIT Press, 1991.

Kwan, C. H., *Economic Interdependence in the Asia Pacific Region,* London and New York, Routledge, 1994.

Landsberg, M.H., PP21: It May Be Positive, But Is It Radical? AMPO Japan-*Asia Quarterly Review*, Vol. 25, No. 1, 1993.

Manila People's Forum on APEC, Brochure on Manila People's Forum on APEC '96, Quezon City, Philippines Host Committee, 1996.

Mendl, W., *Japan's Asia Policy, Regional Security and Global Interests,* London, Routledge, 1995.

Motayama, Y., Politics of Liberalization: A Japanese Perspective on APEC, AMPO-Japan, *Asia Quarterly Review*, Vol. 26, No. 34, 1993.

Muto, I., PP21: A Step in the Process, AMPO Japan-*Asia Quarterly Review*, Vol. 25, No. 2, 1993.

Muto, I., International Civil Society, *Asian Action*, July-September Issue, Bangkok, Asian Cultural Forum on Development, 1993.

Nederveen-Pieterse, J., *Empire and Emancipation*, London, Pluto Press, 1990.

Nederveen-Pieterse, J., Globalization and Emancipation. From Local Empowerment to Global Reform, *New Political Economy*, Vol. 2, No.1, Carfax Pub. Hants, 1997.

Nerfin, M., *Neither Prince nor Merchant*: Citizen—An Introduction to the Third System in World Economy in Transition, K. Ahooja-Patel ed., Oxford, Pergamon Press, 1986.

NGO Forum on APEC, Kyoto Declaration, Statement from the 1995 NGO Forum on APEC, 1995.

Noor, P., ASEM Avoids the Issue, Commentary, No.12, May Issue, Selangor, International Movement for a Just World, 1998.

Ohmae, K., *The End of the Nation State, The Rise of Regional Economics*, New York, Free Press, 1995.

Philippines Rural Reconstruction Movement, The Way of Power: Development in the Hands of the People, Manila, PRRM, 1994.

Polanyi-Levitt, K., *The Life and Work of Karl Polanyi,* Montreal, Black Rose Books, 1990.

Robertson, R., *Globalization: Social Theory's Global Culture*, London Sage, 1992.

Serrano, I., *Reimagining Civil Society*, Manila, PRRM, 1993.

Serrano, I., *Civil Society in the Asia Pacific*, Washington D.C., CIVICUS, 1994.

Spero, J., US Policy Toward APEC, Challenging the Mainstream, Hong Kong, Asian Regional Network for Alternatives—ARENA, 1995.

Stallings, B. (ed.), *Global Change, Regional Response: The New International Context of Development*, Cambridge, Cambridge University Press, 1995.

Thomas, H., *Globalization and Third World Trade Unions*: *The Challenge of Rapid Economic Change*, London, Zed Books, 1995.

Transnational Institute, Asia's Wake-Up Call to Europe: The Perspective for the Philippines. Conference document. 13-14 March Royal Tropical Institute, Amsterdam, 1995.

United Nations Development Programme (UNDP), Human Development Report, New York, Oxford University Press, 1995.

United Nations Development Programme (UNDP), Poverty Report, New York, Oxford University Press, 1998.

Varona, R., Reflections on Regional Networking and PP21. Paper presented to the 6th General Assembly of PP21 held in Kathmandu, Nepal. 8-10 March 1996.

Wallerstein, I., *The Politics of the World Economy*, Cambridge, Cambridge University Press, 1984.

Waterman, P., *A New World View: Globalization, Civil Society, and Solidarity* The Hague, Institute of Social Studies, 1995.

Waterman, P., Beijing and Huairou: Approaches and Departures. Second Thoughts on Researching Women, Feminism and the New Global Solidarity.Conference Paper presented at the Conference on Women, Citizenship and Difference 16-18 July 1996, University of Greenwich, London.

Yun-han, C., The East Asian NICs: A State-led Path to the Developed World, Global Change, Regional Response (Stallings, ed.), Cambridge University Press, 1995.

28

Canadian Foreign Policy in a Globalizing World:

The Role of Canadian Provinces

NALINI KANT JHA

Surely, globalization has influenced the nation-state system in several ways. One of the significant impacts of globalization on the working of the nation-state system can be clearly seen in federal states. All indicators suggest that global interdependence is accelerating the role of states and provinces in the international economy, in essence mirroring a process that occurred earlier at the level of the nation-state. In federal states such as Canada, the US, and India, etc., the states and provinces have become major interveners in economic domain and have never before been so exposed to the competitive forces of international competition. This competition is so fierce that those constituent Governments that choose not to participate may find their economic futures threatened. Framed within these developments, the thrust of state-provincial activities has increasingly been towards direct involvement in the international economy, as compared to the more indirect means of attempting to influence the external economic policy of the federal Government.

International activities of provincial Governments have arisen concern among federal Governments like Canada, because these activities may be a vehicle for some form of trans sovereign meddling, fragmentation of foreign policy, or may be used as venue to express reservations regarding the federal Government's degree of international legitimacy. On the other hand, the export and investment promotion activities of states help reduce Canada's current account deficit that is incurred by its Cdn $ 250 billion net international liabilities. It is, therefore, highly relevant to examine the dimensions as well as limitations of provincial role in the making of Canadian foreign policy and the response of the federal Government to growing provincial activities in foreign affairs to suggest a policy frame for a better management of provincial activities in this regard. Before beginning this exercise, it is however, useful to briefly discuss the Canadian federal structure.

II

It would be stressing the obvious to mention that like India, Canada too has a federal political system having a written Constitution. As against the Indian Constitution, however, the Canadian Constitution does not elaborate the issue of external relations. While the Indian Constitution confers on the Union of India legislative and executive powers, which embrace the total field of external sovereignty, the Canadian Constitutional provisions, like those of Australia, are most primitive in this regard. This is because of the fact that Canada's primary constituent document, the British North America Act of 1867, was drafted at a time when it was not anticipated that any indigenous Canadian authority would possess significant international capacity. Rather, responsibility for managing foreign relations of Canada continued to vest in the imperial Government.[1] Accordingly, the only direct relevant provision inserted into the British North America Act was Section 132, which allowed the federal Government to make laws for implementing in Canada treaties by the British Empire—legislative implementation of treaties being indispensable in Anglo-Canadian legal theory. But this provision conferred no power upon any Canadian authority to make and implement treaties on its own behalf.

The evolution of dominion independence during the twentieth century saw through the development of a full Canadian treaty-making power, which (at least primarily) came to reside in the executive branch of the Canadian federal Government. This evolution of Canadian constitution law in relation to external relation opened up two potential controversies concerning the operation of Canada as a federal state. The first relates to the legislative capacity to implement treaties. Evan assuming that the Canadian federal authorities have an unlimited power to make treaties, it is not clear as to whether the federal Government can make implementing law that is necessary in Canada in accordance with its inherited British constitutional theory. In other words, can

Parliament of Canada enact required implementing legislation if it relates to provincial matters or will a series of provincial laws be required with the corresponding risk that Canada will be unable to fulfil its federal obligations in foreign sphere? Canadian courts answer this question in negative. As classified in the labour conventions case, the powers of the federal Government to make a treaty does not carry with it a power to implement that treaty independently of its other constitutional heads of power.[2] As a result, while the Canadian Government can make a treaty, it cannot implement it through legislation on matters related to provincial jurisdiction. Unlike India, the Canadian Constitution thus represents clearly enough a choice in favour of safeguarding the federal-provincial balance at the possible expense of significant foreign relations considerations.

The overlooking of the foreign policy concerns in the Canadian Constitution has led to avoidable controversies in Canada over the constitutional capacity of the provinces to engage in foreign policy formulation, and especially over their ability to enter into international agreements. As Canada's primary constituent documents are not clear on this point, some Quebecois argue that the capacity to enter into treaties logically must be regarded as concurrent with the powers to implement those treaties. Accordingly, they claim that responsibility for entering into international agreements is divided in Canada between the federal Government and those of the Provinces.[3] Understandably this position has been rejected by Federal Government as well as by commentators of different constitutional viewpoints, who argue that the provinces possess, at best, a very limited capacity in the field of external relations.[4] The vagueness of constitutional documents of Canada concerning the interaction of federalism and external relations thus exaggerates controversies and difficulties in delineating the role of provincial Governments in the making of Canadian foreign policy.

It must however be noted that the above discussion of Canadian Constitutional provisions regarding the management of Canada's foreign policy be taken merely as a starting point of enquiry. The provisions of federal constitutions dealing with external relations are, in a purely technical sense, far from adequate as pieces of constitutional drafting. The best examples are, of course, the Australian and Canadian Constitutions, which effectively fail to make provision in relation to external affairs. But even the vastly more detailed Constitutions of India and Germany, etc., contain their own points of vagueness and confusion in this matter. In fact, the entire relationship between federalism and foreign policy is so fluid, varied and complicated that it is exceedingly difficult for any federal Constitution to adequately deal with this subject. Accordingly, the 'real' regimes for the management of external relations are all too often located outside the Constitutions concerned. We therefore now propose to examine how and to what extent the actual interplay of various forces enable Canadian provinces to guide and mould the external behaviour of Canada.

III

The above-mentioned question appears very simple, as it is manifestly obvious that Canada's provincial Governments engage in considerable activity in the international realm. Not only the Canadian Constitution, unlike India, does not authorize Ottawa to exercise exclusive control over foreign relations, but in practice also, provincial and even city Governments have demonstrated keen willingness to press for their interests in the international activities. To cite only a few examples: the chorus by the Quebec Government to gain a representative role in Francophonic, the attempts by a several Alberta premiers to boost foreign investment in that province, the attempts by Ontario (and Toronto) to secure the 1996 Olympic Games, the agreements signed between British Columbia and Washington on policing, and the winning agreement between the city of Vancouver and strategic cities in the Pacific Rim.[5] The most notable example of the role of provinces in Canada's foreign policy is, however, their role in the shaping of relations with the United States.[6]

Though Canadian provinces have shown keen interest in foreign affairs earlier as well, their international activities have steady increased over the last two decades.[7] The fact that the federal Government in Ottawa has felt the need for the evolution of new institutional mechanisms to enable it effectively co-ordinate the international activities of provinces shows their increasing international ambitions and role.[8]

As elaborated by a leading Canadian scholar, five distinct but related interests propel provincial Governments in Canada into the international sphere: constitutional, material, functional, political and breaucratic.[9] The lack of constitutional clarity over the Federal Government's authority concerning Canadian foreign affairs is, of course, the principal explanation of provincial activities in the international sphere. But other factors have also contributed to role of provinces in the shaping of Canadian foreign policy. Firstly, the 'localization' of international politics and the concomitant 'domesticization of Canada's foreign policy has given impetus to provincial involvement in international affairs. In other words, the shifting of focus in international relations from larger matters of peace, war and alliance building to matters affecting local and provincial Governments such as environment, women's right, etc., has necessitated their foreign activities. The emergence of interdependent issues affecting provincial Governments such as human rights, environment protection, women's right, etc., in the globalizing world has thus created a conducive environment for a increasing role of the provinces in Canada's foreign policy.

Secondly, the changing power relationship in Canada evident from new responsibilities assumed by provinces in important areas of natural resources like water projects for international river developments has promoted the provincial presence in international dealings. Thirdly, the increasing size of the provincial bureaucracies has also contributed to the emergence of the provinces as international actors.[10] For, the increasing number of civil servants improves provincial Governments' capability to perform a more active role in the society. This expands the attention that can be devoted to a particular subject (including international ones) by the civil service.[11]

Whatever may be the cause(s) for the increasing international role of constituent Governments in Canada, their assertiveness in this regard cannot be denied. Examples of this phenomenon are fairly common: the sporadic pronouncements of the *Party Quebecois Government of Rene Lévesque* on the Palestinian issue in the late 1970s; the numerous declarations of municipal council across Canada in the early 1980s[12] that their cities were nuclear free zones; the involvement of the Ontario Government in the apartheid issue in the mid-1980s; the involvement of the city of Vancouver in a development assistance programme; the participation of various provincial and municipal politicians in anti-Beijing protests following the Tiananmen massacre in 1989; the call by the Premier of Alberta for international recognition of Ukraine in August 1991, and so on.[13] The international activities of the provinces thus provide excellent examples of the intersection of domestic and international politics or "intermestic" politics.[14]

IV

While there are some areas of policy in which the provincial

Governments play a critical role, the enhancement of trade investment and finance is an obvious example, there are also many spheres where the provincial Governments play no role at all in shaping policy responses. Numerous crucial areas of global politics are all formulated, decided and pronounced in Canada's name by the federal authorities in Ottawa alone. Whether it be responses to starvation in north-eastern Africa; mal-development in Latin America; American military interventions in Central America; Japanese-American trade conflicts; human rights violations in China and Tibet; the arms control front in Europe; ethno nationalist clashes in the south of the former Soviet region; destruction of chemical/biological weapons in the pacific; interest relief for G-7 or debt relief for G-77 in all of these issues Canada's provincial and local Governments are not even players much less players of consequences.[15]

The above-mentioned descriptioned of the significance as well as limits of provincial inputs in the shaping of Canadian foreign policy presents an inconsistent picture in this regard. This inconsistency emanates from the fact that the Government in Ottawa seems to make sharp distinctions about different types of foreign policy. As a result of provincial initiations since 1960s and comparable moves by constituents units in other federations, Ottawa accepts, on the one hand, that there are policy issues that legitimately engage provinces and require co-ordination between the federal and provincial Governments. On the other hand, Ottawa perceives that subjects like military/security policy, the politics of the changing relations of the great powers, the North-South relations, etc., fall within the *vires* of the Central Government alone. These are the issues over which, the constituent governments do not play any role at all. In this era of globalization when it is popular to deny the monolithic assumptions of statism, and assert instead the "multidimensionality," "perforatedness," "multivocality" or simply the "evanescence" of the nation-state, one can thus safely assert that however abstract the concepts of nation and state might be, and however essentially contested such terms may be,[16] the federal state in Canada remains quite concrete and quite sovereign. Quite contrary to the assertions of globalites who preach the advent of such fanciful notions as borderless worlds and morbidity—if not imminent demise—of the nation-state, it thus appear that there should be one central authority to make foreign policy decision on Canada's behalf in the international system remains widely shared among Canadians, including provincial Government officials themselves.[17]

It is this tendency of the federal Government in Canada to retain its hold over the making of foreign policy that the Government in Ottawa responds in three different ways to the provincial activities in external fields, all depending on the degree to which the constituent Government involvement clashes with Ottawa's perception of national interest. The next section of this article, therefore, discusses how the Canadian federal Government has respondent to the provincial Government's foreign policy demands with a variety of bureaucratic and political mechanisms.

V

As most of the provincial Governments implicitly or explicitly recognize federal pre-eminence in the tailoring of Canadian foreign policy, their international activities are usually not seen as a threat by federal elites. As such, much of the provincial activities concerning external field do not engender political conflict between the levels of Government. Provincial officials abroad, wishing to promote tourism and investment, etc., tend to work cooperatively with their local counterparts. To cite more specific examples; Ottawa did little to discourage widespread involvement of politicians from Canada's provincial and municipal Governments in the condemnation of China's Government after the Tiananmen massacre in June 1989. For, the airing of voice on this issue by local and provincial politicians strengthened Ottawa's voice of protest in this regard. Similarly, the involvement of provincial Governments in efforts to assist the transition to a market economy in Central and Eastern Europe after 1989 fitted broadly into Ottawa's own policy priorities.[18]

In case of differences over foreign policy issues between the two levels of Governments, however, Ottawa may respond in three ways, namely, co-option, neglect or opposition of provincial stands. To cite the example of co-option first, when views of provincial leaders differed with those in Ottawa over the Tokyo Round of multilateral trade negotiations in Ottawa, the Central Government first tried to ensure that the interests of provincial Governments were represented in the overall Canadian position. By 1980, this co-option was given an institutional shape through regularization of federal provincial consultations on trade policy.[19]

Secondly, Ottawa tends to ignore the attempts of provincial Governments to intrude into federal government's policy space. To cite only a few instances, when Bill Davis, the Ontario Premier, called for greater defence spending during the 1979-80 election campaign, or when Don Getty, the Premier of Alberta, called for international recognition of Ukrainian independence following the coup in the Soviet Union in August 1991, the reaction from the federal Government was silence. Likewise silence was the fate of the profusion of nuclear-free declarations by numerous provincial and local Governments in the early 1980s—though in this case the silence was accompanied by condescension. The reaction to these declarations from Ottawa was indicative of the federal Government's apparent calculus that such initiatives fell so far outside the understood boundaries of constituent Government policy space that there was little to be gained by spending serious political energy responding to them.[20]

Thirdly, when federal authorities feel that international activities of constituent Governments threaten Canadian integrity, they oppose such moves, as the Trudeau Government did in the case of some provincial attempts to sanction South Africa in the 1970s, or as Ottawa did in the case of a number of initiatives taken by the provincial Government of Quebec in pursuit of independence in world politics.[21] Even in the area of Canada's foreign trade, which falls within provincial vires, Ottawa could not countenance provincial foreign activities beyond a limit. Thus as stated earlier, while Ottawa tried to co-opt provincial views on trade policy, the Mulroney Government refused to permit the provincial premiers to participate in the actual process of negotiating free trade with the US. Similarly, the federal Government has consistently opposed the opening of separate offices in Washington by the constituent Governments.[22]

It is however instructive to contrast how the attitudes of both the federal and provincial Governments undergo a marked change when it is a matter of policy issues that fall more clearly within their constitutional or legislative domain. If one examines, for instance, the involvement of provincial Governments in trade and economic affairs, which do fall within provincial *vires*, it will be clear the Ottawa has the same range of responses—tolerance, co-option, condescension, or opposition—to the foreign policy initiatives of the constituent units. But when these units have a legitimate claim for involvement, the attitudes of all concerned differ drastically, with the intensity of federal-provincial conflict escalating in a manner not normally present in other spheres of foreign policy. The free trade negotiations with the US, which cut close to core provincial interest in economic development, provide another example of how federal-provincial (and indeed inter-provincial) conflict will become markedly more intense when there is conflict over core issues that clearly fall into legitimate areas of competence.[23] And finally, the politics of Quebec-Paris-Ottawa triangle show how the contending (and frequently incompatible) conceptions of political community held by Canadians of all sorts can generate deep controversy between various levels of Government.

VI

To sum up, if there are areas where Canadian provinces are both active and influential and thereby play significant role in the international political economy in the era of globalization, there are at the same time also those fields of policy, where constituent Governments are simply not players, much less players with influence.

To recapitulate the effectiveness of provincial inputs in Canadian foreign policy first, though the federal Government could have insisted, for example, that since it alone should speak for all Canadians in the international system, it alone could present the bid to have the International Olympic Committee Award for the 1996 Summer Games to Toronto. But such an exclusionary stance, which might have been correct on purely technical ground, would have been seen as illegitimate due to widespread expectation of the concerned cities and provinces about their natural involvement in this process. Whenever, therefore, a Canadian city seeks to host the Olympic games, the lobbying tends to be a three-way effort by the city, the province and the federal Government. Also, Ottawa has recognized that where issues are regional or local in character, the regional or local political forces may have a better chance of finding compromise agreement. Ottawa cannot ignore the fact that while antagonism between it and Washington grew over acid rain co-operation between New England and eastern Canadian provinces matured. British Columbia and its West-coast partners such as Ontario and the Great Lakes states, New England and New York and their Northern partners—all signed agreements and are developing relations that recognized their mutual and regional interests, whatever the international disagreements. On the other hand, there seems to be a wide range of policy issues that the federal Government in Canada perceives as falling within its exclusive jurisdiction. As such, Ottawa resists those foreign initiations of constituent units that conflict with its policies.

These apparent inconsistencies in the levels of activity and influence of provincial Governments of foreign policy require re-examination of the issue of jurisdiction and the claims that provincial Governments make for legitimate involvement in foreign policy areas, as a guide to understanding when and why provincial and municipal Governments may involve themselves in external activities.

Now it is widely recognized that while the federal Government should manage matters involving defence and security of the country, the provinces must be allowed required autonomy to mobilize foreign investment and conduct commercial dealings with foreign countries due to the compulsions of globalization and liberalisation of economy. This emerging consensus notwithstanding, both the levels of Governments must seek to create a common policy to avoid conflict by institutionalising consultative and co-ordinating procedure, anticipating problems, and trying to accommodate each other's legitimate interests.

NOTES

1. Mahler, G., *New Dimensions of Canadian Federalism*, Rutherford, NJ, F. Dickinson University Press, 1987, p. 5; and P. Hogg, *Constitutional Law of Canada,* Toronto: Carswell, 1985, p. 242.
2. (1937), AC 326.
3. Morin, J.Y., "La Conclusion d'Accords Internationseaux Par Les Provinces Canadiennes a la Lumiere du Droit Compare," *Canadian Yearbook of International Law*, vol. 3, 1967.
4. Hogg, No. 2, pp. 254-55.
5. For an overview of the role of provinces in the making of Canada's foreign policy see Kim Richard Nossal, *The Politics of Canadian Foreign Policy*, (Scarborough, Ontario: Prentice Hall, 1997); and his, "The Impact of Provincial Governments on Canadian Foreign Policy," in Dauglas M. Brown and Earl H. Fray eds., *States and Provinces in the International Economy*, Berkeley, California, 1993, pp. 233-43; Elliot J. Feldman and Lily Gardner Feldman, "The Impact of Federalism on the Organisation of Canadian Foreign Policy," *Publius: The Journal of Federalism*, Vol. 14, 1984; P.R. Johannson, "Provincial International Activities," Toronto, *International Journal*, Vol. 33, No. 1, Winter 1977-78, pp. 128-49; and Jha, Nalini Kant, "Foreign Policy Making in Federal States: The Indian and Canadian Experiences," *India Quarterly*, New Delhi, Vol. 55, Nos. 3-4, July-December 1999, pp. 1-16.
6. Brown, Douglas M., "The Evolving Role of the Provinces in Canada-US

Trade Relations," in Brown and Fry eds., *States and Provinces in the International Economy*, ibid., pp. 93-144.

7. A comparison of the perspectives in the literature on the role of federalism in Canadian foreign policy over the last 20 years shows the increasing role of provinces in this regard. See, for example, Ronald G. Atkey, "The Role of the Provinces in International Affairs," *International Journal*, Vol. 26, Winter 1970-71, pp. 249-73; Howard A. Leeson and Wilfried Vanderelst, eds, *External Affairs and Canadian Federalism: The History of a Dilemma* (Toronto: Holt, Rhinehart and Winston, 1973); Johannson "Provincial International Activities," No. 5; Feldman and Feldman "The Impact of Federalism on the Organisation of Canadian Foreign Policy", No. 5; Hans J. Michelmann, "Federalism and International Relations in Canada and the Federal Republic of Germany," *International Journal*, Vol. 41, Summer 1986, pp. 539-71; contributions on Canada in I. Duchacek, D. Latouche and G. Stevenson, eds., *Perforated Sovereignties and International Relations: Trans Sovereign Contacts and Sub-national governments* (New York; Greenwood Press, 1988); Annemarie Jacomy-Millette, "Les activities international's des provinces Canadiennes," in Paul Painchaud ed. de Mackenzie King a Pierre Trudeau Quarante Ans de Diplomatic Canadienne (Quebec: Les Presses de L'Universite Laval, 1989), pp. 81-104; and the Canadian selections in Hans J. Michelmann and Panayotis Soldatos, eds., *Federalism and International Relations: The Role of Sub-national Units*, 1990, Oxford: Clarendon Press.
8. See for details, Feldman, and Feldman, "Impact of Federalism," No. 5.
9. Kim Rachard Nossal, *The Politics of Canadian Foreign Policy*, Scarborough, Ont.: Prentice Hall, 1977, pp. 293-314.
10. Thomas Levy and Don Munton, "Federal-Provincial Dimensions of State-Provincial Relations," *International Perspectives*, March-April 1976, p. 24.
11. Johanson, "Provincial International Activities," No. 5, pp. 363-64.
12. See, for instance, Kim Rachard Nossal, "Micro-diplomacy: The case of Ontario and Economic Sanctions against South Africa", in W.M. Chandler and C.W. Zollner, eds., *Challenges to Federalism: Policy Making in Canada and the Federal Republic of Germany*, Kingston: Queen's University, 1989, pp. 235-50.
13. Nossal, The Impact of Provincial Governments on Canadian Foreign Policy," No. 5, p. 236.
14. The term "intermestic" is usually attributed to Beyless Manning "The Congress, the Executive and Intermestic Affairs," *Foreign Affairs* (New York), Vol. 55, January 1977. For an overview of literature on domestic politics and foreign policy linkages, see Nalini Kant Jha, *Domestic Imperatives in India's Foreign Policy*, New Delhi: South Asian Publishers, 2002, Chapter 1.
15. Nossal, "The Impact of Provincial Governments on Canadian Foreign Policy," No. 5, pp. 234-35.

16. For a sensitive argument on the continuing importance of the state in international relations, see Tom Keating, "The State and International Relations," in David G. Haglund and Michael K. Hawes, *World Politics: Power, Independence and Dependence*, Toronto: Harcourt Brace Jovanovich, 1990, pp. 16-37.
17. For an interesting statement of such assumptions by a senior provincial official, see Wayne Clifford, "A Perspective on the Question with Particular Reference to the Case of the Province of Alberta," *Choix,* Vol. 14, 1982, pp. 108-09.
18. Nossal, "The Impact of Provincial Governments on Canadian Foreign Policy," No. 5, p. 239.
19. Hart, Michael, Dymond Bill and Robertson Colin, *Decision at Midnight: Inside the Canada-US Free Trade Negotiations*, Vancouver, University of British Columbia, 1994, p. 139.
20. Nossal, "The Impact of Provincial Governments on Canadian Foreign Policy," No. 5, p. 239.
21. The Politics of Quebec-Paris-Ottawa triangle show how the contending conceptions of political community held by Canadian of all sorts can generate deep controversy between levels of Government. For details, see J.L. Granatstein and Robert Bothwell, *Pirouette: Pierre Trudeau and Canadian Foreign Policy*, Toronto, University of Toronto Press, 1990, Chapter·5.
22. Despite Ottawa's opposition, Quebec maintains a tourist office in Washington since 1978 and which has done more than merely dispensing tourist information about Quebec. For details, see Gorden Mace, Louis Belanger, and Ivan Bernier, "Canadian Foreign Policy and Quebec," In Maxwell A. Cameron and Maureen Appeal Molot, eds; *Canada Among Nations: Democracy and Foreign Policy*, Ottawa: Carleton University Press, 1995, p. 127. For a discussion of Ottawa's differences with Canadian provinces over their claim of representation in Washington DC and the Ottawa's insistence that Canada must speak with one Hobbesian voice in the field of internal affairs in general and in Washington in particular, see Stephen Clarkson, *Canada and the Reagon Challenge*, Toronto: James Lorimer, 1985, revised edition, pp. 301-10.
23. Nosall, "The Impact of Provincial Governments on Canadian Foreign Policy," No. 5, p. 240.
24. The best history of this triangle during the Trudeau period is to be found in J.L. Granatstein and Robert Bothwell, *Pirouette: Pierre Trudeau and Canadian Foreign Policy*, Toronto: University of Toronto Press, 1990, Chapter 5.

Bibliography

SUNITA GULATI

Abdul Aziz, *Implications of Globalisation: Empowering Women Economically*, Deccan Herald, 6 Oct 2000, p. 12.

Acharyya, Rajat and Marjit, Sugata, *Globalisation and Inequality: An Analytical Perspective*, Economic and Political Weekly, 35(39), 23 Sep 2000, p. 3503-510.

Adiseshiah Malcolm S., *Fiscal Policies and Globalisation*, Bulletin: Madras Development Seminar Series, 23(7) Jul. 93, pp. 308-11.

Adiseshiah Malcolm S., *Globalisation: A Description,* Bulltetin Madras Development Seminar Series, 23(10), Oct. 93, pp. 423-30.

Agrawal, Raj, *Globalization of Higher Education and WTO*, University News, 40(34), 26 Aug. 2002, pp. 1-9.

Ahooja Patel, Krishna, *Globalisation: An Impressionistic View*, Mainstream, 38(19), 29 Apr. 2000. pp. 20-24.

Aijaz Ahmad, *Globalization and the Nation-state*, Seminar, (437), Jan. 1995, pp.43-48.

Aiyar, Swaminathan S. Anklesaria, *Globalisation and Poverty*, Liberal, 10(2) 2002, pp. 41-43.

Alam, Jayanti, *The Other Side of Globalisation: China's Experiments withSocialist Market Economy*, Mainstream, 40(31), 20 Jul 2002, pp. 27-30.

Alderson, Arthur S., *Explaining Deindustrialization: Globalization, Failure, or Success?,* American Sociological Review, 64(5), Oct 1999, pp. 701-21.

Ali Farazmand, *Globalization and Public Administration,* Public Administration Review, 59(6), Nov-Dec 1999, pp. 509-22.

Altbach, Philip G., *Higher Education and the WTO: Globalization Run Amok*, University News, 39(37), 10 Sep 2001, pp. 1-4.

Ambirajan, S., *Globalisation, Media and Culture*, Economic and Political Weekly, 35(25), 17 Jun 2000, pp. 2141-147.

Ananth, V. Krishna, *Globalisation, the left and Marx,* Hindu, 2 Apr 2001, p. 10.

Anderson, Cynthia A., Schulman, Michael D. and Wood, Phillip J., *Globalization and Uncertainity: the Restructuring of Southern Textiles*, Social Problems, 48(4), Nov 2001, pp. 478-98.

Antrobus, Peggy, *Women and Children's well being in the Age of Globalization: A Focus on St Vincent and Grenadines and Small Island Developing States*, Development, 44(2), Jun 2001, pp. 53-57.

Apffelmarglin, Frederique and Parajuli, Pramod, *Geographies of Difference and the Resilence of Ecological Ethnicities*: *'Place' and the Global Motion of Capital*, Development, 41(2), Jun 1998, pp. 14-21.

Apodaca, Clair, *The Globalization of Capital in East and Southeast Asia*: *Measuring the Impact on Human Rights Standards*, Asian Survey, 42(6), Nov-Dec 2002, pp. 883-905.

Aravinda, L.S., *Globalisation and Narmada People's Struggle*, Economic and Political Weekly, 35(46), 11 Nov 2000, pp. 4002-005.

Arora D.S., *Globalisation of Indian Business*, Financial Express, 25 Oct 93, p. 6.

Arora, Dolly, *Globalization, Governance and Rights Struggles*, Mainstream, 40(19), 27 Apr. 2002, pp. 9-13.

Arora, Dolly, *In Times of Globalisation: Democracy, Development and the 'Dirty' Economy*, Mainstream, 36(46), 7 Nov 1998, pp. 13-18.

Arrighi, Giovanni, *Globalization and the Rise of East Asia: Lessons from the Past, Prospects for the Future*, International Sociology, 13(1), Nov. 1998, pp. 59-77.

Assadi, Muzaffar, *Globalisation and the State: Interrogating the Farmers' Movement in India*, Journal of Social and Economic Development, 4(1), Jan.-Jun. 2002, pp. 42-54.

Bagchi, Amiya Kumar, *Globalisation, Liberalisation and Vulnerability: India and Third World*, Economic and Political Weekly, 34(45), 6 Nov. 1999, pp. 3219-230.

Bagchi, Amiya Kumar, *Globalising India: the Fantasy and the Reality*, Social Scientist, 22(7-8), Jul.-Aug. 1994, pp. 18-27.

Bairoch, Paul, *The Constituent Economic Principles of Globalization in Historical Perspective*, International Sociology, 15(2), Jun. 2000, pp. 197-214.

Balaramulu, Ch. and Prasad, Ch. R.R.M., *Managerial Ethics of the Government vis-a-vis the Globalised Economy*, Indian Journal of Public Administration, 47(1), Jan.-Mar. 2001, pp. 1-10.

Balkrishnan, Pulapre, *Globalisation and Keynesian Reach*, Economic and Political Weekly, 37(33), 17 Aug 2002, pp. 3412-413.

Banarji, Jairus, *Globalisation and Restructuring in the Indian Food Industry*, Journal of Peasant Studies, 24(1-2), Oct. 96-Jan. 97, pp. 191-209.

Banerjee, Subhabrata Bobby and Limstead, Stephen, *Globalization, Multiculturalism and Other Fictions: Colonialism for the New Millennium?* Organization, 8(4), Nov 2001, pp. 683-722.

Banerjee-Guha, Swapna, *Critical Geographical Praxis: Globalisation and Socio-Spatial Disorder*, Economic and Political Weekly, 37(44-45), 2 Nov. 2002, pp. 4503-509.

Barber, Benjamin R., *Can Democracy Survive Globalization?* Government and Opposition, 35(3), Summer 2000, pp. 275-301.

Barkin, David, *Mexico: Towards a New Understanding*, Economic and Political Weekly, 38(1), 4 Jan 2003, pp. 29-31.

Barnabas, A.P., *Globalisation and Transformation of Indian Rural Social Structure*, Indian Journal of Public Administration, 45(4), Oct.-Dec. 1999, pp. 801-07.

Bartels, Frank L. and Pavier, H. Barry, *Enron in India: Developing Political Capability—An Imperative for Multi-national Enterprise in an Era of Globalisation*, Economic and Political Weekly, 32(8), 22-28 Feb. 1997, pp. M-11-20.

Bartelson, Jens, *Three Concepts of Globalization*, International Sociology, 15(2), Jun 2000, pp. 180-96.

Basant, Rakesh and Morris, Sebastian, *Competition Policy in India: Issues for a Globalising Economy*, Economic and Political Weekly, 35(31), 29 Jul 2000, pp. 2735-747.

Basu, Kaushik, *The politics of Economics*, Business Standard, 15 May 2002, p. 15.

Bawa, R.S., *Challenges and Opportunities of Globalisation-Implications for India*, Indian Economic Journal, 49(3), Jan.-Mar. 2001-2002, pp. 1-8.

Baxi, Upendra, *Judicial Activism, Legal Education and Research in Globalising India*, Mainstream, 34(12), 24 Feb. 1996, pp. 11-

16; 2 Mar. 1996, 34(13), pp.11-19; 9 Mar. 1996, 34(14), pp. 15-19.

Baxi, Upendra, *Power and Social Action*, Seminar, (437), Jan 1995, pp. 49-52.

Bayne, Nicholas, *Why did Seattle Fail? Globalization and the Politics of Trade*, Government and Opposition, 35(2), Spring 2000, pp. 131-51.

Beaglehole, Robert and McMichael, Anthony J., *The Future of Public Health in a Changing Global Context*, Development, 42(4), Dec. 1999, pp. 12-16.

Berezin, Mabel, *Democracy and its Others in a Global Polity*, International Sociology, 14(3), Sept. 1999, pp. 227-43.

Bernal, Gloria Elena, Bissell, Sharon and Cortes, Ana, *Effects of Globalization on the Efforts to Discriminalize Abortion in Mexico*, Development, 42(4), Dec. 1999, pp. 130-33.

Beyer, Peter, *Globalizing Systems, Global Cultural Models and Religion(s)*, International Sociology, 13(1), Nov. 1998, pp. 79-94.

Bhagat, Manju, Jayashree, S. and Suneeta Singh, *Indian Managers in an Era of Globalisation—Some Considerations*, Management and Labour Studies, 20(4), Oct. 1995, pp. 224-32.

Bhalla, G.S., *Globalisation and Agricultural Policy in India,* Indian Journal of Agricultural Economics, 50(1), Jan.-Mar. 1995, pp. 7-26.

Bhambhri, C.P., *Globalisation, Liberalisation and the Welfare State*, Indian Journal of Public Administration, 42(3), Jul.-Sept. 1996, pp. 258-63.

Bharucha, Rustom, *Politics of Culturalism in an Age of Globalisation: Discrimination, Discontent and Dialogue*, Economic and Political Weekly, 34(8), 20 Feb. 1999, pp. 477-89.

Bhattacharjee, Debashish, *Globalising Economy, Localising Labour*, Economic and Political Weekly, 35(42), Oct. 2000, pp. 3758-764.

Bhavani, T.A., *Small-Scale Units in the Era of Globalisation: Problems and Prospects*, Economic and Political Weekly, 37(29), 20 Jul. 2002, pp. 3041-052.

Bijlert, Victor A. Van, *Some thoughts on Indian Ethics for a Globalizing World*, Journal of Human Values, 6(2), Jul.-Dec. 2000, pp. 145-53.

Bissessar, Anni Marie, *Globalization, Domestic Politics and the*

Introduction of New Public Management in the Commonwealth Caribbean, International Review of Administrative Science, 68(1), Mar. 2002, pp. 113-25.

Bose, A.N., *Regional Planning in India in the Current Phase of Globalisation*, Indian Journal of Regional Science, 31(1) 1999, pp. 1-12.

Bose, Ashish, *Globalising Family Planning*, Financial Express, 3 Nov. 92, p. 6.

Boyd, Susan, *Globalisation and the Public Sector: Changes for Australia—The 1994 Reid Oration*, Australian Journal of Public Administration, 54(1), Mar. 1995, pp. 1-8.

Brecher, Jeremy, *Globalization and Economic Alternatives*, Development, (3) 1995, pp. 30-31.

Breman, Jan, *The end of globalisation?* Economic and Political Weekly, 33(7), 14 Feb 1998, pp. 333-36.

Briceno-Leon, Roberto and Zubillaga, Veronica, *Violence and Globalization in Latin America,* Current Sociology, 50(1), Jan. 2002, pp. 19-37.

Brinkerhoff, Derick W. and Coston, Jennifer M., *International Development Management in a Globalized World*, Public Administration Review, 59(4), Jul.-Aug. 1999, pp. 346-61.

Briones, Leonor Magtolis, *Globalization, Nationalism and Public Administration: Challenge and Response*, Philippine Journal of Public Administration, 41(1-4), Jan.-Oct. 1997, pp. 1-32.

Broad, Dave, *Globalization versus Labour*, Monthly Review, 47(7), Dec. 1995, pp. 20-31.

Budd, Leslie, *Territorial Competition and Globalisation: Scylla and Charybdis of European Cities*, Urban Studies, 35(4), Apr. 1998, pp. 663-85.

Budget for 1992-93, Quarterly Economic Report of the Indian Institute of Public Opinion, 35(1), Jan.-Mar. 92, pp. 3-54.

Business Alliances, California Management Review, 35(1) Fall 92, pp. 7-130.

Callaghan, John, *Social Democracy and Globalisation: The Limits of Social Democracy in Historical Perspective*, British Journal of Politics and International Relations, 4(3), Oct. 2002, pp. 429-51.

Campanella, Miriam L., *Getting the Core: A Neo-Institutionalist Approach to the EMU*, Government and Opposition, 30(3), Summer 1995, pp. 347-69.

Chakrabarti, B.B., *Globalisation and Indian Industry*, Management Accountant, 34(4), Apr. 1999, pp. 264-65.

Chakravorty, Manas, *Two Faces of Globalisation*, Business Standard, 17 Jul. 1996, p. 8.

Chalam, K.S., *Globalisation of Education and Indegenisation of Knowledge*, University News, 40(16), Apr. 2002, pp. 1-3.

Chandiramani, Nilima, *Balance Sheet of Globalisation in India*, Mainstream, Annual 1995, p. 91-98.

Chandra, Nirmal Kumar, *China's Tryst with Globalisation*, Economic and Political Weekly, 30(4), 28 Jan. 1995, pp. PE2-19

Chandra, Sanjay, *Globalisation of Mineral Resources and India*, Mainstream, 31(23) 17 Apr. 93, pp. 27-9.

Chandran, T.R. Satish, *Globalisation: Impact on India and the Southern States*, Journal of Social and Economic Development, 3(1), Jan.-Jun. 2000, pp. 1-41.

Chandrasekhar, C.P., *External Vulnerability and Industrial Policy in the Era of Globalization*, Social Scientist, 24(11-12), Nov.-Dec. 1996, pp. 92-110.

Chandrasekhar, C.P. and Ghosh, Jayati, *The World Economy: A Futile Search for Order*, Hindu(Business Line), 4 May 1999, p. 15.

Chapman, Jennifer, *The Response of Civil Society to the Globalization of the Marketing of Breast Milk Substitutes in Ghana*, Development, 42(4), Dec. 1999, pp. 103-07.

Chatt, Zahoor Ahmad, *Globalisation of Financial Markets: Implications forIndia*, Business Review, 8(1-2), Mar. 2002, pp. 112-16.

Chatterjee, Biswajit and Kundu, Amit, *Rural Non-farm Employment in India and Globalisation: A Critical Analysis*, Indian Journal of Labour Economics, 45(4), Oct.-Dec. 2002, pp. 771-81.

Chattopadhyay, Paresh, *Marx on Capital's Globalisation: The Dialectic of Negativity*, Economic and Political Weekly, 37(19), 11 May 2002, pp. 1839-842.

Chaudhri, D.D. and Nyland, Chris, *Globalisation, Demographic Pressures and Child Labour Standards*, Indian Journal of Labour Economics, 45(3), Jul.-Sept. 2002, pp. 537-60.

Chawla, A.S. and Batra, G.S., *Indian Financial Markets towards Globalisation,* Journal of Accounting and Finance, 9(2), Fall 1995, pp. 217-33.

Chawla, K.L., *Globalisation and Nation State: South Asian Perspective*, India Quarterly, 57(1), Jan.-Mar. 2001, pp. 147-60.

Chernotsky, Harry I., *The Growing Impact of Globalization upon City Policies*, Policy Studies Review, 18(3), Autumn 2001, pp. 29-48.

Clapham, Christopher, *The Challenge to the State in a Globalized World*, Development and Change, 33(5), Nov. 2002, p. 775-95.

Clark, Cal, Green, Johnny and Grenell, Keenan, *Local Regimes: Does Globalization Challenge the "Growth Machine"?* Policy Studies Review, 18(3), Autumn 2001, pp. 49-62.

Clark, Terry Nichols, *Old and New Paradigms for Urban Research: Globalization and the Fiscal Austerity and Urban Innovation Project*, Urban Affairs, 36(1), Sept. 2000: pp. 3-45.

Clift, Ben, *Social Democracy and Globalization: The Cases of France and the UK*, Government and Opposition, 37(4), Autumn 2002, pp. 466-500.

Coclanis, Peter A. and Doshi, Tilak, *Globalization in Southeast Asia*, Annals of the American Academy of Political and Social Science, 570, Jul. 2000, pp. 49-64.

Correa, Sonia, *A DAWN Genderscape on Globalization and Fundamentalism*, Development, 45(2), Jun. 2002, pp. 68-70.

Cukier, Wendy, Chapdelaine, Antoine and Collins, Cindy, *Globalization and Small/Firearms: A Public Health Perspective*, Development, 42(4), Dec. 1999, pp. 40-44.

Das, Hari, *Refining Human Resource Management Systems to Meet the Globalization Challenge: Some Action Guidelines*, Management Accountant, 33(7), Jul. 1998, pp. 485-90, 496.

Dasgupta, Amit, *Globalisation and the East Asian Crisis: Rethinking the Role of State in the New Millennium*, South Asian Survey, 7(2), Jul.-Dec. 2000, pp. 247-55.

Dasgupta, Gurudas, *Globalisation Evil: Indian Working Masses in Peril*, Statesman, 22 Nov. 2000, p. 6.

Dasgupta, Subhoranjan, *A Novel Protest Against Globalisation*, Social Scientist, 30(1-2), Jan.-Feb. 2002, pp. 50-60.

Datt, Ruddar, *Globalisation: Who are the Real Beneficiaries?* Mainstream, 35(31), 12 Jul. 1997, pp. 15-17.

Datta, Soumyendra Kishore, *Globalisation, Education and Productivity*, Asian Economic Review, 40(1), Apr. 1998, pp. 108-16.

Daulaire, Nils, *Globalization and Health*, Development, 42(4), Dec. 1999, pp. 22-24.

Debroy, Bibek, *The East Asian Crisis: Globalisation Conundrum*, Chartered Accountant, 47(4), Oct. 1998, pp. 19-23.

Denis, G., *Food Security and Globalisation*, Productivity, 43(1), Apr.-Jun. 2002, pp. 1-4.

Deshpande, H.V., *Quality and Administration of Higher Education Under Globalisation: Challenges and Remedies*, University News, 41(10), 10 Mar. 2002, pp. 3-5.

Devi, S. Uma, *Globalisation, Information Technology and Asian Indian Women in US*, Economic and Political Weekly, 37(43), 26 Oct. 2002, pp. 4421-428.

Diawara, Mamadou, *Globalization, Development Politics and Local Knowledge*, International Sociology, 15(2), Jun. 2000, pp. 361-71.

Dirlik, Arif, *Globalism and the Politics of Place*, Development, 41(2), Jun. 1998, pp. 7-13.

Diwan, Romesh, *Essentiality of Swadeshi*, Hindustan Times, 10 Feb. 1998, p. 13.

Dohlman, Ebba and Halvorson-Quevedo, Raundi, *Globalisation and Development*, OECD Observer, (204), Feb.-Mar. 1997, pp. 36-39.

Domingo, Ma Oliva Z., *Globalization, Organizations, and Public Administration*, Philippine Journal of Public Administration, 42(3-4), July-Oct. 1998, pp. 157-83.

Drager, Nick *et al.*, *Globalization and Health of the Poor*, Development, 44(1), Mar. 2001, pp. 73-76.

Drower, Sandra J., *Globalisation: An Ppportunity for Dialogue Between South African and Asian Social Work Educators*, Indian Journal of Social Work, 61(1), Jan. 2000, pp. 12-31.

Dubhashi, P.R., *Globalisation and Local Roots*, University News, 33(14), 3 Apr. 1995. pp. 13-14.

Easterlin, Richard A., *The Globalization of Human Development*, Annals of the American Academy of Political and Social Science, 570, Jul. 2000, pp. 32-48.

ECONOMIC reforms, *Yojana*, 38(14-15), 15 Aug. 1994, pp. 8-83.

Eichenberger, Reiner and Frey, Bruno S., *Democratic Governance for a Globalized World*, Kyklos, 55(2) 2002, pp. 265-87.

Ekbladh, David, *Globalisation and the Language of Modernisation*, World Affairs, 6(2), Apr.-Jun. 2002, pp. 52-64.

Elsenhans, Hartmut, *Intensifying Globalisation to make it Socially Acceptable,* India Quarterly, 57(1), Jan.-Mar. 2001, pp. 51-74.

Elsenhans, Hartmut, *Political Economy or Economic Politics? Prospects of Civil Society in Era of Globalisation*, Indian Journal of Public Administration, 46(4), Oct.-Dec. 2000, pp. 567-600.

Emami, Aristotle and Tarzi, Shah M., *Globalization, Trade and LDCs: Reflections on the Consequences and Opportunities of Trade Liberalization*, Asian Economic Review, 44(2), Aug. 2002, pp. 177-92.

Embony, Abdul Rahman, *Globalization and Transnational Class Relations: Some Problems of Conceptualization*, Third World Quarterly, 21(6), Dec. 2000, pp. 989-1000.

Engineer, Asghar Ali, *Globalisation, Democracy and Threat to Diversity*, Mainstream, 35(47), 1 Nov. 1997, pp. 9-14, 26.

Etienne, Gilbert, *Globalisation: Myths and Facts*, Hindu, 8 Jan. 2001, p. 10.

Etzioni-Halevy, Eva, *Linkage Deficits in Transnational Politics*, International Political Science Review, 23(2), Apr. 2002, pp. 203-22.

Evans, Tony, *Citizenship and Human Rights in the Age of Globalization*, Alternatives, 25(4), Oct.-Dec. 2000, pp. 415-38.

Farazmand, Ali, *Privatization and Globalization: A Critical Analysis with Implications for Public Management Education and Training*, International Review of Administrative Sciences, 68(3), Sept. 2002, pp. 355-71.

Feenstra, Robert C. and Hauson, Gordon H., *Globalization, Outsouring, and Wage Inequality*, American Economic Review, 86(2), May 1996, pp. 240-45.

Felbinger, Clarie L. and Robey, James E., *Globalizations Impact on State and Local Policy: The Rise of Regional Cluster Based Economic Development Strategies*, Policy Studies Review, 18(3), Autumn 2001, pp. 63-79.

Focus on globalisation experience, Political Economy Journal of India, 2(3-4), Jul.-Dec. 93, pp. 83-170.

Forrant, Robert and Pyle, Jean L., *Globalization, Universities and Sustainable Human Development*, Development, 45(3), Sept. 2002, pp. 102-06.

Foster, John Bellamy, *The Age of Planetary Crisis: The Unsustainable Development of Capitalism*, Review of Radical Political Economics, 29(4), Fall 1997, pp. 113-42.

Frowen, Stephen F. and Karakitsos, Elias, *Monetary and Fiscal Policy Under Conditions of Globalised Money and Capital Markets: Lessons for the U.K. Personal Sector*, Public Finance, 51(3) 1996, pp. 305-24.

Fulcher, James, *Globalisation, the Nation-State and Global Society*, Sociological Review, 48(4), Nov. 2000, pp. 522-43.

Galbraith, James K., *A Perfect Crime: Inequality in the Age of Globalization*, Daedalus, Winter 2002, pp. 11-25.

Garg, I.K., *Basic Inputs for Globalising Banks*, Political Economy Journal of India, 7(1-2), Jan.-Jun. 1998, pp. 57-59.

Gatade, Subhash, *Chakwara: The Other Silences*, Mainstream, 50(44), 19 Oct. 2002, pp. 24-28.

George, Varughese, *Globalisation and Kerala Society*, Janata, 56(38), 9 Dec. 2001, pp. 5-6.

George, Vic, Political Ideology, Globalisation and Welfare Future in Europe, Journal of Social Policy, 27(1), Jan. 1998, pp. 17-36.

Ghosh, Arun, *Globalisation and its Paradoxes*, Hindu (Business Line), 9 Jan. 2001, p. 14.

Ghosh, Arun, *Globalization and WTO*, India Quarterly, 44(3-4), Jul.-Dec. 1998, p. 9-112.

Ghosh, Arun, *India is a Globalised World: Issues of Growth with Equity and Justice*, Mainstream, Annual 1998, pp. 45-67.

Ghosh, Arun, *Role of Planning in a Globalised Economy*, Economic and Political Weekly, 31(35-37), Sept. 1996, pp. 2355-359.

Ghosh, Buddhadeb and De, Prabir, *Indian Ports and Globalisation: Grounding Economics in Geography*, Economic and Political Weekly, 36(34), 25 Aug. 2001, pp. 3271-283.

Ghosh, Jayati, *Globalization, Export-Oriented Employment for Women and Social Policy: A Case Study of India*, Social Scientist, 30(11-12), Nov.-Dec. 2002, pp. 17-60.

Ghosh, Saibal, *Competition, Globalisation and Bargaining: A Theoretical Analysis*, Labour and Development, 7(2), Dec. 2001, pp. 53-64.

Ghosh, Shekhar, *Poverty Alleviation and Human Rights: Implications of Globalization*, India Quarterly, 57(1), Jan.-Mar. 2001, pp. 75-88.

Gibbon, Peter, *Civil Society, Locality and Globalization in Rural Tanzania: A Forty-Year Perspective*, Development and Change, 32(5), Nov. 2001, pp. 819-44.

Gindin, Sam, *Social Justice and Globalization: Are they Compatible?* Monthly Review, 54(2), Jun. 2002, pp. 1-11.

Globalisation, Government and Opposition, 28(2), Spring 93, pp. 143-288.

Globalisation, *Technology Upgradation and Human Resource*

Development, Indian Journal of Training and Development, 28(3), Jul.-Sept. 1998, pp. 28-41.

Globalization and identity dialects of flows and closures, Development and Change, 29(4), Oct 1998, pp. 601-925.

Globalization: A Symposium on the Challenges of Closer Global Integration, Seminar, (503), Jul. 2001, pp. 12-85.

Go, Julian, *A Globalizing Constitutionalism?* views from the Postcolony, 1945-2000, International Sociology, 18(1), Mar. 2003, pp. 71-95.

Gonsalves, Eric, *Anticipating Globalization*, IIC Quarterly, 26(2), Summer 1999, pp. 81-86.

Gonsalves, Eric, *Meeting the Challenge of Globalisation*, Mainstream, 37(46), 6 Nov. 1999, pp. 13-15.

Goss, Jasper and Burch, David, *From Agricultural Modernisation to Agri-Food Globalisation: The Waning of National Development in Thailand*, Third World Quarterly, 22(6), Dec. 2001, pp. 969-86.

Gouliquer, Lynne, *Pandora's Box: The Paradox of Flexibility in Today's Workplace*, Current Sociology, 48(1), Jan. 2000, pp. 29-38.

Gouri, Geetha, *Globalisation of PSUs*, Hindu (Business Line), 2 May 1997, pp. 8; 3 May 1997, p. 8.

Grueso, Libia, *Territory, Culture and Biodiversity: The Black Communities of the Pacific Coast of Colombia Qualify Globalization*, Development, 41(2), Jun. 1998, pp. 65-69.

Guillen, Mauro F., *Is Globalization Civilizing, Destructive or Feeble? A Critique of Five Key Debates in the Social Science Literature*, Annual Review of Sociology, 27 2001, pp. 235-60.

Gujral, I.K., *Championing the Agenda of those Marginalised by Globalisation*, Mainstream, 38(24), 3 Jun. 2000, pp. 5-7.

Gujral, Inder Kumar, *Globalisation will Succeed only if it is Equitable and Just*, Mainstream, 35(49), 15 Nov. 1997, pp. 25-26.

Gulati, Ashok, Mehta, Rajesh and Narayanan, Sudha, *From Marrakesh to Seattle: Indian Agriculture in a Globalising World*, Economic and Political Weekly, 34(4), 9 Oct. 1999, pp. 2931-942.

Gupta, Asha, *Global Development and Global Welfare*, Yojana, 40(2), Feb. 1996, pp. 26-30.

Gupta, Deepak, *Economic Liberalisation with Endogenous Values: A Marraige not Made in Heaven*, Journal of Institute of Public Enterprises, 18(1-2), Jan.-Jun. 1995, pp. 36-45.

Guptara, Prabhu, *Age of Globalisation: Problems and Prospects* (A review essay), World Affairs, 4(4), Oct.-Dec. 2000, pp. 114-24.

Hamilton, Gary G. *et al.*, *Neither State nor Markets: The Role of Economic Organization in Asian Development*. International Sociology, 15(2), Jun. 2000, pp. 288-305.

Hamm, Bernd, *Thinking Globally and Acting Locally: Global Arguments for Local Reforms*. Nagarlok, 25(1), Jan.-Mar.93, pp. 1-13.

Hansda, Sanjay K. and Ray, Partha, *BSE and Nasdaq: Globalisation, Information Technology and Stock Prices*, Economic and Political Weekly, 37(5), 2 Feb. 2002, pp. 459-68.

Hansen, Randall, *Globalization, Embedded Realism, and Path Dependence: The Other Immigrants to Europe*, Comparative Political Studies, 35(3), Apr. 2002, pp. 259-83.

Harcourt, Wendy, *Women's Health, Poverty and Globalization*, Development, 44(1), Mar. 2001, pp. 85-90.

Harish Kumar, *Globalisation of Business Education*, University News, 35(32), 11 Aug 1997, pp. 10-11.

Harsolekar, Dinesh D., *Globalisation of Indian Higher Education: Putting the Issues in Perspective*, University News, 38(28), 10 Jul. 2000, pp. 1-3.

Hasan, Mubashr, *The Agenda for Good Governance in a Globalised World*, South Asian Survey, 7(2), Jul.-Dec. 2000, pp. 175-86.

Hay, Colin, Globalisation, *'Eu-Isation' and the Space for Social Democratic Alternatives: Pessimism of the Intellect: A Reply to Coates*, British Journal of Politics and International Relations, 4(3), Oct. 2002, pp. 452-64.

Haynes, Michael and Pinnock, Katherine, *Towards a deeper and wider European union?* Economic and Political Weekly, 33(8), 21 Feb. 1998, pp. 415-30.

Heijden, Hein-Auton Van Der, *Political Parties and NGOs in Global Environmental Politics*, International Political Science Review, 23(2), Apr. 2002, pp. 187-201.

Held, David, *Regulating Globalization?: The Reinvention of Politics*, International Sociology, 15(2), Jun. 2000, pp. 394-408.

Helvacioglu, Banu, *Globalization in the Neighborhood: From the Nation-State to Bilkent Center*, International Sociology, 15(2), Jun. 2000, pp. 326-42.

Henry, Cassis and Farmer, Paul, *Risk Analysis: Infections and Inequalities in a Globalizing Era*, Development, 42(4), Dec. 1999, pp. 31-34.

Hensman, Rohini, Globalisation and Informalisation, Economic and Political Weekly, 36(13), 31 Mar. 2001, pp. 1073-074.

Hersh, Jacques and Brun, Ellen, *Globalisation and the Communist Manifesto*, Economic and Political Weekly, 35(3), 15 Jan. 2000, pp. 105-08.

Hochschild, Adam, *Globalisation and Culture*, Economic and Political Weekly, 33(21), 23 May 1998, pp. 1235-238.

Hodos, Jerome I., *Globalization, Regionalism, and Urban Restructuring: The Case of Philadelphia*, Urban Affairs Review, 37(3), Jan. 2002, pp. 358-79.

Hoen, Ellen T., *Access to Essential Drugs and Globalization*, Development, 42(4), Dec. 1999, pp. 87-91.

Holton, Robert, *Globalization's Cultural Consequences*, Annals of the American Academy of Political and Social Science, 570, Jul. 2000, pp. 140-52.

Hountondji, Paulin J., *African Cultures and Globalisation: A Call to Resistance*, Development and Cooperation, (6), Nov.-Dec. 1997, pp. 24-26.

Houtart, Francois, *Sub-Contracting as an Element of Globalisation of the Economy*, ISDA Journal, 9(2), Apr.-Jun. 1999, pp. 83-94.

Howard, James, *The Lessons of Seattle for Social Development*, Development, 43(2), Jun. 2000, pp. 91-93.

Iranzo, Consuelo and Patruyo, Thanali, *Trade Unionism and Globalization: Thoughts from Latin America*, Current Sociology, 50(1), Jan. 2002, pp. 7-74.

Islam, Azizul, *Globalization and Development Revisited in the Light of Asian Experience*, Asia-Pacific Development Journal, 6(2), Dec. 1999, pp. 1-21.

Jain, Arun Kumar, *The Making of an Entrepreneurial Global Manager*, Vikalpa, 21(1), Jan.-Mar. 1996, pp. 15-21.

Jain, R.B., *Globalisation, Market Economy and Human Security: The Indian Experience*, Indian Journal of Public Administration, 42(3), Jul.-Sept. 1996, pp. 309-20.

Jalan, Bimal, *India and the Challenge of Globalisation*, Indian Economic Journal, 49(3), Jan.-Mar. 2001-2002, pp. 9-12.

Janardhan, V., *Globalisation of Capital, Multinational Corporations and Labour: Towards a Perspective*, Economic and Political Weekly, 32(35), 30 Aug. 1997, pp. L2-L9.

Jha, Brajesh and Debroy, Bibek. *Towards Globalising Indian Dairy Sector*, Asian Economic Review, 42(2), Aug. 2000, pp. 306-19.

Jha, Prem Shankar, *Democracy, Globalisation and War: New Myths to Save the West from the Rest*, World Affairs, 5(2), Apr.-Jun. 2001, pp. 26-47.

Jhunjhunwala, Bharat, *Why Bureaucracy Loves Globalisation*, Tribune, 19 Jan. 2001, pp. 10.

Job, Sebastian, *Globalising Russia? The Neoliberal/Nationalist Two Step and the Russification of the West*, Third World Quarterly, 22(6), Dec. 2001, pp. 931-49.

Johri, C.K., *Work Ethos and Globalisation of Indian Economy*, Indian Journal of Industrial Relations, 30(3), Jan. 1995, pp. 297-307.

Joshi, Akshay, *Globalisation and Technology: Lessons for India*, Strategic Analysis, 23(11), Feb. 2000, pp. 1933-955.

Kabra, Kamal Nayan, *Globalisation and Governance: Cloning the New Millennium*, Mainstream, 38(31), 22 Jul. 2000, pp. 11-16.

Kacowicz, Arie M., *Regionalization, Globalization, and Nationalism: Convergent, Divergent, or Overlapping?* Alternatives, 24(4), Oct.-Dec. 1999, pp. 527-56.

Kamo, Toshio, *An Aftermath of Globalisation? East Asian Economic Turmoil and Japanese Cities Adrift*, Urban Studies, 37(12), Nov. 2000, pp. 2145-165.

Kaplinsky, Raphael, *Globalisation and Unequalisation: What can be Learned from Value Chain Analysis*, Journal of Development Studies, 17(2), Dec. 2000, pp. 117-46.

Kaushal, Neeraj, *Globalisation and CTBT*, Economic Times, 15 Jun. 1999, p. 6.

Kentor, Jeffrey, *The Longterm Effects of Globalization on Income Inequality, Population Growth and Economic Development*, Social Problems, 48(4), Nov. 2001, pp. 435-55.

Kessler, Clive S., *Globalization: Another False Universalism*? Third World Quarterly, 21(6), Dec. 2000, pp. 931-42.

Khader, S.A., *Productivity in the Age of Globalization*, Yojana, 46, Jun. 2002, pp. 4-8.

Khanna, Perminder, *Globalization and Agricultural Exports: Indian Scenario*, Political Economy Journal of India, 10(3-4), Jul.-Dec. 2001, pp. 156-59.

Khor, Martin, *Facing up to Globalisation*, Encounter, 4(2), Mar.-Apr. 2001, pp. 68-72.

Kiely, Ray, *Globalization, Post-Fordism and the Contemporary Context Development*, International Sociology, 13(1), Nov. 1998, pp. 95-115.

Kiely, Ray, *Globalization: from Domination to Resistance* (A review article), Third World Quarterly, 21(6), Dec. 2000, pp. 1059-070.

Kim, Pan Suk, *Globalization of Human Resource Management: A Cross Cultural Perspective for the Public Sector Globalization*, Management in Government, 33(1), Apr.-Jun. 2001, pp. 27-47.

Kline, John M., *Australian Federalism Confronts Globalisation: A New Challenge at the Centenary*, Australian Journal of Public Administration, 61(3), Sept. 2002, pp. 27-37.

Koshy, Ninan, *Political Dimensions of Globalisation*, Economic and Political Weekly, 36(18), 5 May 2001, pp. 1513-517.

Kothari, Rajni, *Globalisation and Revival of Tradition: Dual Attack on Model of Democratic Nation Building*, Economic and Political Weekly, 30(12), 25 Mar. 1995, pp. 625-33.

Kothari, Rajni, Globalisation and 'New World Order': What Future for the United Nations? Economic and Political Weekly, 30(40), 7 Oct. 1995, pp. 2513-517.

Kothari, Rajni, *Globalization: A World Adrift*, Alternatives, 22(2), Apr.-Jun. 1997, pp. 227-67.

Kothari, Rajni, *Under Globalisation: Will Nation State Hold?* Economic and Political Weekly, 30(26), 1 Jul. 1995, pp. 1593-1603.

Kozlarek, Oliver, *Critical Theory and the Challenge of Globalization*, International Sociology, 16(4), Dec. 2001, pp. 607-22.

Kripa Shankar, *Indian Economic Crisis and Globalisation*, Mainstream, Annual 2001, pp. 99-103.

Kumaratunga, Chandrika, *Consequence of Globalisation without Corrective Steps*, Mainstream, 35(49), 15 Nov. 1997, pp. 27-29.

Kundu, Amitabh, *Globalising Gujarat: Urbanisation, Employment and Poverty*, Economic and Political Weekly, 35(35-36), 26 Aug. and 2 Sept. 2000, pp. 3172-182.

Kurian, N.J. and Hajela, J.D., *Indian Economy: Liberalisation, Globalisation and Privatisation*, Journal of the Institute of Public Enterprise, 24(1-2), Jan.-Mar.; Apr.-Jun. 2001, pp. 9-12.

Kurian, Tessy, *Women and Globalisation*, Social Welfare, 48(11), Feb. 2002, pp. 6-9.

Lacy, William B., *Empowering Communities through Public Work Science, and Local Food Systems: Revisiting Democracy and Globalization*, Rural Sociology, 65(1), Mar. 2000, pp. 3-26.

Lakshmy Devi K.R., *Globalisation and International Migration of Women Workers: The Unforeseen Challenges with Special*

Reference to the Indian Immigrants in the Middle East, Labour and Development, 7(2), Dec. 2001, pp. 108-25.

Lambert, Rom, *Globalization and the Erosion of Class Compromise in Contemporary Australia*, American Political Science Review, 94(1), Mar. 2000, pp. 93-118.

Lane, Christel, *Globalization and the German Model of Capitalism-Erosion or Survival*, British Journal of Sociology, 51(2), Jun. 2000, pp. 207-34.

Laurell, Asa Cristina, *Structural Adjustment and the Globalization of Social Policy in Latin America*, International Sociology, 15(2), Jun. 2000, pp. 306-25.

Lee, Eddy, *Globalization and Employment: The New Policy Agenda*, Development, 43(2), Jun. 2000, pp. 18-20.

Lee, Kelley, *Globalization, Communicable Disease and Equity: A Look Back and Forth*, Development, 42(4), Dec. 1999, pp. 35-39.

Li Xing, *Capitalism and Globalisation in the Light of the Communist Manifesto*, Economic and Political Weekly, 33(33-34), 15 Aug 1998, pp. 2223-227.

Limaye Madhu, *Globalisation and Third World*, Mainstream, 32(21), 9 Apr. 1994, pp. 5, 35.

Lin, Jan, *Globalization and the Revalorizing of Ethnic Places in Immigration Gateway Cities*, Urban Affairs Review, 34(2), Nov. 1998, pp. 313-39.

Little, Paul E., *Globalization and the Struggles Over Places in Amozonia*, Development, 41(2), Jun. 1998, pp. 70-75.

MacEwan Arthur, *Globalisation and Stagnation*, Mainstream, 32(25), 7 May 1994, pp. 15-19, 27.

Madunagu, Bene E., *The Impact of Globalization on Women's Health and Rights in Nigeria*, Development, 43(2), Jun. 2000, pp. 74-76.

Maitra, Priyotosh, *The Globalization of Capitalism and Economic Transition in China*, Regional Development Dialogue, 18(1), Spring 1997, pp. 52-69.

Majumdar, Bhaskar, *The Global Power Structure and Globalization: Any Choice for the Third World*, Management and Change, 3(1), Jan.-Jun. 1999, pp. 29-51.

Majumdar, Bhaskar, *Globalization of Highly Indebted Countries: Some Issues*, Asian Economic Review, 40(3), Dec. 1998, pp. 351-68.

Majumdar, Bhaskar, *Globalization of the Third World: Some Reflections*, Indian Journal of Economics, 76(303), Apr. 1996, pp. 477-97.

Majumdar, Bhaskar, *India's Trade Link with G-7: An Analysis in the Context of Globalization*, Review of Development and Change, 4(1), Jan.-Jun. 1999, pp. 25-50.

Majumdar, Bhaskar, *Who are the Marginalized Countries in Globalization*? Young Indian, 10(36), 15 Apr. 2000, pp. 7-8.

Majumdar, Bhaskar, *Why is Post-Cold War Globalization Relevant for the Us*? Young Indian, 10(39), 6 May 2000, pp. 4-5.

Majumder, Bhaskar, *Capitalist Globalization: Wanted Manpower Planning*, Productivity, 36(3), Oct.-Dec. 1995, pp. 457-62.

Majumder, Bhaskar, *Regional Integration with the European Union as a Case: Any Lesson for the Third World*, Journal of Social and Economic Development, 2(2), Jul.-Dec. 2000, pp. 208-27.

Majumder, Bhaskar, *Transnational Globalization: Conditions of Production Relocation and Development of Firms*, Asian Economic Review, 42(2), Aug 2000, pp. 188-202.

Majumder, Bhaskar, *Where do the Small Economies of the Third World Go in a Globalized Economy?* Young Indian, 11(18), 2 Dec. 2000, pp. 8-9.

Majumder, Bhasker, *Globalization and Marginalization of Countries: Facts and Possibilities*, Management and Change, 4(2), Jul.-Dec. 2000, pp. 369-85.

Malyadri, P., *Globalization of Indian Agriculture: Some Strategies in the Ninth Plan*, Kurukshetra, 45(6-7), Mar.-Apr. 1997, pp. 83-86.

Mandle, Jon, *Globalization and Justice*, Annals of the American Academy of Political and Social Science, 570, Jul. 2000, pp. 126-39.

Martinelli, Alberto, *Global Order or Divided World*? Introduction, Current Sociology, 51(2), Mar. 2003, pp. 95-100.

Maull, Hanns W., *Containing Entropy, Rebuilding the State: Challenges to International Order in the Age of Globalisation*, International Politics and Society, 2 2002, pp. 9-28.

McBride, Stephen, *Globalization, Employment and Work* (A review essay), Canadian Public Administration, 45(1), Spring 2002, pp. 98-111.

McLaren, John, *Globalization and Vertical Structure*, American Economic Review, 90(5), Dec. 2000, pp. 1239-254.

McNally, David, *Globalization on Trial: Crisis and Class Struggle in East Asia*, Monthly Review, 5(4), Sept. 1998, pp. 1-13.

Meer, Fatima, *The Global Crisis—A Crisis of Values and the Domination of the Weak by the Strong*, Journal of Human Values, 5(1), Jan.-Jun. 1999, pp. 65-74.

Mehra, Ajay K., *Revolution in the Age of Globalisation*, Mainstream, 38(19), 29 Apr. 2000, pp. 7-15.

Mehta, Balraj, *Indian Agriculture and Globalisation Process*, Financial Express, 12 Jun.92, p. 6.

Mele, Christopher, *Globalization, Culture, and Neighborhood Change: Reinventing the Lower East Side of New York*, Urban Affairs Review, 32(1), Sept. 1996, pp. 3-22.

Menezes, Francisco, *Food Sovereignty: A Vital Requirement for Food Security in the Context of Globalization*, Development, 44(4), Dec. 2001, pp. 29-33.

Menon-Sen, Kalyani, *Bridges Over Troubled Waters: South Asian Women's Movement Confronting Globalization*, Development, 45(1), Mar. 2002, pp. 132-36.

Metcalfe, Les, *Linking Levels of Government: European Integration and Globalization*, International Review of Administrative Sciences, 66(1), Mar. 2000, pp. 119-42.

Meyer, John W., *Globalization: Sources and Effects on National States and Societies*, International Sociology, 15(2), Jun. 2000, pp. 233-48.

Minocha, A.C., *Globalisation of Indian Agriculture*, Economic and Political Weekly, 30(15), 15 Apr. 1995, pp. 833.

Mittal, L.N., *Sen's Views on Globalisation and Social Welfare*, Social Welfare, 45(9), Dec. 1998, pp. 7-8.

Mittelman, James H., Globalization: Captors and Captive, Third World Quarterly, 21(6), Dec. 2000, pp. 917-29.

Mizra, Zafar, *Globalization, Health and Poverty: The Role of Civil Society*, Development, 44(1), Mar. 2001, pp. 91-92.

Moghadam, Valentine M., *Transnational Feminist Networks: Collective Action in an Era of Globalization*, International Sociology, 15(1), Mar. 2000, pp. 57-85.

Mohanan, B., *From Economic Globalisation to Post-Globalised Societal Order and the Indian State*, ISDA Journal, 10(3), Jul.-Sept. 2000, pp. 135-64.

Montanari, Ingalill, Modernization, *Globalization and the Welfare State: A Comparative Analysis of Old and New Convergence of*

Social Insurance since 1930, British Journal of Sociology, 32(3), Sept. 2001, pp. 469-94.

Moore, David, *Neoliberal Globalisation and the Triple Crisis of 'Modernisation' in Africa: Zimbabwe, the Democratic Republic of the Congo and South Africa*, Third World Quarterly, 22(6), Dec. 2001, pp. 909-29.

Morrissey, Oliver and Filatotchev, Igor, *Globalisation and Trade: The Implications for Exports from Marginalised Economics*, Journal of Development Studies, 17(2), Dec. 2000, pp. 1-12.

Mukherjee, R., *Changing Scenario of Indian Banking and Finance under Globalisation*, Political Economy Journal of India, 6(3-4), Jul.-Dec. 1997, pp. 149-51.

Mukherjee, Sampat, *Financial Globalisation*, Hindu (Business Line), 13 Jun. 1996, pp. 6; 14 Jun. 1996, p. 6.

Mukhopadhyay, Sukumar, *Globalisation and Indian Services Sector*, Economic and Political Weekly, 37(40), 5 Oct. 2002, pp. 4097-098.

Mungekar, Bhatchaandra L., *The Political Economy of Globalisation*, Janata, 56(38), 9 Dec. 2001, pp. 7-11.

Murthy, Gautam, *Strategies for Effective Indian Globalisation*, Management and Labour Studies, 20(3), Jul. 1995, pp. 161-69.

Nabudere, Dani W., *The Impact of Globalisation on Africa*, Development and Cooperation, 4, Jul.-Aug 1995, pp. 4-5.

Naik, B.M., *The Challenge of Globalization for Indian Universities*, University News, 37(30), 26 Jul. 1999, pp. 5-7.

Nair, M.D., *Global Trade Regime World Trade Organization: Is its Credibility in Peril?* Hindu, 2 Jun. 1999, pp. 21.

Naohisa Nagata, *The Development of Japanese Local Government and its Reform towards the Globalized Age*, International Review of Administrative Sciences, 64(2), Jun. 1998, pp. 219-33.

Narasimham, M., *Globalisation of Financial Market and India*, ASCI Journal of Management, 19(1), Sept. 1989, pp. 1-15.

Narayan, Jandhyala, *Globalisation: Some Strategic Implications*, ASCI Journal of Management, 24(2), Mar. 1995, pp. 123-36.

Narayanan, K.R., *Befiting Answer to Blind Globalisation*, Mainstream, 38(38), 9 Sept. 2000, pp. 5-7.

Narayanan, K.R., *Our Concept of Globalisation*, Mainstream, 38(14), 25 Mar. 2000, pp. 4-6.

Nath, D.C., *Globalisation of Terrorism*, Politics India, 4(1), Jul. 1999, pp. 37-38.

Nayar, Baldev Raj, *Globalisation, Nationalism and Economic Policy Reform*, Economic and Political Weekly, 32(30), 26 Jul. 1997, pp. PE93-104.

Nayyar, Deepak, *Globalisation: The Part in our Present*, Indian Economic Journal, 43(3), Jan.-Mar. 1996, pp. 1-18.

Nayyar, Deepak, *Globalisation and Migration: Retrospect and Prospect*, Yojana, 44(5), May 2000, pp. 18-27.

Neelamegam, R. and Gopathy, V., Globalisation and Corporate Governance in India, Management Accountant, 35(7), Jul. 2000, pp. 492-98.

Nolan, Peter and Wang Xiaogiang, *Reorganising Amidst Turbulence: China's Large-Scale Industry in the Midst of Changing International Distribution of Power, Restructuring and Globalisation of Capitalist Big Business*, Economic and Political Weekly, 33(13), 28 Mar. 1998, pp. 707-16.

Nuevo, Shirley, *Vietnam and Philippines: Globalising of Land Rights*, Encounter, 4(3), May-Jun. 2001, pp. 127-50.

O'hearn, Denis, *Globalization, "New Tigers", and the End of the Developmental State?: The Case of the Celtic tiger*, American Political Science Review, 94(1), Mar. 2000, pp. 67-92.

O'sullivan, Mary, *Corporate Governance and Globalization*, Annals of the American Academy of Political and Social Science, 570, Jul. 2000, pp. 153-72.

Ojha, A.K., *Globalisation and Liberalisation: Prospects of New World Order*, Third Concept, 16(186), Aug 2002, pp. 13-16.

Oomen, M.A., *Anatomy of Globalisation: More a Moral Crisis than a Development Dilemma*, Mainstream, Annual 1995, pp. 75-83.

Oommen, M.A., *Globalization and Poverty in India: Some Explanatory Hypotheses*, Man and Development, 22(3), Sept. 2000, pp. 17-36.

Oomment M.A., *The Political Economy of Globalisation*, Other Side, (109), Jun. 93, pp. 9-26.

Osman, Sabihah, *Globalization and Democratization: The Response of the Indigenous Peoples of Sarawak*, Third World Quarterly, 21(6), Dec. 2000, pp. 977-88.

Othman, Norani and Kessler, Clive S., *Capturing Globalization: Prospects and Projects*, Third World Quarterly, 21(6), Dec. 2000, pp. 1013-026.

Padayachee, Vishnu, *Less Ideology, more Common Sense: Financial Globalisation and the Currency Crisis*, Economic and Political Weekly, 33(46), 14 Nov. 1998, pp. 2929-932.

Paliwal, Dinesh K., *Globalisation of Indian Education*, University News, 40(39), 30 Sept. 2002, pp. 9-15.

Palo, Anil Kumar, *Globalisation and Health Care: New International Economic Environment*. Third Concept, 15(175), Sept. 2001, pp. 43-46.

Panikkar, K.N., *Culture and Globalisaton: A Non-Issue at World Summit on Social Development*, Economic and Political Weekly, 30(7&8), 18-25 Feb. 1995, pp. 374, 375.'

Panini, M.N., *Trends in Cultural Globalisation: From Agriculture to Agribusiness in Karnataka*, Economic and Political Weekly, 34(31), 31 Jul. 1999, pp. 2168-173.

Panitch, Leo, *The New Imperial State*, New Left Review, (2), Mar.-Apr. 2000, pp. 5-20.

Parasher, S.C., *Politics of Globalization: Liberalization*, India Quarterly, 44(3-4), Jul.-Dec. 1998, pp. 114-30.

Pasanski, Milan, *The Globalization of Terrorism*, Review of International Affairs, 42(980), 5 Feb.91, pp. 3-6.

Patil, S.H., *Collapse of Communism and Emergence of Global Economy: India's Experiment with New Economic Policy*, India Quarterly, 49(4), Oct.-Dec. 1993, pp. 17-30.

Patnaik, Prabhat, Globalization and the Emerging Global Politics, Social Scientist, 30(11-12), Nov.-Dec. 2002, pp. 2-16.

Patnaik, Prabhat, Globalization of Capital and the Theory of Imperialism, Social Scientist, 24(11-12), Nov.-Dec. 1996, pp. 5-17.

Patnaik, Prabhat and Chandrasekhar, C.P., *Indian Economy under 'Structural Adjustment'*, Economic and Political Weekly, 30(47), 25 Nov. 1995, pp. 3001-013.

Patnaik, Prabhat, *Nation-State in the Era of 'Globalisation'*, Economic and Political Weekly, 30(33), 19 Aug 1995, pp. 2049-053.

Petras, James, *China in the Context of Globalization*, Journal of Contemporary Asia, 30(1) 2000, pp. 108-16.

Petras, James and Polychroniou, Chronis, *Critical Reflections on Globalisation*, Economic and Political Weekly, 32(36), 6 Sept. 1997, pp. 2249-252.

Petras, James, *Globalisation: A Socialist Perspective*, Economic and Political Weekly, 34(8), 20 Feb. 1999, pp. 459-63.

Petras, James, *Globalization: A Critical Analysis*, Journal of Contemporary Asia, 29(1) 1999, pp. 3-37.

Phelps, Nicholas A. and Tewdwr-Jones, Mark, *Globalisation, Regions and the State: Exploring the Limitations of Economic Modernisation through Inward Investment*, Urban Studies, 38(8), Jul. 2001, pp. 1253-272.

Piper, Nicola and Ball, Rochelle, *Globalisation of Asian Migrant Labour: The Philippine—Japan Connection*, Journal of Contemporary Asia, 31(4) 2001, pp. 533-54.

Powar, K.B., *Globalisation of Distance Learning System: Implications for Developing Countries*, University News, 35(4), 27 Jan. 1997, pp. 4-6.

Prabhash, J., *Globalisation and De-Empowerment*, ISDA Journal, 4(4), Dec. 1994, pp. 153-64.

Prabhu, Ganesh, *Globalisation and Localisation Strategies: A Conceptual Integration*, Management Review, 8(1), Jan.-Jun. 1996, pp. 88-103.

Prasad, Eswar *et al.*, *Effects of Financial Globalization on Developing Countries: Some Empirical Evidence*, Young Indian, 13(34), 22 Mar. 2003, pp. 17-20.

Prasad, Pradhan H., *Globalisation: A Saga of Poor Understanding*, Economic and Political Weekly, 36(3), 20 Jan. 2001, pp. 205-07.

Pratap, Vijay, *Vasudhaiva Kutumbakam: A New Alliance for Democracy in the Era of Globalisation*, Encounter, 4(5), Sept.-Oct. 2001, pp. 11-35.

Purkayastha, Gautam, *Globalisation: Challenges to Tribal Identity of Northeast*, Yojana, 46, Sept. 2002, pp. 39-41.

Quah, Stella, *Values and Development in Asia: A Historical Illustration of the Role of the State,* International sociology, 12(3), Sept. 1997, pp. 295-328.

Quiggin, John, *Neo-Liberal Globalization and the Scope for Employment Policy*, Development, 43(2), Jun. 2000, pp. 15-17.

Radhakrishnan, P. and Swaminathan, C.R., *Revamping Manufacturing Education in the Context of Globalisation*, University News, 40(46), 18 Nov. 2002, pp. 6-9.

Raghavan, Chakravarthi, *Globalisation Model Means Uneven Development*, Mainstream, 34(32), 13 Jul. 1996, pp. 9-12.

Rajagopalan, T., *Higher Education and Globalisation: A New Order has to be Culved*, Tribune, 19 May 2001, p. 10.

Rajan, Ajay and Dhunna, Mukesh, *Globalisation and Management Education*, University News, 36(35), 31 Aug 1998, pp. 3-5, 9.

Ramachandran, B., Globalizing and Galvanizing India's Economy, Third Concept, 9(100), Jun. 1995, pp. 19-21.

Ramachandran, Vimala, *NGOs in the Time of Globalisation*, Seminar, (447), Nov. 1996, pp. 54-59.

Ramakrishna Reddy, K., *Globalisation, Management and Human Values*, Management Review, 8(1), Jan.-Jun. 1996, pp. 104-13.

Ramakrishna, G.V., *How is India Coping with Globalisation*? Financial Express, 11 Jan. 2001, p. 8.

Raman, P., *Ill-Effects of Globalisation on Third World*, Tribune, 1 Jun. 1999, p. 9.

Ramaswamy, P.R., *The Challenges of Globalisation for Civil Servants*, Indian Journal of Public Administration, 48(1), Jan.-Mar. 2002, pp. 50-60.

Rampersad, Frank B., *Coping with Globalization: A Suggested Policy Package for Small Countries*, Annals of the American Academy of Political and Social Science, 570, Jul. 2000, pp. 115-25.

Rangarajan, C., *Globalisation and its Impact*, Money and Finance, 2(8), Jan.-Mar. 2002, pp. 36-54.

Rao, P. Srinivas Subba and Murthy, K.G.K., *The Unfolding Future of Agriculture in Third World Nations in an Era of Globalisation: Lessons from India*, Asian Economic Review, 43(2), Aug 2001, pp. 160-68.

Rasiah, Rajah, *Globalization and Private Capital Movements*, Third World Quarterly, 21(6), Dec. 2000, pp. 943-61.'

Rastogi, Savita, *Globalisation of Higher Education*, University News, 39(35), 27 Aug. 2001, pp. 11-16.

Rastogi, T.N., *Re-Tooling Apparatus of Liberalisation with Social Concerns in Shifting Paradigm of Globalised Indian Economy*, Indian Journal of Public Administration, 42(3), Jul.-Sept. 1996, pp. 434-40.

Ratnam, N. Vijaya, *Globalisation in Developing Economics: A Welfare Perspective*, Third Concept, 15(169), Mar. 2001, pp. 27-30.

Rau, Johannes, *Opportunity, Not Fate: Giving Globalization Political Shape*, Development and Cooperation, (5) 2002, pp. 4-5, 28.

Reddy, C. Rammanohar, *Rocky Road to Seattle*, Hindu, 1 Jun. 1999, p. 10.

Reddy, Y. Venugopal, *Put Growth to Work for the Poor*, Financial Express, 17 Oct. 2000, p. 6.

Reddy, Y.V., *Globalisation, for People and Governments*, Financial Express, 29 May 2001, p. 6.

Regini, Marino, *Between Deregulation and Social Pacts: The Responses of European Economies to Globalization*, American Political Science Review, 94(1), Mar. 2000, pp. 5-33.

Reis, Elisa P., *A Global World, Multiple Angles, One Sociological Community*, Current Sociology, 51(2), Mar. 2003, pp. 113-22.

Riain, Sean O., *The Flexible Developmental State: Globalization, Information Technology and the "Celtic Tiger"*, Politics and Society, 28(2), Jun. 2000, pp. 157-93.

Rian, Sean O., *States and Markets in an Era of Globalization*, Annual Review of Sociology, 26 2000, pp. 187-213.

Rieger, Elmar and Leibfried, Stephen, *Welfare State Limits to Globalization*, Politics and Society, 26(3), Sept. 1998, pp. 363-90.

Rifkin, Jeremy, *Globalisation and Identity: Cultures in Collision*, Deccan Herald, 3 Aug 2001, p. 10.

Robertson, Roland and Khondker, Habib Haque, *Discourses of Globalization: Preliminary Considerations*, International Sociology, 13(1), Nov. 1998, pp. 25-40.

Robinson, William I., (Mal) *Development in Central America: Globalization and Social Change*, Development and Change, 29(3), Jul. 1998, pp. 467-97.

Rodrik, Dani, *Has Globalization Gone too Far?* California Management Review, 39(3), Spring 1997, pp. 29-53.

Ronki Ram, *Afro-Asian Dialogue: Understanding Globalisation in the Periphery*, Social Science Research Journal, 9(1) 2001, pp. 83-95.

Ross, George., *Labour versus Globalization*, Annals of the American Academy of Political and Social Science, 570, Jul. 2000, pp. 78-91.

Roxborough, Ian, *Globalization, Unreason and the Dilemmas of American Military Strategy*, International Sociology, 17(3), Sept. 2002, pp. 339-59.

Ruddar Datt, *Globalisation—Who are the Real Beneficiaries?* Janata, 52(1), Ann. Number 1997, pp. 25-27.

Sabanna, Talwar, Patil, Doddanagouda and Bulla, Bhagwantappa, *Women Workers and Globalisation*, Social Welfare, 49(3), Jun. 2002, pp. 30-34.

Sally, Razeen, *Globalization and Policy Responses: Three*

Perspectives (A review article), Government and Opposition, 35(2), Spring 2000, pp. 237-53.

Sandbrook, Richard, *Globalization and the Limits of Neoliberal Development Doctrine*, Third World Quarterly, 21(6), Dec. 2000, pp. 1071-080.

Saner, Raymond, *Globalization and its Impact on Leadership Qualification in Public Administration*, International Review of Administrative Sciences, 67(4), Dec. 2001, pp. 649-61.

Sanyal Kalyan K., *Paradox of Competitiveness and Globalisation of Underdevelopment*, Economic and Political Weekly, 28(25), 19 Jun. 93, pp. 1326-326.

Sarma, Atul, *Economic Development of the Northeastern States in the Context of Globalisation*, Strategic Analysis, 25(2), May 2001, pp. 295-312.

Sassen, Saskia, *Regulating Immigration in a Global Age: A New Policy Landscape*, Annals of the American Academy of Political and Social Science, 570, Jul. 2000, pp. 65-77.

Sassen, Saskia, *Territory and Territoriality in the Global Economy*, International Sociology, 15(2), Jun. 2000, pp. 372-93.

Sattyamurthy, T.V., *Nationalism in the Era of Globalisation*, Economic and Political Weekly, 33(33-34), 15 Aug 1998, pp. 2247-252.

Savio, Roberto, *Post-September 11th: New Concepts of Information*, Development, 45(4), Dec. 2002, pp. 17-22.

Savitch, H.V., *What is New About Globalisation and what does it Portend for Cities*? International Social Science Journal, 172, 2002, pp. 179-89.

Schild, Veronica, *Beyond the 'Passive State' and other Globalism Myths: Nation States, Social Movements and Gendered Market Citizens*, Development, 41(2), Jun. 1998, pp. 13-37.

Schwettmann, Jurgen, *Co-Operatives and Globalisation: An ILO Perspective*, Review of International Cooperation, 95(1) 2002, pp. 26-30.

Seguiti, Maria Laura, *The Development of Public Administration from a Global Perspective: The Case of Italy*, International Journal of Public Administration, 22(7), Jul. 1999, pp. 1093-114.

Sen, Amartya, *Globalization, Inequality and Global Protest*, Development, 45(2), Jun. 2002, pp. 11-16.

Sen, Sunanda, *Growth Centres in South Asia in the Era of Globalization*, Social Scientist, 24(11-12), Nov.-Dec. 1996, pp. 62-91.

Senarclens, Pierre de, *International Organisations and the Challenges of Globlisation*, International Social Science Journal, 170, Dec. 2001, pp. 509-22.

Sengupta, Arjun, *Financial Management of Globalisation: IMF and Developing Countries*, Economic and Political Weekly, 35(3), 15 Jan. 2000, pp. 115-29.

Sengupta, Arjun, *New Realities of Globalisation*, Business Standard, 16 Jan. 1999, p. 9.

Sengupta, Chandan, *Conceptualising Globalisation: Issues and Implications*, Economic and Political Weekly, 36(33), 18 Aug 2001, pp. 3137-143.

Sengupta, Nitish, *New Economic Policy and its Administration*, Administrator, 40(1), Jan.-Mar. 1995, pp. 143-54.

Seoane, Jose and Taddei, Emilio, *From Seattle to Porto Alegre: The Anti-Neoliberal Globalization Movement*, Current Sociology, 50(1), Jan. 2002, pp. 99-122.

Sethuraman, S., *Managing the Risks of Globalisation*, Hindu (Business Line), 5 Jun. 2001, p. 15.

Sewell, Bill, *New Zealand, Globalisation, and the Growing Importance of International Law*, Public Sector, 19(3), Sept. 1996, pp. 17-19.

Shari, Ishak, *Globalization and Economic Disparities In East and Southeast Asia: New Dilemmas*, Third World Quarterly, 21(6), Dec. 2000, pp. 963-75.

Shariff, Ismail and Littig, David M., *Globalisation: Old Wine into New Bottles*? World Affairs, 6(2), Apr.-Jun. 2002, pp. 38-51.

Sharma, O.P., *The New Plan and Globalisation*, Yojana, 47, Jan. 2003, pp. 229, 30-36.

Sharma, R.K., Kumar, M. Satish and Meher, Surendra, *Education, Skills and the Labour Market in a Globalised World: A Case of India*, Indian Journal of Labour Economics, 45(4), Oct.-Dec. 2002, pp. 1129-147.

Sharma, S.K., *Globalisation of Indian Business Education: To be or not to be, That's the Question*, University News, 35(17), 28 Apr. 1997, pp. 5-8.

Sharma, Subhash, *Social Discourse in a Globalised Era: Towards the Concept of Development Matrix*, Indian Journal of Public Administration, 44(3), Jul.-Sept. 1998, pp. 328-38.

Shiva, Vandana, Emani, Ashok and Jafri, Afsar H., *Globalisation and Threat to Seed Security: Case of Transgenic Cotton Trials in India*, Economic and Political Weekly, 34(10-11), 6 and 13 Mar. 1999, pp. 601-13.

Shiva, Vandana, Globalisation, *Gandhi and Swadeshi: What is Economic Freedom? Whose Wconomic Freedom*, Mainstream, 36(22), 23 May 1998, pp. 13-23.

Shoch, James, *Contesting Globalization: Organized Labor, Nafta, and the 1997 and 1998 Fast-Track Fights*, American Political Science Review, 94(1), Mar. 2000, pp. 119-50.

Short, Clare, *Agenda for Humanity: Globalisation can Work for the Poor*, Times of India, 16 Jan. 2001, p. 12.

Shroff, Manu, *Globalisation: A Stock-Taking*, Economic and Political Weekly, 34(40), 2 Oct. 1999, pp. 2845-849.

Siddharthan, N.S., *Globalisation and the Budget: Urgent Need for Institutional Reforms*, Economic and Political Weekly, 36(11), 17 Mar. 2001, pp. 889-92.

Siddharthan, N.S., *Multinationals and Liberalisation*, Hindu, 11 Jun. 1999, p. 10.

Siddharthan, N.S., *WTO and the Globalisation of Enterprises*, Economic and Political Weekly, 35(21), 22 May 1999, pp. 1287-291.

Siddiqui, Kalim, *Globalisation of the Third World Economy*, Third Concept, 6(69) Nov., 92 pp. 7-13.

Singh Rajendra Prasad, *Globalization of Indian Economy Implications for Export and Employment*, Gandhian Perspectives, 6(1) Spring 93, pp. 75-86.

Singh, Jaspal, *Impact of Globalisation on Society*, Punjab Journal of Politics, 25(2) 2001, pp. 119-37.

Singh, Manmohan, *Globalization and the Asia-Pacific Region: Challenges and Opportunities in the Twenty First Century*, Asia-Pacific Development Journal, 4(2), Dec. 1997, pp. 1-7.

Singh, Purnima, *Understanding Swadeshi in the Age of Globalization*, Third Concept, 15(172), Jun. 2001, pp. 30-33.

Singh, Randhir, *The End of a National Project, an Agreement*, Mainstream, 35(47), 1 Nov. 1997, pp. 21-26.

Sivaraman, Mythily, *Women and Globalisation*, Hindu, 17 Oct. 2000, p. 10.

Sklair, Leslie, *The Transnational Capitalist Class and Global Politics: Deconstructing the Corporate-State Connection*, International Political Science Review, 23(2), Apr. 2002, pp. 159-74.

Slater, David, *The Spatialities of Demoralization in Global Times*, Development, 41(2), Jun. 1998, pp. 22-29.

Smelser, Neil J., *Pressures for Continuity in the Context of Globalization*, Current Sociology, 51(2), Mar. 2003, pp. 101-12.

Smith, Mart, *Globalisation and Local Experience: Encounters with Difference in a UK School*, Sociological Review, 50(1), Feb. 2002, pp. 117-35.

Soederberg, Susanne, *Grafting Stability onto Globalisation? Deconstructing the IMF's Recent Bid for Transparency*, Third World Quarterly, 22(5), Oct. 2001, pp. 849-64.

Special Issue Capturing Globalization, Third World Quarterly, 21(6), Dec. 2000, pp. 917-1080.

Special Issue on Globalisation, World Cities and the Randstad, Urban Studies, 31(3), Apr. 1994, pp. 357-534.

Special Issue: Globalization and Trade, Journal of Development Studies, 17(2), Dec. 2000, pp. 1-205.

Sshankar Gopal, *American Anti-Globalisation Movement: Re-Examining Seattle Protests*, Economic and Political Weekly, 36(34), 25 Aug 2001, pp. 3226-232.

Steinmo, Sven, *Globalization and Taxation: Challenges to the Swedish Welfare State*, Comparative Political Studies, 35(7), Sept. 2002, pp. 839-62.

Stiwell, Frank, *Globalization and Cities: An Australian Perspective*, Review of Radical Political Economics, 30(4), Fall 1998, pp. 139-67.

Streeten, Paul, *Globalisation: International Integration and Disintegration*, Political Economy Journal of India, 9(3-4), Jul.-Dec. 2000, pp. 1-40.

Streeten, Paul, *Globalization, Integration and Interdependence*, Political Economy Journal of India, 8(3-4), Jul.-Dec. 1999, pp. 89-104.

Subramaniam, Vanitha, *The Impact of Globalization on Women's Reproductive Health and Rights: A Regional Perspective*, Development, 42(4), Dec. 1999, pp. 145-49.

Sundar, I., Globalization: Road Way to World Capitalism: Problems and Challenges, Third Concept, 16(187), Sept. 2002, pp. 34-39.

Symposium on Public Administration and Globalization: Inter National and Supranational Organizations, International Review of Administrative Sciences, 67(3), Sept. 2001, pp. 379-570.

Tabb, William K., *Globalization is an Issue, The Power of Capital is the Issue*, Monthly Review, 49(2), Jun. 1997, pp. 20-30.

Tabb, William K., *Progressive Globalism: Challenging the Audacity of Capital*, Review of the Month, 50(9), Feb. 1999, pp. 1-11.

Tallman, Stephen and Fladmoe-Lindquist, Karin, *Internationalization, Globalization, and Capability-Based Strategy*, California Management Review, 45(1), Fall 2002, pp. 116-35.

Tanaka, Keiko and Busch, Lawrence, *Standardization as a Means for Globalizing a Commodity: The Case of Rapeseed in China*, Rural Sociology, 68(1), Mar. 2003, pp. 25-45.

Tandon, B.B., Agnihotri, V.K. and Ramachandran, H., *Globalizatoin and Decentralization: Emerging Issues from the Indian Experience*, International Review of Administrative Sciences, 67(3), Sept. 2001, pp. 505-23.

Tandon, Yash, *Globalization and the South: The Logic of Exploitation*, International Politics and Society, (4) 1997, pp. 389-98.

Tanzer, Michael, *Globalizing the Economy: The Influence of the International Monetary Fund and the World Bank*, Monthly Review, 47(4), Sept. 1995, pp. 1-15.

Tanzi, Vito, *Globalization and the Future of Tax Systems*, D+C Development and Cooperation, (3), May-Jun. 1997, pp. 14-17.

Thakur, K.S., *Indian Economy after Globalisation*, Third Concept, 11(124), Jun. 1997, pp. 51-52.

Thampy, M.M., *Loka Samastha Sukhino Bhavathu—Kerala Health Tourism in the Context of Globalization*, ISDA Journal, 12(3), Jul.-Sept. 2002, pp. 283-89.

Therborn, Goran, *Globalizations: Dimensions, Historical Waves, Regional Effects, Normative Governance*, International Sociology, 15(2), Jun. 2000, pp. 151-79.

Thimmaiah, G., *Globalisation : Back to the Future*? Hindu(Business Line), 7 Mar. 2002, p. 14.

Thomas, Vinod, *Globalization: Implications for Development Learning*, Public Administration and Development, 19(1), Feb. 1999, pp. 5-17.

Thomas, Vinod, *Globalization: Implications for Development Learning*, Public Administration and Development, 19(1), Feb. 1999, pp. 5-17.

Thurow, Lester C., *Globalization: The Product of a Knowledge-Based*

Economy, Annals of the American Academy of Political and Social Scien, 570, Jul. 2000, pp. 19-31.

Tremblay, Reeta C., *Globalisation and Indian Federalism*, Indian Journal of Public Administration, 47(2), Apr.-Jun. 2001, pp. 208-21.

Turmen, Tomris, *Making Globalization Work for Better Health*, Development, 42(4), Dec. 1999, pp. 8-11.

Unni, Jeemol and Rani, Uma, *Globalisation, Information Technology Revolution and Service Sector in India*, Indian Journal of Labour Economics, 43(4), Oct.-Dec. 2000, pp. 803-27.

Upadhyay, V., *The Political Economy of Globalization*, Productivity, 40(1), Apr.-Jun. 1999, pp. 85-91.

Urquhart, Brian, *Between Sovereignty and Globalisation: Where does the United Nations Fit in?* Development Dialogue, 1-2 2000, pp. 5-14.

Valsan, E.H., *Globalization and Public Administration*, Administrative Change, 25(2 and 26(1)), Jan.-Dec. 1998, pp. 9-15.

Vas, Eric A., *India's Respose to Globalisation*, Janata, 5(1), Annual 2000, pp. 51-59.

Verdier, Daniel and Breen, Richard, *Europeanization and Globalization: Politics against Markets in the European Union*, Comparative Political Studies, 34(3), Apr. 2001, pp. 227-62.

Vijayan, M.J., *Something Fishy about Globalisation*, Hindustan Times, 17 Jan. 2001, p. 10.

Vliet, Willem Van, *Cities in a Globalizing World: From Engines of Growth to Agents of Change*, Environment and Urbanization, 14(1), Apr. 2002, pp. 31-40.

Vyas, V.S., *Globalisation: Hopes, Realities and Coping Strategy*, Economic and Political Weekly, 37(12), 23 Mar. 2002, pp. 1109-114.

Wallerstein, Immanuel, *Globalization or the Age of Transition?: A Long Term View of the Trajectory of the World System*, International Sociology, 15(2), Jun. 2000, pp. 249-65.

Wallgren, Thomas, *Political Semantics of 'Globalization': A Brief Note*, Development, 41(2), Jun. 1998, pp. 30-32.

Waltz, Kenneth N., *Globalization and Governance*, PS: Political Science and Politics, 32(4), Dec. 1999, pp. 693-700.

Waterman, Peter, *Beyond Globalism and Developmentalism: Other Voices in World Politics* (Review article), Development and Change, 27(1), Jan. 1996, pp. 165-80.

Watkins, Kevin, *A Skewed Globalisation Regions: Thrust against the Poor*, Deccan Herald, 27 Jan. 2001, p. 8.

Watts, Ronald, *Introduction: Federalism in an Era of Globalisation*, International Social Science Journal, (167), Mar. 2001, pp. 9-12.

Went, Robert, *Globalization in the Perspective of Imperalism*, Science and Society, 66(4), Winter 2002, pp. 473-97.

Wilenius, Markku, *Sociology, Modernity and the Globalization of Environmental Change*, International Sociology, 14(1), Mar. 1999, pp. 33-57.

Williamson, Jeffrey G., *Globalization and Inequality: Past and Present*, World Bank Research Observer, 12(2), Aug 1997, pp. 117-461

Wolfensohn, James D., *Act and Economise Globally*, Pioneer, 8 Apr. 2000, p. 9.

Wong, Lloyd L., *Globalization and Transnational Migration: A Study of Recent Chinese Capitalist Migration from the Asian Pacific to Canada*, International Sociology, 12(3), Sept. 1997, pp. 329-51.

Yach, Derek and Bettcher, Douglas, *Globalization of Tobacco Marketing, Research and Industry Influence: Perspectives, Trends and Impacts on Human Welfare*, Development, 42(4), Dec. 1999, pp. 25-30.

Yadav, J.S., *Globalization and Information Society: Development Perspective-II*, Young Indian, 13(39), 26 Apr. 2003, pp. 16-17.

Yeung, Henry Wai-Chung, *Economic Globalization, Crisis and the Emergence of Chinese Business Communities in Southeast Asia*, International Sociology, 15(2), Jun. 2000, pp. 266-87.

Yogarajah, Anusuya, *Globalisation and Foreign Direct Investment in India*, Journal of Accounting and Finance, 15(1), Mar. 1999, pp. 54-69.

Zafar Husain, *Technological Response of Indian Industry to Globalisation and Liberalisation: Educational Imperatives*, University News, 36(7), 16 Feb. 1998, pp. 1-6.

INDEX

86th Amendment Act, Constitution of India 180
93rd Amendment Bill, Constitution of India 180
AIDS/HIV 150-151, 161
APEC 246, 379, 392, 395-400, 403, 408
ASEAN 20, 258, 385, 390, 392, 396, 400
ASEAN Free Trade Area 390, 396
ASEAN Industrial complementation Scheme 396
ASEM II 409-411
ASEM NGO Working Group 410-11, 423
ASEM Trust Fund 410
ATM 203-205
Academic Institutes 114
Acceleration of process of globalisation xxx
Acharya, R. 233
"Action Agenda" for free trade 402
Action for Children's Television (U.S.A.) 293
Actual integration of economic fundamentals xliii
Advanced Industrialism under Capitalism, Communism or Fascism 40
Advertising and Publicity Campaign in Canada xxxix
Advertising text used in job advertisements for females 331
Afghanistan 149, 257
Africa xxii, xxvi, xxix, 5, 21, 25, 72, 74, 96, 148-149, 162, 183, 211, 259, 376, 383
Agriculture, commercialization of 24
Agricultural Census, 1985-86, xxxiii 24
Ahmad, K. 324
Ahmedabad 282
Aid agencies 225
Aijaz Ahmad 146
Ajmer 129
Akali Dal 366
Akindele, S.T. 135
Al Qaeda 140
Alagappa, M. 416
Albrow, Martin 168
Alcan Aluminium 342
Alienation xxiv, 42
Alka Seltzer 199
Alternative world vision, Gandhian Scheme 42
Ambani, Anil 209
America's Federal Trade Commission 292
American Capitalism 137
American Corporations —MNCs xxiii
American financial institutions 137
American food 137
American popular culture 137
American print and satellite media 137
American Technology and military 137
Amin, S. 223
Amnesty International 139
Amoroso, Bruno 155, 223
Amount raised through Euro Issues 352
Anand Rao, R. 45
Ancient Alhens xliii
Anderson, M.L. 321
Andhra Pradesh 17, 64, 364
Anglophone world 338
Anglo-Saxon economies 191
Anglo-Saxon Group 399
Anxieties of globalization 85
Argentina 9, 246
Aristotle 115
Arrighi, G. 391
Artha 43
Arthus, P.J. 165
Arunachal Pradesh, xxxiv, 24, 227
Arunachala population 227-29
Asia xxii, xxvi, xxix, xliii, 5, 21, 25, 76, 96-98, 149, 183, 211, 248, 255, 259, 262, 270, 279, 302, 240, 345, 347, 352, 376, 383, 387-88, 390-91, 395, 400, 408, 412, 416, 422
Asia Co-prosperity Sphere Project 392

Asia-Europe Environmental Technology Centre 409
Asia-Pacific Business Advisory Group 406
Civil Society Forum 401, 416
Economic Co-operation 341, 390, 398
Forum xxxv, 247, 401, 406, 416, 423
Labour Network 407
Region xxxv, 246, 253-54, 271, 338-39, 345, 350-59, 387-431
Regionalism : Bubbles gone burst 395
Stock Exchange xl, xliii, 353
Summit 405
Manila, 1996 421
Seattle 394
Vancouver, 1997 421
Asian Cultural Forum on Development 411
Asian Development Bank 415
Asian Regional Exchange for New Alternation 414, 424
Asian Regional Network for Alternatives 411
Asian Social Forum, Hyderabad, 2003 129
Asian social movement leaders 413
"Asian Way or Capitalism" 391
Attitude towards television advertising 291
Auroville of Pondicherry 375
Australia 253, 257, 259, 274, 351, 377-78, 398-400, 402, 407, 434
Australian Stock Exchange 357

Babylonian Empire 188
Badla 355
Bairoch, Paul 311
Bajpai, Anupam 18
Bajpai, N. 224
Baker, Gideon 115-16
Bal Manchs 128
Balance of Payment Crisis of India, 1991 xxvi, xxxvi, 95, 275
Bales, R.F. 214
Bangladesh 12, 128, 373, 415
Bank for International Settlement 144, 380
Bankruptcy 84
Bansal, Gaurav 172
Barbara, Santa 301
Barber, R. 116, 128, 129, 374
Bardhan, Pranab 123
Barnard, A. 226
Barnet, R.J. 168
Barthakur, I.K. 231
Baruah, Sanjib 366
Basu, D.D. 366
Basu, Kaushik 108
Bata Industries 342
Beck, Ulrich 36, 38, 40, 41
Behera, M.C. 227, 233-35
Belch, Raymond 302
Belgium 257, 351
Belgium Stock Exchange xli, 350
Bellamy, C. 171
Bello, Walden 224, 393-94, 399, 400, 414, 417, 420
Benevolent, Globalization xxxi
Bergstan, C.F. 390
Berry, J.M. 100
Beteille, Andre 115, 127
Bhaduri, Anita 62-63, 224
Bhagidari Associations 128
Bhagwati, Jagdish 69, 76-79, 148, 153, 384
Bhalla, A.S., 31
Bharat Petroleum Corporation Ltd. 108
Bharatiya Janata Party 108
Bharatiya Majdoor Sangh 108
Bhattacharya, Mohit 58
Bifani-Richard, P. 323
Bihar 17-18, 186, 224
Bisht, Pushpa 93-112
Black, Sandra 78-79
Blair, Harry 56
Blair, Tony 65
Blake Island Summit, 1994 401
Board for Industrial and Financial Reconstruction, India 15, 17
Bogor Declaration 402, 405
Bogor Summit, 393, 401
Boli, John 39
Bolivia 129
Bonded Labour System Act, 1976 180-81
Bonding Associations in Panama 128
Bosnia 374
Bothwell, Robert 337
Boyd, H.W. 215
Brainerd, Elizabeth 78-79
Brass, Paul 361
Brathwaite, John 120, 124
Brazil 9, 12, 160, 262, 351
Brettonwoods Institution 9
Brettonwoods System 27, 373
British Constitutional theory 433
British North America Act of 1867 433
Brown, C. 334

Brown, Douglas M. 435
Brunei 253, 396, 398, 400
Bryan, D. 223
Buchanan, Tollock 7
Buddhism 281, 374
Bureaucracy 226
Bush, Victoria D. 301
Business associations 114
Business standard 283

CIDA Industrial Co-operation Program 342
CNN Real-time global news 134
Cairns, Alan C. 368
Cabinet Committee on Disinvestment, India 108
Cable TV 204
Callaghy, Thomas R. 56
Callahan, David 118, 126-27
Cambodia 253, 396-97, 408
Canada xxvi, xxxi, xxxiii-xxxviii, xii, 93, 96-97, 196-97, 212, 241-51, 253, 257, 273-78, 308-48, 350-51, 360-71, 377-78, 380, 398, 400, 404, 407, 432-43
Canada-India Business Council 269
Canada -India Economic Partnership Agreements 269
Canada's International Market Access Priorities 249
Canada's Merchandise Trade with India, 2001 346-47
Canada's Aid Transfers in India 344
Canadian Constitutional provisions 433
Canadian Consumers realistic and practical in nature xxxviii
Canadian foreign policy 337, 341, 432-43
Canadian household-Income and expenditure 284
Canadian Manufacturers Association 342
Canadian population migratory xxxix
Capital Agency 356
Capital investment flows xxix
Capitalism xxviii, 134, 211
Capitalist world system endangers world integration 39
Cardiff Law School, Cardiff University, (U.K.) 265
Cardoso, Fernando Henrique 384
Caribbean 245-46
Carlson, Lee 300, 303
Castells, Manuel 384
'Catch-up' industrialization 33
Catholic Institute for International Relations 411
Cavanagh, J. 168
Cayman Island 257
Cellular phones 5
Census of India, 1991 230
Centre for Science and Environment 283
Cerny, P. 50, 53
Challenge for administration to recast the role of State 59
Changes in the Social and Political structures of societies xxiv, xxx, xxxii
Challenges to Stock Exchanges 353
Chambers, R. 224, 226
Chandhoke, Neera 117, 119, 122-24, 127
Changes in income distribution, Canada 249
Changing complexion of public administration 49-68
Changing role of the state in globalization propagating 52
Chaudhri, D.P. 184
Chauhan, Ramesh 283
Chauhan, S.S.S. 172
Chhatisgarh 128
Chelliah Committee on Tax Reforms 15
Chicago School 7
Child Labour Act, 1986 (India) xxx, 181
Children, India 289-307
Children, Television advertising xxxvii
Children, United States 289-307
Children's Advertising Review Unit of the Better Business Bureau (US) 302
Children's Consumer Socialisation 292, 302
Children's growing maturity and parent—child interaction 304
Chile 245, 398, 407
Chile Free Trade Agreement 246
China xxvi, xxxvii, 12, 32-33, 84, 96-97, 102-03, 134, 140, 143-44, 148, 160, 183, 253, 256, 262, 281, 290, 299, 301, 305, 318, 338-39, 345, 351-53, 356, 380, 395, 398, 400, 402, 408
Chinese Commuism 147
Chipko Movement 128
Chodorow, N.J. 321
Chowdhury, A. 391
Chretien, Jean xxxv, 269
'Civil Society against the State, Poland 119
Civil Society Organisations xxvii, 122, 125

Civil Society's Alternative Regionalism 419
Clash of globalization 71
Clinton, Bill 191
Clinton, Hillary 292
Coca Cola 4
Coca-Cola's Kinley 283
Coca-Colonization 137
Cohen, Jean L. 117, 125, 127, 412
Cold War 396
Collapse of gold standard 94
Collective life more genial, varied and fruitful—Gandhi 45-46
Combating state minimalism 102
Committee on Trade & Environment (India) 158
Common Effective Preferential Tariff Scheme 397
Commonwealth of Independent States 134
Commonwealth of Nations 340
Communism xxiv, xxviii, xxix, 134
Community Based Organizations 114, 130
Community development 415
'Community Economic Action' 64
Comparative perspective : Globalization 221-443
Comparative study of Canadian & Indian job market xxxix
Competitive markets 20
Competitive Media Reporting 290
Complexion of public administration undergoing transformation 51
Conceptual paradigm : Globalization 1-89
Confederation of Enginerring Industries (India) 342
Conformist agenda xxvii
Confucianism 374
Consequences of globalisation 190
Consumer behaviour 309
Consumer education 312
Consumer expectation from the market 316
Consumer guidance 314
Consumer in Globalized World 198-209
Consumer Protection Act, 1986 (India) 114, 315
Consumer socialisation of the child, television xxxvii
Consumerism and Globalization xxii, xxxii, xxxviii
Contradictions and Challenges, Globalization 36-48, 376
Contribution of women in national wars of independence xxx
Cornia, Giovannni Andree 181
Corporate Globalization 215
Corporate governance 84
"Correct policies" of public governance 18
Cox, R. 389
Creating State—Community Synergy 63
Cree population of Canada 196
Crowe, Bill 290
Cultural aspect—Negative aspects, Globalization 196
Cultural globalization of India and Canada xxxvi
Current fiscal position of Canadian economy xxxv
Current Regional Networks 422
Current trends in Canadian economy in the Era of Globalization 241-51
Customs Cooperation Meeting 409
Czinkota, Iikka 280

DAGA 399
DEMAT 203
DMK 366
Darussalam 396
Davis, Kathy 321
Davos fiction 13
De Oliviera . 412
De Sowsa Santos, B. 389
Decentralisation both a means and an end', Gandhi 45
Deceptive advertisements xxxii
Declaration of Common Resolve 402
Degree of transnationalisation of production 7
Dehin 43
Dehumanization xxiv, 39, 42
Delhi 282
Demand for more power by Regions of India 366
Demand for Regional Autonomy in an Era of globalisation 360-71
Democracy xxvii
Democratic decentralization 44
Democratic global system 20
Demutualised the stock exchange 353
Denhardt, Janet Vingent 66

Denhardt, Robert B. 66
Department of Foreign Affairs and International Trade, Canada 241
Deregulation, privatisation, introduction of market oriented reforms in public services 53
Devaluation of rupee 19
Developed Countries xxxii, xliv, 5, 14, 27, 185, 257, 351
Developing World xxi—xxii, xxix—xxx, xli, xiv, 11, 14, 19, 21, 24, 26, 51, 79, 84-85, 148, 161, 183, 186, 235, 253, 256, 351, 379-80, 382, 391, 420
Development of Civil Society Organisations as growth of communitarianism 56
Development of Derivative Products 353
'Development sound' of trade negotiations 86
Dhaneja, Alka 113-32
Dharma 43
Diamond, Larry, 57
Dibb, Paul 97
Dichotomous view 116
Difference in parental attitudes towards television advertising xxxvii
Diseases xxii, 4
Disinvestments Commission (India) 19
Disneyfication 137
Disparities in wealth and income 21
Distinction between possession and possessiveness 44
Distribution of Canadian ODA by Type of Aid, 1999-2000 344
Distribution of Industrial categories of Arunachalee Main workers 236
Distribution of powers between the Central Government and Governments of States in India 363, 367
Distribution of World FDI inflows during 1985-2001 256
Division of labour xxiii, 13, 24, 28, 39, 168
Donahue, John D. 336
Doordarshan 302
Doornbos, Martin 225
Downgrading in international credit rating of India 19
Doyal, L. 172
Dreze, Jean 110, 225
Drucker, Peter 58
Dubushi, Jay 40
Dutch Stock Exchange xii 350
E-Commerce 203
E-Mail 203
EPG's 2020 Plan 402
ERA Consumer, Malaysia 411
Eade, Deborah 126
Early Voluntary Sectoral Liberalization—15 Sectors xxxv
Early Voluntary Sectoral Liberalization Agreement 246, 247, 404
East Asia 60-61, 64, 148, 224, 265, 382, 384, 391-92, 400, 408
East Asia Crisis 224
East Asia Economic Group 390
East Asia and Asia Europe Meeting 408
East European Countries xxvii, 9, 119, 134, 136, 144
East Indian Ethnic Organizations 343
Ecological aspect—Negative aspect, Globalization 193, 197
Ecological threat xxiv
Ecological violence 42
Economic and Social dimension of attitude toward advertising 291
Economic cooperation 216
Economic development 225
Economic globalization 30, 102
Economic growth 4, 37
Economic inequality xxix
Economic policy reforms xxii
Economic prospects and environmental problems of globalization 155
Economic Survey, India 253, 261
Economic Times Research 16
'Economics of information' 83
Education and gender 171
Edward, a secular Christian Palestinian Nationalist 13
Effects of television on children controversial 292
Egyptian Empire 188
Eighth Five Year Plan (India) 228
Elder, S. 173
Electronic Clearing Service 203, 205
Electronic Fund Transfer 355
Elimination of Child Labour Programme, 1994 181
Elsenhans, Hartmut 361
Elwin, V. 227
Emergence of Civil Society as a Supplementary Democratic Model 56

Emergence of 'Competition State' 52
Eminent Persons Group 400, 402
Employment 78, 173, 231
Empowerment 172
Empowerment of Women xxix
Enron/Dabhol 263
Environment Summit (RIO) 385
Environmental Campaigns 114
Environmental goods & services, Canada 248
Environmental impacts of globalization 161
Environmental pollution xxiv, xxvii, xxix 42
Escert, Reid 340
Essential of Village Republics, Gandhi: 45
Establishing State-market cooperation 62
Establishment of transnational networks 289
Ete, Micnto 229
Eurasian Continent 26
EURONEXT Stock Exchange xli, 351
Europe xxx, 24, 25, 27, 121, 188, 259, 279, 292, 338, 350, 385, 387-88, 408
European Civilization 27
European colonial settlement 25
European Community 376
European Economic Commission 283
European powers 25
European Union xxvi, 96, 155, 163-64, 242, 251, 256, 351, 380, 411-12
Eusuf, Mohammed Abuy 120
Evans, Peter 64
Evolution of civil society 115
Exchanges between Canadian and Indian universities 343
Expanding media xxii-xxiii, 4
Explosion of knowledge 37
Export Processing Zones 173
Export promotion and openness xxx
Extent of state control on capital movements 7
External Commercial Borrowings 352
External liberalization 14
in India —Trade, foreign exchange, capital and technology 16

FICCI 269, 356
Factories Act, 1881 (India) 180
Factors influencing consumer decisions 317
Fair protection for investors, Canada xxxv
Falk, Richard 418
Fall of the Berlin Wall, 1989 134, 137
Family-Communication Theory 300-303
Family communication pattern and advertising related parental practicies xxxvii
Farazmand, Ali 52, 59
Farida, Akhtar 226
Fascism xxviii
Faster economic growth xxii
Federal government xliv
Feldman, and Feldman, 435
Female consumer in the Globalised world 210-20
Ferlie, Ewan 57
Ferranti, Mare 339
Ferree, M.M. 321
Fertilizers xxxiii
Financial relations between the Centre and the States (India) 363
First Five Year Plan 228
Fiscal crisis of India, 1991 xxxvi
Fish and Fish products, Canada 248
Fisher, Julie 117, 121, 125, 128
Fishing industry, Canada 248
Focus India 341
Focus on Global South 414
Focus on Management Orientation in Public Administration 54
Fodder Banks 128
Food and Agriculture Organization 183, 411
Foreign Capital 224
Foreign Convertibility Bonds 16
Foreign direct investment xxxix-xxxvi, 4, 7, 106, 157, 164, 231, 241, 253-72, 352
in Canada 259
in India 260, 353
inflows in selected Asian Developing Countries, 2001 256
in some Asia-Pacific countries during 1995-99 353
outflows from major economies 351
Foreign Institutional Investors 16
Foreign investors in India 40
Foreign policy, Canada 241, 432-43
Foreign Trade 24
Forestry, Canada 248
Forgacs, D. 390
Formation of Global Capital and Market Organization 358
Forward Trading 355
Fox, K. 323
France 12, 14, 247, 257, 351, 380
Francophone world 338

Free competition 101
Free market economy xxvi, 94
Free trade xxxiv, 12, 70
Free Trade Area of America xxxv, 242, 245
Freedom from Debt Coalition 415
Freedom Struggle 18
French Stock Exchange xIi, 350
Friedman, Thomas 7, 72, 93
Front de Liberation du Quebec 368
Fukuyama, Francis 3, 71, 124, 374
Fundamental Rights, India 180, 366
Futuristic Perspective of Civil Society Organizations 125

G-7 Countries xIi, 193, 338, 380, 383, 437
G-8 Countries 97, 161, 257
G-20 Countries 381
G-77 Countries 144, 385, 437
GAP 151
GATT 27, 144, 157, 381, 387-88, 393, 395, 399, 404
GATT-Uruguay Round 401
Gaebler, Ted 60
Galbraith's affluent society 86
Gamble, A. 390, 400
Gandhi, Indira 364
Gandhi, M.K. 42-46, 281, 287
Gandhian alternative 42
Gandhian ideas 38
Gandhian model 46
Gandhian philosophy centres around individual 43-46
Gates, Bill 151
Gender inequity in the job market 320-35
Gender Development Index xxxi, 186
Gender Issues 167-77
Gender Violence 174
General Motors, USA 12, 206
General perception of jobs for women 323
George, Vix 167, 169-71, 173, 175
Gerald, Lesser 292
German Model of 'Social Partnership' 105
German Stock Exchange xIi, 350
Germany 93, 96-97, 246, 257, 345, 351, 377, 380, 387, 434
Ghana 382
Gilpin, Robert 27, 41, 360, 389, 392
Gita 43
Global advertising 290
Global capitalism 36
Global Civil Society Organizations 121
Global consciousness 375
Global Depository Receipts 16, 352
Global Equity Market 4, 350, 357
Global Report on Child Labour, 2002 180
Global Solidarity xxi, 4
Global stock exchange 350
Global terrorism 143
Globalist ideology 133
Globalization : Concept and nature 3-23
Globalization : Its Clashes, contents and discontents 69-89
Globalization : The nature and its dynamics 24-35
Globalization—Centre of diverse intellectual and political agenda xxiv
Globalization, a multidimentional phenomena 49
  a new international system replacing Cold War System xxiv, xxvi
  a process of integrationalism xxxviii
  Human Insecurity and Human Rights 149-50
  modern day phenomena, transcends boundaries and borders 94
  sovereighnty and Human Rights 133-54
Globalization affects different categories 13
Globalization and Advertising 289-307
  and Child Labour 178-87
  and Consumerism 188-97, 308-19
  and its discountents : A pretence of global institutions - Stiglet's approach 83
  and economic impacts 160
  and Foreign Direct Investment : India and Canada 252-72
  and Gender Issues in India 167-77
  and Human Rights 147
  and Indo-Canadian Economic Partnership 267
  and Regionalism in Asia Pacific Region 387-431
Globalization and the changing Dynamics of Indo-Canadian relations 336-49
Globalization more as a threat than as a promise 37
Globalization of banking 235
Globalization of Equity Market 350-59
Globalization of Investment 235
Globalization of Trade 235

Globalization poses new challenges to South-South Solidarity 372-86
Globalizing Tribal Economy 223-40
Gold Standard 94
Golden Eye 203
Goldman, J.100
Gonas, L. 174
Good governance xxviii
Government by market 53
Government deregulation 289
Government, key role towards restructuring of markets 60
Govind Prasad 252-72
Grain Banks 128
Gram Sabhas 128
Gramsci, Antonio 115, 390
Grassroot Support Organizations 117
Great Britain 12, 25, 53, 64, 93, 96, 241, 257, 291, 345, 351, 380, 382
'Great Depression' 94, 139
Greater Volume of Foreign aid 86
Creat City States 115
Greek Empires 188
Green Revolution 17-18
'Green' Signals and Globalization 164
Gross Domestic Product (GDP) 7, 97-98
Grossbart, Stanford 300, 303
Guatemala 128
Gujarat 17-18, 197
Gulati, Sunita 444-74
Gulf 202
Gulf Wars 252
Gupta, Dipankar 117, 123

Haffkins, N. 331
Hamilton, Alexander 25
Hansen, H. 225
Hanumantha Rao, C.H. 104
Harijan 46
Harison, Ann 79
Harmonising Securities Laws 357
Harnessing Globalization for Children : A Report to UNICEF 182
Harris, John 137
Harris, Pater 134-135
Harry Potter Series 138
Hart, Michael 438
Haryana 17-18
Hawke, Bob 399
He, Baogang 118-19, 124
Health and Gender 171
Held, David xliii, 40-41, 49, 178, 361
Heredia, Rudolph C. 37
Hereditary monarchy xxviii
Hermes, N. 225
Hewelett-Packard 203
The Hidden cost of Trade 405
Highlighting the importance of tackhing green house gases global warning 86
Hillmen, John 337
The Hindu 64, 129, 159
Hinduism 281, 374
Hindustan Petroleum Corporation Ltd. 108
Hines, Colin 64
Hirst, Paul 125
Hoffmann, Stanley 138-42
Hogg, P.W. 368
Holland, Hanrich D.161
Holloway, Richard 416
Hollywood movies 134, 374
Holm, H.H. 168
Holton, Robert J. 168
Homegeneity vs. heterogeneity 37
Hong Kong 60, 62, 253, 256, 259, 262, 352, 356, 398, 400, 407, 427
Hong Kong Stock Exchange xl, 350
Horta, Ramos 417
Human advance 4
Human Development in South Asia 126
Human Development Index xxvi, 186
Human Development Report, 1999 19, , 59, 143-44, 148, 150
Human Poverty Index 186
Human Resources Development, Canada 327
Human Rights xvii-xxviii, 3, 133-54
Human rights advocates 114
Human welfare 30
Hume, David 138
Hungary 9, 160, 340
Hunger xxiv, 42
Huntington, Samuel 374

IADEA Workshop Report, 1997 415
IBM 375
IFC xxv, 74, 85
Ian, Thynne 65
Illiteracy xxii, 3
Impact of background factors, socialisation agents 293
Impact of Globalization 12, 338

India and Canada 273-78
on Public Administration 50-51
Impact of Information Technology xl
Impact of job opportunities for women, Globalization xxi
Impact of national boundaries reduced xli
Impact of Globalization on India's rural life 40
Impact upon Indigenous people — Negative aspects, Globalization 196
Imperialism 25
Import of foreign goods, India xxxii
Import Substitution policies xxx
Import of of political - military factors and viewpoints 41
Importance of good delivery of health and education 86
Importance of Technological Globalization 41
Improving the investment climate 86
Inclusive world economy 85
Income inequality xxxi
Income Tax Act, 1961 286
Increased choices of products xxii
Increased trade xxi
Increasing fiscal deficit 19
India xxiv, xxvi, xxix, xxxi—xxxiii, xxxv—xxxviii, xli, xliv, 10, 12, 14, 37, 41, 93, 95, 100-03, 122, 160, 167-77, 180, 183, 202, 224, 253, 256, 258, 260-72, 289-91, 378, 380, 415, 432-34
India : Awakening to Globalized world 95
India-Canada Investment and Collaboration 270
India and Canada Trade, 1990-91 to 2001-02 268
India and Liberalization 14
India Economic Summit 271
India Today International Conclave, New Delhi 110
India under Globalization 93-112
India's economic transition and Canadian business interests 345
Indian Association for Canadian Studies 343
Indian Capital Market xli, 353-54
Indian Constitution 102, 362-65
Indian Consumer Financing Satisfaction Study 285
Indian Culture 4
Indian Household-Income, Expenditure habits 282
Indian National Congress 18, 366
Indian Stock Exchange xl
Indo-Canadian relations 340
Indo-China 340
Indonesia 62, 148, 183, 256, 353, 355-56, 396-98, 400, 402, 427
Industrialized Countries 351
Industrialization, Great Britain 25
Ineffectiveness of nation-states 39
Inequality xxii, 3
Information Technology xxvii
Insecticides xxxiii
Institute for Popular Democracy, Philippines 411
Internal Liberalization 14
International Bank for Reconstruction and Development 157
International Congress of Free Trade Unions 407
International Credit Insurance Corporation 81
International development 225
International Division of Labour 373
International Government Organizations 121
International integration 30
International investment 7
International Labour Organization 137, 173, 179-80, 183, 186, 226
International Monetary Fund (IMF) xxv, xxix, xii, 5-6, 10, 19-21, 74-75, 80, 83, 85, 95, 101, 104, 122, 140, 144-45, 150, 156-60, 164, 193-94, 216, 223-24, 226, 275, 338, 373, 380-81, 383, 393, 409
International Olympic Committee Award, 1996 440
International Trade xxix, 7, 26, 94
Internationalisation 336
Internet, Networking 5, 203
Intra-Asian Trade 409
Iraq 72, 143, 149, 257
Islam 374
Islam, I. 391
Israel 257
Israel Batista of the World Council of Churches 412
Issues and impact Globalization 91-220
Italy xxvii, 12, 257, 351, 380

Jacques, Derrida 78
Jain, R.B. 63
Jainism 281
James Bay Hydro-electric complex in Canada 197
Jameson, Frederic 223, 375
Jammu & Kashmir 364
Janata Party 364
Janda, K. 100
Japan xxxvii, 12, 26, 32, 60-62, 99, 101, 103, 155, 163-64, 248, 253, 256-57, 259, 274, 279, 290-91, 299, 302-03, 305, 318, 345, 350-51, 356, 376-77, 380, 392-93, 395, 398-99, 400, 402, 404, 406-08, 416, 426
"JapaNIEsation" 394
Japanese Development Model 392
Japanese Ministry of Trade and Industry 399
Jayakumar, S. 396
Jayal, Nirija 41
Jennings, Edward T. Jr. 54
Jha, Nalini Kant 432-43
Jharkhand 224
Jhum Cultivation, Arunachal Pradesh 232
Ji, Mindy F. 301
"Jihad" vs. "McWorld" 374
Job market xxxi
Jobs for women on Canadian and Indian Job Sites on the Internet 320-35
Johanson, L.J. 173, 436
Joint Venture xxxiv

Kaboolian, L. 55
Kahle, Lynn 301
Kama 43
Kapiya 281
Kapoor, Neeru 289-307
Kapur, A.C. 368
Kapur, Ashok 340
Karlson, Nils 115
Karnataka 17
Karunanidhi, M. 364
Kaushik, Asha 41-42
Keating, Paul 400
Kelkar Committee 286
Kelsey, J. 400
Kennedy, John F. 289
Kennedy, Paul 29, 394
Kenya 128
Keohane, R.O. 387
Keynes, John Maynard 94, 100
Keynesian Phase, Full Employment xxxi, 190
Kerala 17, 186, 281, 364
Khan, Sonia 320-35
Kissinger, Henry 71, 97
Kono, Yahei 402
Korea 60-61, 99, 223, 256, 340, 382, 395, 400, 404, 420
Korten, David 51, 416
Koshy, Ninan 38
Kosovo, 149
Kravchuk, Robert S. 55
Kuala Lumpur Action Programme on Still Development 403
Kumar, A. 224
Kuri, P.K. 230
Kurien, N.J. 367
Kwan, C.H. 397
Kyoto People's NGO Forum 405-06
Kyoto People's Summit 426
Kyoto Protocol 143

LSE Stock Exchange xii, 351, 356, 358
Labour intensive technology 233
Labour laws, India 108
Labour unions 114
Labour market 78
Labour mobility xxix
Laffer, Gilder 7
Laos 253, 396-97, 408
Latin America xxii, xxvi, xxix, 5, 96, 162, 183, 245, 258, 338, 351, 376, 383
'Latin American Financial Crutch' 80
Least Developed Countries 14, 160
Lechner, Frank J. 39
Lenin, V.I. 26
Lensink, R. 225
Less Globalized Countries xxv
Level of jobs advertised for females 329
Levy, S.J. 215
Levy, Thomas 436
Lewis, P.G. 49
Lewis, Stephen 383
Liberal Capitalism 94
Liberal democracy xxviii
Liberalization, Privatisation and Globalization xxvi, 93, 100-07, 253
Liberalization of National & Global Markets 36
Lindsay, Linda L. 322

List, Fredrich 25
Literacy level of Consumers compared of Indians and Canadians xxxviii
Local Credit Networks in Guatemala 128
Locke, John 115, 138
Lofdahl, Corey L. 162
Lok Sabha 109
London Stock Exchange xli, 350, 353
Low level of Parent-Child interaction 298
Luke, J. 51

MAI 424
MLX Market Edge xl, 350
MTV Europe 290
Madhya Pradesh 17, 197
Maharashtra 17-18
Mahathir, Mohammed 393, 395, 401, 408
Mahler, G. 433
Make use of latest Information Technology 354
Making Globalization work for the poor 133
Making State Institutions responsive to needs of people 61
Maleria 161
Malysia 253, 256-57, 259, 262, 352-53, 356, 395, 398-99, 400, 402, 407-08, 422, 427
Malevolent, Globalization xxxi
Malik, Saroj 36-48
Malnutrition xxii, 3
Manila Action Plan for APEC 403
Manila People's Summit of 1996 403, 405, 407, 426
Manmohan Singh 18
Mantaw, H. 230
Manufacturing industries xxxiii
Maren, Lars 292
Marginalization 31
Marjit, S. 233
Marshal, Don 373
Marx, Karl 27
Marx-Engeles dilemma 72
Massive and reckless industrialization 39
Master Card 208
Matsuura, Koichiro 281
Mauritius 257
Maurya, Chandra Gupta 281
McCorquodale, Robert 134, 145
McDonald 4, 134, 137, 138, 374
McDonald's Pizza 40-41
McGann, James G. 118
McGraw, A.G. 49
McLauhan, Marshall 303, 375
McNeal, James U. 290-91, 303-04
"McWorld" 374
Media networks 5
Medury, Loma 48-68
Megasthenes 281
Memorandum of Understanding 15, 358
Mendl, W. 392, 396
Mercosur 20
Merrill, Lynch xl, 350
Methodological netionalism 38
Mexico 9, 12, 160, 224, 242, 253, 351, 373, 381, 398, 400, 407
Mexico Stock Exchange xl, 350
Meyer, John W. 311
Miami Summit of the Americans, 1994 xxxv, 245
Michael, R. 280
Michael Jackson T-shirts 374
Macklethwait, John 137, 147, 383
Micro-credit Societies in Bangladesh 128
Micro-financing Sector 64
Middle Ages 211
Middle Asian power 98
Middle East xxvi, 74, 96, 252, 259
Migdal, Joel S. 117
Miji People in Nafra Circle 229
Military power rests on economic capabilities 29
Mill, John Stuart 100
Millenium Development Goals 258
Mines Act, 1901 180
Ministry of Disinvestment (India) 19
Mishra, Anil Dutta 3-23, 170, 174
Mishra, L. 186
Mishra, Pramod 372-86
Mishra, Sweta 167-77
Mitsubishi 12
Mittal, Banwari 292
Mobility of Labour 233
Modernization Theory 32
Modified Value Added Tax 15
Moffet, Michael H. 280
Mohamed, Naina Shaih 273-78
Mohiadeen, P.M. Meera 350-59
Mohaman, B. 37
Mohanty. P.K. 227
Mongolia 144

Moore, Mike 191, 303
Moore, Richard K. 216
Moral progress, Gandhi 44
Morality, an acquisition of virtues 43
Morgan Stanley xI, 350
Morin, J.Y. 434
Morris-Hale, Walter 362
Moschis, George P. 300
Moscow fiction 13
Motoyama, Y. 400, 402
Moyinhan, Euzzeno 280
Mukherji, K.P. 365
Mulroney Government 439
Multi-cultural, Canada 97
Multilateral Agreement on Investment, Canada xxxv, 243
Multilateral Agreements on Trade 6
Multinational Companies in India 40
Multinational Corporations xxiii, xxviii, xxxiv, 6, 10, 18, 27, 30, 78, 147, 150-53, 167, 173, 186, 223, 227, 231-36, 258, 373, 381
Multinational Enterprises 290
Multinationals and financial markets xxiii, 36
Mumbai 282
Munton, Don 436
Muralivallabhan, T.V. 155-66
Myanmar 173, 396-97
Myrdal, Gunnar 105

NAFRA Chemicals 229
NAFTA 97, 276, 376, 395, 399
NAM xi
NASDAQ Stock Exchange xIi, 350, 356, 358
NATO 149
NEEPCO Hydel Project, Yazuli 229
NGOs xxvii—xxviii, 5-6, 70, 74, 114, 117-18, 120-21, 123-27, 130, 139, 145, 165, 179, 203, 405, 411-12,417-19, 421-23
NGO Working Group on ASEM 411
NYSE Stock Exchange xIi, 350, 356-58
Naidu, M.V. 39, 235
Napoleonic Wars 26
Narang, A.S. 369
Narmada Bachao Andolan 128
Narrow economic nationalism 94
National boundaries xxvii
National Capital Territory of Delhi Survey 294
National Citizen and Global Citizen 378
National Conference 366
National Democratic Alliance 108
National Development Council 364
National Economic Policy, India 95
National Regulatory Changes, 1991-2003 255
National Renewal Fund 277
National Sample Survey Organization 17
National Security xxii, 29
National Specialization in agricultural activities 24
National Stock Exchange (India) 354, 357-58
Nayanar, E.K. 365
Nayar, Baldev Raj 30
Nayyar, Deepak 62-63, 168, 224
Nefrin, M. 412
Nehru, Jawaharlal 97, 104, 227, 323, 334, 339
Neo-Liberal Capitalism 37
Neo-Liberal Consensus 124
Neo-Liberalism 53
Neo-Marxists 116
The Netherlands 257, 351
New Challenges 379
New Communitarian perspective 116
New Delhi Television Channel 128
New Economic Policy, India xxvi, 253
Newfangled consumerism 39
New Industrial Policy, India 15
New Public Management 54
New Right Schools of Thought 7
New technologies xxi
New World Order xxxiii, 7, 134, 215, 320
New York Times 72
New Zealand 253, 259, 398, 400, 407
New Zealand Stock Exchange 357
Newly industrialised country 390
Nicaragua 377
Nielson Media Research 302
Nigeria 12, 373
Nigmoi Fruit Processing Unit 229
Ninth Five Year Plan 105
Noland, M. 390
Nomenclature of Globalization 373
Non-discrimination for investors, Canada xxxv
Non-Profit Organizations 114
Noor, P.M. 409

North America 387-88, 408
North American Free Trade Agreement 216, 242, 341, 388
North Atlantic Powers 25-26
North-South Dichotomy 383
Northern Hemisphere 11
Nossal, Kim Richard 435
Nye, Joseph S. Jr. 97, 336

OECD xxiii, xxxiv, 13, 27, 50, 148, 243, 379, 399, 424
Oceania 259
Offered an alternative life style, Gandhian Scheme 42
Official Development Assistance (Canada) 340
Ohmae, K. 413
Okinawa faction 13
Oomen, T.K. 362
Open General License 107
Open Market 19
Open Society Endangered Soros's Approach 80
Orissa 18
Orwell, George 322
Osaka Ministerial Summit 401, 402, 405
Osborne, David 60
Outward investment xxxiv
Outward Orientation 33
Overdevelopment vs. Underdevelopment 37
Overproduction vs. Undernourishment 37
Overseas Corporate Bodies 16

Pacific xiiii, 259
Pacific Asia Regional Coalition 411
Pacific Asia Research Centre, Japan 411
Pacific Century and the Asian Crisis 390
Pacific Rim 435
Packaged/Mineral Water 283
Pai, Sudha 41
Pakistan 12, 99
Panama 128
Panchayati Raj 44
Panchayati Raj Institutions 128
Panda, A.N. 360-71
Papua New Guinea 398, 400, 407
Parashar, Utpal 174
Parent-Child interaction and influence of Audio-Visual Tchniques 293, 297-98
Parsons, T. 214
Participatory Rural Appraisal 224
Pasricha, Ashu 210-20
Payne, A. 390, 400
Peaceful methods of eliminating dehumanized globalization, Gandhian Schema 42
Pechman, Joseph 334
Pentagon virtus of Truth, Non-violence, Non-possession, Celibacy and Fearlessness 43
People's Solidarity for Participatory Democracy in South Korea 411
People's Summit on APEC, Vancouver 426
Perlmutter, Hv. 374
Person, D. 174
Peru 398
Pesticides xxxiii, 283
Peters, Guy 57
Peters, James 36
Petersons, Utrich 161
Pettigrew, Pierre S. 249
Pfaff—Czarnecka, Joanne, Raja Singham—Senanayake, Darimi 361
Phases of Globalization xxiii
Phenomena of female consumption marked by two principles — Massive and Extensive xxxiii
Philippines 253, 256, 259, 397-98, 400, 404, 407, 415-16, 420, 425-27
Pietesse, Nederveen 389-90, 420
Pizza Hut 138
Plannign Commission of India 18-19, 106, 364
Plaza Accord in 1985 395
Plural Societies 362
Poland 9, 119, 134, 378
Polanyi-Levitt, K. 387
Polarized World 12
Political aspect — Negative aspects, Globalization 194
Political decentralisation, Gandhi 45
Political fallout of globalization 40
Political Globalization 139
Political participation of women xxix
'Political realism' 33
Polly, Richard W. 292
Pondicherry 375
Popper, Karl 80
Population explosion 183
Populist — Fallacious and Discontents of Globalization 73
Pornography xxxiv

Positive and Negative aspects of Globalization 192, 374
Post-1991 Model of India, Foreign Investment 40
Post-Cold War period xxviii, 120, 143
Post-Globalization Period 253, 270
Post-War Multinational Institutions 100
Post-War Years 94
Poverty xxii, xxiv, 3, 31, 37, 42, 149, 265, 415
Poverty Report of UNDP, 1998 391
Powar, J.D. 285
Preferential Trade Agreement 396
Principal - Agent Relationship 7
Principle of Non-Possession, Gandhi 44
Private electronic trading 350
Private Sector xxvii
Private Voluntary Organizations 114
Privatization xxix, 5, 7, 8
Priyadarshini, Priyanka 223-40
Production by masses in place of mass production, Gandhi 45
Production Controls, India 107
Professional bodies 114
Progressive Internationalism 134
Property Rights Literature 7
Prostitution xxxiv
Public Administration : Emerging issues 52, 58
Public Choice School 7
Public governance 18
Public Sector Undertakings xIi
Punjab 17-18
Purana 281
Pursuit of 'Beggar your Neighbour' policies 94
Putnam, Robert xxvii, 116, 120, 123, 125

Quadra Focus 203
Quintanila, Tammy 152

ROI 18
Radical Agenda xxvii
Radical Groups in the South 191
Raghavulu, C.V. 45
Rehman, Atiur 120
Rahamathulla, B. 241-51
Raikhi Committee on Tax Reforms 15
Raja Singham - Senanayake, Darini and Pfaff-Czarnecka, Joanna 361
Rajasthan 18
Ramiah, Annabhi 18
Ramkothi Block, District Durg 128
Rangriz, Hassan 24-35
Rank and Amount of FDI in different countries, 1998-99 257
Rao, S.L. 107
Recasting the role of the State 59
Re-emergence of Civil Society in the Globalization Context 119
Reformist Agenda xxvii
Reforms in economies xxxvi
Regional Civil Society xiiii, 418
Regional Civil Society's initiatives on APEC 404
Regional Imbalances 362
Regional Integration and the Japanese Dominance in Asia 392
Regional International Market 24
Regionalism in an Era of Globalization 361
Regulatory Authorities-Telecom, Power and Insurance 19
Reid, Leonard N. 299
Related elements of Level of Tariffs 7
Relationship between the State Market and Civil Society 116
Relative Autonomy Approach 116
Reliance 352
Relief Organizations 114
Religious institutions 114
Renan, Earnest 378
Replaces the image of Separate individual society with one world system 39
Reservation of jobs, Arunachal Pradesh 232, 234
Reserve Bank of India 16, 355
Reserve Bank of India Bulletion 261
Resource exhaustion xxiv, 42
Results of Globalization 11
Rhyme, Rethan : Cultural Globalization in India and Canada 279-88
Ricardo, 184
Riesman, D. 215
Right of Consumers 317
Rise in Industrialization xxiii
Rise of Capitalism xxiii
Robertson, David 41, 291, 362
Robertson, R. 168, 387
Robins, Kelvin 41
Rodrik, Dani 30
Roedy, William 290

Role of Civil Society Organizations in the Era of Globalization 113-32
Role of Nation-State xxx
Roman Empire 188
Ronald, D.B. 292
Ronkarnen, Michael H. 280
Rose, Gregory M. 301
Roseborough, H. 215
Rosenau, James N. 41, 374
Rosenbloom, David H. 55
Roy, N.C. 230
Rural Development 226
Russia 9, 12, 32, 84, 97, 134, 136, 148, 338, 398
Russian Melting 80
Rwanda 140

SAARC 20, 98
SADC 20
SAP 172
SARS 161, 252
SPAR 151
Sachs, J.D. 224
Sachs, Jeffery 18
Sangharsh Samritis 128
Sankaran, S.R. 227
Sao Paulo Stock Exchange xl, 350
Sardar Sarovar Project 197
Satish Kumar 43
Satyam Online 352
Savings habit, Canadian situation 285, 286
Schechter, Michael G. 121, 124
Scholte, Jan Aart 119, 126, 135
Scotward, Wackam 292
Search for liberation implies self-development 43
Sebastain, Tin 209
Second Summit of the Americans, Santiago, Chile xxxv, 245
Seattle faction 13
Securities and Exchange Board of India 355-56
Sekar, I. Francis Gnana 279-88
Self, Peter 53
Self development, Gandhian Scheme 42
Self government of communities 42
Self Help Groups 64
Sen, Amartya 110, 225
Sen, Sumanda 170
Sen Gupta, Arindam 108
Senior Officials Meeting on Trading and Investment 401
Seoul Declaration 400
Serrano, I. 415-16
Services and intellectual property 6
Sethi, J.D. 45
Seven major areas of action—World Bank Policy Research Report xxv
Sex trafficking xxxiv
Shaikh, A.A. 69-89
Sharma, Jai Narain 198-209
Sharma, M.L. 44
Shastri Indo-Canadian Institute for Educational Exchanges 343
Shitole, G.Y. 308-19
Shiv Sena 366
Shiva, Vandana 148
'Shock Therapy' 84
Shriman Narayan 44
Shukla, S.P. 231
Significance of the Sectors in the management of public affairs 65
Sikhism 281
Sillicon Valley 383
Singapore 62, 103, 253, 256-57, 259, 345, 351-53, 355, 394-95, 398, 400, 407, 427
Singh, Arun Kumar 133-54
Sinha, Manoj 188-97
Sinha, Yashwant 110
Sinocentric Tribute-Trade System 391
Sivanandan, A. 168
Smajda, Clande 50
Smith, A.D. 38
Smith, Adam 29, 101, 109, 138
Sobhan, Rehman 60, 120, 123
Social aspect—Negative aspects, Globalization 195
'Social Capital' xxvii, 120
Social cohesion 30
Social disintegration 30
Social inequality xxix
Social movements 114
Social Sector expenditure, Arunacahal Pradesh 232
Socialization agents of Children 293
Socialism, India 101, 105
Socialist framework, India 105
Socially Responsible Market Economy 62

Society of Canadian Women in Science and Technology 327
Soja, Edward 375
Somalia 149, 257
Sondhi, Sunil 387-431
Sorensen, G. 168
South Asian Financial Crisis 80
South - South Co-operation 385
South - South Solidarity 372-86
South Africa 378, 439
South America 21
South Asia xxxi, 126, 339, 342, 344, 348, 377
South Bank xli
South East Asia 162, 258, 345, 376
South Korea 32, 103, 173, 253, 257, 259, 290, 351-52, 382, 398, 400, 402, 407, 411, 416, 425
Sovereignty 133-54
Spain 351
Sri Lanka 72, 256, 263, 415-16
Srivastava, B.N. 227
Standard of living of Consumers of India compared with Canadians xxxviii
State - Society interaction 64
State Domestic Product, Arunachal Pradesh 231
State of Civil Society in Asia 412
Statistical Abstracts, Arunachal Pradesh 234
Statutory Liquidity Ratio, India 15
Steward, Frances 174
Steward, Maxianne C. 369
Stiglitz, Joseph 69, 83, 224, 234
Stiglitz's Discontentment on Globalization 84
Stock Exchange 350-59
Storm, Servaas 162
Straight Trough Processing 355
Strang, Heather 120
Strange, Susan 168, 375
Strategies for building sysnergy between state and society 65
Streeten, Paul 136
Structural Adjustment and Global Poverty 394
Structural Adjustment Policies 51, 64, 84
Structural Adjustment Programme xxx, 104, 169, 391
Sub-Saharan Africa 258, 339, 377, 384
Subrahmanyam, K. 366
Success of Political Decentralisation depends on Economic Decentralisation, Gandhi 45
Suharto, President 402
Sunday Times 286
Supply Side of Economics School 7
'Supranational' borderless Global economy 24
Supra-natural borderless economy xxiii
Sustainable development xxvii, 107
Swadeshi 45, 108
Swadeshi Jagran Manch 108
Sweden 351
Swiss Stock Exchange xl, 350
Switzerland 13, 97, 257, 351, 382
Sydney Stock Exchange xl, 350
Szmbarsky, Wistawa 379

'TINA' School of Thought 133, 384
TNC 5
TRIPS 150
TV Advertising Standards Council of India xxxvii, 302
Taiwan 32, 60, 62, 103, 253, 259, 318, 351-52, 356, 395, 398, 402, 407, 420
Taliban 140
Tamil Nadu 17, 364
Tandon, R. 412
Tata Singapore Airlines 263
Taylor, F.W. 54
Team Canada Mission to India 346
Technological Change 289
Technological inequity xxix
Technological transfers xxix
Tehran fiction 13
Tehranian, Majid 38
Tehri Dam Movement 128
Television Advertising & Children's Consumer Socialisation in the United States, Japan and China xxxvii, 289-307
Telugu Desam 366
Tenth Five Year Plan 106, 266
Thailand 23, 45, 51, 72, 148, 179, 223, 253, 256-57, 351, 355, 397-99, 400, 402, 407, 411, 415, 420
Theory of Embedded Autonomy 64
Theory of World Risk Society 40
Third Millenium xxxiv
'Third Party Sector' xxvii, 114, 118

Third United Nations Conference on Least Developed Countries, 2001 160
Third World xxviii, xxxi, xli, 11, 14, 48, 147, 151-53, 156, 164, 179, 226, 392
Third World Globalization 252
Thomas, H. 391
Thomas, Phil 265
Thompson, Grahame 24, 168, 233
Three Discontents of Globalization : (Bhagwati) — Capitalism System, Process of Globalization and Behaviour of Corporations 77
Tilly, Charles, Ed. 27
Times of India 260, 364
Tiwari, R.S. 334
Todaro, M.P. 172
Toffer's 'Cultural Stock' 86
Tokyo Stock Exchange xl, 350
Toronto Stock Exchange xl, 350
Torre, Edicio 417
Tourism, Arunachal Pradesh 233
Tourism industries xxxiv
Trade Facilitation Action Plan 409
Trade related aspects of Intellectual Property Rights 145
Trade relations between India and Canada xl
Trade Unions xxxi, 83, 105
Transformation of Global economic activity 289
Transnational Corporations xxxi, xxxiii, 10, 12, 103, 157, 163-64, 191, 382, 385
Transnational Institute 411
Transnational terrorism 142
"Transnationalism" 336
Trap, F. 225
Trands in Foreign Trade, Canada 241-42
Triadic Forces of Globalization 163-64
Triadic Superpowers of the world 164
Tribal economy xxxiv
Tribal Panchashila 227
Trinity of Globalization, Liberalization and Privatization 162
Triology of Discontents - Jagdish Bhagwati's approach 76
Trudeau Government 439
Turner, L. 105

U.K. Government's White Paper on Globalization of December, 2000 133
UNCED Process 417
UNDP 17, 27, 30, 74, 109-10, 121, 136, 226, 266, 332, 391-92, 415
Human Development Report 133, 136, 266
UNESCO 281
UNICEF 171, 179, 183
US Free Trade Agenda 393
US influence in the Pacific 394
US Securities and Exchange Commission 355
US Trade Act of 1988 395
Uganda 160
Ukraine 9
Underdeveloped Countries 211, 224
Undernourished people, India 260
Unemployment xxiv, 31, 42
Uneven process, unequal distribution of benefits and losses 12
Unification of Settlement 357
Union Carbide 151
United Nations xxvii, xlii, 121, 141-42, 144, 149, 160, 169, 183, 210, 340, 392
United Nations Children Emergency Fund 121
United Nations Conference on Environment and Development 417
United Nations Convention on Rights of the Child, 1992 180
United Nations Conference on Trade and Development 13, 30, 255, 408
United Nations Economic and Social Council 411
United Nations World Summits 407
United States xxiii, xxvi, xxviii, xxxiii, xxxv-xxxvii, xliv, 9, 12, 25-27, 32, 53-54, 73, 83, 93, 95, 97, 101, 107, 121, 139-43, 147, 149, 155-56, 163-64, 206, 209, 211-12, 241-46, 251-52, 257, 259, 270, 279, 289-307, 337, 345, 351, 353, 374, 377-78, 380, 382, 387, 392-94, 398-99, 400-01, 406-07, 432, 435, 439
Universalisation vs. intense parochialism 37
Urry, John 116
Uruguay Round Agreement 10, 381
Uruguay Round Negotiations 71
Ushering in new societal expectations, changing value system 50
Uttar Pradesh 17-18, 186

Vajpayee, Atal Bihari 106

Vasco da Gama 280
Vasudhiv Kutumbhum xiiv
Veltmeyer, Henry 36
Viable set of Strategies, Gandhian Scheme 42
Vietnam 134, 144, 253, 398, 408
Vietnam War 396
Village Republic's Gandhi 43-44
Vinodan, C. 336-49
Violence and War xxiv
Vyasulu, P. 235
Vyasulu, V. 235

Wackman 302
Wadhwa, Charan D. 109
Wadia, A.R. 323
Wadood, Sayed Naimul 120
Wage differentials 78
Wallerstein, Immanuel 24, 41
Wallerstein, J. 387
Walsh, Ann 300
War Measures Act, Canada 368
Waterman, P. 418
Walts, Ronald L. 367-68
Way out for South-South Solidarity 385
'Wealth of Nations', Smith 101
Weapons of Mass Destruction 71
Weaver, R. Kent 118
Webber, Andrew Lloyd 138
Weiner, Myron 181
Weiss, Linda 96
Welch Development Agency 265
Welsch, Eric 51
West African proverb 289
West Bengal 17
West Germany 119
Western Europe 11, 387
Weter, Philop 42
Whaites, Alan 121, 124
Wheare, K.C. 365
Wilding, Paul 167, 169-70, 173, 175
Wilkins, P. 169
Wolfensohn, James 62
Women 64, 320-35
Women Groups in Kenya 128
Women hold key to sustainable development xxx
Women's Enslavement 217
Women's networks 114
Wong, Wilson 51
Wood, Adrian 185
Woodbridge, Adrian 137, 147
Woolridge, Andrian 383
World xxi, xxvi, xxviii, xxxv, 4, 27, 30, 37, 86, 95, 253, 351
World Bank xxv, xxix, xli, 5-6, 12, 19-21, 61-62, 74-75, 79, 85, 95, 101, 104, 122, 144-45, 150, 156, 158-60 164, 193-94, 216-17, 225-26, 345, 381, 383, 409, 416
World Bank and IMF 158
World Bank Policy Research Report, 2002 xv, 85
World Bank Report, 1999 16, 145, 160
World Civil Society Forum, Geneva, 2002 126
World Development Report, 6, 59, 61, 65, 102, 122, 159
World Economic Forum 271
World economy 7, 160
World Food Summit 11
World Health Organization 172, 183
World Social Forum 129
World Summit on Social Development, Manila, 1994 418
World War I xxiii, 26, 94, 368
World War II xxiii, xxx, xxxvii, 26, 73, 94, 169, 183, 189, 216
Wright, Robert 384
WTO xxv, xxix, xxxi, xli, 6-7, 10, 12-14, 20-21, 70, 75, 83, 85, 95, 144-45, 149-50, 155-57, 164, 191, 193, 216-17, 245, 280, 339, 341, 358, 379, 381, 388, 395, 403-04, 408, 412
WTO Globalization and Environment 157

Yadav, Sushma 170, 174, 178-87
Yavan Suvang 281
Yeats, Alexander 346
Yeh 303-04
Young, Fort 322
Young, John A. 203
Youth Campaigns 114
Yu-han, C. 392
Yugoslavia 72

Zoher, Abdoolcarim 290
Zoninsein, Jones 127